A Companion to the Huguenots

Brill's Companions to the Christian Tradition

A SERIES OF HANDBOOKS AND REFERENCE WORKS ON THE
INTELLECTUAL AND RELIGIOUS LIFE OF EUROPE, 500–1800

Edited by

Christopher M. Bellitto (*Kean University*)

VOLUME 68

The titles published in this series are listed at *brill.com/bcct*

A Companion to the Huguenots

Edited by

Raymond A. Mentzer
Bertrand Van Ruymbeke

BRILL

LEIDEN | BOSTON

Cover illustration: Communion token (méreau) of the Reformed Church of Montauban (18th-century, lead, 34 mm). Courtesy of the Bibliothèque de la Société de l'Histoire du Protestantisme Français, Paris.

An elaborate 18th-century communion token from Montauban in southwestern France depicting the shepherd, a time-honored symbol of Christ, with a staff in his right hand and horn in his left. He is flanked on each side by a tree and surrounded by his flock of nine sheep. A large bird, perhaps a protective presence, hovers above. Members of the faithful received communion tokens from their elders upon condition of correct belief and proper behavior. They subsequently presented them for admission to the Lord's Supper.

Library of Congress Cataloging-in-Publication Data

Names: Mentzer, Raymond A., editor.
Title: A companion to the Huguenots / edited by Raymond A. Mentzer, Bertrand Van Ruymbeke.
Description: Boston : Brill, 2016. | Series: Brill's companions to the Christian tradition, ISSN 1871-6377 ; VOLUME 68 | Includes bibliographical references and index. | Description based on print version record and CIP data provided by publisher; resource not viewed.
Identifiers: LCCN 2015045581 (print) | LCCN 2015044151 (ebook) | ISBN 9789004310377 (E-book) | ISBN 9789004310353 (hardback : alk. paper)
Subjects: LCSH: Huguenots.
Classification: LCC BX9454.3 (print) | LCC BX9454.3 .C66 2016 (ebook) | DDC 284/.5--dc23
LC record available at http://lccn.loc.gov/2015045581

Want or need Open Access? Brill Open offers you the choice to make your research freely accessible online in exchange for a publication charge. Review your various options on brill.com/brill-open.

Typeface for the Latin, Greek, and Cyrillic scripts: "Brill". See and download: brill.com/brill-typeface.

ISSN 1871-6377
ISBN 978-90-04-31035-3 (hardback)
ISBN 978-90-04-31037-7 (e-book)

Copyright 2016 by Koninklijke Brill NV, Leiden, The Netherlands.
Koninklijke Brill NV incorporates the imprints Brill, Brill Hes & De Graaf, Brill Nijhoff, Brill Rodopi and Hotei Publishing.
All rights reserved. No part of this publication may be reproduced, translated, stored in a retrieval system, or transmitted in any form or by any means, electronic, mechanical, photocopying, recording or otherwise, without prior written permission from the publisher.
Authorization to photocopy items for internal or personal use is granted by Koninklijke Brill NV provided that the appropriate fees are paid directly to The Copyright Clearance Center, 222 Rosewood Drive, Suite 910, Danvers, MA 01923, USA.
Fees are subject to change.

This book is printed on acid-free paper and produced in a sustainable manner.

In Memory of Myriam Yardeni (1932–2015)

Contents

List of Illustrations and Tables IX
Abbreviations XI
Notes on Contributors XII

Introduction 1
  Raymond A. Mentzer and Bertrand Van Ruymbeke

PART 1
France

1 Organizing the Churches and Reforming Society 17
    Philippe Chareyre and Raymond A. Mentzer

2 Doctrine and Liturgy of the Reformed Churches of France 43
    Marianne Carbonnier-Burkard

3 Huguenot Political Thought and Activities 66
    Hugues Daussy

4 Pacifying the Kingdom of France at the Beginning of the Wars of Religion: Historiography, Sources, and Examples 90
    Jérémie Foa

5 Women in the Huguenot Community 118
    Amanda Eurich

6 Pulpit and Pen: Pastors and Professors as Shapers of the Huguenot Tradition 150
    Karin Maag

7 The Huguenots and Art, c. 1560–1685 170
    Andrew Spicer

8 The Revocation of the Edict of Nantes and the *Désert* 221
    Didier Boisson

PART 2
The Diaspora

9   Diasporic Networks and Immigration Policies   249
    Susanne Lachenicht

10 Assimilation and Integration   273
    Myriam Yardeni

11 Sociolinguistics of the Huguenot Communities in German-Speaking Territories   291
    Manuela Böhm

12 Huguenot Memoirs   323
    Carolyn Chappell Lougee

13 Histories of Martyrdom and Suffering in the Huguenot Diaspora   348
    David van der Linden

14 Huguenot Congregations in Colonial New York and Massachusetts: Reassessing the Paradigm of Anglican Conformity   371
    Paula Wheeler Carlo

15 The Huguenot Refuge and European Imperialism   394
    Owen Stanwood

16 *Le Refuge*: History and Memory from the 1770s to the Present   422
    Bertrand Van Ruymbeke

Bibliography   443
Index   471

List of Illustrations and Tables

Illustrations

7.1   Jean Perrissin, *The Massacre at Tours, July 1562*   180
7.2   Jean Perrissin (?), *Temple of Lyon*   181
7.3   François Dubois, *The Massacre of St Bartholomew*, (c. 1572–1584)   182
7.4   Jacques le Moyne de Morgues, *Laudonnierus et rex athore ante columnam a praefecto prima navigatione locatam quamque venerantur floridenses*   184
7.5   Jacques le Moyne, *Studies of Flowers: A Rose, a Heartsease, a Sweet Pea, a Garden Pea, and a Lax-flowered Orchid*   186
7.6   Sébastien Bourdon, *Crucifixion of St Andrew*   189
7.7   Sébastien Bourdon, *Solomon's Sacrifices to the Idols*   191
7.8   Jacob Bunel, *Henry IV*   196
7.9   Jean Morin after Ferdinand Elle, *Henry IV*   197
7.10   Ferdinand Elle, *Louis XIII*   198
7.11   Ferdinand Elle, *Anne of Austria*   199
7.12   Henri Testelin, *Louis XIV*   200
7.13   Louis Du Guernier, *Miniature of James II, later King of England, as a Young Man* (1656)   203
7.14   Robert Nanteuil after Sébastien Bourdon, *Queen Christina of Sweden*   204
7.15   Sébastien Bourdon, *Queen Christina of Sweden*   205
7.16   Louis Ferdinand Elle, *Samuel Bernard*   206
7.17   Louise Moillon, *Plate of Cherries, Grapes and a Melon*   208
7.18   Jacques Rousseau, *Preliminary sketch for painted decoration probably for a drum or building of circular plan in the Great Greenhouse or the Orangery at the Chateau of St. Cloud in France*   210
7.19   Louis Testelin, *The Holy Family with St Anne*   212
7.20   Abraham Bosse, *Benediction of the Table*   213
7.21   Abraham Bosse, *The Wise Virgins at their Devotions*   214
7.22   Abraham Bosse, *Vows of the King and Queen to the Virgin*   216
7.23   Abraham Bosse, *David with the head of Goliath*   217

13.1 Frontispiece of Pierre Jurieu's *Histoire du Calvinisme,* depicting the crucifixion of the true Church in the form of a woman. The Latin text encourages martyrdom: "If we suffer with Him, we shall be glorified together" (Rom. 8:17)   354
13.2 Frontispiece to the first volume of the *Histoire de l'Edit de Nantes*, depicting French Protestantism as a woman assailed from all sides   362
13.3 Jan Luyken, The whipping of Louis de Neuville in Orange, engraving from Elie Benoist, *Historie der Gereformeerde Kerken van Vrankryk* (Amsterdam: 1696), vol. 2   367

Tables

4.1 The *départments* of the commissioners of the Edict of Amboise (March 1563)   105
4.2 The *départments* of the commissioners of the Edict of Saint-Germain (August 1570)   106
13.1 Contents of the *Histoire de l'Edit de Nantes* by volume   361

Abbreviations

AD	Archives Départementales
AM	Archives Municipales
AN	Archives Nationales (Paris)
BCEW	*Bulletin de la Commission pour l'Histoire des Églises Wallonnes*
BGE	Bibliothèque de Genève (Geneva)
BL	British Library (London)
BnF	Bibliothèque nationale de France (Paris)
BPF	Bibliothèque de la Société de l'Histoire du Protestantisme Français (Paris)
BSHPF	*Bulletin de la Société de l'Histoire du Protestantisme Français*
PHSL	*Proceedings of the Huguenot Society of London* (later *Great Britain and Ireland*)
SCJ	*Sixteenth Century Journal*
TNA	The National Archives (Kew)

Notes on Contributors

Manuela Böhm
is Visiting Professor in German Linguistics at the Universität Kassel, Germany. Her research focuses on sociolinguistics, multilingualism and literacy studies. She recently edited with Olaf Gätje, *Handschreiben—Handschriften—Handschriftlichkeit. Osnabrücker Beiträge zur Sprachtheorie* 85 (2014). She has published widely on the linguistic dimensions of the German Refuge. The volumes include *Sprachenwechsel. Akkulturation und Mehrsprachigkeit der Brandenburger Hugenotten vom 17. bis 19. Jahrhundert* (Berlin: 2010) and a collection edited with Jens Häseler and Robert Violet, *Hugenotten zwischen Migration und Integration: Neue Forschungen zum Refuge in Berlin und Brandenburg* (Berlin: 2005).

Didier Boisson
is Professor of Early Modern History at the Université d'Angers, France. He recently published *La Conversion. Textes et réalités* (Rennes: 2014) and is currently preparing an edition of the proceedings of the provincial synods of the province of Orléanais-Berry.

Marianne Carbonnier-Burkard
is Associate Professor Emerita (*maître de conférences honoraire*) at the Paris Institut Protestant de Théologie. Her publications focus on John Calvin (*Jean Calvin: une vie*. Paris: 2009), on Reformed piety literature from the 16th to the 18th centuries (her book in progress examines "death in Reformed writings"), and on Huguenot memory practices in France.

Paula Wheeler Carlo
is Professor of History at Nassau Community College, State University of New York. Her most recent publication is "The Tyranny of the Consistory? Consistories and Conflicts with Huguenot Ministers in Colonial New York," in *Agir pour l'Eglise: Ministères et charges ecclésiastiques dans les églises réformées (XVIe—XIXe siècles)*, eds. R. Mentzer and D. Poton (Paris: 2014). She is currently working on a scholarly monograph about the Huguenot experience in colonial New England.

Philippe Chareyre
is Professor of Early Modern History at the Université de Pau et des Pays de l'Adour. He specializes in the History of the Reformation in France with

particular attention to the Reformed consistory. His most recent books are *La construction d'un Etat protestant. Le Béarn au XVIe siècle* (Pau: 2010) and several edited volumes: *L'hérétique au village. Les minorités religieuses dans l'Europe médiévale et moderne* (Toulouse: 2011), *Huguenots et protestants francophones au Québec. Fragments d'histoire*, co-edited with Marie-Claude Rocher, Marc Pelchat and Didier Poton (Novalis, Québec: 2014), and *Le protestantisme et la cité*, co-edited with Guy Astoul (Montauban: 2013).

Hugues Daussy
is Professor of Early Modern History at the University of Franche-Comté in Besançon, France. His most recent book is *Le parti Huguenot. Chronique d'une désillusion (1557–1572)* (Geneva: 2014). He is currently working on a political history of the French Reformation from 1557 to 1629.

Amanda Eurich
is Professor of History at Western Washington University. She is the author of *The Economic of Power: The Private Fortunes of the House of Foix-Navarre-Albret* (Kirksville, Mo.: 1994) as well as a number of articles on confessional identity and community in early modern France. She is currently writing a book on the Toulousan jurist, Jean de Coras, and his double life as agent and polemicist for the Huguenot party in southern France during the Wars of Religion.

Jérémie Foa
is Associate Professor (*maître de conférences*) in Early Modern History at Aix-Marseille Université and the Centre National de Recherche Scientifique. He recently published *Le tombeau de la paix. Une histoire des édits de pacification* (Limoges: 2015). His research centers on the ordeals associated with the civil wars (1559–1610) and the resources mobilized by the various players during these troubled times.

Susanne Lachenicht
is Professor of Early Modern History at the Universität Bayreuth, Germany. Her latest publication is an edited collection *Europeans Engaging the Atlantic. Knowledge and Trade, ca. 1500–1800* (Frankfurt/Main, New York and Chicago: 2014). She is currently preparing a monograph entitled *Negotiating Asylum in Europe and the Atlantic World*.

Carolyn Chappell Lougee
is the Frances and Charles Field Professor in History Emerita at Stanford University. She has published widely on Huguenot memoirs from the era of the

Revocation. Her book tentatively entitled *Facing the Revocation* will be published in 2015 by Oxford University Press.

Karin Maag
is Director of the H. Henry Meeter Center for Calvin Studies and Professor of History at Calvin College in Grand Rapids, Michigan. Her most recent publication is a co-edited volume of essays honoring the late Robert Kingdon, *Politics, Gender, and Belief* (Geneva: 2014). Her current research focuses on France and Geneva in the later 16th and early 17th centuries.

Raymond A. Mentzer
holds the Daniel J. Krumm Family Chair in Reformation Studies in the Department of Religious Studies, University of Iowa. His most recent book is *Les registres des consistoires des Églises réformées de France, XVIe—XVIIe siècles. Un inventaire* (Geneva: 2014). He is currently preparing a study of material culture and the liturgy in the French Reformed tradition.

Andrew Spicer
is Professor of Early Modern European History at Oxford Brookes University. His publications include *Calvinist Churches in Early Modern Europe* (Manchester: 2007) and among the edited volumes *Society and Culture in the Huguenot World, c. 1559–1685* (Cambridge: 2002); *Ritual and Violence. Natalie Zemon Davis and Early Modern France* (Oxford: 2012); *Lutheran Churches in Early Modern Europe* (Aldershot: 2012) and *Parish Churches in the Early Modern World* (forthcoming). He is currently completing a monograph entitled *Conflict and the Religious Landscape. Cambrai and the Southern Netherlands, c. 1566–1621*.

Owen Stanwood
is Associate Professor of History at Boston College. A historian of colonial America and the Atlantic world, he is the author of *The Empire Reformed: English America in the Age of the Glorious Revolution* (Philadelphia: 2011). He is currently at work on a book tentatively titled *Dreams of Silk and Wine: Huguenot Refugees and the Promise of New Worlds*, under contract with Oxford University Press.

David van der Linden
is a lecturer and post-doctoral researcher at the University of Groningen. His most recent book is *Experiencing Exile: Huguenot Refugees in the Dutch Republic, 1680–1700* (Aldershot: 2015). He is currently working on a project that

investigates Protestant and Catholic memories about the French Wars of Religion.

Bertrand Van Ruymbeke

is Professor of American Civilization and History at the Université de Paris 8 (Vincennes-Saint-Denis) and senior member of the Institut Universitaire de France (IUF). He is the author of *From New Babylon to Eden. The Huguenots and Their Migration to Colonial South Carolina* (2006) and *L'Amérique avant les Etats-Unis. Une histoire de l'Amérique anglaise 1497–1776* (2013). He also co-edited *Memory and Identity. The Huguenots in France and the Atlantic Diaspora* (2003), *Protestantisme et autorité* (2005), *Les Huguenots et l'Atlantique*, 2 vols. (2009–2012), *Réforme et Révolutions* (2012) and *The Atlantic World of Anthony Benezet, 1713–1784* (forthcoming).

Myriam Yardeni

was, at the time of her death on 8 May 2015, Professor of Early Modern European History Emerita, University of Haifa, Israel. Her recent publications include "Fissures et paradoxes dans la théologie politique d'Elie Merlat," *Revue de l'histoire des Religions* 230 (2013), 67–84 and "Assimilation et intégration dans le Refuge huguenot (fin XVIIe–XVIIIe siècles). Nouvelles possibilités, nouvelles méthodologies," *Diasporas. Circulations, migrations, histoire*, n. 23–24 (2015), "Retour au temps long." At the time of her death, she was preparing a book entitled *Between Faith, Religion and Ethics. The Metamorphoses of the Huguenot "Refugee" Faith*.

Introduction

Raymond A. Mentzer and Bertrand Van Ruymbeke

The Huguenots are among the best known of early modern European religious minorities. Their brutal mistreatment during the 16th-century Wars of Religion is a story familiar to nearly all students of European history. The St. Bartholomew's Day massacre of August 1572—a horrific episode borne of intense religious hatred—is surely the most notorious Reformation bloodbath. The Huguenots' expulsion from France toward the end of the following century conferred upon them a preeminent place in the numerous accounts of forced religious migrations. Their history has become synonymous with repression and carnage, intolerance and discrimination. At the same time, Huguenot accomplishments and contributions in France and the lands to which they eventually fled have long been celebrated. They are distinguished by their theological formulations and ecclesiastical polity, political thought and activities, intellectual and artistic achievements. Political and religious opponents have, for their part, characterized these French Protestants as seditious, disruptive and destabilizing, particularly within the French kingdom. The propaganda campaigns continued well into the 20th century. Only recently have strongly held opinions favorable and hostile given way to more dispassionate reflection. And while this volume's purpose is not to assess the confessional tensions of the modern era, the editors and contributors do seek to present an accurate portrait of the Huguenot past, investigate the principal lines of historical development, and suggest the most recent interpretative frameworks that scholars have advanced for appreciating the Huguenot experience. This is hardly the first book or collection of essays on the Huguenots and it will not be the last. It can, however, underscore those developments in which scholars have taken greatest interest, why this is so, and where the direction of future studies is likely to lead.

While "Huguenot" is now the appellation most frequently applied to members of the early modern French Reformed Churches, the word's etymology remains obscure and controversial.[1] The explanation with widest currency holds that the word was a corruption of the German *Eidgenossen* (confederates bound together by oath), referring to the Genevan protective alliance with Protestant Bern in the struggle against the Duke of Savoy for political and religious

---

[1] Janet G. Gray, "The Origin of the Word Huguenot," *SCJ* 14 (1983), 349–59. Hugues Daussy, *Le parti huguenot. Chronique d'une désillusion (1557–1572)* (Geneva: 2014), 11–13.

independence.[2] French Catholic critics subsequently applied the term to rebellious French Reformed Protestants who, much like their Genevan co-religionists, were deemed unruly and subversive. Not all scholars, however, are convinced. Another interpretation insists upon an indigenous French source linked to the central province of Touraine and its capital, Tours. Proponents of this view look to the myth of King Hugues or Hugon. He was, according to legend, a cruel spirit or phantom who chased about the streets of Tours at night. The tale had its roots in a distant memory of the unpleasant Hugues, count of Tours during Charlemagne's time. The association with French Protestants appears to derive from their clandestine existence and initial tendency to worship at night under the protection of darkness. This was the very moment when King Hugues, the prince of darkness, reigned. Again, the hostile characterization of Reformed Protestants is obvious. Though there is little apparent consensus regarding the genesis of "Huguenot," the designation in the two principal accounts originally had highly pejorative connotations. The *Eidgenossen* version and its connection to Geneva focused, in a Catholic telling, on that city's role as the fountainhead of heresy and iniquity. It also invested French Reformed Protestants with the unsavory quality of political disloyalty. The detestable Hugues and his offensive behavior advanced an equally unflattering account.

Whatever the origins, the first widespread and, at this point, negative application of the term to the reformers appeared about the time of the March 1560 conspiracy of Amboise. It was an ill-fated attempt by Protestant nobles to capture the young king Francis II, arrest or slay the leaders of the ultra-Catholic Guise family, and assert Reformed control over France. Thus, Catholics initially employed "Huguenot" as an insult, much as Protestants called their Catholic adversaries "papists." Over time, terminological refinements and transformations occurred. In a confessional sense, the faithful came to understand themselves as devoted Christians and members of a true Church—the Reformed Churches of France. The ensemble of political, military and diplomatic structures that soon emerged from the religious movement were assumed under the broad designation of Huguenot cause or party.

Though scattered, small pockets of Huguenots were to be found in nearly every corner of the realm, the greatest concentration—some four-fifths of all French Protestants—lived within a crescent of provinces running westward

---

2 For a discussion of the evolution of the term *Eidgenossen* to *eyguenot* and then *huguenot*, see, in particular, Henri Naef, "'Huguenot' ou le procès d'un mot," *Bibliothèque d'Humanisme et Renaissance* 12 (1950), 208–27.

INTRODUCTION

from Dauphiné across Languedoc and Guyenne and up the Atlantic coast.[3] Urban agglomerations, in particular, were celebrated centers of Huguenot strength and activity. Accordingly, towns in the western and southern reaches of the kingdom have been the subject of considerable historical research.[4] Smaller Huguenot communities also dotted the rural landscape, although they did not match the cities in terms of influence. Not surprisingly, these smaller communes have gone largely unstudied, perhaps the result of an absence of readily apparent documentation, perhaps the consequence of scholarly bias in favor of urban settings. Protestantism in France possessed a rural as well as urban topography. Thus, the Cévennes Mountains in southern France were home to a dense network of Reformed villages and small towns.[5] Some local historians have written helpful if brief descriptive accounts of these rural Protestant communities and their churches.[6] Only recently, however, have scholars begun to undertake more systematic investigation.[7]

---

3 Samuel Mours, *Les Églises réformées en France: tableaux et cartes* (Paris: 1958) remains an older yet valuable survey of the complex geography of French Protestantism. See also, his *Essai sommaire de géographie du Protestantisme réformé français au XVIIe siècle* (Paris: 1966).
4 Notable among recent studies are Philip Benedict, *Rouen during the Wars of Religion* (Cambridge: 1981); Edwin Bezzina, *After the Wars of Religion: Protestant-Catholic Accommodation in the French Town of Loudun, 1598–1665* (PhD diss., University of Toronto, 2004); Philippe Chareyre, *Le consistoire de Nîmes 1561–1685*, 4 vols. (Doctoral diss., Université de Montpellier III, 1987); Philip Conner, *Huguenot Heartland: Montauban and Southern French Calvinism during the Wars of Religion* (Aldershot: 2002); Judith Pugh Meyer, *Reformation in La Rochelle: Tradition and Change in Early Modern Europe, 1500–1568* (Geneva: 1996); Kevin Robbins, *City on the Ocean Sea: La Rochelle, 1530–1650. Urban Society, Religion, and Politics on the French Atlantic Frontier* (Leiden: 1997).
5 Alain Molinier, "Aux origines de la Réformation cévenole," *Annales : économies, société, civilisations* 39 (1984), 240–64.
6 See, for example, Maurice Oudot de Dainville, "Le consistoire de Ganges à la fin du XVIe siècle," *Revue d'histoire de l'Église de France* (1932), 464–85; François Martin, "Ganges, action de son consistoire et vie de son Église aux 16e et 17e siècles," *Revue de théologie et d'actions évangéliques* 2 (1942), 17–40 and 130–59; Frank Delteil, "Institutions et vie de l'Église réformée de Pont de Camarès," in *Les Églises et leurs institutions au XVIe siècle. Actes du Vème Colloque de Centre d'Histoire de la Réforme et du Protestantisme*, ed. Michel Péronnet (Montpellier: 1978), 95–113.
7 Christopher McFadin, *The Fiscal Reformation in Rural France, 1598–1685* (PhD diss., University of Iowa, 2015); Raymond A. Mentzer, "Le consistoire et la pacification du monde rural," *BSHPF* 135 (1989), 373–89; Didier Poton, *Saint-Jean-de-Gardonnenque. Une communauté réformée à la veille de la Révocation (1663–1685)* (Gap: 1985). Pascal Rambeaud, *De La Rochelle vers l'Aunis: l'histoire des réformés et de leurs Églises dans une province française au XVIe siècle* (Paris: 2003).

While Emmanuel Le Roy Ladurie's classic division into *cardeurs huguenots et laboureurs catholiques*—Protestant artisans (textile workers in this example) of the town and Catholic peasants (or farmers) of the countryside—may be too facile a characterization of the confessional divide in early modern France, it does serve to evoke the general contours.[8] Members of the artisan and professional groupings certainly formed the backbone of French Protestantism, whether urban or rural. They worked in the leather and textile trades, pursued commercial and mercantile activities, practiced the various legal professions, functioned as notaries, and enjoyed careers as physicians and teachers. Women taught their children to pray in the French vernacular. Men served as elders and deacons. Families contributed to the financial wellbeing of the Church, owned Bibles and Psalters, attended sermon service on Sunday morning, and held regular private worship in their homes with evening Psalm-singing and Scriptural readings.[9]

In all of this, we must remember that Protestants in France were fundamentally a religious minority.[10] Although their situation had political and legal repercussions, the Huguenots possessed none of the reinforcing distinctions—race, ethnicity, language, or unique cultural traditions—that we typically associate with religious minorities in our contemporary world. Reformed congregations thought of themselves as a moral community distinguished by a biblically sanctioned understanding of Christianity. They were, in the ideal, the community of saints, who sought to differentiate their religious beliefs and ritual forms from the "superstitious" views and "idolatrous" practices of a scandalous Catholic Church. This situation changed with the flight of Huguenots from France in the mid-1680s. The emigrants were "strangers" in foreign lands and were recognized as such, principally by virtue of language and culture. Indeed, many refugees tenaciously clung to their unique Huguenot identity as they sought asylum in Switzerland, the Netherlands, Germany, the British Isles, North America and elsewhere. Assimilation, whether welcomed or resisted, could be a difficult process. Altogether, the Huguenots encountered formidable challenges and obstacles both at home and abroad even as they contributed to the enrichment of France and their foreign hosts. It is to this

---

8 Emmanuel Le Roy Ladurie, *Les paysans de Languedoc*, vol. 2 (Paris: 1966), 341–56.

9 Ezra L. Plank, *Creating Perfect Families: French Reformed Churches and Family Formation, 1559–1685* (PhD diss., University of Iowa, 2013).

10 For an extended discussion of the Huguenots as a minority, see Bertrand Van Ruymbeke, "Minority Survival: The Huguenot Paradigm in France and the Diaspora," in *Memory and Identity: The Huguenots in France and the Atlantic Diaspora*, eds. Bertrand Van Ruymbeke and Randy J. Sparks (Columbia, SC: 2003), 1–25.

remarkable community, its origins, painful history and manifest achievements that we turn.

The essays in the present collection focus on the initial Huguenot experience in the French homeland, the later 17th-century diaspora and resettlement in scattered exile communities across Europe, the Atlantic world and Southern Africa, and the close associations between the two developments. Who were the Huguenots and what were the features that distinguished them from other religious and political groups in France? What was their relationship to the French monarchy and the dominant, indeed overbearing Catholic ecclesiastical authorities? What roles did Huguenot women from the humblest to highest station assume within this highly patriarchal society? How did members of the educated Huguenot elite construct an intellectual tradition? And what of artistic achievements? Finally, how did those Huguenots who remained in France after the Revocation survive and eventually reconstruct their community and church? The late-17th-century diaspora poses a different, though hardly unrelated series of queries. What were the principal features of the Huguenot diaspora? And how do they accord with the general contours of other early modern religious migrations? How did the immigrants understand and narrate their experiences? What exactly do scholars mean in their employ of the terms assimilation and integration whether in continental Europe or the wider Atlantic world? What were the language shifts over time and how ought we to interpret them? To what extent was the diaspora linked to a concurrent yet broader imperial project? Finally, how did the Huguenot preserve the memory of their intense religious suffering and, in longer perspective, celebrate a cultural identity that persists to the present?

The historiography of the Huguenot movement within and without the French realm is longstanding and wide-ranging. Over the past century, historians have described and analyzed in detail the tortured history of the Huguenots in France and the subsequent emigration of a sizeable portion of the community seeking sanctuary abroad after 1685. These earlier studies have tended to privilege political and military events, theological and intellectual developments. They are not unimportant matters. On the other hand, recognizing the requirements for precision and concision, the present collection of essays consciously concentrates on the most recent and promising advances in scholarship on the movement in both France and the later Refuge. What are the freshest and most original questions with which scholars have engaged? To what sources have they turned in their exploration of these matters? What methodologies have they adopted? What are the results thus far? In keeping with this approach, each essayist has provided comprehensive bibliographic suggestions regarding the themes and issues under discussion. Readers seeking an extended treatment of the over-arching historiographical trends or bibliographic information for more traditional topics not specifically evaluated in this volume may wish to consult several recent surveys. They include, for France, Patrick Cabanel, *Histoire des protestants en France: XVIe–XXIe siècle* (Paris: 2012), Raymond Mentzer and Andrew Spicer (eds.), *Society and Culture in the Huguenot World, 1559–1685* (Cambridge: 2002) and Geoffrey Treasure, *The Huguenots* (New Haven: 2013). In addition, the final chapter in the present collection—Bertrand Van Ruymbeke's *"Le Refuge*: History and Memory from the 1770s to the Present"—offers an extensive and informative synthesis of the writing of Huguenot history and the various historical phases, stages, and attempts to preserve this history. It discusses fully and in detail the historiographic trends for the Huguenot dispersion.

Philippe Chareyre and Raymond Mentzer initiate the discussion at hand in tracing the formative decades of the Reformation in France. A variety of impulses for religious reform gradually coalesced around the Reformed views espoused by John Calvin and his associates. By the late-1550s and early 1560s, French Reformed Protestants, never more than a minority in an overwhelmingly Catholic kingdom, began to organize their churches in the so-called consistorial-synodal system. The emerging arrangements recognized the fundamental importance of the local church, while maintaining an elaborate hierarchy of colloquies and synods. How did the various institutions—individual churches and their consistories, regional colloquies (or presbyteries), and provincial and national synods—function? What were the responsibilities assigned to the three essential ministries: pastor, elder and deacon? What are the sources for studying these ecclesiastical structures and the officials who staffed them as well as the members of the congregation whom they served? How have scholars understood and explored the Huguenot project to reform both Church and society? What topics, methodologies and interpretive frameworks hold special promise for future study?

Marianne Carbonnier-Burkard addresses a complementary set of issues surrounding the theological precepts and liturgical practices associated with the Reformed tradition in France. The first national synod of the Reformed Churches of France, meeting at Paris in 1559, elaborated the doctrinal standards in a succinct yet comprehensive national Confession of Faith. Its 40 articles were, in many ways, a distillation of Calvin's *Institutes of the Christian Religion*. The Confession of Faith was soon added to the printed Psalter which, in turn, became a Huguenot "Book of Common Prayer." Pastors and elders inculcated these tenets of faith through rudimentary catechism lessons. Calvin, Charles Drelincourt and others published catechisms to guide pastors in their instruction of children and adults. The standard liturgical handbook, the *Forme des prières et chants ecclésiastiques*, contained the order for the sermon service, liturgies for the Supper, baptism and marriage, and instructions for visiting the sick. Overall, this was a highly structured and encompassing system with precise textual guidelines. Scholarly questions certainly remain. The details of catechism instruction and liturgical practices in the local churches, for instance, are not always as well understood as the prescriptive texts. Subtle differences in the various catechetical texts and the customs associated with household worship, especially after 1685, have not been fully sorted out. In general, how were these doctrinal views and related liturgical customs, above all the celebration of the two sacraments—Baptism and the Supper—understood and observed by the faithful?

Alongside these elaborations in the area of ecclesiastical polity and Church discipline, theology and liturgy, the Huguenots developed an important body of political thought and established distinct political institutions. Hugues Daussy takes as his starting point the conversion of noble men and women—the social and political, military and diplomatic elite of the ancien régime—to Protestantism. Once a leadership cadre was in place, political engagement, undergirded by the development of increasingly extreme political theory, followed. These elements of the enterprise effectively functioned as the midwife to a remarkable Huguenot political system. The Huguenot political assemblies and their role in the Wars of Religion hold particular interest. The assemblies have previously attracted historians' attention, but few scholars have been willing or able to undertake the painstaking research that their close, thorough examination project entails. Yet the assemblies and their activities are central to appreciating the Huguenot political party and its military endeavors. Here as elsewhere throughout the essay, Daussy evokes the myriad of rich possibilities for the further close scrutiny of the spectacular rise and equally stunning collapse of the Huguenot cause. What was the system and how did it evolve? What inspired it? How did it function? When and why did it dissolve?

Ending the destructive religious wars and encouraging all sides to coexist peacefully was, naturally enough, a critical concern, especially for the king among whose chief responsibilities were the safeguard of his subjects. "Making peace" and reducing conflict was, according to Jérémie Foa, a major objective for the crown throughout the Wars of Religion. Thus, Charles IX appointed and dispatched commissioners for the application of the edicts of pacification already in the 1560s. They modified the rhetoric of opposition, identified the key objects of contention, and sought to nudge everyone toward forgetting and reconciling. While more commonly associated with Henry IV's efforts to pacify the kingdom at the end of the 16th century, this initial effort to develop and utilize commissioners to resolve heated confessional differences proved an invaluable experiment. If Charles IX's goals were never realized, Henry IV profited enormously from the earlier attempts to use royal officials to mediate religious strife within the realm. That scholars have long neglected the subject is due, in part, to the scattered nature of the documentation and, in part, to the spectacular nature of war. If the violence of conflict has far too often mesmerized scholars, Foa's analysis of the intricacies of 16th-century peacemaking opens an original, central and enlightening avenue of inquiry.

The place and role of women in the extended Huguenot experience has been woefully neglected until the past several decades. Amanda Eurich adeptly demonstrates that women's involvement and agency was fundamental at every level of Huguenot society. Initial attention to women from the elites has now broadened to include individuals from all economic, political and social strata. Powerful figures such as Jeanne d'Albret, Queen of Navarre, provided crucial support and protection. Less prominent women assumed new roles, while continually adapting established traditions. The Reformed community offered fresh opportunities, whether in taking up arms, acting as spies and couriers, or protecting family property during the Wars of Religion. Though the Reformed Churches sought to circumscribe their liturgical roles and closely monitor their behavior, women soon found ways to use the consistory and other institutions to advantage. Wives suffering at the hands of abusive husbands or servant women treated unfairly by their employers might turn to the consistory as a court of appeal. The consistory could also serve to maintain or restore female sexual honor. Women, not unexpectedly, remained the primary vector for the religious education of their children and with the benefit of increased literacy entered the world of letters. Yet as Eurich notes, the meaning of the Reformation for women remains a subject of considerable debate. At the very least, the history of women in Huguenot communities is rich with additional, crucial research possibilities.

In all of this, Huguenot contributions in the intellectual and artistic spheres are particularly noteworthy. Cultural accomplishment was, of course, cherished for its own sake. In addition, these achievements helped to validate the broader religious commitment from which the Huguenots drew strength and purpose. Karin Maag addresses the issue directly in her essay on the manner by which an educated pastorate and distinguished professoriate molded the spiritual and moral outlook of the faithful. The pastors and professors were a relatively small, albeit cohesive group. They were bound together by familial ties and marriage. Many were the sons and grandsons of pastors. In addition, young pastors frequently married the daughters of pastors. These men trained together, following a uniform program at the various academies. They also shared standards of Christian conduct and mutual oversight. Inevitably, these intellectual leaders evinced a common agenda in their regular pronouncements from the pulpit and in their writings on the dangers of sin and the need for atonement. Carefully utilizing the wealth of primary materials accessible through Post-Reformation Digital Library, Maag offers a close reading of the pastors' published sermons and other writings. Her detailed explication of several key texts conveys their powerful theological and moral message that, in turn, served to shape the Huguenot community.

As pastors labored through their sermons and related published works to fashion a godly society, Huguenot artists and artisans sought to create an aesthetic standard. Following its 1648 founding, the Royal Academy of Painting and Sculpture had, during its early decades, a disproportionally large number of Huguenot members. Indeed, their influence within both Protestant and Catholic cultural circles far outweighed their numerical strength. Andrew Spicer points out that despite Calvin and other Reformed theologians' cautions regarding the promotion of idolatry, there was never an absolute prohibition on artistic endeavor. Huguenot artists flourished, receiving and accepting a variety of commissions from Protestant, but also Catholic patrons. Some of the earliest works depicted the horrors of the Wars of Religion; the engravings of Jean Perrissin and Jacques Tortorel are perhaps the best known. Later, 17th-century paintings fastened on biblical stories and religious events, many of them involving strikingly Catholic themes. Portraiture, including paintings of the Catholic monarchs and members of the royal court, was also an important element in Huguenot artistic achievement. Finally, landscape and still-life paintings as well as print production reveal the extent to which these artists worked across a wide spectrum of genres. Their contribution was significant and they obviously did not limit themselves to a Protestant audience. Catholic churches and nobles were among their prominent patrons. Indeed, Spicer concludes that Huguenot artists were pragmatists and professionals who were not constrained by confessional affiliation.

By the end of the 17th century and after decades of increasing pressure on the Huguenots, the monarchy proscribed Reformed worship, razed the temples and dismantled the institutional framework of the churches. Some Huguenots famously immigrated to other countries. The majority, however, chose to remain in their native kingdom, perhaps underestimating the tenacity of royal oppression. Who among them would have predicted that the *Désert*, terminology that established a vivid association with the Biblical ordeal of God's chosen people wandering in the wilderness, would endure so long and that the campaign to eradicate the Reformed religion would be so severe? Didier Boisson meticulously dissects developments over the long and painful century of religious proscription and persecution that followed the 1685 revocation of the Edict of Nantes. Tracing the evolution of the *Désert*, he divides it into three distinct eras: an initial period of intense persecution and unorganized secret worship; a subsequent age dominated by clandestine attempts to restructure and reestablish the churches; and, finally, a time of growing yet grudging toleration in which the Huguenots received civil status, but were not at liberty to worship openly. The faithful endured these difficulties by adopting a variety of strategies, ranging from armed resistance to passive disobedience. The approaches, some more successful than others, differed between the northern and southern reaches of the kingdom as well as between rural and urban churches. Responses to discrimination, mistreatment and cruelty also varied depending on social and economic status. Regrettably, friction between Protestant and Catholic did not end with the Revolution and, understandably, the memory of the rigors of the *Désert* persists to the present.

The traditional Huguenot unities of geography, language, culture and even confessional practices began to dissolve or, at the very least, were deeply challenged in the Refuge. The 150,000 to 200,000 French Reformed Protestants who fled abroad during the last decades of the 17th century were at once sincerely attached to their French homeland and deeply grateful to their hosts. The result was a predictable ambiguity toward political and legal institutions, different forms of worship, and integration into what was for them, at least initially, a "foreign" culture. How did individuals and communities accommodate themselves to the new surroundings and circumstances without compromising completely their own character and distinctive culture? In addition, many refugees soon discovered that they were at best cautiously welcomed by their hosts. In short, the tensions between the desire to maintain Huguenot identity and the practical need to assimilate was an ongoing problem that admitted no facile solution.

Susanne Lachenicht introduces the Refuge and its many elements with a comprehensive overview of diaspora studies. She then carefully explains the Huguenot networks that assisted flight and organized re-settlement. Finally, Lachenicht examines the immigration policies of the various states who received these religious refugees. Early modern diasporic studies, which Lachenicht characterizes as a young and promising research field, focuses on specific issues such as the terms and conditions for migrations, expulsions and re-settlement, and the legal status of ethnic and religious minorities. Integrating the Huguenot Refuge into the broader field of diaspora studies helps scholars to appreciate better the Huguenot experience as well as the role that religious migrations and religious minorities played in historical change during the early modern period. Certainly French Protestant networks existed from the earliest decades of the Reformation when many Huguenots, suffering persecution in their homeland, fled abroad. By the late 17th century an assemblage of networks—military and diplomatic, ecclesiastical, familial, literary and commercial—acted to aid a dramatically larger wave of refugees. How precisely these complex systems intertwined and what purposes they served awaits further investigation. Settlement conditions inevitably differed across the European landscape and Atlantic world, and immigration policies, over which refugee groups ultimately had less control than they wished, evolved according to the changing situation and interests of the host states.

Recurrent throughout the discussion of the diverse aspects of the Refuge are the processes of assimilation and integration. Myriam Yardeni begins with the observation that scholars have frequently underestimated the number of refugees. Here she takes issue with the figures proposed by other contributors to this volume. The immigrants tended, moreover, to be young, single and male. Most historians have viewed their assimilation and integration along linguistic and religious, social and political axes. For her part, Yardeni cautions that although assimilation and integration are strongly related terms, distinctions are necessary and useful. Assimilation is a process of accommodation and acculturation, involving language, dress and diet. Integration is an economic and political phenomenon. In England, the two experiences—assimilation and integration—joined together for the Huguenots. In the Netherlands, on the other hand, an ongoing economic crisis made economic integration difficult. Sometimes integration occurred faster than assimilation. In Prussia, for example, integration was almost immediate, whereas assimilation proceeded at a far slower pace. The multiplicity of different experiences makes it difficult if not impossible to construct a single model or paradigm. Perhaps the one common factor was the determinative role of government policies in the rhythm of assimilation and integration. Here Yardeni's survey of developments in England, Ireland, the Dutch Republic, Germany, Switzerland and the Atlantic colonies provides abundant evidence.

A key feature of Huguenot identity in exile was the French language. Its retention (or erosion) and the circumstances under which it functioned (or ceased to operate) are the subject of Manuela Böhm's chapter on the sociolinguistics of Huguenot communities in German-speaking lands. Noting the shift from a "national" to a "cultural" paradigm in conceptual and theoretical approaches in the study of the Huguenot diaspora, Böhm fastens upon the way in which language can be used as an indicator of acculturation. What were the languages uses, language changes and language policy strategies of the Huguenot communities in the German Refuge? Concentrating on four settlements—two urban and two rural—in Brandenburg-Prussia and Hesse, Böhm carefully elucidates the many complexities of language transformation for the refugees.

The Huguenots experienced a language shift, though at different paces in different parts of the German world, and their language repertoire gradually changed to that of the majority. The retention of the minority language (French) lasted longer in places where it functioned as a sacred language or, as in urban areas, where it conferred social and cultural distinction. Still, language choice was always an act of identity and the last Huguenot communities to adopt German did so in the course of the formation of a modern German national identity.

How then did the men and women who fled France understand and recount their experiences? Carolyn Chappell Lougee's careful reading of Huguenot memoirs suggests several fruitful lines of inquiry. Although the memoir was a popular practice in 17th-century France, these narrative recollections of personal experience were slow to emerge within the Huguenot orbit. The Revocation and ensuing Refuge were the obvious occasion for a number of Huguenot memoirs. Turning principally to the memoirs of Isaac Dumont de Bostaquet, Jacques Fontaine and Jean Migault, Lougee poses two critical queries and offers some preliminary responses. What in the experience of persecution, emigration and exile pushed Huguenots to write private histories? And how did the forms in which they wrote their memoirs make them congruent with Protestant doctrine despite Calvin's own disapproval of personal histories? Certain common features emerge in examining these Huguenot memoirs. They express a distinctively Huguenot religiosity, focus on everyday life, and celebrate family. These elements become the main trajectories for exploring the manner in which Huguenots memorialists transformed personal experience into a central part of their Reformed faith.

The notion that the vast majority of Huguenots who fled France did so for religious reasons permeates the contributions at hand. Not unexpectedly, narratives of martyrdom and suffering have always been central to the Huguenot exile experience. How scholars read these stories is of course crucial. Whereas an earlier generation tended to accept them at face value, historians have now adopted a more critical attitude. Centering his attention on the Dutch Refuge, David van der Linden approaches these refugee histories and martyrologies with an eye to the construction and employ of "vocabulary of victimhood." Some authors, the pastor Pierre Jurieu in his *Lettres pastorales* for instance, were concerned with a more traditional sort of martyrdom. Jurieu systematically collected and published in the *Lettres* individual accounts of the brutalities endured by Huguenots—whether men condemned to the galleys or women locked away in Catholic convents. Elie Benoist's five-volume *Histoire de l'Edit de Nantes* took a fresh and innovative approach—a method van der Linden dubs the archeology of persecution—by tracing the lengthy royal legal assault aimed at destroying Huguenot communities and demolishing their temples. Benoist systematically deconstructed the origins, mechanisms and effects of the judiciary's campaign against French Protestants These stories of Huguenot victimhood have beyond all doubt marked Huguenot identity for centuries. At the same time, van der Linden, much like Yardeni, stresses the need for future research comparing the Huguenot experience with other early modern religious diasporas.

Studies of Huguenot assimilation in the British Atlantic colonies have long underscored the refugees' rapid integration and willing conformity to the Church of England. Paula Carlo in her scrutiny of Huguenot congregations in New York and Massachusetts challenges or perhaps more accurately offers a more nuanced view of this widely accepted paradigm. While fully acknowledging our indebtedness to the interpretative models advanced by Jon Butler and Robert Kingdon, she and other scholars of a newer generation suggest that the issues are far from settled. The Huguenot embrace of the Church of England, such as it was, remains a complex matter. A rigorous evaluation of pastors' sermons and various ecclesiastical records quickly makes this clear. Conditions differed considerably from one settlement to another and no single explanation can be readily applied to explain Huguenot assimilation and religious conformity. New England Huguenots typically did not conform, whereas in New York the situation varied from one congregation to another. Accordingly, Carlo concludes that a more accurate understanding of the complexities of the Huguenot experience in the British North American colonies depends upon further study.

Though historians have long recognized that the Huguenot Refuge was a global phenomenon, they have, as Owen Stanwood notes, been less than systematic in investigating its dimensions. A few settlements have been examined minutely, while others have been neglected—as has the larger structure and purpose of these overseas communities. The flood of French religious immigrants sparked a crisis at the end of the 17th century as local Protestant authorities from to Rotterdam and London sought to accommodate them. At the same time, this influx of Huguenots created new opportunities for European expansion abroad as the British and Dutch attempted to strengthen and expand their empires. From the 1680s well into the 18th century, Huguenots featured prominently in British and Dutch imperial designs. British leaders, for instance, envisioned the refugees securing lands vacated by Catholics in Ireland, making silk or growing vines in the Carolinas, populating way stations along the route to the East Indies, and acting as evangelists to native people in the North American backcountry. The Dutch, meanwhile, tried to use Huguenots to create provisioning stations in South Africa and the Mascarene Islands for their East India ships, and to build up a plantation economy in Suriname. Most of these plans, which were often imbued with an additional distinctly utopian element, ended in failure. Yet when examined together, Stanwood argues, they demonstrate both the global nature of the Refuge and the ways in which state priorities helped to determine where the refugees went and what kinds of communities they built.

The institutionalization of the memory and history of the Refuge occurred in the second half of the 19th century. Bertrand Van Ruymbeke locates its beginnings in France with the 1852 founding of the Paris-based *Société de l'Histoire du Protestantisme Français* along with the Society's journal the *Bulletin*. The following year Charles Weiss published his seminal two-volume study of the Refuge, entitled *Histoire des réfugiés protestants de France depuis la Révocation de l'Edit de Nantes jusqu'à nos jours*. Later, on the occasion of celebrations commemorating the bicentennial of the Revocation in 1885, various Huguenot Societies were founded: the Huguenot Society of London (now Huguenot Society of Great Britain and Ireland), the Huguenot Society of America (based in New York), the Huguenot Society of South Carolina (based in Charleston) and the *Deutsch Hugenotten-Verein* (based in Frankfurt). Unfortunately, a prolonged period of disinterest in Huguenot history followed. Renewed academic treatment of the Huguenot dispersal coincided with the 1985 tercentenary of the Revocation and the 1998 quatercentenary commemoration of the Edict of Nantes. In recent years, the development of migration studies along with the concept of ethnicity has completely revitalized the historiography of the diaspora. Finally, in the 21st century historians are increasingly attentive to the Atlantic and global dimensions of the Refuge.

Taken together, these essays witness the rich and diverse history of the Huguenots in France and beyond. It is a complicated and tangled story of a religious minority whose members endured terrible hardships in the creation and preservation of their Church in France. This deplorable situation worsened dramatically by the late 17th century. The choices were few and unpleasant. Most French Reformed Protestants remained in the homeland and suffered through the *Désert*, yet another ordeal of Biblical proportions visited upon God's people. Others left the kingdom and became *réfugiés* in a diaspora that again appropriated time-honored Scriptural imagery. The Huguenot story is powerful and important in itself as well as in comparison with other diasporic histories. As the essays gathered here repeatedly suggest, rewarding paths of ongoing investigation await scholars. Unexplored sources in addition to already known materials read with fresh eyes, new historical themes and topics, creative approaches, recent methodologies and innovative interpretative frameworks will surely advance the field in unanticipated and productive ways.

PART 1

France

CHAPTER 1

Organizing the Churches and Reforming Society

Philippe Chareyre and Raymond A. Mentzer

1 Introduction: A Religious Minority without Magisterial Support

The Reformed Churches of France[1] never represented more than a minority of French Christians. They and their members, however, had substantial influence within the realm and eventually well beyond its frontiers. Beginning in the 1540s and intensifying over the course of the ensuing decade, Reformed propaganda in the form of printed treatises and itinerant preachers found a ready audience. Communities of belief secretly established the first churches by the mid-1550s. Yet Protestantism, despite initial promising growth, was far from dominant. To be sure, at the end of 1562, there were well over 800 congregations, and by 1570 more than 1200 churches. Huguenot numerical and political strength likely reached a high point on the eve of the Saint Bartholomew's Day massacre of August 1572; a precipitous decline followed thereafter. By the initial decade of the following century, the Huguenot population was less than a million persons.[2] On the other hand, the force and effect of Protestantism, notwithstanding the existence of rural churches, tended to be concentrated urban areas, above all in towns such as Castres, La Rochelle, Montpellier, Montauban and Nîmes in the southern and western provinces. In these and other localities, Huguenots exercised a powerful voice. Still, the Reformed Churches were at no time near to becoming an official Church; that role was reserved for Catholicism. The result was a tense, often violent relationship with the monarchical state. The Wars of Religion, which raged from 1562 until 1598 and then re-erupted briefly during the second and third decades of the following century, left their deadly mark on the Huguenot community. Even promises

---

1   The French Reformed Churches consistently used the plural, suggesting the federative nature of their organization with its emphasis on the local church.
2   Jonathan A. Reid, "French Evangelical Networks before 1555: Proto-Churches," in *La Réforme en France et en Italie. Contacts, comparaisons et contrastes*, (eds.) Philip Benedict, Silvana Seidel Menchi and Alain Tallon (Rome: 2007), 108. Philip Benedict, "The Dynamics of Protestant Militancy. France, 1555–1563," in *Reformation, Revolt and Civil War in France and the Netherlands, 1555–85*, (eds.) Philip Benedict, Guido Marnef, Henk van Nierop and Marc Venard (Amsterdam: 1999), 37; Philip Benedict, *The Huguenot Population of France, 1600–1685: The Demographic Fate and Customs of a Religious Minority* (Philadelphia: 1991), 75–8.

of peace and limited toleration proved ephemeral. The guarantee of civil status and political rights contained in the Edict of Nantes of 1598 was illusory. The monarchy gradually and relentlessly reduced opportunities for Protestants and eroded the protections that the Edict granted to Protestants.[3] Louis XIV revoked the legislation entirely in 1685. Not only was sustained state support for Protestants and their churches virtually nonexistent, the crown in close concert with the Catholic ecclesiastical authorities worked actively for their eradication.

Absent state backing and confronted by intense hostility, Reformed Protestants in France developed robust institutional structures that functioned independently from the magistrate. These forms—local churches and consistories, regional colloquies, and provincial and national synods—served to promote the reform of the individual and of society through the inculcation of correct belief and the encouragement of virtuous behavior. They also fortified the community in the face of continuing harsh treatment and regular persecution. In the century following the revocation of the Edict of Nantes, distinctive Reformed ecclesiastical polity along with its characteristic institutions bolstered and assisted Huguenots in their survival whether clandestinely in France or as refugees abroad.

The French Reformation had its origins around 1520, when Humanists and others, both on their own and in small groups, took an increased interest in spiritual and ecclesiastical renewal. In some cases, individuals were inspired by a reading of Martin Luther's works. In sum, they began to explore possibilities for reinvigorating the Christian Church and restoring its original pristine splendor. Sometimes dubbed an era of "evangelism,"[4] these developments did not constitute an organized movement, although they clearly underscored dissatisfaction with existing theological views, devotional practices and ecclesiastical organization. Not until the mid-1550s did the first Reformed Churches organize.[5] The Reformed Church of Paris, for example, was founded in 1555. There and elsewhere the new churches displayed a robust institutional character. The arrangement, best described as consistorial-synodal, flowed from

---

3   Raymond A. Mentzer, "The Edict of Nantes and its Institutions," in *Society and Culture in the Huguenot World, 1559–1685*, (eds.) Raymond A. Mentzer and Andrew Spicer (Cambridge: 2002), 98–116.

4   At the beginning of the last century, Pierre Imbart de Tour, *Les origines de la réforme*, vol. 3, *L'Évangélisme* (Paris: 1914) invoked the term evangelism—signaling a movement aimed at reform without seeking a break with Rome—to characterize the initial years of the French Reformation.

5   Reid, "French Evangelical Networks before 1555," in *La Réforme en France et en Italie*, 105–24.

longstanding Christian tradition as well as the Scriptural recoveries associated with John Calvin and others in the Protestant leadership. French Reformed ecclesiastical polity was in some ways patterned on, yet in other respects diverged from Genevan practices. While Gallican originality was prominent, the effect of Geneva ought not to be underestimated. The French model was, in turn, highly influential throughout the Reformed world.[6]

Although he spent the greater portion of his adult life at Geneva where he directed the transformation of that city's church, Calvin was in fact French and always considered the reform of his native land a major priority. Geneva's well-known *Ecclesiastical Ordinances* of 1541, whose preparation Calvin personally supervised, elaborated the institutions of the Christian Church with care and precision. This lucid articulation of the four ecclesiastical ministries—pastor, doctor, elder and deacon—along with the consistory served not only as the foundation for the Church of Geneva, but in time became a blueprint for Reformed churches elsewhere.[7] Not surprisingly, when Reformed Protestantism emerged in France during the late 1550s and early 1560s, its leaders generally followed Calvin's Genevan example in the constitution of the local church and its consistory. At the same time, the sheer size of the French kingdom—the geographically largest and most heavily populated dynastic state in Western Europe—pushed Protestants to develop a synodal structure to orchestrate unity and uniformity among the many individual churches.

Reformed Churches firmly rejected the notion of governance by bishops. They found the medieval episcopal system debased and distasteful. Their attitude was part of an overall critique of the Church during the Middle Ages. It had drifted dangerously, as they interpreted developments, from the model of a true Church as found in Scripture; the result was the wholesale corruption of the Roman Church and its hierarchy. Still, as a practical matter, French Calvinists needed a governing structure and they found the synodal system with its strong roots in early Christianity highly appealing.

A small group of pastors meeting at Poitiers in 1557 to settle certain issues relating to belief and governance formulated a set of elementary regulations

---

6 Glenn S. Sunshine, *Reforming French Protestantism: The Development of Huguenot Ecclesiastical Institutions, 1557–1572* (Kirksville, Mo.: 2003) traces the give and take between France and Geneva in the development of French Reformed ecclesiology.

7 The text of the *Ordonnances Ecclésiastiques* can be found in the *Registres de la Compagnie des Pasteurs de Genève du temps de Calvin*, (ed.) J.-F. Bergier, vol. 1, 1546–1553 (Geneva: 1964), 1–3 and 6–8; in English translation: "Ecclesiastical Ordinances," in *The Register of the Company of Pastors of Geneva in the Time of Calvin*, (ed.) and trans. Philip Edgcumbe Hughes (Grand Rapids, Mich.: 1966), 35–49.

entitled the *Articles polytiques pour l'Église réformée selon le Saint-Évangile*. The very first article detailed the new organization with precision and force:

> Because any notion of primacy is dangerous and leads to tyranny, as the papal example demonstrates, we shall guard against, indeed forbid, resolving matters that concern other churches without their consent; a legitimately assembled synod, whose delegates will be named by each church, shall deal with these questions.[8]

The later *Discipline of the Reformed Churches of France*, a church order adopted by Reformed ecclesiastical authorities at the initial meeting of the national synod at Paris in 1559, reinforced this opinion, declaring that "No church shall exercise primacy or power over another."[9] This sense of the fundamental equality of all churches and the prohibition against one church making decisions for another was also understood to mean the equality of ministers, and it eventually expanded to preclude any ecclesiastical province from exercising control over another. Altogether, the arrangement vested considerable authority and independence in the separate churches and their consistories, while maintaining a sophisticated synodal organization.

The delegates—pastors and elders—who assembled clandestinely at the 1559 gathering of the national synod in Paris formulated the text of the Gallican *Confession of Faith*[10] and also drafted regulations for the proper administration of the churches. Known literally as the *Discipline*, the latter document constituted instructions to the churches as well as their membership. The 1559 *Discipline*, which was regularly updated by successive meetings of the national synod, laid out the various principles and practices governing the organization of the churches. It prescribed the manner for administering baptism and celebrating the Lord's Supper, described institutional structures such as the consistory, colloquy and synod, defined the

---

8 "Articles politiques de Poitier," in *L'organisation et l'action des Églises réformées de France (1557–1563): synodes provinciaux et autres documents*, (eds.) Philip Benedict and Nicolas Fornerod, (Geneva: 2012), 1–7, citation p. 5.

9 Isaac d'Huisseau, *La Discipline des Eglises réformées de France ou l'ordre par lequel elles sont conduites et gouvernées* (Geneva: 1666), 117; and in the modern edition: François Méjan, *Discipline de l'Eglise Réformée de France annotée et précédée d'une introduction historique* (Paris: 1947), 241 and 301.

10 Jacques Pannier, *Les origines de la Confession de foi et de la Discipline des Églises réformées de France* (Paris: 1936). Richard Stauffer, "Brève histoire de la Confession de La Rochelle," BSHPF 117 (1971), 355–66. See the chapter by Marianne Carbonnier-Burkard, "Doctrine and Liturgy of the Reformed Churches of France" in this volume.

duties of pastors, elders and deacons, and explained Church financial administration. The *Discipline* also enumerated a variety of moral shortcomings and offered explicit directions to ecclesiastical officials for dealing with these problems and punishing offenders.

The key to the French consistorial-synodal model was the local community of faith. The structure vested substantial authority and considerable autonomy within the local Church, while maintaining an elaborate hierarchy of colloquies and synods. According to the *Discipline*:

> In each church there will be a consistory composed of individuals, notably the pastors and elders, who will conduct its proceedings. The pastors will preside over this company...[11]

The *Discipline* also indicated that in addition to the pastors and elders, the deacons were an integral part of the consistory's operation:

> As for the deacons, seeing that the churches, given the needs of the times, have until now successfully utilized them in the administration of the Church...[they] will normally be present...in the consistory.[12]

Calvin had, in the 1541 Genevan *Ecclesiastical Ordinances*, outlined the essential responsibilities of these three ministries.[13] The pastors preached. They were to "proclaim the Word of God...administer the sacraments, and...exercise fraternal discipline together with the elders..." The elders had the controversial duty to "watch over the life of each person, to admonish in a friendly manner those...at fault...[and]...to administer fraternal discipline." Elders were typically assigned a neighborhood over which they kept a careful daily supervision and were even expected to conduct annual visitations to every household in these districts. Finally, the deacons cared for the needs of the poor and other members of the congregation who were in distress.[14] Beyond the local congregation was an elaborate hierarchy of colloquies, provincial synods and national

---

11 D'Huisseau, *Discipline*, 84. Méjan, *Discipline*, 228.
12 D'Huisseau, *Discipline*, 84–85. Méjan, *Discipline*, 228–29.
13 The Genevan Church included a fourth ministry, that of doctor or teacher, whose task was to "instruct the faithful in sound doctrine..." In reality, the doctors trained future pastors in educational institutions such as the Academy of Geneva. The office of doctor never developed in the French churches.
14 "Ordonnances ecclésiastiques," in *Registres de la Compagnie des Pasteurs de Genève*, vol 1, 1546–1553, 1–13; "Ecclesiastical Ordinances," in *The Register of the Company of Pastors of Geneva in the Time of Calvin*, 35–49.

synods. Thorny issues, whose solution defied the local Church, were forwarded to the colloquies and provincial synods, and failing resolution by these bodies or if they seemed of broad significance, the matters passed to the national synod which had the option of integrating its decision into the national *Discipline*.

The Reformed consistory has become famous for its attempts to correct and improve people's everyday habits and ways of conducting themselves. Yet this aspect of consistorial engagement can be easily exaggerated. In reality, the French consistories were first and foremost ecclesiastical councils whose responsibilities stretched beyond morals control to include ecclesiastical administration, management of financial affairs, and assistance to the poor. In addition, scholars have come to understand that even in its seemingly coercive disciplinary pursuits, the consistory might be properly characterized as a compulsory counseling service as well as a morals court. Two specialists on the Genevan consistory—Robert M. Kingdon and Scott M. Manetsch—have presented the argument in its fullest elaboration. While far from discounting the importance of disciplinary endeavors, they have emphasized the pastoral efforts of the Genevan consistory. It sought to strengthen the family and marriage, pacify a disputatious society, and advance complex rituals of reconciliation. The ministers, according to Manetsch, were "spiritual shepherds" who strove to change "inward attitude[s] of the heart."[15]

While not exclusively a morals tribunal, the role of the consistory in implementing Church discipline cannot be ignored. According to Calvin, the marks of a true Church were "the Word of God purely preached and heard, and the sacraments administered according to Christ's institution." Discipline stood alongside these two identifying marks, though it was more a mark of the Christian and went to the wellbeing of the earthly Church. Thus, in addressing the Apostolic model of the Church in his 1539 debate with Cardinal Sadoleto, Calvin argued that "there are three things upon which the safety of the Church is founded, namely, doctrine, discipline, and the sacraments."[16] Calvin's fellow Frenchman and chief assistant at Geneva, Theodore Beza, was more emphatic

---

15   Robert M. Kingdon and Thomas Lambert, *Reforming Geneva: Discipline, Faith and Anger in Calvin's Geneva* (Geneva: 2012). Scott M. Manetsch, *Calvin's Company of Pastors: Pastoral Care and the Emerging Reformed Church, 1536–1609* (Oxford: 2013), 214–20.

16   John Calvin and Jacopo Sadoleto, *A Reformation Debate*, (ed.) John C. Olin (New York: 1966), 63. John Calvin, *Institutes of the Christian Religion*, 4.1.10. *Ioannis Calvini Opera quae supersunt omnia*, (eds.) G. Baum, E. Cunitz and E. Reuss, vol. 2 (Brunswick: 1863–1900), col 754. *Institutes of the Christian Religion*, (ed.) John T. McNeill and trans. Ford Lewis Battles, vol. 2 (Philadelphia: 1960), 1024.

in his approach, deeming discipline—the promotion of virtue and punishment of sin—an important mark of the church.[17]

As noted, a highly structured synodal arrangement built upon the French churches and their consistories. A pastor and elder from each of a dozen or so local churches gathered in the colloquy two to four times each year. The frequency seems to have varied over time. A pastor unaccompanied by an elder, or vice-versa, was not to be received. Churches with more than one pastor were expected to have them attend on a rotational basis. The local churches were required to reimburse their deputies' expenses. Both pastors and elders were voting delegates. Similar delegations from the churches within each of the sixteen French ecclesiastical provinces met once or twice a year in the provincial synod. The provinces, in turn, appointed two pastors and two elders to attend the national synod, which initially convened annually, but as time wore on and pressure from the French Catholic monarchy increased, met irregularly. Twenty-nine national synods convened in France between May 1559, when delegates from a dozen churches assembled in Paris, and November 1659–January 1660, the occasion for thirty pastors and twenty elders to gather at Loudun.[18] The provincial and national synods elected "in a low voice"—presumably each delegate whispered his choice to the person conducting the election—and by "common accord" a pastor to serve as moderator and one or two men to record the proceedings. An official copy of the acts of each national synod was to be confided to the delegation from the province where the next meeting was to occur. The colloquies and synods settled both administrative and theological matters. They clarified belief, fixed policy, developed comprehensive ecclesiastical regulations, regulated financial affairs, and resolved a variety of disputes.

Individual consistories were subject to the authority of the colloquy, which, in turn, was subject to the jurisdiction of the provincial synod. The French national synod, which stood atop this hierarchy of assemblies, had the power to "definitively decide and resolve" all ecclesiastical questions.[19] The national synod, in particular, possessed considerable legislative and judicial powers. In

---

17 Théodore de Bèze, *Confession de la foy chrestienne, contenant la confirmation d'icelle, et la refutation des superstitions contraires* (Geneva: 1559), 156–57. Glenn Sunshine, "Discipline as the Third Mark of the Church: Three Views," *Calvin Theological Journal* 33 (1998), 469–80.

18 Bernard Roussel and Solange Deyon, "Pour un nouvel 'Aymon.' Les premiers Synodes nationaux des Eglises réformées en France (1559–1567)," *BSHPF* 139 (1993), 545–46.

19 D'Huisseau, *Discipline*, 122–53. Méjan, *Discipline*, 244–56. Paul de Félice, *Les protestants d'autrefois. Vie intérieure des églises. Mœurs et usages. Les conseils ecclésiastiques. Consistoires, colloques, synodes* (Paris: 1899), 264–360.

addition to composing a national confession of faith and adopting detailed ecclesiastical regulations, it acted, along with the colloquies and provincial synods, as a board of appeal for the resolution of difficult questions and disagreements arising within local churches, colloquies and provincial synods.

2   The Manuscript Sources and Publication Projects

The surviving documentation for the study of the French Reformed Churches is certainly less abundant than scholars might wish, but probably richer than commonly assumed. Pastors and elders were diligent record keepers. The Reformed Churches pioneered in the maintenance of baptismal, marriage and burial registers. These efforts in the realm of vital statistics were matched by lists of persons received into the church, rolls of worthy and unworthy communicants, and records of impoverished men and women eligible for assistance. Local consistories kept a written record of their weekly deliberations as well as financial receipts and expenditures. Churches typically saved official correspondence, and delegates to colloquies and various synods both provincial and national often returned to their home communities with copies of the official proceedings. The archives of the Church of Montauban at the end of the 17th century provide instructive insight.

Subsequent to the Revocation, royal officials, working under explicit direction from Louis XIV's government, systematically identified and largely destroyed the archives of the churches. Thus, the king's agents gathered the records of the Reformed Church of Montauban, sorted through them with remarkable care, and drew up an "Inventory of books, registers and papers."[20] This inventory contained a substantial number of financial ledgers: nineteen account books of funds collected for the poor, fifteen rolls of levies imposed on members of the congregation, and thirty-five registers detailing receipts and expenditures. There were also proceedings from various colloquies as well as provincial and national synods, a copy of the *Discipline des Églises réformées de France*, and three registers of conversions from the mid-1560s to the 1580s. Royal officers also counted fifty-five registers of baptisms, marriages and burials. Finally, the inventory listed twenty-one registers of consistory deliberations beginning in 1566 and ending in 1663. The officer in charge of this endeavor to collect and enumerate the Montauban papers then ordered the burning of all the materials with the notable exception of the birth, marriage and death records. The latter were spared because they served a vital public

---

20   AN, TT 255, dossier 35.

interest. The determined, albeit selective destruction of the church archives at Montauban suggests the general contours of the surviving manuscript sources.

The registers of baptism, marriages and funerals are the most voluminous. Though they remain almost exclusively in manuscript form, recent developments make them increasingly accessible. Gildas Bernard, former Inspector General of the Archives of France, edited an extremely helpful guide and inventory of the Protestant *état-civil* for the Ancien Régime.[21] In addition, departmental archives throughout France have increasingly digitalized and made available on their individual web sites the manuscript registers of Reformed births, marriages and deaths.

If the demographic sources are relatively plentiful, the records of the deliberations of the consistories are decidedly sparse. Relatively few survived the devastation associated with the Revocation. The documentation exists largely in manuscript form; only a handful of registers have been published. The manuscripts, moreover, are fragmentary and are widely scattered in archival repositories and libraries across France. Raymond Mentzer has recently published an inventory of the extant registers for the period between the early 1560s, from which the earliest registers date, and the proscription of Protestantism in 1685.[22] He has identified 309 surviving registers from 156 different churches. About one-third are housed in Paris at the Archives Nationales, the Bibliothèque du Protestantisme Français, the Bibliothèque de l'Arsenal and the Bibliothèque Nationale. The remainder are located in the provinces, mostly in the various departmental and municipal archives, but also in the hands of local churches and private individuals. One quarter of the registers are from the period prior to the Edict of Nantes, the remainder cover the years between 1598 and 1685. The oldest are from the 1560s. The deliberations of the consistory of Le Mans, for instance, begin in January 1561 and those from the consistory of Nîmes commence on March of the same year.[23] The 309 surviving registers appear to represent about 10 per cent of the original materials.[24]

---

21   Gildas Bernard, *Les familles protestantes en France, XVIe siècle-1792. Guide des recherches biographiques et généalogiques* (Paris: 1987).

22   Raymond A. Mentzer, *Les registres des consistoires des Églises réformées de France, XVIe–XVIIe siècles. Un inventaire* (Geneva: 2014).

23   Médiathèque Louis Aragon, Le Mans, Ms. 66ter (microfilm Mi 115), Registre des délibérations du consistoire du Mans, du 1er janvier 1561 au 26 février 1562. BnF, Ms. fr. 8666, Registre du consistoire de l'Église chrétienne de la ville de Nîmes (1561–1562) du 23 mars 1561 au 27 janvier 1563.

24   This impression is confirmed by Eugène Arnaud who noted on 15 July 1871: "On n'a retrouvé pour le Dauphiné que les registres des consistoires de Gap, L'Albenc,

No more than a tiny fraction of the consistory registers has been edited and published. In 1998, François Francillon published the five registers of the Reformed Church of L'Albenc, covering the years 1606–82. L'Albenc was the site where the faithful from Grenoble gathered regularly for worship. More recently, Philip Benedict and Nicolas Fornerod have made available one of the earliest consistory registers, that of Le Mans from 1561–62.[25] The other earliest surviving register comes from Nîmes and encompasses the period 1561–63. Philippe Chareyre is presently preparing an edition of this initial register from the Nîmes consistory.

The paucity of records for the colloquies, provincial synods and even the national synods is equally striking. Colloquies and synods at every level in the French Reformed Churches had no permanent bureaucratic staff or offices. Their decisions were carefully recorded by scribes, but the acts were not published except for the national synods. Even then publication occurred much later, and on an unofficial and incomplete basis. There was an English edition by John Quick in 1692 and a subsequent French edition by Jean Aymon in 1710.[26] The local churches often maintained, for their own use, transcripts of the articles passed by the national synods. As a result, the surviving manuscript copies are scattered in a variety of repositories. In an attempt to draw the sources together and make them available in critical editions, a number of publication projects are underway. Françoise Chevalier recently edited the acts of the two final national synods held at Charenton in 1644 and at Loudun in 1659.[27] Didier Boisson has established a critical edition of the acts of the provincial synods of Anjou, Touraine and Maine for the period 1594–1683.[28] Philip Benedict and Nicolas Fornerod have published a variety of documents from the formative period of the late-1550s and early 1560s. They include

---

Die, Dieulefit et Beaumont. Or il y avait plus de 70 consistoires dans la province." AD, Drôme, J 710.

25   François Francillon (ed.), *Livre des délibérations de l'Eglise réformée de l'Albenc (1606–1682). Edition du manuscrit conservé à la Bibliothèque d'Etude et d'Information Fonds Dauphinois. Grenoble Cote R 9723* (Paris: 1998). "Registre du Consistoire de l'Église du Mans," in *L'organisation et l'action des Églises reformées de France*, (eds.) Benedict and Fornerod, 176–253.

26   John Quick (ed.), *Synodicon in Gallia Reformata, or the acts, decisions, decrees, and canons of those famous national councils of the Reformed churches in France* (2 vols. London: 1692). Jean Aymon (ed.), *Tous les synodes des Eglises réformées de France* (2 vols. The Hague: 1710).

27   Françoise Chevalier (ed.), *Actes des synodes nationaux. Charenton (1644)—Loudun (1659)* (Geneva: 2012).

28   Didier Boisson (ed.), *Actes des synodes provinciaux. Anjou-Touraine-Maine (1594–1683)* (Geneva: 2012).

numerous records from provincial synods.[29] Inevitably, additional manuscripts remain to be consulted and compared, edited and published, a task which Bernard Roussel and other scholars have begun.[30] Finally, colloquies also kept written summaries, whose survival is at best random and fragmentary. Often the best sources for these documents are the consistorial registers of local churches wherein the decisions were occasionally recorded.

3   The Evolution of Institutional Functions and Procedures

Given the absence of support from the state in the development of the institutional structure of the Reformed Churches of France, consistories throughout the realm differed in their composition and function. Mentzer's inventory of consistory registers amply displays the differing practices among local churches.[31] Despite the directives of the national *Discipline* of the Reformed Churches, consistorial arrangements were the result of the circumstances surrounding the establishment of the Reformation in each locale, the relationship between Reformed communities and local civil authorities, differences between rural and urban adaptations, and finally the minority status or, less commonly, majority status of Protestant communities in a kingdom that remained overwhelmingly Catholic.

Still, the institutional flexibility of the consistory fit within the broader framework of the consistorial-synodal system which accorded the elders charge over the daily administration of the church. They were usually assisted by the deacons who had responsibility over the management of charitable assistance. The number and function of the elders and deacons varied from one church to another. At Nîmes, there was a deacon for every two elders, but the ratio was different in nearby rural communities. There were ten elders and two deacons at Gallargues, and six elders and two deacons at Aimargues. Some towns, Aigues-Mortes for instance, had no deacons. The Church at Pau had ten elders, but did not designate precise supervisory districts. The Churches of Alès and Montauban had twenty elders, while that of Albenc had sixteen.[32]

---

29   Benedict and Fornerod (eds.), *L'organisation et l'action des Églises reformées de France*.
30   Roussel and Deyon, "Pour un nouvel 'Aymon'," BSHPF 139 (1993), 545–595. Françoise Chevalier, "Les Actes des synodes nationaux: éditions et études. Un bilan historiographique," BSHPF 150 (2004), 63–83.
31   Mentzer, *Les registres des consistoires*.
32   Suzanne Tucoo-Chala, "L'Eglise réformée de Pau au XVIIe siècle," *Revue de Pau et du Béarn* 15 (1988), 75–104. Francillon, *Livre des délibérations de l'Albenc*, 26, 172–73, 198–99.

This quick overview makes clear the extent to which Reformed polity adapted to the size of the local community and its administrative traditions. Thus, at Nîmes and the surrounding region as well as at Metz, the deacons occupied an influential position in the conduct of consistorial business, well beyond their initial role in supervising poor relief.[33] Finally, members of the consistory also performed additional functions, serving as collector of funds for the ministry (*receveur des deniers du ministère*), collector of funds for the poor (*receveur des deniers des pauvres*), auditor of the church's financial accounts, and scribe or secretary.

Deacons and elders, lay persons who held crucial positions in keeping with the notion of the priesthood of all believers, were limited in their tenure. The members of these ministries were typically selected from among the heads of families within the community. In theory, they served an annual term, but in practice their charge could be renewed for longer periods, in some cases for three or four years, or even longer in smaller communities where the candidate pool was limited. The consistory generally met in the temple, or somewhat exceptionally in a designated consistory chamber. Meetings occurred weekly in the larger cities, less often in rural churches, where much depended on the size of the community and the urgency of the matters to be discussed.

Urban churches had salaried officials whose roles have yet to be examined thoroughly. They performed non-ministerial functions for which they were poorly paid. They were cantors and bell-ringers, who might also serve as caretakers for the temple. In some southern towns such as Nîmes, there was also a summoner (*advertisseur*), generally selected from the artisan milieu. He was responsible for the regular upkeep of the temple, and the maintenance of the registers of baptism, marriage, burial and conversion. Yet his principal function, which explains the name, was to inform individuals of their summons to appear before the consistory and to accompany them to the door of the chamber on the appointed day. At Nîmes, the summoner kept a register of summons, which adds significantly to our understanding of consistorial activity because a substantial number of those summoned, particular for minor matters, do not appear in the consistory registers.[34]

The consistory had complete charge over the management of the material and financial affairs of the local Church (payment of pastors, and construction

---

33 Philippe Chareyre, "'La fleur de tous les anciens' ou le ministère des diacres à Nîmes XVIe–XVIIe," in *Agir pour l'Eglise. Ministères et charges ecclésiastiques dans les Eglises réformées (XVIe–XVIIe)*, (eds.) Didier Poton and Raymond A. Mentzer (Paris: 2014), 95–115.

34 Philippe Chareyre, "Le consistoire et l'advertisseur: étude croisée de deux séries de registres nîmois XVIe–XVIIe siècles," *BSHPF* 153 (2007), 525–42.

and maintenance of the temples), liturgical arrangements (the Wednesday and Sunday sermon services, catechism, fasts and services of thanksgiving). Yet it was the administration and distribution of social assistance as well as religious and moral supervision that constituted the bulk of the consistory's activity and dominates the cases and concerns recorded in its registers. To this end, the consistory established a geographic grid, dividing municipal space into "surveillance" districts, "quarters," or "cantons" depending upon the locality, for the close supervision of the faithful. The initial model was the Church of Geneva where the creation of supervisory districts dated from 1537. The Genevan ordinances of 1541 set their number at twelve. An elder had responsibility for each district and was assisted by the *dizeniers*, who were assigned to the twenty-five *dizaines*, originally a military territorial arrangement that predated the Reformation. Together, the elders and *dizeniers* worked to settle endless neighborhood quarrels.[35]

Within France, scholars are best informed for the town of Nîmes, due mainly to the existence of a near complete set of consistory registers for the period 1561–1685.[36] The first register begins with the 23 March 1561 deliberation and the selection of elders and deacons. At this same session, consistory members divided the town into ten districts for the purpose of close supervision of the faithful.[37] In light of subsequent demographic growth, a special consistory session of 12 December 1619, modified the original plan and authorized the establishment of two additional districts within the city's walls. The Nîmes consistory simultaneously increased the number of deacons to six and the number of elders to twelve. The elders now corresponded to the highly symbolic number of Apostles, an arrangement that had long existed in Geneva.[38]

Practices surrounding the division of urban space varied considerably. At Le Mans, there were five supervisors or elders, one for each "canton," along with two deacons.[39] Loudun, whose consistorial activities are well-documented in a substantial series of registers, had eight elders, each assigned to a specific

---

35 Christian Grosse, *Les rituels de la Cène. Le culte eucharistique réformé à Genève, XVIe–XVIIe siècles*, (Geneva: 2008), 249–50.

36 Philippe Chareyre, *Le consistoire de Nîmes 1561–1685* (Doctoral diss., Université de Montpellier III, 1987).

37 Philippe Chareyre, *Premier registre du consistoire de Nîmes* (Geneva: forthcoming). BnF, Ms. 8666, f°1 v°.

38 Philippe Chareyre, "Protestantisme et structuration de l'espace urbain: Nîmes 1561–1685," in *Le protestantisme et la cité*, (eds.) Guy Astoul and P. Chareyre (Montauban: 2013), 111–30.

39 "Registre du Consistoire de l'Église du Mans," in *L'organisation et l'action des Églises reformées de France*, (eds.) Benedict and Fornerod, 178–79.

"canton."[40] The situation at Sainte-Marie-aux-Mines in Alsace was highly unusual. The Church there created four "quarters," each with two elders, one German and one French; and two deacons served the entire community.[41] The eight elders who sat on the consistory of Saint-Jean-du-Gard were in 1672 joined by eleven additional ones for the surrounding villages.[42]

The partition of urban space by the consistory was wholly different from the traditional geography laid down by Catholic parish boundaries. As such, the new rendering allowed the Reformed Church to lay claim to this space and to imbue it with its own standards. This was the world of daily Christian life, which complemented the communal gathering in the temple to hear the preaching of the Word. This space became the indisputable everyday structure for morals control and the formation of the new Christian. The street and the square were the public locales where the faithful took notice of one another's behavior and where the elders learned of the "disorders" that had occurred in the private sphere. This religious investment of public space served to sacralize the ordinary and as such sanctified the street.

4   The Institutions and the Faithful: The Creation of Reformed Identity and Social Cohesion

The extreme importance that consistories accorded to the individual and collective supervision of the faithful has led historians to situate their analysis in a wider European context. They have focused on the development of a society in which the individual was subject to new standards decreed by an ever more powerful state even as the new churches imposed practices and behavior that represented a rupture with traditional customs. Within the framework of this double supervision, the handling of morals offenses—in excruciating detail and often in great number—made the consistory the most active agent in the construction of a modern mannered society. Characterized originally in the 1970s as "social discipline" (*Sozialdisziplinierung*),[43] the

---

40   Edwin Bezzina, *After the Wars of Religion: Protestant-Catholic Accommodation in the French Town of Loudun, 1598–1665* (PhD diss., University of Toronto, 2004).

41   Michelle Magdelaine, "Censurer-exclure dans un environnement pluriconfessionnel, l'exemple de Sainte-Marie-aux-Mines au dix-septième siècle," in *Dire l'interdit: The Vocabulary of Censure and Exclusion in the Early Modern Reformed Tradition*, (eds.) Raymond A. Mentzer, Françoise Moreil and Philippe Chareyre (Leiden: 2010), 309–32.

42   Didier Poton, *Saint-Jean-de-Gardonnenque. Une communauté réformée à la veille de la Révocation (1663–1685)* (Paris: 1985), 80 and 107.

43   Gerhard Oestreich, *Neostoicism and the Early Modern State* (Cambridge: 1982).

concept was extended during the following decade by Wolfgang Reinhard and Heinz Schilling. They proposed the paradigmatic process of confessionalization (*Konfessionalisierung*), into which the pedagogical dimension of the consistory's task was integrated, leading to the construction of a new Christian identity in Europe.[44]

The consistory assumed a double task: the reform of gesture and belief as well as of behavior. The individual, the family, and social groupings, deprived of other intercessors, were forced to conform to this new mold, the only one capable of bestowing upon them divine beneficence. Quantitative analysis of the registers of the Nîmes consistory displays a strong differentiation among consistorial preoccupations. Attendance at sermon service, participation in the Lord's Supper and good behavior during the worship services were ultimately lesser concerns, as were worries over enforcing Reformed theological orthodoxy, condemning the contamination of belief by contact with Catholicism, or eliminating resort to magical practices. The principal interest of the consistory was the moral supervision of society, the establishment of a fraternal Christian community, and the elimination of violent behavior.

French consistories, which did not have the support of the secular authorities, could only impose ecclesiastical sanctions. They ranged, according to the national *Discipline*, from simple admonition to censure, and ultimately excommunication. The consistorial procedure unfolded in four stages: the gathering of information, an acknowledgement of guilt by the sinner, administration of punishment, and finally penitential reparation. The process was fairly rapid in the case of a simple admonition followed by censure; it could be more protracted for grave offenses that involved suspension from the Supper.

The first phase began when the consistory received a report that a transgression had occurred. The information could come directly from the elders or by rumor, often relayed by women. Suzannah Lipscomb has shown that women, though excluded from holding ecclesiastical offices, could, as witnesses to

---

[44] Wolfgang Reinhard, "Reformation, Counter-Reformation and the Early Modern State: A Reassessment," *Catholic Historical Review* 75 (1989), 383–404. Heinz Schilling, "Confessionalization in the Empire: Religious and Societal Change in Germany between 1555 and 1620," in H. Schilling *Religion, Political Culture and the Emergence of Early Modern Society: Essays in German and Dutch History* (Leiden: 1992), 205–45. Joel F. Harrington and H.W. Smith, "Confessionalization, Community, and State Building in Germany, 1555–1870," *Journal of Modern History* 69 (1997), 77–101. Gérald Chaix, "La confessionnalisation. Note critique," BSHPF 148 (2002), 851–65. Philip Benedict, "Confessionalization in France? Critical Reflections and New Evidence," in *Society and Culture*, (eds.) Mentzer and Spicer, 44–61.

events in the public square, demonstrate their ability to influence, perhaps even manipulate, the workings of the consistory.[45]

The second phase involved the appearance of the presumed sinner before the elders. The sinner received a stern warning never to repeat the offense or, if he or she denied fault, was told to reappear at a later date to be confronted by the witnesses to the misdeed. In most instances, the individual repented immediately and was subject to a simple censure. In the case of grievous failings, the consistory imposed a temporary suspension from the Supper. This could also be a preventative measure in instances where the inquiry into the matter had not yet concluded. Depending upon the gravity and the degree of public knowledge of the transgression, the suspension could be private and pronounced within the consistory chambers, or public and announced from the pulpit on Sunday.

The final phase was reparation, private or public depending upon the nature of the suspension. Penance, whether private on one's knees in the consistory chambers or public in front of the entire congregation at the conclusion of the Sunday sermon service, served as both an element of dissuasion and a means of edification; its role ought not to be underestimated. Integrated into the Reformed liturgy, the penitential ritual was meant as much to reconcile the sinner with the Church as to leave its mark on the spirit of the faithful, reaffirming the legitimacy of Reformed discipline and, in a larger sense, the Reformation itself.

This sort of excommunication generally lasted for no more than one or two celebrations of the Supper, an event which occurred four times a year. Following late-medieval practices,[46] suspension was more often than not imposed when the sinner refused to make amends, resisted the consistory, and thereby rebelled against the authority of the Church.[47] The French *Discipline* envisioned temporary suspension from the Supper as a means to "humble sinners and move them to repentance, and also to prompt a sense of dread among others."[48] Suspension was applied variously—regularly and effectively by the

---

45 Suzannah Lipscomb, "Refractory Women: the limit of power in the French Reformed Church," in *Dire l'interdit*, 13–28.

46 Raymond A. Mentzer, "The Reformed Churches of France and Medieval Canon Law," in *Canon Law in Protestant Lands*, (ed.) R.H. Helmholz (Berlin: 1992), 165–85 and idem, "*Disciplina nervus ecclesiae*: The Calvinist Reform of Morals at Nîmes," SCJ 18 (1987), 110.

47 Salomon Rizzo, "*Qui refusera la réconciliation sera interdit de la Sainte Cène*. Entre exclusion et intégration, La régulation consistoriale des conflits sociaux à Genève, dix-sept, dix-huitième siècles," *Dire l'interdit*, 178–99.

48 D'Huisseau, *Discipline*, 96. Méjan, *Discipline*, 233.

southern consistories, but far less often at Loudun in central France.[49] The frequency of suspension should be understood as a function of context. In strong and secure churches such as Nîmes, suspensions from the Supper were common, while in isolated or weaker ones, the consistory hesitated to stigmatize the faithful lest the excommunicated convert to Catholicism and thereby diminish the Reformed community.

Full excommunication remained rare, representing only 3 per cent of the suspensions in the sample of southern French churches studied by Mentzer.[50] It was reserved for the "obstinate and impenitent following a long waiting period" and was only imposed after have been announced from the pulpit on four successive Sundays.[51] Since the consistory organized the liturgy, it was charged with the material preparation of the Supper as well as its spiritual supervision. It possessed three instruments for the discharge of this latter task. The first was the register of deliberations which recorded the cases that had been discussed and the sanctions imposed. The second was the lists or "rolls," notably those which contained the names of suspect persons in instances of collective faults such as participation in dances, charivaris and carnival or, more seriously, the list of individuals suspended from the Supper. The third and final elements was the token (*méreau*), fashioned of lead or tin, which each elder delivered on the eve of the Supper to those in his district deemed worthy of participation.

All of these procedures along with their written documentation had the double goal of reforming the faithful and presenting a united, sanctified community to the Creator. The consistory sought to demonstrate that it had fulfilled its task as guardian of the flock and prevented the faults of a few from bringing divine judgment upon the entire community.

The very first mission of consistories everywhere was to insure the passage from the old to the new Church, then when Catholicism was not completely supplanted, to prevent contact with former beliefs and practices, now considered impure and idolatrous. The elders watched, in particular, for those who continued to attend Mass and participate in other Catholic ceremonies, whether out of curiosity or through attraction to the renewed splendor initiated by Tridentine reforms. They also labored to curb cross-confessional social

---

49   Edwin Bezzina, "The Consistory of Loudun, 1589–1602: Seeking an Equilibrium between Utility, Compassion and Social Discipline in Uncertain Times," in *Dire l'interdit*, 239–71.
50   Raymond A. Mentzer, "Marking the Taboo: Excommunication in the French Reformed Churches," in *Sin and the Calvinists: Morals Control and the Consistory in the Reformed Tradition*, (ed.) Raymond A. Mentzer (Kirksville, Mo.: 1994), 104; 22 of 531 cases.
51   D'Huisseau, *Discipline*, 96. Méjan, *Discipline*, 233.

ties in condemning participation in Catholic baptisms (especially as godparents), betrothals, marriages and burials, and sending children to study at Jesuit schools. To thwart confessional contamination and further demographic weakening of a community that was already a minority, the consistory repeatedly denounced mixed marriages.[52] The principal fear was the abjuration, if only temporary, of faith that was usually required to marry someone of "contrary religion" (a Catholic), followed by uncertainty regarding the confessional upbringing of the couple's future children.[53]

Consistories were equally dedicated to defending the Church against the temptations of Satan. His manifestations included blasphemous oaths invoking the devil, divination, white magic, poisonings and spells such as the notorious satanic ligature, a widely accepted late-sixteenth and early 17th century magical spell that was thought to doom a newly married couple to sterility.[54] The maintenance of religious orthodoxy occupied consistories most everywhere far less. Still, these admittedly rare affairs tend to figure in scholarly analyses because they were often referred to the synod where matters of general interest to the churches were discussed.

The consistory was ever attentive to the family and the institution of marriage, suppressing attempts to break betrothal promises and marital engagements, and cracking down on illicit sexual affairs before and after marriage. Extramarital liaisons only created household discord. The consistory spared no effort in its inquiries; multiple discussions and a variety of testimony, often highly detailed and colorful, lent these matters a prominent place in consistorial proceedings. The elders' intervention in family matters was not limited to these external problems. They also sought to insure that the family cell was a pacified and tranquil space. Thus, the elders worked to end disputes between husbands and wives, and between parents and children; they chastised violent spouses and strongly discouraged harsh treatment of servants. The desire for familial peace and harmony was part of a broader goal to establish public order. Both were essential for the advance of Christ's reign. Love of one's neighbor was inseparable from the love of God, as all were reminded by the

---

52 Elisabeth Labrousse, "Les mariages bigarrés," in *Le couple interdit. Entretiens sur le racisme*, (ed.) Léon Poliakov (Paris: 1980), 159–176. Didier Boisson and Yves Krumenacker (eds.), *La coexistence confessionnelle à l'épreuve. Etudes sur les relations entre protestants et catholiques dans la France moderne* (Lyon: 2009).

53 Philippe Chareyre, "Les réceptions dans l'Église réformée de Nîmes au XVIIe siècle: entre incorporation civique et religieuse," in *La religion vécue. Les laïcs dans l'Europe moderne*, (eds.) Laurence Croq and David Garrioch (Rennes: 2013), 97–119 and 253–61.

54 Raymond A. Mentzer, "The Persistence of 'Superstition and Idolatry' among French Rural Calvinists," *Church History* 5 (1991), 1629.

inscription in the temple at Calvisson, a village near Nîmes: "Love thy God and thy neighbor as thyself. May 1597" (*Aime ton Dieu et ton prochain come toy meme. 1597 de may*).

The pacifying activity of the consistory extended to the whole of society and existed throughout Europe. This social role is clear at Nîmes[55] and in the ten southern French communities studied by Mentzer. In the latter instances, 22 per cent of suspensions from the Supper resulted from violent comportment.[56] Aggressive behavior was also the leading reason for censure at Loudun. This was again the case in the rural world of southern France where 41 per cent of censures were for fighting and other forms of combative conduct.[57] Reconciliation in these situations followed several models. The most common was a mutual renunciation of all animosity, which was sealed with a handshake or kissing of one another's hands. A reciprocal declaration that the parties now regarded one another as "respectable men of good lineage" (*homme de bien et bonne race*) followed. To resist reconciliation was to court suspension from the Supper. The difficult task of reconciling feuding persons, in which the consistory became the restorer of offended honor, was a sphere where it enjoyed considerable success and where its authority was least contested. It was this function of "non-judicial" justice and the daily pacification of society that Church members most readily accepted and which endured for a very long period in consistorial operations across Europe. The consistory's goal of pacifying families and establishing a fraternal society responded to a need for social regulation and assured the Reformed community of cohesion during periods of religious conflict and persecution.

Consistories, however, did not operate uniformly in the realm of morals control. A comparative study of the consistories of Languedoc and the German Palatinate demonstrated that the targets of censure were dependent upon local habits and could vary from one place to another.[58] Thus, in the German

---

55 Philippe Chareyre, "The Great Difficulties One Must Bear to Follow Jesus-Christ: Morality at Sixteenth Century, Nîmes," in *Sin and the Calvinists*, 63–97.

56 Mentzer, "Marking the Taboo," 107; idem, "*Disciplina nervus ecclesiae*," 100–02; idem, "Sociability and Culpability: Conventions of Mediation and Reconciliation within the Sixteenth-Century Huguenot Community," *Memory and Identity: The Huguenots in France and the Atlantic Diaspora*, (eds.) Bertrand Van Ruymbeke and Randy J. Sparks (Columbia, SC: 2003), 45–57.

57 Raymond A. Mentzer, "Le consistoire et la pacification du monde rural," *BSHPF* 135 (1989), 373–89.

58 Janine Estèbe and Bernard Vogler, "La genèse d'une société protestante : étude comparée de quelques registres consistoriaux languedociens et palatins vers 1600," *Annales: économies, sociétés, civilisations* 31 (1976), 352–88.

world, the elders took close aim at drunkenness, while in the Mediterranean arena, inappropriate dress and dancing predominated. The power relationships within urban society could also mean that practices were differentiated according to time and place. Accordingly, dancing, affectation in dress, and games were often behaviors attributed to the elite and might well have been considered a matter of contestation by artisans and members of the legal professions who frequently served as elders in the urban setting. Finally, it would seem that the condemnation of games was a phenomenon of the late-16th-century, while the campaign against dancing was strongest in the early 17th and then lessened several decades later. As for consistorial interest in magical practices, they should be understood as part of the wider upsurge of witch hunts across Europe in the late late-16th and early 17th centuries. These observations of course raise questions of whether the cases recorded in the consistory registers are representative of larger social patterns and how historians ought to interpret the content of the registers in their chronological dimension.

Quantitative studies of the content of the consistory registers suggest an evolution toward fewer censures. The trend is perhaps a reflection of the adaptation of the consistory to its institutional environment as well as new, more efficient forms of control. The development appears to have had a double dynamic, moving principally in the direction of lending pastors greater authority, but also toward heads of household who were given new responsibilities over their members. In 1670 at Nîmes, the cases noted exclusively on the lists kept by the summoner and absent from the pages of the consistory register correspond to the sinners called to appear directly before the pastor. The consistory seems to have accorded less importance to morals offenses, which from now on were resolved in private, excepting prominent persons and theology students whose transgressions demanded public resolution in order to set an example.[59]

The prestige of the pastors was particularly great in the larger towns that had an academy where some of the pastors held professional positions and participated in the drive to defend the Reformed churches through religious polemic. In this regard, the many works authored by Pastor Paul Ferry of Metz are a prime example.[60] Pastors published moral treatises, such as that on witches and games of chance written by Lambert Daneau, who taught at the

---

59 Philippe Chareyre, "Les derniers feux de l'académie de Nîmes," *Le collège royal et l'académie protestante de Nîmes aux XVIe et XVIIe siècles* (Nîmes: 1998), 257–97.

60 Julien Léonard, *Être pasteur au XVIIe siècle. Le ministère de Paul Ferry à Metz (1612–1669)* (Rennes: 2015).

University of Leiden and the Academy of Béarn, or the *Traicté de l'amendement de vie* of Jean Taffin, chaplain to William of Orange and minister of the Walloon Church of Amsterdam in 1584. Both works went through many editions.[61] The pastors fed a literature of edification by printing and distributing their best sermons. These include the sermons of Jean Daillé, Pierre Du Moulin, Jean Mestrezat, and Jean Claude at the Church of Charenton.[62] Finally, there is the example of Charles Drelincourt, the author of numerous catechisms and books of piety.

In France, as in Switzerland and Germany,[63] pastors in visiting their fold reminded families and, in particular, heads of household of their responsibility for domestic piety. The pastors' various publications supported edifying readings and prayer; their sermons, naturally enough, encouraged readings from Scripture.[64] Thus, in 1665 the provincial synod of Nîmes assigned pastors the task of visiting as often as possible the families in their congregations to inquire about the diligence of fathers and mothers in the regular practice of family piety and the proper discharge of their duties in domestic education or training.[65] Wealthier families even had private, if modest libraries of religious books.[66]

The quantitative decline in the consistorial deliberations centering on moral and ecclesiastical censure was accompanied by an increase and reorganization of the practices surrounding catechism. In the educational sphere, pastors had a primary role. This transformation of consistorial activity bears witness to a redefinition not only of institutional functioning, but also of the edification of the entire Church, to the point that Fred van Lieburg and others,

---

61   Philippe Chareyre, "Jeux interdits, jeux tolérés," in *Le plaisir et la transgression en France et en Espagne aux XVIe et XVIIe siècles*, (ed.) Maurice Daumas (Orthez: 1999), 385–418.

62   Ghislaine Sicard-Arpin, "Le sermon protestant: un enracinement dans la parole de Dieu," *Le temps des beaux sermons*, (ed.) J.-P. Landry (Geneva: 2006), 51–59 and Julien Goery, "Y a-t-il eu une querelle de l'éloquence dans les temples à l'âge classique?" *Le temps des beaux sermons*, 29–49. These and similar published materials can be consulted through the Post-Reformation Digital Library (www.prdl.org.).

63   Steven E. Ozment, *When Fathers Ruled. Family Life in Reformation Europe*, (Cambridge, Mass.: 1983).

64   Françoise Chevalier, *Prêcher sous l'édit de Nantes* (Genève: 1994), 361.

65   Raymond A. Mentzer, "The Printed Catechism and Religious Instruction in the French Reformed Churches," in *Habent sua fata libelli. Books Have Their Own Destiny*, (eds.) Robin Barnes, Robert Kolb and Paula Presley, (Kirksville, Mo.: 1998), 93–101. Philippe Chareyre, "Consistoire et catéchèse: L'exemple de Nîmes XVI–XVIIèmes siècles," in *Catéchismes et confessions de foi*, (eds.) M.-M. Fragonard and M. Péronnet (Montpellier: 1995), 403–23.

66   Philip Benedict, "Bibliothèques catholiques et protestantes à Metz au XVIIe siècle," *Annales: économies, sociétés, civilisations* 40 (1985), 343–70.

in discussing events in the Netherlands, invoke the phrase "the Further Reformation."[67] The terminology is equally applicable to the French situation.

Assistance to the less fortunate members of the Church was an activity in the French consistories that, contrary to developments in the Netherlands or in Switzerland, took second place only to morals control. It was, of course, vital that funds earmarked for the poor be spent only on those who were worthy of assistance; aid to the impoverished could not become a pretext for idleness. Its distribution was dependent upon the recipient's good behavior and thus it became an additional means of supervision. Beginning in the second third of the 17th century and especially in Languedoc—at Nîmes and at Saint-Jean-du-Gard—charitable assistance took precedence over other aspects of consistorial activity. At Loudun, management of financial matters represented 706 of the 3,421 recorded actions of the consistory, or 20 per cent of its total activity in the years between 1589 and 1685.[68] At Nîmes, it accounted for 27 per cent of consistorial activity at the end of the 16th century. These financial concerns grew to fully half of recorded activity during the 1640s, and became the principal undertaking twenty years later. The development hardly left time for the elders to attend to misbehavior.

The competition from the Catholic Church in the domain of social welfare and the concern to avoid abjurations in the face of a Tridentine Catholicism that sought to regain lost ground may also help to explain these developments. Nonetheless, the exercise of charity remained a means for supervising the weakest members of the community by conditioning the receipt of assistance upon obedience to the moral standards established by ecclesiastical discipline.

5 Methodologies, Interpretative Structures and Future Research

Specialists in the French Reformed tradition had long concentrated their efforts on institutional accounts[69] or the history of local churches.[70] Interest

---

67   Fred A. Van Lieburg, "From Pure Church to Pious Culture: The Further Reformation in the Seventeenth-Century Dutch Republic," in *Later Calvinism: International Perspectives*, (ed.) Fred W. Graham (Kirksville, Mo.: 1994), 409–30.

68   Edwin Bezzina, "'La foi sans les œuvres est inutile': Les protestants de Loudun et la pratique de la charité (1589–1685)," in *Les œuvres protestantes en Europe*, (ed.) Céline Borello (Rennes: 2013), 133–47.

69   For instance, Paul de Félice, *Les protestants d'autrefois: vie intérieure des Églises, mœurs et usages* (4 vols. Paris: 1896–1902).

70   The list is long. Representative examples are Maurice Oudot de Dainville, "Le consistoire de Ganges à la fin du XVIe siècle," *Revue d'histoire de l'Église de France* (1932),

has now shifted to the study of "lived religion." The consistorial sources with their detailed accounts of daily life have proven exceptionally helpful. They offer a rich tableau of people's familiar routines and experiences both sacred and profane. As we have noted, the religious transformations associated with the Reformation involved far more than an altered set of theological tenets or the introduction of new modes of prayer and liturgical practice. The developments also meant a careful reordering and supervision of the entire community. This was a monumental attempt to translate belief and ideology into a system of everyday attitudes and practices. Assessing individual and collective responses has been challenging.

Scholars have adopted a number of methodological approaches in exploring the issues; and while the synodal institutions have not been ignored, attention thus far has focused primarily on the consistory. Studies that utilize quantitative methods were among the first and most enduring. The best known of these early investigations is Janine Garrisson's 1977 thesis and later book that analyzed more than a dozen Reformed communities in southern France.[71] She collected considerable serial data through close scrutiny of records from southern churches large and small. The goal of the consistory, Garrisson argued, was the religious and moral transformation of the individual through religious instruction and edification as well as the reform of everyday life. By quantifying these activities she sought to measure the impact and evolution of the disciplinary initiative undertaken by local Protestant communities and their churches. This perspective obviously accentuated the consistory as a morals tribunal.

Towards the end of the 1980s, two doctoral theses presented at the University of Montpellier employed quantitative methods to explore long-term consistorial action. Philippe Chareyre in his 1987 dissertation focused on the consistory of Nîmes from its establishment in 1561 to its demise in 1685. The following year, Didier Poton presented a study of the community of Saint-Jean-du-Gard from

---

464–85; François Martin, "Ganges, action de son consistoire et vie de son Église aux 16e et 17e siècles," *Revue de théologie et d'actions évangéliques* 2 (1942), 17–40 and 130–59; Frank Delteil, "Institutions et vie de l'Église réformée de Pont de Camarès," in *Les Églises et leurs institutions au XVIe siècle. Actes du Vème Colloque de Centre d'Histoire de la Réforme et du Protestantisme*, (ed.) Michel Péronnet (Montpellier: 1978), 95–113.

71 Janine Garrisson-Estèbe, *Protestants du Midi, 1559–1598* (Toulouse: 1980, 2nd ed. 1991). See also her comparative study of consistorial activity in Languedoc and the Palatinate undertaken with Bernard Vogler. Estèbe and Vogler, "La genèse d'une société protestante," *Annales: économies, sociétés, civilisations* 31 (1976), 352–88.

the 1598 Edict of Nantes until its revocation.[72] Both investigations benefited from exceptional series of consistory registers, encompassing long time periods and without undue breaks in the documentation. Chareyre meticulously went through the eighteen extant consistorial registers from the Church of Nîmes. They cover more than one hundred and twenty years, beginning in 1561 and ending in 1685. Nearly all the proceedings, dutifully recorded by a trained scribe, have survived. Only the deliberations from 1563–1578 have been lost. Careful use of serial data allowed Chareyre to trace the evolution of consistorial concerns. As previously noted, after 1598 the pastors and elders were less preoccupied with behavioral matters. Their attention turned increasingly to poor relief and the confessional struggle with the Catholics. Poton also had access to an impressive series of consistory registers from Saint-Jean-du-Gard, embracing almost eighty years from 1605 to 1684. He too utilized quantitative analysis to reveal a slow but troublesome transformation in consistorial activity. Early endeavors to correct moral failings gave way over the course of the 17th century to political preoccupations and attempts to safeguard the Church from destruction.

Others since have pursued similar, though not always equally ambitious projects. Mentzer, in the late 1980s, examined the activities of the Nîmes consistory based on the two earliest surviving registers of its deliberations (1561–63 and 1578–83). The analysis involved, in part, a statistical survey of the various "sins" for which the consistory summoned men and women; it also included a breakdown of "sinners" according to gender. He subsequently published a quantitative analysis of excommunication for ten Reformed churches in southern France.[73] Edwin Bezzina, in his 2004 University of Toronto dissertation, made impressive use of data quantification to assess the Reformation at Loudun.[74] His thorough mining of the *état-civil* allowed him to evaluate the frequency of religiously mixed marriages and inter-confessional godparentage. The data bank also yielded valuable information regarding demographic trends at Loudun and hence the delicate balance between Protestants and Catholics in this bi-confessional town. The demographic realities, in turn, help to explain certain aspects of consistorial activity.

---

72 Philippe Chareyre, *Le consistoire de Nîmes, 1561–1685* (4 vols. Doctoral diss., Université Paul Valéry—Montpellier III, 1987). Didier Poton, *De l'Edit à sa Révocation: Saint Jean de Gardonnenque 1598–1686* (2 vols. Doctoral diss., Université Paul-Valéry—Montpellier III, 1988).

73 Raymond A. Mentzer, "*Disciplina nervus ecclesiae*: The Calvinist Reform of Morals at Nîmes," *SCJ* 18 (1987), 89–115; idem, "Marking the Taboo," 97–128.

74 Bezzina, *After the Wars of Religion*; idem, "The Consistory of Loudun," in *Dire l'interdit*, 239–71.

The quantitative methodology employed by Garrisson, Chareyre, Poton, Mentzer, Bezzina and others has shown great promise. Still, it is not without risk. Judith Pollmann, in a celebrated article detailing Church discipline at the Dutch city of Utrecht during the 1620s, raised serious questions about the reliability, meaning and value of these quantitative studies. Astonishingly, the Reformed Church of Utrecht kept no record of roughly 70 per cent of the disciplinary cases that it handled, thus casting doubt on the assumption that the records of deliberations are representative of consistorial activity. Pollmann's critique has led, in turn, to a more general discussion, perhaps best articulated by the participants in a conference held at Pau in 2005. Again, the exchange centered on the relevance and limitations of quantitative analysis for assessing consistorial interest and endeavor.[75]

Other methodological approaches have found favor as of late. Microhistorical studies of particular incidents or anthropological approaches to liturgical rites have, in some cases, been informative of people's devotional habits, routine aspirations, and recurring anxieties.[76] Along these same lines, historians of gender, notably Suzannah Lipscomb, have found the consistorial proceedings invaluable for investigating Protestant women in early modern France. In her 2009 Oxford dissertation and several published articles, Lipscomb has explored the manner in which the Reformed disciplinary system offered women unexpected opportunities to exercise their influence. Female communication networks could readily be deployed to insure that the consistory received information aimed at restoring the honor and reputation of a falsely accused woman.[77]

---

[75]   Judith Pollmann, "Off the Record: Problems in the Quantification of Calvinist Church Discipline," *SCJ* 33 (2002), 423–38. *La mesure du fait religieux: L'approche méthodologique des registres consistoriaux dans l'espace calvinien XVI–XVIIIe siècle*, (eds.) Philippe Chareyre and Raymond A. Mentzer, special issue of the *BSHPF* 153: 4 (octobre-novembre-décembre 2007).

[76]   Mentzer, "The Persistence of 'Superstition and Idolatry,'" 220–33. Françoise Chevalier, Christian Grosse, Raymond A. Mentzer and Bernard Roussel, "Anthropologie historique: les rituels réformés (XVIe–XVIIe siècles)," *BSHPF* 148 (2002), 979–1009. Raymond A. Mentzer, "Fasting, Piety and Political Anxiety among French Reformed Protestants," *Church History* 76 (2007), 330–62.

[77]   Suzannah Lipscomb, *Maids, Wives and Mistresses: Disciplined Women in Reformation Languedoc* (D.Phil., University of Oxford, 2009); idem, "Refractory Women: The Limits of Power in the French Reformed Church," in *Dire l'interdit*, 13–28; idem, "Crossing Boundaries: Women's Gossip, Insults and Violence in Sixteenth-Century France," *French History* 25 (2011), 408–26.

The extraordinary richness of the documentation, growing body of secondary literature, and fresh interpretative perspectives suggest the diverse array of promising possibilities for future research. How did the personal objectives of the faithful differ from those of Church authorities? To what extent did wives and mothers see the consistory as a means to exercise a measure of control over their husbands and children? Did churches, consistories and synods act as agents for the codification of social values such as honor, status and virtue? Did the concerns exhibited by pastors, elders and deacons mirror the overall realities of society? Or were they simply the focused preoccupations of Church authorities? Was ecclesiastical and social discipline a system imposed by the elite of the community? Or was it an occasion for negotiation among different social groups? Finally and perhaps most importantly, how did a minority religion and its institutions function within a bi-confessional, indeed predominantly Catholic world? Was coexistence an illusion? Was the maintenance of Reformed confessional identity and avoidance of contaminating contact with Catholicism, through mixed marriages for instance, impossible? These and other, yet to be formulated questions await future scholars of the Reformation in France.

CHAPTER 2

Doctrine and Liturgy of the Reformed Churches of France

Marianne Carbonnier-Burkard

1   Introduction

Deeply influenced by John Calvin's model of the Reformation and, at the same time, a prime target of intense royal repression, the Reformed Churches of France cemented their unity in 1559 by affirming doctrinal accord in the form of a Confession of Faith, occasionally called a rule of faith. This was soon published and added to the "Geneva Psalter," also known as the "Huguenot Psalter." This collection, completed in 1562, included, besides the "150 Psalms of David put into French verse" by Clément Marot (1496–1544) and Theodore Beza (1519–1605) and the Confession of Faith, Calvin's liturgy for the Church of Geneva, entitled the *Forme des prières et chants ecclésiastiques*, and Calvin's *Catechism*. With the support of successive national synods these three texts became the common doctrinal and liturgical standard for the French Reformed Churches and French Protestants, even after the revocation of the Edict of Nantes (1685).

The Psalter[1] served as a "Book of Common Prayer" for the Huguenots for almost two centuries and made possible the wide diffusion of the "French Confession of Faith" and of Calvin's liturgy and catechism.[2] Although normative, these texts were not unalterable. At the beginning of the 17th century, demands for change were expressed in the synods, and other catechisms and forms of prayer were used in the Reformed Churches of France. These might have modified slightly the meaning and use of the text of the Geneva Psalter, but it was not replaced until the first decades of the 18th century.

---

1 The classic study of the Huguenot Psalter remains Pierre Pidoux, *Le psautier huguenot du XVIe siècle, mélodies et documents* (2 vols., Basel: 1962).

2 The national synod of La Rochelle in 1581 promoted the spread of the Psalter by making it an obligatory manual for the faithful (with a further reminder at the synod of Montauban in 1594).

2 The Doctrinal Standard in Two Forms: The French Confession of Faith and the Genevan Catechism

2.1 *The French Confession of Faith*

The "first synod" of the French Reformed Churches met in Paris at the end of May 1559 to adopt a common Confession of Faith.[3] It was in fact a small clandestine gathering of pastors from the Paris-Geneva network, assembled at the initiative of Antoine de Chandieu (1534–1591). The aim of the pastors was to present the king, assumed to be misinformed, with the confession of faith of those Frenchmen stigmatized as heretics. They also sought to assure the doctrinal unity of all the Reformed churches scattered through the kingdom. The text they adopted had 40 articles and was almost a duplicate of a shorter version that Calvin had sent from Geneva; it was largely his own work.[4] Like all the "modern" confessions of faith after the Augsburg Confession (1530), the "French Confession of Faith" (in Latin, *Confessio gallicana*) was written in the vernacular, in a series of articles each beginning with "We believe." It was also annotated with many scriptural references intended to demonstrate its truth. The 40 articles recognizably possessed the structure Calvin had adopted for the revised edition of his *Institutes of the Christian Religion*, composed during the winter of 1558–59 in four parts.[5]

I.   The Knowledge of God the Creator.
II. The Knowledge of God the Redeemer in Christ.
III. The Way in which we receive the Grace of Christ. What Benefits Come to Us from It? What Effects Follow?
IV. The External Means or Aids by Which God Invites Us into the Society of Christ and Holds Us Therein.

---

3 For a modern edition of the 1559 "Confession de foi des Eglises réformées de France," see Olivier Fatio (ed.), *Confessions et catéchismes de la foi réformée* (Geneva: 1986), 111–27. In English translation, Philip Schaff, (ed.), *Creeds of Christendom*, vol. 3 (1931; repr. Grand Rapids, Mich.: 1998), 356–82. A starting point for the decisions of the national synods is John Quick (ed.), *Synodicon in Gallia Reformata, or the acts, decisions, decrees, and canons of those famous national councils of the Reformed churches in France* (2 vols. London: 1692); and Jean Aymon (ed.), *Tous les synodes des Eglises réformées de France* (2 vols. The Hague: 1710).

4 The text sent by Calvin was printed in Geneva in the form of 35 articles in 1559 and reprinted, along with the version in 40 articles, in several editions of the Geneva psalter until 1566.

5 John Calvin, *Institution de la religion chrétienne (1559)*, in *Ioannis Calvini Opera quae supersunt omnia*, (eds.) G. Baum, E. Cunitz and E. Reuss, vol. 2 (59 vols., Brunswick: 1863–1900). In English translation, John Calvin, *Institutes of the Christian Religion*, ed. John T. McNeill, trans. Ford Lewis Battles (2 vols. Philadelphia: 1960).

Articles 1 to 8

- "We believe and confess that there is but one God, who is one sole and simple essence, spiritual, eternal…infinite, incomprehensible…all-wise, all-good, all-just, and all-merciful." (art.1)
- The revelation of God, first in the order of nature, more clearly through his Word in Scripture. (art. 2)
- The Scriptures (art. 3–5):

    They comprise "the canonical books of the Old and New Testaments," listed according to the order in the Geneva Bible, different from the Vulgate (the "apocryphal" books, while useful to read, are placed separately, outside the Biblical canon).

- The authority of the Scriptures depends on the Word of God "which is contained in these books" and is acknowledged as such by "the testimony and inward illumination of the Holy Spirit." The Scriptures are thus the ultimate standard, according to which "all things should be examined, regulated, and reformed."
- If the three traditional creeds—the Apostles,' the Nicene, and the Athanasian—are formally acknowledged as authoritative, this is "because they are in accordance with the Word of God." Thus, the Word of God expressed in Scripture is the sole authority.
- The Trinity (art. 6): The article declares steadfast adherence to the doctrine set out at the Councils of Nicaea and Constantinople, and "detests" the heretics condemned by the Fathers of the Church.
- The Creation (art. 7): God created "all things, not only the heavens and the earth and all that is in them, but also the invisible spirits," otherwise known as angels.
- Providence (art. 8): It is not only universal, but individual. "God, who has all things in subjection to him, watches over us with a Father's care, so that not a hair of our heads will fall without his will." The emphasis on individual Providence is a unique characteristic of Calvin's piety, in line with the situation of minority Churches in a hostile environment.

Articles 9 to 16

- Man, "created pure and perfect in the image of God…by his own fault he fell from the grace which he had received, and is thus alienated from God…so that his nature is totally corrupt." (art. 9)

- The transmission of original sin to "all the posterity of Adam." (art. 10)
- The condemnation of the entire human race, even little children (even after baptism); even the most holy are stained with sin. (art. 11)
- Election: "From this corruption and general condemnation into which all men are plunged, God, according to his eternal and immutable counsel, calls those whom he has chosen by his goodness and mercy alone in our Lord Jesus Christ, without consideration of their works...leaving the rest in this same corruption and condemnation to show in them his justice." (art. 12)
- While this is the Calvinist doctrine of predestination, the word itself, a source of confessional polemics, was avoided and the formulation of non-election attenuated (the "condemnation" of the "rest" was not an act of the divine will, but the consequence of universal sin).
- Jesus Christ (art. 13–16): "given to us for our salvation" (art. 13), God and man (in conformity with the Nicene Creed, contrary to "the diabolical conceits of Servetus") (art. 14–15), died and rose from the dead for us (art. 16).

Articles 17 to 24

- Justification (art. 17–21): This is justification freely acquired in Jesus Christ, through the unique sacrifice of the cross (art. 17); this justification "rests upon the remission of our sins" without "any virtues or merits" on our part (art. 18); "we are made partakers [in it]...by faith alone," understood as "full confidence" in the promise of salvation (art. 19–20).

    Regeneration "in newness of life" (or sanctification) is also achieved through faith; "we receive by faith grace to live holily;" "the good works which we do proceed from [God's] Spirit, and cannot be accounted to us for justification" or merit. (art. 22)

- The close connection between justification and the important place of sanctification is characteristic of Calvinist doctrine (while for Luther justification was central and good works followed).
- The end of the Law of Moses since the coming of Jesus Christ: Although the ceremonies of the Old Testament are no longer followed, the (moral) Law remains the rule of life for believers, who have received justification through faith. (art. 23)
- Prayer: All prayer must be addressed to God the Father through Jesus Christ, "our only advocate." Prayers to saints and the doctrine of purgatory, "an illusion coming from the same shop" from which have sprung so many abuses,

are condemned. (art. 24) The article rejects other "human inventions" of the Church, such as fasting, auricular confession, and ecclesiastical celibacy, "for the false idea of merit which is attached to them" and because they impose "a yoke upon the conscience."

Articles 25 to 40

- The nature of the Church (art. 25–28).

The "true Church:" "According to the Word of God, it is the company of the faithful who agree to follow his Word and the pure religion which it teaches and who advance in it all their lives," even if among the faithful there are "hypocrites and reprobates" (art. 27). It is the place where the Word of God is received and where there is the use of the sacraments (an echo of the Augsburg Confession). The status of the Catholic Church (the "papacy") is uncertain. On the one hand, it is disqualified because "superstitions and idolatries are in it," but on the other, "some trace of the Church is left in the papacy," in particular baptism, recognized as valid (art. 28).

The purpose of the Church, the preaching of the Gospel, requires "that there be pastors" to exercise the "ministry" of preaching and the sacraments (art. 25). This article, attacking those "enthusiasts" (*fantastiques*) who wanted to do away with pastors, did not contradict the principle, not explicitly stated in the Confession of Faith, of the "priesthood of all Christians," according to which all baptized persons are "priests" (in the sense that all, clerics and lay persons, are members of the body of Christ, but with different functions or services).

- The governance of the Church (art. 29–33).

In the "true Church" three "offices," or charges, are necessary: the teaching of the "pure doctrine" (office of the pastors), the collective moral order or "discipline" (office of the elders), and assistance to the poor and other afflicted persons (office of the deacons) (art. 29).

The pastors are in principle equal, under the unique bishop Jesus Christ, with equality of the Churches as a corollary (art. 30).

Pastors are appointed by "election," except in extraordinary circumstances, "because sometimes, and even in our own days, when the state of the Church has been interrupted, it has been necessary for God to raise men in an extraordinary manner to restore the Church which was in ruin and desolation," but even in this case a "calling" by the Church (assembly) is the rule (art. 31).

The Calvinist model of the Church was based on a plurality of offices, collegial, not hierarchical, and elective. The *Discipline*[6] (or regulations) adopted at the same time as the Confession of Faith at the first synod of 1559, specified the conditions of eligibility for each office and the functions of the "consistory," a body composed of the pastors, elders, and deacons of each Church. The consistory enforced "ecclesiastical discipline" following the rules for "excommunication" in Matthew 18: "scandalous sinners" are to be censured, and if necessary barred from the Supper, in order to bring them to repentance (art. 33).

- The sacraments (art. 34–38).

They do not confer salvation but are "outward signs," visible, which confirm the promise of salvation (art. 34). They are "added to the Word…to aid and comfort our faith, because of the infirmity which is in us." "Only two" are "common to the entire Church," baptism and the Lord's Supper.

Baptism (art. 35) is "a pledge of our adoption," of our "grafting into the body of Christ." Although it is "a sacrament of faith and of repentance, yet as God receives little children into his Church with their fathers…the children of believing parents should be baptized." This article alludes to the analogy between baptism and circumcision, an argument Calvin used against the Anabaptists.

The "Supper" (*cène*) is the sacrament of the "Eucharist." The word *cène*, from the Latin *coena*, "meal," shows that its significance is chiefly as a memorial of Christ's last meal, and therefore centers on the collective act of eating and drinking.

[Jesus Christ] nourishes us truly with his flesh and blood, so that we may be one in him, and that our life is in common. Although he be in heaven until he comes to judge all the earth, still we believe that by the secret and incomprehensible power of his Spirit he feeds and strengthens us with the substance of his body and of his blood. (art. 36)

Those who partake of the Supper with "pure faith…receive truly," through the Spirit, the reality ("substance") to which the signs witness (art. 37). Focused on the question of the nature of the presence of the body of Christ, these articles on the Supper established the opposition of the Reformed to the "enthusiasts and sacramentarians" who regarded the bread and wine as mere symbols (art. 38).

---

6 Isaac d'Huisseau (ed.), *La Discipline des Eglises réformées de France ou l'ordre par lequel elles sont conduites et gouvernées* (Geneva: 1666). For the modern edition to which is appended the 1559 text of the *Discipline* see François Méjan, *Discipline de l'Église réformée de France annotée et précédée d'une introduction historique*. (Paris: 1947).

- Political authority (art. 39–40).

According to Calvin's doctrine, based on the Epistle to the Romans (ch. 13), political authorities are established by God; they hold the "sword" "to suppress crimes committed, not only against the second table of the Commandments of God" (the moral ones), "but also against the first" (the religious ones), including the crime of heresy. Like that of the pastors, the office of the magistrates is "legitimate and holy" (art. 39).

We hold then that we must obey their laws and statutes, customs, taxes and other dues, and bear the yoke of subjection with a good and free will, even if they are unbelievers, provided that the sovereign empire of God remains intact [Acts 4: 19]. Therefore we detest all those who would like to reject authority, to establish community and confusion of property, and overthrow the order of justice (art. 40).

The confession of faith thus ends with a protestation of almost unlimited political obedience, underlined by an attack on Anabaptists.

Not surprisingly, the "French Confession of Faith" staunchly reflects Calvin's ideas, with some hints of Theodore Beza, all the while skillfully composed. Its general tone was meant to defuse the king's hostility toward the Reformed by exalting political authority, and secondarily to gain the trust of the Lutherans. Thus, it emphasized the conformity of Reformed doctrine to that of the universal (Catholic) Church, the Church of the Fathers, both in a profession of Nicene orthodoxy and in a denunciation of heresies. The mention (art. 5) of "the three creeds" of "the Catholic Church" also made it possible to demonstrate closeness to the Augsburg Confession, important for an agreement that Beza sought with the Lutherans and all supporters of religious "concord."[7] The listing of common enemies ran to the same effect: Michael Servetus (art. 14), burned at Geneva in 1553 and defended against Calvin by Sebastian Castellio, who had supporters in France; the "enthusiastic" Anabaptists (art. 25, 38, 40); and also the "sacramentarians" (art. 38), a sobriquet aimed at the Zwinglians, here caricatured in order to dispel any identification with them, which would have been fatal for the Reformed (the Edict of Compiègne of July 1557 prescribed death for all "sacramentarian" heretics).

On the other hand, polemics against the Catholic Church were muted (being explicit only in art. 28), and limited to attacks on "abuses" and "human inventions." Thus nothing was said about the "horror of the Mass" or the "false sacraments," described for example in Beza's *Confession de la foy* (1558). Still, the

---

7 See Mario Turchetti, "Une question mal posée: la Confession d'Augsbourg, le cardinal de Lorraine et les Moyenneurs au Colloque de Poissy en 1561," *Zwingliana* 20 (1993), 53–101.

"French Confession of Faith" did not hesitate to denounce the "assemblies of the Papacy" (art. 28) in order to encourage participation in Huguenot assemblies despite their illegality (art. 26).

Intended to be presented to King Henry II, the Confession of Faith of the Reformed Churches had to wait until the regency of Catherine de Medici, who in 1561 favored a policy of religious concord. On two occasions during 1561, it was officially presented to King Charles IX in connection with Huguenot political petitions. For Beza, however, engaged in political and ecclesiastical diplomacy with the Lutherans in the Empire, the absence of a royal signature weakened the French Confession of Faith. This was why it was important for him to have it publicly authenticated at the national synod held at La Rochelle in 1571 in the presence of the princes of the blood. This synod confirmed the authenticity of the confession and its 40 articles as the "true Confession of Faith of our Reformed Churches of France," drafted at the first national synod of Paris in 1559. After having verified the agreement of all to the formulas of certain articles, the synod made three parchment copies, signed by the deputies of the churches at the synod and "the Queen of Navarre and the Princes of Navarre and Condé and the other lords." This text, with authentic support and princely endorsement, then seemed canonical.

Besides its apologetic function in a context of confessional conflict or agreement, every confession of faith had a function of internal doctrinal regulation. In this case, this function was demonstrated by several practices.

The first usage of the confession, which the *Discipline* anticipated already in 1559, focused on doctrinal control of the ministers. On entering upon their duties in the "churches to which they have been elected," the ministers were to sign the confession of faith (art. 8). The second national synod of Poitiers in 1561 extended this provision to the elders and deacons, in other words to the members of the consistories that regulated the lives of the faithful in the local congregations. The synod of 1571 extended the requirement to professors of theology and the schoolmasters. The French Confession of Faith, also called the *Confession of Faith of La Rochelle* after the 1571 synod that confirmed it, was not only the standard for preaching from the pulpits and for teaching in the schools and academies, but also that for the *Discipline* of the churches, which the various synods elaborated and the consistories put into effect.

Beginning with the synod of 1561, a reading of the confession of faith was the first order of business at the beginning of each national synod, to verify and affirm the agreement of the deputies of the churches. In fact, as the supreme legislature in matters of faith and discipline of the Reformed Churches of France and the appellate court in disputes, the national synod was the interpreter of the *Discipline* as well as the confession of faith to which the deputies swore their adherence (a formal oath was also included beginning with the synod of 1602). In the course of these periodical reviews by the national synods, clarifications and updates were proposed as late as 1612, but they were almost always rejected.[8] The French seem to have adopted the position of Beza, who stated at the beginning of his own *Confession de foy* that the "Scriptural doctrines" stated in the confession of faith were not subject to change, in contrast to the "Church order" (or discipline). When in 1620 the synod of Alès endorsed in the name of all the Reformed Churches the *Canons* of the synod of Dordrecht, which crafted a forceful formulation of predestination, it declared these canons "in conformity with the Word of God and the Confession of Faith," but did not integrate them into the 40 articles of the existing Confession of Faith. The new articles that the pastors and professors had to sign in the future were considered an interpretative appendix to the unchanged Confession of Faith.

Although formal adherence to the 40 articles of the Confession of Faith was not required for all the faithful, it was nevertheless presumed. Placed at the end of the Genevan Psalter, the Confession of Faith was meant to be read repeatedly. Was this distillation of the *Institutes of the Christian Religion*, like that masterful volume, not a guide for the reading of Scripture? Still, pedagogical usage was more specifically expected of the other doctrinal text included in the Psalter, Calvin's *Catechism*.

2.2 *The Genevan Catechism*

In the *Catéchisme de l'Eglise de Genève*,[9] published regularly in Geneva beginning in 1542 and also printed in the Psalter, the French Reformed faithful had direct contact with the doctrines of Calvin. It was a catechism designed according to question and response, a method pioneered by Luther in his *Small Catechism* of 1529, targeting above all children. Here the play of questions (by the minister or teacher) and answers (by the child) is set forth in detail. It is designed for use in the weekly collective catechism sessions on Sunday at noon, and followed an annual cycle. In contrast with the confession of faith, the catechism did not treat questions in systematic order, but followed the three great traditional catechetical texts: the Apostles' Creed, the Decalogue (or Ten Commandments) along with the Summary of the Law, and the Lord's

---

8 See Bernard Roussel, "Le texte et les usages de la Confession de foi des Eglises réformées de France d'après les Actes des Synodes Nationaux (1559–1659)," in *Catéchismes et Confessions de foi*, (eds.) M.-M. Fragonard and M. Péronnet (Montpellier: 1995), 30–60.

9 For a recent edition of this text, Fatio (ed.), *Confessions et catéchismes*, 25–110.

Prayer, adding a fourth section on the sacraments—baptism and the Supper. The goal of the catechism lessons was not only memorization, but informed assimilation of the contents of the faith. A child was meant to be able to "give an account of his faith" before participating in the Supper.[10]

The four parts of the catechism were to form an integrated framework involving the child as a believer. The child was addressed directly, beginning with an initial question about the meaning of human life:

> Minister: What is the chief end of human life?
> Child: To know God.
> M. Why do you say this?
> C. Because he created us and placed us into the world to be glorified in us…without this our condition is worse than that of the brute beasts.
> M. But what is the true and right knowledge of God?
> C. When one knows him in order to honor him.

The following question:

> "What is the proper way to honor him?" gave the child the opportunity to repeat the plan of the catechism.
> C. It is when we place our whole confidence in him [faith: the Creed], when we serve him by obeying his will [the Law: the Decalogue], when we call upon him in all our necessities, seeking salvation and every good thing that can be desired in him [prayer: the Lord's Prayer], and when we acknowledge him both with heart and lips, as the sole author of all blessings [the work of the Holy Spirit in us, through the Word and the sacraments].

Since the catechism was addressed only to the Reformed faithful (children as well as adults) for their instruction and edification, its concerns were above all pedagogical. Thus the doctrine of predestination was too learned to be discussed as such, even though there was occasional mention of the elect and the reprobate. Yet instruction did not exclude all polemic, all the more because the question-and-answer format easily lent itself to doctrinal controversy. The questions were often formulations of the objections of Catholic controversialists. Thus on the subject of the Lord's Supper:

---

10   Olivier Millet, "Rendre raison de la foi: le Catéchisme de Calvin (1542)," in *Aux origines du catéchisme en France* (Paris: 1989), 188–207.

M. Was the Supper then not established to make an oblation [sacrifice] of the body of Jesus to God his Father?

C. No. Because he, himself alone, has this privilege as he is the eternal sacrificer (Hebrews 5:5). But he commands us not to offer his body, but only to receive it (Matthew 26:26).

Again regarding the Supper and the form of Christ's presence:

M. You do not understand then, either that the body is enclosed in the bread or the blood in the chalice?

C. No. But on the contrary to truly receive the sacrament we must raise our hearts to heaven, where Jesus Christ is in glory with his Father...and not look for him in these corruptible elements.

The national synods of the Reformed Churches of France, down to the last gathering at Loudun in 1659, privileged Calvin's catechism. It was the only one to appear in the Psalter. Yet, as a practical matter, authorities encouraged the secondary use of other catechisms, better adapted to the "capacity of small children" or to the changing requirements of confessional controversy. Among the numerous catechisms published by French pastors in the 17th century, the best-seller was Charles Drelincourt's *Catéchisme ou Instruction familière sur les principaux points de la religion chrestienne* (1642). Drelincourt (1595–1669), pastor of the Paris Church at Charenton, did not intend to replace Calvin's catechism, but to explain it point by point in a "familiar" fashion, initially for his own children. In fact, his catechism served to equip the French Reformed in their controversies with Catholic curates and religious, especially in the *collèges*, by supplying them with tools that were both clear and learned. It argued methodically, with the aid of numerous citations from Scripture, and when appropriate from experience or reason. Drelincourt reformulated Calvin's doctrine, shifting it more to pastoral use. He not only avoided the subject of predestination but also the word "damnation." He elided over the biblical figure of God as the punisher of children for their parents' faults, emphasizing instead a merciful God and Jesus the Savior. And again, while proclaiming salvation through faith alone, he also included discussion of works.

Drelincourt's catechism was accompanied by an "abridged version for small children" that was easy to memorize and continued to be used after the Revocation. The first synods of the Desert, under the guidance of Antoine Court (1695–1760), recommended its use, resulting in numerous reprintings at Geneva. The national synod of 1744 officially replaced it with the abridged catechism of the Neuchâtel theologian J.-F. Ostervald (1663–1747). It offered a new model of enlightened Protestant piety that was distinct from Calvin's catechism.

2.3 The Liturgical Standard: The Forme des prières et chants ecclésiastiques

At Geneva beginning in 1542, the liturgy and other public ceremonies of the Church were established by the *Forme des prières et chants ecclésiastiques*.[11] Drafted by Calvin, this liturgical guide, written in the French vernacular, drew upon similar manuals drafted by Martin Bucer for the Church of Strasbourg, containing the psalms to be sung by the faithful, and by Guillaume Farel for the first Reformed churches in French-speaking Switzerland (1533, 1538).[12] The *Form of Prayer* included the order for the sermon service, liturgies for the Supper, baptism and marriage, and instructions for visiting the sick. It was introduced into France clandestinely, at first as separate pieces printed in short collections of prayers, then beginning in 1555 it was inserted into the psalter of Marot and Beza and carried in the baggage of ministers coming from Geneva. Although not formally adopted by the first national synods, the liturgy of Geneva, along with the psalms, was confirmed by the synod of Montpellier in 1598 as the common and unalterable liturgy of the Reformed Churches of France. While the *Form of Prayer* left the officiating ministers some latitude, the synods were careful to preserve this common system by restraining any local attempts at modification. The national synod of Loudun of 1659 barely yielded to demands for the modernization of the language of the psalms, which was considered outmoded. The psalms appeared in 1679 in a version revised by Valentin Conrart (1603–1675) and Marc-Antoine La Bastide (1624–1704), and the entire Psalter, with the liturgy in language "accommodated to the times and current practice," in 1689.

If the Church was, as the Reformers described it, the assembly where the Word of God was proclaimed and preached, and the sacraments administered according to the Word, its highlight was the Sunday service. The French Reformed, like the Genevans and French-speaking Swiss, called this community service not "Mass," but "preaching" (the sermon service). The change in words was significant; the Mass was a Latin liturgy entirely centered on the celebration of the Eucharist, where the bread and wine were "transubstantiated" into the body of Christ, and offered in sacrifice, while preaching, done in the

---

11   Calvin, *Calvini Opera*, 6: col. 165–224. The modern critical edition is Bruno Bürki, "La Sainte Cène selon l'ordre de Jean Calvin, 1542," in *Coena Domini I. Die Abendmahlsliturgie der Reformationskirchen in 16./17. Jahrhundert*, (ed.) Irmgard Pahl (Freiburg: 1983), 347–67. An English translation is available in Bard Thompson, *Liturgies of the Western Church* (New York: 1961), 197–210.

12   On the creation of the Geneva liturgy, see Christian Grosse, *Les rituels de la cène. Le culte eucharistique réformé à Genève (XVIe–XVIIe siècles)* (Geneva: 2008), 117–51.

vernacular, was solely preaching. It ordinarily included no Eucharistic celebration. This liturgical revolution, begun in Zurich and Strasbourg in the 1520s, brought about changes in the architecture and the furnishings of the churches, now called "temples" to distinguish them from Catholic ones. Their plan was now "basilican" and no longer cruciform, with a pulpit facing rows of benches for the worshipers who listened in the ideal attentively.[13]

During the preaching service, the readings from Scripture and the sermon were framed by prayers and songs. While the *Form of Prayer* was originally associated with the psalms put into verse by Marot, and later with the complete Psalter of Marot and Beza (1562), with original melodies supplied by Geneva musicians, this was because the preaching advocated by Calvin involved the participation of the people through the congregational singing of psalms. Calvin was forced to justify the novelty of this "vernacular" service in an address to the reader at the beginning of the *Form of Prayer*. The singing of the "celestial songs of good King David" in the language of all the people had "great force and strength to move and inflame the hearts of men to invoke and praise God with a more vehement and ardent zeal." A table placed in the Psalter at the end of the psalms divided them into a cycle of twenty-five weeks, so that all the psalms would be sung twice a year (at a rate of three per Sunday).[14] The *Form of Prayer* specified only the order of the sermon service for Sunday morning (the main service, since that on Sunday afternoon was devoted to teaching the catechism, and those on "workdays" were less elaborate).

The pastor began with the service with an invocation and a prayer for confession of sins, adopted from a prayer in the Strasbourg liturgy:

> Lord God, eternal and all-powerful father, we confess and acknowledge without pretense before your holy Majesty that we are poor sinners, conceived and born in iniquity and corruption, inclined to evil, unable to do good.

The singing of a psalm by the assembly came next and then the sermon, preceded by the reading of supporting verses and of a prayer composed by the minister. The *Form of Prayer* said nothing about the sermon, but the Geneva practice, which was recommended by the national synod of Sainte-Foy in 1578,

---

13 For the social, cultural, and material impact of preaching in the language of the people, and more broadly for the reception and effects of Reformed liturgical norms in France, see Raymond A. Mentzer, "Laity and Liturgy in the French Reformed Tradition," in *History Has Many Voices*, (ed.) Lee P. Wandel (Kirksville, MO.: 2003), 71–92.

14 Grosse, *Les rituels de la* cène, 163–66.

involved the *lectio continua* (continuous reading) of a book of Scripture. It was an exegetical commentary extending over several months. In the course of the 17th century, this practice competed with offering sermons on particular topics, a practice authorized by the national synod of Charenton in 1644. The pastor was free to choose his text, specifying a topic as the subject of his sermon, particularly on days when celebrating the Supper.[15] However, a different sort of "continuous reading" endured in the French churches by the early 17th century, just as in Geneva. It involved the recitation of successive chapters of Scripture by a reader before the singing of a psalm and before the entrance of the pastor.[16]

The sermon was followed by a long "universal prayer" for all men, in particular the political authorities, the pastors, and the afflicted. This prayer for intercession was followed by a paraphrase interpreting the Lord's Prayer (or by the Lord's Prayer itself). After the singing of a psalm, Aaron's prayer of benediction (Numbers 6:24–26) closed the service.

At Easter and Pentecost, a Sunday in September, and a Sunday during Christmastide, the Lord's Supper was celebrated at the conclusion of the sermon service. Four times a year: this was Zwingli's model established at Zurich and followed by the magistrates of Geneva. The national synod of Paris recommended it in 1565 as a common rule for the French Reformed Churches.[17] This somewhat infrequent reception occurred, however, more often than in Catholic circles, where people typically received the Eucharist but once a year at Easter.[18] On the Sunday preceding the Supper, it was announced from the pulpit "so everyone can prepare to receive it properly." The preparation was carried out during the service on the day of the Supper. According to the *Form of Prayer* the pastor was "to touch on it" in his sermon, that is to interrupt the *lectio continua* of the Scriptural chapter at hand and to take up the Eucharist, a memorial to Christ, as his subject. In any case, a specified order was introduced following the "universal prayer," with a prayer in preparation for the Supper. Although added to the service as a final element, "the manner of celebrating the Supper" was presented separately in the *Form of Prayer*, as the liturgy of a

---

15 Huisseau, *Discipline*, ch. I, art. 12.
16 Grosse, *Les rituels de la cène*, 617.
17 See Huisseau, *Discipline*, ch. XII, art. 14. In fact, in "populous" churches, for practical reasons the Supper was celebrated two Sundays in a row (Grosse, *Les rituels de la cène*, 293–94).
18 Marianne Carbonnier-Burkard, "Le temps de la cène chez les réformés français (milieu du XVIe—début du XVIIIe siècle)," in *Edifier ou instruire? Les avatars de la liturgie réformée du XVIe au XVIIIe siècle*, (ed.) Maria-Cristina Pitassi (Paris: 2000), 57–73.

sacrament. It was specified that the prayer was to be followed by the confession of faith (the Apostles' Creed), then by the account of the establishment of the Supper in Paul's First Epistle to the Corinthians (ch. 11). This account, coupled with a warning against those who celebrate the Supper "unworthily," served as a form of excommunication of scandalous sinners and an exhortation to "test oneself" before communing. Everyone was to verify that he or she felt "true repentance for his faults," "trust in the mercy of Christ" and "the courage to live in concord and fraternal charity with his neighbors." There was also an exhortation at the Supper, which involved an understanding of the sacrament and a comprehension of its spiritual truth:

> Let us lift our spirits and hearts on high, where Jesus Christ is in the glory of his Father... And let us not be fascinated by these earthly and corruptible elements that we see with our eyes and touch with our hands, seeking him there as though he were enclosed in the bread or wine... Therefore let us be content to have the bread and wine as signs and witnesses, seeking for the truth spiritually where the Word of God promises that we shall find it.

The minister then distributed the bread and the cup to the faithful, who processed to the Communion table. Meanwhile, "a psalm will be sung or something from the Scripture read." The Supper ended with a prayer of thanksgiving (then, after 1545 with the Song of Simeon), before the final benediction.[19]

In a brief comment following the "manner of celebrating the Supper" in the *Form of Prayer*, Calvin responded to his critics regarding the changes from the traditional Mass. The use of the language of the people, the distribution of both the bread and the wine to the people, and the instructions denying the doctrine of transubstantiation and the sacrifice carried out by the priest for the salvation of the living and the dead were all tended to desacralize the principal sacrament of the Church. He explained that the changes were simply a return to "the pure institution of Jesus Christ" after centuries of corruption.

Over the course of the 17th century, this "manner of celebrating the Supper," like a second "sermon service," was accompanied by a new individual Eucharistic devotion connected with the examination of the conscience and with the Savior, expressed in manuals such as *La pratique de piété* by the English Puritan

---

19   On the practice of the Supper in the Reformed Churches, see Bernard Roussel, "'Faire la Cène' dans les Eglises réformées du Royaume de France au seizième siècle," *Archives de Sciences Sociales des Religions* 85 (1994), 99–119. On the practice of the Supper and its evolution in Geneva see Grosse, *Les rituels de la cène*.

Lewis Bayly, available in French by 1625. The synod of Loudun in 1659 restored instructions for reading biblical passages and singing psalms during the Supper "in order to bind more closely the devotion of individuals." But a *Recueil des Pseaumes qui se chantent aux jours de la S. Cène*, with prayers in preparing for Eucharist and while receiving it, was published in Charenton in 1661 and had a great success.

Apart from the Sundays for celebration of the Supper, three of which corresponded to the three great Christian feasts, all Sundays were the same. No traditional feast is mentioned in the *Form of Prayer* or in the calendars sometimes printed at the beginning of the Geneva Psalter.[20] The rejection of feast days in the name of "Christian liberty" and for ethical reasons was a constant element in the evangelical Reformation of the cities, adopted for example by Geneva in 1536 and reiterated in 1550. No special liturgy was provided for Easter, Pentecost or Christmas, even if on those days the preacher reminded people of the great events of salvation. In principle, the French Reformed adopted the same position as the Genevans; the Confession of Faith of La Rochelle rejects "the ceremonial observance of days." However, the successive royal edicts establishing the status of the "new religion" in France, beginning in 1562 and ending with the Edict of Nantes of 1598, required abstention from work on the holy days of the Catholic Church. To prevent dangerous inactivity among the Reformed faithful, who were conscious of the attraction of their neighbors' holidays, the national synod of Gergeau (1601) acknowledged that the churches were free to "hold public prayers and preaching on the days of solemn feasts of the Roman Church." All these feast days were not, however, considered the same. The feasts associated with Christ (the Circumcision, the Passion, and the Ascension) approved in the *Confession helvétique postérieure* (1566) were allowed, with the reservation that they be purified of "superstition," while the feasts of the Virgin and the saints were generally the objects of polemic, and in any event a teaching moment for the faithful in a French environment.[21]

Other specific services for particular days were set apart in the *Form of Prayer*. These were services of weekly prayers in connection with times of

---

20 Composed at Geneva during the 1550s, the "*calendrier historial huguenot*" lists, along with their dates, events of sacred (biblical) history mingled with those of profane history. On this calendar see Eugénie Droz, "Le calendrier genevois, agent de la propagande," in *Chemins de l'hérésie*, vol. 2 (Geneva: 1971–1974), 433–59; on its creation, see Max Engammare, *L'Ordre du temps. L'invention de la ponctualité au XVIe siècle* (Geneva: 2004), 127–57.

21 Marianne Carbonnier-Burkard, "Jours de fête dans les Eglises réformées de France au XVIIe siècle," *Etudes théologiques et religieuses* 68:3 (1993), 347–58.

"plague, war, and other such hardships," inspired by the *Bettag* (Day of Repentance and Prayer) that Bucer had initiated at Strasbourg. The exhortations and prayers in the services on these days, a model for which was provided, were to note that these misfortunes were "visitations of God, through which he punishes our sins." During the French Wars of Religion, the Reformed Churches of several provinces put into effect the practice of weekly public prayers. When the synods were later consulted, they hesitated to encourage them, leaving them at the discretion of the local churches.[22] On the other hand, beginning in 1559 the *Discipline* of the Reformed Churches recommended "public and extraordinary prayers...in times of severe persecution or of war, plague or famine, or other great affliction," together with fasts. Calvin had justified the practice of fasts in times of calamity in imitation of the prophet Joel (2:12), on condition they were interpreted as exercises supporting prayers for repentance and not as meritorious acts.[23] According to the *Discipline*, occasional "days of fasting" were to be initiated by the provincial or national synod, or by the local church "after taking advice from its neighbors, and only for great and urgent causes" (1607).[24] They were mostly occasions for concentrated sermons; abstaining from food and drink was secondary. A complete liturgy was printed for the day of fasting observed at Charenton on 19 April 1658, on the occasion of catastrophic floods, set against the background of rumors of war, threats from the Turks, and the "lack of improvement" in the faithful. Three sermons by the pastors were accompanied by the singing of psalms and the reading of whole chapters from the prophets Jonah, Daniel, Isaiah, Ezekiel, and Jeremiah and from Lamentations, Deuteronomy, Revelation, and Matthew's Gospel (ch. 6–7).[25]

In the *Form of Prayer*, the liturgy for the Supper was logically placed after that of baptism. Like the Supper, baptism was to be performed by a "minister," the administration of the sacraments being part of the service ("ministry") of the Word. Baptism, as "a solemn acceptance into the church," should occur "in the presence of the congregation" after the sermon on Sunday or some other day (which necessarily excluded, at least in principle, "emergency baptisms," a traditional medieval practice connected to the notion of Limbo). The *Discipline* of the French Reformed Churches followed a simple rule: "No baptism is to occur except in an ecclesiastical assembly" (1559), and the ceremony was to

---

22 Huisseau, *Discipline*, ch. x, art. 4.
23 Calvin, *Institutes*, III, III, 27.
24 Huisseau, *Discipline*, ch. x, art. 3.
25 Raymond A. Mentzer, "Fasting, Piety and Political Anxiety among French Reformed Protestants," *Church History* 76 (2007), 330–62.

take place "before the final benediction" concluding the service (1583).[26] The liturgy began with a long explanation of baptism, which justified the baptism of infants, followed by a prayer. Promises by the godparents followed, then the baptism itself, the pouring of water on the child's head "in the name of the Father and the Son and the Holy Spirit." The *Form of Prayer* emphasized that "everything is to be said aloud, in the vernacular," for two reasons: first so the people will be witnesses to the baptism, and also so everyone will be "reminded" of her or his own baptism. The solemnity of the ceremony was emphasized. There was no holy oil or candles or "other such pomps," which are all "human inventions," far from "the form of baptism commanded by Jesus Christ [and] employed by the primitive church."

The national synod of Charenton in 1645 adopted a formula for baptism specific to adults, "pagans, Jews, Mohammedans, and Anabaptists" who had been newly converted. The baptism was preceded by the candidate's confession of faith, in the form of a catechetical examination appropriate to each individual case.[27]

Although in Protestant doctrine marriage was not a sacrament but a "temporal affair" or a "mixture" of civil and ecclesiastical, it was always celebrated publicly in the temple according to an ecclesiastical ritual. The marriage liturgy had its place in the *Form of Prayer*. It was to be announced at the beginning of the sermon (on Sunday or a weekday) and was to begin with a discussion of marriage and its treatment in Genesis and as reiterated in the Gospels and the Pauline epistles. After inquiries to verify the volition of the engaged couple and the absence of any impediment, the minister presided over the exchange of vows. This was followed by the reading of the passage from Matthew's Gospel (ch. 19) describing "the holy state of marriage." There followed an exhortation to the spouses "to live devoutly together, in love, peace and union, preserving true charity, faith, and loyalty to each other, according to the Word of God." A prayer of benediction closed the ceremony.

No liturgy for the "consecration of a minister" is provided in the *Form of Prayer*, any more than in the other Reformed formularies of the 16th century. The *Ordonnances ecclésiastiques* of Geneva justified a minimal ceremony in rejecting past practices as superstitious.

It will suffice that a declaration explaining the office to which he is being ordained should be made by one of the ministers, and then that prayers and

---

26   Huisseau, *Discipline*, ch. XI, art. 6 and 15.
27   Huisseau, *Discipline*, ch. XI, art. 19.

intercessions should be offered to the end that the Lord may grant him grace to acquit himself faithfully in it.[28]

The *Discipline* of the Reformed Churches, beginning with the 1559 synod, added the imposition of the hands of the ministers, "without any superstition, however." This practice, recommended by Calvin as conforming to a practice of the apostolic Church, was not used in Geneva because of the hostility of the magistrates to any rite tending to sacralize the pastoral ministry. In reestablishing a pastoral succession linked to the early church, the imposition of hands acquired special meaning for the clandestine and scattered French churches. A formula for the imposition of hands, drafted by the pastor Antoine de Chandieu, was adopted by the synod of La Rochelle in 1571 and added to the *Discipline*.[29]

Like the other liturgical manuals of the early Protestant churches, both Lutheran and Reformed, the *Form of Prayer* ended with instructions for visiting the sick. The Reformers had changed the meaning of visiting the sick, first by removing it from a system of meritorious "works of mercy," and also by freeing it from Jean Gerson's *ars moriendi* (art of dying), which was directed toward "final ends" (death, judgment, Hell, and Paradise). It is the sick person himself, suffering in body and spirit, with guilt and anguish, who receives the visitor's attention. It is this "brother" whom the visitor seeks to console and reassure as well as to convert, all the more because the sinner's salvation depends on his own faith and trust. In France, the Reformed manuals for consoling the sick, with many editions in the 17th century, were addressed to pastors as well as to elders and the faithful in the countryside where no pastor was close at hand.

Like the liturgical collections produced by the Swiss Reformed (differing on this point from the Lutheran Reformation), the *Form of Prayer* is silent on the subject of funerals. This silence voiced a radical desacralization of death. Prayers and Masses for the dead were rejected by Luther and the other reformers as practices derived from a misinterpretation of the Gospel (the Mass as a sacrifice, penitence as a work of satisfaction, purgatory as the site of exchanges between the living and the souls of the dead). In the Lutheran churches, Masses for the dead were replaced by funeral sermons, justified as consolation for the living, purged of any proposed intervention for the salvation of souls. In the Swiss churches inspired by Zwingli's Reformation—the Humanist Reformation of the cities—the rejection was radical. Based on the authority of Scripture, they swept aside Masses and all funeral pomp as "inventions" of the clergy.

---

28 *Ordonnances Ecclésiastiques*, in the *Registres de la Compagnie des Pasteurs de Genève du temps de Calvin*, (ed.) J.-F. Bergier, vol. 1, *1546–1553* (Geneva: 1964), 3.

29 Huisseau, *Discipline*, ch. I, art. 8.

A minority in a hostile environment, the francophone Reformed churches, including that of Geneva beginning already in 1536 even before Calvin's arrival, adopted an aggressive posture toward "superstition" and thus demanded funerals take place without the slightest ritual or prayer that could be interpreted as a "requiem." In France, the Reformed Churches followed the Genevan practice of "lay" funerals, which the national synod of Orléans reaffirmed in 1562: "Ministers shall not offer any prayer at the burial of the dead, to prevent all superstition." This rule, included in the *Discipline of the Reformed Churches*, was again reiterated at the synod of Figeac in 1579; "the article concerning the burial of the dead" was restated and interpreted broadly as a prohibition "of offering any exhortations or prayers there."[30]

The rigorous rule of the total absence of any ecclesiastical rite received some support from royal legislation down to the Edict of Nantes (1598). The various edicts of pacification did not provide for the "supposedly Reformed" (declared heretics by the canons of the Council of Trent) to be buried except "*à la sauvette*"—"in haste," by night and with a restricted audience—and in separate locations outside "consecrated ground" (Catholic cemeteries). Beginning in the 1590s, two national synods echoed demands for the relaxation of the *Discipline* to permit a pastoral presence at burials. In the 17th century, the practice of preaching at funerals, in the deceased's house or at the cemetery, seems to have become common in some provinces. Beginning in 1666, the new restraints imposed on the Reformed regarding conditions of burial excluded any possibility of public preaching, but not pastoral exhortations and consolations at the family's home.[31] Thus, the pastor Charles Drelincourt's *Visites pastorales* (published in multiples volumes at several locations over the years 1665–1669) proposed, alongside models of consolation for the sick and the dying, other models for the bereaved, to be used by pastors or elders. These contained varying lists of Scriptural citations and prayers, to be chosen and adapted according to the concrete situation.

Though it was a handbook for public worship, Calvin intended the *Form of Prayer* to be a guide for the faithful to read in private "so that everyone may recognize what should be said and done in the gathering of the Christian

---

30 Huisseau, *Discipline*, ch. x, art. 5. For a discussion of funerals, see Bernard Roussel, "'Ensevelir honnestement les corps': Funeral Corteges and Huguenot Culture," in *Society and Culture in the Huguenot World, 1559–1685*, (eds.) Raymond A. Mentzer and Andrew Spicer (Cambridge: 2002), 193–208.

31 Marianne Carbonnier-Burkard, "Les morts sans Purgatoire. L'impact de la Réformation sur les pratiques funéraires à l'époque moderne," in *Pratiques autour de la mort. Enjeux œcuméniques*, (ed.) Jacques-Noël Pérès (Paris: 2012), 101–28.

faithful." This democratization of the liturgy for worship was further reinforced by the practice of private worship. In Geneva, as in the Reformed Churches of France, this was encouraged by the insertion into the Psalter, after Calvin's catechism, of not only prayers for morning, evening, and before and after meals, but models for complete family services for the morning and evening, entitled "the service of the father of the family and of all his domestics." The "service of the father" for the morning included an exhortation, a confession of sins (which was the same as in the public service), the morning prayer, which could end with the Lord's Prayer, and the confession of faith (the Apostles' Creed).

The national synod of Paris in 1565 asked pastors to convey the standard for family worship: "The ministers should carefully exhort the heads of families to hold regular prayers in their houses at evening and morning." On Sunday, to prepare for or to extend experience of assisting at the morning public sermon service, "sacred domestic exercises" were recommended to the faithful. Starting with these models of prayer, fervent Reformed even constructed their own family liturgy. This was the case for Baron, a lawyer (*avocat au Conseil*) and author of a *Dialogue entre un père et son fils* (1658). The son in talking to his father describes the family worship:

> You have established this order in your family, that morning and evening you have me read two or three chapters [from Scripture]... But before beginning the morning reading, I offer this prayer... Afterwards I begin reading, we sing a psalm or the last three verses of Psalm 50, and you have us note the most important doctrines encountered there. The reading over, we kneel on the floor, raise our hands and hearts to heaven, and, since we are three, you have composed a prayer, undoubtedly so all three of us may be involved, so that one begins with a general confession of sins, to which he adds the prayer for morning or evening, then another continues with the Lord's Prayer and the Apostles' Creed, and the third offers this prayer:
>
> "Lord, we offer you thanks for all the good things you have given us." When evening comes we finish the day as we began it, by reading of the Word of God, by singing a psalm, and by prayer.[32]

As the Revocation approached and places for worship were razed one after another, family worship on Sunday tended to take the place of community

---

32 *Dialogue entre un père et son fils* (n.p.: 1658), 278. On this book see Marianne Carbonnier-Burkard, "Dialogue entre un père et son fils," in *Mélanges à la mémoire de Michel Péronnet*, (eds.) Joël Fouilleron and Henri Michel, vol. 2 (Montpellier: 2003–2006), 199–213.

worship. In 1684, there appeared at Geneva a small anonymous work, *La pratique de la religion chrétienne pour les fidèles qui sont privés du S. ministère* (often attributed to the pastor Jean Claude, 1619–1687),[33] with an entire chapter devoted to the "practice of domestic piety." "Necessary at all times," the practice of domestic piety is "especially so when the flock is without a shepherd, without preaching, without a temple, without public assemblies or services." Then "every family becomes a church and every father of a family a pastor." The author distinguishes the "ordinary practice" of such piety—morning and evening—from "extraordinary practice" twice a week. For the latter, the father of the family should "imitate the public actions (worship) he has seen performed by the ministers of the Gospel." Thus, first he should "read the confession of sins that is printed at the end of the psalms or the beginning of the liturgy" (the *Form of Prayer*). Then "he should have a psalm sung proper to the season," "in a low voice, because of the rigor of the times." Then "the whole family will kneel and the father of the family will offer a prayer imploring the assistance of the Holy Spirit," for which the author provides a model. After this, the father will read the Scriptural text discussed in the selected sermon. He will "read the sermon with singular application, without undue haste and stopping at the end of the paragraphs, trying to imitate the pronunciation of a preacher." Finally "he will read the extraordinary prayer Calvin has composed for times of affliction for the church and that is printed in our liturgy," or another, entitled "Prayer on the condition of a desolate flock." This private service was an imitation of the public Sunday service, substituting for that prohibited practice. Based on the *Form of Prayer* in the Psalter, while adapting it to the present crisis, this *Pratique chrétienne* offered the French Reformed a privatization of worship born of necessity.

The "necessity" enveloped the entire kingdom in 1685 and was to last for a century. This manual, together with a prayer by Jean Claude "asking God to preserve the public exercise of religion," was reprinted on numerous occasions at Geneva and The Hague until 1779. In fact, the model it presented for private worship, based on the Genevan Psalter, was used by the first "preachers" of the Desert in their clandestine assemblies.[34] The *Form of Prayer* included in the Psalter served as a direct support for the forbidden preaching or as a framework for the new prayers "written in the Desert" spread by Claude Brousson

---

33   *La Pratique chrétienne pour les fidèles qui sont privez du S. Ministère* (Geneva: 1685).
34   See Charles Bost, *Les prédicants des Cévennes et du Bas-Languedoc, 1684–1700* (Paris: 1912), 1: 78–80, 2: 373–98.

(1647–1698).[35] Beginning in 1725 the psalters printed in Geneva adopted the Geneva liturgical modernizations inspired by J.-F. Ostervald. They emphasized the edification of the faithful more than instruction, and prayer more than the sermon. The *Forme des prières*, rebaptized as the *Prières ecclésiastiques* or *Liturgie*, was revised and enriched with a repertory of prayers for the different "solemn occasions" of the Christian calendar.[36] But it was only at the end of the 1730s that books and pastors coming from Lausanne, entering France illegally, allowed these innovations to permeate the Desert.[37]

The abandonment of the doctrinal and liturgical structure inherited from Calvin, under the influence of the Swiss "Enlightenment," came later among the French Protestants than in the stronghold of Geneva itself. Undoubtedly, the prohibition of all expression of the Reformed religion in France after 1685 contributed to prolonging the use of the old Geneva Psalter, both in the Desert and in the numerous churches of the Refuge. For the Huguenots, deprived of temples and pastors or of their native land itself, this small book, combining the *Confession of Faith* and the Geneva *Catechism*, the *Form of Prayer*, and the metrical psalms, took the place of temples and pastors or even of their homeland.

---

35 "Instruction pour les exercices de piété. Du Désert, 10 octobre 1693," in Claude Brousson, *Lettres et opuscules de feu Mons. Brousson, ministre et martyr du saint Evangile* (Utrecht: 1701), 217–44.

36 Maria-Cristina Pitassi, "De l'instruction à la piété: le débat liturgique à Genève au début du XVIIIe siècle," in *Edifier ou instruire*, 91–110.

37 Yves Krumenacker, "La liturgie, un enjeu dans la renaissance des Eglises françaises au XVIIIe siècle," in *Edifier ou instruire*, 111–26.

CHAPTER 3

Huguenot Political Thought and Activities

Hugues Daussy

1   Introduction

The appearance and spectacular expansion of the Reformed Churches, which emerged from the shadows after 1555, briefly gave the most fervent of the faithful hope that by its truth alone the Gospel would prevail in the kingdom of France. But the reaction organized by the civil and ecclesiastical authorities with the support of the *parlements* quickly convinced even the most optimistic that divine providence would have to be aided by human effort. In order to continue the spread of the "true religion" and make the light of truth shine in the highest spheres of power, Calvin and the pastors trained in Geneva resolved to politicize the spiritual conquest of the kingdom.[1] The conversion of the most eminent members of the nobility and also a part of the municipal elite henceforth became a primary objective of pastoral activity. Within a few years, between 1557, the date of the first conversions among the highest strata of the social hierarchy, and the beginning of the first civil war in 1562, a vast process of politicization of the Huguenot struggle was put into gear, laying the basis for the future development of a genuine party, conceived as both a political and a military instrument designed to assure the protection and if possible the victory of the churches of France, confronted, as they were, with the steadily increasing hostility of the Catholic zealots.

2   Conversion of Nobles and Politicization

The massive conversion to Calvinism among the kingdom's nobility toward the close of the 1550s was decisive for the politicization of the French Reformed movement. While the pastors from Geneva played an important role in these conversions, especially those who like Nicolas Des Gallars, Antoine de Chandieu and François de Morel came from the second estate, it was particularly along the axis of kinship that the new ideas traveled.

---

[1] For a detailed description of this process see Hugues Daussy, *Le parti huguenot. Chronique d'une désillusion (1557–1572)* (Geneva: 2014). See also Robert M. Kingdon, *Geneva and the Coming of the Wars of Religion in France, 1555–1563* (1956; repr. Geneva: 2007).

Much has been written about the crucial role of the mothers and wives of prominent men of the kingdom in their conversion to the Reformed religion.[2] Despite important gaps in documentation that often force historians to depend on mere conjecture, the reconstruction of the chains of conversions confirms their influence, although some of these women had never officially broken with the Roman Church. This is the case with Louise de Montmorency, sister of the constable, who was the source of two of the most enduring branches of the Reformed nobility.

Twice married and twice widowed, she saw to it that the children born of her union with Gaspard I de Coligny received a humanist education, which may not have been without significance for the later shift of the Coligny brothers to heterodoxy. The first of them to embrace Calvinism was François d'Andelot, most likely in 1555 or 1556 during his long captivity in the castle of Milan. But he waited until 1558 to profess it publicly.[3] The religious journey of his brother Gaspard, count of Coligny and admiral of France, appears less clear, but it was probably after the defeat at Saint-Quentin that his interest in the Reform increased, stimulated by the greater and greater appeal of Calvin. As for Odet, cardinal of Châtillon, known for religious moderation possibly somewhat tinctured with Erasmianism, his spiritual course remains harder to decipher. He did not actually commit himself to the Huguenot cause until after the beginning of the civil wars.

Madeleine de Mailly, a widow by 1552 and half-sister of the Coligny brothers by the same mother, seems to have declared herself earlier, although little can be stated with certainty. She probably played a decisive role in the religious instruction of her daughters, Éléonore and Charlotte de Roye, believed to have actively contributed to the conversion of their husbands. The former married Louis de Bourbon, prince of Condé, in June 1551. We do not know when or under what circumstances the latter first manifested interest in the Reformed religion. Still, we do know that he passed through Geneva in October 1555 when returning from Italy and that he heard a sermon there. As a prince of the blood his conversion was of capital importance for the political awakening of

---

2   Nancy L. Roelker, "The Appeal of Calvinism to French Noblewomen in the Sixteenth Century," *Journal of Interdisciplinary History* 2 (1972), 391–418; idem., "The Role of Noblewomen in the French Reformation," *Archiv für Reformationsgeschichte* 63 (1972), 168–95. See also the essay by Amanda Eurich in this volume.

3   Hugues Daussy, "Les enjeux politiques d'une conversion. Les relations épistolaires entre Jean Calvin, Jean Macar et François d'Andelot en 1558," in *La foi dans le siècle. Mélanges offerts à Brigitte Waché*, (eds.) Hervé Guillemain, Stéphane Tison and Nadine Vivier (Rennes: 2009), 253–61.

the French Reformed minority. The second of the sisters married in 1557 François de La Rochefoucauld, the most powerful nobleman in Poitou, whose spiritual course remains mysterious until his commitment to the Reformed movement in 1562. Jeanne d'Albret, queen of Navarre, had probably been Reformed at heart since 1555,[4] but she did not officially convert until Christmas 1560, carrying her son the young prince Henry of Navarre with her. On the other hand, her husband Antoine de Bourbon, king of Navarre and first prince of the blood, whose conversion might have disposed royal policy to favor the Reformed camp, after long hesitation ended by reaffirming his loyalty to Catholicism. His genuine sympathy for the evangelical movement was trumped by his political ambition.[5]

These conversions by the high nobility were accompanied by numerous others among the lesser nobility. A partial yet precise picture of the importance of these religious changes among the military nobility is provided by an *Estat de partie des princes, seigneurs, chevalliers de l'ordre, gentilshommes, capitaynes de l'association de Monseigneur le prince de Condé qui ont résolu de vivre et mourir ensemble pour maintenir l'evangille en France*[6] addressed to William Cecil in 1562. While it focuses almost entirely on the provinces north of the Loire, it allows us to identify 232 members of the upper and middle nobility by name and to set at more than 5000 the number of *gentilshommes* willing to serve under the Huguenot banner. It also evidences the support from persons of distinction, some of whom held offices in the service of the king in Picardy, Normandy, Poitou, Saintonge, Angoumois and the Ile-de-France. In southern provinces such as Guyenne, Languedoc, and Dauphiné, which were deeply affected by the phenomenon of noble conversions, we again find strong support among the most powerful *gentilshommes*.

Historians have discussed at length the basic motivations that led to these religious changes. The debates have generally set the proponents of sincere adherence to the Reformed faith against those who argue for actions guided by political or economic interest.[7] Any answer to a question that will undoubtedly always remain an enigma, since it is difficult to plumb consciences at a distance

---

4   Kingdon, *Geneva and the Coming*, 61.
5   Daussy, *Le parti huguenot*, 278–9.
6   Public Record Office, SP 70/41, fols. 50–56. Document published by David Potter, "The French Protestant Nobility in 1562: The Association de Monseigneur le Prince de Condé," *French History* 15 (2001), 307–28.
7   Mack P. Holt, "Putting Religion Back into the Wars of Religion," *French Historical Studies* 18 (1993), 524–51; Hugues Daussy, "Les élites face à la Réforme dans le royaume de France (ca. 1520–ca. 1570)," in *La Réforme en France et en Italie: contacts, comparaisons et contrastes*, (eds.) Philip Benedict, Silvana Seidel Menchi and Alain Tallon (Rome: 2007), 331–49.

of centuries, should certainly be highly qualified. At the top of the noble hierarchy it seems possible to claim that conversions to the Reformation were usually the result of a spiritual impulse. For these eminent individuals, near the summit of power and occupying prestigious offices, there was far more to lose than to gain by abandoning the king's religion. On the other hand, among the middling nobility it is probable that ties of clientage and personal fidelity played a more determinative role.

However this may be, the rising Huguenot tide among the nobility was decisive for the future of the French Reformation as it provided the Reformed minority with a means of political action. Among the converts, those closest to the king were available to serve as vectors for the grievances of their co-religionists and to form a sort of pressure group at the court. This new course of action was suggested by the monarchy itself, which in an edict of 16 March 1560, authorized the Reformed subjects of the king to address petitions to him. It was not until 23 August 1560, when an assembly of notables was meeting at Fontainebleau, that Coligny inaugurated the new procedure by presenting Francis II and Catherine de Medici with two petitions submitted by the Reformed of Normandy and Picardy.[8] This initiative caused a great stir, since the Admiral of France for the first time officially took the side of the Reformed cause. It was followed several months later by a project of greater scope initiated by the participants at the national synod of Poitiers, meeting in March 1561. They decided to establish a permanent deputation from the Reformed Churches to the king. Each synodal province was told to designate a person to represent it at court, and by early June 1561 there were between twelve and fifteen deputies who made up the anticipated deputation. While this group was composed about half-and-half of men from the legal professions and members of the nobility, it was invariably the latter who were designated to speak for the delegation. Gervais Barbier de Francourt, François de Barbançon de Canny, Simon de Piennes de Moigneville, Antoine de Chandieu, and Jean Raguier d'Esternay were the standard-bearers of this delegation, submitting at least four *requêtes* and one *supplique* to the king and queen mother between 11 June 1561 and 2 January 1562. The outbreak of the first civil war in March 1562 led to the dispersion of this deputation, whose members left the court.[9]

---

8 *Deux requestes de le part des fidèles de France, qui desirent vivre selon la reformation de l'Evangile, données pour présenter au Conseil tenu à Fontainebleau au mois d'aoust 1560* (n.p.: n.d.).

9 Philip Benedict and Nicolas Fornerod, "Les députés des Églises réformées à la cour en 1561–1562," *Revue Historique* 315 (2013), 289–332.

The Reformed strove simultaneously to influence the decisions taken by the Estates-General that met at Orléans in December 1560 and at Pontoise in August 1561. As the result of a remarkable effort at coordination and thanks to the conception of a genuine political program, developed in March 1561 at the national synod of Poitiers, the Huguenots sought to have themselves designated as deputies in the electoral assemblies preparatory to the Estates, or if they could not, to have their proposals inserted into the registers of grievances so they might be presented to the political establishment of the kingdom. While these attempts suffered a variety of fates, it should be noted that in the Estates of Pontoise a number of deputies from the nobility and the third estate advanced political claims similar to those defined in Poitiers.

3   The Creation of a Body of Political Thought

This activism, designed to influence royal policy in favor of the Reformed, was only one aspect of the Huguenot struggle. Beginning in 1558, there was also a gradual change in the polemical literature penned by Reformed authors. Alongside works of religious controversy appeared works with political contents, meant to refute Catholic propaganda that strove to confound heresy with sedition. The first three publications whose contents reflected this new argument were a "letter" to the king,[10] a "remonstrance" to the king,[11] and the *Apologie ou defence des bons chrestiens*.[12] All three were anonymous, but were doubtless written by pastors living in Paris, in particular Antoine de Chandieu and Nicolas Des Gallars.[13] While the themes were still in part apologetic, they also contained political arguments designed to refute the accusations of sedition that weighed on the faithful. Basing themselves on the course of conduct advocated by Calvin in his *Institutes of the Christian Religion*, the authors announced the guiding principle that was to be one of the cornerstones of their political position: fidelity to a king ordained by God, whatever the religious differences that divided them from him on a spiritual level.

---

10 Reproduced in Pierre de La Place, *Commentaires de l'estat de la religion et république sous les rois Henry et François seconds et Charles neufieme* (n.p. [Orléans]: 1565), 6–10.
11 The full text has been lost. It is summarized in Antoine de Chandieu, *Histoire des persecutions et martyrs de l'Eglise de Paris, depuis l'an 1557 iusques au temps du Roy Charles neufviesme* (Lyon: 1563), 15–17.
12 *Apologie ou defence des bons chrestiens contre les ennemis de l'Eglise catholique* (n.p.: 1558).
13 See Hugues Daussy, *Le parti huguenot*, 44–56.

These early stages in the politicization of Reformed propaganda became clearer in the waning months of 1559. The embryonic political position advanced a year earlier was expanded considerably in the Huguenot efforts to discredit the ultra-Catholic Guises before and after the Conspiracy of Amboise. Several works with distinct political content, which are known only from later descriptions,[14] were circulated throughout the kingdom. They constructed for the first time a coherent systematic argument opposing the Guise activity that they sought to condemn. By drafting a severe indictment of the two brothers, the cardinal of Lorraine and Duke François, and by denouncing their procedures and claims, the Reformed made themselves the defenders of the ancient law and constitution of the kingdom against those who wished to subvert these matters for their own profit. The creators of this argument again included the Paris pastors, notably François de Morel. Yet they above all drew inspiration from a work sent to them from Strasbourg by François Hotman. Entitled *Discours sur l'affaire Thémistyque*,[15] it was a treasure trove of arguments to bolster political polemics against the Guise, and it contained numerous examples destined to be repeated endlessly in Huguenot pamphlets.

Some months later, between March and July 1560, the development of this political argument reached a decisive stage with the publication of a dozen works justifying the Conspiracy of Amboise. They were all anonymous, but we know that François Hotman wrote the most important of them, *L'histoire du tumulte d'Amboyse* and *Epistre envoiée au Tigre de la France*.[16] Apart from a few details, all these works were copies and repetitions of each other, and displayed a wholly coherent body of doctrine. The themes advanced in 1558–59 were now repeated and developed.[17] The political fiction of the captivity of the king, a prisoner of his evil Catholic counselors, namely the Guises, against whom all this combative literature was directed, is fully elaborated. This interpretation permitted the Huguenots to excuse the sovereign from all responsibility for the royal policy hostile toward Reformed Protestants carried on by his perverse counselors, who were accused of usurping his power and reigning in his place.

---

14 La Place, *Commentaires de l'estat*, fol. 38v°-43; Louis Régnier de La Planche, *Histoire de l'Estat de France, tant de la République que de la Religion sous le règne de François II* (n.p.: 1576), 98–105; Jacques-Auguste de Thou, *Histoire universelle*, vol. 3 (London: 1734), 388–94.

15 "Thémistyque" undoubtedly means "judicial." This work has been partially published in Henri Naef, *La conjuration d'Amboise et Genève* (Paris: 1922), 166–69.

16 *L'histoire du tumulte d'Amboyse advenu au moys de mars 1560. Ensemble un avertissement et une complainte au peuple François* (n.p.: 1560); *Epistre envoiée au Tigre de la France* (n.p.: n.d. [Strasbourg: 1560]).

17 See the detailed analysis of these works in Daussy, *Le parti huguenot*, 152–66.

Accordingly, their determination to free the monarch from those who were forcing him to act against his will justified their recourse to arms. The fact that the Guises were originally from Lorraine, which was outside the kingdom, and were therefore foreigners was also underscored in order to discredit them. Thus, even before the civil wars began the foundations of the Reformed political edifice were firmly implanted and the political portrait of the Huguenot subject drawn: he was faithful to his king who was ordained by God, he submitted to the laws of the kingdom which he deeply respected, he was hostile to tyranny, he was a patriot, and he was ready to die to guarantee his prince the exercise of power according to his own free will.[18]

This theoretical foundation was taken up again and extended beginning in April 1562 in order to justify the recourse to arms by the prince of Condé and the Huguenot nobility. According to the necessities of the moment, the works written by the Reformed polemicists pragmatically alternated between or combined emphasis on the political and religious dimensions, thus demonstrating the complete mixing of motives, constitutional as well as confessional, in the Huguenot revolt. Twelve texts printed during the first civil war came directly from the entourage of the prince of Condé.[19] The political argument was enriched with some refinements based on "constitutional" grounds. Thus, Condé asserted that as a prince of the blood the captivity of Charles IX and his mother, Catherine de Medici, reputed prisoners of the Catholic triumvirate, the duke of Guise, the constable de Montmorency, and the marshal de Saint-André, had forced him to act in conformity with the obligations of his status. Deriving his justification from the theory of the king's two bodies, Condé clothed himself in the legitimacy conferred on him by his rank and in the obligations he claimed to have with respect to the crown. As one of the most eminent members of the *corps politique* of the kingdom, it was his duty to come to the aid of the king who was its head and who found himself deprived of all freedom of action.[20] In short, under his direction the Huguenots were not taking up arms solely for their religion but also in the service of the king and for the wellbeing of the state. Pursuant to an argument that had now been

---

18   Hugues Daussy, "L'invention du citoyen réformé. L'expression de l'identité politique huguenote dans la littérature polémique et les premiers ouvrages historiques réformés," in *L'identité huguenote: faire mémoire et écrire l'histoire (XVIe–XXIe siècles)*, (eds.) Philip Benedict, Hugues Daussy and Pierre-Olivier Léchot (Geneva: 2013), 37–48.

19   Complete list and detailed analysis of these works in Daussy, *Le parti huguenot*, 292–311; 789–92.

20   Arlette Jouanna, *Le devoir de révolte. La noblesse française et la gestation de l'État moderne, 1559–1661* (Paris: 1989), 288 and 294.

thoroughly refined, the defense of royal authority and the protection of the Reformed Churches of France were combined harmoniously and apparently without contradiction.

During the second and third civil wars—between September 1567 and August 1570—more than fifty pamphlets with strong political connotations emerged from the Reformed presses.[21] Tirelessly repeating the recurrent themes of the Huguenot arguments, they again emphasized the necessity of liberating the king from his wicked entourage. Yet in order to attract more sympathizers to the Reformed cause they also insisted on their desire to defend the political interests of the French nobility as a whole, whether Catholic or Reformed, against the foreign favorites who swarmed about the royal entourage. It was no longer only the Lorrainers, but also the Italians who benefited from royal favor thanks to the queen mother, herself a Florentine. This defense of the interests of the nobility was combined with that of the "public good," since the foreign favorites were accused of burdening the people with taxes in order to satisfy their own lust for power.

4 The Birth of the Huguenot Political System

Parallel to the development of this combative thinking, a genuine political organization soon developed. By 1561, its creation was essential for the Huguenots, since their ecclesiastical institutions, which were not intended to play a political role, could not continue to provide the necessary impetus in this domain. Still, the transfer of political initiative to decision-making bodies separate from the consistorial-synodal system was accomplished only gradually.

In initiating the dispatch of deputies from the French Churches to the court in March 1561, the national synod of Poitiers had laid the first foundation block of a Reformed political organization on a national scale. In the following months, all the energy of the nascent Huguenot party was absorbed by the Estates-General of Pontoise and the Colloquy of Poissy. But in the provinces, and especially in the southern reaches, Reformed Protestants had to confront the increasingly violent aggressiveness of their Catholic neighbors. Beginning in the autumn of 1561, the difficulty of living together led them to take measures to protect themselves. Unfortunately, only a handful of documents preserve

---

21 For a complete list and detailed analysis of these works see Daussy, *Le parti huguenot*, 638–71; 794–8.

any trace of the developments.²² Locally, in those few towns where the Huguenots retained political power, such as Nîmes, Castres, Montpellier and Montauban, close collaboration was established between the consistory and the consulate, between the spiritual and the temporal, both established by God in order to uphold his Word. This conjunction of political action and religious requirements was often facilitated by the presence of certain town councilors in the consistories. Their dual membership in the city's two executive institutions fostered the merger of interests in the defense of the faith. Parallel to these attempts at organization on a local scale, which ended in the creation of institutions of ephemeral duration, closely connected with the present emergency, the provincial synods undertook more general measures beginning in the fall of 1561.²³ At Sainte-Foy in November, several *gentilshommes* participated in the synod of Upper Guyenne, contrary to the rules that governed the composition of these assemblies. With their urging, the foundations were laid for a military organization closely modeled on the consistorial-synodal system, whose different levels it reproduced. At the top, two "general chiefs called protectors" were placed over the "two provinces of the *parlements* of Bordeaux and Toulouse," which corresponded to the synodal provinces of Upper and Lower Guyenne, and Upper Languedoc. The colloquies, each provided with a "colonel," were the second level of the pyramidal chain of command. Finally, a "local captain" was to be designated for each church.²⁴ On a national scale, Coligny took the initiative by counting the churches in order to show the queen mother the strength of the nascent Huguenot party and its ability to aid the king in case of need. At the very end of 1561, he asked that a list be made of forces that could be mobilized immediately by the Huguenots in case of war.²⁵

In several provinces, informal assemblies composed of *gentilshommes*, local notables, and sometimes pastors also met in the spring of 1562 to designate military commanders and set up an embryonic organization. Meetings were

---

22   Philip Benedict, "The Dynamics of Protestant Militancy: France, 1555–1563," in *Reformation, Revolt and Civil War in France and the Netherlands, 1555–1585*, (eds.) Philip Benedict, Guido Marnef, Henk van Nierop and Marc Venard (Amsterdam: 1999), 42–45; Daussy, *Le parti huguenot*, 351–55.

23   Contrary to the assertion of Lucien Romier, *Le royaume de Catherine de Médicis. La France à la veille des guerres de religion*, vol. 2 (Paris: 1925), 264–65, the synod of Clairac, which met on 19 November 1560, took no military measures.

24   *Histoire ecclésiastique des Eglises reformées au royaume de France*, (eds.) Johann Wilhelm Baum, Edouard Cunitz, and Rodolphe Reuss, vol. 1 (Paris: 1884), 888.

25   Philip Benedict and Nicolas Fornerod, "Les 2150 'églises' réformées de France en 1561–1562," *Revue historique* 311 (2009), 529–60.

held at Valence in Dauphiné, at Nîmes in Languedoc, and at Saint-Jean-d'Angély in Saintonge. More ambitious was the provincial synod held in Paris on 16 and 17 September 1561. It announced the principle of mutual aid among the Reformed from the different synodal provinces, always within a strict framework of obedience to the king. These developments were the beginning of a movement for political and military coordination among groups of neighboring provinces, if not within the kingdom as a whole. However, this intervention of national and provincial synods in political and military affairs arose only from the force of circumstances. These ecclesiastical assemblies, theoretically composed only of pastors and elders designated by the churches in their jurisdictions, were not authorized to intrude in the political and military realms, and the actions just mentioned represent only a tiny part of their work, which was mainly devoted to questions of Church discipline. The acts of the synod held at Lyon on 25 November 1561 show these assemblies' determination to avoid the administration of these problems. It was decided "that at those synods held in the future we will treat only affairs that concern matters of religion."[26]

While this withdrawal from political affairs was not entirely successful, it nevertheless solidified substantially as a result of the first civil war. A structured and organized Huguenot party, heretofore only in gestation, now began to emerge. This political organization had two levels. At the summit of the Huguenot social pyramid the higher Reformed nobility held the political and military reins of the party, under the direction of the prince of Condé, Admiral Coligny, François d'Andelot, and François de La Rochefoucauld. Based at Orléans, these noble elite entered into a dialogue with the court in the hope of finding grounds for an agreement leading to the return of peace, negotiated with foreign Protestant princes to obtain military aid, and ended by fighting the royal army commanded by the duke of Guise. They envisioned carrying out the struggle on the scale of the kingdom as a whole. But at the same time the southern Reformers established in Languedoc and Dauphiné new institutions whose purpose was to organize the defense of the churches in those provinces where the Huguenots had great numerical strength. Thus, beginning in November 1562 there appeared what is customarily described under the general heading of Huguenot political assemblies. They were not strictly speaking new institutions, created *ex nihilo*, but a confessional version of the provincial

---

26 "Articles arrestez au Synode tenu à Lyon le xxv novembre 1561, auquel Monsieur d'Anduze a presidé," in *L'organisation et l'action des Églises réformées de France (1557–1563). Synodes provinciaux et autres documents*, (eds.) Philip Benedict and Nicolas Fornerod (Geneva: 2012), 116–23.

estates of Languedoc and Dauphiné, where the deep religious division was expressed in a provisional institutional schism during a period of confrontation. In Languedoc, they were also, at a lower territorial level, confessionalized adaptations of the local estates of Vivarais, as well as of assemblies for tax assessment and local assemblies held in the civil dioceses dominated by the Huguenots, especially that of Castres in Upper Languedoc.

The study of these assemblies remains fragmentary,[27] as the incomplete and scattered documentation remains largely neglected.[28] Studies currently being carried out nevertheless permit us to reconstitute the principal stages in the evolution of the political system of which they formed an essential element.[29] The founding assembly was held at Nîmes in November 1562. Composed of deputies from fifteen towns and members of the nobility, it inaugurated a series of seven assemblies that met in Languedoc and Dauphiné during the first civil war, and then thirty others held for Languedoc alone during the two ensuing conflicts.[30] The work accomplished by the assemblies that met during these first three wars responded to the need that had led to their creation: to devise the political, military, and financial structure the Huguenots lacked in order to organize their resistance in the southern provinces. On the political front, the first decisions concerned the command organization in the areas dominated by the Reformed. The assemblies designated the military and political head for each province involved and appointed the members of a political council and a council of war to assist them. Count Antoine de Crussol was the first to receive the title of "chief, defender, and preserver" of the churches of Languedoc, then of those of Dauphiné and Lyonnais when a draft of a confederation among the Reformed of these provinces was created in December 1562. In the financial area, the assemblies took many decisions in order to mobilize their resources. Confiscations and taxes accumulated, allowing them to gather large sums of money that attracted the envy of the great personages of the

---

27 Only some very incomplete studies exist: Léonce Anquez, *Histoire des assemblées politiques des réformés de France (1573–1622)* (1859; repr. Geneva: 1970); Emma Lorimer, *Huguenot General Assemblies in France, 1579–1622* (PhD diss., Oxford University: 2004).

28 Most of the minutes of these assemblies are preserved in the departmental archives of Gard, Hérault, Ardèche and Tarn, as well as in the Bibliothèque nationale de France and the Bibliothèque Mazarine.

29 The author of this chapter is currently studying this political system. For the assemblies before 1572 see Daussy, *Le parti huguenot, passim*. For an overview see Hugues Daussy, "Les assemblées et le système politique huguenots (1562–1598)," in *La France huguenote. Histoire institutionnelle d'une minorité religieuse (XVIe–XVIIIe siècles)*, (eds.) Philippe Chareyre and Hugues Daussy (Rennes: 2016).

30 List and detailed analysis in Daussy, *Le parti huguenot*, 360–86; 593–8; 630–8.

party. The latter, ensconced at La Rochelle during the third war, negotiated with the assemblies of Languedoc for the payment of subsidies to finance their troops. Although relations between the two wings of the Huguenot party were sometimes tense, important financial contributions were nevertheless made to Coligny, Jeanne d'Albret, and the young princes Henry of Navarre and Henry of Condé, who had become the official heads of the party after the death of Louis of Condé at Jarnac in March 1569.[31]

5   The Radicalization of Huguenot Political Thought

After the Saint Bartholomew's Day massacre, which was deeply traumatic for the Huguenot minority, some Reformed theoreticians openly expressed a radical political program. This did not appear out of nowhere, however, since the presence of a marginal and subterranean current of thought in the French evangelical movement was not a novelty. During the first civil war, attacks and iconoclastic depredations of royal tombs and effigies had been reported. In Orléans, busts of Louis XI and Louis XII were torn from the façade of the town hall, and the heart of Francis II, which had been deposited in the cathedral of Saint-Croix, was profaned and burned. In Notre-Dame de Cléry the tomb of Louis XI was also profaned, his copper statue decapitated, his bones thrown to the dogs, and his ashes scattered in the wind.[32]

From 1563 on, defiance of the monarchy began to be expressed in writing. The *Sentence redoutable et arrest rigoureux du jugement de Dieu, à l'encontre de l'impiété des tyrans*, written in Huguenot circles at Lyon, clearly formulated the idea of conditional obedience subject to the prince's respect of his duties to God and the people. If he shirked them and acted as a tyrant he could be dethroned.[33] The prince thus derived his legitimacy from the manner in which he exercised his power, a revolutionary assertion calling into question God's ordaining of the prince. In his address to the king some months later, François

---

31   On these financial questions see Hugues Daussy, "Financing the Huguenot War Effort during the Early Wars of Religion, 1562–1570," *French Historical Studies* (forthcoming); and Mark Greengrass, "Financing the Cause: Protestant Mobilization and Accountability in France," in *Reformation, Revolt and Civil War*, 233–54.

32   Denis Crouzet, "Calvinism and the Uses of the Political and the Religious," in *Reformation, Revolt and Civil War*, 111, and *Les guerriers de Dieu. La violence au temps des troubles de religion, vers 1525–vers 1610*, vol. 1 (Seyssel: 1989), 757–58.

33   *Sentence redoutable et arrest rigoureux du jugement de Dieu, à l'encontre de l'impiété des tyrans, recueillies tant des sainctes escriptures, comme de toutes autres histoires* (Lyon: 1564), 21.

de Boucard also sketched out the idea of a contract, based on the prince's obligation to guarantee to all his subjects the just and equal application of the law. The prize for subversion, however, goes to another work entitled *La Defense civile et militaire des innocents et de l'Eglise de Christ*, published at Lyon in June 1563 and attributed to the jurist Charles Du Moulin. Unanimously condemned by the Lyon Reformed pastors, with Pierre Viret at their head, it was so violent that Soubise ordered it burned and all those possessing it condemned to death. Thus, there is no existing copy, but its contents are known thanks to the justification published by Du Moulin, who, to clear himself, refuted the work at issue.[34] This refutation reveals the central and highly subversive idea of the *Defense civile*: numerous examples drawn from the Bible authorize subjects to undertake armed resistance when their prince oppresses their consciences and commands them to act against God and his Word. This was an assertion that the Reformed, careful to clear themselves of any inclination to sedition, could not possibly endorse.

Beginning in October 1567 and as the result of the two successive wars that disturbed the kingdom until the Peace of Saint-Germain, Huguenot political ideas were pushed farther along the road to radicalism. Like their predecessors, the authors of this literature drew part of their inspiration from the subtle consideration Calvin, Beza, and Viret had given to the appropriateness of and the conditions for resistance to tyrants.[35] The theological and political foundation provided by the conclusions these men had reached on this delicate question was of immense value for the later authors' arguments. Jean de La Haize of La Rochelle, to whom one of the most eloquent pamphlets is attributed,[36] was also the author of the preface of the edition of Calvin's sermons on Daniel printed by Barthélemy Berton in 1565.[37] In this posthumous work, Calvin emphasized that Daniel did not sin by disobeying the king. He thus affirmed that princes are *de facto* deprived of their authority when they cease to serve God and that they should not thereafter be considered princes. Not only should

---

34   Charles Du Moulin, *Apologie de M. Charles Du Moulin, contre un livret intitulé: "la Deffense civile et militaire des innocens et de l'Église de Christ"* (Lyon: 1563).

35   See especially Quentin Skinner, *The Foundations of Modern Political Thought*, vol. 2 (Cambridge: 1978), 225–38. Also Hugues Daussy, "Les huguenots entre l'obéissance au roi et l'obéissance à Dieu," *Nouvelle Revue du XVIe siècle* 22 (2004), 49–69; Robert D. Linder, "Pierre Viret and the Sixteenth-Century French Protestant Revolutionary Tradition," *Journal of Modern History* 38 (1966), 125–37.

36   *Declaration et Protestation de ceux de la religion reformee de La Rochelle, sur la prise et capture des armes qu'ils ont fait le neufieme de Ianuier dernier* (La Rochelle: 1568).

37   *Quarante-sept sermons de M. Jean Calvin sur les huict derniers chapitres des prophéties de Daniel, recueillis fidèlement de sa bouche, selon qu'il les preschoit* (La Rochelle: 1565).

one cease to obey them, he should "bring them down." La Haize relied upon this assertion when arguing in favor of a right of armed resistance granted to inferior magistrates.

Even if this group of authors generally agreed in reaffirming that Charles IX was not responsible for the tyrannical acts committed in his name, mention of royal innocence gradually tended to disappear and be replaced by warnings. Several pieces in verse were more menacing and seemed to have had the audacity to address the king directly. *Cato ou reproche à Pompée* compared Charles IX to Pompey, while Condé was compared to Caesar, the restorer of the state. The defeat of the former was certain unless he drove away the evil counselors from his entourage to make way for the virtuous nobility.[38] Another important theme emerged in the most daring pamphlets, that of the nature of royal power and the relationship of the monarch to his subjects. Here again the theories advanced were innovative, since the sacred character of the sovereign and his power were brought into question. The author of the *Requeste et remonstrance du peuple* did not hesitate to state that historically the people preceded the king, whom they freely consented to recognize because God had inspired them with the desire for obedience. Thus, royalty was not divinely delegated. It was the people, the keepers of sovereignty, who delegated it at God's instigation and who could retrieve it at any moment if God chose to remove their disposition to obey. It therefore became impossible for any sovereign who displeased God to preserve his power. The deposition of a bad king presented no other major difficulties, since numerous historical precedents were cited to demonstrate that the very existence of a monarch was not indispensable.[39] The right to resist a tyrant was thereby further legitimized by removing the sacred character of the sovereign.

The idea of consent as the source of monarchical power appeared again in one of the most famous pamphlets, published at La Rochelle during the third civil war. It was by Jean de Coras and bore the eloquent title *Question politique: s'il est licite aux subjects de capituler avec leur prince*.[40] Coras developed the idea that subjects have the right to "*capituler*" with their sovereign, that is, to negotiate with him. But the author of the *Question politique* gave "*capituler*" a still more subversive meaning, because according to him it also involved a reference to the idea of a contract. This contract, an agreement between the king

---

38   *Cato ou reproche à Pompée, se rapportant aux troubles présentes: avec une imprécation à Dieu vengeur* (Orléans: 1568).
39   *Requeste et remonstrance du peuple, addressante au Roy* (Orléans: 1567).
40   Jean de Coras, *Question politique: s'il est licite aux subjects de capituler avec leur prince*, (ed.) Robert M. Kingdon (Geneva: 1989).

and the people, had its source in a primitive election and must be scrupulously respected. In virtue of that original engagement, the subjects were required to obey the king and the king to look after his subjects. The monarch must avoid at any price adopting a tyrannical attitude that would lead him to cease to *"capituler"* with his people by imposing his will on them arbitrarily. Although the Huguenots out of political necessity stubbornly continued to deny any sort of revolt against the king, continually assigning all guilt to his entourage, an evolution in the concept of the relationship between the monarch and his subjects was certainly under way.

In the years immediately following the Saint Bartholomew's Day massacre, these theories, which the early publications expressed in fragmentary form, developed into a coherent ideological system. Several Reformed thinkers, among them François Hotman, Theodore Beza and Philippe Duplessis-Mornay, published anonymously ten or so treatises with "revolutionary" political contents. The most famous were the *Francogallia* (1573), *Du droit des magistrats sur leurs sujets* (1574), *Le Réveille-Matin des François et de leurs voisins* (1574), and the *Vindiciae contra tyrannos* (1579).[41] Called monarchomachs (those who wish to kill monarchs) by their detractors, these authors did not in fact wish to fight against the monarchy, but against tyranny, whether religious or political. These treatises redefined the relationship of obedience to a prince who tyrannized his subjects. The basis of the argument was the assertion of the sovereignty the people as a body (represented by the Estates-General) and not of the populace in general. The people have the power to choose their kings and to depose them by virtue of a double contract. The first contract, invoking the image of the biblical covenant, was concluded between God and the whole of the people, who in turn contracted with the king. This was the principle of the double covenant. The second contract imposed unequal obligations. The people were required to obey their prince only when the latter respected the engagements he had made to them. In case of the king's tyrannical behavior, whether it involved political or spiritual tyranny, it became legitimate to resist him, by resort to arms if required. All these treatises insisted on the necessity of adhering to legal resistance, founded upon a "constitutional" basis, following a well-established process. A mere private person could not rise up against a tyrant, since this right was reserved to the Estates of the kingdom or the inferior magistrates (all those who possessed public authority). It was their duty to admonish the king and if he was obstinate to take up arms against him and to depose him. However, there was no question of authorizing tyrannicide against what

---

41 Paul-Alexis Mellet, *Les traités monarchomaques. Confusion des temps, résistance armée et monarchie parfaite (1560–1600)* (Geneva: 2007).

these authors called a "tyrant by exercise," that is a legitimate prince who had sunk into tyranny. On the other hand, when dealing with a tyrant by usurpation, it might be legitimate to kill him. These works do not reject monarchy, but rather the gradual slide of the method of governing the kingdom toward the solitary exercise of monarchical power. They condemned a system that, by giving too much power to a king supported by a handful of evil counselors, had led to so tragic an event as the Saint Bartholomew's Day massacre. These theories were extremely subversive, and although these treatises clearly emerged from their ranks, it is important to note that the Huguenots never officially approved them as an authorized expression of their views. Such an avowal would indeed have given the most intransigent Catholics an ideal argument to justify their extermination as subjects rebelling against royal authority and criminals guilty of *lèse-majesté*.[42]

6   The Creation of a Confederal Political System

Among the consequences of the Saint Bartholomew's Day massacre was the strengthening of the Huguenot political system. It developed rapidly with the reestablishment of the political assemblies, which had not met since the Peace of Saint-Germain. A more complex system quickly emerged. The political assemblies henceforth became so numerous in Languedoc that the fragmentary and inexact character of the available sources makes the compiling of an exhaustive list impossible. For the period between 1572 and the signing of the Edict of Nantes, a provisional count allows the identification for the southern provinces of more than 200 assemblies that deserve to be called "political."[43]

It is nonetheless possible to trace the history of the gradual development of a confederal structure whose purpose was ultimately to represent all the Reformed of the kingdom. The first assemblies that included deputies from several provinces met at the end of the winter of 1573. The practice seems to have been inaugurated at Anduze in February 1573. Some months later, at Millau in December 1573, the "general assembly of the Reformed Churches of France held both by the nobility and other estates" recruited delegates from farther afield, since it had a genuinely national dimension. Besides the southern provinces, areas such as Normandy, the Cotentin, the Duchy of Alençon, Maine, the Pays Chartrain, Beauce, Perche, the Ile-de-France, Picardy, the

---

42   Skinner, *The Foundations*, 2: 302–48.
43   Daussy, "Les assemblées et le système politique huguenot."

Vexin, and the Pays de Caux also sent deputies.[44] The general assemblies that followed did not recruit as widely, because until August 1575 they only involved representatives from the southern half of the kingdom, mainly from Languedoc, but also from La Rochelle and Angoumois, which did not prevent them from taking measures that were obligatory for all the churches of France. Beginning in 1579, the scope widened, with an increasingly "national" representation at the assemblies, but the development was gradual. At Montauban in 1584, only six deputies out of thirty-seven had come from north of the Loire. Ten years later at Sainte-Foy, the delegates from the more northerly provinces of the kingdom constituted 50 per cent of the assembly. It marked the completion of the evolution of a system for the effective representation of all the Reformed Churches of France.

Over the course of the nine general assemblies held between February 1573 and August 1575 the first decisions aimed at establishing an effective Reformed political organization were taken. The system was federal in nature, but it would be going too far to call it, as some historians have, the "United Provinces of the Midi."[45] In the first place, it was not restricted to the south of the kingdom. More importantly, the term seems to imply, by analogy with the United Provinces that were established in 1579 with the division of the Spanish Netherlands, that the French Reformers planned this political system as a basis for secession. This was not the case. All the texts originating with the political assemblies that met after December 1573 reaffirmed the obedience of the French Reformers to their king and their inclusion in the kingdom. In describing the Huguenot federal system, it is more appropriate to call them the "Provinces of the Union," an expression the Reformed themselves used in certain of their works.[46]

The overarching principles that governed the structure and the functioning of the system were defined in the regulations approved at Millau and Nîmes in 1573 and 1575, then at La Rochelle in 1588. In the course of an ongoing evolution, a pyramidal system of assemblies, modeled on the consistorial-synodal one, was created throughout the kingdom, which itself was divided into *généralités*. At the local level, the town or village councils elected for each *généralité* deputies to sit in the provincial assemblies, which in turn sent two

---

44 "Organisation du parti protestant délibérée à Millau le 17 décembre 1573," BSHPF 10 (1861), 351–53.

45 Janine Garrisson, *Protestants du Midi* (Toulouse: 1980), 177–95.

46 Arlette Jouanna, "Les 'Provinces de l'Union,' un État dans l'État?," in *Jean Calvin. Les visages multiples d'une réforme et de sa réception*, (eds.) Daniel Bolliger, Marc Boss, Mireille Hébert, and Jean-François Zorn (Lyon: 2009), 155–75.

of their members, one noble and one from the third estate, to the general assembly representing all the churches of the country. The intervals between meetings of these assemblies varied initially, but were eventually set at once each year for provincial assemblies and every two years for the general assemblies. These assemblies retained sovereign power over the Huguenot political system, but delegated the exercise of executive and military power to the most eminent members of the party. A protector of the Reformed Churches of France was designated to exercise supreme authority in these domains. After 1576, this was Henry of Navarre, the first prince of the blood. He was assisted by a council whose members were appointed by the assemblies and who were supposed to monitor his actions so as to keep him from the temptation to act tyrannically. The protector was also supposed to designate a "*général*" in charge of each *généralité*. The "*général*" was assisted by a provincial council whose members were designated by the provincial assembly. Finally, at the sub-provincial level, governors, also assisted by councils, were appointed by the generals to head smaller districts, and commissioners were chosen to represent Huguenot power in each key town. This closely-woven structure was intended to exercise very strict supervision over the areas that had fallen into Huguenot hands, and therefore it actually happened only in some southern regions. Apart from this political structure, the assemblies also established various institutions charged with financial administration and with raising funds to support Huguenot resistance. In practice the civil wars made it impossible to follow the proposed schedule for holding meetings, and the protector's council never actually existed because of the king of Navarre's reluctance to submit to any oversight by the assemblies. In general, however, the system functioned sufficiently well to organize the defenses of the party in the southern regions of the kingdom and to sustain the king of Navarre's military efforts.[47]

Despite the theoretical prohibition on interference by ecclesiastical assemblies in political affairs, there was no air-tight barrier between the consistorial-synodal system and the Huguenot political organization. The desire to separate the two organizations entirely was expressed on 20 July 1567 in regulations probably drafted by the higher Huguenot nobility to establish a system capable of rapidly raising and financing troops in all the provinces of the kingdom.[48] But it is clear that this decision remained relatively theoretical and that pragmatism prevailed when the need arose to provide the electoral procedures

---

47 Daussy, "Les assemblées et le système politique huguenot."
48 Regulations of 20 July 1567, BnF, ms fr. 3174, fol. 109–112 v°. See Daussy, *Le parti huguenot*, 578–83.

with a legitimate institutional underpinning. Many deputies to the various political assemblies were elected within the framework of the ecclesiastical institutions, and pastors also often sat on them.

Gaps in the archival records prevent us from establishing reliable statistics to describe precisely and over time the number and social composition of the different categories of political assemblies. We have enough data for the general assemblies, however, for whom the number of deputies varied from eighteen at Saint-Jean-d'Angély in 1582 to seventy-nine for the assembly of Millau at the end of 1573. Calculations drawn from a sample of five of the eleven general assemblies between December 1573 and November 1588 show that half (51 per cent) of the deputies belonged to the nobility, while 29 per cent were bourgeois and 20 per cent pastors.[49] Among the urban deputies, men from the legal professions and municipal magistrates monopolized almost all the positions. At the lower level of the provincial assemblies the percentage of these deputies coming from towns controlled by the Huguenots was probably greater, while nobles were fewer. If anything is certain, it is that a concern for the representative character of the assemblies was a central preoccupation of the deputies, who were determined to confer indisputable legitimacy on the decisions taken at every level of the system.[50]

7 The Political Campaign for Henry of Navarre

The death on 10 June 1584 of François d'Alençon, duke of Anjou and the king's sole living brother, made Henry of Navarre the presumptive heir to the throne of France under Salic law. Confronted with the determination of intransigent Catholics, foremost among them the Guises, to prevent the succession of a Protestant king, the Huguenots did not back down. In defending the legitimate rights of their protector, they were not content with responding to the military challenge of the Catholic League; they also entered unreservedly into political combat, which they carried on by means of dozens of pamphlets and other polemical treatises published in response to Catholic works. In this struggle, Philippe Duplessis-Mornay, principal councilor to the heir to the throne, displayed remarkable energy. Between March 1585 and August 1589 he wrote no

---

49 Garrisson, *Protestants du Midi*, 205.
50 Hugues Daussy, "Le problème de la représentativité dans le système politique huguenot. Premières recherches," in *La période des guerres de religion: historiographie, histoire des idées politiques*, (eds.) Isabelle Bouvignies, Frédéric Gabriel and Marco Penzi (Lyon, forthcoming).

less than twenty-six works of propaganda, published in the name of the king of Navarre or under cover of anonymity.[51] Other Huguenot pamphleteers also threw themselves into the battle. François Hotman, for example, published his *Brutum fulmen* aimed at the bull of Sixtus V in 1586. These works systematically developed an argument carefully worked out by Mornay and largely inspired by the recurrent themes of the political thought developed by the Huguenots since 1558. The objective was to shift the conflict to the political realm and away from the religious one preferred by the Catholic League. They aimed at demonstrating that the rights of the king of Navarre to the crown of France were incontestable under Salic law, the fundamental law of the kingdom, and that the prince's religion should not figure in a question of a political nature like the succession to the throne. To reinforce his legitimacy, the Huguenot authors presented Henry of Navarre as an ideal prince, replete with all the virtues, kind, "tolerant" of Catholics, and faithful to Henry III. His resort to arms was justified, following the usual rhetoric, as a struggle to help the king and to free him from the ascendancy of the Guises, the evil councilors who prevented him from expressing his true will. The political fiction of the manipulated king was based above all on a line of argumentation aimed at discrediting the heads of the League, who were accused of wishing to keep Henry of Navarre from the throne in order to seize it themselves upon the death of the reigning king. For them religion was only a pretext masking their true objective. Huguenot propaganda also emphasized Guise origins in the Duchy of Lorraine. They were constantly accused of being foreigners allied with Spain. By way of contrast, the king of Navarre and the Huguenots were presented as good Frenchmen and loyal subjects of the king, watchful of the interests of the kingdom and attentive to the needs of the people, upon whom the leaguers had brought suffering by engaging in a civil war. By claiming that one could be both Catholic and criminal, and both Reformed and a faithful subject of the king, the Protestant polemicists strove to extend the distinction between citizen and Christian that they had begun more than twenty-five years earlier. This movement toward the separation of the political and religious spheres, which traditionally had been merged, favored the Huguenot cause. They, of course, sought to obtain from the king civil equality with the Catholics.[52] This campaign was not in vain, since in August 1589 Henry IV became the first Protestant king of France.

---

51   Hugues Daussy, *Les huguenots et le roi. Le combat politique de Philippe Duplessis-Mornay (1572–1600)* (Geneva: 2002), 290–97.
52   Daussy, *Les huguenots et le roi*, 298–346.

8 The Struggle for Recognition

Henry IV's conversion to Catholicism in July 1593 opened a period of intense negotiations between the Reformed and the sovereign. Resolved to obtain the recognition they had sought for so long, the Huguenots engaged in a five-year test of strength with their former protector that ended in the signing of the Edict of Nantes. The first of a series of seven political assemblies opened at Mantes in November 1593. The deputies of the Reformed Churches of France drafted a list of grievances in which they stated their complaints and the remedies they desired in the form of an edict clearly defining their legal status in the kingdom of France. The king and his council proved unreceptive to these proposals, which they considered excessive. A second assembly, meeting in Sainte-Foy in 1594, was hardly more successful in dealing with the king, but its members took a series of important decisions, perfecting the military organization of the Huguenot party and establishing new regulations that substantially altered the functioning of the political system. They divided the kingdom into ten provinces, each headed by a provincial council composed of five to seven members appointed by the provincial assemblies. The latter were to be composed of three representatives from each colloquy—one noble, one pastor, and one member of the third estate. The electoral districts at the basic level were ecclesiastical, confirming the ongoing absence of an air-tight separation of the religious and political domains. At the higher level, the general assembly was reduced in size, since only one deputy per province was to sit on it, thus ten in all. By means of a system of rotation decided by drawing lots, four deputies were to be nobles, two pastors, and four members of the third estate. This division into three "orders," rejected by the general assemblies since 1575, since they had only separated the deputies into the nobility and the third estate, undoubtedly reflected the desire of the Reformed to reproduce the model of the Estates-General and to appropriate its highly representative system, with the major difference that the Huguenot deputies did not vote by order but by province. These elected representatives of the kingdom's churches joined the most eminent members of the party, who were authorized to sit by virtue of their rank.[53] These arrangements were later revised at Saumur in 1595, then at Loudun in 1596. Among the revisions was a doubling of the number of representatives of each province in the general assemblies, which then totaled twenty.

---

53 *Règlement arrêté par l'assemblée de Saincte-Foy, le 30 juillet 1594*, BPF, Ms 710, pièce n° 29(1).

The assembly of Saumur made no progress in the negotiations with the king, and at Loudun in 1596 the Huguenot deputies threatened to break off their dialogue with Henry IV. All the political skill of Duplessis-Mornay, who served as a sort of intermediary between the king and the assemblies, was required to avoid a catastrophe. This crisis marked a decisive turning point in the process of negotiation, which henceforth took on a new character. The king agreed in principle to the drafting of a new edict and named several commissioners to discuss it with the Protestant deputies. Thereafter the deputies sat almost without interruption until the signing of the Edict of Nantes. They suspended their sessions only to change meeting places. There was continuous movement back and forth between the court and the assemblies, with royal commissioners carrying the offers of the council and the Reformed deputies their responses and lists of grievances. On more than one occasion the situation appeared desperate, the king refusing to grant his former co-religionists what they considered indispensable for their survival. In 1597, when the Huguenots were meeting at Saumur there was again nearly a break between Henry IV, who asked the Protestant nobility to come to his aid at Amiens, which had been captured by the Spaniards on 11 March, and the deputies, who did not hesitate to make their obedience conditional upon the satisfaction of their demands. Faced by the need to obtain their military support, the king made numerous concessions. These were the last gains made by the Reformed. After the retaking of Amiens in September 1597 without the help of his Huguenot subjects, Henry IV refused any further changes in the text of the edict, which was signed at Nantes on 30 April 1598.[54] More than an edict freely granted by the king to his Reformed subjects, the Edict of Nantes was in the end a treaty fiercely negotiated between two contracting parties determined to defend their interests.

9 The Gradual Destruction of the Huguenot Political System

After 1598[55] and despite Article 82 of the Edict of Nantes which forbade them, Henry IV regularly authorized the Huguenots to hold political assemblies. Yet the monarch was hesitant to accede to these requests, since he did not want the Reformed of his kingdom to be able to constitute a consistent political

---

54 For a detailed account of these negotiations see Daussy, *Les huguenots et le roi*, 500–64.
55 For a more detailed account of the evolution of the Huguenot political system during this final period see Hugues Daussy and Mark Greengrass, "La fin des institutions politico-militaires (1598–1629)," in *La France huguenote* (forthcoming).

entity. In 1601 the king also allowed his Reformed subjects to establish deputies-general at the court, veritable permanent ambassadors from the churches to the king. Beginning in 1605, these deputies were chosen by the king himself from a list proposed by the Huguenots. Until the assassination of Henry IV in 1610, relations between the king and his Reformed subjects were good and peaceful, despite their determination to obtain permission to hold political assemblies and the various complaints and petitions they regularly addressed to him.

After the apparent tranquility of the last years of Henry IV's reign, the members of the highest Huguenot nobility frequently adopted an ambiguous attitude that contributed substantially to reinforcing the idea, already implanted within the king's council by the activism of members of the Catholic *dévot* party, that the Huguenot political and military power should be suppressed for the good of the royal State. In order to appease the fears expressed by the Reformed through their deputies-general, the regent Marie de Medici published on 22 May 1610 a declaration confirming the Edict of Nantes. She also permitted a new political assembly. Meeting in Saumur from May to September 1611 and presided over by Duplessis-Mornay, the assembly adopted a new set of regulations that refined the organization of the party by the creation of a third level of political assemblies intermediate between the provincial assemblies and the general assembly. These were the assemblies of "circles" that combined three or four provinces. They were conceived as an instrument for rapid defense that could meet in case of aggression. In the course of discussions about the attitude toward the royal power that should be henceforth adopted, two tendencies emerged within the party, which was now divided between the "prudent" and the "firm." According to the latter, it was only by inspiring fear and showing their determination to concede nothing that the party could make itself respected and maintain peace. Among the most resolute defenders of this position were Duke Henri de Rohan and his brother Benjamin de Soubise. Despite these internal dissensions, the party remained united in obedience to the king during the first revolt of the prince of Condé in the spring of 1614. On the other hand, alarmed by the proposed marriage of young Louis XIII with the Spanish infanta, the "firm," and also some "prudent" who changed their views in this instance, participated in the prince's second rebellion in 1615. The peace signed in Loudun on 3 May 1616, however, contained no provisions injurious to the Reformed Churches. In 1617, a new reason for agitation appeared with the *arrêt* of 25 June 1617 that gave the Catholics of Béarn complete freedom of worship and ordered the restitution of all ecclesiastical property. The Protestants of Béarn refused to submit to the royal decision and appealed to the solidarity of all French Reformed Protestants—views expressed in political assemblies of Orthez and then La Rochelle, which met without royal authorization in 1618–19. These assemblies adopted a moderate attitude, however. In 1620, the participation of Rohan and Soubise in the revolt of Marie de Medici against her own son poisoned relations with the crown. The military intervention of Louis XIII in Béarn aggravated tensions further. Despite appeals for calm from Sully, Bouillon, Lesdiguières, and Duplessis-Mornay and the king's strong prohibition, a political assembly met at La Rochelle in early 1621. The deputies protested energetically against the measures taken in Béarn and demanded that Louis XIII restore the status quo ante. Rather than listening to these claims, rudely expressed by an illegal assembly, the king launched a campaign in the spring to subdue the rebellious Huguenots. The La Rochelle assembly organized the party for war and divided the kingdom into eight military districts, raised troops, and put fortresses in a state of defense. Still, only a small part of the Huguenot nobility engaged in this last phase of the Wars of Religion. Rohan and Soubise directed the war, which ended temporarily with the Peace of Montpellier in 1622 before breaking out in a final phase during which Richelieu's determination to "ruin the Huguenot party" ended the resistance of the last diehards. With Rohan and Soubise defeated and La Rochelle captured on 28 October 1628, the Edict of Nîmes, signed on 14 July 1629, put an end to the Huguenot garrisoning of surety towns and also conclusively prohibited the meeting of political assemblies, thus giving the *coup de grâce* to the Huguenot political organization.

This disappearance of the Huguenot party, however, did not toll the death knell of Huguenot political activity, which survived in residual form through the mediating efforts of the deputies general at court. Yet their influence, henceforth negligible, could not prevent the process of gradual erosion of the privileges granted by the Edict of Nantes until its eventual revocation in 1685.

CHAPTER 4

Pacifying the Kingdom of France at the Beginning of the Wars of Religion: Historiography, Sources, and Examples

Jérémie Foa

1   Introduction

Contrary to popular perceptions, the Wars of Religion that disrupted French society from the 1560s to the early 1600s did not constitute an uninterrupted stretch of violence or a relentless parade of battles. Rather, beginning with the reign of Charles IX (1560–1574), the crown thought of itself as an agent of harmony and peace.[1] It tried by every means possible to contain the religious hostilities by devising ambitious programs, often from start to finish, aimed at reducing conflict and enabling its Catholic and Protestant subjects to coexist in the same city, the same street, and sometimes the same house.[2] The task was not easy, since memories were bitter and cried out for vengeance. People were repulsed by the idea of having to live with heretics, enemies but yesterday and a likely future threat to the salvation of all.

For the crown, making peace required distinguishing between faithful Christians and loyal subjects, desacralizing the political community, and detaching, at least partially, the terrestrial and celestial spheres. Although still thought to be mired in religious error, the Huguenots, by virtue of the edicts of pacification (the Edict of Amboise in March 1563, the Peace of Longjumeau in March 1568, and the Edict of Saint-Germain in August 1570),[3] received for the first time the inalienable rights held by all the king's subjects, regardless of their religious position. It meant the guarantee of their persons and property, eligibility for public offices, and freedom of conscience as well as a limited right to

---

1   Denis Crouzet, *Le haut cœur de Catherine de Médicis, une raison politique aux temps de la Saint-Barthélemy* (Paris: 2005).

2   Olivier Christin, *L'autonomisation de la raison politique au XVIe siècle* (Paris:1997); idem, "Citoyenneté ou parité? Deux modèles de coexistence confessionnelle au XVIe siècle," in *La tolérance. Colloque international de Nantes,* (ed.) Guy Saupin (Rennes: 1999), 133–40.

3   The best edition of the edicts of pacification, established under the direction of Bernard Barbiche, can be found online: "L'Edit de Nantes et ses antécédents" (http://elec.enc.sorbonne.fr/editsdepacification/).

public worship. While compelled by "the necessities of the times" to authorize the Reformed religion in his kingdom in the hope of maintaining peace and preserving unity, the young Charles IX encountered intense opposition to this conciliatory policy. The traditional pillars of royal authority (*parlements, bailliages*, governors, municipalities and the like) were especially opposed. Thus, in order to execute his reviled policy and bypass a recalcitrant administration, the king dispatched "commissioners for the application of the edicts of pacification." They were men chosen by him alone from among his most faithful officials, dismissible at will and not accountable except to him. They numbered twenty for the Edict of Amboise and fifteen for the Edict of Saint-Germain.[4] At this singular moment, he played the extraordinary (the new commissioners) against the ordinary (traditional officials). Given the necessities of the times, the king felt authorized to skirt the law and increase his interference. Endowed with substantial executive and judicial power, the commissioners were dispatched in pairs to travel the roads, each in his own "department," and charged with applying the pacification legislation and settling the differences between Protestants and Catholics.[5]

Following a brief historiographical introduction, we will turn to the principal sources for the "process of pacification" in France, focusing on the particular example of the commissioners of the edicts during the reign of Charles IX. The commissioners were witnesses as well as players of the first order in the study of the process that was set in motion to establish peace following the religious conflict. What were the destabilizing issues resulting from the wars that required urgent repair? How were yesterday's belligerents to be reconciled in the absence of common religious points of reference? What balance was to be found between the right to justice and the practical need to forget past offenses? These were questions that vexed the commissioners. They tried to respond step by step through a policy of local accommodation rather than by setting a universal standard devised in the shadowy corridors of power. Put differently, the pacification process enables us to learn what the Huguenots endured during the wars and what their hopes were upon the return of peace. It is an invaluable observation point for understanding what it meant to survive in a civil war.

---

4 Jérémie Foa, *Le tombeau de la paix: Une histoire des édits de pacification, 1560–1572* (Limoges: 2015); idem, "Making Peace: The Commissions for Enforcing the Pacification Edicts in the Reign of Charles IX (1560–1574)," *French History* 18 (2004), 256–74.

5 *Commission expédiée par le Roy pour envoyer par les provinces de ce royaume certains commissaires pour faire entretenir l'edict et traicté sur la pacification des troubles advenuz en iceluy* (Paris: 1563).

2 The Restoration of the History of Peace

For reasons inseparably political,[6] historiographical[7] and archival,[8] the history of war has long been emphasized to the detriment of the history of peace. Hegel wrote that "periods of peace are blank pages in history."[9] Admittedly, violence leaves far more traces in the records than the everyday coexistence between Protestants and Catholics. Extraordinary events—the deployment of troops, the transfer of a sergeant, or a summons by a judge—are the meat of the archives.

What sources, on the other hand, can describe the unobtrusive interaction of a Catholic merchant and a Protestant client or the mechanical routine of daily life? If no one is killed, if no insults are exchanged, what institution will record the event? In other words, are there any records of peaceful coexistence between Catholics and Huguenots? The problem is not simply documentary. It involves the very functioning of memory. Singularity offers a better stimulus to memory than regularity. Beyond the manuscript archives, the other fundamental sources for the study of peace are the printed ones, whether written by chroniclers or historians.[10] Here too the chroniclers overemphasize the periods of conflict; they provide inspiration and material for their pens. While he devotes whole pages to battles, Pierre de Jarrige is suddenly silent after the Peace of Saint-Germain, saying that "in the year 1571 nothing happened in France that deserves to be recorded."[11] That peace scarcely merits ink is

---

6 For Otto Hintze, for example, "war is the *ultima ratio* of modern reason of state"; idem, *Féodalité, capitalisme et Etat moderne en France. Essais d'histoire sociale comparée*, (ed.) Hinnerk Bruhns (Paris: 1991), 314. Charles Tilly emphasizes the links among war, finance, monarchical taxation, and the strengthening of the instruments of government in his *Contrainte et capital dans la formation de l'Europe de 990 à 1990* (Paris: 1992). On this point see Olivier Christin, "L'Etat moderne et la guerre (1550–1750): Note bibliographique," *Actes de la Recherche en Sciences Sociales*, 96–97 (1993), 63–66.

7 Thomas Renna, "The Idea of Peace in the West, 500–1150," *Journal of Medieval Studies* 6 (1980), 143–67.

8 Thus in the Archives Municipales, series AA (municipal correspondence), CC (city accounts), EE (military affairs), and FF (legal affairs) are singularly rich in everything that concerns war, but notoriously poor in matters that concern peace.

9 Cited by Jean-Pierre Azéma, "La guerre," in *Pour une histoire politique*, (ed.) R. Rémond (Paris: 1996), 371.

10 For a preliminary study of these chroniclers see Mathilde Bernard, *Ecrire la peur à l'époque des guerres de Religion. Une étude des historiens et mémorialistes contemporains des guerres civiles en France (1562–1598)* (Paris: 2010).

11 *Journal historique de Pierre de Jarrige, viguier de la ville de St Yrieix (1560–1574)* (Angoulême: 1868), 61.

confirmed by the notorious disproportion between calm and chaos in the historiography of the Wars of Religion, which has long been confined to descriptions of urban riots and fierce battles. When discussing the reign of Charles IX, local scholars always maintained a significant silence for the years between 1563 and 1567 and then again for those from 1570 to 1572. This is all the more regrettable because study of the manner by which cities established peace reveals practices more distinctive than does their engagement in war. Dozens of older monographs bear witness to this. From Cahors to Abbeville, they appear to be mere copies of each other, stringing together in appropriate bits the obligatory passages about the battles of the Wars of Religion.[12] Only Frédéric Kirchner, at the end of the Second World War, was interested in the application of the Peace of Amboise at Lyon, but his unpublished study, not unexpectedly entitled *Entre deux guerres*, remains, by reason of its pessimistic determinism, of limited value for broadening research into the subject of peace.[13]

Over the past thirty years, however, the study of peace has benefited from a profound revival, thanks in particular to the contributions of American, British, German and Scandinavian scholars, who have profited from an older and more institutionally anchored historiographical tradition for the study of peace.[14] We see both in technical papers and in specialized journals,[15] the dynamism of "peace studies," "conflict resolution studies," and "*Friedensforschung*."[16] There is no equivalent in France. Various factors have contributed to the time lag: the relative strength of Protestantism and differing experiences of religious pluralism, the different relationships to the state stemming from experiences with

---

12 For some examples in which peace is not treated, see André Imberdis, *Histoire des guerres religieuses en Auvergne pendant les XVIe et XVIIe siècles* (Riom: 1848); Jean-Baptiste de Vinols, *Histoire des guerres de Religion dans le Velay* (Le Puy:1862); and Henry Ricalens, *Castelnaudary au temps de Catherine de Médicis Comtesse de Lauragais* (Toulouse: 1999).

13 Frédéric Kirchner, *Entre deux guerres 1563–1567. Essai sur la tentative d'application à Lyon de la politique de "Tolérance"* (Lyon: 1952).

14 Alyson Bailes, "La *Peace Research*, les pays nordiques et la sécurité en Europe," *Nordiques* 11 (2006), 9–24.

15 The best known are *The International Journal of Peace Studies*; *The Canadian Journal of Peace Studies*; *The Journal for the Study of Peace and Conflict*; *The Journal of Conflict Resolution*; *Journal of Peace Research*; *Bulletin of Peace Proposals*. On this subject see Ian M. Harris, Larry J. Fisk, and Carol Rank, "A Portrait of University Peace Studies in North America and Western Europe at the End of the Millennium," *The International Journal of Peace Studies* 3:1 (1998), 91–112; Thomas Keefe and Ron Roberts, *Realizing Peace: An Introduction to Peace Studies* (Ames, IA: 1991); Linda R. Forcey, "Introduction to Peace Studies," in *Peace: Meanings, Politics, Strategies*, (ed.) L. Forcey (New York: 1989), 3–14.

16 Ekkehart Krippendorff (ed.), *Friedensforschung* (Cologne and Berlin: 1968).

more or less authoritarian regimes, and the presence or absence of militant campaigns for peace, which were particularly strong in England and the United States. These are factors that led German historians to an early recognition of the links between pacification, religious pluralism, and state consolidation.[17] In the tradition of Max Weber and Norbert Elias (all too late translated into French[18]) German historiography has emphasized how the state developed through a process of the monopolization of violence, but also through a constant effort to control emotions, which could lead it to see peace as the result of a successful process of political intervention. Likewise, from Thomas Hobbes to Carl Schmitt and Reinhart Koselleck, an influential philosophical tradition has situated the necessary outcome of civil war, namely the consolidation of peace, as the birth certificate of the sovereign state.

> A new political order, the result of the settling of the confessional civil wars, developed on the European continent: the sovereign state, an *imperium rationis*, as Hobbes calls it, an empire of objective reason as Hegel says, henceforth independent of theology and whose *ratio* put an end to the heroic epoch, heroic law, and heroic tragedy.[19]

This delay among French historians in the study of peace only underlines the value of the pioneering work of Arlette Jouanna[20] on the subject, or that of Marc Venard, who in 1995 directed a doctoral dissertation on the application of the Edict of Amboise in Poitou and Dauphiné.[21]

---

17   Among numerous examples, see Heinz Schilling, "The European Crisis of the 1590s: The Situation in German Towns," in *The Crisis of the 1590s*, (ed.) Peter Clark (London: 1985), 135–56; see also the remarks of Stuart Caroll, "The Peace in the Feud in Sixteenth and Seventeenth-Century France," *Past and Present* 178:1 (2003), 74–114.

18   Norbert Elias, *Über den Prozess der Zivilisation* (Basel: 1939), English translation *The Civilizing Process* (Oxford: 1994).

19   Carl Schmitt, *Hamlet ou Hécube* (1956) (French translation Paris: 1992), 104–5, quoted by Olivier Christin in *La Paix de religion. L'autonomisation de la raison politique au XVIe siècle* (Paris: 1997), 12; see also Roman Schnur, *Die französischen Juristen im konfessionellen Bürgerkrieg d. 16. Jh.s. Ein Beitrag z. Entstehungsgeschichte d. modernen Staates* (Berlin: 1962); Ilja Mieck, *Toleranzedikt und Bartholomäusnacht. Französische Politik und europäische Diplomatie, 1570–1572* (Göttingen: 1969).

20   Arlette Jouanna, "Les conjurations de paix pendant les guerres de Religion," in Arlette Jouanna and Michel Péronnet (eds.), *L'Edit de Nantes: sa genèse, son application en Languedoc*. Special issue of the *Bulletin historique de Montpellier* 23 (1999), 31–52.

21   Nam Soo Kang, *La Première période de coexistence religieuse en France: entre la paix d'Amboise (mars 1563) et la deuxième guerre de religion (septembre 1567)* (Doctoral diss.: Paris X-Nanterre, 1995).

By focusing his study on two areas with different political and university traditions, France and the Empire, Olivier Christin has shown in *La paix de religion* the great advantage of paying attention to questions of peace in investigating the emergence of the modern state, usually regarded as almost exclusively a consequence of war.[22] This work not only encouraged the study of the contribution of the religious peace settlements to the emergence of the state, but it suggested for this purpose turning away temporarily from the court and the intellectual's library or study to sources less involved with policy, such as city halls, popular assemblies, or simple petitions addressed by the humble to the powerful—in a word to places where the need to make peace by distinguishing the faithful from the citizens was felt with unprecedented intensity.[23] By emphasizing the essential role of men of law, among them the commissioners of the edicts, in the consolidation of peace, this work made possible an investigation aimed less at the words than at the acts of peacemaking. It was, in sum, oriented more toward pacification. A year earlier Michel Cassan's book on the Limousin brought to light a possible municipal peace agreement in the midst of the Wars of Religion, by showing in Limoges the priority of a *"raison de ville"* over the *"raisons religieuses."*[24] Rather than assume a special character for Limoges, this work called on the contrary for an analysis of the mechanisms of secularization in municipal politics, of the reasons for the emergence of this symbolic realm ruled by mutually agreed norms, and by procedures for making decisions apart from confessional violence and religious passions. A few years later, Thierry Wanegffelen demonstrated the presence of peaceful confessional coexistence at Lectoure in Gascony, while refusing to see in it "any sort of secularization, but rather a true 'non-confessional' purpose."[25]

The value of these works as guides has been fully established over the past decade. They have legitimized the study of "confessional coexistence" in France and supported the development of an interest in the reasons for the maintenance or the collapse of community solidarity in the midst of the civil wars.[26]

---

22 Olivier Christin, *La paix de religion. L'autonomisation de la raison politique au XVIe siècle* (Paris:1997). See also the synthesis covering all of Europe: David El Kenz and Claire Gantet, *Guerres et paix de religion en Europe, XVIe–XVIIe siècles* (Paris: 2003).

23 Olivier Christin and Jérémie Foa, "Politique de la plainte," introduction to a special issue *Pétitions et suppliques, Annales de l'Est* 57 (2007), 5–19.

24 Michel Cassan, *Le temps des guerres de Religion. Le cas du Limousin (vers 1530–vers 1630)* (Paris: 1996).

25 Thierry Wanegffelen, *Ni Rome ni Genève. Des fidèles entre deux chaires en France au XVIe siècle* (Paris: 2000), 329.

26 Olivier Christin, "La coexistence confessionnelle, 1563–1567," BSHPF 141 (1995), 483–504; idem, "Citoyenneté ou parité? Deux modèles de coexistence confessionnelle au XVIe

Interest in the question of "confessional coexistence" soon attracted American, British and German scholars, partly because themes of religious pluralism and "multiculturalism" were more in tune with their general concerns.[27] Supported by a long historiographical tradition, several scholars have extended the study of confessional coexistence and have shown the pertinence of examining the mechanisms for stabilizing the social order in zones of religious cohabitation on a national scale[28] as well as at the municipal level.[29] To punctuate this historiographical development, Penny Roberts proposed in a recent article a reversal of traditional views of the beginning of the Wars of Religion, affirming that "ritualized confessional violence in the cities...now appears only one aspect of their history, indeed the exception rather than the rule."[30]

---

siècle," in *La tolérance*, (ed.) Saupin, 133–40; Arlette Jouanna, "Coexister dans la différence. Expériences de l'union avant Coutras," in *Avènement d'Henri IV. Quatrième centenaire, Coutras, 1987* (Pau: 1989), 149–66.

[27] Fritz Dickmann, "Das Problem der Gleichberechtigung der Konfessionen im Reich im 16. und 17. Jahrhundert," *Historische Zeitschrift* 201 (1965), 203–51; Willem Frijhoff, "La coexistence confessionnelle: complicités, méfiances et ruptures aux Provinces-Unies," in *Histoire vécue du peuple chrétien*, (ed.) Jean Delumeau, vol.1 (Toulouse: 1979), 229–57; Etienne François, *Protestants et Catholiques en Allemagne. Identités et pluralisme, Augsbourg, 1648–1806* (Paris: 1993); Benjamin Kaplan, *Calvinists and Libertines: Confession and Community in Utrecht, 1578–1620* (Oxford: 1995); idem, *Divided by the Faith. Religious Conflict and the Practice of Toleration in Early Modern Europe* (Cambridge: 2007); Claire Gantet, *Discours et images de la paix dans les villes d'Allemagne du Sud aux XVIIe et XVIIIe siècles* (Doctoral diss.: Université de Paris I, 1999); Paul Warmbrunn, *Zwei Konfessionen in Einer Stadt: Das Zusammenleben von Katholiken und Protestanten in den paritätischen Reichsstädten Augsburg, Biberbach, Ravensburg, und Dinkelsbühl von 1548 bis 1648* (Wiesbaden: 1983); Joachim Whaley, *Religious Toleration and Social Change in Hamburg, 1529–1819* (Cambridge: 1985).

[28] Philip Benedict, "Un roi, une loi, deux fois: Parameters for the History of Catholic-Protestant Co-existence in France, 1555–1685," in *Tolerance and Intolerance in the European Reformation*, (eds.) Ole P. Grell and Bob Scribner (Cambridge: 1996), 65–93; Keith Luria, *Sacred Boundaries. Religious Coexistence and Conflict in Early Modern France* (Washington: 2005); Mark Konnert, *Civic Agendas and Religious Passion: Châlons-sur-Marne during the French Wars of Religion* (Kirksville, Mo.: 1997).

[29] Gregory Hanlon, *Confession and Community in Seventeenth Century France. Catholic and Protestant in Aquitaine* (Philadephia: 1993); Thierry Amalou, *Une Concorde urbaine: Senlis au temps des Réformes, vers 1520–vers 1580* (Limoges: 2007).

[30] Penny Roberts, "Faire l'histoire des villes au temps des guerres de Religion en France," *Moreana* 43 (2006), 141. See also *Living With Religious Diversity in Early Modern Europe*, (eds.) C. Scott Dixon, Dagmar Freist, and Mark Greengrass (Aldershot: 2009).

3 The Chronic Difficulty of Returning to One's Native Land

If, very much under the influence of contemporary processes of reconciliation in Northern Ireland, South Africa and elsewhere, historiography has taken an interest in peace and reconciliation processes,[31] the sources for the study of the process of pacification at the beginning of the Wars of Religion present paleographic difficulties and are, above all, extremely scattered. The National Archives are singularly meager for treating this question. The series TT of the Archives Nationales, the famous collection of documents regarding Protestants during the Ancien Régime, has preserved only a few items concerning pacification, and the 16th century in general is poorly represented. Those who wish to study the history of peace during the Wars of Religion must draw on two types of sources: the local archives (Municipal and Departmental) and correspondence (the "*manuscrits français*" are preserved in the Bibliothèque Nationale de France, Richelieu site). The ensuing discussion of the existing sources will invoke the example of the commissioners of the edicts of pacification, the inescapable port of entry for writing the history of the Huguenots at the time of the "Peace [Settlements] of Religion."

Exile was, for the Huguenots, the tragic result of religious confrontation. During the reign of Charles IX, in every new war religious minorities were almost everywhere expelled; they began the "dance of the exiles," the appropriation by some of the expropriation from others. The Municipal Archives, and especially the series BB (consular decisions), hold traces of this everywhere. In July 1562, at the midst of the first War of Religion, the *échevins* (municipal consuls) of Clermont ordered "all seditious persons and all those who belong to the new sect and religion" to "clear out" of the city within three days.[32] But, if it was easy to leave, it was much rarer to be welcomed with open arms upon one's return. The documents from the Catholic clergy, held in the Departmental Archives, preserve the records of this opposition (series G and H). At Langres, for example, the city's Catholics, aided by the Cathedral Chapter, displayed a dogged determination to hinder the return of the Huguenots to the city between 1562 and 1566.[33]

---

31 Michel de Waele (ed.), *Lendemains de guerre civile: Réconciliations et restaurations en France sous Henri IV* (Quebec: 2011).
32 AM, Clermont-Ferrand, BB 33, 8 juillet 1562.
33 AD, Haute-Marne, 2 G 136, quatre pièces (1562–1566).

4   Closed Gates at Mâcon

The return from exile of the Protestants of Mâcon, for which we have invaluable evidence in the correspondence held at the Bibliothèque Nationale, is in this respect particularly revealing of the stakes of peace. On 8 June 1563, the guards at the gates of Mâcon saw in the distance the silhouettes of three men, among whom they quickly recognized Philibert Barjot, one of the most influential Reformed notables of the city. These men on foot were returning from a long exile that had begun eleven months after the opening of the first civil war (February 1562–March 1563), during which time they had wandered through "foreign lands" with their companions in misfortune. Behind the approaching trio, the guards caught sight of a faceless crowd of Mâconnais Protestants who hoped to enter the city by virtue of provisions of the Edict of Amboise. There were "a great number of people, both on horse and foot, coming from the direction of Bauge-en-Bresse, estimated to number three hundred persons." They halted "at the entrance to the Saône bridge" in the meadow that marked the frontier of the kingdom of France.[34] The guards, following the orders of the governor Tavannes, kept the gates closed despite the peace arrangements. Still, they could see and almost count the mass of people. The returning exiles sincerely believed that they had nothing to fear. They had always lived here and saw no future elsewhere.[35]

"Who is this troop of people we see in the meadow?" the guards shouted to the three men who had moved forward and appeared to be the group's delegates. "They responded that they were those who were absent from Mâcon [and] who wished to reenter the said city." Philibert Barjot then spoke up and addressed the *échevins*, who had rushed to the gate on hearing the rumor of the return of the exiles. "He said it had pleased the king to order through his edict of pacification that all those absent from their cities will return freely to their homes. He asked the said *échevins* to let them enter the said city and live there in their houses." The gatekeepers and the *échevins* chose not to give way; Tavannes's orders were strict. After having offered in vain to let only the three delegates pass, the guards bolted the gates and watched from a distance the troop of exiles, who resolved to camp in the

---

34   Jean de Coras evoked the figure of Ulysses in discussing the return of exiles in his treatise on Martin Guerre, *Arrest memorable du parlement de Tholose contenant une Histoire prodigieuse d'un supposé mary, adveniïe de nostre temps: enrichie de cent & onze belles & doctes annotations* (Paris: 1572; lst ed. 1560), 2, 16, 75.

35   BnF, Ms. fr. 4048, fol. 147v°-148 (8 juin 1563).

meadow for the moment.[36] Thus the exiles, among them prominent people within the city, experienced the dramatic reversibility of the social order. In the course of civil war, the privileged could lose everything, while the humble might suddenly benefit.

Following the fratricidal conflicts the possibility of return for the exiles depended on mutual recognition—and the good faith—of those who had remained behind. Only they were capable of recognizing the exiles. The guards stationed at the gate knew very well who those trying to enter Mâcon were but pretended not to recognize them. The city had become Catholic thanks to the war and the authorities demanded "a list of the names of those who want to reenter in order to inquire whether they are all from the said city." The Protestants refused to state their identity, claiming that "there is no need to give the names of those absent, because those in the said city know them well."[37] If the Reformed refused to objectivize their identity because it traditionally depended on implicit recognition by neighbors, the religious conflict required the invention of new methods for identifying persons.[38] What characterizes societies engulfed in civil war is the tragic collapse of confidence and community cohesion. The Protestants were readily described as "suspect." Thus the guards just stood around and pretended not to recognize the beneficiaries of government acts. The religious conflict had altered the balance of power and the political and economic hierarchies, producing spectacular social ascents but also unexpected declines. It was partly the business of the crown to legitimize or, on the contrary, to challenge this acquired status, these new situations born of the latest war.

This is why the commissioners, mediators by definition, played an essential role in the reintegration of the returning exiles. While the return of Catholic ecclesiastics to Huguenot cities rarely posed problems, that of the Reformed to Catholic cities was never a matter of course. The Edict of Amboise lacked clarity, stating that henceforth "everyone everywhere may live and stay in *his* house."[39] The Catholic cities took advantage of this parochial formulation by affirming that only native inhabitants of the city with long-established roots could return to their own residences, while in no case could strangers install themselves at their leisure. In a petition addressed to

---

36   BnF, Ms. fr. 4048, fol. 147 (8 juin 1563). On Mâcon during the Wars of Religion, see Ami Bost, *Histoire de l'église protestante de Mâcon* (Mâcon: 1977).
37   BnF, Ms. fr. 4048, fol. 147v°-148 (8 juin 1563).
38   Vincent Denis, *Une Histoire de l'Identité. France, 1715–1815* (Seyssel: 2008).
39   Edict of Amboise, article 2.

the commissioners, the *échevins* of Mâcon, anxious over the situation, asked "whether, following the said edict of pacification...strangers will be freely permitted to come and reside in this said city."[40] In reply to a negative response restricting entry to natives only, the cities assumed the right to examine entrants, since in the absence of baptismal, marriage and death registers only the native inhabitants were able to decide who local residents were. This border control produced in turn numerous conflicts at city gates that impeded a return of calm. It is why in February 1564 Charles IX tried to make an adjustment, specifying that "the king's cities are open to his subjects."[41] Charles IX thus left the choice of domicile entirely to his subjects' wishes and removed all obstacles (guards at gates as well as confessional barriers) to people's movement within the kingdom. The mere fact of being a royal subject conferred a right of access to all cities of the kingdom, regardless of religion. The criterion of membership in the nation sufficed; essential for pacification, it also gave hope to rallying French people around their king and exporting the conflicts outside the frontiers of the realm.[42] Charles IX very explicitly answered the Huguenots of Languedoc that "the subjects of the king" might reside "in all the provinces of his kingdom as seems good to them."[43] The Reformed of Montpellier invoked this statement in 1565 in recalling "the free access it has pleased His Majesty to give all his subjects to all the cities of this kingdom."[44]

Once the exiles had been reintegrated by the commissioners, the complaints began. They provide a vital source for the study of not only the reality but above all the memory of religious clashes, the manner by which in the grievances the conflicts were reconstructed *a posteriori* as legitimate (and therefore to be forgotten) or illegitimate (and therefore to be prosecuted). Most of these written grievances are now housed in the municipal archives. They are indispensable testimony for the history of the situation of the Huguenots during the initial Wars of Religion.

---

40 AM, Mâcon, EE 49, pièce n° 12 (fin janvier 1571).
41 BnF, Ms. fr. 15879, fol. 58v° (février 1564).
42 Pacifist poetry in particular invoked nationalist sentiment and the unity of France in trying to bridge the religious chasm. See, for example, the verses of Jacques Grévin during the second civil war: "L'avare Italien, l'Espagnol fin et caut / Le paresseus Angloys et la trouppe estourdie / Des mutins Allemans que la France mandie / Regardent ce théatre, et bien peu leur en chaut." Jacques Grévin, sonnet XVI (automne 1567) in his *Sonnets d'Angleterre et de Flandre* (Paris: 1898), 17.
43 BnF, Ms. fr. 15879, fol. 106 (1564–1565?).
44 Louise Guiraud, *La Réforme à Montpellier*, Mémoires de la société archéologique de Montpellier 7 (1919), 397.

5 The Period of the Grievances

Upon their arrival in a city or village, the commissioners summoned a general assembly of the inhabitants drawn from the two confessions and asked them present their grievances.[45] Although many of the written records have disappeared, we know from several accounts that the inhabitants virtually stampeded the commissioners to make formal complaints.[46] At Valence in February 1572, for example, an inhabitant was alarmed at the mass "of affairs that are presented every day before the commissioners," and described the plaintiffs' desire to gain the ear of the prince.[47] The commissioners thus were part of a broader movement that has been dubbed the "judicial conversion" of the religious conflict.

5.1 The Grammar of the Grievances

The religious conflict was not diminished by the peace itself, but it changed strategies and pursued its goals by other means, notably judicial ones. In other words, the adversaries did not give up on "reducing" or bringing down their enemies, but the preferred weapon henceforth, the one that promised the best results, was the law. The religious struggles were thus the occasion for a greater employ of judicial proceedings, favoring the skills of new agents, no longer theologians or soldiers but jurists. The followers of both confessions hired lawyers, solicited advice from legal specialists in order to formulate their grievances properly, and demanded judgments against their adversaries. In writing the history of this process, the series CC of the municipal archives, which contains the municipal accounts, is particularly valuable. The *maire* and *échevins* of Tours, for example, asked five lawyers of the *présidial* court to attend "the assemblies held to consider and to advise what is necessary to claim and request in appearing before the commissioners deputized by the king for the maintenance of the edict of pacification."[48] As Olivier Christin has shown, the pacification was "a stroke of luck for men of law."[49]

But religious conflict was not merely channeled by the complaints. It partly changed its character, since its participants had to submit to a very precise

---

45 Florence Alazard (ed.), *La Plainte à la Renaissance* (Paris: 2008); Olivier Christin and Jérémie Foa (eds.), *Suppliques et pétitions de l'époque moderne à nos jours. Annales de l'Est* (April 2008).
46 For a detailed analysis of the body of complaints see Foa, *Le tombeau de la paix*, 225–74.
47 AM Montélimar, BB 53, fol. 41 (23 février 1572).
48 AM Tours, CC 79, fol. 66v° (2 décembre 1563).
49 Christin, *La paix de religion*, 104.

grammar, meticulously formulated by the commissioners. The conditions that the latter established for accepting petitions included the removal of insults and a declaration in the complaint that the intention was to seek the common good and not just the advancement of a confessional group. At Amiens on 14 August 1563, the commissioners Le Cirier and Lamoignon prohibited "insults in deed or word."[50] Accordingly, the body of complaints addressed to the agents of the crown omitted all offensive terms. Huguenots were never called "heretics," but always those of the "pretended religion," which contrasted sharply with the contemporary pamphlet literature. Catholics likewise were not described as "papists." In the same way, the arguments of the plaintiffs were dressed in strictly secular clothing; one could no longer hope to win in court because one was the better Christian, but only because the argument advanced was more convincing and conformed better to the law.

5.2   The Struggle for the Temples

Penny Roberts has shown clearly that the most important battles of the Wars of Religion were not fought on military terrain but around places of worship.[51] It was in fact in the laws that established the physical boundaries of confessional coexistence that the defeat of the Huguenots occurred. Their spatial removal precipitated a social decline that fortunes on the battlefield never imposed. The principal subject of the complaints addressed to the commissioners (a fifth of the cases) was questions over worship. Charles IX's commissioners were supposed to authorize temples for the Huguenots. Besides two temples within the cities held by the Huguenots upon the conclusion of peace (7 March 1563 for the Edict of Amboise and 1 August 1570 for the Edict of Saint-Germain), the Protestants had the right to one temple in the suburbs of one city in each *bailliage* according to the Edict of Amboise and to two in each *gouvernement* according to the Edict of Saint-Germain. But where was this place of worship to be located? Was it to be in the principal town of the district or, on the contrary, in some distant village? Was it to look like a true place of worship, possessing genuine dignity and manifest visibility, or rather to remain discreet and inconspicuous with the look of a private residence? If the Huguenots' goal was to obtain a site close by, the Catholics strove to keep the worship service as far away as possible. In all the complaints that they addressed to the commissioners on this subject, the Huguenots asked for nearby temples not for their own salvation, but

---

50   AM Amiens, AA 14, fol. 208v.
51   Penny Roberts, "The Most Crucial Battle of the Wars of Religion? The Conflict over Sites for Reformed Worship in Sixteenth-Century France," *Archiv für Reformationsgeschichte* 89 (1998), 247–67.

always for the benefit of public order. A distant site would force them into clandestine worship and consequently incite new troubles. The Catholic arguments for keeping the Protestant temples far away never emphasized the threat their presence would pose to their salvation, or the fear of heretical "pollution." Although these confessional motives remained in the background, the play of counter-argumentation forced the Catholics to emphasize the economic and military risks connected with the establishment of Reformed worship.

To this end, the use of a rhetoric suggesting "perverse effects," that is "warnings" of the unanticipated risks of having a temple nearby, became the preferred weapon of the petitioners opposed to Reformed worship. Series GG of the municipal archives is invaluable in this regard. It frequently includes the subseries "*religionnaires*" that preserves important material on the Huguenots.[52] At Nantes, for example, the commissioners were alerted to the troublesome consequences for commerce if there were a temple in the suburbs ("by the said exercise, the said commerce would be almost entirely interrupted").[53] The object of the argument was to keep the debate outside the religious orbit, to politicize it and give it a technical turn of phrase. This allowed the Catholic opponents, while pretending to respect and indeed applaud the proposed objective—peaceful coexistence—to resist the means for accomplishing it. This technical method of secularizing the arguments is striking at Nantes, where the *échevins*, aided by the clergy, employed their wealth of empirical knowledge of the city to avoid the establishment of Reformed worship. In their petition, they argued that the suburb of Beauregard was not a place of particular sanctity and therefore not incompatible with the practice of Huguenot worship.[54] Though not sullied by Protestant worship, it was "a small island on the bridges," demonstrating at a glance what an "inconvenience it would be to the king and the city [if the Reformed] held the passage on their bridges."[55] The impartial argument of national security thus furnished an acceptable alternative to the unmentionable religious argument.

It therefore matters little that the authors never mentioned their fundamental concern, what offended their souls and consciences and led them to take

---

52 For example, AM Albi, GG 79, pièce non numérotée (huguenots d'Albi); AM Nantes, GG 642–646; AM Lyon, GG 77–80; AM Castelnaudary GG 82 (XVIe siècle-1698); AM Marseille GG 134.
53 AM Nantes, GG 643, pièce 3 (avant le 25 mai 1564).
54 Will Coster and Andrew Spicer (eds.), *Sacred Space in Early Modern Europe* (Cambridge: 2005); Andrew Spicer, "(Re)building the Sacred Landscape: Orléans 1560–1610," *French History* 21 (2007), 247–68.
55 AM Nantes, GG 643, pièce 3 (avant le 25 1564).

action, often with great anguish: their salvation and the damnation of their adversaries. On the other hand, it matters a great deal that they were forced to make a technical and juridical case. Only this approach would convince the commissioners and with them the crown. It matters that they felt they had to remain silent about the confessional motivations of their struggles and to back up their arguments with the secularized standard of the common good, an inverted argument that Jon Elster has called "the civilizing force of hypocrisy."[56] As the preferred issue for converting religious conflicts into political arguments, the question of Reformed worship assisted the judicial, or rather technical, conversion of the religious struggle. Here more than elsewhere it became essential for the faithful to make themselves convincing and to collect the necessary technical information, the neglected details that would prevent or alternatively legitimize the establishment of a temple. The need was not to prove how the salvation of all would be imperiled, but how the terrestrial interests of most of the inhabitants would suffer or conversely benefit from its establishment.[57] Hence the obligatory detour through economics, military strategy ("the neighboring lands are not without suspicion of trouble and reports have recently arrived of attempted ambushes in Lorraine, near and adjacent to this province [of Champagne]"),[58] the behavior of crowds ("the variety of persons of contrary religions being pressed and restricted in such a small place [Nantes] would be the occasion for promoting frequent riots") or of young people ("the students of the two religions might be in constant dissension"), and sociological analysis (the place is "inhabited by boatmen and fishermen").[59]

The commissioners in their decisions were therefore expected to take account of all these "warnings" and of relative Protestant and Catholic strength, and depending on the circumstances to establish a temple nearer to or farther from the principal city. Where the Protestants were numerous, were wealthy, had strong support from or controlled the municipal council, they could establish their place of worship closer. On the other hand, where they were weaker, their worship site was placed farther away in an undesirable location. At Troyes, for instance, the Huguenots had to be satisfied with Séant-en-Othe, "a mean little town" according to the Protestant Nicolas Pithou.[60] In the end,

---

56 Jon Elster, "Argumenter et négocier dans deux Assemblées constituantes," *Revue française de science politique* 44 (1994), 191.
57 Michel Lussault, "L'espace pris aux mots ," *Le Débat* 92 (1996), 99–110.
58 AM Troyes (Fonds Boutiot), A 17, fol. 140 (mars 1571).
59 AM Nantes, GG 643, pièce 3 (avant le 25 mai 1564).
60 Nicolas Pithou, *Chronique de la ville de Troyes et de la Champagne durant les guerres de Religion (1524–1594)*, vol. 2 (Reims: 2000), 539.

the commissioners established justice based on conciliation, an approach closer to medieval traditions than to modern conceptions, more concerned with reconciling the parties than applying the law at any cost.

6 Who were the Commissioners?

It was essential for the letters commissioning the agents of pacification to remain vague and indefinite so they would have the room for maneuver necessary for local adjustments. If they had been restricted by unalterable instructions, they would have been unable to take into account the complexities of the circumstances.[61] At the same time, the crown could not be casual about the dispatch of agents with powers that were both exorbitant (superior to those of a *parlement*) and imprecise.

TABLE 4.1 *The départements of the commissioners of the Edict of Amboise (March 1563)*

Burgundy and Nivernais	Estienne Charlet and Jehan de Monceaux
Brittany	Estienne Lallemant de Voulzay and Pierre de Chantecler
Champagne and Brie	No commissioners appointed
Guyenne	Anthoine Fumée, Jerosme Angenoust, then Jacques Viart
Ile-de-France	Mathieu Chartier and Pierre de Longueil
Languedoc	Jean-Jacques de Mesmes and Jacques de Bauquemare
Lyonnais, Auvergne, Bourbonnais	Michel Quelain and Gabriel Myron
Normandy	Jacques Viole and Jehan de la Guesle
Orléanais and Berry	Baptiste de Machault
Picardy	Charles de Lamoignon and François le Cirier
Poitou, Saintonge, La Rochelle, and Aunis	René de Bourgneuf and Pierre de Masparraulte
Provence and Dauphiné	Jacques Phellypeaux and Jessé de Bauquemare
Touraine, Anjou, and Maine	François Briçonnet, Arnoul Boucher, and Jehan de Lavau

---

61 Ronan de Calan and Jérémie Foa, "Paradoxes sur le commissaire. L'exécution de la politique religieuse de Charles IX (1560–1574)," *Histoire, économie et société* 2 (2008), 3–20.

TABLE 4.2 *The départments of the commissioners of the Edict of Saint-Germain (August 1570)*

Champagne, Burgundy, Auvergne, Bourbonnais	Nicolas Potier and Charles de Lamoignon
Guyenne	Robert de Montdoulcet and René Crespin
Paris and Ile-de-France	Estienne Lallemant and Jessé de Bauquemare
Normandy and Picardy	Anthoine Fumée and Simon Roger
Lyonnais, Dauphiné, Provence, Languedoc	Edouard Molé, Jehan de Belot, then Claude Faulcon
Orléanais, Anjou, Bretagne, Poitou	Philippe Gourreau de la Proustière and François Pain

6.1 Court Favor and the Commissioners

Catherine de Medici, the Queen Mother and regent, took special care to provide safeguards that, on one hand, would guarantee the obedience of the agents to the crown and, on the other, would assure them the necessary creditability with local residents. The status of the commissioners, first of all, increased their submission to the monarchy. Dismissible at will, they were the most striking manifestation of the power of the sovereign. Extraordinary agents intended to short-circuit the overly partisan regular courts, they demonstrate that the religious conflicts—and above all the need to end them—precipitated an executive watershed under the last Valois monarchs. The king departed more and more from the far too narrow framework of the law by creating exceptions. The Chancellor Michel de l'Hôpital, for example, did not hesitate to distance himself from the overly partisan commissioner Gabriel Myron, who was then on assignment at Tours.[62] Still, the commissioners followed the straight and narrow most of the time, and they knew that their mission offered a unique opportunity to come to the attention of the king, with whom they were in daily correspondence. Moreover, on completion of successful commissions, these agents of peace were generously repaid with prestigious offices, such as the presidency of a provincial court. Finally, several of the commissioners were newly arrived and owed everything to royal favor. Thus, Jehan de Belot, a commissioner under the Edict of Saint-Germain, came from a merchant family of the rural Rouergue and had only become a *maître des requêtes* in 1567.[63] The peace process proved to be an ideal opportunity for

---

62 AM Tours, EE 5, pièce 15 (novembre 1564).
63 Jean R. Marboutin, "Un Ami de Ronsard: Jean Dutreuilh de Belot," *Revue de l'Agenais* 39 (1912), 93–110.

the creatures of the prince to continue their advance and for the prince to bestow favor.[64]

6.2 The Impartiality of the Commissioners

The commissioners owed everything to royal favor and it was not conferred at random. It was granted to men endowed with specific qualities that made them suitable for making peace. It was critical that the commissioners not seem in the eyes of the local inhabitants to decide matters according to personal or confessional considerations, but rather for the common good. The first requirement was for the commissioners to be outsiders in the places they sought to pacify so that local power and clientage networks would not influence them.[65] As mercenaries of peace, they resisted all the more the self-serving advice lavished on them by residents. Moreover, they could not be militants committed to any religious cause, manifest clients of the Guise or the Châtillon, or, even worse, members of the clergy. More often than not, they belonged to the *"robins politiques,"* those who, although not Reformed, were opposed to repression of the Huguenots. Many of them, such as Charles de Lamoignon, had had Protestant sympathies at one time but had returned to the Catholic camp. Even more numerous were commissioners with friends, relatives, or allies on the Protestant side. This was the case, for instance, with René Crespin, commissioner in Brittany under the Edict of Saint-Germain. His son was a Huguenot and a citizen of Geneva. This was also true of Jacques Viole, whose wife had "attended sermons" and "did not celebrate Easter last."[66] These men of peace were selected by virtue of their religious moderation or, to use a term from the period, their impartiality. In 1564, the commissioners dispatched to Poitou painted a revealing self-portrait when they denounced to the king the "overdone and excessive affection that some of [his] officers of justice express for their religion, whether one or the other, such that without considering the needs of [his] service and the repose of [his] country, they wish to do whatever [their] zeal for their religion commands them."[67] The crown sought to emerge from the civil wars, as Carl Schmitt has observed, by presenting and seeing itself as a neutral party above the various factions. The

---

64 On the political use of favor, see Nicolas Le Roux, *La faveur du roi. Mignons et courtisans au temps des derniers Valois (vers 1547–vers 1589)* (Seyssel: 2000).

65 The commissioner Myron was denounced in Tours because, besides being a "devout papist" according to the Huguenots, he "is from this city and has his father, mother, brother, and relatives here." AM Tours, EE 15, pièce 5.

66 BnF, Ms. fr. 4047, fol. 49 ff.

67 BnF, Ms. fr. 15878, fol. 141–42 (17 septembre 1564).

image of the state as arbiter, both impartial and absolute, became essential amid the religious clashes.[68]

7 The Commissioners Caught between Reawakening of Conflict and the Need to Forget

7.1 *An Impossible Task?*

As one-man bands in the service of peace, the commissioners had to deal with everything: the reintegration of the exiles, the restitution of Catholic churches, buildings and furnishings, the disarming of the people, the location of Protestant temples and cemeteries, and the reconciliation of the inhabitants as well as the apportionment of municipal offices. This program was all the more ambitious because Charles IX had deprived his *parlements* of jurisdiction over the edicts of pacification and affairs connected with religious coexistence.[69] Peace was an extraordinary process and the decisions of the commissioners were declared equally valid to those of a sovereign court. The commissioners did not have as large a staff, however, and were soon overwhelmed by their task. Forty years later Henry IV took a lesson from Charles IX and supported his agents of pacification with "*chambres de l'édit*," courts which assumed the administrative details of the peace process.[70] In 1563–1564 and 1570–1572 the commissioners were overwhelmed by plaintiffs who, quite aside from disputes over houses, offices and the payment of damages, flooded them with petty claims for restoration of chests and dressers. Theoretically all-powerful, the commissioners were helpless. The hours they spent dealing with the scars of war reduced the time devoted to peace. They expended considerable energy searching for arms, all too carefully hidden away. Although the commissioners constantly appealed for the surrender of arquebuses at city hall, they were unable to shrink the arsenals that people had accumulated during the Wars of

---

68 Thus Carl Schmitt wrote that "a new political order, the result of the settling of the confessional civil wars, developed on the European continent: the sovereign state, an *imperium rationis* as Hobbes calls it, an empire of objective reason as Hegel says, henceforth independent of theology and whose *ratio* put an end to the heroic epoch, heroic law, and heroic tragedy." Carl Schmitt, *Hamlet ou Hécube* (1956) (French edition, Paris: 1992), 104–105, quoted in Christin, *La Paix de religion*, 12. See also, Reinhart Koselleck, *Le règne de la Critique* (French edition, Paris: 1979).

69 Sylvie Daubresse, *Le Parlement de Paris ou la voix de la raison (1559–1589)* (Geneva: 2005).

70 Francis Garrisson, *Essai sur les commissions d'application de l'Edit de Nantes*, part 1: *Le règne d'Henri IV* (Montpellier: 1964). Diane Margolf, *Religion and Royal Justice in Early Modern France: The Paris Chambre de l'Edit, 1598–1665* (Kirksville, Mo.: 2003).

Religion. At Millau in October 1563, for example, the commissioner watched helplessly as the inhabitants offered him "a halberd of little use, another a club, others crossbows without strings…others old explosives."[71] They were passing off the fossilized remnants of a former age, the stockpiles from the Hundred Years' War.

Still worse, the commissioners' zeal in paying off the losses of war often mortgaged the chances of peace. In Lyon, for example, a Catholic writer thought that the efforts at exhaustive restitution of property seized during the wars turned the inhabitants against each other—especially the Catholics against the Protestants—more than had the military clashes. Claude de Rubys claimed that the Catholics regularly assailed the commissioner Jean-Jacques de Mesmes "for trifling matters of little value, such as the restitution of a parrot, an anvil, a pot of grease, a pound of candles, and numerous other things of the same sort."[72] He concluded tragically that the actions of the commissioner "turned the inhabitants of the city against each other more than all the troubles and civil wars of the past had done, and these wounds continued to bleed until the news arrived of the slaughter of the Protestants on St. Bartholomew's Sunday, August 24 of the said year 1572."[73] While we cannot accept Claude de Rubys's accusation of the commissioner responsibility in the massacres, we can at least agree that appeasement and justice rarely go well together.

There were two particular points the commissioners stressed in constructing a future peace: the creation of mixed political structures and oaths of reconciliation.

7.2   A Bipartisan Policy

During the wars, the municipal councils and consulates had become homogeneous from a religious perspective, the dominant confession having banished the members of the minority from the corridors of power. This was the case at Troyes, Lyon and Montauban. As a result, conflict was reduced. Regrettably, the coexistence of two opposing confessions in the same territory generated innumerable conflicts that begged mediation. By default they found expression in the streets, in blood. Ending warfare did not mean denying religious differences, but rather offering them a defined framework of expression, symbolic spaces governed by standards for debating and making decisions without violence and without religious validation of politics. Here again the municipal archives are of great help. At Grenoble, a city violently torn apart by the two

---

71   *Mémoires d'un calviniste de Millau (1560–1582)*, (ed.) J.-L. Rigal (Rodez: 1911), 110–11.
72   Claude de Rubys, *Histoire veritable de la ville de Lyon* (Lyon: 1604), 409.
73   Rubys, *Histoire veritable*, 421.

parties, the consuls at the request of the commissioners decreed in December 1563 that "henceforth those who wish to pray to God in the said special councils should make their prayers quietly and secretly."[74] This need to desacralize the space for decision-making stemmed from the confessional mix put in place by the commissioners.

The commissioners systematically ordered that subjects of the two religions be admitted "into the councils" regardless of their numerical importance. In September 1563 the commissioner Madeleine permitted the Protestants of Briançon to attend the general assemblies regularly "with a voice in decisions," giving them an unhoped-for chance to politicize their opposition—both to demilitarize and deconfessionalize it.[75] About the same time at Blois, Pot de Chemault decreed that when "assemblies for the business of the city meet, those of the said religion are to be called."[76] The commissioners even went so far as to fix quotas, as they did in Aix in October 1564, ordering "that there be included the number of a fourth part [a quarter] from those of the new religion."[77] The measure was doubly extraordinary and testifies to the increased intervention of the crown in municipal political administration. Not only did the commissioner install Huguenots at the center of power in a city with a Catholic majority, but he thereby annulled an election held just a month before on 24 September 1564 "in conformity with the ancient forms."[78] The agents of peace went even further at Lyon, Gap, Millau, Nîmes, Béziers, Montpellier and Vienne—all Huguenot cities—by enforcing the election of equal numbers of Catholic and Protestant consuls. Sometimes, when this sort of interference with "local liberties" seemed impossible, the commissioners tried to bypass the consulate by stripping it of the administration of confessional differences and establishing a bipartisan, parallel body charged with settling conflict. This is what they undertook at Romans by negotiating the creation of an assembly composed of thirty men, fifteen Catholics and fifteen Protestants, charged with the routine handling of problems arising from confessional coexistence.[79] The traditional recourse to members of the clergy for restoring peace having been rendered useless, the commissioners made politics the preferred means for re-creating a social consensus. Since it was impossible to resort as in the

---

74   AM Grenoble, BB 18, fol. 466 (mardi, 28 décembre 1563).
75   Charles Charonnet, *Les guerres de Religion et la société protestante dans les Hautes-Alpes (1560–1789)* (Gap: 1861), 42–43; cf. AM Briançon II, 9, "Livre du roi," 17 septembre 1563.
76   BnF, Ms. fr. 15878, fol. 159 (8 octobre 1563).
77   AM Aix-en-Provence, BB 60, fol. 74 (26 octobre 1564).
78   AM Aix-en-Provence, BB 60, fol. 64 (24 septembre 1564).
79   AM Romans, BB 10, fol. 109 (octobre 1563).

past to processions or Masses of reconciliation, the delegation of the maintenance of peace to God or to sacred objects was, as it were, revoked, and henceforth it was through structures built by men that the community would be asked to rediscover and mend itself. By distinguishing the body of citizens from the body of the faithful, the crown dissolved the unity of the mystical body of the city.[80] Over time, a desacralization of the community ensued. It was "certainly not a breaking of the bond with God, but the recognition of the part played by humans, and thus the contingent in political construction."[81] Matters concerning the salvation of the faithful were no longer to be decided in this empowered realm. They were henceforth turned over to the Churches alone. The only issues decided jointly were henceforth secular. They concerned the allotment of taxes, keeping of arms, repair of the city walls, cleaning the streets, organizing celebrations and so on.

7.3 Living together as "Brothers, Friends, and Fellow-citizens"

Even more than the inhabitants, the commissioners had an acute awareness of the irreversibility of the time of troubles. Through their daily activity they knew that not all was curable, certainly neither deaths nor wounds. More than justice, the commissioners promoted concord. They repeatedly made townspeople swear to a "publicly announced general reconciliation, signed by all the heads of household."[82] They could not bring back to his inconsolable widow Gilbert Douxsaintz, a Huguenot from Clermont, murdered during a Corpus Christi procession in 1568. Despite her request for redress, the commissioners refused to prosecute those responsible.[83] At Lisieux in August 1563, the commissioners Viole and La Guesle had imposed a similar "silence" on Christine Hébert, a Catholic, regarding the death of her husband, killed in a confrontation with some Huguenots during the first civil war.[84] Forgetting thus served to consolidate peace and avoid the renewal of conflicts that would have resulted from too intense an inquiry. At Saint-Maixent, the commissioners described to the king the pacification that resulted from such selectivity, the inhabitants "abandoning

---

80 As Reinhart Koselleck has shown, the political structure of absolutism was designed as a rational solution for the religious conflicts, the latter being nourished by unitary conceptions of "mystical bodies," both of cities and of the kingdom. Besides Koselleck (earlier cited), see Hélène Merlin, *L'absolutisme dans les lettres et la théorie des deux corps. Passions et politique* (Paris: 2000).

81 Arlette Jouanna, "L'Edit de Nantes et le processus de sécularisation de l'Etat," in *Paix des armes, paix des âmes*, (eds.) Paul Mironneau and Isabelle Pébay-Clottes (Paris: 2000), 484.

82 AM Romans, BB 6, fol. 220.

83 AM Clermont, BB 38 (20 novembre 1570).

84 BnF, Ms. fr. 16221, fol. 122v° (27 août 1563).

part of their vengefulness and the hope of finding [satisfaction] by means of the commission."[85]

But did telling people that "what they complain of is pardoned and forgotten" promote peace or offer a pretext to those who, frustrated by justice, would seek through arms the revenge they were refused in court?[86] Naturally, what everyone was supposed to renounce was the reopening of a cycle of vengeance not his particular recollections. But the commissioners always had to take account of the balance of power—far less than the legal norms—when they cast themselves as censors and rewrote the history of the troubles in keeping with their proceedings, moralizing it by making a distinction between legitimate and illegitimate conflicts. People evidently had greater possibility to hold onto the property they had acquired during the troubles and to escape prosecution, if they were powerful rather than weak. The policy of forgetting contributed to the concentration in the hands of the sovereign of a valuable power—that of transforming hostilities into glorious feats of arms, or the inverse, in different circumstances. The king and the commissioners established a sort of capital fund of fidelity among those who had profited by their largesse. The crown and its commissioners hoped that these beneficiaries would devote their efforts to preserving a peace that profited them and they were all the more courted because they were so numerous. The gains from the uncertain boundaries of forgetting could be reinvested and simultaneously serve concord (profits of pacification), the commissioners (profits of social promotion) and also the strongest (profits of domination). Making peace required prioritizing political questions over juridical ones.

The king's agents preferred forgetting to systematic redress of grievances. They were guided by the Edict of Amboise, which decreed that "all injuries and offenses that the iniquities of the times and the opportunities that have arisen from them may have produced among our said subjects, and all other things past and caused by these present disturbances will remain extinguished, as though dead, buried, and not having happened."[87] The expression "not having happened" expressed the magic of the process—going back in time, rewriting history. It was the miracle accomplished by the policy of reconciliation.[88] If they refused to forget, men would be condemned to reproach one another endlessly for the deeds of the past and to see the conflicts endlessly reborn. In

---

85   BnF, Ms. fr. 15878, fol. 110v° (18 août 1563).
86   BnF, Ms. fr. 15878, fol. 110v° (18 août 1563).
87   Edict of Amboise, article 9.
88   Paul Ricoeur, *La Mémoire, l'Histoire, l'Oubli* (Paris: 2000), 587 ff.

Amiens, as everywhere else, the commissioners commanded people to cease "to insult and provoke one another with reproaches over what is past."[89]

The forgetting encouraged by Charles IX was not simply symbolic. It had a material dimension, which was manifested in objects as well as in space—a reified and practical dimension of forgetting. These incarnations of memory, which were to be effaced, were neglected by the Edict of Amboise, but that did not keep the commissioners from trying to erase them. On the other hand, the Edict of Saint-Germain drawing upon the lessons of the past, devoted an entire article to the material aspect of forgetting, revoking the judgments (*arrêts*) issued during the religious troubles:

> [...] which for this reason we wish to be crossed out and removed from the registers of our courts, both sovereign and inferior, as also we order all traces, vestiges and record of the said defamatory executions [of judgments], writings and acts against their persons, memory and posterity all to be removed and effaced, and those places where for this reason demolitions and razing [of buildings] occurred be returned to their owners to use and dispose of according to their wishes.[90]

The episode of the cross of Gastines at Paris in 1571 is undoubtedly the most famous manifestation of the conflict between memory and forgetting in its spatial aspect.[91] Everywhere, the space used in the confessional struggles resounded with the echoes of battles lost and dreams broken, an open history book that the crown claimed to correct. Nothing shows more clearly this constant interconnection between forgetting and the rewriting of history than the action by which the commissioner Jehan de Villeneuve condemned Georges Bosquet's *Histoire de la délivrance de la ville de Toulouse* to burn at the stake. It was an exclusively Catholic reading of the events of May 1562.[92] Villeneuve forbade any new editions of the work and ordered all who possessed copies to turn them in so that they could "also be burned."[93] Authors in the employ of

---

89 AM Amiens, AA 14, fol. 208v.
90 Edict of Saint-Germain, art. 5, 32.
91 Barbara Diefendorf, *Beneath the Cross: Catholics and Huguenots in Sixteenth-Century Paris* (Oxford: 1991), 84–8 and 151–5.
92 Georges Bosquet, *Histoire de la délivrance de la ville de Toulouse* (1562), repr. in *Pièces historiques relatives aux guerres de Religion de Toulouse* (Paris: 1872), 120ff; Pierre-Jean Souriac, *Une guerre civile. Affrontements religieux et militaires en Midi toulousain* (Seyssel: 2008).
93 AM Toulouse, AA 14, fol. 93 (15 septembre 1564).

the government sought to construct an ideal history of the monarchy,[94] while the commissioners labored to destroy the evidence—and the sources—of the actual, but far too contentious, history of the reign. A good history, peaceful albeit fictitious, was thus substituted for a bad polemical history, even if it was truthful. In October 1565 Charles IX wrote to the seneschal of Toulouse ordering him to toss into the flames "everything that might restore to memory the past injuries."[95]

Providing a framework for coexistence required not only the pardon of past offenses but also trust for the future. Thus, while the commissioners hoped to annul the past through forgetting, they undertook to control the future through oaths.[96] When leaving a place, they assembled the inhabitants and had them swear henceforth to live as "brothers, friends, and fellow citizens." They hoped in this way to link the future behavior of the inhabitants to their irrevocable sworn word. In August 1563, for instance, the commissioners had the people of Grenoble swear to respect the edicts of pacification and to forget past animosities.[97] Sanctions no longer descended from heaven and excommunication no longer followed perjury. Whereas in the Middle Ages the Church was always involved in oaths and considered it "legitimate to intervene in any case where their breaking is suspected," now the honor of the person swearing the oath was violated if he falsified it. The dishonor also extended to the one in whose name the oath was taken, the one to whom it was sworn, namely the king.[98] It fell to the latter to guarantee the oath by punishing its violation severely. The burgeoning of oaths sworn to the king to respect the edicts implied an accompanying widening of the scope of royal intervention. Royal governors, magistrates, and officers were henceforth the guarantors of oaths.

The possibility of peace depended on a political negation of the inherent limits of human time (past and future), a denial that obstinately refused to admit that the past was over and that the future was unpredictable. This policy allowed the commissioners to deny the irreversibility of the past through the encouragement of forgiveness, while diminishing the uncertainty of the future through giving one's word. Living together during the religious conflicts

---

94   Myriam Yardeni, "La conception de l'histoire dans l'œuvre de La Popelinière," *Revue d'histoire moderne et contemporaine* 11 (1964), 109–26.

95   AM Toulouse, AA 14, pièce 70 (22 octobre 1565).

96   Paolo Prodi, "De l'analogie à l'histoire: le sacrement du pouvoir," in idem, *Christianisme et monde moderne. Cinquante ans de recherches* (Paris: 2006), 217–46.

97   AM Grenoble, BB 18, fol. 432v.

98   François Billacois, "Rituels du serment: des personnages en quête d'une 'voix off,'" in *Le Serment*, vol. I, *Signes et fonctions*, (ed.) Raymond Verdier (Paris: 1991), 23–33.

required playing human political abilities against its anthropological limits. The situation benefited the state, the prime manipulator of this symbolic transgression of temporal limits. It follows that if, as Hannah Arendt has remarked, living with the "other" is the condition of forgiving as much as one's word (because nothing compels one to pardon oneself and a pledge made to oneself is hardly constraining), religious conflict, in that it was the result of the daily presence of the enemy, precipitated the process of politicization of society.[99] By making the need to forgive and the obligation to commit oneself more pressing, the civil wars advanced the establishment of the modern political state.

8 Conclusion

The question of the failure of the commissioners to reestablish peace haunts every study that seeks to take the measure of their activities. The renewal of conflict in 1567, in 1568–1570, then again after Saint Bartholomew's, meant the end of the hope for peace promoted by the crown and the failure of the commissioners.[100] The isolation of the latter was the primary reason for their failure. It is no doubt an illusion to think that so few men, even if selected with care, could achieve peace. The choice of an extraordinary process reinforced the marginalization of the ordinary courts of justice all the while distancing and separating the agents of peace. By acting in this way the monarchy deprived itself of collaborators who, although apart, remained indispensable.[101] By a single stroke the king assured the total exhaustion of the commissioners and the overburdening of his council. Jules Gassot affirmed the situation when he expressed regret that the handling of business concerning the edict was retained by the "king's privy council and forbidden to the other judges, which

---

99   Hannah Arendt, *La Condition de l'homme moderne* (1961; French edition, Paris: 1983), 301–14.

100 Denis Crouzet, *La Nuit de la Saint-Barthélemy. Un rêve perdu de la Renaissance* (Paris: 1994).

101 *Ordonnance du roy attributive de jurisdiction aux baillifz, seneschaux, prevost des mareschaux à l'encontre des infracteurs de son édit de la paix*, 1563 (BnF F 46823 [19]). It was not until 1566 that conditions were normalized: *Lettres patentes du roy par lesquelles il renvoye et attribue à la chambre du conseil du Parlement de Paris la cognoissance et jugement par de tous et chascuns les procès et differends concernants l'execution et entretenement de l'edict de pacification*, Moulins, 10 février 1566 (BnF, F 27573 [17]).

brought a multitude of suits to the council."[102] In contrast to the Empire, the pacification process in France was more monarchical than judicial, and no court of justice assisted the crown in the business of peace. The prince's isolation speaks eloquently to the originality but also the unpopularity of a policy aimed at reaching beyond religious antagonism. The drumbeat of the confessional rivalry drowned out the delicate refrain of peace.

Within this context, Charles IX's refusal to "confessionalize" his agents—to appoint, as did Henry IV, a Catholic commissioner along with a Protestant one—exposed them to criticism from both sides. It might have been better to dispatch into the provinces commissioners clearly identified from a religious point of view. This refusal to make them members of a particular side, this obstinacy in considering them above all as agents of the king, hindered the commissioners. The Huguenots accused them of being Catholic and the latter accused them of being Reformed. Pacification in France, as contrasted to the Empire, was universalist. It spoke to the king's subjects, not to the faithful.[103]

Was pacification stillborn from the outset, to be set aside with so many other innovations without a future and inventors without talent? The response begs nuance. The royal commissioners undoubtedly contributed to the development of means capable of allowing people of differing faiths to live together. These were techniques of peace that in large part were not embodied in the text of the edicts, but were the fruit of patient consultation between the commissioners and the king's subjects. Numerous chronicles testify, moreover, to the relatively peaceful years 1563–1567 and 1570–1572 during Charles IX's reign. The commissioners certainly deserve some credit for these developments. The pacification was, to be sure, temporary, but it would be wrong to regard the occasions as no more than intervals between wars.

In many respects, pacification during the reign of Charles IX was a model for that put into effect forty years later by Henry IV.[104] Far from starting from scratch, the commissioners of the Edict of Nantes reestablished in many ways the arrangements set up by the commissioners of Charles IX: the division of cemeteries and consulships, restitution of property, settlement of conflict, prohibition or reestablishment of processions, and so on. But the political context, the war-weariness, and the lessons drawn from the earlier failures assisted the first Bourbon monarch. As a sort of entryway for the Edict of Nantes, pacification

---

102   Jules Gassot, *Sommaire mémorial (souvenirs) de Jules Gassot secrétaire du roi (1555–1623)* (Paris: 1934), 58.
103   Olivier Christin, "L'Europe des paix de Religion: semblants et faux-semblants," BSHPF 144 (1998), 489–505.
104   Garrisson, *Essai sur les commissions*. Margolf, *Religion and Royal Justice*.

under Charles IX served as a laboratory and without doubt had fundamental importance.

Although historians now recognize that the process of pacification did not begin with Henry IV, they are not in agreement on the place of the state in the process. Whether they are interested in "reformation," "civilization," "acculturation," "confessionalization," or—the subject that interests us—"pacification," a statist or elitist model of the diffusion of social phenomena still seems the dominant explanation advanced by scholars. According to this interpretation, norms are propagated from the top downward toward the bottom of the social ladder, set in motion by the elites or the state, in a process of social discipline in which ordinary subjects are merely the objects of the techniques of power.

In the case of the return of calm to France after the Wars of Religion, the model of "pacification from above" has enjoyed broad favor. Henry IV, the edicts of pacification, Catherine de Medici, and the commissioners of the edicts have been emphasized as the determining factors in emerging from the crisis. For Arlette Jouanna, coexistence was "imposed from above by the royal edicts, maintained by the governors, and controlled by commissioners expressly appointed for this purpose."[105] In urging his subjects "to live together as brothers, friends, and fellow citizens," Charles IX advocated a solution to the violence that only the crown seemed in a position to administer. By promulgating a series of edicts granting freedom of worship and conscience to the Huguenots and by dispatching "commissioners of the edicts of pacification" to apply them, the king met with opposition from a great number of his subjects. This view, however, tends to ignore the role of the subjects themselves in the pacification process, making them perpetually turbulent juveniles, constantly brawling and unable to restore calm on their own. Did the modern state actually have the ability to impose peace instead of simply reacting to everyday problems? Could it really hope to achieve pacification without taking account of the local people who had, or did not have, a vested interest?[106]

---

105 Jouanna, "Coexister dans la différence," in *L'avènement d'Henri IV*, 151.
106 Jean-Frédéric Schaub, "Le temps et l'État: vers un nouveau régime historiographique de l'Ancien Régime français," *Quaderni Fiorentini per la Storia del Pensiero Giuridico Moderno* 25 (1996), 127–81.

CHAPTER 5

Women in the Huguenot Community

Amanda Eurich

1   Introduction

In 1963 André Bieler published *L'homme et la femme dans la morale calviniste*, and offered perhaps the first serious consideration of the place of women in Calvin's theology.[1] In the two decades following its publication, a number of seminal works on the role and status of women in the Reformed tradition heralded the expansion of opportunities for the female sex. Jane Dempsey Douglass championed the salutary effects of Calvinist doctrines on marriage, election and the priesthood of all believers which she argued "contributed to greater freedom and equality for women," even in the largely masculine preserve of theology and preaching.[2] Nancy Roelker's studies of French noblewomen, who were in the vanguard of the Reformed movement, echoed Douglass' sentiments, suggesting that women embraced the Reformation because it offered them a "sense of purpose" and the opportunity to exercise a leading role as patrons and protectors of the new religious movement.[3] Natalie Davis's examination of the appeal of Calvinism to urban women argued that Calvinism complemented the scope and independence that early modern women's lives already had, even though the promises of spiritual equality and companionate marriage never fully countered the moral restrictions imposed by Reformed tradition and broader social convention.[4]

Scholars of the German Reformation have been considerably less charitable about the benefits that Protestantism afforded early modern women. In the 1980s Merry Wiesner, Susan Karant-Nunn and Lyndal Roper all asserted that the Protestant Reformation reinforced, perhaps even deepened, the misogynist

---

1   André Bieler, *L'Homme et la femme dans la morale calviniste* (Geneva: 1963).
2   Jane Dempsey Douglass, "Women and the Continental Reformation," in *Religion and Sexism: Image of Woman in the Jewish and Christian Traditions*, (ed.) Rosemary Ruether (New York: 1974), 292–318, quoted at 303; idem, *Women, Freedom and Calvin* (Philadelphia: 1985).
3   Nancy Roelker, "The Appeal of Calvinism to French Noblemen," *Journal of Interdisciplinary History* 2 (1972), 391–481; idem, "The Role of Noblewomen in the French Reformation," *Archiv für Reformationgeschichte* 64 (1972), 168–195; idem, *Queen of Navarre: Jeanne d'Albret 1528–572* (Cambridge, Mass: 1968).
4   Natalie Davis, "City Women and Religious Change," in *Society and Culture in Early Modern France* (Stanford: 1975), 65–95.

assumptions and patriarchal ideologies of classical and medieval tradition.⁵ As Wiesner argued, the suppression of convent life limited opportunities for women whose lives were even more firmly inscribed within the household and subjected to male tutelage. Roper's work on Reformation Augsburg went even further, insisting that the "moral reformism" of the Protestant Reformation problematized the presence of autonomous, single women (nuns and prostitutes) in civic life while encouraging the creation of new secular institutions, which placed married women even more fully under male authority in the home as well as in society at large. More recently Karant-Nunn has argued convincingly that the reformation of ritual transformed the sacraments into a vehicle of disciplinary control that perpetuated the misogynist clerical discourse and practice. The preservation of rituals, such as churching in Lutheran tradition, reinforced pervasive cultural anxieties about the female body as a site of impurity and pollution, underscoring women's greater need for moral regulation.⁶

Recent studies on women and their place in Huguenot society have not resolved the debate over the long term effects of religious change on women's lived experience. Much like Davis's pioneering essay written over forty years ago, the broad arc of scholarship on women and the Reformed tradition points to the complicated legacies of medieval tradition and Renaissance humanism, the tensions between the spiritual and pastoral ideals of Calvinist theology and the realities of women's lived experience as well as the ability of many Huguenot women to create a distinctive space for themselves within the church, within their community and within the *longue durée* of Christian history. Some women even recognized fairly readily that the coercive disciplinary system of Reformed church could be manipulated to their advantage as an instrument of empowerment rather than coercion and shame. In the Huguenot communities of early modern France, female activism and agency was a repeated source of contestation and negotiation as well as personal liberation and spiritual fulfillment.

---

5 Merry Wiesner, "Beyond Women and the Family: Toward a Gender Analysis of the Reformation," *SCJ* 18 (1987), 311–21; Susan Karant-Nunn, "Continuity and Change: Some of the Effects of the Reformation on the Women of Zwickau," *SCJ* 13 (1984), 17–42; Lyndal Roper, *Oedipus and the Devil: Witchcraft, Sexuality in Early Modern Europe* (London: 1984); idem, *The Holy Household: Women and Morals in Reformation Augsburg* (Oxford: 1989). For a recent summary of research on gender and the German Reformation, see Wiesner, *Gender, Church and State in Early Modern Germany* (London: 1998), and Heide Wunder, *He is the Sun, She is the Moon: Women in Early Modern Germany*, trans. Thomas Dunlap (Cambridge, Mass.: 1998).

6 Susan Karant-Nunn, *The Reformation of Ritual: An Interpretation of Early Modern Germany* (London: 1997).

2 Women at Court

As Charmarie Blaisdell has shown, French-born Genevan reformer John Calvin recognized that noblewomen were crucial to the diffusion and survival of Reformed ideas in France and deliberately targeted them because of the potent influence they exercised over their husbands, children and far-reaching patronage networks.[7] Calvin also realized that noblewomen often controlled considerable family fortunes and shrewdly tapped his aristocratic correspondents for funding to sustain the increasingly embattled Huguenot churches of France, their pastors, and adherents. Among his early contacts and erstwhile patrons was Marguerite de Navarre, the only sibling of Francis I and an accomplished humanist in her own right. Marguerite has long been a subject of study by historians of the French Reformation because of the protection and support she offered to reform-minded scholars and theologians as well as for her devotional writings, which nourished and legitimated reformist ideas in court circles and among court women.[8] The ongoing interest that Marguerite holds for historians as well as literary scholars is evident in a recent volume in Brill's Companion to Christian Tradition series edited by Gary Ferguson and Mary McKinley.[9] Here and in his two-volume study of the "queen of dissent," Jonathan Reid has burnished Marguerite's image as a staunch promoter of evangelical ideas and protector of reform-minded theologians, such as Guillaume Briçonnet and the Meaux group.[10] Reid's careful reconstruction of Marguerite's epistolary network, her various efforts to protect evangelicals from prosecution in her own territories, and her abortive efforts to realign French diplomatic interests with continental Protestant powers clarifies how Marguerite and her circle helped lay the essential groundwork for formal establishment of the French Reformed Churches in 1559 and thereafter. Literary scholars have also emphasized the militantly innovative and evangelical quality of much of Marguerite's *oeuvre*. Isabelle Garnier, Patricia Cholakian,

---

7   Charmarie Jenkins Blaisdell, "Calvin's Letters to Women: The Courting of Ladies in High Places," SCJ 13 (1982), 67–84.
8   Pierre Jourda, *Marguerite d'Angoulême, duchesse d'Alençon, reine de Navarre (1492–1549): étude biographique et littéraire* (2 vols. Paris: 1930); Barbara Stephenson, *The Power and Patronage of Marguerite of Navarre* (Burlington, Vt.: 2004); Patricia and Rouben Cholakian, *Marguerite de Navarre (1492–459): Mother of the Renaissance* (New York: 2005).
9   Gary Ferguson and Mary McKinley (eds.), *A Companion to Marguerite de Navarre* (Leiden: 2013).
10 Jonathan Reid, *King's Sister—Queen of Dissent: Marguerite de Navarre (1492–1549)* (2 vols. Leiden: 2009); also "Marguerite de Navarre and Evangelical Reform," in *A Companion to Marguerite de Navarre*, (eds.) Ferguson and McKinley, 29–58.

Gary Ferguson and Mary McKinley see in her work a sustained (though often oblique) critique of the church, its clergy and the dangerous antipathies they promoted toward women.[11] Other scholars continue to emphasize Marguerite's deep fascination with Neoplatonic tropes which contributed to her growing rift with Calvin in her later years.[12]

In the first half of the 16th century in France, Marguerite was among the most prominent female supporters of religious reform but certainly not the only one. Renée de France, the daughter of Louis XII, engaged in an active correspondence with a number of prominent reformist intellectuals (among them Pier Paulo Vergerio and John Calvin) and encouraged the reformist ideas in the duchy of Ferrara after her marriage to Ercole II. Charmarie Blaisdell has described how Renée painfully negotiated the confessional dynamics of her marriage to the duke, whose growing enthusiasm for the Counter-Reformation led to the introduction of a special court of the Inquisition in the duchy in 1545, and her arrest and imprisonment nine years later.[13] After Ercole's death in 1559, Renée returned to France where she continued to support the reform of the church, harboring Pierre Viret and Theodore Beza on her estates in Montargis. Blaisdell's analysis of Renée's correspondence with Calvin points to the increasing constraints imposed upon women with the formal establishment of the French Reformed Churches in 1559. While Calvin often praised Renée (in his letters to her and to others) for her steadfast support of reform, he sharply criticized her for meddling in local consistory affairs, an activity which she plainly saw as an extension of the seigneurial patronage and protection she offered to fledging Reformed communities in her territories.[14]

By the 1560s and 1570s a new generation of French noblewomen openly embraced Calvinism, promoted the Reformation in their territories and estates, and negotiated with foreign powers to marshal military support for Protestant

---

11 Isabelle Garnier and Isabelle Pantin, "Opening and Closing Reflections: The *Miroir de l'ame de la pecheresse* and the *Miroir de Jesus Christ crucified*," in *Companion to Marguerite de Navarre*, (eds.) Ferguson and McKinley, 109–59; Patricia Cholakian, *Rape and Writing in the Heptameron of Marguerite de Navarre* (Carbondale, Ill.: 1991).

12 Philip Ford, "Neoplatonic Themes of Ascent in Marguerite de Navarre," in *A Companion to Marguerite*, (eds.) Ferguson and McKinley, 2; John Thompson, *John Calvin and the Daughters of Sarah*, (Geneva: 1992), 39–40.

13 Charmarie Jenkins Blaisdell, "Renée de France between Reform and Counter-Reform," *Archiv für Reformationgeschichte* 63 (1972), 196–226.

14 Blaisdell, "Calvin's Letters to Women," 67–84. As a local minister complained to Calvin, "She is turning everything upside down in our ecclesiastical assembly....our consistory will be the laughing stock of papists and Anabaptists. They'll say we are being ruled by women," as quoted in Davis, "City Women," 84.

armies in the field. Because of their connections to the highest court circles and princely families, high-ranking French aristocrats, such as Jeanne d'Albret and her sister-in-law, Eléanor de Roye, princesse de Condé, were in a position to advance the Calvinist cause at a national level. Nancy Roelker's 1972 biography of Jeanne d'Albret, the daughter of Marguerite de Navarre and Henry d'Albret, is a useful starting point for the study of noblewomen during the French Wars of Religion.[15] Mark Greengrass has closely studied Jeanne's efforts to implement the Reformation in her semi-independent principality of Béarn. Amanda Eurich has traced how Jeanne mobilized her private fortunes to finance the Reformation in her territories and Calvinist armies in the field after she became titular head of the Huguenot party in late 1560s.[16] David Bryson's more recent and controversial study of Queen Jeanne focuses on her militant vision of creating a Protestant promised land in southwestern France, an ideal driven by Old Testament rhetoric as well as dynastic ambition. His analysis of her correspondence with military leaders emphasizes more fully than previous scholarship her strategic involvement in the military and logistical details of war-making as well as high court diplomacy. Lamentably, there still is no modern study of Jeanne's equally powerful sister-in-law, Eléanor, comtesse de Roye, who engaged the support of German princes and Elizabeth I for the fledgling Protestant movement and later played a key role in the Peace of Amboise in March 1563.[17]

After the St Bartholomew's Day massacre in 1572, few noblewomen wielded the central role they had in first decades of the French Reformation and the religious wars. Certainly the death of key female protectors in the 1570s (Jeanne d'Albret, Eléanor de Roye, and Renée de France) deprived the Reformed movement of powerful, independent women with close ties to crown and court; other prominent noblewomen, including Catherine de Parthenay, Charlotte d'Arbaleste and Louise de Coligny, fled Paris in the aftermath of the massacre and sought refuge in Protestant strongholds or with sympathetic Protestant foreign powers. Marie-Hélène Grintchenko has explored the ongoing influence

---

15 Nancy Roelker, *Queen of Navarre: Jeanne d'Albret 1528–1572* (Cambridge, Mass.: 1972); Mark Greengrass, "The Calvinist Experiment in Béarn," in *Calvinism in Europe 1540–1620*, (ed.) Andrew Pettegree (Cambridge: 1996), 119–42; on her protection of churches in Normandy, see Penny Roberts, *Peace and Authority during the French Religious Wars* (Basingstoke: 2013), 149–53. On her broader literary and artistic patronage of Reformed movement, see Philippe Chareyre and Claudie Martin-Ulrich (eds.), *Jeanne d'Albret et sa cour. Actes du colloque international de Pau 17–19 mai 2001* (Paris: 2001).

16 S. Amanda Eurich, *The Economics of Power: The Private Finances of the House of Foix-Navarre-Albret during the Religious Wars* (Kirksville, Mo.: 1994).

17 Jules Delaborde, *Eléanor de Roye, princesse de Condé, 1534–564* (Paris: 1876).

exercised by Catherine de Bourbon, who followed in her mother's footsteps as a stalwart defender of Protestantism in Béarn and Navarre, which she governed independently for the better part of two decades because of her brother Henry IV's pressing concerns on the battlefield.[18] After 1593, Catherine's presence at Henry IV's court bolstered the Protestant party in royal circles and allowed her to marshal literary and artistic talent on behalf of the Bourbon monarchy and religious reform. Catherine's departure from court after her marriage to the Duke of Bar, and her death in 1604, marked the end of Huguenot women's involvement in high court politics and diplomacy. Recent scholarship on court culture and state-building in early modern France has also ascribed the decreasing political influence of women to more than the lack of leadership. The consolidation of male authority at court as well as in the pulpit consigned noblewomen to secondary, supporting parts. As Kathleen Wellman and Michel De Waele have suggested, the masculinization of the Bourbon court as well as the rituals of reconciliation with Catholic *chefs du parti* instituted by Henry IV intensified the exclusion of noblewomen from the informal exercise of political power from the late 16th century onward.[19]

Recent works by Keith Luria, Nicole Vray and others, however, have emphasized the critical role that French noblewomen, such as Charlotte-Brabantine, duchesse de la Trémoille, Marie de la Tour d'Auvergne, and Catherine de Parthenay, duchesse de Rohan, continued to play at the local level as defenders of Huguenot privilege.[20] Their influence was especially important in the mid-17th century as the Bourbon monarchy initiated its legal and administrative assault on Huguenot rights of worship and ordered the destruction of Calvinist temples across France.

3   Women and Religious War

Since the mid-1990s scholars have emphasized the crucial role that women from across the social divide assumed during the religious wars in France. Wars, even in our modern society, often create a power vacuum that disrupts

---

18   Marie-Hélène Grintchenko, *Catherine de Bourbon (1559–1604), influence politique, religieuse et culturelle d'une princesse calviniste* (Paris: 2009).

19   Kathleen Wellman, *Queens and Mistresses of Renaissance France* (New Haven: 2013), 323–71; Michel De Waele, "La fin des guerres de Religion et l'exclusion des femmes de la vie politique française," *French Historical Studies* 29 (2011), 199–230.

20   Keith Luria, *Sacred Boundaries: Religious Coexistence and Conflict in Early Modern France* (Washington, D.C.: 2005), 170–84, 211–29; Nicole Vray, *Catherine de Parthenay, duchesse de Rohan: protestante insoumise, 1554–1631* (Paris: 1998).

traditional patterns of patriarchal authority and privilege, allowing women to transgress established boundaries of gender perceptions and performance.[21] The religious wars of the 16th century brought unique challenges to the task of managing family estates which often fell to women during peacetime as well.[22] As Brian Sandberg has argued, "protecting families and their belongings became a primarily female responsibility during the sieges of the Wars of Religion,"[23] especially as armies on both sides of the conflict targeted wealthy estates for food and other supplies. Kristen Neuschel has suggested that women even assumed traditional male, military duties, mustering saltpeter and muskets to defend their family estates from attack.[24] Contemporary chroniclers were certainly struck by the valiant efforts levied by women in defense of their cities and chateaux. Susan Broomhall and Eliane Viennot have called attention to contemporary accounts that describe women taking up arms themselves and fighting alongside men, sometimes even commandeering military actions.[25] Brantôme famously described the *femmes fortes* of La Rochelle who mounted the ramparts, dramatically dressed in white, "the most virile and robust among them carrying arms" to protect the city during the siege of 1573. The exploits of Claude de la Tour, dame de Turenne, reputed to have led several sieges in the second and third religious wars inspired a contemporary biography by one Jean Villerman published at the conclusion of the conflicts.

Letters, municipal records, and military narratives reveal that women acted as intermediaries and informants, and as power brokers in their own right,

---

21   See, for example, Irène Hermann and Daniel Palmieri, "Between Amazons and Sabines: a Historical Approach to Women and War," *International Review of the Red Cross* 92 (2010), 19–30; Bernard Cook, *Women and War: A Historical Encyclopedia from Antiquity to the Present* (Santa Barbara: 2006).

22   On women's role in estate management, see Robert Kalas, "The Noble Widow's Place in the Patriarchal Household: The Life and Career of Jeanne de Gontault," *SCJ* 24 (1993), 519–39; idem, "Noble Widows and Estate Management during the French Wars of Religion," *SCJ* 49 (2008): 357–70. Sharon Kettering, "The Patronage Power of Early Modern French Noblewomen," *Historical Journal* 32 (1989), 817–26; Kristen Neuschel, "Noblewomen and War in Sixteenth-Century France," in *Changing Identities in Early Modern France*, (ed.) Michael Wolfe (Durham, NC: 1997), 124–44.

23   Brian Sandberg, "Generous Amazons Came to the Breach: Besieged Women, Agency and Subjectivity during the French Wars of Religion," *Gender and History* 16 (2004): 654–88, esp. 670.

24   Neuschel, "Noblewomen and War," 126.

25   Elaine Viennot, "Les femmes dans les troubles du XVI siècle," *Clio: histoire, femmes et sociétés* 5 (1997), 79–96; Penny Richards, "The Guise Women: Politics, War and Peace," in *Gender, Power and Privilege in Early Modern Europe*, (eds.) Jessica Munns and Penny Richards (London: 2003), 159–70; Susan Broomhall, *Women and Religion in Sixteenth-Century France* (London: 2006), 130.

during the French Wars of Religion. By blood, by marriage and by faith, Huguenot women were at the center of important networks which allowed them to transmit political news, smuggle clandestine messages to key figures in the Huguenot party, and defend family properties from the depredation of civil war. As Mark Greengrass has emphasized, informal communication networks were essential to the Protestant movement in France, which was, even in the so-called Huguenot crescent, highly dispersed. Just as in the early church that Protestants revered, letters sustained and reinforced the collective identity of the Reformed movement, its political vision and clandestine endeavors.[26] The Dijonnais women studied by Annette Finley-Crosswhite and Susan Broomhall penetrated enemy lines and checkpoints undetected to pass on information and goods to family members in exile, effectively serving as key co-conspirators in the war effort.[27] As studies by Evelyne Berriot-Salvadore, Jane Couchman, and Susan Broomhall have shown, women did more than ferry letters across enemy lines; they were active and engaged correspondents who involved themselves in the dangerous political machinations of Huguenot party.[28] Huguenot noblewomen such as Louise de Coligny, Charlotte Arbaleste, Charlotte de La Trémoille, and Catherine de Parthenay were clearly conversant with the epistolary conventions of wartime correspondence. They exchanged coded letters with each other and with their spouses on matters of weighty political import within the militant circles of the Calvinist leadership.[29] Embedded in the letters that Jean de Coras, the famed jurist from Toulouse, sent to his second wife, Jacquette de Bussy, are elliptical references, political postscripts and even fully fledged circulars that read like diplomatic or military dispatches. That Jean expected Jacquette to share these with his colleagues

---

26   Mark Greengrass, "Informal Networks in Sixteenth-Century Protestantism," in *Society and Culture in the Huguenot World*, (eds.) Raymond Mentzer and Andrew Spicer (Cambridge: 2002), 78–81.

27   S. Annette Finley-Crosswhite, "Engendering the Wars of Religion: Female Agency during the Catholic League in Dijon," *French Historical Studies* 20 (1997), 127–54; Broomhall, *Women and Religion*, 129.

28   Evelyne Berriot-Salvadore, *Les femmes de la société de la Renaissance* (Geneva: 1999), 213–15, 502–510; Jane Couchman, "'Give birth quickly and then send us your good husband': Informal Political Influence in the Letters of Louise de Coligny," in *Women's Letters Across Europe, 1400–1700: Form and Persuasion*, (eds.) Jane Couchman and Ann Crabb (Aldershot: 2005), 164–84; Susan Broomhall, *Women and the Book Trade in Sixteenth-Century France* (Aldershot: 2002), 111–12.

29   Broomhall, *Women and Religion*, 111–12; Catharine Randall Coats, "Shouting Down Abraham: How Sixteenth-Century Women Found their Voice," *Renaissance Quarterly* 50 (1997), 484.

and co-religionists is often implied in the lengthy commendations with which he ends his missives; other times the expectation is explicitly stated.[30]

High profile Protestant leaders relied heavily on the services of their womenfolk (daughters, wives, and female retainers) who could slip through enemy lines and city gates more easily than their male counterparts, who were publically branded as rebels. In late December 1570, for example, Jacquette de Bussy engaged in a dangerous mission, entering Toulouse after an exhausting three-day journey in hopes of recovering the remnants of family possessions, and Coras' library and papers, confiscated by parlementary decree.[31] The letter she sent from Toulouse to Coras, hunkered down on the family estates in the Protestant stronghold of Réalmont, reveal the complicated strategies that Huguenot women deployed to protect their estates and the elaborate negotiations required to reassemble household goods, papers and provisions dispersed and hidden with family, friends and Huguenot sympathizers or confiscated by city officials. Bussy's efforts to recover their possessions led to the discovery that many had been irretrievably lost or sold, but she proved relentless in her efforts to retrieve Coras' library and papers and to restore some semblance of order to their urban properties and leaseholds in and around Toulouse. Her letters reveal how faithful friends and retainers, many of them female, were instrumental in the preservation of their properties which had been rented out, ransacked, sold off or looted by soldiers.[32]

Women, especially widows, shrewdly manipulated the sympathies of legal authorities, peace commissioners and the crown, playing their maternal hand in the effort to secure the restoration of family property and honor.[33] Susan Broomhall has described how a group of Huguenot widows, with their children in tow, sought an audience with the Queen Mother, Catherine de Medici. In a dramatic gesture that suggests that they clearly understood the power of collective action and maternal imagery, they knelt before the Queen Mother and began weeping and wailing "with one loud and striking voice" begging for mercy and justice.[34] Women also invoked their maternal and familial responsibilities in their petitions before the *chambres de l'Édit*, the special

---

30   Charles Pradel (ed.), *Lettres de Jean de Coras, sa femme et ses amis* (Albi: 1880).

31   On the seizure and sale of Coras' property, see Archives municipales de Toulouse, BB12 (délibérations municipales) and GG825, 826 (confiscations et ventes des biens protestants). See also Pierre-Jean Souriac, *Une Guerre civile: affrontements religieux et militaires dans le midi toulousain (1562–1596)* (Seyssel: 2008), 171.

32   On the financial impact of repeated confiscations of property, punitive fines and taxes levied on the Protestant population of Toulouse, see Joan Davies, "Persecution and Protestantism: Toulouse, 1562–1575," *The Historical Journal* 22 (1979), 31–51.

33   Roberts, *Peace and Authority*, 69.

34   Broomhall, *Women and Religion*, 139.

courts of appeal for Protestants established by the Edict of Nantes. The narratives that women constructed for the courts also mobilized gendered notions of honor and reputation, sometimes detailing brutal sexual assaults by Catholic military commanders or their troops, to make the case that they and by extension their family members were victims of "execrable" war crimes punishable by law.[35]

4 Women and Worship

Calvinist theory and practice significantly reduced the place of women in the liturgical life. The repudiation of the cult of saints, the veneration of the Virgin, and the salvific merits of baptism displaced women as mediators and exemplars of divine grace within the spiritual community, while the Reformed tenet of *sola Scriptura* upheld Pauline proscriptions against female preachers. Nonetheless, in the early days of the Reformation in France and Francophone Geneva, women could be found disseminating the new religious ideas behind the closed doors of convents, schools and their own homes.[36] As Mary McKinley argues in the case of Marie Dentière, the French-born noblewoman and ardent supporter of the Reformation in Geneva, women may well have preached with the complicity of Genevan reformers. Pierre Viret recognized that Dentière's pre-conversion experience as the abbess of an Augustinian convent in Tournai might be particularly valuable to his proselytizing efforts among Geneva's nuns, especially the redoubtable Jeanne de Jussie.[37] Dentière followed her missionizing exploits with an explosive pamphlet, written in the vernacular and dedicated to Marguerite de Navarre. In it, she defended the right of women to preach and

---

35 Diane C. Margolf, *Religion and Royal Justice in Early Modern France: The Paris Chambre de l'Edit, 1598–1665* (Kirksville, Mo.: 2004), 76–85, 104, 114; on the gendered nature of judicial narratives in early modern France, see Natalie Davis, *Fiction in the Archives: Pardon Tellers and Their Tales in Sixteenth-Century France* (Stanford: 1990), 77–110.

36 Broomhall, *Women and Religion*, 81–3; Davis, "City Women," 78–80.

37 Marie Dentière, *Epistle to Marguerite de Navarre and Preface to a Sermon by John Calvin*, trans. Mary B. McKinley (Chicago: 2007); idem, "The Early Modern Teacher—Marie Dentière: An Outspoken Reformer enters the French Literary Canon," *SCJ* 37(2006), 401–12; Thomas Head, "A Propagandist for the Reformation," in *Women Writers of the Renaissance and Reformation*, (ed.) Katharina M. Wilson (Athens, Ga.: 2006), 260–283; on Calvin's views on women's right to preach and on Marie Dentière, see Thompson, *Daughters of Sarah*, 41–45. For Jeanne de Jussie's description of the experience and her virulent opposition to the Reformation, see *The Short Chronicle*, trans. Carrie Klaus (Chicago: 2006).

teach theology.[38] Although Dentière's *Epistle to Marguerite de Navarre* was banned within a few months of its publication in 1539, French women drawn to the new reformist ideas continued to proselytize, although their efforts were often directed toward other women and confined to the domestic sphere. As Susan Broomhall has even suggested, "women may have been more successful preachers of the new ideas than men because they were less likely to attract the suspicions of local authorities."[39]

The fluidity of ritual practice in the underground churches of the early Reformation fuelled Catholic fantasies about Protestant men and women worshipping and singing together in promiscuous proximity.[40] The propriety of clandestine worship services also concerned the male leaders of the Reformed movement. Within two years of the formal constitution of the French Reformed Churches in 1559, the National Synod of French churches sanctioned Huguenot communities in southern France for allowing women to transgress Pauline injunctions by "making public readings or prayers."[41] Women were excluded in other ways from the liturgical traditions of the Reformed church by religious leaders. Jean Morély's suggestion, for example, that women might serve as deaconesses as they had in the early church was roundly rejected by the National Synods.[42] Even the physical organization of worship emphasized women's subordinate status as well as their greater need for regulation and instruction. Raymond Mentzer, for example, has shown how seating arrangements in Huguenot temples underscored patriarchal ideals of order, regulation and control, segregating women and children. In Geneva and presumably in many French Calvinist churches, too, women and children often sat close to the front near the pulpit under the eagle eye of the preacher, where they could receive the especial instruction they needed.[43] Women also attended special catechism classes geared to their level of understanding and concerns.[44]

---

38   Published at Geneva in 1539 and banned the next year, Dentière's *Epistre à Marguerite de Navarre* enjoys the distinction of being the first vernacular theology to be written by a woman.
39   Broomhall, *Women and Religion*, 82.
40   Davis, "City Women," 86.
41   As cited in Broomhall, *Women and Religion*, 83.
42   Davis, "City Women," 84; see also Glenn Sunshine, *Reforming French Protestantism: The Development of Huguenot Institutions, 1557–1572* (Kirksville, Mo.: 2003), 94–119, John Thompson, *Daughters of Sarah*, 58–62. Jean Morély, *Traicté de la Discipline et police chrestien* (1562).
43   Raymond Mentzer, "The Reformed Churches of France and the Visual Arts," in *Seeing Beyond the Word: Visual Arts and the Calvinist Tradition*, (ed.) Paul Corby Finney (Grand Rapids: 1999), 212–13.
44   Davis "City Women," 82.

Consistory registers, notarial records and sermons suggest that Huguenot women found ways to insinuate themselves into the ritual process and even to invest their actions with potent new social meanings. Women's presence at certain liminal moments in the spiritual life of their families and communities may even have been valued by men and seen as an extension of their domestic and maternal responsibilities. Although Calvin's condemnation of emergency baptism eliminated one of the few places were women had exercised an important liturgical role in the medieval church, consistory records reveal how difficult it proved to dispel lingering anxieties over the perils of purgatory. Women were often caught in the crossfire of conflicts over the persistence of popular practices and healing rituals which Calvinist authorities struggled in vain to suppress as papist superstition and folk practices deemed unchristian.[45] In their roles as midwives and healers, women could be charged with idolatry, and even worse, witchcraft. Even so, men and women in Protestant communities throughout France continued to turn to female herbalists and healers, regarded as powerful intermediaries between the natural and supernatural world, for assistance. In the rural communities of southern France studied by Raymond Mentzer, an active traffic in healing rites and most poignantly, the resuscitation of stillborn infants, flourished. The honorific title, Donne Figuieyres dite La Sauvage, given by locals to a controversial healer in the Cévennes, Mentzer has argued, is indicative of deeply embedded tensions over the activities of female practitioners of folk medicine and their contested place within the early modern world.[46]

Nonetheless, Huguenot women managed to mark their presence at the baptismal fount in a number of ways.[47] Both visual and written records suggest that godmothers sometimes not only presented the baby for baptism, but also participated in the baptismal ceremony by pouring the baptismal water into the hands of the officiating minister. Mentzer's exploration of disputes at the communion table underscores how Huguenot women sometimes transformed the sober celebration of the Lord's Supper into a battleground over social precedence. The quarterly celebration of communion so central to Reformed tradition and ritual not only marked an important occasion to demonstrate

---

45   Raymond Mentzer, "The Persistence of 'Superstition and Idolatry' among Rural French Calvinists," *Church History* 65 (1996), 220–33; idem, "La Place et le rôle des femmes dans les églises réformées," *Archives de sciences sociales des religions* 113 (2001), 125–27; idem, "Le consistoire et la pacification du monde rural," BSHPF 135 (1989), 373–89.
46   Mentzer, "La Place des femmes," 126–27; on the vitality of Marian sanctuaries and infant resuscitation, see also Jacques Gélis, *Les Enfants des limbes: mort-nés et parents dans l'Europe chrétienne* (Paris: 2006).
47   Raymond Mentzer, "Laity and Liturgy in Reformed Tradition," in *History Has Many Voices*, (ed.) Lee Palmer Wandel (Kirksville, MO.: 2003), 74–77.

membership among the godly, it also offered elites a highly visible opportunity to establish their social standing within the larger community. In deference to their authority as heads of the household, men were allowed to go first in communion line, followed by their wives. In Ganges, noblewomen were convoked before the consistory because they had pushed and shoved each other in the communion line in a desperate effort "to display superiority of social position."[48] Women were also involved in similar conflicts over seating, rushing to grab benches ahead of neighbors.[49] Sometimes these contests over seating even erupted into violence. In the small town of Saint-Jean-du-Bruel, a prominent female member of the congregation surreptitiously ordered the destruction of a new bench installed for notaries' wives because it had displaced and decentered her own. Moving benches in the tiny community of Aimarges became the catalyst for a catfight between prominent women of the community and the pastor's wife. Complaints over seating and precedence were not only a woman's fight; men proved just as eager to defend their privileged space and engage in various strategies to lay claim to their place within the congregation. These tussles over precedence are a prime example of the polyvalence of ritual tradition, which allowed women to invest liturgical and devotional rituals with their own social meanings that spoke both to their fundamental place within the community and their limited opportunities to express it.[50]

As Susan Broomhall has argued, women's presence at the deathbed (and caring for the body after death) was an extension of their traditional role as caretakers of sick and elderly.[51] Women used their authority as caregivers to preserve the spiritual identity and integrity of their dying family members or to transform the experience into a privileged moment of proselytism.[52] Some women refused priests access to the dying; other lobbied relatives to make a clear expression of their desire to die and be buried in accordance with Reformed tradition.[53] Their frequent involvement in funerary arrangements

---

48 Raymond Mentzer, "Marking the Taboo: Excommunication in Reformed Churches," in *Sin and the Calvinists: Morals Control and the Consistory in the Reformed Tradition*, (ed.) Raymond Mentzer (Kirksville, Mo.: 1994), 115.

49 Mentzer, "The Reformed Churches and the Visual Arts," 213–16.

50 Raymond Mentzer, "Les débats sur les bancs dans les Églises réformées de France," BSHPF 152 (2006), 393–406. Karant-Nunn, *The Reformation of Ritual*, 6.

51 Broomhall, *Women and Religion*, 105–06.

52 Broomhall, *Women and Religion*, 105–06.

53 On these deathbed struggles, see Penny Roberts, "Contesting Sacred Space: Burial Disputes in Sixteenth Century France," in *The Place of the Dead: Death and Remembrance in Late Medieval and Early Modern Europe*, (eds.) Bruce Gordon and Peter Marshall (Cambridge: 2000), 134–40.

also drew Huguenot women into protracted, potentially dangerous struggles with secular authorities as well as family members. Susan Broomhall cites the case of Philippe de Lun who sent her husband's body to a poorhouse in hopes of burying her spouse without the pomp and circumstance of Catholic tradition. This clandestine action brought her to the attention of local officials who rightly suspected her of Reformed sympathies and ultimately charged her with heresy and executed her.[54] The small gifts of cash or clothing that testators often left to their female care-givers is also evidence of an extensive domestic health care system largely orchestrated by women that operated at the margins of the increasingly confessionalized municipal health programs in 17th-century France. Huguenot women were thus instrumental in the development of an early modern version of hospice care which allowed many Protestants to escape the spiritual (as well as physical) dangers of hospitalization.[55]

Wills also provide rich testimony to the pivotal social and financial role that women, especially widows, could exercise in Huguenot communities.[56] Women, even those charged as executors of their husband's estates, were often freed from the kinds of lineage concerns that shaped men's wills and they had considerable discretion in shaping their testamentary legacies. Their posthumous bequests were often vital to the survival of the community and its poorest members. More often than male testators, women reached across generational and familial lines and mobilized their gift-giving to sustain emotional ties among collateral kin, friends and community. Their wills often reveal the gendered network of friends, neighbors, and family which encouraged female sorority and sociability. In the 17th-century Reformed communities of the Midi, women were accorded an increasingly important role in funerary rites. Keith Luria has described how young women bearing garlands sometimes marched in funerary processions, accompanying the bodies of their female friends to the cemetery in touching demonstrations of female sociability and solidarity. Although they clearly did so with the complicity of men in the community, the practice was criticized by synodal authorities who condemned these "novelties," which mimicked the papist rituals of their Catholic neighbors.[57]

---

54   Broomhall, *Women and Religion*, 106–07.
55   Amanda Eurich, "Between the Living and the Dead: Preserving Confessional Identity and Community in Early Modern France," in *Defining Community in Early Modern Europe*, (eds.) Michael Halvorsen and Karen Spierling (Aldershot: 2008), 43–62; see also Broomhall, *Women and Religion*, 115–17 for a discussion of women's charitable activities.
56   Eurich, "Between the Living and the Dead," 54.
57   Luria, *Sacred Boundaries*, 125.

Women were, thus, often at the center of conflicts over ritual innovation and other rites of passage within the Reformed church.

As legal restrictions against the practice of Calvinism (and Calvinists) tightened in the 17th century, women continued to carry out their function as custodians of religious tradition and spiritual identity within the family. From the 1660s (if not earlier in some Protestant strongholds, such as Béarn), the Crown mandated the increasing marginalization and eventual exclusion of Protestants from public life and office-holding. The political consequences of recusancy thus weighed much more heavily on men, who risked their offices and dynastic ambitions, than on women whose confessional allegiance posed little immediate threat to their family's public status.[58] Wives of royal officials did not necessarily follow their husband's lead and renounce their Calvinist faith when political expedience demanded it. This decision, as Raymond Mentzer has suggested, may have been a "deliberate and mutual" strategy on the part of some Huguenot couples to construct a dual family identity in which women conserved religious traditions within the private, domestic world, while their husbands preserved the public face of conformity. Considerable pressure, public and private, was often brought to bear on the wives of *nouveaux convertis* who refused to adopt their husband's religion. Split households could become the focus of intense confessional battles in which Catholic clerics, friends and neighbors relentlessly lobbied the recusant spouse while Protestant ministers struggled to counterbalance the centripetal dynamic of conversion within the family cell.[59] Where some women succumbed; others, such as the celebrated Marie de la Tour studied by Keith Luria, remained stalwart supporters of Protestantism, rearing children and grandchildren in the Reformed faith. Five years after Marie's death in 1665, her son, the prince de Tarente, finally converted to Catholicism, but his Protestant wife and daughter chose instead to seek refuge in Copenhagen.[60] In the decades before the Revocation of the Edict of Nantes, Huguenot women assumed an ever more critical role in the preservation of the faith and family tradition.

---

58 See, for example, Barbara Diefendorf, "House Divided: Religious Schism in Sixteenth-Century Paris," in *Urban Life in the Renaissance*, (eds.) S. Zimmerman and R. Wiseman (Newark: 1989), 80–99; Raymond Mentzer, *Blood and Belief: Family Survival and Confessional Identity among Provincial Huguenot Nobility* (Lafayette, Ind.: 1994), 170–73.

59 Amanda Eurich, "'Speaking the King's Language': The Huguenot Magistrates of Castres and Pau," in *Society and Culture in the Huguenot World (1559–1685)*, (eds.) Mentzer and Spicer, 134–35.

60 Luria, *Sacred Boundaries*, 174–79.

5 Women before the Consistory

No institution more fully embodied the patriarchal ethos of Reformed tradition than the consistory. Devised by Calvin as an instrument of church discipline, the consistory's famously all-male body met weekly to dispense aid, instruction and correction to community members. Historians of the consistory have emphasized its intrusive character and its inordinate preoccupation with regulation, order and sexual control, which often made women among its chief targets.[61] The systematic examination of consistorial records in Geneva and France carried out by Robert Kingdon and his students has tempered the image of consistories as a "savage judicial system."[62] As Kingdon himself suggested more than two decades ago, the Geneva consistory embraced a broad program of reform in its efforts to create a godly society and often acted as a vehicle of instruction, education and reconciliation, offering "social help" as well as social discipline to members of the Reformed community.

Raymond Mentzer's meticulous exploration of the surviving consistorial records of Huguenot communities in early modern France has also encouraged a more nuanced approach to our understanding of church discipline and its gendered execution. In rural communities throughout the Midi, as Mentzer has observed, it is often the absence of women in the consistorial records that is striking.[63] Men, not women, were convoked before the consistory, often in their role as *paterfamilias*, to answer for the misconduct of their wives and daughters as well as their own failure to control their households. Deeply embedded ideals of masculinity and gender performance as well as the patriarchal injunctions of Scripture effaced women, Mentzer writes, "in religious affairs, if not in all facets of public activity."[64]

---

61 William Naphy, *Calvin and the Consolidation of the Genevan Reformation* (Manchester: 1994), 106–11; Jeffrey Watt, "Women and the Consistory in Calvin's Geneva," SCJ 24 (1993), 429–39; Michael F. Graham, "Social Discipline in Scotland, 1560–1610" in *Sin and the Calvinists*, (ed.) Mentzer, 136–37. On France, see Janine Estèbe and Bernard Vogler, "La genèse d'une société protestante: étude comparée de quelques registres consistoriaux languedociens et palatins vers 1600," *Annales: économies, sociétés, civilisations* 31 (1976), 362–88; Raymond Mentzer, "*Disciplina nervus ecclesiae*: The Calvinist Reform of Morals at Nîmes," SCJ 18 (1987), 89–115; idem, "Morals and Moral Regulation in Protestant France," *Journal of Interdisciplinary History* 31 (2000), 1–20.

62 Robert Kingdon, "The Geneva Consistory in the Time of Calvin," in *Calvinism in Europe 1540–1620*, (eds.) Andrew Pettegree, Alaistair Duke and Gillian Lewis (Cambridge: 1994), 21–34.

63 Mentzer, "Le consistoire et la pacification du monde rural," 388–89.

64 Mentzer, "Marking the Taboo," 125.

Nonetheless, studies of consistory records have helped to reclaim the voices and lived experiences of women, especially the poorest and most vulnerable members of the community, who fairly quickly identified the disciplinary body as a source of material succor and social rehabilitation. As Mentzer and others have argued, the consistory empowered women to take on unjust employers, thwart familial marriage strategies, refuse unwanted suitors or sue sexual partners for breach of promise, and bring abusive husbands or sexual predators to some kind of justice. Françoise Moreil and Suzannah Lipscomb have argued that consistories often functioned as a court of appeal for women suffering from domestic abuse.[65] Moreil's study of the consistory of Courthézon near Orange, for example, describes how the consistory intervened on behalf of Laure Cherfils who repeatedly leveled complaints against her husband, David Bertrand, for abusive behavior. Eight years after the initial complaint, Cherfils appeared before the consistory, destitute and pregnant, begging for sustenance and assistance from her wayward husband. Although Bertrand at first refused to answer the consistorial summons and later to attend his child's baptism, his suspension from communion along with pastoral ministrations and threats ultimately led to an apparently satisfactory reconciliation with his wife and family. Two more children were born to the couple following the reunion.[66] Lipscomb has argued that the record of Reformed consistories in family mediation cases is somewhat more checkered than Cherfils's case suggests. Although the French National Synod spoke out early against domestic abuse, Lipscomb emphasizes that consistorial authorities were often reluctant to act. Many church elders still embraced popular beliefs reinforced by humoral theory as well as Scriptural sources that women were by their essential nature more carnal and irrational than men and in greater need of male control and correction. Moreover, the consistory saw the preservation of the family, the essential unit of social and religious life, as one of its key objectives. The goal of reconciliation, thus, often overshadowed the impetus to protect wives and other family members from physical violence.[67] As Nikki Shepardson has so aptly put it, in prescriptive literature as well as practice, wifely forbearance was honored as a kind of "domestic martyrdom."[68]

---

65   Suzannah Lipscomb, "Subjection and Companionship: The French Reformed Marriage," *Renaissance and Reformation* 6 (2004), 349–60; Françoise Moreil, "Chercher consolation: L'exercice de censure dans les consistoires méridionaux," in *Dire l'interdit*, (eds.) Raymond Mentzer, Françoise Moreil and Philippe Chareyre (Leiden: 2010), 283–308.

66   Moreil. "Chercher consolation," 288–89.

67   Suzannah Lipscomb, "Refractory Women: The Limits of Power in the French Reformed Church" in *Dire l'interdit*, (eds.) Mentzer, Moreil and Chareyre, 17–20.

68   Nikki Shepardson, "Gender and the Rhetoric of Martyrdom in Jean Crespin's *Histoire des vrays tesmoins*," SCJ 25 (2005), 167–71.

Women, especially young and single females, often sought moral and material restitution from the consistory in cases of sexual assault, but here again the archival record is complicated. Lipscomb has emphasized how quickly poor women in Reformed communities recognized that the consistory could provide them with the means to restore their sexual honor and reputation. Citing the case of Anne Rocquière who had been brutally beaten and physically assaulted by a gang of young men, Lipscomb argues that poor women with no social or financial capital to enlist lawyers and civil authorities in their case realized early that they could seek some form of redress and reparation from the consistory. As Françoise Moreil asserts, consistorial and synodal authorities took charges of predatory behavior seriously and were willing to proceed against even the most illustrious of community members if necessary. In the Reformed community of Dieulefit, for example, a minister accused by a maid servant of making improper advances (dressed only in his nightshirt) was suspended from his post, although we should hasten to add that he was reinstated by the National Synod some four years later after producing character witnesses who challenged the maid's testimony. Amanda Eurich's case study of Gabrielle Lefevre, a Genevan bookseller's daughter who claimed to have been impregnated by a French theology student boarding with the family, underscores many of the difficulties women faced in the pursuit of the restoration of their sexual reputation.[69] Widely accepted Galenic theories that conception could only take place if the woman had experienced orgasm inextricably linked pregnancy to female consent. This understanding of conception made it nearly impossible for unmarried women to construct convincing narratives of assault; all but the youngest victims of sexual assault or seduction were often considered equally complicit partners in the sinful act of fornication.[70] In Gabrielle's case, the purported father of her child had returned to Béarn, where he had promptly married and taken up a pastorate. Although local pastors and synodal authorities evinced concern over her situation, they ultimately sided with their colleague, who was tied by blood and marriage to important clerical dynasties in the region. For more than two decades, Gabrielle's father sought unsuccessfully to receive some sort of restitution for his daughter's damaged reputation, even taking his case to the French National Synod where distance and politics eventually effaced it from the collective memory. As Joy Schroeder and John Thompson have recently argued, Calvin

---

69 Amanda Eurich, "Le corps violé: la séduction et le rapt à Genève et en France à l'époque moderne," in *L'Anthropologie du protestantisme moderne*, (ed.) Oliver Christin (Rennes: forthcoming).

70 See William Naphy, *Sex Crimes from the Renaissance to the Enlightenment* (Stroud: 2004), 93–94.

and other Protestant reformers were still inclined to see rape as a consequence of female license and seduction.[71]

William Monter's assertion that the moral rigor of the Reformation in Geneva and other Huguenot communities helped to eliminate the sexual double standard begs careful reconsideration.[72] Reformed consistories in France as well as Geneva could and sometimes did level the persistent gender and class distinctions of early modern society in ways that recognized the vulnerability of the women who came before them.[73] Consistories were inclined to punish both unmarried pregnant women and their male partners (if they could find them) and sometimes leveled more serious charges and punishments than municipal authorities toward male offenders, especially toward adulterers whose actions threatened familial stability. Unwed pregnancies, however, were an especially serious and public violation of the strict standards of morality and godliness that defined the Reformed community. The very visible consequences of sexual sin and the scandal it provoked in the community meant that women who gave birth out of wedlock were often submitted to humiliating public rituals of repentance in addition to the normal penalty of suspension from communion.[74] Consistories often compounded the social disgrace of unwed motherhood by insisting on the ritual performance of penance at Sunday service. In a number of articles, Mentzer has sensitively explored the physical and personal toll that unwed pregnancy sometimes took upon women. The threat of public exposure and shaming drove some single mothers to desperate actions, such as infanticide, which only exacerbated their problems.

Judith Pollmann's studies of consistorial discipline in the Reformed communities of the Netherlands have encouraged an even more nuanced reading of the archival record. As she has reminded us, discipline was not just a matter for the consistory alone; many cases were handled by house visits while many other were not entered into the consistory register out of deference or sympathy.[75] Pollmann's recent analysis of gender and discipline in the Reformed

---

71 Joy Schroeder, *Dinah's Lament: The Biblical Legacy of Sexual Violence in Christian Interpretation* (Minneapolis: 2007), 12–51; John Thompson, *Reading the Bible with the Dead* (Grand Rapids: 2007), 185–214.

72 William Monter, "Women in Calvinist Geneva (1550–1800)," *Signs* 6 (1980), 189–209.

73 See for example, the case studies in John Witte and Robert Kingdon (eds.), *Sex, Marriage and the Family in John Calvin's Geneva* (Grand Rapids: 2005).

74 Mentzer, "Marking the Taboo," 122; idem, "Morals and Moral Regulation," 15–17.

75 Judith Pollmann, "Off the Record: Problems in the Quantification of Calvinist Church Discipline," *SCJ* 33 (2002), 423–39.

communities of the Netherlands, where church membership was voluntary as in many Huguenot communities in France, suggests that Dutch women sought membership in the church because it signified their honorable status within the larger social community. They were also more willing to submit to consistorial discipline than men because they had no other institutional mechanism or corporate sodality to mark their social status in the larger social community. For women, the strict vetting of the Reformed community to determine who was "worthy" of participation in the quarterly celebration of the Lord's Supper was an important social marker of honorability. Pollmann thus situates the complicated matrix of consistorial discipline and social reputation within highly gendered understandings of honor. "Women were much quicker than men," she notes, "to see the benefits of making peace … and more willing to accept male mediation during home visits."[76]

Like Pollmann, Suzannah Lipscomb has emphasized how Huguenot women sometimes used the disciplinary mechanisms of the consistory to affirm their membership among the godly.[77] Women, especially older women, were instrumental in policing the sexual behavior of other women, especially single women and widows who were already suspect because they were not subject to male tutelage. Consistories, like the secular courts of early modern France, recognized that women often had access to privileged information that circulated in the intimate female spaces and discursive networks of early modern society. Midwives and other female caregivers were readily tapped by consistories for their professional expertise as witnesses. And as Lipscomb argues, women not only acted as informants, they also were willing to be agents of discipline themselves, dispensing a sort of "rough justice" upon females in the community who transgressed moral norms, which in turn bolstered their own standing as honorable women. Philippe Chareyre's research on the consistory of Nîmes has described how women in this most Protestant stronghold, inspired perhaps by a particularly virulent sermon on prostitution, forced their way into a house suspected of harboring a prostitute and drove her out the community.[78]

Scholars of early modern France have underscored the limitations of consistorial discipline in a Catholic kingdom, where confessional competition

---

76 Judith Pollmann, "Honor, Gender and Discipline in Dutch Reformed Churches," in *Dire l'interdit*, (eds.) Mentzer, Moreil and Chareyre, 29–42, esp. 41.

77 Suzannah Lipscomb, "Crossing Boundaries: Women's Gossip, Insult and Violence in Sixteenth-Century France," *French History* 25 (2011), 408–26.

78 Philippe Chareyre, "'The Great Difficulties One must Bear to Follow Jesus Christ': Morality at Sixteenth-Century Nimes," in *Sin and the Calvinists*, (ed.) Mentzer, 75.

and the minority status of Calvinism generally often moderated consistorial discipline.[79] As Judith Meyer has argued, officials were reluctant to mete out harsh disciplinary measures that might drive members into the bosom of the rival confession. And indeed, consistorial registers are full of many accounts of women willing to protest sanctions against them. These complex stories of conformity, coy manipulation, and on rare occasions, outright resistance suggest that women learned how to use the marginal situation of Huguenot communities within France and the various "appeal mechanisms" in the system to their advantage.[80]

Even the most famous case of opposition to consistorial authority, however, is a cautionary tale that underscores the limits of female powers of resistance. In 1584, Charlotte Arbaleste, the wife of the famous Calvinist statesman and theologian, Philippe Duplessis-Mornay, engaged in an entrenched battle with the pastor and consistory at the Protestant stronghold of Montauban, where the Duplessis-Mornay family was temporarily in residence for the Protestant general assembly. At issue were her fashionable court hairstyles considered by the Montalbanais pastor to be a violation of standards of modesty and moderation in dress unbecoming in a godly woman, especially of her station. Denied communion, Arbaleste launched a skillful campaign to clear her name and restore her honor, deploying her considerable skill as a writer as well as her powerful social networks. She penned a letter to local notables and the consistory to rally support for her position before producing a fully-fledged *mémoire* delineating her argument. Both Catharine Randall Coats and Susan Broomhall have produced fascinating analyses of the Arbaleste's text. Randall Coats' exploration of her linguistic and rhetorical strategies observes that Arbaleste wrote her *Mémoires* in the third person perhaps as a distancing device.[81] In her defense, Arbaleste ventured into the realm of theological speculation and argumentation and articulated her own deeply learned interpretation of Scripture, Calvin's *Institutes*, and the *Ecclesiastical Discipline*, all at variance with the local consistory. She did not hesitate to turn the pastors' words against him, citing a sermon where he had "preached that gold and precious stones were creations of God and indifferent." Her evocation of nuanced arguments over the complicated Calvinist tenet of adiaphora

---

79 On limitation see Judith Meyer, "On the Frontlines of Coexistence: Courthézon's Consistory in the Early Seventeenth Century," *SCJ* 43 (2012), 1037–60; Mentzer, "Morals and Moral Regulation," 18–20.
80 Broomhall, *Women and Religion*, 41.
81 Randall Coats, "Shouting Down Abraham," 411–43; Broomhall, *Women and Religion*, 41–43.

(or indifferent things) demonstrates a remarkable theological nimbleness. As Susan Broomhall argues, Arbaleste "claimed to understand better than the local elders of Montauban the central tenet of the hierarchy's notions of discipline within the church."[82] In her insistence that the affair was a local issue that had no grounding in Scripture or in the ordinances of "a national synod, or of a provincial [synod], or of a colloquy," Arbaleste also recalled her cosmopolitan experience in Reformed communities across Europe where she had been welcomed without problem. Finally, Arbaleste artfully employed patriarchal ideas of authority and submission to evade censure, claiming that she could not answer to the charges without her husband's approval, which would be hard to procure since he was engaged elsewhere on important diplomatic missions for the affairs of the Reformed church. In spite of her vigorous and reasoned defense, Arbaleste failed in her bid to sway consistorial authorities. Ultimately, her only recourse was to move the family to the more hospitable town of Villemur where she was admitted to the Lord's Supper.

Charlotte Arbaleste's experience in Montauban was part of a vigorous crusade against court hairstyles and fashionably low-cut bodices waged by church elders throughout much of southern France in the late-16th century.[83] Graeme Murdock has traced the campaign in the Protestant stronghold of Nîmes where a number of women defiantly ignored private warnings, threats of excommunication and public sermons, even when deacons and elders positioned themselves at the threshold of the temple and called out offenders before they entered. As Murdock explains, events in Nîmes triggered a complex set of reactions which reveal the complicated gendered dynamic of church discipline delineated by Judith Pollmann and others. Some women choose to underscore the membership among the "godly" by submitting relatively quickly to sanctions; others carried on more protracted battles, sometimes even co-opting their husbands in the struggle. The struggle against fashionable *décolletage* did not just pit the wealthy women of Nîmes against male members of the consistory; the women's husbands also took offense at these slights against their familial honor and patriarchal authority within the household. While the campaign against immodest dress, as Murdock asserts, was not a uniquely Calvinist

---

82 Broomhall, *Women and Religion*, 42. Her skillful actions allowed her to engage in the kind of "subversive conformity," a strategy employed with varying effects by many erudite women in early modern France. See Anne Larsen, "Legitimizing the Daughters' Writing: Catherine des Roches' Proverbial Good Wife," *SCJ* 21 (1990), 561.

83 Graeme Murdock, "The Elders' Gaze: Women and Consistorial Discipline in late Sixteenth-Century France," in *John Calvin, Myth and Reality: Images and Impact of Geneva's Reformer*, (ed.) Amy Burnett (Grand Rapid: 2010), 69–90.

battle, it was a struggle that mobilized material as well as sexual constructions of Calvinist identity, one that emphasized that the sober dress and comportment of women were important markers of confessional difference.[84]

6   Women at Home and Education

Calvinist conceptions of marriage as a symbiotic partnership between husband and wife valorized motherhood. Women were instrumental in teaching family retainers as well as their own progeny the fundamental devotional practices of the new religion. Their role in the religious education of children was an important element in the creation and preservation of a holy household. Much of this domestic instruction was necessarily oral—teaching children and household servants to recite Scripture and vernacular prayers according to the new formulae favored by Reformers before they began more formal catechistic training, if indeed they could be spared from household tasks.[85] As Evelyne Berriot-Salvadore has argued, Calvinist memorialists, male and female alike, celebrated this maternal legacy, and often attributed their deep and abiding loyalty to the Reformed faith to their early childhood training.[86]

As a religion of the Word, Calvinism also placed an important value on the ability to read Scripture. To what extent this emphasis on biblical knowledge encouraged literacy, especially among Huguenot women, is still a subject of debate. Marriage contracts, for example, suggest a significant gender gap in literacy rates. In many 16th-century Huguenot communities, the ability of brides to affix their names to the marriage contract was significantly below their future spouse. Although notarial records reinforce the image of a Reformed community that was more urban and literate than its Catholic counterparts, Calvinist women still lagged far behind their male counterparts. As Philip Benedict has argued, this discrepancy persisted into the late 17th century, especially in rural communities where the ability of Calvinist women to sign their name to their wedding contract remained thirty to forty percent lower than men.[87] That said, Benedict and others have argued that signatures

---

84   See also Broomhall, *Women and Religion*, 113–14.
85   Mentzer, "La place et le rôle des femmes," 127.
86   Berriot-Salvadore, *Les femmes de la Renaissance*, 121–26; see also Roberts, *Peace and Authority*, 14; Luria, *Sacred Boundries*, 179–92, 225–30.
87   Philip Benedict, *Christ's Churches Purely Reformed: A Social History of Calvinism* (New Haven: 2002), 515; M.M. Compère, "École et alphabétisation en Languedoc aux XVIIe et XVIIIe siècles," in *Lire et écrire. L'Alphabétisation des Français de Calvin à Jules Ferry*, (eds.) F. Furet and J. Ozouf, vol. 2 (Paris: 1977), 88–89.

may not be a reliable index of biblical literacy. Reformed communities privileged reading over writing, especially for women. There is convincing evidence that many women of relatively modest means and social standing may well have been able to read the Bible and other devotional texts, or at the very least recite passages of Scripture from memory, even though they could not write.[88]

Part of the answer for this persistent dichotomy can be found in the lively debate waged among Reformed circles over the value of a humanist education for women. Where Calvinists were quick to establish a network of colleges and seminaries chiefly geared toward the training of young men for the ministry, they were far more cautious about the creation of schools for women. Natalie Davis and others have emphasized the almost total lack of formal education among city women.[89] The daughters of Calvinist elites fared somewhat better, although they received most of their education at home with their mothers' guidance, and perhaps with the help of private tutors. Much like their Catholic counterparts, Calvinists promoted a gendered curriculum intended to prepare women for marriage and motherhood, often both at a very early age.[90] Some young women received exceptional training in foreign languages as well as other disciplines, such as mathematics, associated with practical domestic skills. Charlotte Arbaleste, for example, offers testimony in her memoirs of her exceptionally broad education which encouraged intellectual interests that prompted Philippe Duplessis-Mornay to identify her as a potential life companion.[91] Evelyne Berriot-Salvadore has described how Louise de Coligny took the education of her six step-daughters seriously, making sure they receiving training in vernacular languages that ultimately prepared them for suitable marriages within the larger network of international Calvinism.[92] As Mentzer and Berriot-Salvadore have shown, noblewomen continue to concern themselves with their sons' education, even after they had left the household.[93]

---

88 Benedict, *Christ's Churches*, 516–18; Broomhall, *Women and Religion*, 82–84.
89 Davis, "City Women," 80; for a broad overview of female education in 16th-century France, see Broomhall, *Women and the Book Trade*, 13–26.
90 Mentzer, *Blood and Belief*, 122–23; Berriot-Salvadore, *Les femmes de la Renaissance*, 134–55.
91 Nadine Kuperty-Tsur, *Se dire à la Renaissance*, (Paris: 1997), 41–44; Berriot-Salvadore, *Les femmes de la Renaissance*, 127–33.
92 Berriot-Salvadore, *Les femmes de la Renaissance*, 134–36.
93 Berriot-Salvadore, *Les femmes de la Renaissance*, 481–501; Mentzer, *Blood and Belief*, 100–01, 144. Berriot-Salvadore, *Les femmes de la Renaissance*, 136, for example, has described how Louise de Coligny consulted Philippe Duplessis-Mornay, who helped her develop a program of study for her son, orphaned after the assassination of his father, William the Silent.

Female learning and literacy were important components of the ideal of companionate marriage among Calvinist elites. For all but "exceptional" women, however, Latinity and logic remained the province of men and one of the great markers of male education. We can detect the gendered ideals of education in the testamentary bequest of the Orangeois pastor, Charles Vielhenx, who divided his precious library among his two children. To his daughter Vielhenx gave his books in French and Italian, while his son received his Latin books and a stipend "should he decide to enter the ministry."[94] The Calvinist memorialist, Agrippa d'Aubigné, expressed the widespread ambivalence toward female learnedness in a letter to his two daughters. Certain disciplines, as he saw it, were unnecessary and undesirable, promoting "the dislike of housework and of thriftiness, condescension toward a less learned husband, and great strife and harmony."[95] The danger of too much learning was the disruption of the natural order of family life, where wives were to be subordinate to their husbands in all things, even intellect.

Seventeenth-century debates on the value of female education rehearsed similar reservations about female learning and humanist training as Joyce Irwin's study of the correspondence between the French minister, André Rivet, and Anna Maria van Schurman, a devout and deeply learned young Dutch woman, has shown.[96] Although Rivet encouraged the young scholar in her intellectual pursuits and put her in contact with other like-minded noblewomen, such as Princess Elizabeth, the daughter of the Calvinist Elector of the Palatinate, his response to Schurman's carefully scripted dissertation on the value of a liberal education for women echoed Aubigné's half a century earlier. Humanist studies were "neither useful nor appropriate" for the majority of women, especially those occupied with family matters. Like Aubigné, Rivet's argument against female learning was rooted in the potential threat that it posed to patriarchal power within the household and beyond. The acquisition of "verbal cleverness," he posits, might encourage women "to take the lead in argument in a crowd of disputants."[97]

Keith Luria, Luc Racaut, Thomas Head and others have also emphasized how Catholic polemicists seized upon the image of the learned woman to

---

94   Eurich, "Between the Living and the Dead," 55.
95   As quoted in Randall Coats, "Shouting Down Abraham," 424.
96   Anna Maria van Schurman, *Whether A Christian Woman Should be Educated and Other Writings from her Intellectual Circle*, trans. Joyce Irwin (Chicago: 2007). Published in France in 1638, and later in England in 1673 under the title, *The Learned Maid: An Essay to Revive the Ancient Education of Gentlemen*.
97   As cited in Irwin, 51.

deride Reformed theology and tradition.[98] Religious polemic on both sides of the confessional divide reveals how fears of gender inversion played out in early modern print culture, where female learning came to symbolize in various ways the threat that Protestant reform posed to the social and moral order. Luria thus puts women at the center of the confessionalization process as symbols as well as agents of religious differentiation and its dangers. Using the work of Joan DeJean and Frances Dolan, he has examined the gendered constructs of polemical literature which often depicted powerful Huguenot women as "amazons," who like their literary counterparts, challenged the conventions of feminine virtues by intruding into the typically male domains of war, politics, and theology.[99] The images of these "virile" women, intransigent protectors of heretical belief and practice, loomed large in Catholic imagination and propaganda. Huguenot women also functioned as objects of ridicule in Catholic polemic, their attraction to the so-called Reformed religion advanced as proof of its faulty theological constructs. As Thomas Head has argued, the *femmelette* (little woman) remained the stock in trade of Catholic polemicists through the 16th and 17th centuries. Luria's analysis of an anonymous dialogue set to verse, *La Ministresse Nicole*, penned in the 17th century in the local dialect of Poitou, illustrates the comedic value of the *femmelette* image in popular vernacular literature.[100] Luria calls the poem a carnivalesque satire in which the servant of a Protestant minister learns to read and is so taken with her new found knowledge and power that she dons her master's clerical robes, engages in disputes with Catholic priests and even performs a mock marriage, transgressing the boundaries of class, gender and clerical status much to the amusement of her rustic interlocutors.

Protestant martyrologists made very different use of the image of female learning. As Marianne Carbonnier-Burkard has observed, women in Jean Crespin's *Histoire des martyrs* resist their male interrogators both physically and spiritually, and even triumph over them with dazzling displays of Scriptural knowledge, thus transforming their private torture into public demonstrations

---

98 Luc Racaut, *Hatred in Print: Propaganda and Huguenot Identity during the French Wars of Religion* (Aldershot: 2002), 94–99; Thomas Head, "The Religion of the *Femmelettes*: Ideals and Experience among Women in Fifteenth and Sixteenth-Century France," in *That Gentle Strength: Historical Perspectives on Women in Christianity*, (eds.) Lynda Coon et al. (Charlottesville: 1990), 149–75; Luria, *Sacred Boundaries*, 197–215; Berriot-Salvadore, *Les femmes de la Renaissance*, 68–73.

99 Frances Dolan, *Whores of Babylon: Catholicism, Gender, and Seventeenth-Century Print Culture* (Ithaca: 1999); Joan DeJean, *Tender Geographies and the Origin of the Novel in France* (New York: 1991).

100 Luria, *Sacred Boundaries*, 205–10.

of the power and authenticity of their faith.¹⁰¹ William Monter's study of heresy trials in early modern France suggests that officials sometimes showed a certain reluctance to execute female offenders.¹⁰² Huguenot women, nevertheless, faced the martyr's stake with the same resolve as their male counterparts. Protestant martyrologies refashioned their stories to accentuate the obvious contrast between their physical and moral fortitude in the face of death and the inherent weaknesses of the female sex.¹⁰³ As Nikki Shepardson has argued, female martyrdom should be understood as a "subversive and destructive act…of social disobedience" that challenged traditional definitions of feminine virtue.¹⁰⁴ "Actual female martyrs as opposed to textual constructions," Shepardson writes, "abandoned their sacred duties as wives and mothers and entered into public positions as religious agitators and rebels."¹⁰⁵ Martyrologists, however, carefully reconstructed their actions in more acceptable terms, casting them as models of wifely submission, encouragement and compassion.¹⁰⁶ Both Marianne Carbonnier-Burkard and Susan Broomhall suggest that Crespin's female martyrs tellingly frame their impending death in particularly gendered terms, as a kind of "divine re-marriage" reuniting them with their true bridegroom, Jesus Christ. Torn between their earthly responsibilities as wives and mothers and their spiritual duty as witnesses to the true faith, their last gestures and valedictions recall the bridal mysticism of apocalyptic and medieval tradition.¹⁰⁷

7   Women, Propaganda and the World of Print

In her landmark essay, "City Women and Religious Change," Natalie Davis argued that the Protestant Reformation meant a narrowing of the literary

---

101   Marianne Carbonnier-Burkard, "La Réforme en langues des femmes," in *La Religion de ma mère: les femmes et la transmission de la foi*, (ed.) Jean Delumeau (Paris: 1992), 179–82.
102   William Monter, *Judging the French Reformation: Heresy Trials in Sixteenth-Century Parlements* (Cambridge, Mass: 2002).
103   On Crespin, see Luc Racaut, "Religious Polemic and Huguenot Self-Perception and Identity, 1554–1619," in *Society and Culture in the Huguenot World*, (eds.) Mentzer and Spicer, 29–43; Catharine Randall Coats, "Reconstituting the Textual Body in Jean Crespin's Histoire des martyrs (1564)," *Renaissance Quarterly* 44 (1991), 62–85.
104   Nikki Shepardson, *Burning Zeal: The Rhetoric of Martyrdom and the Protestant Reformation Community in France, 1520–570* (Bethlehem, PA: 2007), 81–107.
105   Shepardson, *Burning Zeal*, 85.
106   Nikki Shepardson, "Gender and the Rhetoric of Martyrdom," 171.
107   Broomhall, *Women and Religion*, 68; Carbonnier-Burkard, "La Réforme en langue des femmes," 182–83.

landscape for women. A generation of humanist scholars from Marguerite de Navarre to Hélisenne de Crenne, Madeleine and Catherine des Roches, and Louise Labé had produced poetry, dialogues, letters and Latin translations, and had earned the grudging praise of their male counterparts.[108] Even so, as Davis argues, "there was no Protestant counterpart for an urban poet such as Louise Labé."[109]

The discursive turn in history has refocused attention on the literary achievements of erudite Huguenot women who took up the quill in defense of their faith. Although few in number, they waged a war of words against their Catholic opponents as ably as their male counterparts. Jeanne d'Albret penned various public declarations in defense of her actions on behalf of the Protestant party. Jeanne's letters to the Cardinal d'Armagnac and members of the royal family, which carefully delineated Huguenot grievances as well as her own personal concerns, were published and circulated as political pamphlets.[110] Much like her Catholic rival, Catherine de Medici, Jeanne was a shrewd and skillful propagandist, who used the rhetoric of motherhood as well as patriotic duty to justify her actions.[111] In 1568, for example, Jeanne formally announced her entry into the third religious war with a pamphlet entitled, *Ample Declaration on the Joining of Her Arms to those of the Reformers*, often referred to by scholars as her memoirs.[112] As in much of her writing, Jeanne boldly addressed misogynist slurs against her and defended her right as a mother and Queen to take up arms. Where Claudie Martin-Ulrich has insisted that Jeanne's letters and memoirs were an acceptable private venue for the expression of her frustrations and political agenda, Mary Ekman argues that Jeanne "clearly intended to influence the course of events." For Ekman the memoirs are "a discursive effort on the part of the Queen to represent herself and her cause as just and loyal to the French monarchy and also to assert her rights as sovereign of her own

---

108 See, for example, Diane Wood, *Hélisenne de Crenne: At the Crossroads of Renaissance Humanism and Feminism* (Madison, NJ: 2000); Larsen, "Legitimizing the Daughters' Writing," 559–74.
109 Davis, "City Women," 85–96.
110 Roelker, *Queen of Navarre*, 301–311; Broomhall, *Women and Religion*, 97, 120–21. In *Se dire à la Renaissance* (Paris: 1997), Kuperty-Tsur has emphasized the apologetic nature of Renaissance memoirs. Life-writing in the Renaissance was essentially a political act, one of "self-justification" as well as "self-declaration."
111 Katherine Crawford, "Catherine de Médicis and the Performance of Political Motherhood," *SCJ* 31 (2000), 643–73.
112 On Jeanne's literary skill and list of publications, see Broomhall, *Women and the Book Trade*, 19, 152–53, 227–31. On her poetic exchange with Joachim du Bellay in which he lauded her literary ability, 188–89.

land."[113] This debate underscores the hybridity of Renaissance *lettres missives* as well as *belles lettres*.[114] As Jane Couchman has argued, nothing was actually personal in Renaissance correspondence. The epistolary practices of the early modern era intentionally blurred modern distinctions between public and private. Colette Winn, Broomhall, Couchman and others have demonstrated that Huguenot noblewomen deployed considerable political acumen in their epistolary exchanges with family members and political figures, and sought to sway public policy and aid the Calvinist cause.[115] As we have already seen, Charlotte Arbaleste, Catherine de Parthenay, Catherine de Bourbon, Louise de Coligny and her step-daughters all carried on an active epistolary life that demonstrates their engagement with matters of state.

Recent scholarship has also emphasized the remarkable variety of female literary production, even within artistic constraints imposed by Calvinist tradition. Huguenot women penned and published conventional expressions of grief, such as the anonymous tribute written to Eleanor de Roye, princesse de Condé, after her death in 1564, which celebrated her exemplary virtue.[116] Where these concerned a father or husband felled by an assassin's hand, women were quick to recognize the political potential of a daughter or widow's lament. Louise de Coligny, who was no stranger to family tragedy, published grief-filled prose poems for her father, the Admiral Coligny, whose assassination triggered the Saint Bartholomew's Day massacre, and later in 1584, for her husband, William the Silent. In so doing, she effectively created a new martyrological

---

113 Claudie Martin-Ulrich, "Catherine de Médicis et Jeanne d'Albret, la reine-mère et la reine conteuse," in *Devenir roi: Essais sur la literature addressée au Prince*, (eds.) Isabelle Cogitore and Francis Goyet (Grenoble: 2009), 223–33; Mary Ekman, "'Satisfaite de soy en soy-meme:' The Politics of Self-Representation in Jeanne d'Albret's *Ample Declaration*," in *The Rule of Women in Early Modern Europe*, (eds.) Anne Cruz and Michoko Suzuki, (Urbana: 2009), 30–41. On rhetoric of political loyalty and duty, see Arlette Jouanna, *Le Devoir de révolte: la noblesse française et la gestation de l'Etat moderne, 1559–1661* (Paris: 1981). Ekman has also taken David Bryson to task for minimizing the importance of the memoirs which she sees as a continuation of Jeanne's lifelong personal battle to chart an autonomous course in spite of the machinations of familial and court policies.

114 See also Jane Couchman, "What is 'Personal' about Sixteenth-Century French Women's Personal Writings," *Atlantic* 19 (1993), 16–22.

115 Jane Couchman, "Charlotte de Bourbon's Correspondence: Using Words to Implement Emancipation," in *Women Writers in Pre-Revolutionary France: Strategies of Emancipation*, (eds.) Colette Win and Danielle Kuizenga (New York: 1997), 101–15; idem, "'Give birth Quickly,'" 164–84; Susan Broomhall, "Letters Make the Family: Nassau Family Correspondence at the Turn of the Seventeenth Century," in *Early Modern Women and the Transnational community of Letters*, (eds.) Julie Campbell and Anne Larsen (Aldershot: 2009), 27–30.

116 Broomhall, *Women and Religion*, 93.

genre, which enshrined her father and husband's achievements for posterity and vilified the enemies of the Reformed religion who murdered them. Huguenot women also explored the genre of biography and history, writing family memoirs which celebrated the public careers of their fathers and husbands. Even though men are the chief protagonists in these family chronicles, Randall Coats, Kuperty-Tsur and Broomhall contend that the women authors they have studied find a way to insert themselves into the heroic narrative.[117] In her memoir of her illustrious husband, Philippe Duplessis-Mornay, for example, Charlotte Arbaleste emphasized how instrumental her partnership was to her husband's political and literary success. In other ways, women memoirists followed the traditions of the genre, commemorating deeply held Calvinist ideals of divine providence, predestination and election. These kinds of family histories, rooted in narratives of perseverance and suffering, were critical to the survival of the Reformed movement in the 17th century and beyond, helping to forge an even more resolutely Calvinist identity that would transcend the crucible of religious war and the Huguenot diaspora.[118]

Sara Grieco Matthews's research on Georgette de Montenay, an accomplished Huguenot poet in Jeanne d'Albret's entourage, analyzes her mastery of devotional emblem literature favored by early modern theologians and religious writers, including Theodore Beza.[119] First published in 1572, Montenay's *Emblemes chrestiennes* almost immediately attracted international acclaim and ultimately was published in several languages. Its popularity even inspired a Catholic version of the text, created and disseminated by the Jesuit order. Emblem books, such as Montenay's, fused word and image and became an important vehicle of religious and propaganda, crossing both confessional and national boundaries. As Matthews shows, Montenay also championed the ideals of sexual equality, rejecting emblematic traditions that often relied on popular tropes of feminine weakness and inferiority and offering "a more equally, spiritually enlightened view of gender" drawn from Neo-Platonic tradition as well as Reformed doctrine.[120] In Montenay's *Emblemes chrestiennes*, women are envisioned as the pathway to salvation as well as forceful and militant defenders of Reformed tradition, most famously in the emblem of her

---

117   Broomhall, *Women and Religion*, 90.
118   Susan Broomhall and Colette Winn, *Les Femmes et l'histoire familiale XVIe–XVIIe siècle* (Paris: 2005); idem, "The Problematics of Self-Representation in Early Modern Women's Memoirs," *Tangeance* 78 (2005), 11–35.
119   Sara Greico Matthews, "Georgette de Montenay: A Difference Voice in Sixteenth-Century Emblematics," *Renaissance Quarterly* 47 (1994), 793–871.
120   Matthews, "Georgette de Montenay," 802.

patron, Jeanne d'Albret, who is depicted literally laying the foundation of God's "holy temple" with the tools of the architect's craft at her side.

Susan Broomhall and Nicole Vray have called attention to the literary achievements of Catherine de Parthenay, whose close ties to Catherine de Bourbon contributed to her stature in court society.[121] Conversant in Latin, Greek and Hebrew, Parthenay composed poems, plays and ballets that celebrated the female heroes of classical and biblical tradition and championed the importance of female activism to the Protestant cause. In 1573, for example, Parthenay rallied the citizenry of La Rochelle during the infamous siege by royalist forces with her play *Judith and Holofernes*, based on the Old Testament story of the virtuous Hebrew widow, who crept into the tent of the Assyrian general, Holofernes, and behead him, thus saving her people from destruction.[122] Parthenay clearly identified with the Hebrew Amazon in word and deed and conscientiously drew on the emerging Huguenot rhetoric of resistance in which Judith functioned as an exemplar of the righteous tyrannicide.[123] In the 1590s, Parthenay also produced ballets for the royal courts of Henry IV and his sister, Catherine de Bourbon. Raymond Ritter, Marie-Hélène Grintchenko, and Susan Broomhall all have pointed to the highly politicized nature of the ballets which were openly critical of Henry's rapprochement with Catholics and his marginalization of Catherine in court politics and diplomacy.

8   Conclusion

Did Calvinist women have a Reformation? Recent scholars would cast this as *une question mal posée*—one that ignores the diversity of female experience

---

121   Broomhall, *Women and Religion*, 121–22; Vray, *Catherine de Parthenay*.

122   Henriette Goldwin (ed.), *Théâtre de femmes de l'Ancien Régime au XVI siècle* (Saint Etienne: 2006), 24–25. The story recounted in the Book of Judith was relegated by Protestants to the Apocrypha, even though it became an increasingly potent symbol of Huguenot resistance theory in the aftermath of the St. Bartholomew's massacre.

123   The complex iconography of Judith in Renaissance art has drawn the attention of art scholars who have described how Judith's image was increasingly sexualized in the 16th and 17th-century. Protestant commentators, however, glossed over the sexual subtexts of the tale. See Kevin R. Brine, Elena Ciletti and Henrike Lähnemann, *The Sword of Judith: Judith Studies across Disciplines* (Cambridge: 2010), 55–70; see also Katherine S. Maynard, "To the Point: The Needle, the Sword and Female Exemplarity in du Bartas' 'la Judith,'" *Romance Notes* 46 (2006), 69–181. The poem was written at behest of du Bartas' patron, Jeanne d'Albret, and draws connections between Hebrew heroines and contemporary Protestant women.

and women's experience of the Reformation.[124] Scholars have long recognized that social status gave noblewomen considerable room to maneuver and to influence political and religious affairs. Attention to political and social geography as well as social status has further complicated the story of women within the Huguenot movement. It mattered greatly when and where women lived in France—before 1559 or after 1589 or after the reversals to Huguenot political fortunes in the mid-17th century, in urban centers or *la France profonde*, in Protestant strongholds or beleaguered minority communities. More nuanced readings of women's interactions with the patriarchal authorities and institutions of the Reformed church suggest that women found ways to circumvent as well as manipulate its disciplinary agenda to their benefit. Consistories were not always hell bent upon female subordination and subjection, nor did men universally support the condemnation of certain female-centered ritual practices and beliefs. The idea that women found ways to evade, subvert and oppose male authority and create space for themselves, even in the closed liturgical rituals of the Reformed church, reflects a new appreciation of female agency, expressed in both word and deed. The rich and complex history of women in Huguenot communities is still an open field of research. Unlike Catholic women religious, Huguenot women had no claim to a separate corporate identity, no formal sorority, no clearly definable archives that detail the contours of their distinctive spirituality and lived experience. Yet buried in public and private archives are the letters, notarial records, consistorial registers, and other undiscovered or forgotten texts that still speak to their critical contributions to Reformed tradition and Huguenot communities in which they lived.

---

124   For example Merry Wiesner-Hanks, "Society and the Sexes Revisited," in *Reformation and Early Modern Europe: A Guide to Research*, (ed.) David Whitford (Kirksville, Mo.: 2008), 396–407.

CHAPTER 6

Pulpit and Pen: Pastors and Professors as Shapers of the Huguenot Tradition

Karin Maag

In his 17th-century work on how to prepare sermons, the Huguenot pastor and professor Jean Claude laid out the aims of preaching, highlighting how much more effective sermons were than simply reading and meditating on Bible passages:

> Everybody can read Scripture with notes and comments to obtain simply the sense, but we cannot instruct, solve difficulties, unfold mysteries, penetrate into the ways of divine wisdom, establish truth, refute error, comfort, correct, and censure, fill the hearers with an admiration of the wonderful works and ways of God, inflame their souls with zeal, powerfully incline them to piety and holiness, which are the ends of preaching, unless we go farther than barely enabling them to understand Scripture.[1]

Claude's high view of preaching illustrates the significant role Huguenot pastors ascribed to their own work in decisively forming the spiritual and moral outlook of their congregations.

Focusing particularly on printed sermons and other writings by Huguenot pastors and professors in the hundred-year period from 1570 to 1670, this essay will examine how these pastors understood their role in shaping the worldview of the French Reformed communities they served. Indeed, the emergence of the clergy and professoriate as an inter-married and closely-related class, with its own rites of passage, emergent dynasties, internal fissures, and conflicting visions of what the Reformed churches in France could be, played a pivotal role in fashioning the Huguenot tradition. Although many of the pastors and professors discussed here were equally ardent polemicists who regularly clashed with their Catholic adversaries,[2] this essay will concentrate on the

---

1 Jean Claude, *An Essay on the Composition of a Sermon*, trans. Robert Robinson (Cambridge: 1778), 5. The original French version of the work, *Traité de la composition d'un sermon*, was published after Claude's death in his *Oeuvres Posthumes* (Amsterdam: 1688).

2 See, for instance, the work of Paul Ferry, pastor in Metz from 1612 to 1669, and his polemical exchanges with Catholic clergy, in Julien Léonard, *Être pasteur au XVIIe siècle: Le ministère de Paul Ferry à Metz (1612–1669)* (Rennes: 2015), 152–92.

sermons and writings intended for their flocks. Through their sermons, writings, and service as the intellectual leaders of the Church, the Huguenot pastors and professors sought to articulate their vision of the Church, focusing above all on biblically-grounded faith and morals formation for the entire Reformed community. Although their legacy has been overshadowed to a great extent by historiographical attention paid to the political and military struggles of the later French Reformation, the influence of these intellectual leaders on the Reformed communities of their day should in no way be discounted.[3]

At the outset, it is important to point out that the characteristics of the French Reformed pastorate highlighted below were not unique to the Huguenots. Indeed, across early modern Europe in the later 16th and 17th centuries, similar patterns of training, examination, oversight, and inter-marriage helped create a strong esprit de corps among Protestant clergy, whether Reformed or Lutheran. At the same time, the growing emphasis on seminary training for Catholic priests after the Council of Trent also built increasing uniformity among Catholic clergy.[4]

One possible starting point for a consideration of early modern Huguenot pastors and professors' influence on their communities is to examine numerical data. Unfortunately, these numbers are hard to come by, largely because of

---

[3] Recent studies focusing on the political and military aspects of Huguenot history after 1570 include Robert Knecht, *The French Civil Wars, 1562–1598* (Harlow: 2000); Mack Holt, *The French Wars of Religion, 1562–1629*, 2nd ed. (Cambridge: 2005); Scott Manetsch, *Theodore Beza and the Quest for Peace in France, 1572–1598* (Leiden: 2000); Michel Grandjean and Bernard Roussel (eds,), *Coexister dans l'intolérance: l'édit de Nantes (1598)* (Geneva: 1998).

[4] For the Reformed clergy in the German Palatinate, see Bernard Vogler, *Le clergé protestant rhénan au siècle de la réforme, 1555–1619* (Paris: 1976); for Scotland, see John McCallum, *Reforming the Scottish Parish: the Reformation in Fife, 1560–1640* (Farnham: 2010), especially Chapter 5, "The Ministry as a Profession"; for the Netherlands, see Willem Frijhoff, "Inspiration, instruction, compétence? Questions autour de la sélection des pasteurs réformés aux Pays-Bas, XVIe–XVIIe siècles," *Paedagogica Historica* 30 (1994), 13–38. For Lutheran clergy, see Friedrich Wilhelm Kantzenbach, "Das reformatorische Verständnis des Pfarramtes," in *Das Evangelische Pfarrhaus. Eine Kultur- und Sozialgeschichte*, (ed.) Martin Greiffenhagen (Stuttgart: 1984), 23–46; Luise Schorn-Schütte, *Evangelische Geistlichkeit in der Frühneuzeit* (Gütersloh: 1996). For more on Catholic clergy, see Joseph Bergin, "Between Estate and Profession: the Catholic Parish Clergy of Early Modern Western Europe," in *Social Orders and Social Classes in Europe since 1500: Studies in Social Stratification*, (ed.) Michael Bush (London: 1992), 66–85. Comparative works include Luise Schorn-Schütte, "The 'New Clergies' in Europe: Protestant Pastors and Catholic Reform Clergy after the Reformation," in *The Impact of the Reformation. Princes, Clergy, People*, (eds.) Bridget Heal and Ole Peter Grell (Aldershot: 2008), 103–24; and Luise Schorn-Schütte, "Priest, Preacher, Pastor: Research on Clerical Office in Early Modern Europe," *Central European History* 33 (2000), 1–39.

the fragmentary state of surviving records. In by far the best and most thorough recent demographic study of French Protestants from 1600 to 1685, Philip Benedict estimates that the Huguenot population reached 930,000 to 960,000 at the end of Henry IV's reign in 1610, and dropped to around 730,000 by 1681.[5] Yet even these figures are based on extrapolations and calculations founded on birth rates as recorded in baptismal registers. Determining the number of pastors is even more challenging, as exact records have rarely survived. The records of the national synod of Alès in 1620 provide a list of 760 churches served by a total of 729 pastors.[6] Based on the list of churches and pastors established at the national synod of the French Reformed Churches in 1660, there were 663 pastors serving churches in France that year, not counting the neighboring and closely-linked principalities of Béarn (another thirty-four pastors), Sedan (another three pastors) or Metz (another four).[7] The relatively small number of pastors in comparison to the number of the faithful might suggest that the former's influence in shaping their congregations' world-view would be minimal at best. Yet the intellectual leadership provided by the pastors and professors did not reflect their low numbers. Instead, due to their cohesion, training, and control of the chief means of communication, these leaders made an impact that outweighed their small numbers by far.

One of the most important elements that built cohesion among the pastors and professors was their sense of group identity. One strong feature of this identity stemmed from familial and marriage bonds that united men of successive generations in the same careers. For example, consider the Chamier family. Pierre Chamier (also known as Adrien) was born in 1532, and became a pastor, serving five different churches in south-eastern France including Montélimar. His son Daniel Chamier, known as "le grand Chamier," was born in 1565, and married Antoinette Moissard in 1589. Daniel Chamier served as pastor in four different churches, including Montélimar, and also taught theology at the Huguenot academy of Montauban from 1612 to 1621. Of their five children, one son died young, and one daughter married a merchant, but their other two daughters, Madeleine and Marguerite, also married pastors. Daniel and Antoinette's eldest son, Adrien, became a pastor, again in Montélimar, for an impressive fifty-four years. Married to Madeleine Alard, Adrien fathered

---

5 Philip Benedict, "The Huguenot Population of France, 1600–85," in his *The Faith and Fortunes of France's Huguenots, 1600–85* (Aldershot: 2001), 34–120, esp. 92–95.

6 Jean Aymon (ed.), *Tous les synodes nationaux des églises réformées de France*, vol. 2 (The Hague: 1710), 232.

7 These numbers are based on the figures provided by Samuel Mours, *Le Protestantisme en France au dix-septième siècle* (Paris: 1967), 60–85.

four children, the eldest of whom, also called Daniel, became a pastor. Daniel served three churches, ending up as pastor in Montélimar for five years following his father's death. Daniel's marriage to Madeleine Tronchin produced five children, the eldest of whom, again called Daniel (born in 1661), became a pastor, this time in England.[8] So in the course of 150 years, the Chamier family produced five pastors over successive generations, not counting the two pastor sons-in-law who married Chamier daughters. For its part, the church of Montélimar was served by successive pastors of the Chamier family for nearly a hundred years. One could hardly ask for a better example of the ways in which the French Reformed clergy became a self-perpetuating group.

A second strong source of cohesion for Huguenot pastors and professors stemmed from their training. By the first decades of the 17th century, the standard practice for a young man wishing to enter the ministry was to study at one of the Huguenot academies, whose main mission was to provide theological, exegetical, and homiletic training for future pastors. Of the eight academies established between 1562 and 1606, three (Orthez in Béarn, Sedan, and Orange) lay outside France, and two of those within France (Die and Nîmes) were very small foundations that only attracted students from the local area.[9] Future Huguenot pastors also regularly attended Reformed centers of learning that were further outside the French orbit, including the Genevan Academy (established in 1559) and the University of Leiden (established in 1575, but really only beginning to flourish as a center for theological studies after the turn of the century).[10]

The Huguenot academies served as the intellectual flagships for the French Reformed communities. The academies of Sedan (founded in 1602) and Saumur (inaugurated in 1606) in particular had deservedly strong academic

---

[8] Data for this and other genealogical studies of French Reformed pastors comes from http://sitepasteurs.free.fr/. Users can search by name, date, or other information by using the "base de données" and can easily build up a picture of pastoral dynasties and lineages.

[9] For more on the Huguenot academies, see Daniel Bourchenin, *Etude sur les académies protestantes en France au XVIe et au XVIIe siècle* (1882; repr. Geneva: 1969); Karin Maag, "The Huguenot academies: preparing for an uncertain future," in *Society and Culture in the Huguenot World, 1559–1685*, (eds.) Raymond Mentzer and Andrew Spicer (Cambridge: 2002), 139–56; Jean-Paul Pittion, "Les académies réformées de l'Edit de Nantes à la révocation" in *La Révocation de l'Edit de Nantes et le protestantisme français en 1685*, (eds.) Roger Zuber and Laurent Theis (Paris: 1986), 187–208.

[10] On France, Leiden University, and the Genevan Academy, see Karin Maag, *Seminary or University? The Genevan Academy and Reformed Higher Education, 1560–1620* (Aldershot: 1994), 103–28 and 172–85.

reputations, but came at theological issues from divergent perspectives. The chief professors of Saumur, John Cameron and Moïse Amyraut, argued in favor of hypothetical universalism, namely the idea that God made universal grace available to all people but that this salvation is limited only to those to whom God gives faith. The theological outlook of Saumur fostered enquiring minds, but still operated within the boundaries of orthodoxy, at least according to its professors.[11] Meanwhile, the academy of Sedan, and especially its leading professor Pierre Du Moulin, took a more conservative or traditional stance, opposing anything that seemed to deviate from the doctrinal decisions taken at the Synod of Dordt.[12] The end result was conflict, expressed via a sequence of polemical writings on each side of the debate, and only ultimately calmed by mediation at the highest level in the national synod meetings of the Huguenots.[13]

Although each of the three leading academies in terms of scholarly reputation and number of students (Montauban, Sedan, and Saumur) had its own distinctive outlook, the fact that many of the students spent time at more than one institution tended to minimize these differences. In the end, these future pastors were bound to one another by friendship honed during their student years and by the shared experience of studying Greek, Hebrew, philosophy, and biblical studies according to a set curriculum.[14] In 1620, the national synod of Alès set out some common statutes for all the French academies, noting that students admitted to study theology would first have to give evidence of their morals and of their knowledge in philosophy and the humanities before being admitted to the theology lectures. Each academy was to have two or three theology professors, one or two lecturing on scriptural exegesis of the Old and New Testaments, and one teaching Christian doctrine based systematically on the *loci communes* or common-places of theology. Each professor was to teach

---

11 On Saumur and its theological outlook, see Albert Gootjes, *Claude Pajon (1626–1685) and the Academy of Saumur: the First Controversy over Grace* (Brill: 2014), especially Chapter 2. See also François Laplanche, *Orthodoxie et prédication: l'œuvre d'Amyraut et la querelle de la grâce universelle* (Paris: 1965), especially 39–42.

12 Laplanche, *Orthodoxie et prédication*, 118–27. Pierre Du Moulin was born in 1568, and studied in Sedan and at Cambridge. He served as a pastor at Charenton (where the Huguenots of Paris came to worship) from 1599 until 1621. He later accepted a post as professor of theology at the Academy of Sedan. A prolific writer, Du Moulin published numerous works, including many polemical treatises.

13 Laplanche, *Orthodoxie et prédication*, 133–74.

14 For more on the impact of these studies even years later, see Ruth Whelan, "Proposants et hommes de lettres en formation: la correspondance entre Paul Baudry et Élie Bouhéreau (1662–1683)," *BSHPF* 159 (2013), 93–113.

four times a week, and students were to show what they had learned through regular practice sermons and declamations which were assessed by their peers, the faculty, and local pastors.[15] This common curriculum (also largely followed in the other Huguenot academies and in Geneva and Leiden) meant that future pastors had experienced a similar training regimen prior to the start of their ministerial careers, and this shared intellectual frame of reference helped shape their outlook. As Jean-Paul Pittion noted, "the structuring of academic education therefore aimed to ensure the formation of the Reformed, and to create an elite pastoral corps. Its end result was the reinforcement of a national pastoral style."[16]

Following his studies, the future pastor, known as a *proposant*, was examined by his local colloquy or gathering of the pastors and elder delegates of the area, or by the next level up, namely the provincial synod. He had to provide testimonials about his morals and undergo a thorough assessment of his learning, doctrine, and preaching skills. At the national synod of Saint-Maixent in 1609, the delegates clearly laid out the examination process, which is worth quoting at length to get a sense of the common standards candidates for ministry were to attain:

> The candidate's examination will first include trial sermons on the word of God based on texts assigned to him. One of these sermons will have to be in French and the other can be in Latin, if the colloquy or the synod feels it expedient. The candidate will be given twenty-four hours to prepare for each of these. If the company is satisfied, he will be examined on an assigned chapter of the New Testament, to see if he knows enough Greek to be able to interpret it. And as for Hebrew, one should check to see if he knows enough at least to be able to use good books to make the Scriptures clear. To this one should add an examination of his work in the most useful parts of philosophy, all done charitably and without turning to useless and thorny questions. Finally, he will be asked for a succinct Latin confession of faith, on which he should be examined by way of debate. And if after this examination he is considered capable, the company should outline the responsibilities of the charge to which he is called, and should declare to him the power that he has received to preach the Word of God and administer the Sacraments in the name of Jesus Christ.[17]

---

15   Aymon, *Tous les synodes*, 2: 210–11.
16   Pittion, "Les académies réformées," 192.
17   Aymon, *Tous les synodes*, 1: 358.

Candidates who failed to satisfy their examiners in any of the areas under scrutiny, including their preaching skills, were sent back for further study.[18] To ensure yet more unity of outlook among its clergy, the French churches insisted that all new pastors were to sign their agreement to the confession of faith and to the *Discipline* (the ecclesiastical ordinances governing the French Reformed Churches).[19] Securing common consent to confessional teachings and ecclesiological practices helped to create a framework within which pastors could exercise their ministry.[20]

At the same time, the synodical authorities placed significant weight on ensuring common standards of behavior among the future pastors. In 1660, the national synod of Loudun heard complaints from its delegates about the decline in the moral standards and behavior of the *proposants*. Critics voiced concern about the students' long hair, colorful and over-ornamented clothing, visits to taverns and time spent with women, their habit of strolling around while wearing a sword and "that their [preaching] style is more reminiscent of a romance than of the Word of God."[21] Although these critiques should probably be taken with a grain of salt, the synodical authorities took the matter very seriously, showing again how important it was to ensure that future leaders of the Huguenot communities lived lives that reflected their high calling. The synod minutes noted:

> [...] these abuses open the door to a deluge of profanations flooding into the sanctuaries, and furthermore it [the synod] asks them [the professors and Church leaders] to suspend the recalcitrant from the Lord's Table, to delete their names from the student matriculation list, and to take away from them any hope of ever being received into the Office of Holy Ministry. And all students, especially those in theology, are specifically ordered to abstain from all the abuses described above, and to keep away from all things that go against modesty and true holiness. These virtues should shine in the lives of those called by God to serve in Christ's church.[22]

---

18   Karin Maag, "Preaching Practice: Reformed Students' Sermons," in *The Formation of Clerical Confessional Identities in Early Modern Europe*, (eds.) Wim Janse and Barbara Pitkin (Leiden: 2005), 133–48.
19   Aymon, *Tous les synodes*, 1: 101.
20   For an outstanding case study of the steps towards examination and ordination of pastors, and an analysis of the status of the pastorate among the French Reformed, see Léonard, *Être pasteur*, 69–94.
21   Aymon, *Tous les synodes*, 2: 795.
22   Aymon, *Tous les synodes*, 2: 795.

By insisting on common moral standards even for those who were not yet in charge of congregations (and rejecting from ministry those who would not conform to these rules), the synods helped to craft the Huguenot intellectual leaders into a group whose cohesion went beyond a shared academic experience of set courses and examinations.

Indeed, the records of the successive Huguenot national synods from 1559 to 1660 show just how important the moral probity of the pastoral corps was to the French Reformed Churches. There are few more convincing examples of the seriousness with which the synods approached this task than the recurring lists of "vagabond" pastors at the end of synod meeting minutes. Those whose names appeared on these lists were *personae non gratae* in the Church, and congregations were warned not to allow them any place in leadership. While some of the "vagabond" pastors were cited for apostasy (an increasingly serious problem by the first decades of the 17th century), many others had fallen foul of the high moral standards expected of those in ministry. At the national synod of Charenton in 1623, for instance, of the twelve pastors listed who had been deposed from ministry, seven were charged with adultery. Several of these were also condemned for other moral failings, as in the case of Pierre Paloque, who had been dismissed from ministry mainly because of his "unnatural behavior towards his aged parents, and because of grave suspicions of adultery, which he never managed to refute, and because in all of his behavior, he always acted as a man unworthy of Holy Ministry."[23] The stringent supervision of pastoral behavior at all levels of the French Reformed Churches again helped to ensure that professional standards of behavior were highlighted, even in cases where ministers fell well short of the desired norms. Even the fact that the synods took time to provide these lists argues for the strong emphasis in the Huguenot Church on the need to maintain standards in the pastorate, both to edify the faithful and to avoid giving grounds for mockery to their religious opponents.

Indeed, examining the various cases where pastors and professors got into trouble with their colleagues, even for offenses that had nothing to do with moral failings, is instructive. In many cases, the stumbling block was the person's desire to pursue projects or ideas that did not fit within the parameters of the theology or ecclesiology of their peers. In other words, by considering what works or activities challenged the norms of the group, we can gain a better sense of what the Huguenot Church upheld as its core values. For instance, in the mid-1590s, the Huguenot Church wrestled with what to do about pastors and other leaders who advocated for a rapprochement between the Reformed

---

23   Aymon, *Tous les synodes*, 2: 297.

and Catholic communities in France. A case in point is Jean de Serres. Born in France and having studied at the academies of Lausanne and Geneva, Serres began his career in ministry in Jussy, a village outside Geneva. By 1572 he was in trouble with the Genevan Company of Pastors for having wanted to quit his parish without authorization. He taught at the Lausanne Academy and at the academy in Nîmes, where he also served as a pastor from 1578 to 1589.[24] He left Nîmes under a cloud, having had numerous disagreements with the Nîmes consistory. From 1589 to 1596, he served as a pastor and professor of theology in the principality of Orange near Avignon.[25]

In spite of his earlier difficulties with Church authorities, Serres was a well-respected figure in the French Reformed Churches, especially due to his historical writings. Furthermore, alongside his pastoral, teaching, and writing work, Serres had served on several diplomatic missions at the court of Henry of Navarre, who became Henry IV of France in 1589. As it became increasingly clear that the king's conversion to Catholicism was the only way to restore peace and order in France, Serres grew convinced that the way forward for the two divided confessional groups was to find common ground. His attempts to do so found support at the royal court, as Henry IV authorized the printing of two works by Serres in 1597: his *Advis pour la paix de l'Eglise et du Royaume* and his longer Latin treatise on the same subject, *Apparatus ad fidem catholicam*.[26] In both works, Serres attempted to gain consensus on doctrines that the two confessions shared.[27] Yet his attempts at conciliation met with strong disapproval from his peers.

Earlier on, when Serres produced a work showing that the Reformed doctrinal lineage stretched back to the early Church, and that the Catholics were innovators, the delegates to the national synod of Montauban responded very cautiously to his request in 1594 to have some learned colleagues look over his manuscript. They ordered him to have three copies made for inspection by two different sub-sets of French Churches and by Geneva. In the meantime, "according to our Discipline, the said Sieur de Serres must not have any part of

---

24 Sven and Suzanne Stelling-Michaud, *Le Livre du recteur de l'académie de Genève (1559–1878)* (Geneva: 1976) 5, 561.

25 Thierry Wanegffelen, *Ni Rome ni Genève: des fidèles entre deux chaires en France au XVIe siècle* (Paris: 1997), 452.

26 For more on these two works and the important political context of Jean de Serres' attempts at conciliation, see Manetsch, *Theodore Beza*, 294–307.

27 Karin Maag, "Conciliation and the French Huguenots, 1561–1610," in *Conciliation and Confession: The Struggle for Unity in the Age of Reform, 1415–1648*, (eds.) Howard Loutham and Randall Zachman (Notre Dame: 2004), 142–46.

the work printed or published."[28] Two years later, at the national synod held at Saumur, the delegates reiterated the need to have the work inspected by pastors and delegates of whatever province Serres chose as the place of publication; without that inspection, the work was not to appear in print.[29] When his two published works advocating religious reconciliation based on a shared doctrinal foundation appeared in print in 1597, Serres found himself under attack from all sides.

Writing from Geneva, Calvin's successor Theodore Beza sharply criticized Serres for taking on a mediator role to which he had not been called, and for seeking out common doctrinal ground where none existed.[30] Although Serres died in May 1598, posthumous criticism followed him. The national synod of Montpellier, meeting only a week after Serres' death, explicitly condemned his two writings.[31] The synodical delegates also warned against any similar plans to seek unity between the two confessional groups:

> Though the faithful should desire with all their hearts, for the glory of God and the peace of the state, that all the citizens of this realm be brought together in one and the same religion, however, both because our sins make this goal something to be hoped for rather than sought, and because by using this pretext, many ill-intentioned people pretend to unite and mingle the two faiths, pastors are to carefully warn their flocks not to give ear to these people, as there can be no communion between God's temple and the temple of idols. Furthermore, such people are only trying to seduce the credulous, to get them then to abandon their faith in the holy Gospel. Thus all those who attempt such a reconciliation, either orally or in writing, will be very severely censured.[32]

The king's conversion to Catholicism in 1594 had heightened the anxiety of his former co-religionists. In this atmosphere of rising tension and concern, any attempts to suggest that there were not in fact that many significant differences between the Reformed faith and Roman Catholicism were perceived by the Huguenot leadership as a covert strategy to encourage conversion to the majority faith.[33] In this context, it is hardly surprising that the pastors in

---

28 Aymon, *Tous les synodes*, 1: 186–87.
29 Aymon, *Tous les synodes*, 1: 206.
30 Manetsch, *Theodore Beza*, 304–05.
31 Aymon, *Tous les synodes*, 1: 222.
32 Aymon, *Tous les synodes*, 1: 219.
33 Scott Manetsch underscores how far the king did in fact support such a strategy; see *Theodore Beza*, 307.

leadership positions, who were most committed to the continuation of the Reformed faith in France, refused to countenance any proposals to find common ground with their confessional opponents. It is worth noting that the synodical delegates were quick to point to the dangers such proposals posed to the unwary faithful, and that the pastors of the French Reformed Churches were the ones charged with alerting their flocks to these risks. Thus cohesion among the clergy was maintained by condemning writings that went against the agreed-upon norms of the group, and cohesion among the faithful was meant to be maintained by ensuring that the pastors issued identical warnings to their parishioners to pay no heed to any such plans.

By far the best and most effective way for pastors to issue warnings or to teach their congregations was through their sermons.[34] Indeed, hearing (or reading) sermons was the most common and consistent way that the Reformed faithful learned about what God wanted them to do or to avoid in their lives. Françoise Chevalier has estimated that in the period from 1598 to 1685, more than two million sermons were preached in the roughly seven hundred places of Reformed worship in France from 1598 to 1685.[35] That number seems low; if one estimates that only one sermon was preached each week in each of the seven hundred congregations, fifty-two Sundays a year, for eighty-seven years, the figure is over three million. Lasting on average an hour and twenty minutes, these sermons demanded a lot from their hearers in terms of attention and focus.[36] Although most of these sermons were not written down and thus are lost, a number of them have survived in printed form.

Having now laid out the ways in which the Huguenot pastorate was bound together by marriage and familial ties, education and assessment, and by mutual oversight, the remainder of this contribution will analyze a range of surviving sermons from the late 16th to the late 17th century, to explore the moral instruction provided by the French Reformed pastors to their congregations. By analyzing surviving sermon texts and other pastoral writings focused primarily on moral issues, my aim is to investigate how pastors presented these teachings to their flock and what key values they sought to inculcate.[37] Given

---

34 For a case study of sermon preparation and preaching practice, see Léonard, *Être pasteur*, 75–82.
35 Françoise Chevalier, *Prêcher sous l'Edit de Nantes: la prédication réformée au XVIIe siècle en France* (Geneva: 1994), 213.
36 Pittion, "Les académies réformées," 197.
37 Other scholars have been working on similar themes, focusing on pastoral writings; see Marianne Carbonnier-Burkard, "Les pasteurs français auteurs d'une littérature d'édification au XVIIe siècle," *BSHPF* 156 (2011), 37–48.

that historians working on these sermon collections only have access to a small proportion of the total number of sermons preached, and that one cannot be sure that the text mirrors the actual oral rendition, any conclusions need to be drawn with care. Furthermore, a study of surviving sermons is in many ways an analysis of a one-way trajectory: we have the pastor's words, but not his flock's reaction or response. Yet even a survey of surviving sermons can highlight the centrality of morals inculcation as one of the important strands in Huguenot homiletics.

The primary sources for this study are the French sermon collections accessible via the Post-Reformation Digital Library database.[38] I limited the sample to sermons preached in French by pastors who served in France and were born before 1650. The total came to well over four hundred sermons, more than half of which were preached and later published by the very prolific Jean Daillé, who served for over forty years as pastor of Charenton, the closest French Reformed place of worship to Paris.[39]

One key theme that recurred in these pastors' sermons was the importance of harmonious marital relationships, a key component in the survival and flourishing of Huguenot families, and, by extension, in the stability of the wider French Reformed community. Consider for instance two sermons preached by Jean Daillé at Charenton, the first on 22 February 1637 and the second eight months later, on 20 September 1637. In both cases, his text came from 1 Peter 3, a passage that lays out the norms of behavior for wives and husbands. The first sermon focused on 1 Peter 3:1–6, and was directed at wives. Right from the start of his sermon, Daillé emphasized the primordial importance of marriage as a divinely-created institution: "Since marriage is the oldest institution established by God, who wanted Adam to be a husband before he was a father, master, or magistrate, therefore marriage is the most important and most necessary institution for humanity."[40] Having established this clear starting-point, Daillé then noted Satan's role as the enemy of marriage, and mentioned in passing how Jesus, the apostles, and Paul commended marriage and worked to strengthen it by their words and writings. He then quickly reviewed Peter's letter up to Chapter 3, and pointed out that although women

---

38 To access the Post-Reformation Digital Library databases of scanned texts, go to www.prdl.org. The databases can be searched by author, title, genre, date, publisher, and so forth.

39 On Daillé, see http://sitepasteurs.free.fr/.

40 Jean Daillé, "Sermon IX sur la premiere epitre de S. Pierre Chap. III. Vers. 1, 2, 3, 4, 5, 6. Prononcé le 22 Fevrier 1637," in his *Melange de sermons prononcés par Jean Daillé à Charenton pres de Paris, en divers temps, & sur differents sujets* (Amsterdam: 1658), 251.

were the target audience for this part of the chapter, men were to listen attentively as well, both because of the ties that bound them to their wives, and because everyone, whatever their gender, could learn from the instruction provided in the passage.[41]

Daillé's exegesis followed standard interpretations: wifely subjection was the result of Eve's original sin, and wives were to submit to their husbands voluntarily. Daillé did make a strong exception for matters of faith; in such cases, a wife was to subject herself to the higher authority of God and not deny her beliefs even under pressure from her spouse.[42] Indeed, one of the central themes of Daillé's sermon was a vigorous plea for both men and women to do more to bring their spouses to the true faith. "We have lost our zeal; the name of God and of his Christ no longer affects us; the world and the flesh are the focus of our affection; and we feel that it is already a lot to maintain ourselves in the faith, and that attracting others to it would be to take over the task of the pastors."[43] By addressing his congregation directly in the sermon, Daillé reminded them of their vital role in maintaining and spreading the Reformed faith. Clearly he had no interest in fostering a defensive or inward-looking approach within the Huguenot community.

Daillé went on to critique women's tendencies to spend time and money beautifying themselves, not only because of the waste of time and money, but also because they were altering themselves in ways that God had not intended, and were implicitly criticizing his creative work as imperfect, since these women felt the need to make improvements. Based on his exegesis of the biblical text, Daillé recommended that women should instead focus on modesty and the work of enhancing the inner beauty of their souls.

While Daillé's exegesis of 1 Peter 3 did not bring up any particularly innovative interpretations, he did highlight key themes that shaped the Huguenot community's contemporary experience, including an emphasis on modesty and sobriety in apparel, especially for women, and the challenges mixed marriages posed to the survival and spread of the Huguenot faith. These challenges were amplified in an eight-page pamphlet published in 1620 by Pierre Du Moulin, who was a pastor at Charenton at the time.[44] Although this text is a pamphlet rather than a sermon, it is worth analyzing because it addressed and even sharpened many of the same concerns as Daillé noted in his discourse.

---

41 Daillé, "Sermon IX," 255.
42 Daillé, "Sermon IX," 262–63.
43 Daillé, "Sermon IX," 266.
44 Pierre Du Moulin, *Conseil fidele et salutaire sur les mariages entre personnes de contraire religion* (n.p.: 1620).

The pamphlet was clearly directed at the French Reformed community, rather than at a Catholic readership. Already in the second paragraph, Du Moulin compared marriages between Protestants and Catholics to attempts to link Jesus Christ and idols, and later on he spoke of the deep concern that "our children will become idolatrous and be led astray from the path of salvation."[45] Using a range of biblical examples, Du Moulin argued that mixed marriages inevitably brought about God's wrath, including the Flood, because "the children of God, that is, the descendants of Seth, coupled in marriage with the descendants of Cain."[46] Du Moulin was also quick to point out the practical difficulties that resulted from mixed marriages, even as early as the wedding ceremony. If the marriage was celebrated in a Catholic church, then the Protestant spouse had implicitly given credence to the priest's spiritual authority. If the marriage took place in a Protestant church, and if the Catholic spouse had not converted, then he or she was in fact guilty of perjury, by making public promises "to live holy lives, according to the word of God and his Holy Gospel."[47]

Turning to what the couples in such marriages could expect in their daily lives, Du Moulin warned against the dangers of undue influence of Catholic clergy on members of the household, and about the risks of the family's funds being surreptitiously squandered on Catholic devotional and charitable practices.[48] Du Moulin also highlighted the difficulties such couples would encounter in bringing up their children, painting a picture of religious tension in the household with children divided against parents and parents against their children.[49] While Du Moulin was willing to admit that in some cases such marriages did succeed, he was quick both to give all the credit to God, and to define success as a marriage in which the Catholic partner finally converted to the Reformed faith.[50] In his concluding section, Du Moulin put his finger on the reasons why marriages between Huguenots and Catholics in France were matters of such deep concern. A Catholic spouse in France was part of the majority group, with all the advantages and clout this majority status provided. Protestant spouses, already on the defensive outside the home, were to avoid jeopardizing the one safe place they had left.[51]

---

45   Du Moulin, *Conseil fidele*, Ai verso and Aii recto.
46   Du Moulin, *Conseil fidele*, Ai verso.
47   Du Moulin, *Conseil fidele*, Aii verso and Aiii recto.
48   Du Moulin, *Conseil fidele*, Aiii recto.
49   Du Moulin, *Conseil fidele*, Aiii recto-Aiv recto.
50   Du Moulin, *Conseil fidele*, Aiv recto.
51   Du Moulin, *Conseil fidele*, Aiv verso.

Together, Du Moulin's 1620 treatise and Daillé's 1637 sermon show how seriously the Huguenot pastors took the issue of marriages between Catholics and Protestants in France. In an era of static if not declining membership, the very real fear that such marriages would weaken the position of the Huguenot community, if not in the current generation then in the next one, seems valid. This anxiety particularly held sway in cases when a Reformed woman married a Catholic man, since the prevalent trend seemed to be for children to be brought up in their father's faith.[52] Although avoiding such marriages was clearly the main recommendation of the Huguenot clergy, couples who shared the same faith could not simply rest on the security of having made the right confessional choice. Indeed, Daillé's second sermon on 1 Peter 3 shed light on the faithful husband's particular responsibilities in his household.

In his second sermon, Daillé turned his attention more specifically to the males in his congregation. Even though the sermons were preached eight months apart, Daillé reminded his hearers that he had previously preached on the earlier verses of 1 Peter 3 that were addressed to women.[53] In other words, he linked his two sermons and expected a certain degree of recall on the part of his listeners. Daillé's exegesis focused first of all on the duties of a husband towards his wife, and on the need to act lovingly towards her, albeit from his superior position as the leader of the household. Once again connecting the lived experience of his hearers with the subject of his sermon, Daillé warned husbands not to be too conciliatory to their wives, notably if the wife followed Catholic practices: the danger in such instances was not only that the wife would be engaging in idolatry, but that the couple's children could also be drawn into the wrong paths. "There are some who, accommodating their wives' superstition, neglect their children's salvation, allowing them [their wives] to dedicate their children to error, and to bring them up in it."[54] Like Du Moulin in his treatise, Daillé was keenly aware of the repercussions of Catholic influences in the household on the rising generation.

Throughout the sermon, Daillé highlighted the spiritual equality between husbands and wives, and ended with a peroration calling on both partners in

---

52 On mixed marriages and their impact, see Gregory Hanlon, *Confession and Community in Seventeenth-Century France: Catholic and Protestant Coexistence in Aquitaine* (Philadelphia: 1993), 102–11 and Raymond Mentzer, "Les contextes de la conversion à l'époque de la Réforme," *Cahiers d'étude du religieux: recherches interdisciplinaires* 8 (2010), 2–9, especially 6.

53 Daillé, "Sermon X sur la premiere epistre de S. Pierre Chap. III vers. 7 prononcé le 20 septembre 1637," in his *Melange de sermons prononcés par Jean Daillé à Charenton pres de Paris, en divers temps, & sur differents sujets* (Amsterdam:1658), 284.

54 Daillé, "Sermon X," 288.

marriage to bring regularly their entire household before God through family prayers and devotions. Couples were to:

> [...] carry out together all the duties of piety, offer together to the Lord their sacrifices of prayer and charity, read and meditate together on the teachings of his word, and dedicate their room to God, like a small sanctuary, in which they present to God each day and each night two hearts prostrate at his feet, both full of the same zeal and aflame with the same love. Husbands, since God honors you with his image, you are the high priests and the overseers of this domestic sanctuary. You must see to it that divine worship takes place here faithfully, purely, and reverently.[55]

Daillé's call to husbands and wives to ensure regular household Scripture reading, prayer, and worship underscores a vital strand of Huguenot piety. Even making it to church to attend worship regularly was not guaranteed, especially for the Reformed of Paris who had to travel outside the city to do so.[56] Thus, having daily household worship under the leadership of the husband and father offered both regular religious instruction and a partial substitute for Sunday services in weeks when getting to church was impossible.

Du Moulin's treatise and Daillé's two sermons on 1 Peter 3 offer insights into how Huguenot pastors addressed the thorny issue of family and marital relationships within the wider context of pressure put on the French Reformed community to rejoin the Catholic majority. Yet French pastors in this period did not limit themselves to marriage issues when tackling the broader topic of faithfulness to God's commands. A particularly rich source of material in this vein stems from sermons preached during fasting and prayer services, which the Huguenots held at regular intervals to plead for God's mercy and grace, whether in times of natural calamities, persecution, or political uncertainty. Because pastors preached these sermons to awaken their hearers to the dangers of sin and the need for repentance, these texts offer an unparalleled view into the main moral failings that the pastors wanted to address.

In 1667, Pastor Pierre Trouillard published a set of two sermons which he had preached at the fast-day services at Ay in nearby Champagne on 29 June of that year. Trouillard was born in Sedan and studied at the academy in that city.

---

55 Daillé, "Sermon X," 310.
56 Up to 1606, Parisian Huguenots worshipped at Ablon, about fifteen miles away from Paris. After 1606, Henry IV allowed the community to establish itself closer to Paris, at Charenton, about five miles from the capital. Even that distance could be difficult to travel in winter. See Chevalier, *Prêcher sous l'Edit de Nantes*, 24.

Pierre Du Moulin was one of his professors. By the 1660s, the situation of the Huguenots in France was becoming increasingly stressful. In 1661, King Louis XIV appointed commissioners charged with obtaining documentary proof from each Reformed church that it had been holding public worship services legally in 1596 or 1597. Without such proof, churches were closed down and demolished, though the regulations were not applied with equal force in all areas.[57] Given these pressures and the clear sense that the legal space available for Protestants in France was being increasingly eroded, it is hardly surprising that the Huguenots turned to their faith, holding special fast-days and prayer services to implore God's aid. For pastors, however, these services were meant to bring congregations to a clear-eyed awareness of their sin and their need for repentance and amendment of life. Thus, fast-day sermons offered pastors a golden opportunity to point out the reasons why the community was suffering: human sin was the cause, and the pastors were keen to point out exactly how their parishioners were at fault.

Basing himself on Revelation 2:4–5, in which the church of Ephesus was condemned for falling away from its earlier strong practice of the faith, Trouillard began the first of his two sermons by laying out the categories of wrongdoing he saw in his own day: impiety, blasphemy, cheating, debauchery, and quarrels. Added to that list were specific injuries to the faith: "despising the Word of God, neglecting prayer, profaning the sacraments, failing to acknowledge God's blessings and forsaking one's zeal and charity."[58] After an extended analysis of the passage from Revelation and its implications, Trouillard turned specifically to his congregation's failings in their practice of the Reformed faith, especially regarding the sacraments. As Trouillard noted:

> As for Baptism, where are those who, after having received it, actually fulfill the promises that were made in their name? Indeed, we follow through so poorly that in most cases, if baptism could be administered twice, there would be a number who would need rebaptism because they have renounced their first baptism by their works. And if we turn to the other sacrament, what will the Lord not hold against those who, having come to his table, immediately return to the table of debauchery, and who, having been received at a meal of peace and charity, turn back to their quarrels and their hatred.[59]

---

57 Mours, *Le Protestantisme en France*, 153–54.
58 Pierre Trouillard, *Deux sermons faits pour le jeune celebré le 29 Juin 1667* (Sedan: 1667), 6.
59 Trouillard, *Deux sermons*, 47.

Pastor Trouillard's censure of his congregation's behavior was not new or unique to French Reformed Protestantism. What is significant, however, is Trouillard's use of the sacraments as the moral reference points for his flock. The problem was not simply that people were behaving badly, but that they were falling away from their covenant commitments as manifested in their partaking of the sacraments. Thus, although many of the sins listed by Trouillard were individual ones that could affect a person's standing in the eyes of God, the pastor oriented his critique around communal practices during which the faithful came as a group into God's presence. Trouillard went on to charge his congregation with hypocrisy. Although they came to church, sang psalms, prayed, listened to sermons, and partook in the Lord's Supper, their participation was only skin deep, and below the surface, they continued to indulge in their passions without paying heed to God and his commands.[60]

In a similar vein, Josué Le Vasseur, who served as pastor and professor in Sedan from 1646 until his death in 1672, preached a sermon in that city. It was published posthumously in Geneva in 1678. Taking 1 Corinthians 6:10 as his text, Le Vasseur had no hesitation in pointedly laying out all the ways in which his congregation was mired in sin. He spoke freely of members' "deep-rooted malice" and "profound stupidity," condemning his flock with a vigor that shows with what little restraint certain pastors took advantage of their control of the pulpit.[61] Drunkenness, fornication, adultery, usury, theft, blasphemy, gossip, vindictiveness, quarrelling, hatred, pride, and insolence: all were targeted by Le Vasseur in his sermon and apparently he thought that all were being practiced by members of his congregation.[62] Yet the significance of the sermon lay not in its wholesale condemnation of contemporary vices, but in its wrestling with one of the central problems of Protestant theology. As Le Vasseur noted, his congregation seemed to be convinced that God's grace, through which they had been saved, would be more than enough to forgive them their sins after they died, and that therefore they had no particular need to restrain their behavior until the moment of their death. Crucially, he ascribed part of the reason for this misconception to his preaching and that of his colleagues:

> My brothers, my dear brothers, I fear that in all innocence we have given you leave to sin, all the while trying to fulfill our duty before God...I admit that what keeps you in this state of disorder is your hope of impunity,

---

60   Trouillard, *Deux Sermons*, 50–54.
61   Josué Le Vasseur, *Sermon sur la premiere Epistre de Saint Paul Apostre aux Corinthien Chap. 6. Vers. 10. Prononcé à Sedan* (Geneva: 1678), 4.
62   Le Vasseur, *Sermon*, 5–6.

your conviction of God's grace, which we preach to you and whose riches we portray, declaring to you according to his divine word, that there is no sin too great or too numerous for him to overcome, and that those who have once partaken of this grace cannot finally fall away from it. I fear that you are using this doctrine as a cushion for your vices.[63]

Le Vasseur's insight that congregations may have been misled into downplaying the damaging effects of their sin thanks to their pastors' sermons on the centrality of grace is worth further analysis. On the one hand, one could argue that Le Vasseur was simply trying to get his congregation's attention and not repel them from his call for genuine repentance by heaping all the blame for their wrongdoing on them alone. In other words, by having the pastors share the blame, congregations could perhaps more readily see that their misbehavior was rooted in a misunderstanding of what had been preached. On the other hand, if taken seriously, Le Vasseur's claim that pastors bore some of the responsibility for this sorry state of affairs does underscore how important sermons could be in shaping the behavior of French Reformed communities, even in ways the pastors had never intended. From Le Vasseur's perspective, his sermons on God's grace had been too effective; his congregation had taken hold of the message of grace preached to them from the pulpit but had stretched the doctrine to have it cover their transgressions, without understanding the need for genuine and immediate repentance for sin.

Le Vasseur's vigorous use of the pulpit as a podium from which he could critique his parishioners for their misdeeds went further than any other French Reformed pastor studied so far. Yet he shared with his pastoral colleagues the belief that preaching was an effective tool in shedding light both on moral failings and on the path to genuine repentance and amendment of life. One could argue that the ceaseless round of sermons might suggest that this method was in fact ineffective in changing lives, since pastors continued to climb into the pulpit week after week to remind the people of their sins and call them to repentance. However, one should not take the pastors' assessment of their flock's behavior at face value. Since Reformed preachers favored the prophetic mode of discourse in their sermons, the likelihood of getting praise for one's behavior from the pulpit was quite low.[64] For their part, pastors seemed to

---

63　Le Vasseur, *Sermon*, 9–10.
64　The prophetic mode of preaching and generally pessimistic outlook on human behavior was already part of Calvin's repertoire; see Bruce Gordon, *Calvin* (New Haven: 2009), 138–39, 144–46. Later Reformed preachers followed the same strand, even in situations where they were the spokesmen of the official faith. See Andrew Pettegree, "Coming to

put considerable weight on the transformative power of preaching, not so much because of the pastor's words, but because his words were grounded on God's word.

Trained at the same schools, vetted by the same church authorities, and marrying each other's daughters and sisters, French Reformed pastors were a cohesive and well-trained force in leadership of the Huguenot communities by the later 17th century. It is no wonder that these pastors were among the first to be targeted by French Catholic authorities for exile or imprisonment, as both the French government and French Catholic Church knew that without the leadership of the clergy, the Huguenot Church would have a very hard time surviving. Moves to close or demolish places of worship and ban preaching were all efforts to put an end to what had been a highly influential current of theological and moral instruction that decisively shaped the early modern Huguenot experience.

Terms with Victory: the Upbuilding of a Calvinist Church in Holland, 1572–1590," in *Calvinism in Europe, 1540–1620*, (eds.) Andrew Pettegree, Alastair Duke and Gillian Lewis (Cambridge: 1994), 160–80.

CHAPTER 7

The Huguenots and Art, c. 1560–1685*

Andrew Spicer

1   Introduction

At an extraordinary meeting of the Royal Academy of Painting and Sculpture in Paris on 10 October 1681, the president Charles Le Brun read a command from the king's minister Jean-Baptiste Colbert. On the orders of Louis XIV, those who were members of the *Religion Prétendue Reformée* were to be deprived of their positions within the Academy; their places were to be taken by Catholics, and membership in the future was to be restricted to this confession. The measure particularly targeted seven men: Henri Testelin (1616–95), Secretary of the Academy; Jean Michelin (1623–96), Assistant Professor; Louis Ferdinand Elle, *père* (1612–89), Samuel Bernard (1615–87), Jacques Rousseau (1630–93), council members; Mathieu Espagnandel (1616–89) and Louis Ferdinand Elle *fils* (1648–1717), academicians. The secretary, Testelin, who had painted several portraits of the young king during the 1660s, acquiesced to the royal order but requested that the Academy recognize that he was deprived of his position not due to any personal failings concerning his honesty and good conduct. The academicians acknowledged this to be the case and similarly noted that the other Huguenots present—Bernard, Ferdinand Elle and Michelin—had acquitted their charge with probity and to the satisfaction of the company.[1] The following January, the names of Jacob d'Agard and Nicolas Eude were struck from the Academy's registers because they had both sought refuge in England.[2] The expulsion of these artists and sculptors from this learned society was part of the increasing personal and religious restrictions imposed on the Huguenots by Louis XIV, which culminated in the revocation of the Edict of Nantes in October 1685. While some abjured their faith (Bernard, Ferdinand Elle, *père* and *fils*, Lespagnandel) and were readmitted to the

---

* The research and writing of this essay was completed while Faculty Visiting Fellow at the H. Henry Meeter Center, Calvin College, Grand Rapids, Michigan. I am grateful to the Center for its support, as well as to Dr. Margit Thøfner for her helpful comments on an earlier version of this essay.

1   *Procès-verbaux de l'Académie Royale de peinture et de sculpture 1648–1793*, (eds.) Anatole de Montaiglon, Paul Cornu, vol. 2 (11 vols. Paris: 1875–1909), 197–98.

2   *Procès-verbaux de l'Académie Royale*, 2: 215.

Academy, others (Michelin, Rousseau, Testelin) sought exile in Britain, the Dutch Republic and Germany.

When the Academy was founded in 1648, the Huguenots were disproportionately well-represented. At a time when they comprised around five to six per cent of the French population, about a third of the twenty-four founder members were adherents of the Reformed faith. These included Samuel Bernard, Louis Ferdinand Elle *père* and Henri Testelin as well as Sébastien Bourdon (1616–71), Louis du Guernier (1614–59), Thomas Pinagier (c. 1616–53) and Louis Testelin (1615–55).[3] Henri Testelin was later described as "the father of the Academy, having done more than any other towards its establishment."[4] This new institution sought to elevate the status of the arts, from the applied arts of a highly skilled artisan to an intellectual profession. While they eschewed certain activities associated with trade guilds, the academicians provided instruction in drawing as well as other skills such as anatomy and perspective which were considered necessary for producing the higher artistic forms, specifically history painting.[5] Although the Reformed representation in the Academy declined in subsequent decades, a further thirteen Huguenot artists, engravers and sculptors can be identified as members before 1681.[6] The Academy, however, represented the elite of the artistic establishment; Heinich has calculated that between its foundation in 1648 and 1700, only 178 artists were members representing a mere eight per cent of French painters in the

---

3   Nathalie Heinich, *Du peintre à l'artiste. Artisans et académiciens à l'âge classique* (Paris: 1993), 240; Menna Prestwich, "Patronage and the Protestants in France, 1598–1661: Architects and Painters," in *L'âge d'or du Mécénat*, (eds.) Roland Mousnier and Jean Mesnard (Paris: 1985), 82–83; Philip Benedict, "Calvinism as a Culture? Preliminary Remarks on Calvinism and the Visual Arts," in *Seeing Beyond the Word. Visual Arts and the Calvinist Tradition*, (ed.) Paul Corby Finney (Grand Rapids, MI: 1999), 36–37; Jacques Pannier, *L'Église réformée de Paris sous Louis XIII de 1621 à 1629 environ* (Paris: 1932), 416–21.

4   Richard Beresford, "Jacque Bullart on French Artists: Poussin, Le Brun, Testelin, Mignard and Van der Meulen," *The Burlington Magazine* 137 (1995), 23.

5   Paul Duro, *The Academy and the Limits of Painting in Seventeenth-Century France* (Cambridge: 1997).

6   Abraham Bosse (1653), Jean Michelin (1661), Jacques Rousseau (1662), Isaac Moillon (1663), Pierre Du Guernier (1663), Etienne Picart (1664), Mathieu Lespagnandel (1672), Nicolas Heude (1673), Pierre Lombard (1673), Jean Forest (1674), Jacob d'Agard (1675), Jean Ecman (1675) and Louis Ferdinand Elle *fils* (1681). Bosse was only an honorary member as at the time printmaking was regarded as an artisan skill. L. Vitet, *L' l'Académie Royale de peinture et de la sculpture. Étude historique* (Paris: 1861), 330, 332, 334, 336, 337, 339, 340, 341, 344; Pannier, *L'Eglise réformée de Paris*, 416–21; Carl Goldstein, *Print Culture in Early Modern France. Abraham Bosse and the Purposes of Print* (Cambridge: 2012), 6.

same period.⁷ There were other Reformed artists, such as Aaron Bugé, who resided in Paris, who did not enjoy exalted status and for whom there is little or no evidence of their work.⁸

The work of these Huguenot artists has generally been overshadowed by other French painters, in particular Nicolas Poussin (1594–1665) and Charles Le Brun (1619–90).⁹ Furthermore, the influence of the Italian academies on French painting and the role assumed by the Academy in determining the artistic discourse has meant that historical studies have tended to concentrate more on classicism and the contribution of these leading figures rather than other artistic styles and influences.¹⁰ The emulation of artistic styles and the conscious reference to the works of the great masters has led to confusion and the misattribution of the work of some Huguenot painters. This is particularly true of the work of Sébastien Bourdon, but he was also harshly criticized by his contemporary André Félibien for not developing his own style.¹¹ In the past, this criticism has colored attitudes towards his work but recent research has emphasized the range of his talent and contribution to 17th-century French art. Bourdon and other Huguenot artists not only associated with the leading artists of the period, but they received important commissions from the Catholic Church and crown in their own right. Furthermore, through their membership in the Academy, they contributed to the professionalization of the arts in France.¹²

These men were part of the artistic élite in later 17th-century France and provide an important focus for this essay, but it will also consider the contribution made before the Academy's foundation by other Huguenot artists. This overview of their contribution to the graphic arts in late 16th and 17th-century France will also consider whether their Reformed faith influenced their work

---

7   Heinich, *Du peintre à l'artiste*, 241.
8   E. Benezit et al. (eds.), *Dictionary of Artists*, vol. 2 (14 vols, Paris: 2006), 391; Jules Guiffrey, *Histoire de l'Académie de Saint-Luc. Notice sur la communauté des maîtres peintres et sculpteurs parisiens*, Archives de l'Art Français. Recueil de documents inédits, new series 9 (1915), 208.
9   Richard Verdi and Pierre Rosenberg (eds.), *Nicolas Poussin, 1594–1665* (London: 1995), 11–15.
10 Geraldine Elizabeth Fowle, "The Biblical Paintings of Sébastien Bourdon" (Ph.D. thesis, 2 vols, University of Michigan, 1970) 1: 1–2; Duro, *The Academy and the Limits of Painting*, 41–45.
11 André Félibien, *Entretiens sur les vies et sur les ouvrages des plus excellens peintres anciens et modernes*, vol. 4 (1725, repr. Geneva: 1967), 241–42; Fowle, "The Biblical Paintings of Sébastien Bourdon," 1: 2–3.
12 Duro, *The Academy and the Limits of Painting*, 18–35.

and the extent to which it affected their relationship with the crown and other patrons.

Jacques Pannier was the first historian to consider the contribution to the arts made by Huguenot artists as part of his study of the Reformed Church in Paris during the reign of Louis XIII. It was first published in 1922, but was considerably expanded in a second edition that appeared a decade later.[13] This research provided the basis for Menna Prestwich's survey of patronage and Protestantism in France between the reigns of Henry IV and the start of Louis XIV's personal rule in 1661. This essay focused not only on Reformed painters but also architects; the first part of her survey looked at the du Cerceau family and Salomon de Brosse, whose achievements included the design of the Huguenot temple built at Charenton, near Paris. Her approach was mainly biographical, identifying particular artists and engravers as well as their family links and associations, in what was a tight-knit community. It was really only the artistic contributions of Sébastien Bourdon and Abraham Bosse that were studied in any depth.[14]

In the thirty years since the publication of Prestwich's essay, there has been increasing interest in early modern French art. Attention has been paid to 16th-century prints, particularly those generated during the Wars of Religion. This includes Philip Benedict's detailed study of the series produced by Jean Perrissin and Jacques Tortorel in Geneva between 1569 and 1570.[15] There have been major exhibitions on the work of early 17th-century painters such as Nicolas Poussin and Simon Vouet,[16] as well as research into lesser known artists and engravers from this period. As part of this process, there has been a growing awareness of the work of Huguenot artists as well as the reattribution of works to them. A retrospective of the work of Sébastien Bourdon was held in his home city of Montpellier in 2001 and was accompanied by an extensive catalogue of his complete works. In 2004, the 400th anniversary of the birth of the engraver Abraham Bosse at Tours was marked by an exhibition in the city and the Bibliothèque nationale. There has also been an exhibition of the work of Isaac Moillon (2005) and several studies including a catalogue raisonné of

---

13 Pannier, *L'Eglise réformée de Paris*, 403–36.
14 Prestwich, "Patronage and the Protestants in France," 78–88; Pannier, *L'Eglise réformée de Paris*, 403–29.
15 Karen Jacobson (ed.), *The French Renaissance in Prints from the Bibliothèque Nationale de France* (Los Angeles: 1994), 117–19; Philip Benedict, *Graphic History. The Wars, Massacres and Troubles of Tortorel and Perrissin* (Geneva: 2007).
16 Jacques Thuillier et al. (eds.), *Vouet* (Paris: 1990); Verdi and Rosenberg (eds.), *Nicolas Poussin*.

the paintings of his sister Louise.[17] Further research has revealed the work of other lesser known artists, including the Huguenots Samuel Bernard and Louis du Guernier.[18] Outside the elite circles of the Academy, other Protestants such as Daniel Sarrabat, a nephew of Bosse, and Nicolas Tournier have been the focus for recent research and exhibitions.[19] To differing degrees these studies have acknowledged the religious beliefs of the artists but have tended to focus on their artwork. Although the intention of this essay is to provide a broad overview of the Huguenot contribution to the visual arts and its historical context, the range of this assessment has in part been determined by what has survived. The remaining works of Abraham Bosse and Sébastien Bourdon are relatively extensive but other artists are only known through a handful of paintings, engravings of lost pictures or archival references.

This overview also needs to be considered in relation to the longstanding debate over the relationship between Calvin and the visual arts.[20] The condemnation of religious images, the iconoclastic assault during the confessional conflicts of the later 16th century and the plain white interiors of Reformed places of worship have for some seemed to suggest that Calvinist theology and artistic expression were incompatible. Calvin did condemn idolatry and any attempt to represent God, for it was "vanity and falsehood for men to try to fashion God in images," but the Genevan reformer was not opposed to the arts *per se*.[21] He objected to the use of art in religious contexts and in one of his biblical commentaries explained how people's attitudes could alter depending on where a work was viewed:

---

17 Jacques Thuillier (ed.), *Sébastien Bourdon, 1616–1671. Catalogue critique et chronologique de l'œuvre complet* (Paris: 2000); Sophie Join-Lambert and Maxime Préaud (eds.), *Abraham Bosse. Savant graveur. Tours, vers 1604–1676, Paris* (Paris: 2004); Nicole de Reynies and Sylvain Lavessière (eds.), *Isaac Moillon 1614–1673. Un peintre du roi à Aubusson* (Aubusson: 2005); Helen Chastain Sowa, *Louise Moillon: Seventeenth Century Still-Life Artist. An Illustrated Biography* (Chicago: 1998); Dominique Alsina (ed.), *Louyse Moillon: Paris, vers 1610–1696: la nature morte au Grand Siècle: catalogue raisonné* (Dijon: 2009).

18 See for example, Céline Paul, *Les Mystérieux du XVIIe siècle. Une enquête au cabinet d'art graphique* (Paris: 2002).

19 Pascal-François Bertrand (ed.), *Nicolas Tournier et la peinture caravagesque en Italie, en France et en Espagne* (Toulouse: 2003); *Nicolas Tournier, 1590–1639. Un peintre caravagesque* (Toulouse, 2011); François Marandet (ed.), *Daniel Sarrabat (1666–1748)* (Saint-Étienne: 2011).

20 For an overview of the historiographical debate, see Benedict, "Calvinism as a Culture?" in *Seeing Beyond the Word*, (ed.) Finney, 20–25.

21 John Calvin, *Institutes of the Christian Religion*, ed, John T. McNeill, trans. Ford Lewis Battles, vol. 1 (Philadelphia: 1960), 105.

There was certainly always a liberal use of pictures, but God wanted his temple to be free of images, so that people would not be captivated by such enticements and directly turn to superstition. If we see a picture of a human being or animal in some unconsecrated place, no religious feeling affects our souls. Everyone acknowledges it to be a picture. Even idols themselves are not worshipped as long as they are in studios or workshops. If a painter's studio is filled with images, everyone walks by; if they delight in looking, they still show no sign of reverence for pictures. But as soon as a picture is moved into another place, its sacredness blinds people and transports their minds into a stupor. They do not stop to think that they just saw a picture in an ordinary studio.

This is why God would not allow any pictures in his temple. Certainly when a place has been consecrated, it is inevitable that an image bemuses people as if some arcane divinity lurked therein.[22]

In his *Institutes of the Christian Religion*, after condemning the use of religious imagery, Calvin went on to argue that "because sculpture and painting are gifts from God, I seek a pure and legitimate use of each." "Therefore it remains that only those things are to be sculpted or painted which the eyes are capable of seeing" as well as "histories and events" represented acceptable forms of art.[23] It was therefore permissible for artists to depict narrative biblical scenes as well as history paintings together with those which reflected a close observation of the natural world such as landscapes, still life painting and portraiture.

In France, Reformed theologians had condemned the presence of religious imagery in places of worship at the colloquy of Saint-Germain-en-Laye in February 1562 and the iconoclastic assault from the late 1550s had seen churches purged as they were taken over for Reformed worship.[24] The early synods of

---

22   John Calvin, *Calvin's Old Testament Commentaries. Ezekiel 1 (Chapters 1–12)*, trans. D. Foxgrover and D. Martin (Grand Rapids, Mich.: 1994), 203.

23   Calvin, *Institutes of the Christian Religion*, 1: 112. For a full discussion, see Sergiusz Michalski, *The Reformation and the Visual Arts. The Protestant Image Question in Western and Eastern Europe* (London: 1993), 59–74; Carlos M.N. Eire, *War Against the Idols. The Reformation of Worship from Erasmus to Calvin* (Cambridge: 1986), 195–233; Jérôme Cottin, *Le Regard et la Parole. Une théologie protestante de l'image* (Geneva: 1994); Christopher Richard Joby, *Calvinism and the Arts: A Re-assessment* (Leuven: 2007), 1–28.

24   David Willis-Watkins, *The Second Commandment and Church Reform. The Colloquy of St. Germain-en-Laye, 1562* (Princeton: 1994); Philip Benedict, "The Dynamics of Protestant Militancy: France, 1555–1563," in *Reformation, Revolt and Civil War in France and the Netherlands 1555–585*, (eds.) Philip Benedict, Guido Marnef, Henk van Nierop and Marc Venard (Amsterdam: 1999), 35–50.

the French Reformed Churches went further and sought to prevent artists from undertaking commissions that might be regarded as furthering Catholicism. At Orléans in 1562, the synod ordered:

> Printers, Booksellers, Painters and other Artificers and in general all the faithful, particularly such as bear office in the Church shall be admonished, not to exercise their Arts, Office or calling in or about the superstitions of the Romish Church or their dependencies, nor in the least favour of them: and the cognisance of particular matters, that may happen thereupon, and their correction and reformation shall belong unto the consistories.[25]

Five years later, the synod repeated its admonition and in explaining the earlier injunction ordered the abstention "from all manner of work in their respective trades that may in the least favor idolatry; and if after admonition they continued in such practices, they shall be subjected to censure."[26] These principles became enshrined in the Discipline or church order for the Reformed Churches in France that was agreed at the synod of La Rochelle in 1572.[27] Further clarification had been sought in 1598 by the synod of Lower Languedoc meeting in Montpellier regarding "those who were engaged in activities that furthered idolatry." They requested that the article of the Discipline concerning painters, carpenters, masons and others should be made clearer and amplified.[28] What is not evident is how far this injunction was enforced by consistories into the 17th century. Certainly ministers continued to condemn idolatry; it was in this context that a minister in Dauphiné, Daniel Chamier asserted in 1618 that any "Church that teaches & encourages the painting of God…teaches and encourages Idolatry," adding that to paint God was "the greatest devotional crime there can be."[29] Further research into sermons as well as extant consistory records might provide insights into the attitudes of the church authorities in the 17th century towards the visual arts.

---

25   John Quick, *Synodicon in Gallia Reformata. Or the Acts, Decisions, Decrees, and Canons of those Famous National Councils of the Reformed Churches of France*, vol. 1 (London: 1692), 25.
26   Quick, *Synodicon in Gallia Reformata*, 1: 74–75.
27   Quick, *Synodicon in Gallia Reformata*, 1: liv.
28   BPF, MS 534², f. 24.
29   Cited in Matthew Koch, "Calvinism and the Visual Arts in Southern France, 1561 to 1685," in *Seeing Beyond the Word*, (ed.) Finney, 177.

An assessment of the Reformed contribution to the visual arts in France is complicated, in some cases, by uncertainty as to whether a particular artist was actually a Huguenot or not. Before 1685, interment in the Huguenot cemetery in Paris provides relatively compelling evidence of the religious convictions of the deceased, as in the case of Sébastien Bourdon and Abraham Bosse.[30] The interment of a spouse or children who died in infancy might provide an indication but not conclusive proof of the artist's religious stance, due to the possibility of a confessionally-mixed marriage. In other instances, there has been speculation about the religious beliefs of certain artists based on their work. This is true of the Le Nain brothers, who painted realistic scenes of everyday life and lived in the Saint-Germain district of Paris, which was home to a number of Huguenot artists.[31] Such attributions represent an attempt to confessionalize particular genres; in reality these rustic scenes or *bambochades* also appealed to a Catholic audience. There are other artists such as Jean Perrissin whose adherence to the Reformed faith appears to have been short lived.[32] While Sébastien Bourdon appears to have remained true to the Reformed faith while in Rome, to the extent that the threat of being denounced to the Inquisition hastened his departure, Nicolas Tournier converted, regularly receiving Easter communion before his return to France.[33] As has been seen, some of the academicians who were expelled in 1681 subsequently abjured and were later readmitted. In other instances, for example Daniel Sarrabat, it is only possible to presume that the decision to remain in France after 1685 was an indication of acceptance of the changed religious climate and conversion to Catholicism. What might be concluded from the career of Louis Chéron, who was baptized at Charenton but completed several important commissions after the Revocation, yet finally left France during the 1690s for England where he became a member of an exiled French congregation?[34] Or that of Etienne Picart, academician and *graveur du roi* specializing in

---

30   Henri Herluison, *Actes d'état-civil d'artistes, musiciens et comédiens extraits des registres de l'Hôtel-de-Ville de Paris, détruits dans l'incendie du 24 mai, 1871* (Orléans: 1876), 47, 53–54.

31   Jacques Pannier, "Les frères Le Nain ont-ils été protestants?" BSHPF 83 (1934), 496–506; Pierre-Michel Bertrand, "Question d'iconologie: A propos de la soi-disant Victoire de le Nain au Musée du Louvre," *Gazette des Beaux-Arts* 1576–77 (2000), 283–94.

32   See below, p. 181.

33   Félibien, *Entretiens sur les vies*, 4: 265; Thuillier (ed.), *Sébastien Bourdon*, 33, 39; Jean Louis H. Bonnet, "Nicolas Tournier, peintre montbéliardais en Languedoc," in *Nicolas Tournier, 1590–1639*, 65; Luisa Vertova, "La religiosità di Nicolas Tournier a Roma," in *Nicolas Tournier et la peinture caravagesque*, (ed.) Bertrand, 91–102.

34   "Cheron, Louis," in *Oxford Dictionary of National Biography*, (eds.) H.C.G. Matthew, B. Harrison et al., vol. 11 (Oxford: 2004–), 310–11.

portraits and Catholic subjects, who migrated with his better-known son, the engraver Bernard Picart, to the Dutch Republic in 1710?[35] Due to these difficulties in establishing the confessional identity of some artists, this essay will focus on those who were regarded as Huguenots by their contemporaries, as well as the works completed by others when they were adherents of the Reformed faith. This, inevitably, means a mainly Parisian focus on the artistic elite whose careers are better documented than others.

2 War and Exploration

During the early 16th century, the French Protestant movement made limited use of visual imagery to attack the Catholic Church, its religious practices and adherents, when compared to the widespread production of woodcuts and prints as part of the German Reformation. Some prints were adapted for a French audience such as Lucas Cranach the Elder's *Passional Christi und Antichristi*, which contrasted the passion of Christ with the Antichrist/Papacy. The reworked series included new prints heightening the attack on the clergy and the Mass, published in both French and Latin editions, which proved to be particularly popular during the late 16th and 17th centuries. Pierre Eskrich's edition, which was published in Lyon, went through nine different printings between 1557 and 1600. Relatively few other German prints were similarly adapted to advance the Protestant cause in France.[36] Furthermore, only a limited number of prints by French artists attacking Catholicism were produced. One by Jacques le Challeux, a probable victim of the St. Bartholomew's Day massacre, depicted the "Tree of Jesse" emerging from the bowels of the Papacy and bearing as its fruit the corruption of the Catholic Church, symbolized by ecclesiastical figures.[37] Perhaps the most remarkable image was *Mappe-monde nouvelle papistique*, also printed by Eskrich, at Geneva in 1566. The picture is

---

35   Eugène and Emile Haag, *La France Protestante, ou Vies des Protestants Français*, vol. 8 (9 vols. Paris: 1846–59), 228; Lynn Hunt, Margaret C. Jacob, and Wijnand Mijnhardt, *The Book that Changed Europe: Picart & Bernard's Religious Ceremonies of the World* (London: 2010), 45.

36   Philip Benedict, "Of Marmites and Martyrs: Images and Polemics in the Wars of Religion," in *The French Renaissance in Prints*, (ed.) Jacobson, 117–19; Philip Benedict, *Graphic History*, 17; Vanessa Selbach, "Artisan ou artiste? La carrière de Pierre Eskrich, brodeur, peintre et graveur, dans les milieux humanistes de Lyon et Genève (ca. 1550–1580)," in *Le Calvinisme et les arts*, (ed.) Yves Krumenacker (Chrétiens et Sociétés XVIe–XXIe siècles, numéro spécial, 2011), 37–55.

37   Benedict, *Graphic History*, 63–65.

formed from sixteen folios that are placed together to form a large map of a world created by the Papacy, which sits within the jaws of hell. The image is so detailed that it required the publication of an accompanying book to explain the iconography.[38]

Similarly, the confessional conflicts of the later 16th century did not generate a substantial degree of polemical imagery. Atypical is the print of *Le renversement de la grande marmite*, which projected a Reformed message and was produced as a single sheet intended for sale or display. The print depicts a cooking pot with ecclesiastical vestments and the trappings of Catholicism being overturned by the power of the Holy Spirit through the Bible and the flames of burning martyrs. Catholic clergy attempt to shore up the pot to prevent it from toppling, although their corruption undermines their efforts. Produced in 1562, the image manifests the enthusiasm and optimism of the Reformed movement of the period and it was a theme repeated in other works.[39] It was, however, the Catholics who became the principal exponents of this form of print, with the allegorical as well as narrative images that were produced relating to Henry III, the assassination of the Guises and the king.[40]

Rather than adopting a straightforwardly polemical approach, one of the most important French Protestant works sought to provide a visual account of the first stages of the religious wars. The full title of the *Quarante Tableaux* explained that it included "divers memorable histories concerning the wars, massacres and troubles that have occurred in France during these last years. All gathered from the testimony of those who were there in person and saw them, and truly portrayed." The series of prints were commissioned at Geneva in April 1569 from the Lyon artist Jean Perrissin with Jacques Tortorel employed to etch the scenes.[41] The resulting series of prints sought not merely to depict recent episodes in the developing confessional conflict but also to provide a visual explanation of what had happened. Beginning with the 1559 meeting of the *parlement* of Paris to discuss heresy, the series of 39 prints recorded events such as sieges, battles and skirmishes as well as massacres (Figure 7.1) and

---

38 Benedict, "Of Marmites and Martyrs," 119; [Jean-Baptiste Trento and Pierre Eskrich], *Mappe-Monde Nouvelle Papistique. Histoire de la Mappe-Monde Papistique, en laquelle est declairé tout ce qui est contenu et pourtraict en la grande table, ou carte de la Mappe-Monde* (Geneva: 1566), (eds.) Frank Lestringant and Alessandra Preda (Geneva: 2009); Selbach, "Artisan ou artiste? La carrière de Pierre Eskrich," 37–55.
39 Benedict, "Of Marmites and Martyrs," 109–17.
40 Benedict, "Of Marmites and Martyrs," 127–30; Keith Cameron, *Henri III, a Maligned or Malignant king?: (Aspects of the Satirical Iconography of Henri de Valois)* (Exeter: 1978).
41 Benedict, *Graphic History*, 4, 15–24.

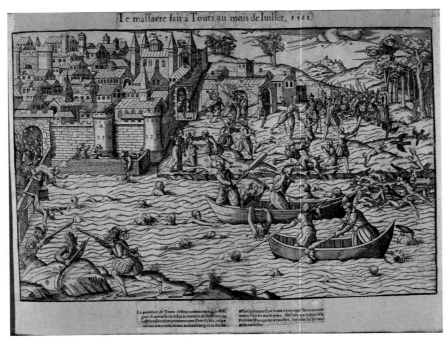

FIGURE 7.1   *Jean Perrissin*, The Massacre at Tours, July 1562.
              © RIJKSMUSEUM, AMSTERDAM

peace agreements up to 1570.[42] The format of each of these prints was similar, with a title of the scene being depicted, an image which recorded a number of incidents or individuals which were then identified in the key underneath. The image therefore attempted to encapsulate the whole event rather than portraying just one moment. The *Quarante Tableaux* were intended "to represent these varied events according to the reports of those who were eyewitnesses and who have faithfully and dispassionately recounted all of the circumstances." In spite of such claims of impartiality, this was not simply a narrative of events as it emerged out of the Huguenot tradition of historical accounts and martyrologies of the period.[43] Nonetheless, the series should not be regarded as solely Reformed propaganda; it becomes more objective as it progresses; some events are included because they were regarded as significant and they also include scenes which do not necessarily create a favorable impression of the Huguenot cause. While these prints do not offer a completely

---

42   Benedict, *Graphic History*, 6, 22–23, part 2.
43   Benedict, *Graphic History*, 123–49.

FIGURE 7.2   *Jean Perrissin (?)*, Temple of Lyon, called Le Paradis.
COURTESY OF BGE (BIBLIOTHÈQUE DE GENÈVE), CENTRE D'ICONOGRAPHIE GENEVOISE

impartial view of the period, they might nonetheless be considered with other French news prints as an attempt to record recent events.[44]

Although Perrissin had sought refuge in Geneva during the late 1560s, he subsequently returned to Lyon and appears to have abjured the Reformed faith and even remained in the city during the time when it was under the control of the Catholic League. His later paintings included a number of municipal commissions among them civic entries as well as a portrait of Henry IV. One work, which since the 19th century has been attributed to Perrissin, is the view of the interior of the Huguenot temple of Le Paradis in Lyon (Figure 7.2), which had been erected in 1564 but was razed by the Catholic mob in 1567. Although

---

44 Benedict, *Graphic History*, 86–111, 151–69.

FIGURE 7.3   *François Dubois,* The Massacre of St Bartholomew, *(c. 1572–1584).*
COURTESY OF MUSÉE CANTONAL DES BEAUX-ARTS DE LAUSANNE. DON DE
LA MUNICIPALITÉ DE LAUSANNE, 1862. INV. 729. PHOTO: N. RUPP

drawings of the exterior and interior of the temple were signed by Perrissin, the differences between them and the painting of the inside of the building have raised questions as to its attribution. Even if the painting is not the work of Perrissin, what may have initially been intended as an allegory of Reformed worship, has nevertheless become an iconic image of French Reformed preaching.[45]

Alongside the prints of the *Quarante Tableaux*, probably the most well-known depiction of the religious conflict that wracked late 16th-century France is François Dubois's *The Saint Bartholomew's Massacre* (Figure 7.3). Dubois is believed to have fled to Geneva in the wake of the massacre in August 1572, in which he lost several relatives. The painting was completed before 1584 and is the only known signed work by the artist. It continued the form of "visual reporting" of the *Quarante Tableaux* and its graphic depiction of atrocities and bloodshed offers parallels with the massacre scenes in these prints. The painting may have been based on a written account of the massacre and it assumes a sense of authenticity through depiction of an urban landscape that

---

45   Benedict, *Graphic History*, 55–61; Bernard Reymond, "'Temple de Lyon nommé Paradis:' que représente au juste le tableau conservé à Genève?" *BSHPF* 155 (2009), 781–94. On Le Paradis, see Andrew Spicer, *Calvinist Churches in Early Modern Europe* (Manchester: 2007), 172–73.

is recognizable as Paris, even if it is not topographically accurate. Amidst the horrors of the massacre, the body of Coligny is thrown to the ground from an upstairs room and is then hacked to pieces, while in the background the figure of Catherine de Medici inspects the corpses.[46] This was not a subject, which generally found favor with other Reformed artists, perhaps due to the *oubliance* clauses of the peace agreements, although Philippe Duplessis-Mornay did own a painting of the murder of Coligny.[47] Nonetheless, there were a number of paintings depicting massacres in a classical setting after Anthoine Caron's *Massacre of the Triumvirate* (1566) but the attribution of one of these to Dubois is disputed.[48]

Alongside the depiction of the religious conflict, the work of another artist sought to provide a visual record of the French expedition to Florida in 1564–65. The mission took place under the patronage of Gaspard de Coligny and was intended to establish a Huguenot colony in the New World. Although his background is unclear, Jacques le Moyne appears to have been sufficiently well-known in court circles to be commissioned to record the expedition.[49] His illustrated narrative of the Florida expedition of 1562–64, was published by Theodor de Bry at Frankfurt in 1591: *Brevis narration eorum quae in Florida Americae provincial Gallis acciderunt*. It included forty-two engravings and a map, depicting aspects of the French expedition and their dealings with the indigenous Indian population.[50] Le Moyne recorded the customs, religious practices as well as the conflicts of the local population. Only one of the original paintings survives (Figure 7.4) but it recalls the remarkable moment when the French expedition's commander Laudonnière was led by the Indian chief Authore to the column that had been erected by Jean Ribault in 1562 during his earlier expedition, claiming the territory for France.[51] The explanatory text to the engraving of this image stated:

46   Benedict, *Graphic History*, 188–89; Ralf Beil (ed.), *Le Monde selon François Dubois: peintre de la Saint-Barthélemy* (Lausanne: 2003).
47   Benedict, *Graphic History*, 189; Benjamin Fillon, "La Gallerie de portraits de Du Plessis-Mornay au château de Saumur,"*Gazette des Beaux-Arts* 2nd series, 20 (1879), 168.
48   Jean Ehrmann, "Massacre and Persecution Pictures in Sixteenth-Century France," *The Journal of the Warburg and Courtauld Institute* 8 (1945), 196–97; Neil Cox and Mark Greengrass, "Painting Power: Anthoine Caron's *Massacres of the Triumvirate*," in Graeme Murdock, Penny Roberts and Andrew Spicer (eds.), *Ritual and Violence. Natalie Zemon Davis and Early Modern France,* Past and Present Supplement 7 (Oxford: 2012), 241–74; Beil (ed.), *Le monde selon François Dubois*, 10–11, 21–23.
49   Paul Hulton (ed.), *The Work of Jacques Le Moyne de Morgues. A Huguenot Artist in France, Florida and England*, vol. 1 (London: 1977), 3–4, 75.
50   Hulton (ed.), *The Work of Jacques Le Moyne de Morgues*, 1: 3, 11.
51   Hulton (ed.), *The Work of Jacques Le Moyne de Morgues*, 1: 162–64.

FIGURE 7.4　*Jacques le Moyne de Morgues,* Laudonnierus et rex Athore ante columnam a praefecto prima navigatione locatam quamque venerantur floridenses.
COURTESY OF THE PRINT COLLECTION, MIRIAM AND IRA D. WALLACH DIVISION OF ART, PRINTS AND PHOTOGRAPHS, THE NEW YORK PUBLIC LIBRARY, ASTOR, LENNOX AND TILDEN FOUNDATIONS

…he [Authore] led them to the island on which Ribault had placed on top of a certain mound a marker of rock carved with the arms of the King of France. Drawing close they noticed that the Indians were worshipping this stone as if it were an idol. For when the chief himself had saluted it and shown it the sort of reverence he was accustomed to receive of his subjects, he kissed it; his people copied him and encouraged us to do the same. In front of the stone were lying various offerings of fruits of the district and roots that were either good to eat or medicinally useful, dishes full of fragrant oils, and bows and arrows; it was also encircled from top to bottom with garlands of all kinds of flowers, and with branches of their most prized trees. After witnessing the rites of these poor savage people they returned to their comrades with the intent to search out the most suitable site for building a fort.[52]

In view of the iconoclastic attacks that had taken place in France during the early 1560s, Le Moyne's depiction of idolatrous worship is particularly striking.

52　Quoted in Hulton (ed.), *The Work of Jacques Le Moyne de Morgues,* 1: 141.

It would appear to support the assertion that de Bry's publications on the New World were more focused on Reformed concerns in Europe than attempting to record and understand Native American customs.[53] Recent research has suggested that de Bry, rather than pursuing an avowedly Reformed agenda, sought to avoid alienating a potential Catholic readership. Le Moyne's painting could be read allegorically by Protestants but it could just as easily be considered by Catholics as portraying the pagan religious practices of the Native Americans.[54] Besides his Florida paintings, Le Moyne is also known for his carefully observed studies of plants and fruit which were completed in France and later England, after his move to London "for religion" (Figure 7.5).[55]

The work of Dubois, Le Moyne, Perrissin and Tortorel took place against the background of the confessional conflicts of the late 16th century, which had forced all of them to leave France at some point for exile in either England or Geneva. These were not the only artists who were affected by the conflict. Nicolas Tournier was born in 1590 at Montbéliard in the territory of the duke of Württemberg. His father, who was also a painter, fled there from Besançon.[56] The grandfather of the academician Louis du Guernier had held a position in the *parlement* at Rouen but was killed during the wars, leading his son, Alexander, to seek exile in England. With the end of the wars, he returned to France and established himself as a miniature painter in Paris.[57] The concessions granted to the Huguenots under the Edict of Nantes established a degree of religious co-existence, which allowed artists of the Reformed faith to work at the highest levels of French society for much of the 17th century.

3   History Painting

Recording the religious wars and overseas exploration belonged to the broader field of historical painting for which Calvin expressed his approval in the *Institutes of the Christian Religion*.[58] This genre was not confined to recent

---

53 Bernadette Bucher, *Icon and Conquest. A Structural Analysis of the Illustrations of the De Bry's Great Voyages* (Chicago: 1981); Anthony Grafton, *New Worlds, Ancient Texts. The Power of Tradition and the Shock of Discovery* (Cambridge, Mass.: 1992), 128–29; Michiel van Groesen, "The De Bry Collection of Voyages (1590–1634): Early America Reconsidered," *Journal of Early Modern History* 12 (2008), 3–4.
54 Van Groesen, "The De Bry Collection," 1–24.
55 Hulton (ed.), *The Work of Jacques Le Moyne de Morgues*, 1: 13–14, 58–59, 77–80, 154–62, 165–84, 2: plates 1–33.
56 Bonnet, "Nicolas Tournier," 65.
57 Félibien, *Entretiens sur les vies*, 4: 209–10; Benezit, *Dictionary of Artists*, 4: 1188.
58 Calvin, *Institutes*, 1: 112.

FIGURE 7.5   *Jacques le Moyne,* Studies of Flowers: A Rose, a Heartsease, a Sweet Pea, a Garden Pea, and a Lax-flowered Orchid.
COURTESY OF THE METROPOLITAN MUSEUM OF ART, NEW YORK

events but also incorporated episodes from classical antiquity and the Bible. The work of the leading Huguenot artist of the 17th century, Sébastien Bourdon, for example, included *Augustus at the Tomb of Alexander* and two versions of *The Meeting of Anthony and Cleopatra,* but the majority of his painting depicted religious scenes or episodes from the Bible. In view of the range of subjects that could be defined as history painting and because of the number of Bourdon's works that survive compared to other Huguenot artists, this section will focus primarily on the representation of biblical stories and religious events.

Probably the most significant religious works completed by Huguenot artists were their contributions to a series known as the "Mays." Between 1630 and 1707 the goldsmiths' guild in Paris presented "to the most holy and glorious

Virgin, each year on the first day of May, an eleven foot high votive painting, to decorate the great pillars of the nave of the church [Notre Dame Cathedral]; the paintings were to depict the Acts of the Apostles."[59] The painting, together with a specially commissioned sonnet, was displayed publicly outside Notre Dame Cathedral on the eve of 1 May and was presented to the cathedral authorities the following day. The presentation was an important civic event but the celebrations were also often attended by the king and members of the court. The goldsmiths appointed the leading painters of the day to complete the commissions and, particularly after 1648, members of the Academy.[60]

Sébastien Bourdon was the first Huguenot to complete one of these paintings; his *The Crucifixion of St. Peter* was presented in May 1643. Two paintings were completed by Louis Testelin—*St. Peter Resurrecting the Widow Tabitha* (1652) and *The Flagellation of Paul and Silas* (1655)—and were described by his contemporary André Félibien as being his best work. Remarkably, considering the significance of the occasion, Louis Chéron completed two further paintings—*Prophet Agabus Preaching to St. Paul* and *Salome Bearing the Head of St. John the Baptist*—after the Revocation in 1687 and 1689.[61] Although Bourdon and Testelin were, unlike Chéron, both members of the Academy, it is possible that their commissions may have owed something to their connections with the goldsmiths' guild.[62]

The general theme of the paintings is the lives of the apostles, especially the missionary activities of the early Christians as recorded in the Acts of the Apostles, although occasionally artists negotiated with the cathedral chapter to paint another subject.[63] Bourdon's *The Crucifixion of St. Peter* was therefore unusual because it did not depict a biblical scene but the martyrdom of St. Peter which had become an important theme in the reassertion of the authority and origins of the Catholic Church in the wake of the Reformation. In particular, the Catholic Church sought to refute Reformed accusations that St. Peter had died in Jerusalem rather than Rome. Recently returned from Italy,

---

59 Annick Notter (ed.), *Les Mays de Notre Dame de Paris* (Arras: 1999), 43. See also Olivier Christin, "Le May des orfèvres. Contribution à l'histoire de la genèse du sentiment esthétique," *Actes de la recherche en sciences sociales* 105 (1994), 75–90.

60 Todd P. Olson, *Poussin and France. Painting, Humanism and the 'Politics of Style'* (New Haven: 2002), 204; Notter (ed.), *Les Mays de Notre Dame*, 13–15, 29–30, 39.

61 P.M. Auzas, "Les Grands Mays de Notre-Dame de Paris," *Gazette des Beaux-Arts* 36 (1949), 177–79, 181–83, 186–87, 198; Félibien, *Entretiens sur les vies*, 4: 202; François Marandet, "'The Pool of Bethesda' by Louis Chéron: a *modello* discovered at the Wellcome Library, London," *The Burlington Magazine* 156 (2014), 162.

62 Thuillier (ed.), *Sébastien Bourdon*, 214; Pannier, *L'Église réformée de Paris*, 418.

63 Olson, *Poussin and France*, 204; Notter (ed.), *Les Mays de Notre Dame*, 15, 18, 43.

Bourdon's painting was influenced by Caravaggio's *Crucifixion of St. Peter* (1600) and in its final form dramatically depicted the saint nailed to the upturned cross as it was raised into an upright position.[64] The paintings of the other Huguenot artists engaged more directly with Acts, depicting the preaching mission and miracles of the apostles, such as Testelin's portrayal of the resurrection of Tabitha. The themes and form of the five paintings completed by Huguenot artists were not distinct from the work of Catholic artists, some of whom chose to paint the apostles preaching.[65] The "Mays" also engaged a wider audience as prints were produced from the paintings.[66]

Although only twenty-six when the painting was presented, Bourdon's "May" painting established his reputation in Paris and led to a number of other commissions for Catholic churches.[67] These included the *Crucifixion of St. Andrew* at Chartres in 1647 (Figure 7.6), which unlike the Notre Dame canvas was painted for the cathedral's main altar. This painting is not as violent and aggressive as the "May" painting, the composition is less crowded, and the attention of the figures as well as the viewer is drawn to the outstretched arms of the apostle. As only one of these has been tied to the X-shaped cross, the position of his body echoes that of the crucified Christ. St. Andrew's gaze is directed towards the heavens and thereby engages with a separate panel in which angels reach down to bestow a martyr's garland and palm. Above the angels, Christ sits amidst the clouds looking towards the apostle, his figure and white robes conceal all but the uppermost portion of his crucifix on which he rests, so that only a diagonal cross is visible directly above that on which the apostle is being martyred. While according to tradition St. Andrew requested that he be executed on a diagonal cross as he considered himself unworthy of being crucified like Christ, Bourdon's portrayal of the two crosses makes St. Andrew's crucifixion like that of Christ.

While the martyrdom of St. Andrew is not recorded in the Bible, it was a subject that related to the lives of the Apostles. The same could not be said of another important commission, *The Beheading of St. Protase* (c. 1655) for the Parisian church of Saint-Gervais, depicting the martyrdom of a saint whose

---

64 Thuillier (ed.), *Sébastien Bourdon*, 214–20; Jean-Luc Bordeaux, "Sebastien Bourdon's First Idea for his 'Crucifixion of St Peter'—the 'May' of 1643," *The Burlington Magazine* 121 (1979), 30–33; Fowle, "The Biblical Paintings of Sébastien Bourdon," 1: 41–50, 2: 125–28.

65 For example, Jacques de Létin, *Saint Paul preaching to the Aeropagite* (1636); Charles Poerson, *Preaching of St. Peter at Jerusalem* (1642); Eustache Le Sueur, *Preaching of Saint Paul at Ephesus* (1649).

66 Hélène Guicharnaud, "Louis Testelin (1615–1655), *Saint Pierre ressuscite la veuve Tabitha*," *L'Estampille/L'Objet d'Art* 127 (October 2002), 83–84; Notter (ed.), *Les Mays de Notre Dame*, 92–93.

67 Thuillier (ed.), *Sébastien Bourdon*, 218.

FIGURE 7.6 *Sébastien Bourdon,* Crucifixion of St Andrew *(1647).*
COURTESY OF THE PALAIS DES BEAUX-ARTS, LILLE. PHOTO © RMN-GRAND PALAIS/RENÉ-GABRIEL OJÉDA

actual existence was uncertain. The remains of the martyred St. Protase and his elder brother St. Gervais had purportedly been discovered in Milan in the 4th century, but their medieval hagiography remained relatively slight. Bourdon's painting was one of a series depicting the lives of these martyrs, which served as a cartoon for a tapestry on the subject.[68] While this might be considered an unusual subject for a Huguenot artist, even more remarkable is

68 Thuillier (ed.), *Sébastien Bourdon*, 341–43.

the painting of the vision of St. Ignatius of Loyola, founder of the Jesuits, of the Virgin and Child. As the work is only known from a preparatory *modello*, it is unclear whether it was actually completed.[69]

One of the most remarkable altar paintings completed by Bourdon was for the cathedral in his native Montpellier, where confessional tensions had a long and violent history. In February 1657, the cathedral chapter commissioned Bourdon to paint a retable for their main altar. Bourdon had completed the *Fall of Simon the Magician* by the following year. In one sense this might be regarded as an unusual subject for the high altar. The dispute between St. Peter and Simon Magus appears in Acts, but there are varying accounts of his death in the Apocrypha. The altarpiece shows St. Peter and Simon the Magician in the context of a debate before the emperor Nero. During the disputation, the magician levitated but fell to the ground due, according to one account, to St. Peter's prayers to halt his flying. The legend had little credence until the pontificate of Clement VIII, when it was included as one of the six mysteries that decorated St. Peter's basilica in Rome. The theme had come to represent the defeat of superstition and corruption by the Early Church, and in the post-Tridentine era it could also be read as St. Peter, the personification of the Catholic Church, defeating heresy.[70]

While it is surprising that the cathedral selected Bourdon to complete such an important religious work, the artist's acceptance of the commission indicates that he was able to separate his own religious convictions from his professional activities. Furthermore, altarpieces were an important way in which artists could demonstrate their skills to a much wider audience than might be possible in fulfilling private commissions. There is nonetheless a suggestion in the Montpellier altarpiece that Bourdon sought to detach himself from the underlying sense of Catholic triumphalism. While the gaze of the emperor and the other figures are looking skyward towards the magician falling head first towards the earth, a face resembling that of Bourdon in his self-portraits, looks out towards the viewer instead. With his marginalized figure on the edge of the canvas amidst the infidels below the emperor's dais rather than in close proximity to St. Peter, it suggests that Bourdon was distancing himself from the triumph of Catholicism and associating himself with the infidels with whom the Catholic Church usually associated heretics.

Bourdon's religious paintings included a number of other works depicting scenes from the Old and New Testament, amongst which were *The Presentation*

---

69 Thuillier (ed.), *Sébastien Bourdon*, 236.
70 Thuillier (ed.), *Sébastien Bourdon*, 39, 360–61; Fowle, "The Biblical Paintings of Sébastien Bourdon," 2: 123–25.

FIGURE 7.7   Sébastien Bourdon, Solomon's Sacrifices to the Idols.
COURTESY OF THE MUSÉE DU LOUVRE, PARIS. PHOTO © RMN-GRAND
PALAIS (MUSÉE DU LOUVRE)/STÉPHANE MARÉCHALLE

at the Temple and *The Flight to Egypt* completed in 1644–45 for the Queen's oratory.[71] He also painted several works that related to biblical accounts of idolatry. They included two versions of *Solomon's Sacrifices to the Idols* (Figure 7.7). The subject related the account in I Kings 11 of how Solomon in his old age had turned away from God and was persuaded by his many foreign wives to build temples around Jerusalem where incense was burned and

---

71   Thuillier (ed.), *Sébastien Bourdon*, 232–35.

sacrifices made to the pagan gods. Bourdon portrays the kneeling figure of the old king with his hands clasped across his chest in the center of the composition; a young woman wearing a diadem directs his attention towards an idol, beneath which incense is being burnt. This was not a common theme in French painting and Bourdon's first version was painted in Italy but the second was probably completed around 1646 for Louis Phélypeaux, a Catholic patron of the arts. Phélypeaux was also secretary of state for Protestant affairs which meant he was responsible for the implementation of the Edict of Nantes in France and the resolution of any problems that arose. It has been argued that *Solomon's Sacrifices to the Idols* was meant to convey a moral message about an aged king being led astray by his attractive young wives or as a contrast between youth and old age.[72] Or was there intended to be a Protestant message about the consequences of idolatry? The Bible recounts how God's punishment for Solomon's actions was to raise up his enemies to destroy his kingdom after his death.[73] Two other Old Testament passages relating to idolatry provided Bourdon with the subject for several other paintings: *Laban looking for his Idols* (Genesis 31: 34–35) and *Jacob Burying the Idols* (Genesis 35: 4).[74] In his commentary on Genesis, Calvin attacked Laban's veneration of images and his daughter's "obstinate love of idolatrie," while drawing parallels with Catholic religious practices.[75] The second passage has been seen as representing the end of idolatry. As these alternative interpretations suggest, Bourdon's paintings could appeal to either a Catholic or a Protestant audience; he did not limit his market by painting with an overtly confessional agenda.

Bourdon was certainly not the only Huguenot who completed paintings for Catholic churches and religious orders. In the early 17th century, Jacob Bunel had painted works for several churches and ecclesiastical institutions in Paris and the provinces. These works included a commission from Marie de Medici of the *Assumption of the Virgin Mary*, although the story that his religious convictions prevented him from painting the Madonna's face may be apocryphal.[76] Amongst Bourdon's contemporaries, as has been seen, Louis Testelin

---

72 Thuillier (ed.), *Sébastien Bourdon*, 151–52, 244–45; Fowle, "The Biblical Paintings of Sébastien Bourdon," 2: 49–51.

73 I Kings 11: 11–13.

74 Thuillier (ed.), *Sébastien Bourdon*, 42, 167, 169–70, 381.

75 John Calvin, *A Commentarie of John Calvine, upon the first booke of Moses called Genesis* (London: 1578), 652, 654.

76 Jean Bernier, *Histoire de Blois, contenant les antiquitez et singularitez du comté de Blois* (Paris: 1682), 522–23; Félibien, *Entretiens sur les vies*, 3: 127; Paul Lafond, "François et Jacob Bunel. Peintres de Henri IV," *Réunion des sociétés des beaux-arts des départements* 22 (1898), 590–92; Sylvie Béguin, "Pour Jacob Bunel," in *Claude Vignon en son temps: actes du*

painted two "Mays" for Notre Dame. He also completed a series of paintings for the Sisters of the Assumption in Paris and was commissioned to produce a twelve-foot painting of the Circumcision for the Jesuits at Tours.[77] An extant painting of *Saint Louis tending to the Christian Plague Sufferers* (c. 1655), depicts the monarch presenting the plague victims to the Virgin Mary who is interceding on their behalf with Christ.[78] A decade later, Isaac Moillon painted the *Death of St. Louis* for the Hôtel-Dieu at Beaune. The artist was responsible for a series of paintings, which were completed between 1645 and 1646 for a newly created ward. These included a ceiling painting and nine panels showing the healing miracles of Christ. There were also two *grisailles* depicting the patron St. Hugh as a Carthusian and as a bishop, as well as a retable of *St. Hugh Resuscitating a Drowned Boy*. Moillon produced a number of other works for the hospital, including *Mary Magdalen at the foot of the Cross*, *Pentecost or the Descent of the Holy Spirit*, *The Resurrection*; other paintings were completed for some of the local churches and religious houses: *The Body of Christ at the foot of the Cross*; *St. Yves the Advocate*; *The Adolescent Christ between the Virgin and St. Joseph or The Earthly Trinity*.[79]

As this survey indicates, the range of religious paintings produced by Huguenot artists was very broad. While there was certainly a preponderance of biblical themes, they did not rely solely on the Scriptures but also drew upon the Apocrypha for inspiration for their paintings. Their work also included depictions of scenes, the historical veracity of which were less than certain, such as the lives of the saints. This was not only contrary to Calvin's statements on the appropriate forms of religious art but was also at odds with the condemnation by the Reformed synods about the production of work that furthered what they regarded as the superstition and idolatry of the Catholic faith. Religious themes were however only one aspect of historical painting and the work of these Huguenot artists also extended to the portrayal of scenes from ancient history and classical mythology. The nature of these commissions as well as the subjects that were painted indicate how these Huguenot artists focused on the higher forms of French art. Their professional commitments

---

colloque international de l'université de Tours (28–29 janvier 1994), (eds.) Claude Mignot and Paola Pacht Bassani (Paris: 1998), 84–85.

[77] Guillet de Saint-Georges, "Louis Testelin," in *Mémoires inédits sur la vie et les ouvrages des membres de l'Académie royale de peinture et de sculpture*, (eds.) L. Dussieux, E. Soulié, Ph. de Chennevières, Paul Mantz and A. de Montaiglon, vol. 1 (Paris: 1854), 219–20, 223.

[78] David Sinnoneau, "Louis Testelin dessinateur," in *Dessins français aux XVIIe et XVIIIe siècles : Actes des colloque Ecole du Louvre 24 et 25 juin 1999*, (ed.) Nicholas Sainte Fare Garnot (Paris: 2003), 169.

[79] Reynies and Laveissière, *Isaac Moillon*, 60–80, 101–102.

were not impeded by their own personal religious convictions and adherence to the Reformed Church.

4   Portraiture

Peter Burke, in his *Fabrication of Louis XIV*, points out that while the crown sought to depict the monarchy in ways that enhanced its status, there was also a prevailing counter-culture that adopted less flattering visual imagery. "For the biblically-minded Protestants, he was not Solomon or David, but Herod of Phaeton."[80] Yet even up to the Revocation there were Huguenot artists at court who portrayed the majesty and authority of the French king. To an extent this reflected the loyalty of the principal Huguenot artists towards the crown, but it was also more generally characteristic of their co-religionists, who regarded the monarch as the defender and protector of their privileges. This was also a continuation of a long-standing association of the Huguenot artists with royal portraiture and images of kingship which began in the late 16th century at the court of Henry of Navarre.

While only a limited number of portraits survive from the late 16th and early 17th century, this genre of painting became increasingly popular. Collectors began to amass portraits and drawings; from 1561, Catherine de Medici formed the first collection in France, which included likenesses of members of the court as well as historical portraits. An inventory of the paintings of one of the Huguenot leaders, Philippe du Plessis-Mornay in 1619, included portraits of Protestant Reformers and princes from France and abroad, as well as the royal family, friends, his own family and ancestors.[81] Although portraiture was initially a rather elite genre, its appeal broadened with the production of prints derived from these paintings. This became increasingly important during the religious wars as they were used to promote the interests of Henry of Navarre, particularly after 1589 when they were used to emphasize the legitimacy of his claim to the French throne against the challenges of the Catholic League.[82]

Even before his accession, Henry of Navarre as the Huguenot leader recognized the importance of portraiture. During the 1580s, François Bunel painted a number of works at the court of Navarre, including portraits of the king and

---

80   Peter Burke, *The Fabrication of Louis XIV* (London: 1992), 135.
81   Cynthia Burlingham, "Portraiture as Propaganda. Printmaking during the Reign of Henri IV," in *The French Renaissance in Prints*, (ed.) Jacobson, 140; Fillon, "Galerie de portraits de Du Plessis-Mornay," 163–68, 212–16.
82   Burlingham, "Portraiture as Propaganda," 139–40.

his family; they included ten paintings of the monarch.[83] Some of Bunel's now lost portraits are only known through the later prints that were based on them. Some twenty-six prints of the king have been identified from between 1587 and 1595, all based on Bunel's work.[84] Although historians have been unable to establish conclusively whether François Bunel was a Huguenot, the fact that he was a member of the king of Navarre's household suggests that this was highly likely; the Protestant credentials of his brother Jacob are, however, more certain.[85]

Jacob Bunel became painter to the king and lodged at the Louvre from 1604 until his death a decade later. Following his accession, Henry IV commissioned a number of artistic projects including portraits and decorative schemes for the royal palaces. These included the depiction of the king as mythic heroes, and the portrait of *Henry IV as Mars* has been attributed to Bunel. It depicts the seated monarch in Roman dress with a laurel wreath, his feet symbolically resting on plates of armor and the weapons of war.[86] These classical allusions can also be seen in an engraving based on a lost Bunel painting, which depicts a bust of the king wearing armor but crowned with a laurel wreath like a triumphant Roman general.[87] At the Louvre, Bunel also worked on a series of paintings of the kings and queens of France. A drawing completed after 1607 reveals Bunel's portrayal of the king in a classical setting flanked by portraits of his two children (Figure 7.8). In this full length portrait, the king is standing, wearing a robe decorated with fleur-de-lis. His sword is sheathed at his side but at his feet are his breastplate, gauntlets and helmet. The image served to underscore the legitimacy of the Bourbon regime and its future continuity.[88] Although Bunel's art was not confined to this genre, his portraits of the monarch tend to be allegorical and focus on the attributes of kingship. Through prints, these paintings became an important part of the visual idealization of the crown that evolved more fully during the reign of Louis XIV.

The prevailing influence in French art in the early 17th century was Flemish, especially after the arrival of Frans Pourbus in Paris in 1609. One of these artists from the southern Netherlands was Ferdinand Elle, who originated from Mechelen and became painter in ordinary to the king. Whether Elle was a

---

83 Lafond, "François et Jacob Bunel," 560–73.
84 E.g. François Bunel, *Portrait of Henri of Navarre* (1589), British Museum, London (BM 1848, 0911.571); Burlingham, "Portraiture as Propaganda," 142.
85 Lafond, "François et Jacob Bunel," 578–79; Béguin, "Pour Jacob Bunel," 84.
86 Béguin, "Pour Jacob Bunel," 85; Burlingham, "Portraiture as Propaganda," 139, 142.
87 Jacob Bunel, *Henricus IV Franc. et Nava. Rex* (1605), British Museum, London (BM 1927, 1008.175).
88 Béguin, "Pour Jacob Bunel," 86–87.

FIGURE 7.8　　*Jacob Bunel*, Portrait of Henry IV.
COURTESY OF THE MUSÉE DU LOUVRE, PARIS. D.A.G.
PHOTO © RMN-GRAND PALAIS (MUSÉE DU LOUVRE)/
MICHÈLE BELLOT

convert to Protestantism is unclear, but all of his seven children were baptized at the Reformed temple at Charenton; his son and grandson, both named Louis Ferdinand Elle, were, as we saw, expelled from the Academy in 1681 for their faith.[89] Portraiture appears to have been their particular specialism, but as some of their careers overlapped there has been some confusion over the attribution of paintings to particular members of the family. Although Ferdinand Elle was a successful artist, only a limited number of his paintings have survived, but his commissions included works such as the group portrait of civic

---

89　　Benezit, *Dictionary of Artists*, 5: 161–62; Pannier, *L'Eglise réformée de Paris*, 414–15.

FIGURE 7.9 *Jean Morin after Ferdinand Elle,* Henry IV.
AILSA MELLON BRUCE FUND, ACCESSION NO.1984.25.20.
COURTESY NATIONAL GALLERY OF ART, WASHINGTON

dignitaries for which he received 400 francs in 1609 and a portrait of Henry IV (Figure 7.9). Furthermore, portraits of Louis XIII and Anne of Austria which were once considered the work of his son are now attributed to him (Figures 7.10 and 7.11). The two full-length portraits of the king and his consort depict them facing and looking directly at the viewer against an opulent but theatrical background. Behind the figures, rich red full-length curtains are parted to reveal a classical architectural setting reminiscent of an Italian loggia with the landscape beyond. The figure of the king partly conceals a classical façade, which could be that of Saint-Paul-Saint-Louis, the Jesuit church built on the orders of the monarch. Its inclusion emphasized the Catholicity of the French crown as

FIGURE 7.10 *Ferdinand Elle*, Louis XIII.
COURTESY CHISWICK HOUSE, LONDON. © ENGLISH HERITAGE

well as the significance of royal patronage of the Church. Although there are no overt symbols of monarchy, such as a crown or scepter, the confident gaze of the king and the richness of the setting emphasized their status and authority.

Although Ferdinand Elle's son, Louis, had a long career as a court painter, the significance of his work has only recently been recognized. Amongst the works of Louis Ferdinand Elle *père* is a portrait of Louis XIV from *c.* 1665; the king is shown as a military leader dressed in armor, while in the background there is a battle scene, probably a reference to the Flanders campaigns. His other works include portraits of members of the court and royal family, such as the queen Marie-Thérèse of Austria as St. Helena holding the cross; the king's cousin, La Grande Mademoiselle, before a garden; and his nephew Philippe d'Orléans. Probably his most important painting was commissioned by Louis XIV for a girls' school established by his second (and secret) wife, Madame de Maintenon, at Saint-Cyr in 1684. The portrait depicts Madame de Maintenon and her niece, with the institution in the background. It was completed shortly

FIGURE 7.11   *Ferdinand Elle,* Anne of Austria.
COURTESY OF CHISWICK HOUSE, LONDON. © ENGLISH HERITAGE

before Ferdinand Elle's death in 1689 but probably after he abjured his faith and was readmitted to the Academy in January 1686.[90]

The Elles were not the only Huguenot portraitists who painted the Catholic monarchs and members of their court. Henri Testelin completed several

---

90   Benezit, *Dictionary of Artists*, 5: 161–62; *Visages du Grand Siècle. Le portrait français sous le règne de Louis XIV, 1660–1715* (Paris: 1997), 55, 83, 93, 204–7.

FIGURE 7.12   *Henri Testelin,* Louis XIV.
COURTESY OF CHÂTEAUX DE VERSAILLES ET DE TRIANON, VERSAILLES.
PHOTO © RMN-GRAND PALAIS (CHÂTEAU DE VERSAILLES)/GÉRARD BLOT

portraits of Louis XIV. In fact, he submitted his *Louis XIV as a Child* at his admission to the Academy. This was one of the two portraits of the monarch executed by Testelin on the eve of the Fronde. Both depict the young king looking directly at the viewer, in the one portrait he is seated (Figure 7.12) and in the other standing, against a classical background, although this is partially concealed from the viewer by the rich hanging behind. The predominant feature of these two paintings is the ermine and rich blue of the velvet robe with gold fleurs-de-lis, which in the seated portrait cascades down on to a similar carpet in a different shade. Besides this robe, the young king also wears the gold chain of the Order of St. Michael around his neck and is holding either a baton or a scepter. In the seated portrait, Louis is also portrayed as protector of the arts with the foundation of the Academy, his scepter points to a globe and musical instrument, while in the foreground is an artist's palette.[91] These attributes are even more apparent in a portrait that Testelin completed for the Academy some twenty years later following the confirmation of their privileges by the king. In *Louis XIV as Protector of the Royal Academy of Painting and Sculpture*, the monarch is again seated on a dais with his flowing royal robes, his gaze engaging the viewer. Testelin has portrayed the king at the center of the portrait and provided a more elaborate setting with a classical arch in the background through which can be seen a fountain reminiscent of Rome while in the foreground are a sculptor's tools, a bust and drawings. The painting indicates the importance of the monarch but also evokes the classicism being advanced in France by the Academy.[92] In contrast, *Colbert Presenting to Louis XIV the Members of the Royal Academy of Sciences created in 1667* is a much more crowded painting as Testelin included the academicians being presented as well as Colbert and the king. Although the monarch is resplendent at the center of the painting, he is not wearing the royal robes; his gaze looks at the viewer while for Colbert and the academicians, he is the focus of their attention. In 1673, Testelin also exhibited portraits of the king and queen at the salon in Paris.[93] These royal portraits reinforced the status and authority of the French monarchy but several of them also underscored the importance of Louis XIV's patronage of the arts and in particular his support for the Academy in which Testelin played an important role.

While the political symbolism and the projection of a particular image of monarchy meant that these portraits were often an idealized representation of their subjects, the use of allegory meant that some painters stepped even further away from Calvin's ideal of realism or historical accuracy. During the early 1640s, Isaac Moillon painted *The Triumph of the French Monarchy* or *An Allegory of French Magnificence*, which continued the Flemish allegorical tradition, which was best represented by Rubens's Medici cycle of paintings for the Luxembourg Palace. Although Moillon's work is only known from a modello, it either relates to a specific event or to the good government of the regency of

---

91   Christopher Wright, *The French Painters of the Seventeenth Century* (London: 1985), 264.
92   Duro, *The Academy and the Limits of Painting*, 59–60.
93   *Visages du Grand Siècle*, 305.

Anne of Austria. Enthroned in the center is a female figure, the personification of France wearing the royal robes and holding a scepter in one hand and gesturing to the figure of justice. In the foreground, St. Michael wields his bloody sword, killing not only the dragon but crushing underfoot the symbol of discord. The painting also hints at the restoration of prosperity after the exhaustion of war. Although the particular circumstances behind this commission are unknown, the meaning of this eulogy to the French crown is clear.[94] Several later paintings by Huguenot artists demonstrate the importance of classical influences on the arts during the 17th century. In particular, these paintings depicted portraits being presented by Roman gods or mythological figures, thereby elevating the status of their subject. *Fame presenting France with the Portrait of Louis XIV* from about 1665 has been attributed to Ferdinand Elle *père*. It depicts an idealized portrait of the king being borne aloft and displayed by the allegorical figure of Fame.[95] A similar approach can be seen in a portrait of the Grand Condé which Nicolas Eude presented to the Academy in 1672; it depicts the prince's portrait being painted by Hercules, the canvas being borne by cherubs, while in the background is the figure of Victory. These paintings went beyond the political iconography of royal portraits to depict these princes as lauded by the gods for their achievements.[96]

Not all royal portraiture undertaken by Huguenot artists was quite so grandiose, such as the portrait of James, Duke of York by the miniaturist Louis du Guernier's dated 1656 (Figure 7.13). This is a relatively simple and understated portrait for someone associated with the court and the only indication that this was a person of quality is inferred by the elaborate embroidery of his gown. This may have been due to the prince's status at the time. Although James was heir presumptive to the English crown following the execution of his father Charles I, he was in exile and serving in the army of his cousin Louis XIV.

Unlike some of his co-religionists, Sébastien Bourdon did not paint members of the French court. Rather, in 1652 towards the end of the Fronde, the artist left for Stockholm. For a short period, he was painter to the court of the Lutheran Queen Christina of Sweden. He painted three portraits of the queen, which were also published as prints (Figure 7.14). The most significant of his Swedish portraits of Queen Christina was commissioned by the Spanish ambassador, and had been finished by June 1653. Bourdon showed the queen on horseback, in a hunting scene with a hawk, dogs, and a richly dressed page (Figure 7.15). While portrayal on horseback was an indication of high

---

94 Reynies and Laveissière (eds.), *Isaac Moillon*, 52–54.
95 *Visages du Grand Siècle*, 204.
96 *Visages du Grand Siècle*, 126, 208.

FIGURE 7.13
Louis Du Guernier, James, Duke of York, later James II, King of England, as a Young Man *(1656).*
© RIJKSMUSEUM, AMSTERDAM

social status and has been considered as a metaphor for monarchical power, Bourdon's other portraits of the queen reflected the difficulty that early modern painters found in conveying the authority of female rulers. The paintings generally lack monarchical symbols and even in the one that includes a scepter, it is barely visible. By contrast Bourdon's depiction of the heir apparent, Carolus Gustavus, reveals a much more martial and flamboyant figure wearing armor, with a rich blue sash across the breastplate, holding a baton with his hand resting on a helmet. Bourdon had returned to Paris by late 1653 and the following year Queen Christina abdicated, subsequently converting to Catholicism.[97] Bourdon was not the only Huguenot artist to work at the Scandinavian courts; a generation later Jacques d'Agar was invited to the Danish court by King Christian V. D'Agar had become a member of the Academy in 1675 and painter to the king but following his expulsion with other academicians he went into exile.[98]

The less formal style of portraiture in Bourdon's depictions of Queen Christina as well as the Italian influences regarding the modeling and lighting became the established form for middle-class French portraiture for the rest of the century.[99] Typical are the several portraits of the city consuls that Bourdon completed while in Montpellier in the late 1650s.[100] Besides this form of

---

97 Thuillier (ed.), *Sébastien Bourdon,* 292–306.
98 Benezit, *Dictionary of Artists,* 1: 149–50.
99 Wright, *The French Painters,* 81.
100 Thuillier, *Sébastien Bourdon,* 356–59.

FIGURE 7.14   *Robert Nanteuil after Sébastien Bourdon,* Queen Christina of Sweden.
© RIJKSMUSEUM, AMSTERDAM

portrait, the close links and family relationships between the Huguenot artists meant that they painted or engraved portraits of each other. The execution and presentation of these works was probably also a token of friendship between the artist and the sitter. Louis Ferdinand Elle *fils* even presented his portrait of the miniaturist and engraver Samuel Bernard as his piece for admission to the

FIGURE 7.15   *Sébastien Bourdon,* Queen Christina of Sweden.
COURTESY OF PRADO MUSEUM, MADRID. PHOTO © MUSEO NACIONAL DEL PRADO, MADRID. DIST. RMN-GP/IMAGE DU PRADO

Academy in 1681 (Figure 7.16). The artist is portrayed seated at his desk with a paintbrush or stylus in his hand. The portrait conveys the sense of his status as a successful artist through the rich gown that he is wearing. Bernard himself was responsible for the print of the painter and miniaturist Louis du Guernier, who is portrayed simply wearing a dark gown and resting against a plinth. This simplicity can also be seen in the self-portrait of Sébastien Bourdon. These paintings lack the bombastic approach of royal portraiture but conveyed a sense of the professionalism of these Huguenot artists.

FIGURE 7.16 *Louis Ferdinand Elle,* Samuel Bernard.
COURTESY OF CHÂTEAUX DE VERSAILLES ET DE TRIANON, VERSAILLES. PHOTO © RMN-GRAND PALAIS (CHÂTEAU DE VERSAILLES)/DANIEL ARNAUDET/JEAN SCHORMANS

5 Landscape and Still-life Painting

Two genres that were regarded as being particularly appropriate for Protestant painters were still life and landscape paintings. These would appear to conform to Calvin's injunction "that only those things are to be sculpted or painted which eyes are capable of seeing."[101] The two forms were popular in France, although they were not particularly significant genres for Huguenot artists. This may in part have been due to the influence of the Academy, which regarded

---

101 Calvin, *Institutes*, 1: 112.

still-life painting as being the lowest form of artistic representation.[102] It was therefore an entirely appropriate form of painting for an unmarried woman, such as Louise Moillon, but not for aspiring professional artists who were members of the Academy.

The principal still-life painters of the early 17th century were François Garnier and his step-daughter Louise Moillon. There is no doubt about Moillon's commitment to the Reformed faith, although in spite of her resistance and resilience following the Revocation she was forced to convert and died a Catholic in 1696. Garnier's religious adherence is principally inferred from his marriage into the Huguenot Moillon family and the baptism of his children at the Reformed temple near Paris.[103] About a dozen works have been identified as being by Garnier or have been attributed to the artist. These include his *Fruit on the Table: Gooseberries and Cherries* in the Louvre; the work is clearly signed and dated 1644. Lit from the foreground, the focal point of the painting is the two short branches of fruit. The leaves partly obscure the gooseberries underneath. While there are only a few leaves on the sprig of cherries, the foliage is as carefully observed. The creamy coloring of the table is suggestive of a tablecloth but is completely without any detail to distract from the depiction of the fruit.[104]

Garnier's work is overshadowed by that of his step-daughter, Louise Moillon.[105] The inventory of her mother's possessions at her death in 1630 included thirteen works by her young daughter.[106] Much of Moillon's *oeuvre* dates to the period before her marriage to the Huguenot timber merchant Etienne Girardot. Of the surviving sixty-nine signed works, forty-nine of them date to before 1641.[107] Moillon's still-life paintings are generally sparse. The dark background and simple foreground both with very few distinguishing features mean that the focus is on the center of the canvas. The baskets or Delft bowls containing different fruits—peaches, plums, strawberries, and grapes—are executed in precise detail (Figure 7.17). Some paintings include an extensive range of fruits, while some are much simpler compositions with just one or two items.[108] Although accomplished as an artist of still-life works, some of her paintings depicted fruits and vegetables in context. This can be seen in the 1630 painting *The Fruit Merchant* where the table is laden with apples, grapes,

---

102 Wright, *French Painters*, 96, 101.
103 Benezit, *Dictionary of Artists*, 5: 1350; Alsina, *Louyse Moillon*, 36.
104 Michel Faré, *La Nature morte en France. Son histoire et son évolution du XVIIe au XXe siècle* (Geneva: 1962), 1: 100, 2: figs. 3: 66, 67; Wright, *French Painters*, 186.
105 Alsina, *Louyse Moillon*, 41, 60.
106 Faré, *La Nature morte*, 1: 42; Alsina, *Louyse Moillon*, 334.
107 Alsina, *Louyse Moillon*, 60, 67, 326–29.
108 Alsina, *Louyse Moillon*, 67, *passim*.

FIGURE 7.17   *Louise Moillon,* Plate of Cherries, Grapes and a Melon.
COURTESY OF MUSÉE DU LOUVRE, PARIS. PHOTO © RMN-GRAND PALAIS
(MUSÉE DU LOUVRE)/MICHEL URTADO

melons, plums but also artichokes, cauliflower, cucumbers, pumpkins and a marrow. The focus of this composition, however, is the woman selecting peaches from the basket presented by the fruit seller.[109] Several others of her work around this date also contextualized the displays of fruit and vegetables.[110] It is an indication of Moillon's status that five of her paintings depicting various fruits entered the collection of the English king Charles I.[111]

Although Moillon sometimes contextualized these displays of fruit and vegetables, in neither her work nor that of Garnier was there an attempt to add symbolic elements beyond those needed to hold or display the fruit. Markedly different were the still life paintings of Samuel Bernard, a member of the Academy who in spite of its disdain for the genre painted several pictures of flowers in the mid-17th century. The opulence of his *Still Life with Violin, Ewer, and Bouquet of Flowers* is very different from the paintings of Garnier and Moillon. Unlike their work, the subject fills almost the entire canvas, while the

---

109   Alsina, *Louyse Moillon*, 114–16.
110   Alsina, *Louyse Moillon*, 118–21.
111   Alsina, *Louyse Moillon*, 335.

fruit and flowers are placed in a much richer and decorative context.[112] The contrast between the simple rendition of fruit and vegetables by Garnier and Moillon and the more flamboyant still life of Bernard underscores the problem of attempting to see this genre as representing a particularly Reformed artistic tradition.[113]

In contrast to the still-life paintings, the landscapes and architectural views painted by Jacques Rousseau were more fantastic than closely observed realism. He had been admitted to the Academy in 1662, later becoming treasurer, and exhibited three landscape paintings at the salon of 1673 as well as another work of architectural perspective. However, Rousseau is comparatively unknown as an artist. Some of his drawings have been attributed to his "tutor" and brother-in-law Herman van Swanevelt, while a number of his major commissions have been lost. Rousseau established his reputation in Paris through painting a number of landscape murals as decorative schemes for royal palaces and noble townhouses. These included "perspectives" which were painted on external walls, particularly in the Marais district, to create an illusion of greater distance and space in city gardens. While the vagaries of the northern climate led to the loss of many of these external views, a number of the interior murals were lost with the demolition or destruction of the buildings that they had enhanced. Rousseau's talents were recognized with several royal commissions including eight canvases for the Tuileries palace as well as *trompe l'oeil* architectural perspectives for Versailles. Even after his expulsion from the Academy in 1681 for his faith, he was called upon to decorate Louis XIV's new palace at Marly and in September 1686, he received his final sum of the 22,000 livres that he had been paid for his work on the king's orangery at Saint-Cloud (Figure 7.18). His drawings for the Saint-Cloud project depict a classical colonnade through which the garden beyond can be glimpsed. Another impression of Rousseau's decorative landscapes can be gleaned from a 19th-century view of the staircase that he completed at Montagu House, after the first duke had invited him to England in 1690. It emphasizes the Arcadian landscape he created but also the *trompe l'oeil* effect with its classical architectural details on the far wall. A contemporary observer regarded his work there as demonstrating "his excellentcy in the Art of painting & his great skill in Architecture and Landskipe." Besides several other noble commissions, Rousseau also worked at Hampton Court

---

112   Pierre Rosenberg, *France in the Golden Age. Seventeenth-Century Paintings in American Collections* (New York: 1982), 207, 222; Wright, *The French* Painters, 96, 101; Faré, *La Nature morte*, 1: 67, 2: plate 212.

113   Alain Mérot, *French Painting in the Seventeenth Century* (New Haven: 1995), 241.

FIGURE 7.18 *Jacques Rousseau*, Preliminary sketch for painted decoration probably for a drum or building of circular plan in the Great Greenhouse or the Orangery at the Chateau of Saint-Cloud in France.
© V&A

Palace for William III.[114] In the end, the Huguenot contribution to landscape and still life painting was limited and even the achievements of the greatest exponent of the latter form, Louise Moillon, were mainly produced over a short period.

6 Prints

During the early 17th century, there was a revolution in print production in France and at the forefront of this burgeoning industry was the Huguenot Abraham Bosse. In particular, he explored the various possibilities of this medium producing single sheet prints, broadsides, placards, almanacs, theses, book illustrations, books and pamphlets. Bosse's first dated works appeared in 1622 and it is estimated that by his death in 1676, he was responsible for more than 1500 such works and for illustrating some 120 books. In addition, he was the author of a treatise on etching and engraving, published in 1645. Although this drew on the technical innovations of Jacques Callot, it was the first such treatise on the subject and went through a number of editions as well as being translated into English and other languages. He published a treatise on perspective in 1648 and shortly afterwards was invited to teach this subject at the academy, although as engraving was regarded at the time as an artisan craft, he

---

114   "Rousseau, Jacques," in *Oxford Dictionary of National Biography*, 47: 965; Elspeth A. Evans, "Jacques Rousseau: A Huguenot Decorative Artist at the Courts of Louis XIV and William III," *PHSL* 22 (1970–76), 142–61; Cécile Bouleau, "Jacques Rousseau (1630–1693): un peintre de perspective aux Tuileries," *Bulletin de la Société de l'Histoire de l'Art Français* 1993 (1994), 52–61; Anne Charlotte Steland, "Early Drawings by Jacques Rousseau in the Manner of Herman van Swanevelt," *Master Drawings* 45 (2007), 167–86; Ulysse Robert, "Quittances de Peintres, Sculpteurs et Architectes Français (1555–1711)," *Nouvelles Archives de l'Art Français. Recueil de documents inédits* 4 (1876), 64; George Scharf, *Staircase of the Old British Museum* (1845), British Museum, London (BM 1862, 0614.311).

only became an honorary member. Differences with the academy over the importance of perspective led to his expulsion in 1661 and the start of his most significant period of print production and publishing.[115] Bosse's prominence and the scale of his production have tended to overshadow the work of some other Huguenot printmakers, such as Samuel Bernard and Etienne Picart, who also made an important contribution in the dissemination of images.

While Bosse tends to be labeled as the Huguenot printer, as Goldstein has recently shown, the importance of religious printmaking in this period meant that he did not confine himself to producing works aimed at an exclusively Protestant market. In fact, Bosse regularly produced prints of similar subjects to those of Catholic printers, such as images of the Virgin, the saints and religious scenes.[116] There were also frontispieces and title pages for divine offices and devotional works, such as the *Imitation of Christ* and St. Ignatius of Loyola's *Spiritual Exercises*, but he also produced them for Protestant books. These included French and Italian Bibles (1641), which had been translated by Jean Diodati, a refugee in Geneva, as well as a New Testament and two editions of the psalms.[117] He was also responsible for the frontispiece to *Consolation of the Soul against the Fears of Death* (1651) written by the Reformed minister at Charenton, Charles Drelincourt. Here Bosse drew upon the traditions of the *danse macabre* with the faithful before the grave, with the skeletal figure of death reaching with his scythe to gather them in.[118] Medieval themes, such as this, were used by Bosse in other prints to convey a religious message that had a resonance for both Catholics and Protestants.[119] Probably Bosse's most iconic and well-known image was the title-page for Thomas Hobbes' *Leviathan* published in 1651.[120]

The work of other Huguenot engravers also reflected the demand for Catholic prints, with works such as Samuel Bernard's engraving of Guido Reni's *Flight into Egypt* and Louis Testelin's *The Holy Family* (Figure 7.19). The latter included the non-biblical figure of the Virgin's mother, St. Anne. Unlike Bosse, Etienne Picart actually lived in Rome for several years, even signing some of his prints "Romanus."[121] His engravings also drew upon the city's religious art, such as his *Birth of the Virgin*, *Virgin Sewing*, and *Virgin in Glory* from Guido Reni's series of frescoes depicting the life of Virgin Mary in the chapel of the Annunciation in the Quirinal Palace. His other engravings advanced aspects of Catholic devotion,

---

115 Goldstein, *Print Culture in Early Modern France*, 1, 6.
116 Goldstein, *Print Culture in Early Modern France*, 86–87.
117 Join-Lambert and Préaud (ed.), *Abraham Bosse*, 21–22, 50–52, 216, 255, 296.
118 Join-Lambert and Préaud (ed.), *Abraham Bosse*, 52, 259.
119 Goldstein, *Print Culture in Early Modern France*, 87–88.
120 Join-Lambert and Préaud (ed.), *Abraham Bosse*, 258–59.
121 Haag, *La France Protestante*, 8: 228; Benezit, *Dictionary of Artists*, 10: 1357; Hunt, Jacob, and Mijnhardt, *The Book that Changed Europe*, 116–18.

FIGURE 7.19   *Louis Testelin,* The Holy Family with St. Anne.
AILSA MELLON BRUCE FUND 2014.37.4. COURTESY OF THE NATIONAL
GALLERY OF ART, WASHINGTON

such as Antonio Corregio's *Mystic Marriage of St. Catherine*. This showed the infant Christ sitting on the Virgin's knees placing a ring on St. Catherine's finger, with St. Sebastian looking on. (This was also the subject of a print by Bourdon.) Another print was of Carlo Maratti's *The Virgin of the Immaculate Conception* (1665), in which the Virgin stands on a globe holding the infant Christ who spears a serpent with a cross, surrounded by angels in the clouds. It was dedicated to the queen as the founder of the order of the Immaculate Conception.[122]

There were certainly some religious themes that were more attractive to Protestant audiences and this was particularly the case with some of the moralizing subjects printed by Bosse. The etching *The Benediction* has been regarded as having Protestant overtones; it depicts a family in a relatively simple setting gathered around a table saying grace before a meal (Figure 7.20).

122   M. Huber and C.C.H. Rost, *Manuel des curieux et des amateurs de l'art, contenant une notice des principaux graveurs,* vol. 7 (9 vols. Zurich: 1797–1808), 259–60; British Museum, London: Prints 1874,0808.1836, 1837,0408.176, 1874,0808.1689; Thuillier (ed.), *Sébastien Bourdon,* 350.

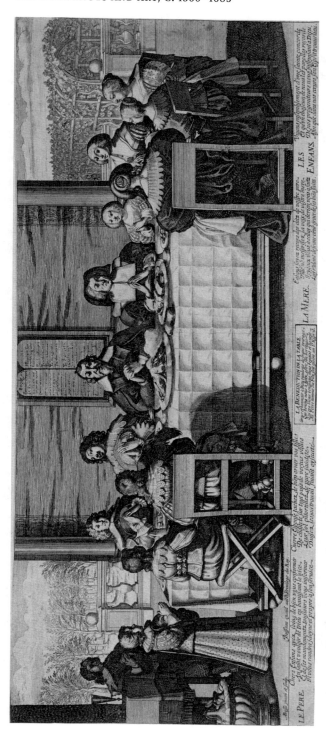

FIGURE 7.20 *Abraham Bosse*, Benediction of the Table.
© RIJKSMUSEUM, AMSTERDAM

FIGURE 7.21   *Abraham Bosse*, The Wise Virgins at their Devotions.
AILSA MELLON BRUCE FUND 2003.127.1.1. COURTESY OF THE NATIONAL
GALLERY OF ART, WASHINGTON

The head of the household is seated in the center of the composition beneath the tablets of the Ten Commandments and the accompanying verse suggests that he is fulfilling his responsibilities by reminding them of their moral and spiritual obligations.[123] The Ten Commandments also appear in a less Spartan interior in an etching in the series on the Wise and Foolish Virgins (Figure 7.21). In *The Wise Virgins at their Devotions*, the Ten Commandments appear above the fireplace presented by Moses, in a manner not unlike the Decalogue boards in Huguenot temples, although before it there is a crucifix suggesting a more Catholic environment. While this might suggest a degree of confessional ambiguity in the scene, here and also in *The Benediction*, the biblical reference to Exodus 20 can be clearly seen. This accorded the Reformed enumeration of the Ten Commandments with its condemnation of making graven images as the second commandment, in contrast to the Catholic text based on Deuteronomy. It is a subtle distinction but nonetheless an indication of Bosse's Huguenot faith, but not one which probably exercised many viewers as the Ten Commandments were fundamental to both confessions.

123   Goldstein, *Print Culture in Early Modern France*, 89–90.

There was also a religious dimension to some of the prints that Bosse produced relating to the French monarchy. Some of them served to demonstrate the piety and Catholicity of the crown such as *Saint Louis appearing to Louis XIII* (c. 1628), which included the façade of the Parisian church of Saint-Paul-Saint-Louis, or the king kneeling in prayer before a crucifix (1642). Following the birth of the dauphin in 1638, Louis XIII consecrated the nation to the Virgin Mary (Figure 7.22). In an image—*The Joy of France*—which may have been intended for an almanac, Bosse portrayed the king and queen kneeling in their royal robes before an altar above which appears the Virgin Mary amidst billowing clouds and rays of light. The king presents the crown and scepter, while the queen lifts up the heir to the throne. The dauphin's birth, so many years after the royal marriage, led to his being given the epithet Dieudonné (God-given).[124] Such religious allegory also accompanied the birth of Louis XIV's son, with Bosse's *The Dauphin in the Arms of Faith and between Might and Justice* (1662).[125]

As has been seen, political portraits were important in asserting the power and authority of the crown. Not all of the prints produced, however, conveyed a positive image of the monarchy. During the Fronde, Bosse and Louis Testelin were responsible for engravings that were critical of the regency government of the Queen Mother and Cardinal Mazarin. Testelin's drawing *Return of the Bread of Gonesse* (1649) was engraved by Samuel Bernard and depicted the defeat of the Prince of Condé's attempted blockade of Paris. Bread is brought into the city from Gonesse in a triumphal procession by the armed peasants, who rather than the royal forces are the victorious figures. The print fitted the contemporary evocation of the peasantry during the period of the Fronde.[126] Bosse's etching *David and Goliath* (1651) portrayed the head of Goliath on the ground beside his sword while the young victor holds up his slingshot or *fronde* (Figure 7.23). The accompanying verse attacked what the *frondeurs* considered Cardinal Mazarin's exploitation of the French state by reference to his alleged homosexuality.[127] While the prevailing theme in Huguenot print production reflected loyalty to the monarchy, there were moments of crisis when Reformed artists were prepared to criticize France's political leaders.

The sheer diversity and range of print production in early 17th-century France means that only some of the areas in which Huguenot printmakers

---

124   Join-Lambert and Préaud (ed.), *Abraham Bosse*, 84, 199–200, 220; Goldstein, *Print Culture in Early Modern France*, 108–10.
125   Join-Lambert and Préaud (ed.), *Abraham Bosse*, 273–74.
126   Olson, *Poussin and France*. 196.
127   Join-Lambert and Préaud (ed.), *Abraham Bosse*, 256–57; Goldstein, *Print Culture in Early Modern France*, 116–17.

FIGURE 7.22 *Abraham Bosse*, Vows of the King and Queen to the Virgin.
COURTESY OF THE ELISHA WHITTELSEY COLLECTION, THE ELISHA WHITTELSEY FUND, 1951, THE METROPOLITAN MUSEUM OF ART, NEW YORK

FIGURE 7.23 *Abraham Bosse,* David with the head of Goliath.
JOSEPH PULITZER BEQUEST, 1917, COURTESY OF THE
METROPOLITAN MUSEUM OF ART, NEW YORK

made a contribution can be explored here. A pivotal figure in this industry was Abraham Bosse, whose own output exemplified the rapid growth and breadth of print production during the 17th century. Although Bosse is the best known of the Huguenot printmakers, the contribution of his co-religionists to this field should also not be overlooked. This focus on religious themes as well as political imagery has shown that Bosse and others did not limit themselves to a Protestant market, but also printed images that appealed to Catholics. As the Huguenots were only a minority of the population, this must have made sound commercial sense. In the political field, their work continued to express Huguenot loyalties although this was not unequivocal as some prints published at the time of the Fronde illustrated. There were therefore some clear parallels between print production and the work of Huguenot artists, some of whose paintings circulated more widely in the form of prints.

7   Conclusion

This survey of Huguenot artists and their work has shown that their output was not limited to a particular artistic genre. They made significant contributions to a number of different areas of 17th-century painting. The most talented and skilled painters aspired to, and produced, works that depicted historical themes, which was regarded as the highest form in the artistic hierarchy, as well in the slightly less well-esteemed area of portraiture. Relatively few Huguenot artists worked on still-life painting, considered to be the lowest level of artistic production. This was a classification of painting that was reinforced during the second half of the 17th century by the Academy, in which a number of Huguenots played a role, as part of their professionalization of the arts. Like other artists, the Huguenots painted according to their particular talents as well as the commercial demands and artistic conventions of the period, and were not constrained by their own religious beliefs. They did not refuse important commissions from Catholic churches and institutions. To have done so would have closed off from them one of the most important sources of artistic patronage in this period. There are occasional hints that the artists sought to disassociate themselves from overt statements of Catholic triumphalism, such as Bourdon's altarpiece for Montpellier cathedral, but it did not prevent them from completing similar projects. In other genres, these artists appear to have been aware of the commercial importance of producing devotional prints and paintings for a primarily Catholic audience, as their own co-religionists formed only a small minority of the population. There were, however, other works which could be seen as appealing to both confessions. Paintings such as Bourdon's *Solomon Sacrifices to the Idols* or Bosse's moralizing prints could be seen as depictions of particular events, but they were also capable of various interpretations that appealed to either a Protestant or a Catholic audience.

The religious beliefs of the Huguenot artists do not seem to have prevented them being chosen to undertake significant commissions not only for the Catholic Church, such as the "Mays," but also the crown. These included paintings for royal chapels and palaces as well as portraits of the Bourbon kings, their family and members of the court. While there were some critical prints produced by Huguenot artists at the time of the Fronde, they generally recognized the importance of royal patronage and were still painting portraits up to the eve of the Revocation. This may also reflect the fundamental loyalty of the Huguenots to the crown as the guardian of their religious privileges. It appears that even after his expulsion from the Academy, Jacques Rousseau's talent led him to be employed in the decoration of Marly and Saint-Cloud in spite of his religious convictions. Similar attitudes may explain Louis Chéron's completion of "Mays" in 1687 and 1689. Their particular artistic skills appear to have outweighed any difficulties that may have been posed by their religious convictions in the minds of their clients.

The work of these Huguenot artists suggests that they were able to separate their own religious convictions from their professional career. Contrary to the decrees of the Reformed Churches, they produced work that advanced the Catholic faith or depicted scenes of questionable veracity from the lives of the saints. It is unclear how this compartmentalization of their lives affected the relationship of these artists with the Reformed Churches. Certainly Bosse, Bourdon and others continued to baptize their children at the Huguenot temple at Charenton, stood as godparents to each other's children and were eventually interred in the Reformed cemetery. The comments of some contemporaries suggest that these artists were able to adopt a pragmatic approach that balanced their religious convictions and their art. André Félibien noted, for example, that the miniaturist Louis du Guernier "never spoke of his religion; if he spoke of ours, it was in a wise and honest manner." In a *mémoire* read to the academy after the Revocation, in 1692, Louis Testelin was observed to have had "the misfortune of having always lived in the Calvinist religion, but he had not the stubborn impulses that are common to people infected by these errors, and avoided seditious controversy."[128] In the early 1680s, the pragmatic approach taken by these artists was challenged first by their expulsion from the Academy in 1681 and then by the revocation of the Edict of Nantes four years later. This forced these artists to make a choice between their professional careers and their religious faith. As has been noted some artists did abjure their faith after being expelled from the Academy and were subsequently readmitted, but others such as Jean Michelin, Henri Testelin and Jacob d'Agard sought exile. Louise Moillon remained in France but her family was persecuted for its continued adherence to the Reformed faith.

---

128 Félibien, *Entretien sur les Vies*, 4: 209–10; De Saint-Georges, "Louis Testelin," 224. The accuracy of the *mémoire* has led to the suggestion that Testelin's widow might have provided some of the information. Simonneau, "Louis Testelin," in *Dessins français aux XVIIe et XVIIIe siècles*, (ed.) Sainte Fare Garnot 181–82, fn. 4.

Although this survey has necessarily concentrated on the Parisian artistic elite, it has illustrated the significance of the Huguenots for the visual arts in 17th-century France. Their contribution was not confined to a single genre but encompassed a range of different forms of painting that reflected their particular skills and professional aspirations. Their artistic production illustrates the difficulties that exist in attempts to relate Calvin's comments on the visual arts to the work of adherents of the Reformed faith. There is no commonalty that allows their work to be defined as "Reformed" or "Huguenot" art. The Huguenot artists were pragmatists and professionals whose religion did not constrain their production until they were forced in the early 1680s to choose between their faith and their careers.

CHAPTER 8

The Revocation of the Edict of Nantes and the *Désert*

Didier Boisson

1   Introduction

In October 1685, the Edict of Fontainebleau rescinded the Edict of Nantes and put an end to an unprecedented period of more than eighty years of coexistence between the French Catholic majority and the Reformed minority. Still, the rights of the Huguenots had undergone two periods of considerable reevaluation at the hands of royal authorities. First, during the reign of Louis XIII, the decade of the 1620s ended with the signing of the Peace of Alès and the Edict of Nîmes which, while confirming the Edict of Nantes, henceforth prohibited the Huguenots from possessing fortified places and from holding their political assemblies. This marked the end of the so-called Huguenot party. Secondly, beginning in 1656 the government of Louis XIV progressively robbed the Edict of Nantes of real meaning through both legislative measures and the use of violence.[1]

The revocation of the Edict of Nantes marked for the Huguenots the beginning of more than a century during which the Reformed Church had no legal existence, an ordeal that only ended with the French Revolution. This was the period called the Desert, a reference to the wandering and suffering of the Israelites after their departure from Egypt. A *Désert improvisé* (improvised Desert) (1685–1715) was characterized by energetic persecution and unorganized clandestine Reformed worship. It was followed by a *Désert discipliné* (disciplined Desert) (from 1715 to the 1760s), distinguished by the clandestine campaign to reestablish the Reformed Churches of France despite government repression. Finally, there was a *Désert toléré* (tolerated Desert) (from about 1770 to 1789) following the Calas affair, which led Louis XVI to sign an edict of toleration in 1787, granting the Reformed not freedom of worship, but at least civil

---

1   Regarding these developments, see Jean Orcibal, *Louis XIV et les protestants* (Paris: 1951); Janine Garrisson, *L'édit de Nantes et sa révocation* (Paris: 1985); Élisabeth Labrousse, *"Une foi, une loi, un roi?" Essai sur la Révocation de l'édit de Nantes* (Paris: 1985); Roger Zuber and Laurent Theis (eds.), *La Révocation de l'édit de Nantes et le protestantisme français en 1685* (Paris: 1985).

status.[2] These years, from 1656 to 1789, stand at the heart of this essay. To understand them better it is important to keep in mind the differences, unmistakable in the sources, between northern and southern France, urban and rural Protestantism, the notables and the common people, and also between the two groups enforcing the repression, namely the royal government (and its representatives) and the Catholic Church.

2   The Revocation of the Edict of Nantes

Following the death of Cardinal Mazarin in 1661, Louis XIV was not excessively occupied with religious issues. Although uniformity of faith was desirable, royal policy initially focused on foreign matters. Still, the king was aware of the economic importance of the Reformed community and its loyalty to the crown during the Fronde. He also understood that Protestants no longer posed a threat to the kingdom. In his *Memoirs* Louis XIV nevertheless expressed a wish to adhere scrupulously to the Edict of Nantes, by which he meant that whatever was not expressly allowed by law would be prohibited.[3] The king thus decided that the best way to secure uniformity of faith was through legal means, particularly as the Catholic Church was putting pressure on him. Also, throughout the 1660s and 1670s, the assemblies of clergy were demanding greater legal strictures on Protestants. The Catholic clergy saw the Edict of Nantes as a set of privileges favoring Huguenots and that the king had the right to withdraw them.[4] The *parlements* and the intendants were two other effective conduits for royal power. The *parlements*, convinced of the ideas undergirding the Catholic Reformation, intensified their rulings against Protestants within their particular jurisdictions. The intendants, for their part, were generally faithful executors of royal decisions. Between 1661 and 1679, those most noted for their anti-Protestant zeal were Nicolas Foucault, intendant of Montauban from 1674 to 1684, Henri Daguesseau, who held office in Languedoc

---

2   Samuel Mours and Daniel Robert, *Le protestantisme en France du XVIIIe siècle à nos jours* (Paris: 1972); Didier Boisson and Hugues Daussy, *Les protestants dans la France moderne* (Paris: 2006); Patrick Cabanel, *Histoire des protestants en France, XVIe-XXIe siècle* (Paris: 2012).

3   Louis XIV, *Mémoires pour l'instruction du Dauphin*, (ed.) Pierre Goubert (Paris: 1992). See also the works of Jacques-Bénigne Bossuet, particularly his *Discours sur l'histoire universelle* (1681).

4   Bernard Dompnier, *Le venin de l'hérésie. Image du protestantisme et combat politique au XVIIe siècle* (Paris: 1985); Pierre Blet, *Les Assemblées du clergé et Louis XIV, de 1670 à 1693* (Rome: 1972).

from 1673 to 1685, and René de Marillac in Poitiers from 1673 to 1684.[5] This same zeal flourished among the *dévots*, all the more because they felt themselves to be supported and encouraged by the authorities.

The royal declaration of 18 July 1656 marked a turning-point in the monarchy's anti-Protestant policy, even though the decree was not put into effect until April 1661. Upon the request of any Catholic clergyman, two commissioners, one Catholic and one Protestant, would be sent to a site of Reformed worship. They would be accompanied by a member of the Catholic clergy and charged with application of the Edict of Nantes "*à la rigueur*."[6] Their task was to determine whether worship was being conducted according to the terms of the Edict. Catholics hoped thereby to eliminate places of Reformed worship.[7] Some Protestant temples were razed to the ground on the pretext that they were too close to the Catholic parish church, since hearing Psalm singing might offend Catholics. Others had to be demolished because they were "illegally" built within the town walls. The various Reformed churches had to provide written proof of their right to exist under the provisions of the Edict of Nantes. Some found it impossible to comply. When the two commissioners disagreed, the king's council had the power to act.[8] It frequently decided in favor of the Catholic commissioner, but in some cases it made no decision and the temple's fate remained "*en partage*," in effect, at a stalemate. Some temples remained in this state of suspension for more than a decade, until they were destroyed just before the Revocation.[9]

There was also extensive legislation between 1661 and 1669 aimed at restricting the rights of Protestants. Pastors were forbidden to preach except in the localities where they lived; the Reformed faithful could not sing Psalms in the

---

[5] The activity of the intendants can be studied above all in the Archives Nationales (série G⁷) and in the Archives Départementales (série C). See also Anette Smedley-Weill, *Les intendants de Louis XIV* (Paris: 1995).

[6] On the subject of the commissioners of the Edict, see the essay by Jérémie Foa in this volume.

[7] For the anti-Protestant legislation see Léon Pilatte, *Édits, déclarations et arrests concernans la Religion P. Réformée (1662–1751)* (Paris: 1885).

[8] The royal decisions have been published and are also found in the online catalogue in the Bibliothèque nationale de France. See also Luc Daireaux, "'Ceux de la RPR.' Les protestants vus à travers les actes royaux, XVIᵉ-XVIIᵉ siècles," in *Enoncer/dénoncer l'autre. Discours et représentations du différend confessionnel à l'époque moderne*, (ed.) Chrystel Bernat (Turnhout: 2012), 251–63. The numerous prosecutions of Reformed communities are mostly found particularly in the Archives Nationales, série TT.

[9] Solange Deyon, "La destruction des temples," in *La Révocation*, (eds.) Zuber and Theis, 239–58.

streets; burials could take place only at dawn or dusk and the number of those attending was limited first to 30, then to 10.[10] The Protestant school system was also attacked. Pont-de-Veyle's school was closed in 1662, and those at Castres and Nîmes instructed to be shared with the Jesuits. All these restrictions were reiterated in the declaration of 2 April 1666. Three years later there was a brief respite. Persecution, both of the Catholic Jansenists and the Protestants diminished. The declaration of 1 February 1669 also revoked certain measures taken since 1661. Preparations for war with the United Provinces and, after 1672, the war itself diverted the king's attention from domestic concerns. But this did not mean that persecution ceased entirely. For example, Paul Pellisson, a Huguenot who had converted to Catholicism in 1670, established a conversion fund, officially known as the *Caisse des Économats*, in 1676. The notion was that by financially compensating "New Converts" or "New Catholics," that is those who had renounced Protestantism, conversions would be more readily obtainable. But this attempt at "buying consciences" proved a failure.[11] And amid these developments, Protestants did not remain inactive. They defended themselves by sending delegates to the royal court, by having their deputy general, the Marquis de Ruvigny,[12] intervene on their behalf, and, when he was considered too timid, by drafting their own memoirs or ultimately by emigrating.

In 1679, with the return of peace after the Dutch War, recourse to legal oppression resumed with considerable intensity. Between 1679 and 1685, anti-Protestant legislation followed several paths. The authorities attacked institutions first, with surveillance of the churches' provincial synods by a Catholic commissioner, then suppression of the Reformed academies between 1681 and 1685. Next, discriminatory measures were enacted: a ban on mixed marriages in 1680, permission for judges to visit sick Huguenots to determine in which faith they wished to die, and a prohibition on emigration. Then the professions open to Huguenots were limited. The Reformed faithful were progressively excluded from all administrative and judicial offices, from the army and navy, and from numerous occupations. They had to abjure if they wished to continue in their profession.[13] Legislation on conversions also became still more restrictive. In 1680 Catholics were forbidden to convert to the Reformed faith.

---

10   Pilatte, *Edits, declarations* 9–28.
11   On this question, see the various studies by Janine Garrisson and Élisabeth Labrousse.
12   Solange Deyon, *Du loyalisme au refus: les protestants français et leur député général entre la Fronde et la Révocation de l'édit de Nantes* (Lille: 1976).
13   In his study *Professions et métiers interdits, un aspect de l'histoire de la Révocation de l'édit de Nantes* (Groningen: 1960), A.T. van Deursen examines the various professions and carefully cites his sources.

Finally, pastors were targeted. In 1683 penalties were established for pastors who accepted abjurations from Catholicism.[14] Each time, the objective was the same: to force the Huguenots to convert by limiting the practice of the Calvinist faith when a violation of the law occurred. And the suppression of places of worship intensified.[15]

The role of the intendants was important in implementing the royal legislation. In 1681 the intendant of Poitou, Marillac, asked that dragoons be brought in and lodged with Protestant families to prompt their conversion. These were the infamous *dragonnades*. From May to November 1681, soldiers crisscrossed Poitou. According to witnesses, they sought to elicit a family's conversion, and were often accompanied by Capuchins. Once their objective was reached, they moved into the house next door. Numerous Huguenots were ruined by the soldiers, who stole and vandalized. The results were impressive; perhaps 30,000 abjurations occurred within a few months. Even in areas not visited by the dragoons, abjurations were obtained simply out of fear of their arrival.[16] The royal authorities also found a willing ally in the clergy. On 1 July 1682, an extraordinary assembly of the clergy published the *Avertissement pastoral*. This text was an appeal for the conversion of Protestants and received the support of the monarchy. It was to be read to each Reformed church's consistory in the presence of the intendant and the bishop of the locale or their representatives. It was read first to the consistory of Charenton near Paris on 20 September 1682. In their response, the pastors contested the power that the bishops were usurping over the Reformed faithful. The *Avertissement pastoral* had no effect on the conversion of Huguenots, however.[17]

Another reaction was that of the Nîmes attorney Claude Brousson. He proposed that worship be conducted, beginning on the last Sunday in June 1683, in

---

14   Pilatte, *Edits, declarations* 133–34.

15   The legal actions are found chiefly in série TT of the Archives Nationales. Numerous regional studies have also been published. See, for example, Luc Daireaux, *"Réduire les huguenots." Protestants et pouvoirs en Normandie au XVIIe siècle* (Paris: 2010).

16   *Journal de Jean Migault ou malheurs d'une famille protestante du Poitou victime de la révocation de l'édit de Nantes (1682–1689)* (Paris: 1995); Yves Krumenacker, *Les protestants du Poitou au XVIIIe siècle (1681–1789)* (Paris: 1998); Élie Benoist, *Histoire de l'édit de Nantes* 5 vols. (Delft: 1693–1695).

17   Élisabeth Labrousse (ed.), *Avertissement aux protestants des provinces* (Paris: 1986); Didier Boisson, "Un affrontement religieux feutré: la lecture de l'*Avertissement pastoral* devant les consistoires," in *Les affrontements. Usages, discours et rituels*, (eds.) Frédérique Pitou and Jacqueline Sainclivier (Rennes: 2008), 215–26. One of the major texts is Claude Pajon, *Remarques sur l'Avertissement pastoral, avec une Relation de ce qui se passa au consistoire d'Orléans assemblé à Bionne, quand il y fut signifié* (Amsterdam: 1685).

all the places where it had been forbidden in Languedoc and Dauphiné. But this proved a failure. Repression was not slowed, especially in Dauphiné, Vivarais and the Cévennes. Pastors, in particular, were targeted. Some went into exile or abjured, while others were imprisoned or executed.[18] In fact, the developments revealed a distinction between the communities in the north of the kingdom and those in the south, the so-called Midi. While the former, more dispersed among a Catholic majority, certainly condemned this initiative, the Huguenots of the Midi appeared more inclined toward active resistance. The division between these two major Protestant groupings in France was not only geographical, but also social, between the north dominated by the notables and southern communities where ordinary folk had a powerful voice.

The pace of events accelerated in 1685. Legislative acts proliferated and penalties became heavier. Prosecutions were more numerous, the result of infractions committed by communities. Worship would then be proscribed and the temples closed, indeed destroyed. Worse still, the *dragonnades* returned and spread. In May 1685, they proliferated in Béarn. Other regions, such as Languedoc, Aunis, Saintonge, Dauphiné and Burgundy, were affected between June and September. Violence induced mass conversions everywhere. The situation appeared favorable for the chancellor Le Tellier to propose the Edict of Fontainebleau to the King on 17 October; it was signed the next day. The preamble justified the Revocation by the statement that "the majority of our adherents to the *Religion Prétendue Réformée* (RPR or So-called Reformed Religion) have embraced Catholicism." The text comprised twelve short articles. Article 1 revoked the Edicts of Nantes and Nîmes and ordered the destruction of all Protestant temples. All exercise of the Reformed religion was forbidden, along with the conduct of schools. Parents were required to have their children baptized by the local parish priest. Reformed pastors had the choice of emigrating or converting, but exile was forbidden to all other Huguenots. Penalties were established for relapse into Protestantism. The edict ended with an ambiguous promise:

> Moreover, the aforesaid members of the *Religion Prétendue Réformée*, while we wait until it pleases God to enlighten them like the rest, may remain in the towns and villages of our kingdom and continue their business and retain their property here without being troubled or hindered on account of the said *Religion Prétendue Réformée*, on condition of their

---

18   See the works of Claude Brousson, in particular *Estat des Reformez de France* (Cologne: 1684), but also those published after the Revocation, such as *La manne mystique du désert* (Amsterdam: 1695).

not practicing it nor meeting under the pretext of prayers or worship in the said religion.[19]

According to Élisabeth Labrousse, this article was nothing but "deceit" and "dust in the eyes," and had no objective other than letting people "believe that *devotio privata* could continue in France," and "moderating the indignation" that the Revocation inspired among the foreign Protestant powers.[20] The *Parlement* of Paris registered the Edict of Fontainebleau on 22 October. Only Alsace escaped the effect of the legislation because of the Treaty of Westphalia (1648), which was still in force and which the King promised to respect.

The Revocation came into its own when Louis XIV was at the height of his power and influence in Europe. The Truce of Regensburg signed with Spain and the Empire in 1684 was a resounding diplomatic victory, allowing Louis XIV to retain the principal annexations he had made since 1679, Strasbourg in particular. The King and his court subsequently lived in an atmosphere of increasing piety. In 1683, Louis XIV secretly married Madame de Maintenon, "who succeeded in transforming the sovereign into a devout despot."[21] Finally, the death of Colbert in the same year altered the governmental equilibrium. From then on, the chancellor Michel Le Tellier and his son, the Marquis de Louvois, secretary of state for war, were the decisive influences in favor of a harsher anti-Protestant policy.

The European Protestant states unanimously condemned the revocation of the Edict of Nantes. In the immediate aftermath of the Revocation, various published accounts examined the pre-Revocation repression. Elie Benoist, the former pastor of Alençon exiled in the United Provinces, wrote the most famous.[22] Written pleas by pastors and Reformed literary figures increased–even before the Edict of Fontainebleau–asking that freedom of conscience be maintained in the realm. Henri Basnage de Beauval, an attorney at Rouen, published *La tolérance des religions* in 1684 in Amsterdam; it emphasized the need for confessional competitiveness, since, as he wrote, a church "that has no enemies to repel...necessarily falls as soon as it imagines it cannot fall."[23] In 1686 Pierre Bayle, a refugee in Rotterdam since 1681, published a pamphlet

---

19   Pilatte, *Edits, déclarations* 244–45.
20   Labrousse, "Une foi, une loi, un roi?" 184.
21   Pierre Chaunu, "La décision royale (?): un système de la Révocation," in *La Révocation*, (eds.) Zuber and Theis, 13–28.
22   Benoist, *Histoire de l'édit de Nantes*. See also the chapter by David van der Linden in the present volume.
23   Henri Basnage de Beauval, *Tolérance des religions*, (ed.) É. Labrousse (New York: 1970).

Ce que c'est que la France toute catholique sous le règne de Louis le Grand, in which he denounced the attitude of the Catholics toward the "dragoon violence," and later his *Commentaire philosophique sur ces paroles de Jésus-Christ*, "*Contrains-les d'entrer.*" He made the distinction between an informed understanding (that of the Calvinists) and an erroneous understanding, but he thought it essential to grant freedom of conscience and freedom of worship to those who had an erroneous understanding, namely to the other Christian confessions, to Judaism, to Islam and even to atheism. It was the state's duty to establish this civil toleration.[24]

3   The *Désert improvisé*

The revocation of the Edict of Nantes, the *dragonnades*, the conversions and the departures abroad to Refuge left Reformed communities significantly weakened and without substantial guidance due to the abjuration or emigration of pastors and the proscription of Reformed institutions. Yet despite the persecution, which certainly did not diminish after the Edict of Fontainebleau, there emerged various forms of resistance.

Officially, uniformity of belief had been reestablished in France. But the authorities were well aware that this uniformity was only a façade. The Edict of Fontainebleau was therefore only another stage in the anti-Protestant repression; the legislative offensive quickened. The declaration of 29 April 1686 again condemned individuals who relapsed. During the War of the League of Augsburg, Louis XIV, fearing a revolt, decided to disarm the New Converts. The ordinance of 16 October 1688 required them to surrender their arms. The declaration of 13 December 1698 acknowledged the failure of the Edict of Fontainebleau in that the authorities recognized the persistence of Reformed worship. It asked bishops to take action to ensure the genuine conversion of New Converts and to establish schools to educate their children. Finally, after a legislative hiatus from 1702 to 1713, the final years of Louis XIV's reign saw a resurgence of repressive measures, in particular the declaration of 8 March 1715. Henceforth for a person to be designated as relapsed, it was not necessary

---

24   The bibliography for Pierre Bayle is immense. Two principal works are Élisabeth Labrousse, *Pierre Bayle* (Paris: 1996) and Hubert Bost, *Pierre Bayle* (Paris: 2006). Numerous editions of Pierre Bayle have been published; see *Ce que c'est que la France toute catholique*, (ed.) É. Labrousse (Paris: 1973); *De la tolérance. Commentaire philosophique sur ces paroles de Jésus-Christ "Contrains-les d'entrer,"* (ed.) Jean-Michel Gros (Paris: 1992). The Voltaire Foundation of Oxford is editing his correspondence.

to have abjured the *Religion Prétendue Réformée* and then returned to it. Individuals only needed to be among those "subjects born of parents who were of the *Religion Prétendue Réformée* before or after the revocation of the Edict of Nantes, and who, during their illnesses, had refused to receive the sacraments of the Church from *curés*, vicars, or other priests and had declared that they wished to continue and die in the *Religion Prétendue Réformée*."[25]

The relapsed were especially persecuted. They were mostly individuals who refused to receive the Catholic last sacrament from a *curé* on their deathbeds. After 1686, the corpses of relapsed Protestants were tried and condemned to be dragged through the streets on a rack and thrown on the refuse heap. In addition, their property was confiscated. After 1700, the spectacle of dragging a dead body on a rack ended, but the prosecutions continued.[26] There were also constant searches for clandestine assemblies. The authorities sought to arrest the preachers who conducted them and the pastors who were crisscrossing the kingdom. Preachers and pastors could be condemned to death, or sent to the galleys or to prison (for example the fortress of Ham in the north, the castles at Saint-Malo, Angers and Niort, and the Tour de Constance at Aigues-Mortes). Parents, moreover, who did not send their children to catechism or to Mass, could be imprisoned. Children could be seized and delivered to Catholic relatives, to hospitals, or to convents.[27] Finally, some 1,550 Protestants were sent to the galleys "for the faith" between 1680 and 1748, although most of the sentencing took place before 1715. Participation in a clandestine assembly was the foremost reason for condemnation (52.6 per cent). The "obstinate," that is those who refused to convert, were the ones who were in particular dispatched to the galleys. The authorities aimed at "selective" repression by condemning some in order to discourage others who might wish to follow their example. Most of the Protestants in the galleys refused to renounce their faith. This was the case with Isaac Lefèvre and Jean Marteilhe, both of whom left moving accounts.[28]

---

25   Pilatte, *Edits, declarations* 482–84. The sources on the persecution are still widely scattered in the Archives Nationales (série TT) and the Archives Départementales (série B).

26   Didier Boisson, "La justice royale et les procès contre les cadavres aux XVIIe et XVIIIe siècles," in *Justice et protestantisme*, (eds.) Didier Boisson and Yves Krumenacker (Lyon: 2011), 113–27.

27   Alain Joblin, *Dieu, le juge et l'enfant. L'enlèvement des enfants protestants en France (XVIIe-XVIIIe siècles)* (Arras: 2010).

28   Numerous accounts of the galleys have been published. See Didier Poton and Bertrand Van Ruymbeke (eds.), *Histoire des souffrances du sieur Élie Neau, sur les galères, et dans les cachots de Marseille* (Paris: 2014); Jean Marteilhe, *Mémoires d'un galérien du Roi-Soleil* (Paris:1982); *Histoire des souffrances et de la mort du fidèle confesseur et martyr M. Isaac Lefèvre, de Chatel Chignon en Nivernois, advocat en Parlement* (Rotterdam: 1703);

Locally, the persecutions depended to a large extent on the attitude of the authorities. The *curés* played a prime role in the repression by denouncing the relapsed, blasphemers and those who did not attend Mass or send their children. But the attitude of each ecclesiastic varied according to his character, to that of the New Converts of the parish, and to royal policy. Thus, while no one condoned Protestant activity, it was not always denounced. It was the same with other authorities, such as the intendants. In the *généralité* of Bourges, the intendant Dey de Séraucourt (1682–1699) had 92 children shut up in the General Hospital of Bourges in 1699, while his successor, Roujault (1699–1705), abandoned this policy. In Dauphiné, Le Bret (1683–1686), practised great severity, while his successor, Bouchu, was less certain about the value of persecution.[29]

Clandestine assemblies took place spontaneously most everywhere within a few months of the Revocation. The first known meeting in Poitou was held on Pentecost in 1686 near Saint-Maixent. The number of participants always varied greatly. Anywhere from a few dozen to several thousand New Converts might gather. These assemblies usually met at night in isolated locations. During the service, a Psalm would be sung, a prayer read and one or more sermons delivered. The preachers conducting these assemblies were men who had decided to take the lead in resistance. The faithful in the secret assemblies came mostly from lower social groups, since members of the elite usually attended private assemblies in the home of one or another Reformed person. The clandestine pastors were often former ministers who had apostatized and subsequently retracted their abjuration. Others were ministers who had fled the kingdom and then returned secretly. Finally, some had become ministers only after the Revocation; Claude Brousson is the best known of the latter. Like many of his fellow pastors, he travelled through the realm in the 1690s before being arrested in October 1698 and executed at Montpellier on 3 November.

Affirming the Protestant faith after 1685 meant refusing the obligatory Catholicism. But between the obstinate, who rejected any concession to the Catholic Church, and the Nicodemites, who hid their attachment to the Reformed faith, a wide range of possible attitudes existed. Many New Converts

---

Pierre-M. Conlon, *Jean-François Bion et sa Relation des tourments soufferts par les forçats protestants* (Geneva: 1966); Gaston Tournier, *Les trois frères Serres de Montauban, forçats pour la foi de 1686 à 1713 et 1714* (Mas-Soubeyran: 1937). For a study of the galleys, see André Zysberg, *Les galériens. Vies et destins de 60,000 forçats sur les galères de France* (Paris: 1987).

29 Besides série TT and G⁷ of the Archives Nationales, see série C of the Archives Départementales. Le Comité des Travaux Historiques et Scientifiques has published numerous accounts of intendants at the end of the 17th century that allude to the Protestant question. See also Jean Lemoine (ed.), *Mémoires des évêques de France sur la conduite à tenir à l'égard des Réformés* (Paris: 1902).

were willing to have their children baptized in the Catholic Church because whether performed by Catholic or Protestant, the sacrament had the same value. As for marriage, the relatively late declaration of 13 December 1698 insisted upon Catholic marriage. Nevertheless, already in the 1690s some Protestant couples spurned this Catholic sacrament. They signed a marriage contract before a notary and eventually had their union blessed by an underground pastor. Some did not hesitate to go abroad to marry. When they had their children baptized, the *curés* declared the infants illegitimate.[30] When a New Convert was dying, his relatives tried to hide his condition in order to keep the *curé* away from his bedside. He would die in the Protestant faith and might be buried secretly in a private plot. The importance of domestic worship in the Calvinist tradition facilitated the dissemination of religious knowledge. Books also circulated. The possession of Calvinist literature, however, was forbidden and numerous volumes were burned. Still, families managed to preserve them.[31] Books imported clandestinely were sold clandestinely. They included printed sermons, Bibles, prayer books and Pierre Jurieu's *Lettres pastorales*.

In March 1686, Pierre Jurieu published *L'Accomplissements des prophéties*, a work in which, interpreting the Book of Revelation, he predicted the end of persecution in 1689.[32] At about the same time, a prophetic movement arose in Dauphiné and then in Languedoc. Near Crest in 1688, Isabeau Vincent, a young shepherdess who could neither read nor write and who spoke only the local *patois*, preached in French while in a trance. Not surprisingly, she attracted crowds. Vincent was arrested in June of that year, but other young people soon began to prophesy. Their gatherings attracted more and more people, and were quickly suppressed. Yet after having seemingly disappeared, the movement spread anew in the Cévennes and Languedoc in 1700. These prophets, who came from artisan and peasant background, predicted the deliverance of the people of Israel (the Huguenots) and the destruction of Babylon (the Catholic Church). During their "inspirations" the prophets were seized with "trembling," or convulsions, and exhorted their listeners in French rather than in the local parlance. The essential message of their prophetic discourse was an appeal for the revival of the faith. The intendant of Languedoc, Bâville, tried once again to suppress the movement. In the spring of 1702, however, under the influence of the prophet Abraham Mazel, an appeal for holy war was launched. The goal was to drive the Catholic clergy from the region and liberate victims of persecution

---

30   These attitudes can be identified by examining parish registers.
31   See, for example, Pauline Duley-Haour (ed.), *Mémoires pour servir à l'histoire et à la vie d'Antoine Court* (Paris: 1995).
32   Pierre Jurieu, *L'accomplissement des prophéties*, (ed.) Jean Delumeau (Paris: 1994).

imprisoned in Pont-de-Montvert. An armed expedition was launched and the abbé du Chaila, considered one of those responsible for the persecution, was killed on 24 July 1702. This marked the beginning of the War of the Camisards.[33]

Up to the end of 1702, the Cévenol rebels (the Camisards) gathered around leaders who came from the prophetic movement: Abraham Mazel, Jean Cavalier, and Elie Marion. They moved through the Cévennes in small armed bands and confronted the royal troops. The war, in fact, was a "trilateral conflict," involving the Camisards, the royal soldiers and various armed Catholic groups (the Florentines and the Cadets of the Cross).[34] Massacres and atrocities by the different camps ensued. But after the defeat of Cavalier in April 1704, the principal Camisard leaders laid down their arms and emigrated. Thereafter, the Camisard movement experienced only sporadic revivals. In the spring of 1705, the "plot of the children of God" was discovered and those responsible arrested. In 1709, Mazel tried to raise Vivarais, then the Cévennes, but failed and was killed in 1710. Camisard success, however limited, can be explained above all by their guerilla tactics. Royal troops were harassed by rebels who knew the terrain well. But the Camisards also profited from the mediocre quality of the opposing soldiers and the support of the local population. Yet the greatest strength of the Camisards was their religious fervor, the "assistance of heaven," as Elie Marion wrote.[35]

From the very beginning of the Protestant Reformation, every wave of persecution was accompanied by departures abroad–to the lands of the Refuge. But never had so many Protestants fled as under Louis XIV. Neither the legislation prohibiting emigration, nor the severe treatment of those arrested, nor the loss of their property discouraged the Huguenots. Between 1680 and 1715 some 150,000 to 180,000 Protestants fled. This exodus went through periods of acceleration and deceleration. Departures increased after 1678, but the most important wave was between 1685 and 1688. The War of the League of Augsburg

---

33 Henri Bosc, *La guerre des Cévennes, 1702–1710* (Montpellier: 1985); Philippe Joutard, *Les Camisards* (Paris: 1976). Many participants published their memoirs: Maximilien Misson, *Le théâtre sacré des Cévennes*, (ed.) Jean-Pierre Richardot (Paris:1996); Élie Marion, *Avertissements prophétiques*, (ed.) Daniel Vidal (Grenoble: 2003); Esprit Fléchier, *Fanatiques et insurgés du Vivarais et des Cévennes*, (ed.) Daniel Vidal (Grenoble: 1997); Élie Salvaire, *Relation sommaire des désordres commis par les Camisards des Cévennes*, (ed.) Didier Poton (Montpellier: 1997).

34 Chrystel Bernat, "La guerre des Cévennes: un conflit trilatéral?," BSHPF 148 (2002), 461–507.

35 Philippe Joutard, *La légende des Camisards. Une sensibilité au passé* (Paris: 1977); Patrick Cabanel and Philippe Joutard (eds.), *Les Camisards et leur mémoire 1702–2002* (Montpellier: 2003).

and that of the Spanish Succession slowed the movement, but the period of peace between these two wars saw emigration pick up.[36] The percentage of the departing Reformed population varied from one region to another. It was high in Normandy, Picardy, Champagne and Aunis, and may have reached 25 per cent in Dauphiné and Poitou, but was lower in some other provinces and in the Cévennes. The regions near the borders or on the coast were those that lost the most inhabitants. Despite numerous checks and controls, the ports of Bordeaux, La Rochelle, Dieppe and Calais were important points of departure. The exodus also seems to have been greater from urban communities than from rural areas.[37] Emigration was the principal cause of the disappearance of Protestantism in certain cities, such as Vitry-le-François in Champagne. An attachment to the land restrained many rural people. Exile also led to the breakup of some families. In Frankfurt-am-Main, "the hinge of the Refuge," (*plaque tournante du Refuge*)[38] between spring 1686 and autumn 1687, more than 60 per cent of the refugees passing through were unaccompanied men. Families were torn apart. A couple might leave without their children, a wife without her husband, and children without their parents.[39] The economic consequences of the departure of the Huguenots are still the subject of discussion. All the testimonies emphasize the economic decline caused by this emigration. The reports drafted by the intendants at the end of the 17th century and the Protestant pamphlets also underline this phenomenon. According to the historian W.C. Scoville, the economic difficulties that preceded the revocation of the Edict of Nantes had already begun in 1683. Thus, the Revocation cannot explain everything. But in both industry and commerce, the businesses of the fleeing Protestants were taken over by New Converts who remained in France, by Catholics, and even by foreigners.[40]

---

36   Myriam Yardeni, *Le refuge protestant* (Paris: 1985); Michelle Magdelaine and Rudolf von Thadden (eds.), *Le Refuge huguenot* (Paris: 1985); Eckart Birnstiel, *La diaspora des Huguenots. Les réfugiés protestants de France et leur dispersion dans le monde (XVIe-XVIIIe siècles)* (Paris: 2001).

37   Among the accounts of departures of refugees are Jacques Fontaine, *Mémoires d'une famille huguenote victime de la révocation de l'édit de Nantes,* (ed.) Bernard Cottret (Montpellier: 1992); and Isaac Dumont de Bostaquet, *Mémoires d'Isaac Dumont de Bostaquet sur les temps qui ont précédé et suivi la Révocation de l'Édit de Nantes,* (ed.) Michel Richard (Paris: 1968).

38   Michelle Magdelaine, "Francfort-sur-le-Main, plaque tournante du Refuge," in *Le Refuge huguenot,* (eds.) Magdelaine and von Thadden.

39   *Le Refuge Huguenot,* (eds.) Magdelaine and von Thadden.

40   Warren C. Scoville, *The Persecution of Huguenots and French Economic Development, 1680–1720* (Berkeley: 1960).

4 The *Désert discipliné*

A double rupture in the historical course of French Protestantism occurred in 1715. To begin with, the death of Louis XIV led to some relief from persecution. Secondly, Antoine Court's project to call the first Synod of the Desert constituted the initial stage in a slow–and incomplete–movement to reestablish the Reformed Churches of France, albeit in the context of underground resistance and persecution.

This period of the "disciplined Desert" was dominated by the personality of Antoine Court, who initiated the reorganization of the "churches under the cross." The expression was invoked at the time of the Revocation to suggest the permanence of the churches despite their persecution. Antoine Court, who was born in 1695 in Vivarais, began to preach in 1713. Together with Pastor Pierre Corteiz, he promoted clandestine assemblies and, in August 1715, convened the first Synod of the Desert in the Cévennes. The decisions taken on this occasion were the basis for the reorganization of the churches: the reestablishment of elders whose duties were to supervise ecclesiastical discipline, to organize assemblies, and to assist clandestine preachers. The newly founded communities were to avoid Catholic practices and refuse baptism, marriage and burial at the hands of the *curés*. This first Synod condemned the prophetic movement and the Camisard revolt.[41] In conjunction with other preachers and pastors of the region, men such as Jacques Roger and Pierre Durand, it trained new preachers. Himself a pastor, Court conducted his mission clandestinely, but in 1729, doggedly pursued by the authorities, he decided to leave the kingdom. Once in Switzerland, he maintained a network of connections, conducting an active correspondence with numerous pastors and churches of the Desert.[42]

Emulating Antoine Court, preachers and pastors convened secret assemblies and proceeded to create new churches, chiefly in the southern provinces such as Vivarais, Dauphiné, the Cévennes and Languedoc. Farther west in Aunis, Saintonge, Poitou and Normandy, the first churches of the Desert were often reestablished, beginning in the 1730s, under the influence of preachers and pastors from the Midi. The spread of the churches gradually allowed for the more regular summoning of provincial and national synods. The first

---

41 Hubert Bost and Claude Lauriol (eds.), *Entre Désert et Europe. Le pasteur Antoine Court 1695–1760* (Paris: 1998).

42 Antoine Court left a voluminous corespondence that can be consulted in Geneva (Bibliothèque Publique et Universitaire, collection Court) and Paris (Bibliothèque de la Société de l'Histoire du Protestantisme Français).

provincial synods were held in the Cévennes, Languedoc, Dauphiné, and Vivarais between 1715 and 1721. But they were delayed until 1740 in Upper Languedoc, 1744 in Poitou and 1757 in Béarn. Eight national synods of the Desert were also held between 1726 and 1763. The national synod of 1744 attested to the progress made in reorganization with representatives from the provinces of Normandy, Poitou, and Saintonge in attendance.[43]

Between 1715 and 1789, the number of judgments, edicts and declarations against Protestants declined in comparison to the reign of Louis XIV. Though these various measures maintained existing anti-Protestant legislation, since the monarchy refused to reverse its decisions, authorities were aware of the ineffectiveness and the failure of repression. The declaration of 14 May 1724 resurrected the old laws and inaugurated a new wave of oppression. It was a reaction to the initial attempts to restore the Reformed churches. The act forbade "the exercise of any religion other than the said Catholic religion and any assembly for that purpose" under penalty of the galleys for men, imprisonment for women, and death for preachers and ministers. Children had to be baptized within 24 hours of their birth, go to Catholic school and catechism until the age of 14, and attend Mass. A certificate of Catholicity was required for admission to public or judicial office.[44] The legislation was theoretically in effect until 1789, but its application was erratic. The authorities tried to limit clandestine assemblies, even though they were mindful that too repressive a policy might prompt Protestants to take up arms or emigrate. The government therefore often wavered between strictness and indulgence. It continued to seek out clandestine meetings, to arrest preachers and pastors, to seize and imprison children, and to re-baptize by force children baptized in the Desert. Yet the prosecution of New Converts who had died as "relapsed" was less frequent and, under the declaration of April 9th 1736, Reformed individuals who had been refused burial by a *curé* were to be buried by their families upon permission from a judge.[45]

Three principal types of worship were practiced in the 18th century. Public assemblies met at night. They occurred mainly when military pressure was not too severe and took place under the auspices of a preacher or pastor.

---

43 Edmond Hugues, *Les synodes du Désert*, 3 vols. (Paris: 1886).

44 Pilatte, *Edits, déclarations*, 534–50.

45 Krumenacker, *Les protestants du Poitou*; Didier Boisson, *Les protestants de l'ancien colloque du Berry de la Révocation de l'édit de Nantes à la Révolution (1679–1789), ou l'inégale résistance de minorités religieuses* (Paris: 2000); Alfred Galland, *Essai sur l'histoire du protestantisme à Caen et en Basse-Normandie de l'édit de Nantes à la Révolution* (Paris: 1991); Jean-Claude Gaussent, "La campagne de rebaptisassions de 1752 dans les diocèses de Nîmes et de Montpellier," *BSHPF* 145 (1999), 729–49.

Out-of-the-way places—a wood, a clearing, an isolated barn—were favorite. The gatherings often drew participants from several different churches. Once the place and time of the meeting had been fixed by the pastor and the elders, the latter undertook to inform likely participants. The area selected for worship was laid out in an arc. This space, which symbolized the parquet of the former temples, was reserved for the Lord's Supper and for the celebration of marriages and baptisms. Items for worship might also be brought: a communion table, some cups, and a wooden pulpit, often one that could be easily dismantled. Public worship was conducted according to rules less precise than in the 17th century, since the liturgy followed two models, English and Genevan. The Anglican liturgy had spread, especially in the west of the kingdom, because of Huguenot contacts with refugees in the British Isles. The Geneva liturgy was probably more widely used, due to the influence of Antoine Court. Whenever possible the faithful participated in the Lord's Supper four times a year, and admission tokens were distributed to eligible communicants.[46]

Private assemblies brought together a limited number of the faithful, above all notables, both noble and bourgeois. The point of such meetings was to avoid mingling with the public assemblies of the common people, and to avoid persecution by virtue of these more discreet gatherings. This was "society" worship and which included the Sunday liturgy and the reading of sermons. This sort of worship often persisted until the eve of the Revolution and these assemblies often met without a pastor.

Although important to Calvinism, family worship was little known in the 18th century. It permitted isolated households without recourse to a preacher or pastor to continue the practice of their faith by reading sermons, prayers, Psalms, and other devotional works.[47] Collections of prayers, often published in England, Switzerland or the United Provinces, circulated in the kingdom. Some titles, such as the works of Charles Drelincourt or Jean Claude, dated from before 1685, but were reprinted later. More recent ones were written by pastors, especially foreign ministers such as Jean-Rodolphe Ostervald and Bénédict Pictet. The practice of family worship was controversial, however. The notables, less inclined to participate in public worship, favored it, while the pastors and preachers preferred to emphasize participation in public assemblies. Thus, the different forms of worship, complementary in the 17th century, eventually became rivals.

---

46   Yves Krumenacker, "La liturgie, un enjeu dans la renaissance des Eglises françaises au XVIIIe siècle," in *Edifier ou instruire? Les avatars de la liturgie réformée du XVIe au XVIIIe siècle*, (ed.) Maria-Cristina Pitassi (Paris: 2000), 111–26.

47   Yves Krumenacker, "La place du culte privé chez les protestants français au XVIIIe siècle," *Revue de l'histoire des religions* 217 (2000), 623–38.

The pastoral corps, an essential element in the movement to restore the churches of the Desert, underwent an important transformation in the 18th century. At the end of the reign of Louis XIV and during the Regency, the first pastors of the Desert, educated in the French and foreign Protestant academies prior to 1685, gave way to a generation of self-appointed preachers who were ordained either in Switzerland or in France by ministers who had been to Switzerland. Originally from the south and southwest reaches of the kingdom (Dauphiné, Vivarais, the Cévennes and Languedoc), members of this new generation were self-taught, and came from less affluent and artisan backgrounds, much like Antoine Court. The need to train new pastors, the desire to ensure their religious orthodoxy and the specific nature of preaching "under the cross" led to the creation of the Seminary of Lausanne. As from 1726, the Academy of Lausanne accepted French candidates whose studies its professors supervised for one to two years. Antoine Court tried to keep the candidates recruited by the Seminary from being linked to a particular province so as to able to dispatch them later to any region where the Church had been restored, and not simply to the Midi. He was in constant contact with the candidates, oversaw their conduct and corresponded with the churches that had sent them.[48]

The Seminary of Lausanne allowed for an increase in the number of pastors, which proved indispensable for the restoration of churches. Whereas around 1730 there were only 12 ministers active in France, all in the Midi, there were 28 in 1744, 62 in 1763, 150 in 1783, and finally 180 on the eve of the Revolution. However, even if intellectual recruitment improved during the 18th century, the persecution and the inadequate training resulted in "the complete absence of genuine Reformed pastors and theologians."[49] Caught between the prophetic movement, the restoration of church discipline, and the Enlightenment, the pastors were divided. The acts of the synods expose numerous conflicts whereby the new order established by Antoine Court was opposed by preachers or pastors who refused to obey it, often in the name of a personal internal calling. Thus, the pastoral corps underwent important transformations in the 18th century, without any noticeable decline, as traditional historiography often claims. Still, the faith of the pastors, influenced by a variety of movements, was undoubtedly more fragile.[50]

---

48   Claude Lasserre, *Le Séminaire de Lausanne (1726–1812), instrument de la restauration du protestantisme français* (Lausanne: 1997).

49   Philippe Wolff (ed.), *Histoire des protestants en France de la Réforme à la Révolution* (Toulouse: 2001).

50   Hubert Bost and Claude Lauriol (eds.), *Refuge et Désert. L'évolution théologique des huguenots de la Révocation à la Révolution française* (Paris: 2003).

The Reformed faith was transmitted through participation in the different forms of worship, and also through printed materials. Two cities, Paris and Lyon, were centers for the clandestine circulation of Protestant religious books. The books, especially catechisms, New Testaments, psalters, and devotional works, were sent to the different Protestant provinces. Booksellers and peddlers then distributed them further afield. The principal supply sources were the countries of the Refuge, mainly the printing houses of London, Geneva and Amsterdam. After the Revocation, numerous Protestant printers from Paris, Lyon and Saumur emigrated and pursued their trade abroad. They continued to publish Protestant religious books in French.[51] A network of underground schools developed at the same time as the restoration of the churches. For teaching catechism, Antoine Court asked that Drelincourt's *Catechism*, first published in 1642, be used. Yet Drelincourt's text was quickly deemed to accord well with the *Catechism* of Jean-Frédéric Ostervald, pastor of Neuchâtel, first published in 1731. The national synod officially adopted Ostervald's *Catechism* in 1744. This change was important, because Drelincourt stressed doctrine and polemic, while Ostervald offered a Pietistic orientation.

Few members of the Reformed community left accounts of their faith. It seems however that the traditional polemical themes dividing Protestants and Catholics inspired the Calvinists of the Desert. But their faith evolved. Greater importance was placed on works and, under the influence of Pietism, devotion was accorded a more important role. The change is evident in the writings of Marie Huber. Born at Geneva in 1695, she settled with her family in Lyon in 1711, dying there in 1753. Her principal works, *Écrit sur le Jeu et les plaisirs* (1722) and *Le Monde fou préféré au monde sage* (1731), display this Pietistic influence.[52] These religious itineraries pose the question of what it meant to be a Protestant in the 18th century. Had faith weakened under the pressure of persecution? Or was it at the very least jeopardized? The dangers encountered by those participating in worship in the Desert may have led families to distance themselves from Calvinism and brought them closer, not to Catholicism, but to religious indifference. Was it by virtue of their faith that Protestants defined themselves or, even if they had become detached from their confessional position, was it Protestantism's distinctive character and history with which they identified?

---

51   Yves Krumenacker, "La circulation clandestine des livres protestants au XVIIIe siècle," *La Lettre Clandestine* 13 (2004), 85–101.

52   Maria Cristina Pitassi, "Etre femme et théologienne au XVIIIe siècle. Le cas de Marie Huber," in *De l'humanisme aux Lumières* (Paris and Oxford: 1996), 395–409.

5   The *Désert toléré*

Between 1761 and 1765 three dramatic incidents gave the Protestants the opportunity to denounce the intolerance to which they were subjected. On 19 February 1762, Pastor François Rochette, arrested after having presided over a clandestine assembly, and three brothers accused of having tried to free him, were executed in Toulouse. In the same city on 10 March 1762, the Protestant merchant Jean Calas was also executed. His crime was the alleged murder of his own son because the latter had wished to convert to Catholicism. About the same time, Pierre-Paul Sirven, a jurist from Castres specializing in feudal law, was accused of murdering his daughter. In April 1762, he took refuge in Switzerland with his family. Two years later, he was condemned *in absentia* for the crime of infanticide. These three affairs, thanks to Voltaire's public campaign, led to the firm condemnation of both the judicial errors and the religious repression and intolerance to which this minority was subjected. Voltaire fought to establish the innocence of Calas and Sirven. This was the objective when, in 1763, he published his *Traité sur la tolerance*. Two years later, he secured the rehabilitation of Calas and his family.[53] These affairs led to a significant reduction in persecution. Toleration increased in many provinces. Assemblies could be held more and more openly, and even during the daylight hours. In 1769, the last women imprisoned in the Tour de Constance in Aigues-Mortes were released. A kind of "officialization" of Protestantism gradually evolved. In 1767, for example, a ruling of the *Parlement* of Paris ordered "the removal of the insulting term natural son" from the Catholic baptismal records of children whose parents had married in the Desert.[54]

In 1763, when the final national Synod of the Desert met, nineteen provinces were represented. Yet deputies from the northern provinces as well as those from the major urban centers were largely absent. Many congregations in these areas still suffered from a lack of pastors. In the larger cities, the congregations, dominated by the notables, organized "committees" that negotiated *de facto* toleration with the local authorities. These committees often stood apart

---

[53]   The two principal studies of this affair are those of David Bien, *The Calas Affair: Persecution, Toleration, and Heresy in Eighteenth-Century Toulouse* (Princeton: 1960), and Janine Garrisson, *L'Affaire Calas. Miroir des passions françaises* (Paris: 2004). They provide the essential bibliography of manuscript and printed sources for the case. Voltaire, *Traité sur la tolerance*, (ed.) John Renwick (Oxford: 2000).

[54]   This reduction in persecution can be observed for all the provinces studied, chiefly in the judicial archives (série B) of the Archives Départementales. See, for example, Boisson, *Les protestants de l'ancien colloque du Berry*; Krumenacker, *Les protestants du Poitou*.

from the synodal organization. Thus, a committee was formed in Paris in 1749, and others functioned in Bordeaux, Marseille, La Rochelle and Caen.[55] In the provinces where churches had been restored during the first half of the 18th century, the decisions of synods insisted on several points. While prudence was still advised, assemblies were now to be held during the daytime. The prohibition on contact with the Catholic Church was once again reaffirmed.[56] The General Delegate was responsible for petitions to the King. Antoine Court first held the position and, following his death in 1760, was eventually succeeded (in 1763) by his son Antoine Court de Gébelin. Upon the latter's death, Rabaut Saint-Etienne, son of the Nîmes pastor Paul Rabaut, replaced him. Continuing his predecessor's quest for toleration, Rabaut Saint-Etienne published in 1779 his *Triomphe de l'intolérance ou Anecdotes de la vie d'Ambroise Borély, mort à Londres âgé de 103 ans*, better known under the title *Le vieux Cévenol*. Altogether, many pastors, much like Court de Gébelin and Rabaut de Saint-Etienne, were influenced by the Enlightenment and Pietism.[57]

Apart from persecution, one of the major problems confronting Protestants was the absence of civil status. Regarding marriage, some couples accepted Catholic marriage, while others rejected it. In reality, couples were not observing the prohibition on Catholic marriage that numerous Synods of the Desert had issued. After 1715, some Protestants married in the Catholic Church, often at the price of an insincere abjuration; they abandoned all Catholic practices immediately afterwards. Couples who had married illegally sometimes sought Catholic marriage several years later in order to legitimize their children.[58] Entering into an illegal Catholic marriage, however, is harder to understand. All marriages were supposed to be celebrated by the *curé* of the two future spouses. Yet some couples married outside their own parish, without authorization from their own *curé* but with the complicity of a Catholic priest. Their union was Catholic but illegal.[59] The most common practice, however, was still

---

55 Urban Protestantism is still an understudied subject. See Yves Krumenacker, *Les protestants au siècle des Lumières. Le modèle lyonnais* (Paris: 2002).

56 Hugues, *Les synodes du Désert*; Yves Krumenacker, "L'élaboration d'un 'modèle protestant': les synodes du Désert," *Revue d'Histoire moderne et contemporaine* 42 (1995), 46–70.

57 Jean-Paul Rabaut Saint-Etienne, *Du Désert au Royaume. Parole publique et écriture protestante (1765–1788). Édition critique du "Vieux Cévenol" et de sermons de Rabaut Saint-Étienne*, (ed.) Céline Borello (Paris: 2013).

58 This behavior can be studied only by exhaustive research of the parish registers. Many of these registers have now been digitalized and are accessible on the websites of the various Archives départementales.

59 Records of rehabilitations of marriages after 1787 may make possible the identification of such accommodating *curés*.

illegal Protestant marriage. Even if some couples were satisfied with a marriage contract signed before a notary, many sought to celebrate their union in front of a Protestant pastor. Others did not hesitate to go abroad. The most common destination was somewhere in the Barrière, that is cities such as Namur and Tournai in the Austrian Netherlands where there were Dutch Protestant garrisons. These soldiers were accompanied by ministers of French origin who served as chaplains. The Protestants in the north of the kingdom did not hesitate to make the journey.[60] Other couples married inside the realm and had their marriages blessed by a pastor of the Desert or celebrated in the chapel of a foreign embassy, notably those of the United Provinces and of Sweden.[61] In 1744, the pastors of the Desert were asked to keep baptismal and marital registers. Until the movement to reestablish the churches developed, couples regularly had their children baptized by the *curé*. After 1715, however, baptisms celebrated in the Desert became more common, particularly in the Midi.

The influence of the Huguenot philosopher and writer Pierre Bayle upon the Enlightenment strain in French Protestantism was enormous. His ideas were adopted once more in the 18th century by, for example, the Cévenol Protestant, Laurent Angliviel de La Beaumelle, who in 1748 publicized Bayle's ideas on toleration and freedom of conscience through the vehicle of an exotic tale, *L'Asiatique tolérant*.[62] He sought to demonstrate that intolerance was contrary to the ideals of Christianity. In 1751, Antoine Court wrote a similar piece in defense of religious toleration, *Le Patriote français et impartial ou réponse à la lettre de M. l'évêque d'Agen*.[63] Still, even if they were read, these works exerted little influence until the famous incidents of extreme judicial prejudice during the 1760s. The *philosophes* were not particularly concerned with the Protestant question before this time and their relations with Protestants were marked by disagreements, and even misunderstandings. Why? Protestantism was unquestionably tarnished by the revolt of the Camisards. Authors such as Voltaire offered a negative image of the Camisards, who were considered fanatics. It was not until the publication of Antoine Court's *Histoire des troubles des Cévennes ou de la guerre des Camisards* in 1760 that Protestants offered a lucid

---

60   D. Ollier, *Eglises wallonnes de la Barrière, Tournai, Armentières, Menin, Ypres et Namur* (Le Cateau: 1894).

61   BPF, Ms. 1610 (Chapel of the Swedish Embassy) and Ms. 410-410bis (United Provinces).

62   Laurent Angliviel de La Beaumelle, *Deux traités sur la tolérance. L'Asiatique tolérant (1748)*. *Requête des protestants français au roi (1763)*, (ed.) H. Bost (Paris: 2012); Claude Lauriol, *La Beaumelle. Un protestant cévenol entre Montesquieu et Voltaire* (Geneva: 1978). The Voltaire Foundation of Oxford is publishing La Beaumelle's correspondence.

63   Antoine Court, *Le Patriote français et impartial*, (ed.) Otto H. Selles (Paris: 2002).

analysis of the causes of the revolt. The miscarriages of justice in the 1760s also changed perceptions and understandings of the Protestants' situation. Jean-Jacques Rousseau's *Du Contract social* denounced the mistreatment of Protestants. Voltaire's *Traité sur la tolérance*, dating back to 1763, had a substantial impact on public opinion as well as on the royal court. Volume sixteen of the *Encyclopédie* appeared in 1766 and included an entry on "Toleration" written between 1762 and 1764 by the Geneva pastor Romilly, who took his inspiration principally from Locke and Bayle.

In 1752 Joly de Fleury, *procureur général* of the *Parlement* of Paris, published a memoir in which he argued for the superiority of civil authority over religious authority in matters of civil status. Similar views followed from Antoine Court, author of *Lettre d'un patriote sur la tolérance civile en France* (1753), Turgot in *Lettres à un grand vicaire sur la tolérance* (1753), and Loménie de Brienne in *Le Conciliateur* (1754). In 1766, upon the request of Louis XV, Gilbert de Voisins, *conseiller d'État*, drafted a memoir in which he proposed authorizing private worship and legalizing Protestant marriages celebrated either before a magistrate or before a *curé*, acting not as a priest but in the name of the king as an officer of the civil state. Court de Gébelin opposed this proposal because it did not legalize public worship and Louis XV abandoned the reform initiative. Matters came to a head during the reign of Louis XVI. Various authors, ministers and magistrates, such as Condorcet and the Baron de Breteuil, sought to move public opinion and above all the court. In the spring of 1787 Malesherbes was named *ministre d'État*. He had drafted a *Mémoire sur le mariage des Protestants* in 1785, then in 1787 a *Second mémoire sur le mariage des Protestants*. He negotiated the text of a law with Rabaut Saint-Etienne.[64] Louis XVI signed the edict on 17 November 1787. Although called an edict of toleration, this legislation did not in any sense grant Protestants religious toleration, only civil status. Why? Possibly because Rabaut Saint-Etienne, aware of the progress of toleration in the kingdom, preferred this concession in order to settle the question of civil status.[65] The preamble of the edict recounted the failure of the policies of Louis XIV and Louis XV. Article 1 authorized public

---

[64] An assessment of the sources regarding the debates over the civil status of the Protestants has been published by Jacques Poujol, "Aux sources de l'Édit de 1787: une étude bibliographique," *BSHPF* 133 (1987), 343–84; and 142 (1996), 293–309.

[65] On the edict of toleration, see André Encrevé and Claude Lauriol (eds.), "Actes des Journées d'études sur l'Édit de 1787," *BSHPF* 134 (1988); Hubert Bost, "Vers la tolérance ou vers l'édit (1750–1787)," in *Ces Messieurs de la R.P.R. Histoires et écritures de huguenots, XVIIe-XVIIIe siècles*, (ed.) H. Bost (Paris: 2001), 365–76. Rabaut Saint-Etienne, *Du Désert au Royaume*, (ed.) Borello.

worship only for the Catholic religion, but did not expressly forbid any other form of worship. For a declaration of marriage, couples were to present themselves before a *curé* or judge; the marriage would then be legal and indissoluble. In addition, Protestant couples who had married illegally could always present themselves to a *curé* or judge and validate a marriage contracted illegally and thereby legitimize their children. The birth of children was to be declared to a *curé* or judge. In the event of a death, two relatives of the deceased were to appear before a *curé* or judge. Finally, ground was to be set aside for the burial of non-Catholics. The application of this edict, in particular the rehabilitation of marriages, varied according to location. Some communities allowed them to be rehabilitated before a *curé* because the nearest judge was a substantial distance away. In other cases, it was the result of good relations between the Protestants and the local representative of the Catholic Church. In yet other instances, people travelled to the judge or else the judge visited the community. Many couples chose this solution, but others decided that even if their union was illegal under the law, it was in fact acknowledged by everyone in the community.[66]

In 1685 French Protestantism in the north was composed mainly of communities of notables, while that in the south was much more "ordinary" in its social character. A century later and regardless of region, winegrowers, peasants, workers and artisans were in the majority. They probably represented more than 80 per cent of Reformed Protestants in 1789. This social transformation of Protestantism primarily affected the northern provinces. In Picardy, the greatest concentrations of Protestants were in Vermandois and Thiérarche. Many were *mulquiniers*, workers employed in the production of linen cloth, especially in the Saint-Quentin area. In the nearby Brie region, the great majority were winegrowers. The situation was the same in Normandy, just as in the region of the Norman Bocage (around Condé-sur-Noireau), where textile workers and peasants were in the majority. The regions of the Reformed crescent, from Poitou to Dauphiné, did not experience so strong a sociological upheaval, because the influence of the notables was already much weaker. While the great majority of Protestants were ordinary folk, their history is less known than that of the elite who have held the attention of historians.[67]

---

66 As required by law, rehabilitations and declarations under the edict of toleration are found principally in the parish registers if the *curé* recorded them, or in série B of the Archives départementales if the judge did so. Some registers can also be found in the Archives nationales (U 1338).

67 Didier Boisson and Christian Lippold, "Les protestants du centre de la France et du Bassin Parisien et la Révocation de l'édit de Nantes," *BSHPF* 148 (2002), 337–83; idem, "La survie

The Protestant elite, whose economic success was due to trade in textiles, the international maritime trade, and banking, lived in the kingdom's larger towns. In Saint-Quentin, families such as the Dumoustiers or the Frizeaux built their fortune on trade in linen cloth. It was the same in Sedan with the Pouparts and the Labauches. The prosperity of the city of Bordeaux was due principally to the growth in colonial trade and here Protestant merchants played a vital role, whether they were originally foreigners (Bethmanns and Bartons) or from the southwest (Bonnaffés and Barthez). In Marseille, it was above all Genevans (the Vernets), the Swiss (the Scherers and Sollicoffres) and French Protestant merchants from Languedoc and Dauphiné who dominated. But it was in Paris that the Protestant elite was most impressive. Among the principal figures was Christophe-Philippe Oberkampf (1738–1815), originally from Germany, who founded his own textile mill in Jouy, near Paris, in 1760. Protestant banking circles, which included the Thelussons and the Girardots were also prominent. Certain luxury artisans, often German-speaking Lutherans such as J.-H. Riesener, a cabinet-worker for the royal court between 1774 and 1784, made their fortunes thus.[68]

This Protestant elite behaved much like the Catholic elite. Many Protestant merchants sent their children to be educated abroad. Likewise the libraries belonging to these notables resembled those of the Catholics. The culture of the Protestant elite was, furthermore, characterized by membership in the Freemasonry. Protestants were admitted to the many Masonic Lodges. This intellectual society primarily favored integration, assimilation, and social recognition for a minority that was still not already completely integrated. Also, some merchants, whose Reformed faith had weakened and who were drifting toward deism, were looking for "substitute worship." Freemasonry even attracted some pastors, notably Paul Rabaut and Antoine Court de Gébelin.[69]

6 Conclusion

The history of the French Protestants between the Revocation of the Edict of Nantes and the Revolution cannot, in the end, be confined to the War of the Camisards and the long struggle for religious toleration, despite the fact that

---

religieuse des communautés protestantes du centre de la France et du Bassin parisien de la Révocation de l'édit de Nantes à l'édit de tolérance (1685–1787)," *Histoire, Économie et Société* 21 (2002), 227–56.

68   Krumenacker, *Des protestants au siècle des Lumières*.
69   Gérard Gayot, "Les problèmes de la double appartenance: protestants et francs-maçons à Sedan au XVIIIe siècle," *Revue d'Histoire moderne et contemporaine* 18 (1971), 415–29.

historians have placed enormous emphasis on these two themes. The consequences of the Edict of 1787 were felt even after the convocation of the Estates-General in May 1789. During the debates that preceded the vote for the Declaration of the Rights of Man and of the Citizen (26 August 1789), Jean-Paul Rabaut Saint-Etienne, negotiator of the Edict of 1787 and a deputy to the Estates-General from Nîmes, asked for "freedom of religion for all non-Catholics, freedom of worship, and freedom to practice it in edifices designated for that purpose."[70] He was heard in part. Article 10 of the Declaration specified that "no one shall be disquieted on account of his opinions, including his religious views." This freedom was confirmed by the Constitution of 3 September 1791, which guaranteed to every citizen the freedom "to follow the religious worship to which he is attached" (Section 1).

The special civil status of the Protestants disappeared with the Law of 30 September 1792, which assigned to the municipal mayors (*maires*) the responsibility from this point onward for maintaining birth, marriage and death registers. This measure must be seen as both a desire to make practice uniform and as the authorities' wish to discontinue clandestine registers, not only by the Protestants but also by those Catholics who rejected the Revolution's reorganization of the Catholic Church within the framework of the Civil Constitution of the Clergy.

Still, the first years of the Revolution were marked by strong tensions between Catholics and Reformed Protestants due to the official reestablishment of Reformed worship, aspirations among the Reformed bourgeoisie to hold political power, and by the new rights granted to the Protestants. In December 1789, the National Assembly permitted non-Catholics to be admitted to all civil and military offices. As a result, "brawls" broke out in several cities in the spring of 1790. In Montauban on 10 May, during a religious procession, the Catholic populace lashed out against the municipal authorities and the National Guard, composed mainly of Protestants. The riot led to five deaths. In Nîmes, in June, similar outbreaks caused nearly 300 deaths, reminding Catholics of the massacre of their co-religionists in the infamous "Michelade" of 1567.[71] Longstanding animosities and anxieties were not quick to disappear.[72]

---

70   André Dupont, *Rabaut Saint-Etienne, 1743–1793. Un protestant défenseur de la liberté religieuse* (Geneva: 1989).
71   On this subject, see Valérie Sottocasa, *Mémoires affrontées. Protestants et catholiques face à la Révolution dans les montagnes du Languedoc* (Rennes: 2004).
72   Michèle Sacquin, *Entre Bossuet et Maurras. L'antiprotestantisme en France de 1814 à 1870* (Paris: 1998).

PART 2

The Diaspora

CHAPTER 9

Diasporic Networks and Immigration Policies

Susanne Lachenicht

1   Introduction

Diaspora (from the Greek διασπορά: dispersion) originally referred to the ancient Greek colonization in the Mediterranean. Beginning with the first major exile of the Jews, the Babylonian captivity of 587 B.C., the term became closely linked to expulsions of Jews and the forced migrations of ethnic or religious minorities more generally. Diasporas more often than not mean "victim diasporas," ethnic or religious groups, persecuted for their faith, expelled and dispersed to different parts of the world. The lost homeland becomes a focal point, tying together people scattered all over the world, sometimes for centuries. Since the 1990s, diaspora sociologists, such as Robin Cohen, have conceived of diasporas in a broader perspective. In his work, Cohen describes "imperial diasporas" such as the British in India or Africa during the second British Empire, "labor diasporas" such as Indians on Africa's East Coast, or "trade diasporas" as the Chinese or Lebanese in North America. What make those distinct groups comparable to others are typical patterns in narratives and practices: strong ties with the lost homeland, supra-national networks, problems in integrating into new environments, and their role as transcultural agents. The latter connect societies and cultures that would not be linked if those groups were not present.[1]

For a long time, historical narratives have either been written from a confessional or a national perspective. Church history and national historiographies often excluded religious and ethnic minorities, and their contributions to state, culture and society. However, religious and ethnic minorities, such as Sephardi and Ashkenazi Jews, Huguenots, Mennonites and Quakers have developed their own, specific historiography as histories *à part*, as the following examples illustrate:

> Christian charity, Sire, the example of your ancestors and the well-being of your state invite you to meet their [the French refugees] expectations and to support them in their designs, because apart from the blessings of Heaven and the love of all Protestants, of which His Majesty disposes, the

---

[1] Robin Cohen, *Global Diasporas: An Introduction* (London: 1999), ix, 26.

number of your subjects and of the amount of your income could increase with the accession of a nation whose industriousness and labor would produce in little time affluence, riches and safety by cultivating the soil which Your Majesty will allow them, by their application to the trade and their vigilance, and their fidelity.[2]

This *Address from Protestants in France to [the English King] Charles II, praying for liberty to remove into Ireland*, most likely written in the early 1680s, when Huguenots were heavily persecuted in France, is one example, among others, that displays a very self-confident refugee people: Huguenots proud of their French Reformed culture, Huguenots promoting their economic and cultural qualities. A century later, these perceptions of the Huguenot self, had not altered:

The refugees originating from a country, where polished manners are much more developed than anywhere else, whose language is refined and since the century of Louis XIV has manifested refinement in masterpieces of eloquence and poetry, are not likely to take the citizens of their countries of refuge as a model, but hope to serve them as a model in many different ways.[3]

This extract from the *Mémoires pour servir à l'histoire des réfugiés français dans les états du Roi de Prusse*, a nine-volume history of Huguenots in Brandenburg-Prussia, written in the 1780s by the two fourth-generation Huguenot pastors,

---

2 "La charité Chrétienne, Sire, l'exemple de vos ancestres, et le bien de vôtre état vous invitent a leur étre propre et a les encourager [les Protestants français] dans leur dessein car outre les benedictions du ciel et l'amour de tous les protestants, que V.M. peut s'atirer, le nombre de vos sujets et de vos revenus peut s'acroitre notablement par l'accession d'un peuple dont l'industrie, et le travail sera capable d'apporter dans peu de temps l'abondance, la richesse, et la s(o)ureté par la culture des terres que V.M. leur permettra de planter(,) par leur application au commerce et par leur vigilance, et leur fidelité." Oxford, Bodleian Library, *Address from Protestants in France to Charles II, praying for liberty to remove into Ireland*, 17th century, Ms. Rawl. A. 478 (11,352).

3 "Les réfugiés, sortant d'un pays où la politesse des mœurs avoit fait plus de progrès que partout ailleurs, parlant une langue cultivée et dès lors fixée par les chefs-d'œuvre que l'éloquence et la poésie produisirent pendant le beau siècle de Louis XIV, bien loin d'être dans le cas de se modeler sur leurs nouveaux citoyens, pouvaient espérer au contraire de leur servir à plus d'un égard de modèles." Jean-Pierre Erman and Pierre Chrétien Frédéric Reclam, *Mémoires pour servir à l'histoire des réfugiés françois dans les états du Roi de Prusse*, vol. 1 (Berlin: 1782–1799), 302.

Jean Pierre Erman (1735–1814) and Pierre Chrétien Frédéric Reclam (1741–1789), displays an even more self-confident attitude towards the Huguenots' specific qualities and the contributions they made to their host societies.

More recent research on ethnic and religious minorities and migrant groups has made evident that the latter had a rather important impact on historical change in the economy, society, politics and culture. Migrants and diasporas were and are *service agents* moving between two or more different cultures, as British historian Arnold Toynbee (1889–1975) put it. While bringing new goods, ideas and peoples to a variety of regions, most diasporas form "fossil societies" as, more often than not, they try to preserve a distinct ethnic, religious or other cultural group identity. Diasporas therefore are innovative and fossil—and they serve as agents of transculturation.[4] The history of minorities is by no means a history of the margins but central to our understanding of history at large. However, in analyzing the contributions made by minority and diasporic groups, we have to disentangle carefully the multi-faceted relationships between their own myths and their impact on political, economic, cultural and social change.

Diaspora studies, the comparative analysis of minority groups and their contributions to historical change, the study of their entangled histories, bring together parallel narratives. While 19th and 20th-century diasporas have become subject to more historical and sociological enquiry, early modern diaspora studies are a rather young research field. Over the last decade, more and more historians of the early modern period have turned their interest to transnational and entangled histories.[5] No longer solely working on one specific minority group, they integrate their work into a more holistic perspective on early modern agents of historical change.

Early modern diaspora studies deal with a specific set of questions such as the terms and conditions for migrations, expulsions and re-settlement, and the legal status of ethnic and religious minorities. They are concerned with the agency of minority groups in negotiating those terms and conditions. Furthermore, historians of early modern diasporas are interested in how diaspora groups form, how they develop and how they transform notions of their specific identities. Diaspora studies are also interested in the formation of

---

4   Arnold J. Toynbee, *A Study of History*, abridgment of vols. 7–10, (ed.) David Churchill Somervell (London: 1957), 217.
5   See Ina Baghdiantz McCabe, Gelina Harlaftis and Ioanna Pepelasis Minoglou (eds.), *Diaspora Entrepreneurial Networks. Four Centuries of History* (Oxford: 2005), Susanne Lachenicht (ed.), *Religious Refugees in Europe, Asia and North America* (Hamburg: 2007); Susanne Lachenicht and Kirsten Heinsohn (eds.), *Diaspora Identities. Exile, Nationalism and Cosmopolitanism in the Past and Present* (Frankfurt am Main: 2009).

diaspora networks, the so-called strong and weak ties,[6] their purposes and their role for the transfer of ideas, goods and peoples. They deal with the expectations that states and societies entertained when inviting and settling religious and ethnic minorities, with the development of concepts such as "acculturation," "integration" and "assimilation." Integrating the history of the Huguenot Refuge into the broader field of diaspora studies could help us understand both the specificities of the Huguenot experience and patterns of the role diasporas played for historical change in the early modern period.

2   Huguenot Networks

French Protestant or Huguenot networks started forming from the 1540s onwards with John Calvin's successful missionary efforts in France. Calvin and his successors in Geneva established regular communication with Huguenot pastors in the various French provinces. These pastors set out to establish what we call *églises dressées*, fully established Calvinist churches with their specific church discipline (*discipline ecclésiastique*), governed by a consistory (*consistoire*) made up of pastors, church elders (*anciens*) and deacons (*diacres*). French Protestant churches were linked to each other by correspondence networks and by regional and national synods. From the mid-16th century, with the onset of persecution of Protestants in France, the so-called Wars of Religion (1562–1598) and the slaughter of thousands of Calvinists during Saint Bartholomew's Day massacre (23 to 24 August 1572), more and more Huguenots were looking for exile, or a refuge, abroad. Thus, the *premier Refuge* came into place. An estimated 20,000 French Protestants left France between 1562 and 1660.

To what extent this *premier Refuge* could be called a diaspora—a nation abroad, bound together by the loss of the homeland, one common language, ethnic origin and one religion, a nation in exile that forms a distinct and often segregated group—is still being discussed by specialists of the Huguenot Refuge.[7] Prior to the revocation of the Edict of Nantes in 1685, Huguenots

---

6   In the analysis of social contacts and networks we distinguish between "strong" and "weak" ties as the main types of possible relationships. "Strong ties" exist between family members, friends, neighbors, people who entertain regular and close contacts. "Weak ties" are new, more distant connections that might seem less trustworthy in the beginning but can prove rather powerful in commerce and trade. For the concept see Mark Granovetter, "The Strength of Weak Ties: A Network Theory Revisited," *Sociological Theory* 1 (1983), 201–33.

7   Bertrand Van Ruymbeke, "Refuge or Diaspora? Historiographical reflections on the Huguenot dispersion in the Atlantic World," in *Religious Refugees in Europe, Asia and North America, 6th–21st century*, (ed.) Susanne Lachenicht (Hamburg: 2007), 155–69.

outside France might not have been perceived as a nation in exile, as a diaspora *avant la lettre*. Having fled to the Netherlands, the Palatinate, the Reformed Swiss cantons or England, Huguenots, between the 1560s and 1680s, frequently went back and forth, returning to France for trade and commerce, marriage or simply because they entertained hopes that the peace treaties of Longjumeau (1568), Saint-Germain-en-Laye (1570) or Beaulieu (1576) would last. Furthermore, during the *premier Refuge*, the Huguenots of France formed multi-ethnic communities in exile, together with Protestant Walloons, Palatines and other groups who had fled from persecution in the Spanish Netherlands and the Holy Roman Empire.

Between the 1550s and the 1680s England, the Netherlands, the Reformed Swiss cantons and the Palatinate saw the establishment of Huguenot and Walloon churches which served French Protestants in exile as centers of worship, of relief and aid in the establishment of new lives and communities. Huguenot churches of the Refuge corresponded with each other in order to control the influx and on-migration of Huguenots, to provide testimonials or certificates for fellow-Protestants, so the latter could be accommodated in towns and guilds.[8]

During the 16th century, networks of correspondence also emerged between the Huguenots' military leaders in France and Protestant powers in Europe, diplomats of the Elector Palatine, Philip of Hesse, Elizabeth I of England or the early Stuarts. Those diplomatic and military networks mostly linked promoters or defenders of the Protestant cause. What Herbert Luthy, Robin Gwynn, John Bosher and Myriam Yardeni have dubbed the Protestant International was an attempt by Protestant powers in Europe to establish a bulwark against the Counter-Reformation—the Catholic Church's attempts to suppress and extirpate Protestantism in Europe.[9] While political and economic interests often made Protestant powers refrain from concerted all-Protestant military initiatives, some states such as Protestant England or the Netherlands were addressed as protectors of the Protestant cause, as "defenders of the faith" far into the late 18th century.[10]

---

8   Susanne Lachenicht, *Hugenotten in Europa und Nordamerika. Migration und Integration in der Frühen Neuzeit* (Frankfurt am Main: 2010), 47–55.

9   Herbert Luthy, *La banque protestante en France, de la Révocation de l'Édit de Nantes à la Révolution*, vol. 1, *Dispersion et regroupement (1685–1730)* (Paris: 1959); Robin Gwynn, "The Huguenots in Britain, the 'Protestant International' and the defeat of Louis XIV," in *From Strangers to Citizens. The Integration of Immigrant Communities in Britain, Ireland and Colonial America, 1550–1750*, (eds.) Randolph Vigne and Charles Littleton (Brighton: 2001), 412–24; John F. Bosher, "Huguenot Merchants and the Protestant International in the Seventeenth Century," *William and Mary Quarterly* 3rd ser. 52 (1995), 77–102.

10   Lachenicht, *Hugenotten in Europa*, 65.

Huguenots have for a long time been the subject of historical writing. However, very little has been done with regard to an exact analysis of Huguenot networks, how they intertwined and which purposes they served. There was not one single Huguenot network but many networks which included Huguenots and promoted some of their interests back home in France and abroad.

When in 1685, King Louis XIV of France revoked the Edict of Nantes, some 150,000 to 200,000 (of an estimated 750,000) French Protestants left France. Again, they settled in the Netherlands, the Reformed Swiss cantons, the German Palatinate and England, but also, now, in Brandenburg-Prussia, Scandinavia, Ireland, the Americas and South Africa. Estimates vary with regard to the exact number of Huguenot refugees in the countries of Refuge. It is said that Switzerland accommodated some 22,000 refugees, England 40,000 to 50,000, the Netherlands 50,000 to 70,000, Brandenburg-Prussia between 15,000 and 20,000 and Denmark, Sweden and Russia some 2,000 refugees. Ireland might have received 3,500 refugees, the British colonies in North America 2,500.[11]

With the peace treaties of Rijswijk of 1697 and Utrecht of 1713, Huguenot hopes vanished that the anti-French coalition would force Louis XIV to re-establish the Edict of Nantes in France.[12] French Protestantism could only survive in exile or as clandestine crypto-Calvinist churches in France, the *églises du désert*. After 1685, the *Grand* or *Second Refuge* came into place. Huguenots, now, at the very latest, sought to establish a *"France protestante à l'étranger"* (Protestant France abroad), not only in Brandenburg-Prussia, as Etienne François has claimed,[13] but in transcending all (possible) countries of refuge. The Huguenot Refuge became a diaspora.

Heavily persecuted for their faith in the later 16th century and then again during the reign of Louis XIV, Huguenots were dependent on Christian charity and the generosity of European Protestant states to be accommodated after their illegal flight from France following the Edict of Fontainebleau of

---

11   Robin D. Gwynn, *Huguenot Heritage. The History and Contribution of the Huguenots in Britain* (London: 1988), 24, 31. Eckart Birnstiel and Andreas Reinke, "Hugenotten in Berlin," in *Von Zuwanderern zu Einheimischen. Hugenotten, Juden, Böhmen, Polen in Berlin*, (eds.) Stefi Jersch-Wenzel and Barbara John (Berlin: 1990), 16–152. Bertrand Van Ruymbeke, *From New Babylon to Eden. The Huguenots and their Migration to Colonial South Carolina* (Columbia, SC: 2006), 13.
12   Lachenicht, *Hugenotten in Europa*, 46.
13   Etienne François, "La mémoire huguenote en Hesse, en Allemagne et dans les autres pays du Refuge," in *Die Hugenotten und das Refuge. Deutschland und Europa. Beiträge zu einer Tagung*, (eds.) Frédéric Hartweg and Stefi Jersch-Wenzel (Berlin: 1990), 233–39, here 235.

1685. Huguenots and their spiritual, diplomatic and military leaders had to convince the Protestant princes within Europe and the proprietors of their colonies to grant asylum and settlement privileges to those French Protestants fleeing religious persecution in France. Early modern European states and cities were used to offering asylum to a persecuted religious and ethnic minority, such as Sephardi Jews leaving the Spanish territories after the Alhambra Edict of 1492 or the expulsion from Portugal from the 1580s onwards. While many European rulers had some experience in granting asylum to persecuted minorities, the terms and conditions on which these minorities were to be received and accommodated had to be negotiated. The State Papers of England and Acts of Parliament provide ample material that helps us understand what those negotiations looked like. We can see that Huguenots lobbied European states and colonial governments, so the latter would grant minorities most favorable conditions for their settlement. It is also evident that the Huguenots had a rather good knowledge of various minority groups and settlement privileges that the former had been granted within Europe and the Atlantic world. Towards the end of the 17th century, Huguenots claimed to establish autonomous Huguenot colonies in Ireland and "hoped that Ireland would become a prominent place of refuge for their persecuted brethren."[14] When lobbying the English crown for settlement privileges, the Huguenots explicitly drew on the example of the Munster and Ulster plantations of the later 16th and early 17th centuries.[15]

In order to understand how and to what extent Huguenots were able to lobby the Protestant powers in Europe, we need to consider a set of networks forged prior to and after 1685. These either included Huguenots to a large extent, were Huguenot-controlled or exclusively Huguenot. It is important to note that these networks were not separate from but communicated with each other.

2.1 *Diplomatic and Military Networks*

Diplomatic networks were crucial to help establish those Huguenots who had chosen to flee France after 1685. Regular contacts with the Protestant European

---

[14] BPF, Papiers Court, Cote 615 no. 15, 128–36. The document is mentioned in Madame Alexandre de Chambrier, "Projet de Colonisation en Irlande, par les réfugiés français 1692–1699," PHSL VI/3 (1898–1901), 370–431 and Michelle Magdelaine, "L'Irlande huguenote: utopie ou réalité?" in *De l'humanisme aux Lumières, Bayle et le Protestantisme. Mélanges en l'honneur d'Elisabeth Labrousse*, (eds.) Michelle Magdelaine, Maria Cristina Pitassi, Ruth Whelan and Antony McKenna (Paris, Oxford: 1996), 273–87.

[15] BPF, *Projet pour l'établissement des réfugiés en Irlande*, Papiers Court, no. 17 M, M 617, 187.

courts, together with an office as court councilor or special envoy could help to convince Protestant powers in Europe and overseas to grant asylum to the persecuted French Calvinists. Among the most prominent diplomatic and military leaders of the *Grand Refuge* was Henri Massue, Marquis de Ruvigny, later Lord Galway. Born in Paris in 1648 to the first Marquis de Ruvigny, the then Deputy General (the official representative) of the French Huguenots at the Court of Louis XIV, Henri followed his father as Deputy General. The Ruvigny left France after 1685, even though Louis XIV had granted the family freedom of worship on its French estates. With Lady Rachel, widow of the Whig-martyr Lord William Russell and daughter of the older Ruvigny's sister, Rachel Massue de Ruvigny Wriothesley, Countess of Southampton, the French Ruvigny had an important link to the English court. When they moved to England, Ruvigny and his two sons, Henri Massue and Pierre, Sieur de la Caillemotte, were granted accommodation in the royal palace at Greenwich. In 1692 King William III made Ruvigny Lieutenant-General of his army in Ireland and in 1693 one of the Lords Justice of Ireland.[16] The Huguenot cause might not have been the most important concern of William III, but regiments under the command of Huguenot officers such as Du Cambon, La Melonière and La Caillemotte had helped him in his campaign in Ireland. Granting major privileges to his Huguenot officers therefore was a means of repaying them for their services.

Gaspar de Perrinet Marquis d'Arzeliers (1645–1710), with close links to Ruvigny, was another important diplomat in the service of both the English crown and French Huguenots. D'Arzelier's father had also served as Deputy General of the Huguenots at the French court. In 1687 d'Arzeliers left France to find refuge in the Netherlands, later moving to Berne, where he forged contacts with most Protestant courts in Europe. Another of Ruvigny's diplomatic partners in organizing the English and Irish Refuge was Henri de Mirmand. Born at Nîmes in 1650 (died 1721), he tried to organize the ongoing migration of Huguenots who had fled to Zurich, Geneva and Lausanne. In 1686, the Elector of Brandenburg made him Court Councilor, which enabled de Mirmand to go on a diplomatic mission with the aim of convincing other Protestant rulers in Northern Europe to grant asylum and settlement privileges to his Huguenot brethren in Switzerland. On his various missions (1688–99), de Mirmand worked together with the consistory of the Huguenot churches in Switzerland. In the 1690s, Ruvigny, d'Arzeliers and de Mirmand made efforts to establish major Huguenot colonies in Ireland, forging thus a bulwark against the

---

16   Raymond Pierre Hylton, *Ireland's Huguenots and their Refuge, 1662–1745: An Unlikely Haven* (Brighton: 2005), 86.

Jacobites and a possible invasion of England.[17] Forced by other Protestant European states' unwillingness to admit further French refugees to their territories,[18] the military and intellectual leaders had to look for new homes for thousands of Huguenots who had not yet found a safe refuge in Europe. In the end, King William III was not willing to grant major funding for the transport and settlement of 600 Huguenot families. This unwillingness meant that Huguenots in the cantons of Bern and Zurich could not move on to other places of refuge in Europe and her colonies. As, in 1691 and 1693, these Swiss cantons were no longer able to provide for the refugees due to failed harvests, the refugees in Bern and Zurich were close to starvation.[19]

Equally important in establishing diplomatic networks was Armand de Bourbon, Marquis de Miremont (1655–1732), later special envoy of Queen Anne during the peace negotiations at Utrecht.[20] However, Miremont's diplomatic activities were not blessed with success. In 1713, the Protestant powers in Europe showed very little interest in forcing Louis XIV of France to re-establish

---

17   Details of these plans and their failure can be found in BPF, Papiers Court, copies, cote 615, no. 15, cote 617, no. 17 and cote 618 AA, no. 18, pp. 174–181, in the Staatsarchiv Zürich, Französische Angelegenheiten, amtliche Akten 1688–1693, EI 25:14 July 1693–1694, in the Staatsarchiv Bern, Piedmont-Buch, St.A.B. AV 153, *Piedmontesische frantzösische Glaubengenossen Persecution und Exilierung samt ihrer Versorgung von den Evanglischen Orten und diesen armen Leuthen Recomendationis...von 1690–1700*: Letter of the clergy of the city of Zurich to the city of Bern, 21 August 1693, fol. 26, and London, Lambeth Palace Library, Miscelleanous Letters, no. 109: Unsigned letter [to William III], c. 1694, concerning the settlement in Ireland of French Protestant refugees forced to leave Switzerland. Copy 3 ff. See also Chambrier, Projet de Colonisation, 370–431, Magdelaine, L'Irlande huguenote, 273–87. Vivienne Larminie, "Exile and Belonging: Philibert Herwarth, Ambassador to Switzerland and Benefactor of the French Hospital," PHSL 28 (2006), 509–23. Susanne Lachenicht, "New Plantations in Ireland? Antoine Court and the Settlement of French Refugees in the Mid-Eighteenth Century," PHSL 29 (2009), 227–37.
18   Susanne Lachenicht, "Die Freiheitskonzession des Landgrafen von Hessen-Kassel, das Edikt von Potsdam und die Ansiedlung von Hugenotten in Brandenburg-Preußen und Hessen-Kassel," in *Les États allemands et les huguenots. Politique d'immigration et processus d'intégration*, (eds.) Guido Braun and Susanne Lachenicht (Munich: 2007), 71–83, here 79.
19   Rémy Scheurer, "Durchgang, Aufnahme und Integration der Hugenottenflüchtlinge in der Schweiz," *Die Hugenotten, 1685–1985*, (eds.) Rudolf von Thadden and Michelle Magdelaine (Munich: 1985), 38–54.
20   BL *Appointment of Marquis de Miremont to negotiate at Utrecht on Huguenot and Protestant affairs*, Add. Mss., Ch. 76124, of 1711. Matthew Glozier, *The Huguenot Soldiers of William of Orange and the Glorious Revolution of 1688: the Lions of Judah*. (Brighton: 2002), 96–98.

the Edict of Nantes.[21] One of his partners in diplomacy was Ezechiel von Spanheim,[22] from 1680 privy councilor at the court of the Elector of Brandenburg. In 1689 Spanheim became director of the central administration of the Huguenot colonies in Brandenburg-Prussia, crowning his 1685 success in bringing new subjects into that territory.[23]

2.2   Networks among Pastors and Consistories

Networks of Huguenot churches within and outside France were crucial not only in establishing additional Huguenot churches but also in organizing the flight, terms and conditions for asylum and re-settlement and on-migration. The surviving correspondence and consistory minutes of Huguenot churches such as the London Threadneedle Street Church, the New York *Église du Saint Esprit*, the Berlin Friedrichstadtkirche, and the correspondence of the Berlin Huguenot pastor Jean Henri Samuel Formey (1711–1797) and many others show that the Huguenot churches of the Refuge entertained close contacts with other Protestant churches and Huguenot military and diplomatic leaders. Formey, for instance, corresponded with the vast majority of Huguenot pastors in Brandenburg, Prussia and Brandenburg-born Huguenots in Switzerland and Britain.[24] One of the best known networks was that of Antoine Court. Born in 1695 to a Protestant peasant family in the Vivarais, Court was officially raised as a Catholic. At age fourteen, he began to join clandestine meetings of crypto-Calvinists in the Cévennes Mountains. In 1729, Court moved to Switzerland where the *restaurateur du protestantisme français* began to build up a network that aimed for both the restoration of Protestantism in France and the strengthening of French Protestant interests in the Refuge.[25]

21   BL, Add. 36795, 81–82, 100–01 and 138.
22   On Ezechiel Spanheim, see Sven Externbrink, "Internationaler Calvinismus als Familiengeschichte: Die Spanheims (ca. 1550–1710)," in *Grenzüberschreitende Familienbeziehungen. Akteure und Medien des Kulturtransfers in der Frühen Neuzeit*, (eds.) Dorothea Nolde and Claudia Opitz (Cologne: 2008), 137–55.
23   Charles Ancillon, *Mélange critique de littérature recueilli des conversations de feu Monsieur (David) Ancillon avec un Discours sur la vie de feu Monsieur (David) Ancillon et ses dernières heures*, vol. 1 (Basel: 1698), 383–84.
24   Berlin, Staatsbibliothek Preußischer Kulturbesitz, Fonds Formey.
25   Edmond Hugues, *Antoine Court. Histoire de la restauration du protestantisme français au XVIIIe siècle* (2 vols. Paris: 1872). Maurice Boulle, "L'enfance et l'adolescence d'Antoine Court dans l'histoire de Villeneuve-de-Berg," in *Entre Désert et Europe, le pasteur Antoine Court (1695–1760). Actes du Colloque de Nîmes (3–4 novembre 1995)*, (eds.) Hubert Bost and Claude Lauriol (Paris: 1998), 15–29. Pauline Duley-Haour, "Le réseau européen d'Antoine

Internal networks were meant to forge a homogenous religious and social diaspora. They were also about the much disputed orthodoxy of the faith, social control of mobile members of the diaspora community, and as mentioned above, certificates for Huguenots to find a living in diaspora. Through their external networks, the Huguenots sought to find new pastors for their churches, especially when, from the mid-18th century onwards, pastors of French Reformed descent became rare. Networks with other Protestant churches were concerned with constructing and re-enforcing the Protestant International to strengthen contacts with other Protestant communities. Their aim was, as well, to promote other Huguenots' careers through letters of recommendation and the use of the community's members' contacts. It has been claimed that the consistories' networks were at the core of forging *one* Huguenot diaspora identity.[26]

2.3 Family Networks

Family networks served a variety of purposes. They helped to forge family ties, mostly of family members scattered all over Europe and the Atlantic world, through gossip about the local Huguenot community, enquiries into the lives and fortunes of other family members and acquaintances, and even the exchange of cooking recipes. They also helped to arrange marriages for the younger generations, resolve financial problems, and find positions for the youth as pastors, tutors, in the military or in the local administration. In addition, family correspondence clearly served emotional needs. They provided support when family members were sick, dying or depressed not the least in situations where the Huguenot pastor or tutor was the one and only French Protestant, typically in rural settings, in households of the local elites or among ever diminishing flocks of former French Protestants.

2.4 Correspondence Networks and the Republic of Letters

French Protestants in the diaspora, at least those belonging to the educated classes, played an especially significant role as mediators and multipliers of literature, the sciences and culture at large within the Republic of Letters. The latter included French Protestants, Lutherans, Catholics, and a few Muslims and Jews. Huguenot networks stretched from St. Petersburg to the German lands, Sweden, Denmark, Britain and Ireland, and crossed the Atlantic to New

---

Court. Moteur financier de l'émigration de 1752," in *Entre Désert et Europe*, (eds.) Bost and Lauriol, 363–77. Lachenicht, "New Plantations."

26 Myriam Yardeni, *Le Refuge huguenot. Assimilation et culture* (Paris: 2002), 40–21, Lachenicht, *Hugenotten in Europa*, 48.

York, Pennsylvania, Surinam and finally South Africa. It would be wrong to say that the Republic of Letters and the exchange of ideas and knowledge would not have worked without the Huguenots, but their role was crucial. The Republic of Letters depended heavily on the Huguenots networks to collect, publish and disseminate the knowledge available within late 17th and 18th-century Europe.[27] Huguenots enhanced the exchange of knowledge within the Republic of Letters not only through correspondence but even more so through learned journals such as the *Bibliothèque britannique*, the *Bibliothèque germanique*, or the *Bibliothèque impartiale*. However, these so-called cosmopolitan networks of learned Huguenots did not merely serve the free and impartial exchange of knowledge in the sciences, philosophy, medicine, literature and theology within Europe and the Atlantic world.[28] French Protestants used them, as much as their learned journals, in large extent to serve the Protestant, more precisely the Huguenot cause. In their letters and journals, Huguenots kept telling their correspondence partners about the situation of French Protestants in exile, on the French galleys and of those back home in France, suffering from persecution and forced conversion efforts. Huguenots urged their correspondence partners to use their networks to convince the public and ultimately the governments of Protestant states to assist French galley slaves, exiles and those Huguenots who stayed behind in France. Networks, moreover, served to promote their qualities as a diaspora, as a nation of French Protestants, superior to other nations. Finally, Huguenots used their Republic of Letters networks in order to promote their brethren's careers. The correspondence of Jean Henri Samuel Formey, some 17,000 letters from more than 2400 correspondence partners, shows that his contacts with the German philosopher Christian Wolff or the Swiss poet Albrecht von Haller, were not exclusively devoted to matters of "erudition" but were also valuable in finding jobs and positions for young Berlin Huguenots and for non-Huguenot pupils growing up in Formey's Berlin household.

---

27 Christiane Berkvens-Stevelinck, "De la Haye à Berlin en passant par Londres," in *La vie intellectuelle aux refuges protestants: actes de la Table ronde de Munster du 25 juillet 1995*, (eds.) Jens Haeseler and Antony McKenna (Paris: 1999), 85–89.

28 Gerald Cerny, *Theology, Politics and Letters at the Crossroads of European Civilization. Jacques Basnage and the Baylean Huguenot Refugees in the Dutch Republic* (Dordrecht: 1987). Hubert Bost, *Un intellectuel avant la lettre: le journaliste Pierre Bayle (1647–1706)* (Amsterdam: 1994). Susanne Lachenicht, "Hugenottische Streitkultur in der Gelehrtenrepublik? Oder La mort de l'honnête homme," in *Ordnungen des "Wissens"—Ordnungen des Streitens. Gelehrte Debatten des 17./18. Jahrhunderts in diskursanalytischer Perspektive*, (ed.) Markus Meumann (Tübingen: forthcoming).

2.5 Commercial Networks, Networks of International Trade

Huguenots had already established networks of trade and commerce before the onset of persecution in the 1550s and had intensified their endeavors throughout the 17th century. Prior to the 1680s Huguenot trading posts already existed in New York, Boston, Surinam, Jamaica, Barbados and Charleston. Through the Huguenot Refuge in the Dutch Republic and in England, Huguenot networks encompassed the Atlantic Ocean and stretched, via South Africa, to the Indian Ocean and beyond. French Protestants were active in the *Vereenidge Oostindishe Compagnie* (VOC) (Dutch East India Company), both as merchants in the Far East and as members of international finance funding merchant enterprises.[29] Huguenots not only traded in wine, silk, manufactured goods, grains and salt within Europe and in the Mediterranean world but reached out into the fish, slave, sugar, textile and timber markets far into the Atlantic and the Indian Oceans. People of various ethnic and religious origins were partners with Huguenots active in commerce and trade. Those Huguenots who established themselves as merchants in London, New York, Boston and Charleston strengthened their ties with those who remained in France. Too little research has been carried out so far, but it seems that Huguenot merchant families favored a model where one member of the family converted to Catholicism and stayed behind in France in order to maintain the family's long-established trading contacts and networks in and from France. Economic interests, it seems, were in those cases more important than confessional constraints. The London Huguenot merchant Pierre Albert was thus able to trade wine from Bordeaux with the help of his family in the Bordelais region. With the help of his brother, Baudouin Seignoret successfully organized silk contraband trade from Lyon to London.[30] There is an abundance of primary sources available to study these Huguenot networks. Some scholars of the early modern period, such as John Bosher, Alison Grant and R.C. Nash have started working on the Huguenot networks in trade and commerce.[31] The bulk of analysis, however, remains to be done. Substantial networks in the Atlantic and Pacific trade and

---

29   Matthew Glozier, "Huguenots and the Dutch East India Company (VOC)," *PHSL* 29 (2010), 385–96, here 385.
30   Gwynn, *Huguenot Heritage*, 194–95.
31   Bosher, "Huguenot Merchants," 77–102; idem, "The Imperial Environment of French Trade with Canada, 1660–1685," *English Historical Review* 108 (1993), 50–82. R.C. Nash, "Huguenot Merchants and the Development of South Carolina's Slave-Plantation and Atlantic Trading Economy, 1680–1775," in *Memory and Identity. The Huguenots in France and the Atlantic Diaspora*, (eds.) Bertrand Van Ruymbeke and Randy J. Sparks (Columbia, SC: 2003), 208–40. Alison Grant, "By Sea: Huguenot Maritime Links with 17th Century Devon," *PHSL* 25 (1993), 451–63.

commerce made Huguenots desirable migrants, especially for those European powers endeavoring to establish overseas empires.

3 Immigration Policies

In the 17th and 18th centuries, most European rulers had a major interest in colonization. During much of the 17th century, some continental European states lost a considerable amount of their population, not the least due to the devastating Thirty Years' War. Some princes, such as the Elector of Brandenburg, opted for colonization within their own territories. England chose to establish colonies and plantations in Ireland, in North America and the Caribbean. Colonization and the establishment of plantations were supposed to have a civilizing effect on indigenous peoples. Furthermore, it was thought that colonization would enhance the size of a country's population as well as its military power. Complying with the major "rules" of mercantilism also meant that European powers had some interest in granting asylum to religious minorities, even if the latter did not adhere to the dominant denomination of the host country. Some minorities such as Sephardi Jews with their global networks of trade and commerce[32] or Huguenots with their assumed knowledge in winegrowing and the establishment of manufactures and textiles were thought to improve the economy of the host country or its colonies. For many Protestant European states and their growing overseas empires, fellow-Protestants seemed to be more apt to fulfill the expectations they entertained. In the 1680s, Huguenots, not the least through lobbying on their part, had become "ideal partners" in strengthening the Protestant cause in Europe and in building overseas empires.[33] For the Irish case, this is evident in a later published letter to Robert Molesworth, member of the Irish Privy Council, entitled "The True Way to Render Ireland Happy and Secure" and dating from 1697. The author was convinced that the "remarkably well-bred and civilized French…would help greatly to improve the ruder Irish both in manners and religion."[34]

One of the first European princes to accommodate Huguenot refugees after the Revocation was the Great Elector, Frederick William of Brandenburg.

---

32 See for example, Jonathan I. Israel, *Diasporas within a Diaspora: Jews, Crypto-Jews and the World Maritime Empires, 1540–1740* (Leiden: 2002).

33 See Owen Stanwood's chapter in this volume.

34 Quoted in Grace Lawless Lee, *Huguenot Settlers in Ireland* (1936; repr. Baltimore: 1993), 256. The quotation is from a letter to Robert Molesworth entitled "The True Way to Render Ireland Happy and Secure."

French refugees settling within Brandenburg-Prussia had already enjoyed certain privileges[35] when Frederick William issued the Edict of Potsdam on 29 October 1685.[36] The edict thus confirmed, standardized and enlarged the privileges of the French refugees if they agreed to settle permanently within the Electorate. The edict provided the settlers with legal status, guaranteeing the French Reformed Protestants "a sure and free refuge in all the lands and provinces of (the Brandenburg-Prussian) dominions." More specifically, the edict allowed the establishment of Huguenot colonies, with their own administration, jurisdiction and French law (*Ordonnance française*).[37] For the first ten years, Huguenot colonies in Brandenburg were exempt from paying taxes. Furthermore, they received land assignments and building materials for houses and sheds and were freed from military service and billeting. The edict guaranteed freedom of worship. The colonies were allowed to maintain the discipline, liturgy and ecclesiastical polity of the French Reformed Churches as established in France. In practice, however, the French churches in Brandenburg had to accept the Calvinist Elector as their supreme governor and synods came to be prohibited.[38] In many respects the edict enabled the French refugees to form a "separate nation," the French nation in Brandenburg. By 1692, however, the Elector closed the territory's frontiers to the further influx of French refugees. In a letter to William III of England, Frederick III of Brandenburg expressed the view that Brandenburg had offered sufficient help to the refugees. Now, he argued, other Protestant states in Europe had to provide asylum and settlement privileges.[39] Still in 1698, de Mirmand complained that most Protestant rulers within the Holy Roman Empire, the Calvinist ones in particular, refused to grant further asylum. The situation forced de Mirmand and other Huguenot diplomats to ask Lutheran rulers to accommodate the little-liked Calvinist refugees.[40] Only in 1699 did the Elector of Brandenburg agree to the further demands of Huguenot diplomats and admit Huguenot refugees

---

35 Yardeni, *Le Refuge Huguenot*, 60.
36 According to the Julian calendar, then still used in Brandenburg-Prussia; the date would be 8 November 1685 according to the Gregorian calendar.
37 Legal cases between Germans and French were to be resolved by both the "magistrate" of the German community involved and a French arbiter.
38 Margarete Welge, "Die Französische Kirche zu Berlin," in *Hugenotten in Berlin*, (eds.) Sibylle Badstübner-Gröger, Klaus Brandenburg, Rainer Geissler et al. (Berlin: 1988), 88–132, here 96–99.
39 BPF, Papiers Court, no. 17 M, M 617.
40 BPF, Papiers Court, Mss. 618 AA, 168–71 and 174–81.

coming by way of Berne.[41] Twenty-four years later, in 1709, the King of Prussia[42] confirmed the privileges granted in 1685 and naturalized all French Protestants.[43] In 1720, an act re-confirmed the privileges granted in 1685.[44] The special legal status of Huguenots in Brandenburg-Prussia—that of the French nation—was only dissolved in 1809.

Within the Holy Roman Empire, other Protestant territories followed and some even preceded the famous Edict of Potsdam. In the Landgravate of Hesse-Kassel, three letters patent set the terms and conditions for Huguenot settlement there. The "Freyheits-Concession" of April 1685[45] did not explicitly mention Huguenots as the addressees of this edict. It allowed all Protestant strangers to settle within the country if they were to erect manufactures and contribute to trade and commerce. The edict was clearly motivated by the Landgrave's mercantile interests. According to the *cuius regio, eius religio* principle, all immigrants had to express their willingness to become Calvinists. Huguenots were therefore especially welcome, as the Landgrave himself was a Calvinist. The immigrants were allowed to build churches on condition that they would bear all costs for buildings and their ministers. The Landgrave exempted all immigrants from taxes, fees and services for a period of ten years and also freed them of the compulsory membership in the guilds. The edict allowed immigrants to hire as many "master craftsmen" and "journeymen" as they considered useful for their business. A system rivaling the established guilds had begun.

However, for the Huguenot agents organizing the transport of the refugees to the German states, the "Freyheits-Concession" was anything but satisfactory. Their spokesman in Hesse-Kassel, Jean Feuquier, arranged for the Landgrave to issue letters patent in August 1685 enlarging the privileges granted in April 1685. All French craftsmen arriving in Hesse-Kassel were immediately admitted as master craftsmen and fell under the Landgrave's control and not that of the local guilds. They also enjoyed special protection against competing tradesmen. The letters patent of August 1685 further guaranteed to pay salaries to the French lectors, precentors and school masters. In December 1685, the *Concessions and*

---

41 Christian Otto Mylius, *Recueil des édits, ordonnances, règlements et rescrits contenant les privilèges et les droits attribués aux françois réfugiés dans les États du Roy de Prusse* (Berlin: 1750), 129.

42 In 1701, Frederick III (1657–1713), Elector of Brandenburg, from the Hohenzollern dynasty, and Duke of Prussia in personal union, assumed the title of King of Prussia and ruled from 1701 as King in Prussia.

43 Edouard Muret, *Geschichte der Französischen Kolonie in Brandenburg-Preußen, unter besonderer Berücksichtigung der Berliner Gemeinde* (Berlin: 1885), 307.

44 Muret, *Geschichte der Französischen Kolonie*, 307–10.

45 Lachenicht, "Freiheitskonzession," 71–75.

Privileges followed. They were to explicitly satisfy Feuquier's "demanded privileges." These concessions—this time printed in French, and not, as in many other cases, in French and German—now permitted the refugees to erect manufactures, where they would be free from paying taxes and rendering services for ten to twelve years. While the edict of April 1685 had made very clear that only manufacturers, craftsmen and tradesmen would be welcome, the December concessions also enabled men of private means to be admitted, if they agreed to invest their fortunes in state affairs. Other professions and simple workers were also welcome, if they agreed to commit to "hard work" and to obey the laws of the country.[46]

The German Elector Palatine with some of its territory close to the French border had already started accommodating French exiles from the mid-16th century onwards. The Calvinist Elector Frederick III (1515–1576) was eager to strengthen the Calvinist cause throughout Europe. Already in 1562, he granted asylum and settlement privileges that Brandenburg and other Protestant states were to copy a century later. The letters patent included land assignments. The immigrants had to swear an oath of allegiance to the Elector and were made naturalized subjects of the Elector Palatine. The French and Walloon Calvinists had to accept the Palatine church polity, yet, were allowed to have their own ministers. Services could be held in French or in Dutch. Up to the death of Charles I Louis (1617–1680), Elector Palatine, and the beginning of the Palatine Wars of Succession (1688–97), the Palatine Electorate became a major asylum for French and Piedmontese Protestants and also, to some extent, for Jews. When in 1685, the year of the revocation of the Edict of Nantes, the Catholic line Pfalz-Neuburg succeeded the Calvinist Pfalz-Simmern, re-Catholicization began. The same year marked the end of the Palatinate's pro-Calvinist immigration policies. In 1699, all French Protestants had to leave the Palatinate. Many of them settled in Brandenburg-Prussia, the Netherlands and in Scandinavia.

Within the Holy Roman Empire, the year 1685 saw a number of edicts which favored the settlement of Huguenots fleeing persecution in France. Differing in their details, many of them allowed French Protestants to establish separate communities, if not a "separate nation" within the respective German territory. The Brandenburg case set the example. In the 1680s most Huguenot diplomats lobbied the Protestant rulers in Europe and their overseas territories to grant the refugees privileges similar to the Edict of Potsdam. The Huguenots' aim was to establish separate colonies that would allow French Calvinists to become a fully-fledged diaspora, with their own church organization, administration, jurisdiction and substantial economic privileges.

---

46   Lachenicht, "Freiheitskonzession," 71–75.

Contrary to other Protestant European powers that had lost much of their population in the Thirty Years' War, England was less interested in increasing its population in the home country. However, populating the rising English and later British colonies, Ireland included, as Nicholas Canny would claim,[47] was not supposed to drive too many English people abroad. Granting asylum and settlement privileges in Ireland and the western Atlantic colonies to non-English peoples was therefore *de rigueur*, particularly from the later 17th century onwards. Furthermore, during the wars of Louis XIV and at the very latest with the accession of William of Orange to the English throne, England resumed its role as a protector of the Protestant faith.[48] Within the Protestant International, England was to develop into the protector of all Protestant denominations. Ireland, as England's "oldest colony," became a military base and a bulwark against Jacobite attacks on Protestant England. Youghal, Waterford, Kilkenny, Carlow, Belfast, Birr, Dublin and Portarlington were expected to become home to a large number of French Protestant settlements where Huguenot soldiers could protect the Protestant cause in Ireland and England. Palatine settlements on the Irish west coast, Limerick in particular, were to follow in the early 18th century. In the case of Huguenot colonies in Ireland, French Protestants lobbied the English and Irish governments for favorable privileges and settlement conditions. Huguenot diplomats such as Henri Massue, Marquis de Ruvigny, later Lord Galway, claimed to establish autonomous Huguenot colonies in Ireland,[49] pressed by the needs of a growing number of Huguenot refugees in Switzerland and other Protestant lands when these states refused to admit more French Protestants. In the 1690s, d'Arzeliers, together with Ruvigny and de Mirmand, developed a series of plans for bringing Huguenots, refugees in Switzerland, to Ireland by way of the Netherlands and England. In his *Projet pour l'établissement des Refugiez en Irlande*,[50] d'Arzeliers sought to bring 600 Huguenots from Zurich, Bern and Geneva to Ireland. However, as the *Note sur l'état du pays destiné aux réfugiés* shows, he did not have an accurate understanding of settlement conditions in Ireland. According to the *Note sur l'état du pays destiné aux réfugiés*, Huguenots in Ireland should have been able to grow vines and olive trees, and could have

---

47 Nicholas Canny, *Kingdom and Colony. Ireland in the Atlantic World 1560–1800* (Baltimore: 1988).

48 Graham C. Gibbs, "The reception of the Huguenots in England and the Dutch Republic," in *From Persecution to Toleration. The Glorious Revolution in England*, (eds.) Ole Peter Grell, Jonathan I. Israel and Nicholas Tyacke (Oxford: 1991), 275–306, here 304.

49 BPF, Papiers Court, Cote 615 no. 15, 128–36 and no. 17 Cote 617.

50 BPF Cote 617, no. 17.

produced silk and woolen garments,[51] which would then be shipped by Cork merchants to all parts of the world. D'Arzeliers dreamt that the English crown would grant Huguenots naturalization, lands and building materials, and would bear all costs for transportation to Ireland and the establishment of church, school and hospital buildings. Furthermore, he was sure that French Calvinists in Ireland would enjoy free exercise of their religion. Synods would be permitted and the Huguenots would be exempt from paying taxes and custom duties. D'Arzeliers reminded the English crown that other European rulers such as the Elector of Brandenburg had granted these privileges and had been rewarded by economic success. For d'Arzeliers, Huguenots in Ireland had to be established with their own jurisdiction and local administration. Local magistrates should not be allowed to rule over the refugees.[52] The plans failed as the English government was not willing to support Ruvigny's and d'Arzeliers settlement policies with the necessary funds. In addition, the Irish landowners were not willing to provide the necessary lands and the French refugees in the Swiss cantons did not seem wealthy enough to fulfill the high expectations entertained by the English crown and its advisers. In the end, only a small number of Huguenot soldiers and officers were settled in Portarlington, Waterford, Dublin and a few other towns in Ireland.[53]

Huguenot settlements in the English colonies of North America were, as much as in Ireland, subject to negotiation. England had a keen interest in populating the so-called *terra nullius* and in pushing the frontier further west. In a number of descriptions of the colonies to be settled, refugees, such as the Huguenots René Petit and Jacob Guérard, tried to attract Huguenot settlers to the Carolinas and lobbied the proprietors of the Carolinas to grant Huguenots naturalization. This was also the case in many letters addressed to Henry Compton, Bishop of London, and a petition entitled *Humble proposition faite au Roye et à son Parlément pour donner retraite aux étrangers protestants et aux prosélites dans ses Colonies de l'Amérique et surtout en Caroline.*[54] Many of these *Descriptions du pays* (descriptions of the land) were modeled on privileges granted in Brandenburg-Prussia in 1685: free land for Huguenot settlers, religious freedom, and claims of exemption from taxation for ten years. With

---

51 BPF, Papiers Court, Cote 615 no. 15, 128.
52 BPF, Papiers Court, Cote 615 no. 15, 128–36.
53 Lachenicht, *Hugenotten in Europa*, 133–50.
54 London, British Public Record Office, *Humble proposition faite au Roye et à son Parlément pour donner retraite aux étrangers protestants et aux prosélites dans ses Colonies de l'Amérique et surtout en Caroline*, CO, 1/43/16. The letter to Henry Compton, see Oxford, Bodleian Library, Rawlinson Mss. C 984, 217 ff.

regard to Huguenots and other Protestant settlers, the proprietors of the Carolinas, at least during the 1680s and early 1690s, indeed granted naturalization, the right to vote and to stand for election to public offices, including the colonial Assembly.[55] The Crown also paid for some Huguenots' passage across the Atlantic. French Protestants, much as other non-Conformists, were allowed to establish their own churches. Still, after 1691 the Quaker governor, John Archdale, abolished those privileges.[56] Only in 1712 were French Protestants and other dissenters in the Carolinas allowed naturalization privileges and the right to vote and to stand for election. In the colony of New York, two major Huguenot settlements developed. In New Paltz, the original Huguenot patentees (established in 1677 by Governor Edmund Andros) had their own local administration (into which other European settlers were slowly integrated) and were treated as natural-born Englishmen. In New Rochelle, privileges granted to the French Protestant minority were similar to those granted to Dutch Calvinists or German Lutherans. The heterogeneity reigning in the British colonies in North America was brought to an end by an Act of Parliament in 1740. Then, Parliament enacted legislation for the colonies granting naturalization to all foreign Protestant settlers, provided that they swore an oath of allegiance to the King.[57]

Despite England's efforts to utilize Huguenots in the process of building the first British Empire, most Huguenots were accommodated within England itself. Between 1687 and 1720 an estimated 50,000 French Protestants arrived in England to find a permanent new home. England accommodated foreigners mostly on the basis of Parliamentary acts, favoring apart from the 1689 *Declaration for the Encouraging of French Protestants to transport themselves into this Kingdom* no particular ethnic group but Protestants in general. There are a few exceptions to this pattern, though, as the 1681 *Declaration of Hampton Court* makes evident. In the early 1680s, Huguenots, through a propaganda campaign and a vast number of petitions to Henry Compton, Bishop of London, and King Charles II, were able to impose their needs on the English Crown. Even prior to the harsh *dragonnades* of the 1680s in France, the officially conformist Huguenot Church of London, the Savoy Church (established in 1661), tried to convince Parliament to open all professions in London to

---

55 John Alexander Moore, "Frenchmen to Freemen: The Politics of Naturalization in Early Carolina," *Transactions of the Huguenot Society of South Carolina* 100 (1995), 248–53.

56 Bertrand Van Ruymbeke, "South Carolina: The Home of the Huguenots? (1680–1719)," *Transactions of the Huguenot Society of South Carolina* 96 (1991), 42–80.

57 *The Statutes at Large. From the First Year of King George the First to the Third Year of the Reign of King George the Second*, vol. 6 (London: 1763), 384–86.

Protestant strangers.⁵⁸ In 1681, Huguenots in England addressed a vast number of letters and petitions to the King, Parliament and bishops of the Anglican Church.⁵⁹ Furthermore, pamphlets describing the French Catholic atrocities against Huguenots in France to an English and Dutch-speaking audience flooded the book market. They included a *Humble Petition of the Protestants of France to the French King, to recall his declaration for taking away their children from the age of seven years* (London 1681); the *Present State of the Protestants in France in three letters: Written by a gentleman at London to his friend in the country* (London 1681); *The horrible persecution of the French Protestants in the province of Poitou truly set forth by a gentleman of great quality...*(London 1681); *A Letter from Rochel France: to MR. Demeure, one of the French ministers at the French church in the Savoy, shewing the intolerable persecutions that are there exercised against them* (London 1681); *A Strange but true account of the barbarous usage of three young ladies in France for being Protestants: with a relation also of their wonderful escape from thence into England* (London 1681); and *The Great Pressures and Grievances of the Protestants in France and their Apology to the Late Ordinances made against them; both out of the Edict of Nantes, and several other Fundamental Laws of France; and these new Illegalities, and their Miseries are Contrived by the Pop. Bishops Arbitrary Power* (London 1681). Most of these petitions and pamphlets asked for the following privileges for Huguenots coming into England: denization, if not naturalization, free access to all guilds and professions and to education, no taxes on any goods or possessions brought into England, poor relief for the refugees and equal rights for all nonconformists in England, including French Calvinists.⁶⁰ The *Declaration of Hampton Court*, issued in July 1681, complied with those claims except for equal rights for non-conformists. The London guilds, moreover, were permitted to decide themselves whether they wanted to accept Protestant strangers among their members. In 1686, Henry Compton, Bishop of London, issued a circular on the Huguenot cause echoing the claims made by Huguenots five years earlier.⁶¹ Further campaigns, lobbying the British Crown, Parliament and Church of England representatives can be found in British archives. When between 1709 and 1712, some 12,000 "poor Palatines" came to Britain to

---

58   Robin D. Gwynn (ed.), *Minutes of the Consistory of the French Church of London, Threadneedle Street: 1679–1692* (London: 1994), 45.
59   Lachenicht, *Hugenotten in Europa*, 56–69.
60   Oxford, Bodleian Library, Tanner Mss. 92, 180.
61   Oxford, Bodleian Libray, Tanner Mss. 30, 10, Letter of Henry Compton, Bishop of London (written in April 1686) making an ardent appeal to the clergy of his diocese to help the Huguenots.

be re-settled in the British colonies in North America, Huguenots again urged the British Crown to support the Protestant cause in Europe and the colonies and to force Louis XIV of France to revoke the Edict of Fontainebleau.[62] Huguenot petitions of this period explicitly mention the privileges granted to the Palatines, claiming that the British government should not forget the Huguenot cause. In this case, however, the French Protestant petitioners asked for privileges that had not really been granted to the Palatines. Philipp Otterness has described the failed campaign, failing on the part of the so-called "poor Palatines" and their recruiters, to settle some 12,000 of them in the British colonies. Most Palatines were sent back to the European continent; only a few among them made their way to Ireland and to what is now New York State.[63]

In the Calvinist Netherlands, the seven separate provinces regulated the immigration and accommodation of religious refugees. During the 1680s, a number of provinces and cities issued privileges, some as early as 1681, paralleling the English *Declaration of Hampton Court*. In 1681, the city of Amsterdam made French Protestants free burghers, admitted them to all guilds, helped craftsmen in setting up new workshops and exempted them from taxation. This was echoed by the city of Leiden.[64] However, only a couple of years later, in 1690, the Amsterdam municipal government revoked those privileges making it more difficult for Huguenots to found new lives in Amsterdam.[65] The city of Groningen granted in 1681 free access to the guilds and made Protestant immigrants exempt from paying taxes. Similar privileges can be found in the provinces of Friesland, Geldern and Utrecht.[66]

4   Conclusion

It seems that members of "victim diasporas" such as the Huguenots were capable of lobbying states and governments for asylum and settlement privileges

---

62   Oxford, Bodleian Library, *State Papers of Queen Anne*, vol. XXXIII, 56–80, 94–114, 137–44, 245–46.

63   Philip Otterness, *Becoming German: The 1709 Palatine Migration to New York* (Ithaca: 2004), 57–76.

64   Paul Lucien Nève, "Le statut juridique des réfugiés français huguenots; quelques remarques comparatives," in *La condition juridique de l'étranger hier et aujourd'hui. Actes du Colloque organisé à Nimègue 8–11 mai 1988* (Nijmegen: 1988), 223–46, 235. Hans Bots and René Bastiaanse, "Die Hugenotten und die niederländischen Generalstaaten," in *Die Hugenotten*, (eds.) von Thadden and Magdelaine, 55–72.

65   Bots and Bastiaanse, "Hugenotten," 58, 61. Gibbs, "The Reception," 302–03.

66   Nève, "Statut juridique," 236, 246.

only to a limited extent. While, in some contexts, Huguenots were successful in claiming considerable privileges, emphasizing their value and their possible contributions to the economy, culture and military power of the host states, they failed in others. While Huguenots lobbied all Protestant European states to grant asylum and settlement privileges that would have allowed them to form largely autonomous congregations and colonies, only Brandenburg-Prussia and several other German states allowed the French Reformed refugees to settle as a "French nation" abroad. There, the so-called French colonies had their own administration, a separate jurisdiction under French law, their own churches and educational system. In England, Ireland and North America, the government allowed the Huguenots their own churches and consistories. However, in law, administration, the economy, and to some extent in religious matters, French refugees were expected to integrate into state and society.

Within continental Europe, religious minorities other than Huguenots, such as Mennonites, Moravians, Sephardi and Ashkenazi Jews, lobbied European rulers for asylum and a large degree of autonomy for their communities. Seeking as much as the Huguenots the preservation of their original faith and culture these groups also sought to be vested not only with churches or meeting houses and a system of social aid and control, but also with their own administration, laws, jurisdiction, schools, and at the frontier with their own militia.[67] Within Europe, Brandenburg-Prussia and the rising Russian Empire were eager to accommodate Huguenots, Dutch and Swiss colonists, Mennonites and, in the case of Russia, Moravians.[68] Other European powers such as England were reluctant to grant considerable privileges within their own territories. In British North America, however, at the frontier, German Lutherans, such as the Salzburgers who settled in Georgia, were able to negotiate wide-ranging grants, including Lutheran churches, schools, courts and a militia for self-defense. In the initial years after their settlement in the 1730s, Georgia Salzburgers were directly responsible to the crown in London, not to the authorities in Georgia.[69] At the very periphery of the expanding first British Empire, settlement privileges were particularly generous, even for non-Christian settlers. Between 1652

---

67 Carola Wessel, "'We do not want to introduce anything new.' Transplanting the Communal Life from Herrnhut to the Upper Ohio Valley," in *In Search of Peace and Prosperity: New German Settlements in Eighteenth-Century Europe and America*, (eds.) Hartmut Lehmann, Hermann Wellenreuther and Renate Wilson (University Park, Pa.: 2000), 243–62.

68 Andreas Gestrich, "German Religious Emigration to Russia in the Eighteenth and Early Nineteenth Centuries. Three Case Studies," in *In Search of Peace and Prosperity*, (eds.) Lehmann et al., 77–98, here 78 and 87–88.

69 Renate Wilson, "Land, Population, and Labor. Lutheran Immigrants in Colonial Georgia," in *In Search of Peace and Prosperity*, (eds.) Lehmann et al., 217–45.

and 1667, when Surinam was under English rule (Governor Lord Willoughby), Sephardi Jews enjoyed religious freedom and a high degree of administrative autonomy. They built synagogues and mounted their own militia; they were allowed to settle on land wherever they wanted. In Jamaica, from the 1660s, Sephardi Jews could be endenizened and even naturalized. From 1740 onwards, Sephardi Jews enjoyed, in theory, possible naturalization throughout the British Empire.[70] Even in Europe and the British Isles, drawing on the utility for the economy of France, Britain and the Netherlands, Sephardi Jews were able to build religious and ethnic enclaves with, later in the 17th century, their synagogues, public bath houses, their own administration, jurisdiction and educational system, as the Bordeaux and Amsterdam communities make evident.[71]

Some minority groups, such as Sephardi Jews and Huguenots, seem to have been more successful in negotiating asylum and settlement privileges than others. Looking at the State Papers of Queen Anne, the sheer number of Huguenot petitions from the period between 1704 and 1714, ten times as many documents as those of Palatine "lobbyists," as well as the diplomatic, economic, intellectual and military networks of the Huguenots show that successful lobbying needed special ingredients, intertwining networks and a propaganda machine that helped nourish the European states' need for immigration. However, the case of the Huguenots during the 1690s shows that networks and lobbying did not always prove as successful as the group's diplomatic and military leaders might have wished. Immigration policies were subject to the early modern rulers' ever changing political, military, religious and economic interests that, despite concerted efforts, could not always be controlled by the refugee groups.

---

70   Yitzchak Kerem, "Sephardic Settlement in the British Colonies of the Americas in the 17th and 18th Centuries," in *From Strangers to Citizens*, (eds.) Vigne and Littleton, 285–95, Susanne Lachenicht, "Sephardi Jews: Cosmopolitans in the Atlantic World?" in *Diaspora Identities. Exile, Nationalism and Cosmopolitanism in Past and Present*, (eds.) Susanne Lachenicht and Kirsten Heinsohn (Frankfurt am Main: 2009), 31–51.

71   Esther Benbassa and Aron Rodrigue, *Sephardi Jewry: A History of the Judeo-Spanish Community, 14th–20th Centuries* (Berkeley: 2000). Daniel M. Swetschinski, *Reluctant Cosmopolitans. The Portuguese Jews of Seventeenth-Century Amsterdam* (Oxford: 2004).

CHAPTER 10

Assimilation and Integration

Myriam Yardeni

1   Introduction

Between the years 1681, the beginning of the *dragonnades*, and approximately 1710, a quarter of all Huguenots fled their homeland. They fled to the British Isles, the United Provinces of the Netherlands, various German states and Switzerland. While we find among their number a handful of adventurers and a few emigrants whose main impetus was economic, the vast majority of Huguenots were concerned to save their souls, a fact that stands in flagrant contradiction with what E.-G. Léonard and others have asserted about the depth and intensity of Huguenot belief. Their flight stands alongside the expulsion of the Jews from Spain and Portugal and the Moriscos from Spain as one of the most important mass emigrations of early modern Europe.

The fugitives were convinced that their exile would not last long. They believed that the Sun King, Louis XIV, would soon change his policy of persecution and that they would be able to return to their homeland. For this reason they looked only for a temporarily shelter. Their state of mind is perhaps best described as an attempt to find refuge.[1] But with the Treaty of Ryswick in 1697, most lost hope of returning to their homeland, and with the Peace of Utrecht in 1713, their exile became definitive.

The flight from France was dangerous. The king forbade Huguenots to leave the country. When caught attempting to do so the men were put on galleys or imprisoned and the women were shut up in cloisters.

Their initial faith and conviction that their exile would not last long notwithstanding, the assimilation of the Huguenots began almost immediately upon their arrival in a new country—assimilation in the sense that they had to learn the basic words of greetings in a new language, the elementary customs of their new home, and its rudimentary rules of comportment.

---

1   "Refuge" is a neologism created by Charles Weiss, the first global historian of the Huguenot diaspora of the Revocation era. Weiss distinguished judiciously between exile, emigration and refuge. Charles Weiss, *Histoire des réfugiés protestants de France depuis la Révocation de l'Edit de Nantes à nos jours*, vol. 1 (Paris: 1853), x.

2   Numbers

When Louis XIV revoked the Edict of Nantes on 18 October 1685 there were in France some 700,000 to 1,000,000 Huguenots, approximately 4–5 per cent of the population.[2] We are therefore speaking of about 200,000–250,000 exiles since the Reformation. Nevertheless, nothing is more misleading in the secondary literature than the calculation of the number of the fugitives.

Today the tendency is to reduce drastically the numbers involved. For instance, Mark Greengrass speaks of about 150,000 refugees.[3] Perhaps the most drastic reduction is made by the Dutch economic historian H. Nusteling. Following his calculations for Amsterdam, not only as a case study, but as a source for all his calculations for all the Dutch provinces, the number of the refugees is lowered from between 70,000-90,000 to only 35,000.[4] For Eckart Birnstiel, some 200,000 Huguenot refugees left their homeland during the three centuries between the beginning of the Reformation era and the Revocation, a figure that includes the various migrations between the different diaspora countries themselves.[5] On the other hand, R. Hylton mentions 10,000 Huguenots from the Dauphiné province alone in the seven years immediately following the Revocation.[6] It is quite an impossible task to calculate exactly the number of the fugitives.

We can surmise that this reduction of numbers is exaggerated. True, some fugitives moved from one place to another, registering and receiving help in many communities. Furthermore, some fugitives were registered up to ten times at some of the main points of transition, such as Frankfurt-am-Main and Switzerland. On the other hand, we find Huguenots in villages in which they did not constitute communities and maintained no records.

---

2   Philip Benedict, *The Huguenot Population of France, 1600–1685: the Demographic Fate and Customs of a Religious Minority* (Philadelphia: 1991).
3   Mark Greengrass, "Protestant Exiles and Their Assimilation in Early Modern England," *Immigrants and Minorities* 4 (1985), 68–81.
4   Hubert Nusteling. *Welvaart en werkgelegenheid in Amsterdam, 1540–1860* (Amsterdam: 1985). Willem Frijhoff, "Uncertain Brotherhood: The Huguenots in the Dutch Republic," in *Memory and Identity: The Huguenots in France and the Atlantic Diaspora*, (eds.) Bertrand Van Ruymbeke and Randy J. Sparks (Columbia, SC: 2003), 128–171.
5   Eckart Birnstiel and Chrystel Bernat (eds.), *La diaspora des huguenots: les réfugiés protestants de France et leur dispersion dans le monde, XVIe–XVIIIe siècles* (Paris: 2001).
6   Raymond P. Hylton, "The Huguenot Settlement at Portarlington," in *The Huguenots and Ireland: Anatomy of an Emigration*, (eds.) C.E.J. Caldicott, Hugh Gough and J.P. Pittion (Dublin: 1987), 306.

Sometimes the fugitives arrived—or departed—in small groups with their families and other people from their original villages; occasionally entire villages departed together; it was even known for fugitives representing a certain profession to travel together; but mostly the flight was an individual act, which divided families and friendships and sundered other bonds.

It is very difficult to ascertain the relative ages of the fugitives. Sometimes we have excellent records from the towns and even small villages from where they fled, and sometimes we have documents for the places where they arrived. But it is quite impossible to analyze systematically the numbers because of the great lacunas in the evidence. Nevertheless, one can surmise that the large majority of the fugitives were young, from 15 to 30 years old, single, mostly male although perhaps a third were women. But averages should not blind us to the exceptions; there were also families with small children and some of the refugees were 85 years old.

They are no precise numbers for the British Isles. It is conventional to speak of about 50,000–60,000 fugitives.[7] For the Netherlands the convention, as we have seen, is about 70,000, for Brandenburg-Prussia, 20,000–22,000. But it is very difficult to provide numbers for Switzerland, for which we have gathered more detailed information below.[8] Probably the exact numbers were less important for the assimilation and integration of the refugees than the elements involved in the two processes.

The accepted signs of assimilation and integration for the large majority of historians of the Huguenot emigration are language, religion, social and political integration, enriched by mutual, usually literary exchanges and reciprocal influences between the host nation and the emigrants. The problem is that for most historians of the Huguenot emigration, assimilation and integration are not only interwoven concepts but also interchangeable phenomena.

In the wake of some new trends in cultural and also social history, however, it becomes possible to distinguish various elements in the processes and, indeed, to distinguish clearly between the two concepts of assimilation and integration themselves. For assimilation is a process of accommodation and acculturation, the principle elements of which are language, dress and diet, followed by amalgamation and even a change in the ethnic character of the

---

7   Robin Gwynn, "Conformity, Non-conformity and Huguenot Settlement in England in the Later Seventeenth Century," in *The Religious Culture of the Huguenots, 1600–1750*, (ed.) Anne Dunan-Page (Aldershot: 2006), 33.
8   See below, section 6, Switzerland. Rémy Scheurer, "Passage, accueil et intégration des Huguenots en Suisse," in *Le Refuge huguenot*, (eds.) Michelle Magdelaine and Rudolf von Thadden, (Paris: 1985), 45–62.

emigrant.[9] Integration, on the other hand, is an economic and political process that sometimes runs parallel to assimilation but is sometimes completely distinct in time.

3 British Isles

It is no accident that the two political territories that received the largest contingents of Huguenots in the years of persecution following the Revocation were the British Isles and the Dutch United Provinces. These two countries were already asylum lands for the persecuted—Reformed believers, Lutherans, Calvinists and others in the 16th century and the first half of the 17th—and they both had in place already established French speaking churches, with smoothly functioning structures for community aid. The British Isles[10] contained an already integrated Huguenot community, replete with luxury industry, banqueters and aldermen of the Municipality of London.

In the years following the Revocation, the sparkling success of the first and second generation of émigrés, now born in England, is well captured in the figure of Sir Peter Delmé, who was both Lord Mayor of London and Governor of the Bank of England. Many of the more assimilated Huguenots in later years were probably the descendants of this first generation who willingly melted into their English surroundings, anglicized their names,[11] became conformists who followed Anglican forms of worship and liturgy, and gathered primarily in Westminster and the Savoy Church under the famous and militantly anti-French "Whig" pastor, Jean Armand Dubourdieu.

On the other hand, many of the new emigrants in London underwent similar processes as their refugee brethren in Berlin and became truly "French" only in the second generation.[12] For while perceived on arrival by the locals as French, the emigrants identified as "Languedociens," "Messins" (from Metz), and so on, and it was only their children who understood themselves to be

9   Eileen Barrett, "Huguenot Integration in late 17th-and 18th-century London: Insights from Records of the French Church and Some Relief Agencies," in *From Strangers to Citizens: The Integration of Immigrant Communities in Britain, Ireland, and Colonial America, 1550–1750*, (eds.) Randolph Vigne and Charles Littleton, (Brighton: 2001), 375.

10 Fabienne Chamayou, "Le Refuge dans les îles britanniques," in *La diaspora des huguenots: les réfugiés protestants de France et leur dispersion dans le monde, XVIe–XVIIIe siècles*, (ed.) Eckart Birnstiel (Paris: 2001), 43, criticized by Gwynn, "Conformity, Non-conformity and Huguenot Settlement in England," in *Religious Culture*, (ed.) Dunan-Page, 33.

11 Robin Gwynn, *Huguenot Heritage: The History and Contribution of the Huguenots in Britain* (Brighton: 2001).

12 Myriam Yardeni, *Le Refuge protestant* (Paris: 1985), 47, 101.

French. The first to arrive in London founded aid associations for their brothers and, as later waves arrived, these were regrouped in line with common provincial origins, such as Normandy or Poitou. But even for them, assimilation was rapid. Nathalie Rothstein has shown how the Huguenot master weavers became, in the first half of the 18th century, not only exemplary Englishmen with English partners and apprentices, but also English patriots.[13]

From the 16th century, London attracted the bulk of the Huguenot refugees. In the years of the great persecutions and following them, there were more than 22,000 Huguenot refugees in London, with a total of 50,000 to 60,000 throughout the British Isles. For Robin Gwynn the explanation of these large numbers is in part that London was a capital city that already possessed all the necessary structures for receiving them, and in part the relatively tolerant policy of the last Stuarts and, with the "Glorious Revolution," the subsequent ascendance to the throne of the Calvinist couple William and Mary. Many Huguenot soldiers and officers did indeed follow William and his army. But there was also the openness of the English textile artisans and guilds (economic rivalry and tension notwithstanding). The resultant economic fusion left its mark upon the English language, for example: "denim" from "de Nîmes," and cord back from Caudebec in Normandy.[14] Other important British Huguenot centers of these years were the Channel Islands, Canterbury, Plymouth, Bristol, Dover, and also Norwich in Norfolk.[15]

What really characterizes the Refuge in England is the way that assimilation and integration went together and, indeed, were inseparable. What is standardly emphasized, in the histories of the Huguenots in Britain, is their contribution to the various arts and crafts,[16] from Lloyds insurance company to the rediscovery of Shakespeare by Garrick in the 18th century, and so on. Finally, even the rivalry and tensions between Episcopal conformist Anglican and nonconformist Calvinist churches contributed to and helped perfect the process of assimilation by fostering the progressive disappearance by amalgamation and other ways of the Huguenot churches.[17] As Robin Gwynn has remarked, today there are few Englishmen without some Huguenot traces in their blood.

---

13 Nathalie Rothstein, "Huguenot master weavers: exemplary Englishmen, 1700–1750," in *From Strangers to Citizens*, (eds.) Vigne and Littelton, 160–71.
14 Robin Gwynn, *The Huguenots of London* (Brighton: 1998), 49.
15 Robin Gwynn, "Distribution of Huguenot Refugees in England," Part I in *PHSL* 21 (1970), 404–36, and Part II in *PHSL* 22 (1976), 509–68.
16 For a visual illustration, see Tessa Murdoch, *The Quiet Conquest: The Huguenots, 1685 to 1985, Catalogue of the Museum of London Exhibition, in Association with the Huguenot Society of London* (London: 1985).
17 Refugees could easily choose their church or leave it. For more on this subject, see Myriam Yardeni, *Le Refuge Huguenot: assimilation et culture* (Paris: 2002), 67.

And while the rediscovery of this Huguenot element has contributed to and reinforced a Huguenot concern with family memory and an accompanying "snobbism," fostered by serious scholarly research, often propelled by the Huguenot Society of Great Britain,[18] little or none of this awareness has yet penetrated the textbook histories of England.[19]

4   Ireland

With regard to the 16th and early 17th centuries, and even more so for the 18th, Ireland, with its 10,000 refugees from the "Roi Soleil's" persecution,[20] constitutes a special and in many respects different story. It was the peculiar policy of Ireland to gather and make political capital out of the French Calvinist refugees. Huguenot refugees were encouraged to settle by the grant of privileges, although without establishing linguistic autonomy as in Brandenburg. This new chapter in the history of Irish colonization was intended to aid the economic development of the country, but the colonization system was also intended to promote England's religious (Anglican) interests and to increase English political influence and domination in Catholic Ireland.

The Duke of Ormond, twice Lord Lieutenant of Ireland, initiated petitions to the last Stuart monarchs in order to attract Huguenot refugees, perhaps under the influence of James Harrington, who suggested in *Oceana* (1656) the transformation of Ireland into a new Canaan by the settling of Jews who excelled in arts and agricultures in ancient times. The Huguenots of these years of course also excelled in arts, manufacture, commerce and agriculture, and Ormond details this in his memoires.

Such utopian plans began to be partially realized after Switzerland expelled its refugees, and with the initiative of Lord Galway (Marquis de Ruvigny) under William III.[21] More than 10,000 Huguenots officers and soldiers were now brought and settled in Ireland, together with peasants, artisans, merchants and pastors, the latter mostly from the entourage of William III. Many Huguenot

---

18   *Huguenot Society of London,* since 1986, *Huguenot Society of Great Britain and Ireland*. For more on this subject see Dunan-Page (ed.), *Religious Culture,* Introduction.

19   Among the notable exceptions: Paul Langford, *Englishness Identified. Manners and Character 1650–1850* (Oxford, 2000) and John Marshall, *John Locke, Toleration, and Early Enlightenment Culture* (Cambridge: 2010).

20   For the best discussion of numbers see Hylton who, referring to the totality of Huguenot emigration to Ireland, concludes that the amount "should eventually prove to be neither less than 8000, nor much more than 10,000." Raymond Hylton, *Ireland's Huguenots and their Refuge, 1662–1745: An Unlikely Haven* (Brighton: 2005), 204.

21   See below section 6, Switzerland.

pastors adopted Anglicanism and strengthened conformism, which was even imposed on many of the new Huguenot settlers by Peter Drelincourt, one of the most influential members of Ormond's household. The most important Huguenot centers were Dublin, and the new semi-military settlement and military colony of Portarlington. Other colonies included Cork, Kilkenny and Waterford. But there were also utopian plans to settle Huguenots in Ireland.[22]

The assimilation and integration of the Huguenot refugees in Ireland was not simply a natural or spontaneous process. At times it was also the outcome of the well-planned conformist political machinations of Bishop Moreton, who in 1702 forced the dismissal of Portarlington's beloved non-conformist pastor, Benjamin Daillon. Portarlington's Huguenots passed into local folklore: the image of French veterans in their scarlet cloaks, swords, and knee buckles gathered in the market square and religiously savoring, in tiny china cups, a rare and expensive beverage called "tea" has proven to be an enduring one. Generations of Irish children in Counties Laois and Offaly would fondly recall the grace, elegance and culture of the Huguenots.[23]

Demographically, Dublin was of course the most important Huguenot center, with a population of 4000 Huguenots at its peak around 1720, more than 5 percent of the total city population. When Dublin became a sophisticated social and intellectual center in the 18th century, Huguenot influence in the luxury trades grew considerably,[24] as did also their importance in cultural life.[25] Nevertheless, with the imposed integration of the Huguenot churches in the frame of the Anglicanisation of Ireland, assimilation followed the integration process willy-nilly.

5 The Dutch Republic

A severe economic crisis that beset Amsterdam was accompanied by a dramatic fall in the population in the years immediately preceding the revocation

---

22   Michelle Magdelaine, "L'Irlande huguenote: utopie ou réalité?" in *De L'Humanisme aux Lumières. Bayle et le protestantisme. Mélanges en l'honneur d'Elisabeth Labrousse*, (eds.) Michelle Magdelaine, Maria-Christina Pitassi, Ruth Whelan and Antony McKenna (Paris: 1996), 273–87.
23   Hylton, "The Huguenot Settlement at Portarlington" in *The Huguenots and Ireland*, (eds.) Caldicott, Gough, and Pittion.
24   David Dickson, "Huguenots in the Urban Economy of Eighteenth-Century Dublin and Cork," in *The Huguenots and Ireland*, (eds.) Caldicott, Gough, and Pittion, 321–32.
25   Jane McKee, "The Influence of the Huguenots on Educated Ireland: Huguenot Books in Irish Church Libraries of the Eighteenth Century," in *Religious Culture*, (ed.) Dunan-Page, 121–36.

of the Edict of Nantes. Consequently, local authorities in the Dutch Republic were receptive to an influx of Huguenot refugees from France.

This economic and demographic decline was one of the most important causes that transformed the Dutch Netherlands into the *"Grande arche des fugitifs,"* as Pierre Bayle, the great philosophe of Rotterdam, called the United Provinces. When thousands of native inhabitants left Amsterdam, the regents seized the opportunity to attract French refugees to their city, according them such privileges as exemption from guild duties, land excises and civil rights for life. But it was not only Amsterdam that was active in attracting refugees. Many periodicals, such as the *Gazette de Leyde*, developed methods of publicly inviting refugees to their respective city or town, praising its particular advantages.

In any case, the already existing Walloon churches in the Republic,[26] the high standing of the French language and civilization in the Netherlands, and the solid reputation of the Dutch Republic as a paradise of toleration[27] attracted the largest numbers of Huguenot refugees among all the host countries. In Amsterdam alone there were already 800 Huguenots prior to the Revocation of the Edict of Nantes.

Other Dutch cities and provinces, such as Groningen, followed Amsterdam, according important privileges to the refugees. The number of Walloon churches grew rapidly,[28] and they took under their charge the poor refugees, organizing collections but also receiving important help from the different representative assemblies. In relation to other emigrants, the refugee pastors were relatively privileged. Of 800 exiled pastors, 350 were appointed to a newly founded *"Église"* or joined one of the already existing Walloon churches.[29] Often their former flock from France joined them in the new Refuge. The most important Huguenot centers would include Amsterdam, Rotterdam, Leyden,

---

26   F.H. Gagnebin, "Liste des Eglises wallones des Pays Bas et des pasteurs qui les ont desservies," *Bulletin de la Commission pour l'histoire des Eglises wallonnes* 3 (1888), 25–64, 97–120, 209–40, 313–46.

27   Benjamin J. Kaplan, "'Dutch' Religious Tolerance: Celebration and Revision," in *Calvinism and Religious Toleration in the Dutch Golden Age*, (eds.) R. Po-Chia Hsia and Henk van Nierop (Cambridge: 2002), 8–26.

28   Hans Bots, "Le Refuge Huguenot dans les Provinces-Unies. Orientation bibliographique," in *Conflits politiques, controverses religieuses*, (eds.) Ouzi Elyada and Jacques Le Brun (Paris: 2002), 101–17.

29   For a list of the pastors who settled in the Netherlands, see Hans Bots, "Les pasteurs français au Refuge dans les Provinces-Unies: Un groupe socio-professionnel tout particulier: 1680–1710," in *La Vie intellectuelle aux refuges protestants*, (eds.) Jens Häseler and Antony McKenna (Paris: 1999), 9–68.

The Hague, Middelburg, Haarlem, Arnhem, Zutphen, Zwolle, Deventer, Groningen, Franeker and Sneek.

Depression followed in the wake of the early years of enthusiasm and Christian charity. The Dutch Republic fast became saturated with refugees. Their increasing numbers raised antagonism and heightened economic rivalry. A Dutch cultural nationalism also developed. Associated with Peter Rabus at the end of the 17th century and Justus Van Effen in the 18th, it alleged that the French refugees had invaded Dutch cultural life. Indeed, of 220 bookshops in Amsterdam, 80 were owned by French refugees. French newspapers and periodicals dominated the market and French teachers and educators were hired not only by the nobles but also by the Dutch bourgeoisie.

Economic integration was not easy because of a new economic crisis that beset the Dutch Republic. For many categories of emigrant, economic integration was relatively successful; but even for them assimilation was slow and painful. Few scholars were able to join Dutch universities. Teachers and educators had to adapt themselves quickly to the changing mentalities of the Dutch Republic. Private educators and tutors employed by the merchant bourgeoisie had to abandon the *"français de cour,"* set aside their French mannerisms and adapt themselves to their new middle class employers. On the other hand, hundreds and hundreds of refugee educators from the southern French provinces hardly embodied the mainstream language, ideals and manners of Parisian France. For the successful intellectuals and journalists, assimilation was even more difficult. Their *"République des lettres"* prospered, but they had few contacts with the "backward" Dutch and they formed an artificial French preserve in the Dutch Republic. They lived in a close and isolated French universe, disdaining their Dutch hosts with their seemingly bizarre civilization, customs, and culinary taste (the refugees had many jokes about the Dutch and their herring). Such refugees continued to imitate French fashion in clothing and, even in the second generation, did not learn or understand Dutch.

From 1690, the Dutch cities, with Amsterdam at their head, began to abolish the privileges previously granted to the refugees. Their collections and donations could no longer cover the expenses of refugees in need, and lotteries were organized in order to sustain them. The disillusion was mutual. The Dutch economy suffered a new crisis in the wake of a surplus of production. Many Huguenot artisans and laborers left the Dutch Netherlands, while many soldiers and officers joined William III, and followed him to England. Later, Amsterdam's regents would react to the situation once again. In the mid-18th century all "refugee" pupils were ordered to learn their elementary school materials in Dutch. Willy-nilly assimilation now commenced and only a few French speaking Walloon churches survived into the 19th century. Even the

French ethnic characteristics of the refugees become increasingly Dutch with more and more mixed marriages.

6   Germany

In the late 17th century and the early 18th, the years of the great Huguenot emigration, the German Empire was a huge conglomerate of Catholic, Lutheran and also Calvinist states. These states were sometimes themselves mixed. In 1613, for example, John Sigismund changed his religion from Lutheranism to Calvinism and henceforth the Lutheran population of Brandenburg was ruled by a Calvinist prince. Catholic and Protestant territories were sometimes inextricably mingled, as with the Lutheran city of Worms encircled by the territories of the Catholic Bishopric of Worms.

Almost all the Reformed German states were interested in attracting Huguenots. They wanted to see the refugees definitively settle in their territories as opposed to merely obtaining temporary shelter. This was a major difference between Germany and the other receiving countries, and this despite the animosity, even in Brandenburg-Prussia, displayed against the French Calvinists by a large section of the Lutheran population.

The major German states sent recruiters to the main points of passage of the Huguenots into Switzerland, Frankfurt-am-Main and even the Dutch Republic. These recruiters organized immediate convoys for transport, praising the *Aufnahmenspolitik* of the various German princes,[30] exhorting the privileges and concessions granted to the refugees, which included linguistic autonomy, membership in the guilds and exemption from taxes for a limited period of time. As explained by Etienne François and many others, the preferred pattern of settlement was, for most German rulers, the foundation of special colonies.[31] Among the new "colonies," some of the most important included Erlangen in Bayreuth-Brandenburg, Karlshafen in Hesse-Kassel, and even villages such as Friedrichsdorf[32] in the Uckermark or special suburbs such as Dorotheenstadt and Friedrichstadt in Berlin.

---

30   Susanne Lachenicht, "Die Freiheitskonzession des Landgrafen von Hessen-Kassel, das Edikt von Potsdam und die Ansiedlung von Hugenotten," in *Hugenotten und Deutsche Territorialstaaten. Immigration und Integrationprozesse*, (eds.) Guido Braun and Susanne Lachenicht (Munich: 2007), 71–83.

31   Étienne François, "L'Accueil des refugiés huguenots en Allemagne," in *The Revocation of the Edict of Nantes and the Dutch Republic*, (eds.) J.A.H. Bots and G.H.M. Posthumus Meyjes (Amsterdam: 1986), 207–16.

32   Auguste Descamps, *Un village français en Allemagne* (Lille: 1905).

The initiative in attracting refugees to Germany belonged to Frederic William, the Great Elector of Brandenburg, who in October 1685 published his famous Edict of Potsdam, an immediate and incisive answer to Louis XIV's Edict of Fontainebleau, and issued only three weeks after that of Louis XIV.[33] Frederic William's edict granted the refugees a large package of privileges, thereby decisively influencing the course of the integration and assimilation of the Huguenot refugees. Among the privileges in the context of the assimilation process was the possibility for the refugees to continue without change their liturgies and ceremonies in French. And almost every such church had a French school, closely supervised and controlled of course by the German authorities. The refugees further enjoyed administrative and judicial autonomy, appointing their own judges, as well as many economic and fiscal advantages, such as exemption from taxes over several years and direct reception into most of the guilds. The Edict of Potsdam served as a model for other princes and cities interested in attracting Huguenots. The bulk of these refugees chose Brandenburg, mainly Berlin, in which a French church had existed since 1672. But other French churches were soon established in the new Huguenot quarters specially founded for them in Berlin. Indeed, this is the best illustration of the "colony system" practiced also in many other German cities and principalities.

The system had many advantages. It made it possible for the refugees to teach in French and even to bring with them elements of their lives from their former homeland. The church in Erlangen, for example, was built on the model of that of Vitry-le-François. On the other hand, local rulers were able to closely supervise the refugee colonies, which were totally dependent on them.

The most "French" colony was, of course, that of Berlin, with its 11,500 refugees in 1698. Thanks to the Academy of Sciences and its many Huguenot refugee members, Berlin became a major "French" cultural center. The Huguenot communities and churches also owned and directed such famous institutions as the hospital, the French *collège* and the seminary. The latter allowed them to train their own ministers, thereby avoiding the dearth of pastors that affected practically all the other Huguenot churches of the Refuge and made them totally dependent on Geneva.

The colonies of Berlin and Prussia were the slowest to be assimilated into their German environment. The privileges of the communities were abolished by Friedrich Wilhelm III only in 1809. The French language henceforth survived

---

33   Jürgen Wilke, "Berlin zur Zeit des Edikts von Potsdam. Das Edikts und seine Bedeutung," in *Hugenotten in Berlin*, (ed.) Gottfried Bregulla (Berlin: 1988), 13–53.

only in the churches and the prestigious French Gymnasium.[34] In fact, Friedrich Wilhelm's act merely made official an already long-existing situation. Practically all the descendants of the lower classes among the first and second generation of Huguenot refugees—the artisans and soldiers—had long since melted into their German surrounding and had forgotten the language of their fathers. But this was not the case with the higher classes of pastors and intellectuals. Even the assimilated and integrated foreign minister of Prussia, Jean Pierre Frederic Ancillon, descendent of Charles Ancillon, wrote his books in French. In 1801 there were still 7600 "refugees" in Berlin.

Aside from Berlin, the only other city in Prussia with a high percentage of Huguenot refugees was Magdeburg—2000 in 1720. Other Prussian cities reached a peak of around 1000 refugees. Proportionally to its number of inhabitants, Hesse-Kassel hosted even more Huguenot refugees—4000 for only 140,000 inhabitants, followed closely by Hesse-Darmstadt. Another type of refuge can be found in Lutheran Saxony as Niedersachsen with Hameln, Celle Hannover, Wolfenbüttel—Brunswick and Kursachsen, where refugees were only "protected" (Schutzverwandte) but denied rights or privileges.[35] Many Lutheran "outbreaks" against the Calvinist refugees notwithstanding, the Hansa towns of Hamburg, Bremen and Lübeck were home to a more tolerant tradition toward foreigners, thanks to the merchant and maritime networks of these cities. The pace of assimilation was different in the various German states. Slowest in Prussia and much faster elsewhere, assimilation began usually with the passing of the first generation: mixed marriages and a rapid transition from "Mémoires vécues" to "Mémoires racontées."[36]

Integration, by contrast, was immediate. This was because the Huguenots came as emigrants not as refugees. They came to change their sovereign and to become the loyal subjects of different rulers, or loyal citizens of different states, cities or towns that offered them the possibility of transferring to them their

---

34 On the end of the colony, see Viviane Prest, "La fin de la colonie française de Prusse (1809–1812)," in *Diasporas. Histoire et Sociétés* 18 (2011), 123–42. Prest emphasizes the vehement discussion among the pastors and savants themselves over the issue of the abandonment of the use of French in the "Églises."

35 Wilhelm Beuleke, *Hugenotten in Niedersachsen* (Hildesheim: 1960), Katharina Middell, "Hugenotten in Kursachsen: Einwanderung und Integration," in *Hugenotten und deutsche Territorialstaaten*, (eds.) Braun and Lachenicht, 51–71.

36 For the survival of the memory of French origins, see Catherine Yon, "Sur les traces du passé Français," in *Die Hugenotten und das Refuge. Deutschland und Europa*, (eds.) Fréderic Hartweg and Stefi Jersch Wenzel (Berlin: 1990), 219–32; Susanne Lachenicht, "'Migrations.' Entre mémoire(s) et 'Erinnerungskultur,' XVIIIe–XIXe siècle: le cas des huguenots," in *Francia* 37 (2010), 425–34.

loyalty. All the local differences in the pace of integration were the outcome of this very special situation. Of course, integration by no means always translated into immediate economic success. Furthermore, this unique phenomenon did not always influence the pace of assimilation, and perhaps was obscured by the overwhelming shadow of Prussia. Prussia was the most important state in this respect, taking in more than half of the 44,000 refugees who settled in German territories.

The pattern of assimilation was different in the various German territories. In the culturally more developed states, French mannerism, fashions and traditions of dress and dietetic tastes and habits survived because of the enormous prestige of French civilization or what was called then "l'Europe des Lumières." But eventually the outcome was the same: assimilation, albeit softened, differentiated and embellished by familial memories.

7   Switzerland

The Old Swiss Confederation was composed of sovereign urban cantons and rural cantons, which were linked together by a large network of defensive and mutual assistance treaties. The confederation also included other towns and territories such as the Grisons, Valais, Saint Gall, Geneva and the Principality of Neuchatel, which became "Prussian" in 1707 after the death of the duchesse Marie de Nemours and the locals voted for incorporation into Prussia. In this complicated network of alliances, Zurich played the key role.

Switzerland was the most important transit country for the Huguenot refugees. From there they went on to places such as Brandenburg-Prussia and other German states, the Dutch Netherlands, the British Isles and Ireland. Tens of thousands of refugees passed through Switzerland, but relatively few settled there. It is not easy to fix more precisely the numbers of refugees who crossed Switzerland. In the years preceding and following the Revocation, perhaps some 120,000 or 140,000 or even more. We know that between 1684 and 1692, 26,500 refugees crossed the canton of Neuchâtel, where the total number of inhabitants was 25,000, while the city of Neuchâtel had a population of 3,000 and was crossed by 20,000 refugees.

The most important francophone territory, the Pays de Vaud, was a dependency of Berne and contained among others the cities of Lausanne, Le Locle, Morges, Vevey and Yverdon. Berne and Basel had already an "Église française" with several pastors. But even German "territories," such as Saint Gall and Zurich, played their part in this passage across the land. The refugees received help from the different cities, were looked after with donations of money, shoes, clothes, medical assistance and, if needed, help for provisionary accommodation and transport facilities. One of the best known institutions providing such help was the *Bourse française* of Geneva.[37]

The different cities of the Pays de Vaud could present to the authorities of Berne a list of the refugees whom they wanted to stay. In compiling such lists they were motivated mainly by economic interest. Refugees could also ask the authorities of Berne to stay. On the other hand, it was not easy to expel the refugees once they were asked to leave and we know that many of them remained illegally and melted into the local population. Between the years 1687 and 1720, many of them settled in Le Locle. Of the 7200 inhabitants of Lausanne in 1765, 1500 were French refugees. Morges, Meudon and Yverdon were liberal and willingly received Huguenot refugees, but even here assimilation and integration were not easy, except perhaps for some privileged vocations, such as silk weavers, jewelers and various artisans in the textiles industries who printed *indiennes* and other luxury products.

There were also brilliant successes, such as that of Jacques Louis Pourtalès, who put the city of Neuchâtel at the center of a huge global network of international commerce in *indiennes* and printed silks. He was able to do this thanks to his Huguenot relatives and friends, all descendants of Huguenot refugees with bases in London, Lorient (in France), Hamburg, Philadelphia, Constantinople and Pondicherry.

For most of the refugees, it was cultural assimilation that was the most difficult. Refugees felt antagonism in Zurich, where the Huguenot women were considered too noisy and provocative with their high "coiffure" and even too elegant when they walked on the ramparts. Elsewhere, French pastors were asked not to gesticulate. But there was no complaint raised against their theology and commentaries upon the Holy Scriptures.

The Swiss Confederation was unable to absorb all the Huguenots and made serious efforts to find for them other refuges in alternative host countries. The best known of such efforts were those of Henri de Mirmand,[38] who directed Huguenots to Brandenburg in the winter of 1699, when the refugees were asked to leave Switzerland.

In Geneva, assimilation was the most natural outcome, as the city was the capital of Calvinism, and above all of French Calvinism. Integration was also

---

37   Cécile Holtz, "La Bourse française de Genève et le Refuge de 1684 à 1686," in *Genève au temps de la Révocation de l'Edit de Nantes*, (eds.) Olivier Fatio et al. (Geneva: 1985), 441–500.

38   Madame Alexandre de Chambrier, *Henri de Mirmand et les réfugiés de la Révocation de l'Edit de Nantes, 1650–1721* (Neuchâtel: 1910).

fast, even if, for reasons both of its size and also the controls and pressure of the French authorities, the city was unable to keep so many new refugees. Nevertheless, of the 100,000 or so refugees who passed close to Geneva, scores and even hundreds stayed, as shown by the list of different arts and crafts of Geneva to which they contributed.[39]

8   The Dutch and American Colonies

A part of the Huguenot settlers in the American and Dutch colonies (the Cape and Surinam) were not refugees, but immigrants. They did not choose the colonies because they were persecuted, but because they decided to leave their "Refuge," i.e. Britain or the United Provinces. They were not necessarily the adventurers or the very poor among the refugees who had nowhere to return; nevertheless, they were true immigrants.

The colonies discussed here in a very brief overview are the Dutch Cape Colony and the English colonies of Virginia, South Carolina, Boston and the city of New York;[40] but there were also other Huguenot settlements in Dutch Surinam, in Quebec and the Caribbean. These settlers and immigrants were mostly recruited in Britain and the United Provinces following a propaganda campaign of brochures and pamphlets promoting the advantages of the new "Edens." The Cape Colony was organized and financed by the Dutch East India Company and the first Huguenot immigrants arrived at the end of 1687. These initial settlers were followed by other "transports." The eventual total of about 220 settlers constituted almost a quarter of the "white" population. Their role was to produce the necessary agricultural products for the Dutch settlers of the East India Company and its agents. The Huguenot immigrants of the colony were guaranteed the status of "free burghers." Tensions and crises arose immediately, and in 1702 the militant and erudite pastor, Pierre Simond, left Drakenstein. Integration and forced assimilation followed after a prohibition on the use of French. From free burghers the Huguenot immigrants became true Afrikaners. The need to safeguard their fields from ruin by the nomad Khoikhois eventually transformed them into champions of apartheid.[41]

---

39   Pierre Bertrand, *Genève et la Révocation de l'Edit de Nantes* (Geneva: 1965). Fatio et al. (eds.), *Genève au temps de la Révocation*.

40   Charles Baird, *History of the Huguenot Emigration to America* (1885; repr. Baltimore: 1973). Jon Butler, *The Huguenots in America. A Refugee People in New Word Society* (Cambridge, Mass.: 1983).

41   Eckart Birnstiel, "La Diaspora huguenote dans le nouveau monde," in *La Diaspora*, (ed.) Birnstiel, 115.

The story of the American colonies is much more nuanced and fragmentary. It has been told many times how the first child born in New Amsterdam was the son of a Huguenot. The history of the Huguenot community is less golden. The last survivor of a group of Huguenot settlers who arrived in New York at the end of the 17th century, Daniel Boutecou, died in 1773 at the ripe old age of 92. He was for all of his life devoted to the survival of the French Church. The fortunes of this group and indeed the life of Daniel are illustrations of a slow defeat in a fight for identity. Assimilation was also fostered by biological and demographical factors, with fathers often surviving their sons.[42] Nevertheless, the main cause of their disappearance was that at the beginning of the 18th century most of the New York Huguenots migrated to New Paltz and New Rochelle, with the result that both communities were too small to survive. In Boston, a successful merchant community, mainly originating from La Rochelle, led almost a double "life" and was characterized by a double, divided identity. Perfectly integrated and even assimilated, they could still maintain parallel specific French and Huguenot identities, as illustrated, for example, by Peter and Andrew Faneuil.[43]

The really successful colonies were those of South Carolina and Virginia. They are also the best documented and the best researched. It is a well-known fact that the settlers of South Carolina were planters and huge land owners. They experimented with a long series of crops on their plantations, finally hitting upon the profitable cultivation of indigo. As Van Ruymbeke explains,[44] their integration was dazzlingly successful while their assimilation was rather a process of acculturation and creolization. Slave owners because of their need to work their huge plantations, they ceased, practically, to partake in Calvinist ethics and morals. The immense distances between the properties of the different Huguenot settlers necessitated mixed marriages with the English. It was also extremely difficult to maintain pastors for organized worship. It thus became more and more difficult to organize religious life, and the visits of the pastors and gatherings became increasingly rare.

Another of the elements of the success story were the Huguenot merchants of South Carolina, descendants of nobles and great merchant dynasties, mainly from La Rochelle. Even if they worked on a smaller scale than their English

---

42   Joyce D. Goodfriend, "The Protestants of Colonial New York City: A Demographic Profile," in *Memory and Identity,* (eds.) Van Ruymbeke and Sparks, 241–54.

43   Susanne Lachenicht and Myriam Yardeni (eds.), *Réseaux des diasporas—Identitiés des diasporas* (Rennes: forthcoming 2015).

44   Bertrand Van Ruymbeke, *From New Babylon to Eden, the Huguenots and Their Migration to Colonial South Carolina* (Columbia, SC: 2006), introduction.

counterparts, thanks to their "European" Huguenot network they could maintain their cosmopolite Huguenot identity.

We can also place into the narrative outlined above that of the Virginia settlers of Richmond and Manakintown, whose story followed nearly the same pattern as that of their brethren in South Carolina. Many other and different processes of assimilation and integration took place in other settlements.

9   Conclusion

The difficulty in analyzing the pattern of assimilation and integration in the Huguenot diaspora is that of isolating the weight of the local conditions and their part in the process of general assimilation, integration and disappearance of the Huguenots, and their rebirth, survival and glorification in the different family and historical memories cultivated by the different local and national Huguenot societies.[45]

This rapid survey of the dispersion of the Huguenots throughout a multiplicity of very different countries, provinces, cities, towns and colonies—and the list given is of course not exhaustive[46]—helps us to understand the huge differences between early modern and contemporary assimilation and integration. In the former case, we are concerned with small entities. In the latter, we see the constitution of huge territorial and national states, together with the first signs of globalization, due to the development of the different media of communication, such as telegraphs, telephones, cinema, internet, and so on.

Assimilation and integration are very closely related concepts. Nevertheless we have to distinguish between the two processes. Assimilation is a cultural phenomenon while integration is a social one. Usually, assimilation precedes integration, which begins only when the "refugees" realize that they can no longer survive on donations or acts of charity organized for them in their new home countries and that they have to look after themselves and their families.

The multiplicity and the varieties of different case studies make it difficult if not impossible to construct a single model or paradigm. Perhaps there is but one common factor in all these cases. The initiatives and interventions of kings, governors and ministers in early modern times and that of governments in modern times could change the rhythms of integration, as seen, for example, in the acts of naturalization in England or the decision of the municipal

---

45   For a list see Lachenicht, "Migrations," 584.
46   Huguenots also settled in countries not mentioned in our survey, such as Denmark, Russia, and Turkey, and probably, as individuals, in many others.

authorities of Amsterdam in the 18th century that instruction no longer be given in French in the elementary schools of the different "Églises."[47] Of course, the decision that all school instruction would henceforth take place in Dutch led not only to the integration of the French into their Dutch surroundings, but also entailed cultural assimilation.

It is a well-known fact that from the dawn of history, humanity has had to choose or has had to establish a hierarchy of preferences with regard to our need to act. Thus, decisions are not always rational, not always emotional. Sometimes it is difficult to determine to which category they belong. Of course, people in every age and all circumstances have made all kind of compromises. These choices were also influenced by constrains. Nevertheless, these choices are sometimes determinants of the rhythms of assimilation and integration of the refugees or emigrants and their descendants. One good illustration of such irrational choice is provided by Simon Pelloutier (1694–1757), a theologian, historian and author of the *Histoire des Celtes*. Born in Leipzig, he spoke very faulty French, yet fiercely defended the case for teaching in French rather than in German.[48]

It is not easy to establish the hierarchy of choices or to construct a sociological paradigm. Choice is always an individual process influenced by too many factors to allow the specification of a useful model. We can only resort to the criteria of the frequency of some phenomenon, a clear-cut factor, but at times misleading. This hierarchy of choices changed in the wake of external factors, such as the politics of emigration of some German states. Nevertheless, and as we have shown, we cannot establish a hierarchy of preferences for the assimilation and integration of the Huguenot refugees in their respective new homelands.

The roads leading to assimilation and integration were different, but the outcome was always the same: assimilation and integration. Sometime it was embellished by the historical memory of persecution and martyrdom of the Huguenot fathers, a process which began in the 19th century and the foundation of various "local" Huguenot societies in Great Britain and Ireland, Germany and even in many cities and towns in the United States and elsewhere. In most cases, this outcome was also the continuation of the contribution of the first Huguenot refugees and their descendants to local economies and cultures. And it was always a question of changing and multiple identities, which were the main components not only of assimilation but also integration. But this is another story.

---

47 See above section 4, The Dutch Republic.
48 Christian Velder, *300 Jahre französisches Gymnasium Berlin* (Berlin: 1989), 80–83.

CHAPTER 11

Sociolinguistics of the Huguenot Communities in German-Speaking Territories

Manuela Böhm

1   Introduction

The Huguenots, the largest and best-known early modern group of migrants who sought asylum in German-speaking territories, have been the focus of substantial attention in recent years. It is clear that in the conceptual and theoretical approaches there has been a shift from "national paradigm" to "cultural paradigm."[1] In contrast to the national paradigm, which is very much focused on demographic statistics and immigration policy research, the cultural-historical perspective focuses on the transformation process regarding self-image and external image, group behavior and cultural memory forms. These, in turn, provide information about patterns of perception as well as changing forms of identification and interaction, which were the result of migration. This is relevant to both minority and majority groups. A research perspective employed in this way allows insights into cultural practices, such as language, which are associated with migration. The communicative-pragmatic functions of language, its assigned role in language policy or ideology and its actual use provide information about the social negotiation of identity, symbolic affiliation and the differentiation strategies of speakers.[2] In many respects language can be used as a diagnostic tool: as a communication and structuring medium in cultural and social practices, as a group-forming tool, as a sign for individual and collective identity in flux, and therefore as an indicator of acculturation and/or segregation processes.

This brief overview forms a point of departure for this chapter and provides a framework for that which follows. The essay offers insights from a different perspective, namely the sociolinguistic perspective, into the Francophone Protestants who settled in German-speaking areas. At the heart of the matter

---

[1] Katharina Middell and Matthias Middell, "Migration als Forschungsfeld," *Grenzgänge* 9 (1998), 6–23.
[2] For the variation in language use and choice in an ethnolinguistic point of view, see Robert B. LePage and Andree Tabouret-Keller, *Acts of Identity: Creole-based Approaches to Language and Ethnicity* (New York: 1985).

are language use, language change and language policy strategies of the Huguenot community in the German Refuge. The objective is to use these language relationships to reach conclusions regarding the relationships between the Francophone minority and the German-speaking majority.

From the sociolinguistic perspective, migration is always connected with changes in communication and language situations.[3] From a linguistic viewpoint, in the case of the Huguenots, these changes can be roughly described as follows. The Huguenots, before being forced to flee, lived in a relatively stable language situation and made use of a set of language repertoires which varied according to their locality, region and sociocultural background. As a result of settling in the diaspora, their language repertoires became a minority and this led to a contact-induced language change. This change left its traces on both immigrant speakers and the indigenous population—on both French and German communities—in the form of language contact phenomena and altered language attitudes. These language phenomena are multilingualism in the Huguenot community and diglossia in related domains such as the church. The spoken and written varieties of French or German show evidence of internal changes such as code-switching or borrowing. As multilingualism became increasingly asymmetrical and the plurilingual competence of the Huguenots and their descendants withered, language shift took place. As we will see, there are many examples from the Refuge in German-speaking lands of how Huguenot descendants attempted to counteract or even stop this language shift with various language policy strategies.

The aim of this chapter is to describe in detail fundamental elements of this language contact situation and its transformation, and to explore it in relation to sociocultural conditions. Tackling this question represents a considerable methodological challenge. Firstly, the Huguenots were a language minority who migrated more than three hundred years ago. It means that the processes in question are not easily accessible for analysis and thus the problem of evidence is a very real concern. The difficulties result from the fact that common sociolinguistic methods for collecting data, such as participant observation, interviews, language tests and so forth, cannot not be utilized. Another issue is that the entire language reality, in particular spoken language use, cannot be reconstructed. This is mainly due to the spatiotemporal limits of spoken

---

3 See Paul Kerswill, "Migration and Language," in *Sociolinguistics/Soziolinguistik. An international Handbook of the Science of Language and Society*, (eds.) Ulrich Ammon et al., 2nd ed., vol. 3 (Berlin: 2006), 2271–85; and Joachim Raith, "Religiöse Migration," in *Kontaktlinguistik—Contact Linguistics—Linguistique de contact*, (eds.) Hans Goebl et al., vol. 1 (Berlin: 1996), 311–20.

language and also the quantity and quality of data available. Both matters have been extensively discussed with reference to language history studies as a "bad data problem."[4]

The first part of this essay explores the most important Huguenot settlements in German-speaking areas, while the second part examines the relationship between acculturation processes and language change and shift. In comparing two settlements, Brandenburg and Hesse, the third part seeks to illustrate in detail various scenarios of language adaptation and to identify the key factors.

Altogether, the goal is to demonstrate that, first of all, the analysis of language provides information about processes of sociocultural transformation. Secondly, it suggests that only microsociolinguistic and comparative approaches reveal the complexity and diversity of the language situation of Huguenot communities within the Refuge in German-speaking lands. Thirdly, it points up that general assumptions about language change in minority situations, such as one finds in, for example, sociolinguistic models and historiographical extrapolations, do not go far enough.

2   Huguenot Settlements in German-speaking Lands: A Brief Overview

During the early modern period, the Holy Roman Empire was not a nation state but a historically evolved, loose federation of self-sufficient, independent states with an elected emperor at its head. The territorial rulers (prince electors, princes, bishop princes, counts and lords) and the free and imperial cities had, as a part of their position, a seat and a vote in the Imperial Diet (*Reichstag*).[5] These territorially and politically powerful structures facilitated the Reformation and led, in Germany, to cultural and political splintering. After the Peace of Augsburg in 1555, Lutherans were legally recognized as a second religious denomination in the German Empire. The Peace of Westphalia (1648) extended to the Reformed Church the legal status granted Lutherans in 1555. Each ruler, or magistrates in the free cities, decided the particular territory's religious position. Here it is important to mention that the Huguenots were granted refuge not by the empire but various local Reformed and Lutheran rulers.

---

4   See William Labov, *Principles of Linguistic Change*, vol. 1, *Internal Factors* (Oxford: 1994), 10–11.
5   See Gerhard Köbler, *Historisches Lexikon der deutschen Länder. Die deutschen Territorien und reichsunmittelbaren Geschlechter vom Mittelalter bis zur Gegenwart*, 7th ed. (Munich: 2007).

Francophone Protestants came to German territories already in the 1550s when persecution started. The biggest immigration wave came after the revocation of the Edict of Nantes in 1685. Protestant princes granted the Huguenots refuge, typically asylum, which was sometimes accompanied by generous privileges. The significantly later influxes, such as into Gumbinnen in East Prussia around 1710 or into Potsdam in 1719, were exceptional.

Various migrant groups were known as "Huguenots." They shared a Calvinist faith and French as a *lingua sacra*. Strictly speaking, the term "Huguenot" was first used pejoratively for those Protestants who fled France after the revocation of 1685. They referred to themselves as "*réformés*" and those who had left their homes used the terms "*réfugiés*" or "*français réfugiés.*" Later they referred to themselves as "*descendants de réfugiés*" or as "Huguenots."[6] Other francophone Calvinists in the German diaspora such as Walloons, Waldensians, Orangeois and Palatines are included in the group known as Huguenots in its broadest sense.[7]

The Walloons had already in the 16th century fled areas of the southern Netherlands. Reformed ideas had reached these areas very early. These Protestants, mainly from Flanders, Hainaut, Picardy and Artois, found protection from the Counter-Reformation in England, the northern Protestant provinces of the Netherlands and in German territories where they established colonies such as the Hanau Walloon community which was begun in 1594. The Electoral Palatinate had also taken in many Walloons, but they had to flee this area during the War of the Palatine Succession and re-Catholicization beginning in 1688. The Mannheim Walloons, for instance, resettled at Magdeburg in 1689.[8] These groups from the Palatinate who sought a second Refuge were the descendants of Walloons, Waldensians and Reformed French, and they formed what were known as Palatine colonies on German soil. The Waldensians, who originally came from inaccessible Alpine valleys in Piedmont and Savoy, became Protestants in 1532. Following the flight or exile from Piedmont and Dauphiné, and from the French occupied areas of Savoy, only a part of the group stayed in German territories, mainly in Hesse-Kassel, Hesse-Darmstadt and Brandenburg. It was mainly Savoyard Waldensians who settled in the southern Hessian counties of Württemberg and Baden.[9] The Orangeois were also known as Huguenots; they were exiled from the principality of Orange in

---

6 Eckart Birnstiel and Andreas Reinke, "Hugenotten in Berlin," in *Von Zuwanderern zu Einheimischen. Hugenotten, Juden, Böhmen, Polen in Berlin*, (eds.) Stefi Jersch-Wenzel and Barbara John (Berlin: 1990), 16.
7 Barbara Dölemeyer, *Die Hugenotten* (Stuttgart: 2006), 12–13.
8 Paul Dibon, "Le Refuge wallon, précurseur du Refuge huguenot," *XVIIe Siècle* 76–77 (1967), 53–74.
9 See Gabriel Audisio, *Les vaudois. Histoire d'une dissidence. XIIe-XVIe siècle* (Paris: 1998).

southern France and settled in Geneva and Brandenburg-Prussia in 1703 and 1711–1713.¹⁰

The German-speaking Huguenot diaspora was therefore, with regard to their Reformed traditions and regional influence, very heterogeneous. This was not without consequences for the processes of acculturation and language development in Huguenot communities. Before turning to this question, however, I would like to offer an overview of the most important Huguenot settlements in German-speaking areas and their legal framework.

In total, between 38,000 and 44,000 Huguenots came to Protestant ruled princely states or free cities in the Empire. Their distribution was roughly as follows:¹¹

- Brandenburg-Prussia approx. 18,000–20,000
- Hesse-Kassel approx. 4,000
- Rest of Hesse¹² approx. 3,700
- Electorate of Brunswick-Lüneburg¹³ approx. 1,500
- Margraviate of Brandenburg-Ansbach-Bayreuth approx. 4,000
- Electoral Palatinate approx. 3,400
- Württemberg approx. 3,000
- Hanseatic cities approx. 1,500
- Baden-Durlach approx. 500
- Electorate of Saxony approx. 250

The concessions made to the refugees by the rulers and cities varied enormously from simple tolerance to wide-ranging privileges which meant that the Huguenots had far better status than other immigrant groups. The variation in privileges can be explained in part by the religious persuasion of the welcoming territorial prince. Another factor played a role however, namely mercantile considerations

---

10   Françoise Moreil, "Une arrivée retardée: les Orangeois à Berlin en 1704," in *Hugenotten und deutsche Territorialstaaten. Immigrationspolitik und Integrationsprozesse. Les Etats allemands et les huguenots. Politique d'immigration et processus d'intégration*, (eds.) Guido Braun and Susanne Lachenicht (Munich: 2007), 85–106.

11   These and the following figures are taken from Dölemeyer, *Hugenotten*, 51–52. Johannes E. Bischoff, *Lexikon deutscher Hugenotten-Orte* (Bad Karlshafen: 1994) provides a complete list of all Huguenot settlements in German-speaking territories. For a reference map of these areas, see http://www.hugenottenmuseum.de/hugenotten/karte-siedlungsorte-franz-ref-gemeinden-im-roemischen-reich.pdf.

12   Including Hesse-Darmstadt, Hesse-Homburg, Isenburg Counties, Solms, Nassau and Hanau.

13   Including Brunswick-Lüneburg and Brunswick-Wolfenbüttel.

in the form of repopulation. In Brandenburg-Prussia and Hesse-Kassel, the hope was that the immigrants would provide an important kick start to the economy. Thus, an attempt was made to entice successful merchants and craftsmen by offering attractive conditions.[14] Another idea is suggested by Barbara Dölemeyer who asserts that the concessions corresponded in certain ways to the political, military, cultural and dynastic relations between the individual princedoms and the Protestants in France.[15]

The minimal legal arrangements usually included tolerating the immigrants and allowing religious freedom, although open practice was not always permitted. In this way, the orthodox Lutheran clergy of Leipzig attempted to prevent the Huguenots' petition to be allowed to have their own pastors, Reformed church services and ceremonies (baptisms, marriages and funerals). The Catholic Elector of Saxony complied with the request for the establishment of the Huguenot community; however, this was on condition that church services and all religious activities took place in private residences.[16] Since the Huguenots did not belong to the Lutheran church, in Leipzig they had no civic rights and only received the right of residence if they paid protection money. The situation was similar in Frankfurt where Walloons had settled since the middle of the 16th century and founded a French Reformed community in 1554. The right to practice their religion openly was withdrawn in 1561 by the Frankfurt city council following pressure from Lutherans, indigenous merchants and craftsmen. In 1596, conducting Reformed church services within the city limits was banned completely. Only in 1787 was the Huguenot community permitted to open a church, albeit without tower or bells, within the city area. Still, no marriages or baptisms were allowed to be celebrated in the church.[17]

The widest-ranging privileges in the German territory were enjoyed by the *réfugiés* in Brandenburg-Prussia. The Prince Elector Friedrich Wilhelm, a Hohenzollern and Reformed ruler of a Lutheran population, guaranteed them

---

14   Concerning the motivations of the host countries, see Matthias Asche, *Neusiedler im verheerten Land: Kriegsfolgenbewältigung, Migrationssteuerung und Konfessionspolitik im Zeichen des Landeswiederaufbaus: Die Mark Brandenburg nach den Kriegen des 17. Jahrhunderts* (Münster: 2006); see also Stefi Jersch-Wenzel, *Juden und "Franzosen" in der Wirtschaft des Raumes Berlin/Brandenburg zur Zeit des Merkantilismus* (Berlin: 1978); and Dölemeyer, *Hugenotten*, 84–168.

15   Dölemeyer, *Hugenotten*, 81, 98–100, 149. For details on settlement privileges, specifically the legal status of the Huguenots, see Barbara Dölemeyer, "Rechtliche Aspekte konfessioneller Migration im frühneuzeitlichen Europa am Beispiel der Hugenottenaufnahme," in *Glaubensflüchtlinge: Ursachen, Formen und Auswirkungen frühneuzeitlicher Konfessionsmigration in Europa,* (ed.) Joachim Bahlcke (Münster: 2008), 1–25.

16   Katharina Middell, *Hugenotten in Leipzig* (Leipzig: 1989), 43, 49–51.

17   Dölemeyer, *Hugenotten*, 159–60.

in the Edict of Potsdam of 29 October 1685. The Huguenots had their own church administration with the maintenance of the *Discipline ecclésiastique* and the consistory system, freedom of settlement, economic and tax advantages, freedom of commerce and service, their own separate jurisdiction and the right to establish their own schools. These special rights gave the refugees a particular legal status which differentiated them from the indigenous population but also from other migrants. The legal expression for this minority status was the "French colony." Its members came under a special religious, legal and social order, which remained in place until 1809. It is important to note that in contrast to a "ghetto" as a segregated area, a "colony" was not a topographical reference, but a legal one. However, the legal status also created a (virtual) social space in which the Huguenot minority stayed together until the colony changed due to the integration of its members.[18] The Naturalization Edict of 1709 gave Huguenots the chance to be both French colonists and Prussian subjects.[19] Colonies were also founded in Hesse-Kassel; here the term usually meant rural settlements such as Carlsdorf, Mariendorf, Kelze or Schöneberg, which were established because cities like Kassel or Hofgeismar were unable to take in all the refugees. Even if the Landgrave Karl promised freedom of belief, protection, economic support and the use of French in church and school in December 1685, the legal privileges were not as wide-ranging as in Brandenburg- Prussia.[20]

In very rare cases, the territorial lords were prepared to make political concessions in view of the local, provincial and national organization of the synodal system of the French Reformed Churches. Above all, Reformed territorial leaders insisted on their prerogative regarding the *summus episcopus*.[21] Several Lutheran princes and dukes, including those of Brandenburg-Bayreuth and Württemberg, permitted synod elements.

Isolation and coherence were two elements of immigration policy which had direct consequences for the acculturation of migrants to the majority population. While in Brandenburg-Prussia it was possible to use refugees to a certain extent to repopulate towns and villages that had been ruined during the Thirty Years' War, in Hesse-Kassel new settlements were established in rural areas or were extended, as in the city of Kassel. Secondly, the degree of coherence in the settling groups was very varied. The Waldensian, Walloon and Orangeois settlements often consisted of coherent groups led by pastors, whereas other settlements were formed progressively by small refugees groups.

---

18   Manuela Böhm, *Sprachenwechsel. Akkulturation und Mehrsprachigkeit der Brandenburger Hugenotten vom 17. bis 19. Jahrhundert* (Berlin: 2010), 54–55.
19   Birnstiel and Reinke, "Hugenotten in Berlin," 50–51.
20   Dölemeyer, *Hugenotten*, 102–103.
21   Birnstiel and Reinke, "Hugenotten in Berlin," 79–82.

3 Acculturation and Language: Modeling Language Shift

It is clear from the previous section that local settlement conditions varied. Still, the process generally meant the establishment of self-administrated Reformed communities with very different rights. These locally varying conditions, which above all differed in the legal and social status of migrants, the scale of the communities, their topographical isolation or integration, and group or individual settlements, were significant parameters that defined the acculturation of these Huguenot communities.

The term acculturation, which refers to the signs of adaptation in social and cultural contact, is, like the other two categorizing terms—integration and assimilation, used inconsistently in historical migration research. In American terminology integration and assimilation are often used synonymously; in German, integration is usually used as a generic term for convergent processes.[22] In contrast to assimilation, acculturation means "transforming" into the accepting culture and this is how I am using the term. It invokes an anthropological understanding of culture which questions the effects of contact on socio-cultural patterns such as traditions, values, attitudes, communication and interaction.[23] In addition, when employing the concept of acculturation, I assume that continuous cultural contact changes both cultures and not simply the minority culture.[24] Assimilation is occasionally understood as the final phase of acculturation during which the values and cultural patterns of the minority culture disappear almost completely, and this leads to the complete loss of differentness.[25]

Acculturation is expressed in many ways, and in the case of the Huguenots who fled to the German world the various indicators for acculturation have been closely observed and described. Intermarriage,[26] where Huguenots married non-Huguenots, could mean conversion from the French Reformed

---

22   Marita Krauss, "Integration und Akkulturation. Eine methodische Annäherung an ein vielschichtiges Phänomen," *Migration und Integration. Aufnahme und Eingliederung im historischen Wandel,* (eds.) Mathias Beer, et al. (Stuttgart: 1997), 14.

23   Krauss, "Integration und Akkulturation," 15.

24   Robert Redfield et al., "Memorandum for the Study of Acculturation," *American Anthropologist* 38 (1936), 149–52.

25   Redfield et al., "Memorandum for the Study of Acculturation," 150.

26   For intermarriages in different French colonies, see Wilhelm Beuleke, "Wiederheirat und Mischehe, Verlobung und Scheidung bei den Hugenotten," *Der Deutsche Hugenott* 42 (1978), 2–20, for Brandenburg-Prussia: Asche, *Neusiedler im verheerten Land,* 562–82; and Susanne Lachenicht, *Hugenotten in Europa und Nordamerika. Migration und Integration in der Frühen Neuzeit* (Frankfurt: 2010), 376–84.

church to German Reformed or Lutheran churches[27] and accompanying demographic declines in the Huguenot colony's population.[28] A fundamental indicator of acculturation is language, more precisely multilingualism, which demonstrates that the language of the majority culture is used alongside the minority language. It also points to language shift (whether in the individual or in a collective form). Despite the importance attributed to language as a means of group formation and securing identity, it is astonishing how little research has been done on the language situation of Huguenot communities. Most research has examined no more than isolated features, brought together results from other individual studies, or only dealt selectively with language aspects. Linguistically based, systematic and methodological-theoretical original studies on the diaspora in the Empire are rare.[29]

Acculturation and/or integration are most noticeable when a community gives up the internally used language varieties which the members brought with them and takes on those of the majority. This process has been labeled "language shift" by Uriel Weinreich and describes the change in the habitual use of one language to another. He also advocates examining the accompanying social aspects as a part of language contact.[30] Language shift is not a sudden event and one language is not abruptly "gone." Language shift is a more complex, long term phenomenon which takes place over generations. In modern linguistics, the general assumption is that a language shift is completed in three generations.[31]

---

27 Concerning Huguenots joining the German Reformed and Lutheran churches in Hamelin, see Thomas Klingebiel, *Weserfranzosen. Studien zur Geschichte der Hugenottengemeinschaft in Hameln. 1690–1757* (Göttingen 1992), 228–31; for the Berlin colony: François David, "Refuge huguenot et assimilation: Le cas de la colonie française de Berlin," in *La Diaspora des Huguenots. Les réfugiés protestants de France et leur dispersion dans le monde (XVIe-XVIIIe siècles)*, (ed.) Eckart Birnstiel (Paris: 2001), 75–97.

28 For the demographic evolution of the Huguenot population in Hamelin, see Klingebiel, *Weserfranzosen*, 171–76; for Berlin: Jürgen Wilke, "Die Französische Kolonie in Berlin," in *Berlin 1650–1800. Sozialgeschichte einer Residenz*, (ed.) Helga Schultz (Berlin: 1992), 353–431.

29 Concerning language policy of the Berlin Huguenots, see several studies by Frédéric Hartweg, "Sprachwechsel und Sprachpolitik der Französisch-Reformierten Kirche in Berlin im 18. Jahrhundert," *Jahrbuch für die Geschichte Mittel- und Ostdeutschlands* 30 (1981), 162–76; and "Französisch als Kultsprache? Zur Sprachpolitik der französisch-reformierten Kirche in Berlin 1744–1814," *Beiträge zur Romanischen Philologie*, 34 (1985), 5–42. For German as second language among the Huguenots, see Helmut Glück, *Deutsch als Fremdsprache in Europa vom Mittelalter bis zur Barockzeit* (Berlin: 2002), 158–232; for the multilingualism and language shift of the Brandenburg-Prussian Huguenots, see Böhm, *Sprachenwechsel*.

30 Uriel Weinreich, *Languages in Contact. Findings and Problems* (New York: 1953), 68.

31 Helmut Glück (ed.), *Metzler-Lexikon Sprache* (Stuttgart: 2000), 675. Also a classic among the contact linguistics models language shift within three generations: Joshua A. Fishman, "Language maintenance and language shift as a field of inquiry," *Linguistics* 9 (1964), 32–70.

This assumption does not accord with the Huguenot experience (and in my view is not very plausible anyway) and we will return to this in our conclusion.

It should not be forgotten that it is the language users who set this process in motion. Generally, it is the case that more and more speakers in a multilingual community start using language B, the language of the majority community, in more and more situations over the period of observation rather than what had previously been the dominant language, language A.[32] This means that language shift is heralded by changes in the function and domain distribution of the minority language. Regarding the Huguenots, the question is therefore in which situations did they use which language, or when did they begin to switch from the language they learned from previous generations to that of the surrounding indigenous community.

To answer this question, let us turn to the Graded Intergenerational Disruption Scale Model (GIDS) of Joshua Fishman. This is used as an analytical tool in modern sociolinguistics in order to define the level of threat to minority languages.[33] The GIDS is, like the well-known Richter scale, an implication scale. Below I have provided a condensed version adapted to our purposes. It indicates the typology of eight stages measuring the level to which the language of a minority has been damaged or is threatened by a language shift.

Stage	Typology of stages	
8	Users of minority language are old people and language is taught as second language mostly to adults	**Language shift most likely**
7	Users of minority language are beyond child-bearing age	*Weak side*
6	Attainment of informal, intergenerational orality	
5	Literacy in minority language in home and community	
4	Minority language is used in children's formal education in conjunction with the majority language	*Strong side*
3	Minority language is used in the lower work sphere outside of the minority community or in the neighborhood	
2	Minority language is used in lower governmental services	
1	Use of the minority language in higher educational, governmental, occupational and media activities	**Language shift unlikely**

---

32 Susan Gal, "Language shift," in *Kontaktlinguistik*, (eds.) Goebl et al., 586.
33 Joshua A. Fishman, *Reversing Language Shift. Theoretical and Empirical Foundations of Assistance to Threatened Languages* (Clevedon: 1991), 87–109.

The strength of this model lies in the fact that it accentuates the dynamics of language shift processes and their *longue durée* nature. It also allows, to a certain extent, a diagnostic and prognostic evaluation of the stability of a minority language. Fishman's model achieves two aims. Firstly, it helps identify sociolinguistic factors which are relevant for the stability of a minority language. It is, however, important whether the language is used orally or in a written form, whether it is used in more formal domains (such as an official language, school language and, in the case of the Huguenot church, sacred language) or more in informal situations and domains (for example as a family language). Significantly, minority language survival seems to be more threatened (weak side, stage 5 to 8) if the language is only used within the community, whereas a language becomes stronger (strong side, stages 4 to 1) if it is used in various domains outside the community. Secondly, the model indicates the relevance of intergenerational mother tongue transmission. For a long term stable language situation to occur, there must be bilingual education at school (stage 4).

Applied to the Huguenots, this means that the long term survival of their language could only have been secured if

- they continued using their language both orally and in written form (stage 5 and 6).
- younger generations were brought up to be multilingual and this multilingualism was institutionally anchored in the schools (stage 4).
- their language was shared by at least parts of the majority community. Fishman writes here that the "control [of] certain industries, products or areas of specialization [in order] to provide for themselves…economic foundations" must be secured[34] (stage 3).
- on the one hand their language retained its function as an (internal) official language (stage 2), on the other hand that their language was used to communicate within the political domain and higher education in the majority community (stage 1).

Of course there are disadvantages to using the model for our purposes. It was developed in connection with studying endangered languages and is therefore related to recent language shifts that took place practically in front of

---

34   Fishman, *Reversing Language Shift*, 103.

researchers and was not designed for use in historical contexts. In addition, we also have the problem of bad data which does not allow us to use methods such as questionnaires and language tests, or to draw data systematically and in their entirety from historical sources to provide reliable information on the status of the Huguenot language minority. However, despite all these drawbacks, the GIDS is useful as a diagnostic tool in historic cases such as that of the Huguenots. In the third section of this article we will examine the four very differently structured Huguenot communities in more detail and use Fischman's typology as a guide. Before moving on to this, I would like to make a few basic comments on the difference between spoken and written language among the Huguenots.

In the previous section, the emphasis was on the shift from *one* language to *another* and this suggests in the process of their acculturation into the German diaspora, the francophone refugees exchanged one language, namely the "old" French mother tongue for another, namely the German "new" language. The process was not, however, this simple. Generally, the Huguenots spoke more than one language when they arrived in their German Refuge and they remained multilingual after they lost their competence in French. This is connected with the difference between vernaculars and written language.

The inventory of vernaculars among the refugees, just like that in the language regions of France, was wide-ranging and showed a great deal of vernacular variation. A glance at the French language map makes it clear that, at the lower end of the regional spectrum we are dealing with a dialectal continuum of the *oïl* language region which reaches from the north down to approximately the Loire valley. These varieties are historically linguistically linked with modern French (for example Norman, Walloon and Picard). South of this area, along a virtual border stretching from Bordeaux to Grenoble, we find patois and dialects of the Occitan dialects (as for example, Dauphinois, Auvergnat and Limousin) which are influenced by the northern Spanish varieties. In addition, there are regional and minority languages such as Franco-Provençal, Breton, Alsatian, and the like, which are very different from French and not even typologically related. As a result there was and is great debate over what is a dialect and what is a distinct language. Thirdly, in cities we encounter urban vernaculars (for example, the Paris or Metz urban vernaculars). The answer to the question of what the Huguenots spoke in the German diaspora may therefore also vary according to the regional makeup of their community. To a limited extent, problems such as a lack of direct knowledge of the spoken language can be compensated for through research into metalinguistic commentaries and the reconstruction of spoken language from written sources. This requires, however, appropriate sources.³⁵

The written language of the Huguenots is, in contrast, easy to reconstruct. The spoken languages, dialects, patois which the refugees brought with them into the diaspora was "roofed" by the French written language—if of course, they were literate. The Protestants came into contact with the French written language above all and firstly in the form of religious texts. Just as for all Protestants, a Bible in the vernacular language played an important role for the Huguenots. The three key texts for daily religious practice, education and edification were the French Bible translation by Pierre Robert Olivétan, the Genevan Catechism of Calvin (which was replaced in part by the *Abregé des veritez et des devoirs de la réligion chrétienne* by Daniel de Superville) and the Genevan Psalter. These texts were, without doubt, a stimulus for the development of the French written language used in a supra-regional way. Yet statements such as that of Eckart Birnstiel, that the French Bible resulted in a "uniform, high French sacred language,"³⁶ can be challenged on two essential grounds. For one thing, there have been very few investigations of the effects of this Bible, so it cannot be claimed without further investigation that Olivétan's translation of the Bible had a similarly important catalytic and modeling effect on the French as, for example, the Luther Bible translation had on the development of New High German. The convergence function and importance of the sacred language still needs to be established. Secondly, it is highly questionable how uniform this written French actually was. According to the current state of knowledge among Romance language historians, we can assume that the French language area in the 1530s was far from having, in Susanne Lachenicht's words, a "common standardized language" which had an identity-promoting effect.³⁷ Even if there was a northern French influence through Calvin's writings and Francis I's edict of 1539 (Ordinance of Villers-Cotterêts), which imposed French in all official, public documents, this influence led only later to standardization, when the production of written works increased considerably. In addition, the statement that the "services were held in French Protestant

---

35   For dealing with the bad data problem, see Böhm, *Sprachenwechsel*, 122–24, 185–201.

36   Birnstiel and Reinke, "Hugenotten in Berlin," 110–12; Eckart Birnstiel, "Asyl und Integration der Hugenotten in Brandenburg-Preußen," in *Hugenotten und deutsche Territorialstaaten*, (eds.) Braun and Lachenicht, 141.

37   Susanne Lachenicht, "Huguenot Immigrants and the Formation of National identities, 1548–1787," *The Historical Journal* 50 (2007), 312. Concerning the standardisation process and the tension between vernacular varieties and written French, see Anthony R. Lodge, *French. From Dialect to Standard* (London: 1993).

temples all over France in one and the same French tongue"[38] need to be reconsidered with an eye to the actual language conditions. France, as Andres Kristol so succinctly phrased it, was even into the 19th century only a partially francophone country.[39]

How much variation (or the lack of standard language) existed in written French can be seen from the sources still available to us. Let us take the Waldensians as an example. Their language situation, as it was for all of the Huguenots who came from the Occitan language area, is an excellent example of medial diglossia. The Waldensians spoke one of the Franco-Provençal dialects but wrote, if they were literate, French. They had early access to a Bible which was, at least partially, translated into Occitan, the sacred language. This situation persisted until 1532 when a large number of Waldensians joined the synod of Chanforans which was influenced by the Swiss Reformed Church. This meant the sacred language changed to French.[40] Hans Joachim Schmitt, who examined the written competence of the Waldensians in the German diaspora in the period between 1685 and 1740, found that this language included a large number of archaic forms and dialectal or regional language influences. These were markedly different from contemporary northern French usages and Schmitt came to the conclusion that in the 17th century the standard concept in written language had only penetrated to a limited extent.[41] It is conceivable that the Waldensians were not an exception but in fact the norm.

The language situation in which the refugees in the German-speaking diaspora found themselves was, however, no less complicated and no less multilingual than the situation they had left behind. The German-speaking area was marked by strong dialectal continuum and the dualism of High German and Low German.[42] The Benrath line, an isogloss, running from west to east at the level between about Düsseldorf and Berlin, divided the German language area. In the northern part we encounter medial diglossia (with an endoglossic standard)

---

38   Lachenicht, "Huguenot immigrants," 312.

39   Andres Kristol, "Le plurilinguisme socialisé dans l'espace ‚francophone' du XVIIIᵉ siècle," *Multilinguisme et multiculturalité dans l'europe des lumières*, (eds.) Ursula Haskins Gonthier and Alain Sandrier (Paris: 2007), 25–47.

40   Peter Wunderli, *Die okzitanischen Bibelübersetzungen des Mittelalters. Gelöste und ungelöste Fragen* (Frankfurt: 1969), 35–70. Henri Boyer (ed.), *Dix siècles d'usages et d'images de l'occitan* (Paris: 2001), 177–222.

41   Hans Joachim Schmitt, *Der französische Wortschatz der Waldenser in Deutschland. Archivstudien* (Tübingen: 1996), 77–88, 99.

42   Joseph Salmons, *A History of German: What the Past Reveals about Today's Language* (Oxford: 2012).

from roughly the 16th century: People spoke Low German but wrote High German. The increasing prestige of High German, also due to the influence of the Eastern Middle German spread by Luther, led to the suppression of Low German.

A hypothesis strongly supported by the dialectologist Marie-Carla Lichtenthal-Milléquant assumes that a mixed language would have formed through language contact between the German and French varieties in the communities that she has defined as a "*Dorfsprache*."[43] From a sociolinguistic or dialectology viewpoint this is, as a koineization process, plausible.[44] Given the current state of research, there is, however, no satisfactory data for this assumption and to my knowledge no contemporary statements which would provide evidence of interpersonal use of a mixed language. The material examined regarding the Huguenot language situation in Brandenburg-Prussia does not provide any information regarding this issue and Hans Joachim Schmitt also excludes the status of a "Waldensian, Huguenot or exile French" in his study of the Waldensians.[45] Without doubt, there was contact between quite different varieties in the communities. However, if and how a pidgin formed from these various patois, regional and urban languages, or if one variety became dominant, we cannot say with any authority, based on the current state of research.

4   Acculturation and Language Shift in Comparison: Brandenburg-Prussia and Hesse

In this section I will deal with convergence and divergence in the acculturation and language shift processes within various Huguenot communities. I intend to show which socio-cultural factors aided acculturation and language shift and which delayed these processes. I will pay particular attention to their spatial-social situation as language change and language shift among the Huguenots

---

43   Marie-Carla Lichtenthal-Milléquant, "Französische Sprachinseln auf deutschem Boden am Beispiel einiger Hugenottenkolonien Hessens," *Zeitschrift des Vereins für hessische Geschichte und Landeskunde* 91 (1986), 175–96.

44   For dialect-based koineization, see Paul Kerswill and Peter Trudgill, "The Birth of New Dialects," in *Dialect Change. Convergence and Divergence in European Languages*, (eds.) Peter Auer et al. (Cambridge: 2005), 196–220.

45   Böhm, *Sprachenwechsel*, 189–92. Schmitt, *Der französische Wortschatz der Waldenser in Deutschland*, 82.

was determined by the surroundings in which the process of adaptation was taking place. In order to make a comparison, I have selected four very differently structured communities: two in Brandenburg-Prussia and two in Hesse. Two settlements, namely Friedrichsdorf/Taunus and Strasburg/Uckermark, were small towns with village-like characteristics in very rural areas. The other two settlements, Frankfurt am Main and Berlin, were in dynamically developing cities. If the settlement areas and the spatial-social position of the four colonies were shown relative to one another, the following matrix would be the product.

	Brandenburg-Prussia	Hesse
urban setting	Berlin	Frankfurt am Main
rural setting	Strasburg/U.	Friedrichsdorf/T.

It is important, however, to note in advance that the language situation of the four communities has been subject to varying degrees of research. While Berlin und Strasburg/U. have been the focus of much research, only the dialectology aspect of Friedrichsdorf/T. has been examined and Frankfurt am Main has not been considered at all.[46]

4.1 *Local Settlement Conditions*

Between 1687 and 1712, 55 new families founded "Nouveau Village," later renamed Friedrichsdorf, at the foot of the Taunus, 17 km north of Frankfurt am Main. Friedrichsdorf was a mixed colony with a relatively balanced number of northern and southern French, with the largest group coming from Picardy. At the beginning, the settlement had a relatively broad-based but rather small-town professional structure. Then from the 18th century forward, the Huguenots lived almost exclusively from the textile industry.[47] Under the specially

---

46   For Berlin and Strasburg/U., see Böhm, *Sprachenwechsel*; and for Friedrichsdorf /T. see Lichtenthal-Milléquant, "Französische Sprachinseln auf deutschem Boden" and idem, *Das Französische in einigen hessischen Hugenottenkolonien in sprach- und kulturhistorischer Sicht.* (Frankfurt/M.: 1969 [Typescript]). For a comparison between Strasburg/U. and Friedrichsdorf/T.: Manuela Böhm, "Der Sprachwechsel der Hugenotten im ländlichen Raum. Die französischen Kolonien Strasburg/Uckermark und Friedrichsdorf/Taunus im Vergleich," in *Zuwanderungsland Deutschland. Die Hugenotten. Ausstellungskatalog des Deutschen Historischen Museums,* (eds.) Sabine Beneke and Hans Ottomeyer (Wolfratshausen: 2005), 127–33.

47   Angelika Baeumerth, *300 Jahre Friedrichsdorf 1687–1987* (Friedrichsdorf: 1987), 15–16.

negotiated privileges for Friedrichsdorf, the refugees were segregated from the indigenous population due to differences in language, ethnicity and statutory rights.[48] The *réfugiés* themselves desired this segregation, which was later strengthened by the ban on further immigration for Germans (1731) and the limitation of intermarriage (1746) by Landgrave Friedrich III. Huguenot women were banned from marrying German men from this point forward. Huguenot men who intended to marry German women were allowed to do so, but for a price; the oldest son of such a mixed marriage would be a *"Friedrichsdorfer,"* all the other children had right of residency, but no civil rights.[49]

The *réfugiés* arriving at Strasburg/Uckermark had their own unique story. This group arrived in 1691 as a closed community in the small town, whose population included Swiss immigrants and Jewish inhabitants alongside the French and Germans. Here they were met with inhospitality and poverty because of the Thirty Years' War, which had ravaged the region to the far north of Brandenburg. At the time of emigration, however, it became the German region most heavily populated by Huguenots. There were 55 families who settled here—all descendants of Walloons. They had found their "first Refuge" in the Palatinate and Hesse. They came originally from Flanders, Pas de Calais, Picardy, Artois and Hainaut, and settled in Strasburg under the conditions agreed upon in the Edict of Potsdam. Approximately two-thirds of them had been born in the first Refuge, the Palatinate, and one-third came from Walloon areas. The social structure of the colony during the time of emigration was clearly marked by agrarian influence since almost two-thirds were farmers or specialized in cultivating tobacco. For the rest, the craftsmen's trades illustrate an arrangement closely aligned to local needs: Strasburg/U. needed bricklayers, carpenters, joiners, wheelwrights, brewers and distillers. At the end of the 18th century, the structure of the economy changed from an agricultural base to that of a colony increasingly influenced by small-town crafts.

In Berlin, approximately 140 km away, there had been a French Reformed community since 1672 and after the Revocation this became a contact point for the newly arrived refugees. There were three waves of migration between 1684 and 1710; approximately 7000 Huguenots came to Berlin and its suburbs. The city remained the center of Huguenot life in Brandenburg-Prussia into the 19th

---

48   "Personne ne pourra se mêler avec ceux que le soussigné nous à indiqués pour habiter ou faire communauté avec eux que du consentement des anciens et directeurs... Comme ils seront séparés de langue, d'habitation et ordre politique des originaires, ils auront aussi des notaires ou greffiers... " quoted by Barbara Dölemeyer, *Die hessen-homburgischen Privilegien für französisch-reformierte Glaubensflüchtlinge* (Bad Karlshafen: 1990), 43.

49   Dölemeyer, *Die hessen-homburgischen Privilegien*, 41–44.

century. Between 1700 and 1750 more than a third of all the Huguenots who had migrated to Prussia lived there. By 1700, they numbered around 5500 and thus every fifth Berliner was a Huguenot.

The Berlin community was a mixed colony par excellence in every respect. In terms of regions represented, there was a great deal of variety since the first migration was from the areas around Metz, Sedan, Paris and the rural areas of Dauphiné, Languedoc and Champagne. After this, there followed mainly Walloons, Palatines and finally Orangeois.[50] The social structure was just as varied. Seventy per cent belonged to the petty bourgeoisie (craftsmen, merchants and journeymen), ten per cent were wholesalers, factory owners, lawyers, civil servants and scholars (therefore free professions) and ten per cent were noble—in short, French society *en miniature*, as Jürgen Wilke so fittingly described it.[51] Strikingly, the institutional structure of the French colony varied greatly. From the 1720s, there were four places of worship in addition to the first and most important church, the *Friedrichstadtkirche* which was erected in 1705. At times there were as many as thirteen pastors. Primary schools were founded at the very beginning of the community's establishment: in 1689 the *Collège François*, in 1725 the *Maison des Orphelins*, in 1770 the *Séminaire de théologie* and in 1779 the *Pépinière des Chantres et Maîtres d'École*.[52]

All three of these colonies were founded and developed on the basis of the wide-ranging privileges of the Hesse-Homburg Edict and the Edict of Potsdam. It meant that they not only had access to their own pastors, churches and schools but were largely autonomous in their administration and form in Friedrichsdorf until 1825 and in Prussia until 1809.

The privilege of practicing freely their religion was not extended to the refugees living in Frankfurt. It was here in 1554 that a group of 369 French Protestants founded a community that included mostly Walloons (from Flanders and Hainaut) but also Protestants from the cities of Rouen, Chartres and Orléans.[53] As mentioned above, the Frankfurt Council withdrew the right to practice their religion under pressure from the Lutheran Orthodoxy. In 1561 public church services were banned, and from 1596 until 1787 no services were tolerated at all. This forced the *réfugiés* to hold their services *extra muros*, in the territories of tolerant rulers such as in Offenbach, Hanau or Bockenheim and

---

50   Wilke, "Die Französische Kolonie in Berlin," 356–57.
51   Wilke, "Die Französische Kolonie in Berlin," 366, 363.
52   For these institutions, see Ursula Fuhrich-Grubert, *Die Französische Kirche zu Berlin. Ihre Einrichtungen. 1672–1945* (Bad Karlshafen: 1992).
53   Friedrich K. Ebrard, *Die französisch reformierte Gemeinde in Frankfurt am Main. 1554–1904* (Frankfurt am Main: 1906), 109.

to erect churches there.⁵⁴ Many left the town completely and moved to Hanau or Frankenthal in the Electoral Palatinate.

The influx, however, continued; between 1585 and 1595 approximately 4000 *réfugiés* were living in Frankfurt.⁵⁵ Following the Revocation, the city became a collection area and center for redirecting refugees into the German-speaking diaspora. About 100,000 *réfugiés* moved through Frankfurt, 45,000 between 1685 and 1695 alone.⁵⁶ The enormous number of new arrivals naturally had an effect on the community. One consequence was that the social structure changed and the refugee community gradually shifted from a Walloon collective dominated by weavers to a community based on trade and urban dwellers. The Frankfurters became very rich through this process. This can be seen from the almost 52,000 guilders which the community collected between 1685 and 1705 for needy refugees, or the 84,000 guilders which they mustered in 1792 for building their church.⁵⁷ On the question of legal and political status, the Frankfurt Council was remorseless. Of the first Walloon *réfugiés*, one-third secured civil rights, the rest had the less well-protected status of the so-called "*Beisassen*" (a status with reduced civil rights). From 1628, only Lutherans were able to gain Frankfurt civil rights. Although they were an economically significant group, the Frankfurt Huguenots as Reformed belonged to a non-conformist religion and therefore were only tolerated—and their political status was also reduced to toleration.

That the acculturation of the Huguenots in the four constellations briefly sketched here progressed very differently can be attributed to the disparity in their starting points.

At Friedrichsdorf/T., the acculturation ran in completely the opposite direction. Until 1837, according to Lichtenthal-Milléquant, "it was the *Germans* who were assimilated."⁵⁸ The relationship between the majority and the minority which characterized most of the communities was turned on its head at Friedrichsdorf/T. by immigration policies that promoted segregation. The Strasburg Huguenots also tried many different ways of distinguishing themselves from their surroundings and insisted upon their special status. The experience of migration which they shared, the connection of being from the

---

54 Bettina Strauss, *La Culture française à Francfort au XVIIIᵉ siècle* (Paris: 1914), 5.
55 Dölemeyer, *Die Hugenotten*, 159.
56 Strauss, *La Culture française*, 7; see also Michelle Magdelaine, "Geschichte einer Paradoxie: Frankfurt am Main und das hugenottische 'Refuge,'" in *Migration und Modernisierung*, (eds.) Georg Altrock et al. (Frankfurt am Main: 2006), 146.
57 Ebrard, *Die französisch reformierte Gemeinde in Frankfurt am Main*, 123, 139.
58 Lichtenthal-Milléquant, *Das Französische in einigen hessischen Hugenottenkolonien*, 53.

same country and the new start together in Strasburg would certainly have caused the group to bond. In comparison to the other Brandenburg Huguenots living in a rural setting, they acculturated much later.[59] However, they integrated much faster than their fellow Christians in Friedrichsdorf because they were ethnically and culturally isolated, though not spatially or professionally.

The urban-influenced Huguenot communities of Frankfurt and Berlin acculturated very differently. In view of the fact that there has been no systematic examination of the Frankfurt Huguenots, a tentative yet plausible thesis is that they integrated very quickly because of their economic power, yet as Christine Bierbach writes, they remained a distinct religious group.[60] Their relatively advanced stage of integration, their social ascent and, above all, the avoidance of colony formation speak to rapid acculturation. They influenced the city as successful financiers and merchants. Many Frankfurt Huguenots had achieved an excellent position which is indicated, among other things, by the fact that at the end of the 16th century of the 84 most important wholesalers in Germany, six were French Protestants.[61] On the other hand, their numerous attempts to gain concessions for their faith from the city council failed repeatedly until 1787. The irony of the story is that they owed their entire civil and religious equality, which was finally achieved in 1806, to a Catholic prince-primate.[62]

The situation was somewhat different in Berlin. There the Huguenots, not to put too fine a point on it, had spent the entire 18th century defending their special status which they saw as threatened by signs of acculturation. By the fourth generation, the colony's marriage register shows that a third of all marriages were intermarriages.[63] Also, declining church attendance, switches to the German Reformed communities and the fact that the lower classes above all "drifted" away from the French colony and community indicate cultural and religious acculturation.[64] In 1809, all the Prussian French colonies lost their special status. At this time, the Strasburg Huguenots differed from their fellow citizens in terms of religion at most. In the Berlin upper class at least, things looked different. These people, as we will see, clung unperturbed to their identity as Huguenots.

---

59   Böhm, *Sprachenwechsel*, 150–61.
60   Christine Bierbach, "'Tout le monde parle français ...?' Zur Geschichte und sozialen Rolle des Französischen in Frankfurt am Main," in *Frankophone Sprachvarietäten. Variétés linguistiques francophones*, (ed.) Peter Stein (Tübingen: 2000), 160, 162.
61   Ebrard, *Die französisch reformierte Gemeinde in Frankfurt am Main*, 110.
62   Ebrard, *Die französisch reformierte Gemeinde in Frankfurt am Main*, 140.
63   Lachenicht, *Hugenotten in Europa und Nordamerika*, 376–82.
64   Böhm, *Sprachenwechsel*, 135–51.

What was the effect of these acculturation scenarios on the language situation? Firstly, it should be stated that quite different language shift scenarios (in terms of dynamic and structure) are to be expected. The often-repeated theory that the Huguenot language shift was completed faster in urban-influenced communities may be accurate in the case of Friedrichsdorf/T., but it does not take into account that this was a special case where the Huguenots were successful in delaying the shift to German for a long time.[65] In Brandenburg-Prussia at least, the assumption of an early language shift in the city colonies does not stand up to close examination. Indeed, research shows the opposite to be the case.[66] Sweeping urban-rural dichotomies conceal the differentiated and complex language relationships.

In Friedrichsdorf, the colonists were not obliged to interact with Germans and so French remained among them for a long time. Segregation worked here simultaneously as a kind of language maintenance feature. In Frankfurt, the extensive language contact with German varieties and the marginalization of their worship practices presumably led to a rather fast acquisition of German. Still, French was retained in certain domains. In Berlin, a split in the colony in relation to language behavior can be observed. It was the cultural and social elite among the Huguenots who from the second half of the 18th century clung tightly to French. They maintained their language not only for reasons of religious identity and social distinction, but also used it as a high-level, religious and colloquial language, both in spoken and written form. Language shift was here, as in Strasburg/U., a problem seen as a crisis which was to be fought with language policy. These language policy strategies had more success in Berlin than in Strasburg for many reasons, as we will see.

These abbreviated comments will be elaborated using the categories from Fishman's GIDS model. The following categories will be compared: the intergenerational transmission of language, French vs. German vs. bilingual instruction, French as a sacred language and French as a *lingua franca*.

4.2 *Intergenerational Transmission of Language*

There are many metalinguistic commentaries for Strasburg/U. and Berlin dating from the 1750s and the 1760s which gave warning that the transmission of the "native language" to successive generations was in grave danger. In 1887,

---

65   Glück, *Deutsch als Fremdsprache in Europa vom Mittelalter bis zur Barockzeit*, 185. Fritz Wolff, "Selbstbehauptung und Integration der Hugenottengemeinden in Hessen," in *Die Hugenotten und das Refuge. Deutschland und Europa*, (eds.) Frédéric Hartweg and Stefi Jersch-Wenzel (Berlin: 1990), 209–10.

66   Böhm, *Sprachenwechsel*, 516–35.

the *Friedrichsdorfer Chronik* noted that the "fall of the language of the Father" was nigh. Lichtenthal-Milléquant states that already at the beginning of the 19th century there were noticeable Low German and High German interferences in the sources from Friedrichsdorf/T. They indicate a "retreat" of French, but it remained a colloquial language until around 1897.[67] By this time, French had not been a colloquial language in the others communities for a long time, but at most a symbolically used sacred language.

From 1750 onward, there is evidence in the Strasburg sources of significant Low and High German interference as a result of effective language contact with spoken Low German and written High German—a sign that French was declining.[68] Comments like that of the Strasburg pastor Maréchaux, who in 1785 "a trouvé le françois relativement négligé, qu'il ne voit aucun moyen de le retablir"[69] signaled that the shift to Low German as a colloquial language was complete by the fourth generation. In Berlin, the sources display in the 1830s language phenomena such as code-switching, inter-lingual interferences in speech of High German, Low German and the Berlin vernacular, indicating that the communicative and colloquial language of the Huguenots was no longer French by the sixth generation.[70] Among the Berlin Huguenots, however, there was a difference with regard to language behavior. The language shift proceeded, viewed socially, from the bottom up. It affected the Huguenot underclass first. The school commission convened in 1814 arrived at a similar conclusion:

> [...] c'est principalement sur la classe indigente, à laquelle le françois devient de plus en plus étranger, sur les enfants des pauvres instruits dans nos écoles ou élevés dans nos fondations, qui après qu'ils en sont sortis perdent si facilement l'habitude de la parler, que nous devons fixer notre attention.[71]

As Frédéric Hartweg points out, this phenomenon had worried the consistory and other church councils already in the 1760s.[72] The debates did not lead to agreement, however, that this process would be hard to stop. The introduction

---

67 Lichtenthal-Milléquant, *Das Französische in einigen hessischen Hugenottenkolonien*, 53.
68 Böhm, *Sprachenwechsel*, 192–201.
69 Archiv der französisch reformierten Kirche zu Berlin, AFrD Rep. 32a – 6255, fol. 12.
70 Böhm, *Sprachenwechsel*, 186–92.
71 Archiv der französisch reformierten Kirche zu Berlin, AFrD Rep. 32a – 4, fol. 54r.
72 Frédéric Hartweg, "Französisch als Kultsprache? Zur Sprachpolitik der französisch-reformierten Kirche in Berlin 1744–1814," idem, "Sprachwechsel und Sprachpolitik der Französisch-Reformierten Kirche in Berlin im 18. Jahrhundert."

of German church services, bilingual catechism, and the like was delayed. For the Berlin Huguenots, French had an inner group-bonding strength and was part of their hybrid identity; it also signaled a unique feature to the outside world and was understood to be a guarantee of special status.[73] Because of the existence of German Reformed communities as at Strasburg/U., merging with them was naturally a realistic (if unacceptable) option. Apart from language, there were from a theological standpoint no differences. The upper class for politically strategic and social status reasons took care that French was protected from any kind of erosion. The Huguenot elite in Berlin used French well into the 19th century, at least for those functions which Fishman defined in the GIDS as at least a partial transmission vehicle to following generations, as "language as family interaction, of interaction with playmates, neighbors and acquaintances."[74] It served them as a spoken, colloquial and family language while the rest of the community found itself in a diglossia situation and used the Berlin urban vernacular as colloquial language, High German as written language and French, mostly passively, as a sacred language.

On the basis of current research it is difficult to say whether the Frankfurt Huguenots managed this to the same extent from the 17th to the 19th century. But at least the fact that they, in contrast to the other three communities, had no access to a central, namely educational place of language communication makes it seem difficult for them to have passed all the francophone varieties and registers to following generations.

It is clear that varying amounts of time elapsed within the individual communities between the warning of "threatening" language shift and the point in time at which French actually stopped being the general language of communication. This also means that they had varying degrees of success in influencing language shift. An appropriate tool for exerting an influence was language policy strategies that were perpetuated through the schools, quite in the sense of Fishman, who recognizes in schools a key role in language retention in a minority situation.

4.3 French, German or Bilingual Instruction?

The minority situation of the Huguenots meant that school was an important place for securing identity. Here the language was taught and practiced in both its spoken and written forms, and religious instruction was also provided well

---

73 Concerning the collective cultural identity and the 'lieux de mémoire' of the Berlin Huguenots in the nineteenth century, see Manuela Böhm, "Kollektives Gedächtnis und Erinnerungsorte der Berliner Hugenotten," in *Berlins 19. Jahrhundert. Ein Metropolen-Kompendium*, (eds.) Roland Berbig et al. (Berlin: 2011), 473–90.

74 Fishman, *Reversing Language Shift*, 93.

into the 18th century. In addition, school is the place where not only language acquisition takes place but language shift is also set in motion and influenced. Language use, language policy and school instruction are closely related since in school important community cultural and social practices are acquired and language is the medium of instruction. These functions provide important support not only for the refugee generations but also for the following generations. With progressive acculturation these language and identity securing elements run, however, into danger.

The Frankfurt *réfugiés* were banned from having their own schools in 1592. This fact can be compared to the loss of a focal point to maintain, reproduce and to popularize the French language and a specific Huguenot refugee identity and to diffuse it throughout the community until their legal and denominational equality was declared in 1806. If the Huguenots wanted to send their children to a religious school, they had to go to a boarding school in one of the surrounding Huguenot communities, such as in Hanau or Homburg. French lessons were also hard to come by. Public German schools did not teach French and only in 1784 was the language made an option in the grammar school curriculum.[75] Therefore, if the Frankfurt Huguenots wanted their children to be instructed in the "spirit of the Father," their only choice was private instruction.

The Edict of Potsdam and the Hesse-Homburg privileges secured financing for schools, in part because the territorial ruler paid the teachers. In Berlin, the refugees immediately began establishing schools. Here we find three forms of schools: firstly the "*Écoles paroissiales*"—parochial schools, the communities' own primary schools; secondly the private schools which were independent of the communities but funded and franchised by them; and then the schools belonging to institutions for the poor and needy (primarily the *École de Charité*, the *Maison des Orphelins* and the *Petit Hôpital*).[76] Non-school based private lessons were generally provided by a tutor, *hofmeister* (literally court-master, a tutor responsible for his charges beyond their education) or preceptor. Naturally, this was a socially restricted educational option.

A glance at the orphans' school, the *Maison des Orphelins*, makes clear that it was only at the end of the 18th century that a language shift was noticeable—in any event, 30 or 40 years after the language problem had been discussed in the church councils. One reason for the delay of language shift is that this completely Huguenot institution provided a relatively intact francophone

---

75 Bierbach, "Tout le monde parle français …?" 170.
76 For the Huguenots' primary schools in Berlin, see Franziska Roosen, *"Soutenir notre Église." Hugenottische Erziehungskonzepte und Bildungseinrichtungen im Berlin des 18. Jahrhunderts* (Bad Karlshafen: 2008).

environment. Another reason may be the effect of extensive instruction in reading and writing in French. The most important reason, in my opinion, is that German was taught alongside French, from around 1760. Thus, the situation in the orphanage was radically different from the diglossia found in the middle and lower strata of the rest of the Huguenot community. The children in the orphanage acquired cross-functional multilingualism which weakened the virulence of the language problem. Around 1830, however, the process of language shift was complete in this school. German had become the colloquial and classroom language, whereas French was only taught as a foreign language.[77]

In Strasburg/U., the question of German language at school came up simultaneous to the debate over attrition of French. It is clear from the 1753 school regulations that things were not going well for French in the school; speaking German was banned among both teachers and students in an attempt to halt the loss of competence in French. Insisting on the use of French as the sole language of instruction and banning German from schools was a practice abandoned by the consistory in 1785 and the first German reading book, Rochow's *Kinderfreund* was purchased. In 1796, local school rules stipulated German lessons in reading, writing, penmanship and arithmetic, and French was only taught in a ritualized form, namely for the catechism, psalms and prayers. Finally, in 1832, despite decades of Huguenot resistance, the school was merged with the Lutheran school.

Language lessons and language acquisition in these two schools was characterized by two very different strategies for dealing with teaching language and language policy. Both strategies, which can be summarized using the binary terms monolingualism vs. multilingualism, had despite their differences the same aim: the preservation of a group identity and the French language, which was closely linked with this identity. The loss of this identity was regarded as a danger and, following this logic, something to be averted if possible. The decision reached regarding monolingual or bilingual instruction was, however, different. The latter at the *Maison des Orphelins* promoted multilingualism for a certain time, which probably is also the reason for a delayed language shift.[78]

---

77   For the preceding and following comparison of language acquisition within the primary schools of Strasburg/U. and the *Maison des Orphelins* in Berlin, see Böhm, *Sprachenwechsel*, 435–517.

78   Manuela Böhm, "Stratégies autour des choix linguistiques dans l'enseignement huguenot en Brandebourg-Prusse, " in *Les Huguenots éducateurs dans l'espace européen à l'époque moderne,* (eds.) Geraldine Sheridan and Viviane Prest (Paris: 2011), 275–99.

4.4 Formal Domains of Language Use: French as Sacred Language

The Huguenots were religious migrants. They left their homeland because of their religion and sought a place in which they could practice their Reformed faith unhindered. For this reason, religious practice was an important part of life and in this regard language played an essential role. This is illustrated by the long, bitter and intensely debated loss of French—the sacred language of church services, official business and Scriptural readings.

The religious practice of the Frankfurt Huguenots was characterized by marginalization and disruption. No church services were permitted within the city walls, which necessitated a difficult journey to Hanau and Bockenheim, a trip that was often, especially during the Thirty Years' War, impossible. The community often went years without a francophone pastor and, accordingly, was forced to employ German-speaking pastors. In 1638, the congregation discussed joining the German Reformed Church, but decided against it. Rather, both communities opted to appoint clergymen who would be able to cover for each other.[79] The Huguenot pastors were from this point contractually obliged to be able to speak German. Altogether, the Huguenots had a close and friendly relationship with the German Reformed community.[80] This meant intensive French-German contact in the ecclesiastical domain, above all with the "other" Reformed community who (in contrast to Strasburg or Berlin) did not threaten their special rights or identity and with whom they could feel a certain solidarity.

In Berlin, church services were assured from the beginning and in the 18th century it was possible to choose between five different venues and listen to up to thirteen different pastors. Among the Berlin pastors were well-known theologians, including Abbadie, Gaultier de St. Blancard, Lenfant, Beausobre and Formey. By the 1760s the majority of the community did not understand the worship (which is, in Reformed tradition, concentrated on the speaking and hearing of the Word) and therefore stayed away. Yet the consistory and other church councils were reluctant to make changes because of the significance that French had as a sacred language. The maintenance of French meant also, however, that key tasks, namely pastoral care and sermons, were no longer guaranteed.[81] For this reason, all the debates, attempts and ideas on the introduction of German as the language of church services failed. The situation persisted until 1819 when the Kurmark government brought great pressure to

---

79 Ebrard, *Die französisch reformierte Gemeinde in Frankfurt am Main*, 115–16.
80 Ebrard, *Die französisch reformierte Gemeinde in Frankfurt am Main*, 124.
81 Hartweg, "Sprachwechsel und Sprachpolitik der Französisch-Reformierten Kirche in Berlin im 18. Jahrhundert."

bear on the community and Friedrich Wilhelm III pushed German through as the language of church services in 1831.[82] The Berlin Huguenots kept the consistory proceedings (registres de déliberations de consistoire) in French until 1852 and the parish registers in French until 1896.

Astonishingly, the Frankfurt Huguenots kept French as their sacred language for a long time, despite the difficulties. German was only introduced in 1916 following a long debate. It should not be assumed that at this time French served as a cross-functional and common variety for the Frankfurt Huguenots despite what is known about the language use of Huguenots in other communities. The use of French was limited to sacred affairs, a use which belonged firmly to the religious environment and thus here there was a diglossia like in the Berlin middle and lower classes (the Frankfurt urban vernacular as a spoken language, German as a written language and French as a sacred language). Whether the whole church service or only parts of it were held in French until 1916 requires further investigation. The late change to German, to my knowledge the latest in the German-speaking diaspora, shows, however, how strongly the fight to practice their religion bound the Frankfurt Huguenots to the French language. This is demonstrated by the fact that the last French edition of the Psalter for the community was printed in 1898. From around the 1850, the records and parish registers show that they are transcriptions (and therefore presumably they were written initially in German and then subsequently translated into French). Research into these issues and testing the hypotheses presented here is a general research desideratum.

Let us now turn to the question of sacred language in rural areas. While in the Berlin community the issues were still being discussed and delayed, in the area around Strasburg the language shift even in the domain of church services was long complete. A lack of continuity and long periods without pastors had been a problem since the 1740s, so the change in 1794 to alternating German and French language church services was a pragmatic decision. In Friedrichsdorf, this took place roughly a century later in 1885. Pastors and school teachers who aimed to maintain French and the essential material resources (from 1836 a Sunday school, from 1856 a kindergarten, a library for confirmation candidates, and a church reading group initiated by Pastor Cérésole) allowed the Friedrichsdorfers to maintain their language in the religious arena and also across generations. German only became the official language around 1890.[83]

---

82 For the role of German as the sacred language of the Brandenburg Huguenots, see Böhm, *Sprachenwechsel,* 214–39.

83 Lichtenthal-Milléquant, "Französische Sprachinseln auf deutschem Boden," 190–91.

The Strasburgers made German the official language for consistory records and parish registers in 1818 and 1833 respectively. Joining with the German Reformed was something which they vehemently refused, however. Preventing German from becoming the language of religion for as long as possible and keeping French as sacred language can be clearly seen as important objectives in Berlin and Strasburg at least. This exacted its price; the sacred language only had a symbolic value for many community members.

4.5 *French as Language of the Majority?*

French was in all four communities an internally valid official language which meant it was the language in which administrative tasks were accomplished. The above-mentioned details of the language shift in parish registers and consistory records are an indication of the different dynamics of language shift in this area. In his GIDS model Fishman admits the high probability of retaining the minority language when it fulfills its function as an internally valid and administrative language anchored by its written form. Fishman recognizes a greater guarantee of "vitality" for a minority language when it also has a prestige function for the majority community as, for example, an educational or cultural language. The degree of communicative reach and prestige which French commanded in the environment of individual Huguenot communities differed from area to area and this is where the urban-rural contrast is particularly noticeable.

The Frankfurt Huguenots were, from the perspective of the indigenous population, the wrong religious denomination, but possessed the dominant culture and language. The attraction for other Frankfurters is shown by the private non-denominational schools run by the Huguenots. They were established in the second half of the 18th century by, for example, Maître Roland and Nicolas Paradis. Both aligned their program of instruction with the classical curriculum of the elite academies and were tailored to the bourgeois clientele: the *meilleures familles*. Thus, the children of the Goethe family and those of the Mayor Textor had these institutions to thank for their cultural and linguistic formation.[84] The incredibly varied francophone press also demonstrates the prestige of and support for French in Frankfurt.[85]

The privileged position and the francophone infrastructure of the Berlin Huguenots facilitated not only an existence as a state within a state and the correspondingly prolonged survival of the French language, but also led to a colonizer's consciousness among the Huguenots. They were the central

---

84 Strauss, *La Culture Française*, 83–106.
85 Bierbach, "'Tout le monde parle français …?'," 175–78.

characters in the hegemony of the French-German culture and language transfer. The Berlin Huguenot elite with their French language skills and culture were able to profit greatly from the Francophile trend among the German aristocracy and urban citizenry.[86]

Huguenots in villages and country towns were far removed from any kind of intellectual urban culture. Their language situation is reflected in a letter from the pastor Henri Samuel Catel, who served in Strasburg in the period 1778–1781, to his father-in-law and Berlin pastor and Academy secretary Jean Henri Samuel Formey:

> Je ne parle ici françois qu'en chaire et chez moi. Rarement le parle-t-on chez les Rellstab [the German Reformed pastor] à cause de Monsieur qui le comprend, mais ne le parle pas.[87]

There is ample evidence of well-developed French language skills among the families of the Berlin Huguenot upper class in the same time period as, for example, the Erman family among whom at the beginning of the 19th century French was the colloquial and vernacular language. Pastor Jean Pierre Erman spoke and wrote only French his whole life. It was similar with J.H.S. Formey, J. Henri and C.D. de Lanzicolle whose unblemished competence in the French mother tongue must have been representative of the Berlin upper class of the French colony. The surrounding countryside was completely lacking in these pillars of the French language. At Strasburg/U. there was no francophone infrastructure and no one with whom the Huguenots could have spoken in French. Anyone speaking to the native population would have had to speak Low German.

Friedrichsdorf was also a long way from an environment where French would have had any kind of communicative reach. There, however, speaking French was normal until at least the 19th century which meant that French was the majority language. Those who profited probably the most from this situation of Friedrichsdorf as a linguistic enclave, were the students coming from various nations to the well-known educational institutions such as the Institut Garnier (founded in 1836) and the girls' boarding school (opened in 1849).

---

86   Concerning francophonie in 18th-century Prussia, see Manuela Böhm, "Domains of francophonie and language ideology in Prussia in the eighteenth and early nineteenth century," in *European francophonie: The Social, Political and Cultural History of an International Prestige Language*, (eds.) Derek Offord et al. (forthcoming).

87   Staatsbibliothek zu Berlin, SBB, Nachlass Formey, S.H. Catel and J.H.S. Formey, 30.12.1779.

5 Conclusion

Whenever members of a religious community seek refuge in a new location where they find themselves a religious, linguistic and cultural minority, various scenarios for the further existence of the community are possible: quick and inconspicuous integration, protracted integration, discrimination or even segregation. These are all variants of more or less complete acculturation. Much depends on the local, political and legal framework which gives the migrants a certain status in the social structure.

The Huguenot settlements discussed here have shown that language and acculturation are intertwined in many ways. The one is a consequence of the other and the first has a catalyzing effect on the second. From a linguistic standpoint, the migration of the Huguenots changed several fundamental parameters of the languages involved: the language map (their geographic distribution), the language repertoires themselves and the relationship of the speakers to their languages. The clearest sign of acculturation among the Huguenots was that they went through a language shift, which means that their language repertoire changed to that of the majority society—from a linguistic standpoint generally an irreversible and complex process.

The Huguenots in the German-speaking diaspora completed the language shift at different paces in various domains, language situations and institutions. From all the domains looked at here, it is clear that the religious domain remained untouched by language shift the longest. This fits with the fact that the Huguenot communities examined here scarcely acculturated with regard to their religion. The French Reformed communities in Berlin and Frankfurt am Main still exist today; the group in Strasburg only joined the German Reformed in 1950.

The retention of French as a sacred language in Frankfurt, the multilingualism and cross-functional use as a means of social distinction among the Berliners, and the long ban on German in schools in Strasburg show that the language or languages which the Huguenots brought with them were not only a group-formation identifying element but also acted as a symbol to the outside world. The language choice—the decision for German or French—was always an "act of identity."

Analysis of the language shift among the Huguenots quickly makes clear how little relationship the process has with the theory by which scholars model general language shift in sociolinguistics. There and in several studies of language shift among the Huguenots, the assumption is the following sequence.[88]

---

[88] For modelling the language shift within three generations, see: Frédéric Hartweg, "Die Hugenotten und Deutschland. Eine Minderheit zwischen zwei Kulturen," in *Die*

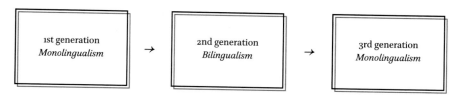

We saw above that "a language shift" does not just happen. Rather, the length of time needed in the various domains, language situations, sociocultural and local conditions, and form (spoken/written) varies. There is another respect in which the model is not appropriate. The change did not occur within the space of three generations in any of the communities studied here, but was in each case a *longue durée* phenomenon. Thirdly, it has become clear that it was more than the simple exchange of one language for another. Due to the multilingual starting situation of the migrants and the multilingualism of the majority community, the change from language varieties used in each of the Huguenot communities to that of the majority community caused a change to the whole linguistic inventory. The reality of this language process is considerably more complex than the model above.

It is much more helpful to use other theories such as Fishman's GIDS model in order to reach conclusions about language shift in Huguenot communities and the acculturation behavior underlying it. On this basis, it is possible to show that the Huguenots kept their linguistic minority situation stable for as long as their language repertoires were able to fulfill all the relevant functions, which means written and spoken language, official language and colloquial language. A litmus test for language maintenance is the question of intergenerational continuation of the language(s) whereby, according to Fishman, the stage of bilingual education anchored in school is the point of no return. Denying language shift, ignoring it and stubbornly clinging to the sole use of French despite being aware of the language reality meant that the Huguenots had to pay the price of language attrition. This is evident in analysis of the purely defensive language policy of the Strasburg school or the hesitation of the Berlin Church councils in the face of language loss among the lower classes.

Hugenotten 1685–1985, (eds.) Rudolf von Thadden and Michelle Magdelaine (Munich: 1985), 173; idem, "Der Sprachwechsel im Berliner Refuge," in *Zuwanderungsland Deutschland. Die Hugenotten. Ausstellungskatalog des Deutschen Historischen Museums*, (eds.) Sabine Beneke and Hans Ottomeyer (Wolfratshausen: 2005), 121; Johannes Kramer, "Die Glaubensflüchtlinge," in *Das Französische in Deutschland. Eine Einführung*, (ed.) Johannes Kramer (Stuttgart: 1992), 71–95; Jürgen Eschmann, "Die Sprache der Hugenotten," in *Hugenottenkultur in Deutschland*, (ed.) Jürgen Eschmann (Tübingen: 1989), 9–35.

In Fishman's words, "Bilingualism is a benefit for all." In contrast, the option of multilingualism chosen by the Berlin Huguenot upper class and at the *Maison des Orphelins* was a guarantee for longer retention of the minority language because, again according to Fishman, the population experiencing language shift has no alternative, by and large, but to be bilingual.[89]

Language shift began significantly later in those communities where French had value for the majority community. In urban settings such as in Berlin and Frankfurt, speaking French was an economic factor because quite simply it conferred social and cultural capital. But even in this area, the social symbolic value of French was not long-lived. Migration and language shift also caused each language to be newly evaluated in terms of its status in society. Thus, it is only logical that the last Huguenot communities to finally take on German did so at the time when in the course of the formation of a German national state German became a factor in identity formation.

---

89   Fishman, *Reversing Language Shift*, 84.

CHAPTER 12

Huguenot Memoirs[1]

Carolyn Chappell Lougee

How little we really know about this practice [of private writing]. The most basic questions—how many and what sort of persons engaged in it, or why they were moved to do so, or how these vectors changed over time— have yet to find even preliminary answers.[2]

1 Introduction

Memoir—a narrative recollection of first-hand experience—became a significant social practice in France in the 17th century. Notations of expenditure and family milestones that were traditionally recorded in *livres de raison*[3] began to take on the form of a story, founding a genre whose exemplars could range from lengthy chronicles of public actions down to a few pages of private memories. Personages with privileged access to important events recorded their political, military, or diplomatic exploits in *mémoires-histoires* that were

---

[1] Portions of this article are drawn from previous publications by the author: "Writing the Diaspora: Escape Memoirs and the Construction of Huguenot Memory," in *L'Identité huguenote. Faire mémoire et écrire l'histoire (XVIe–XXIe siècle)*, (eds.) Philip Benedict, Hugues Daussy and Pierre-Olivier Léchot (Geneva: 2014), 261–77; "Paper Memories and Identity Papers: Why Huguenot Refugees Wrote Memoirs," in *Narrating the Self in Early Modern Europe*, (eds.) Bruno Tribout and Ruth Whelan (Oxford: 2007), 121–38; "Emigration and Memory: After 1685 and After 1789," in *Egodocuments and History: Autobiographical Writing in its Social Context since the Middle Ages*, (ed.) Rudolf Dekker (Hilversum: 2002), 89–106; "'The Pains I Took to Save My/His Family': Escape Accounts of A Huguenot Mother and Daughter After the Revocation of the Edict of Nantes," *French Historical Studies* 22 (1999), 5–67.

[2] James S. Amelang, "A Room of One's Own: Keeping Writings Private," in *Les écrits du for privé en Europe (du moyen âge à l'époque contemporaine)*, (eds.) Jean-Pierre Bardet et al. (Bordeaux: 2010), 184.

[3] *Livres de raison* were day-to-day or episodic family accounts typically recording fragments of financial information and noteworthy family milestones. Often multi-author and multi-generational, they were distinguishable from memoirs, which were single-authored and retrospective, with narrative shaping and continuity. On *livres de raison*, see Nicole Lemaître, "Les livres de raison en France (fin XIIIe–XIXe siècles)," *Bolletino della ricerca sui libri di famiglia* 7 (2006), 1–18.

sometimes published in their lifetimes.⁴ Both Catholics and Protestants penned these *mémoires-histoires*—d'Aubigné and Sully among the Reformed as well as Richelieu, Bassompierre, and Retz among Catholics⁵—but on neither side were these writings specifically oriented to convey religious experience or purpose. By contrast, private memoirs—self-reflective histories tracing the writer's own life course (as distinct from episodes of public import), laying bare emotional experience, and confiding intimate beliefs—often centered on situations or emotions the writer experienced because of his or her adherence to one or the other religion. Across the century, Catholic autobiographical memoirs adopted the deeply interior model of Augustine of Hippo or Teresa of Avila to both retrace and celebrate their writer's conversion, offering readers exempla that might guide their own progression toward faith.

Curiously, autobiographical memoirs⁶ were slower to emerge among Huguenots than among their Catholic neighbors and—more surprisingly—even slower than among Calvinists across the Channel. Whereas English Puritans produced copious confessional memoirs from the very early 17th century onward, only after the reprise of persecution in the 1680s and the Revocation of the Edict of Nantes in 1685 did Huguenots employ personal histories in Calvinist polemics or find memoir a meaningful form of testimony to their personal experience of trying times. That until then Huguenots "lacked a tradition of spiritual journal-keeping,"⁷ that "French Protestants do not seem

---

4   "Memoires, au pluriel, se dit des Livres d'Historiens, écrits par ceux qui ont eu part aux affaires ou qui en ont été témoins oculaires, ou qui contiennent leur vie ou leurs principales actions: Ce qui répond à ce que les Latins appelloient *commentaires*. Ainsi on dit les *Memoires de Sulli, de Villeroy, du Cardinal de Richelieu, des Maréchaux de Themines, et de Bassompierre, de Brantosme, de Montrefort, de la Roche-Foucaut, de Pontis*, &c.": Antoine Furetière, *Dictionaire universel, contenant generalement tous les mots françois tant vieux que modernes, Et les termes de toutes les sciences et des arts*, vol. 2 (The Hague: 1694), 94.

5   Frédéric Charbonneau offers a "Catalogue raisonné des mémoires français du xviiᵉ siècle" listing 79 memoirs in the appendix to his *Les Silences de l'histoire: les mémoires français du XVIIe siècle* (Sainte-Foy, Québec: 2000), 241–46. The only additional Protestant memorialists listed among the 79 are La Force, his son Castelnau, and Dumont de Bostaquet.

6   The distinction between memoir and autobiography has been a staple of autobiography studies. It is fundamental to several of the articles on life-writing in Roger Chartier (ed.), *A History of Private Life: Passions of the Renaissance*, trans. Arthur Goldhammer (Cambridge, Mass.: 1989), and Michael Mascuch's *Origins of the Individualist Self: Autobiography and Self-Identity in England, 1591–1791* (Stanford: 1996) is predicated upon it. But the boundary between memoir and autobiography has come to seem, to many critics, less and less salient or meaningful.

7   Philip Benedict, "Two Calvinisms," in his *The Faith and Fortunes of France's Huguenots, 1600–85* (Burlington, Vt.: 2001), 224.

to have been particularly active in writing diaries, autobiographies, biographies, memoirs, or even accounts of their spiritual lives"[8] has been noted but has yet to be persuasively traced to its origins.

The later emergence of Protestant memoirs in France may well have been rooted in both theology and strategy. Puritans and Huguenots drew contrasting emphases from Calvinist doctrines, emphases that issued in contrary stances on the creation of self-reflective documents. Puritans' emphasis on methodical self-discipline and high self-monitoring as practices of sanctification made autobiographical writing for them a religious act. By contrast, Huguenots privileged threads in Calvin's writings that not only minimized the role of self-remembrance in sanctification but also actively disapproved of self-justifying personal narratives.[9] The New Testament founding of redemption upon remembrance of Jesus delegitimized commemoration of human works and entailed a denial of personal history. Calvin himself said little about his own person,[10] left behind no narration of his life, and even concealed his gravesite so it would not become a *lieu de mémoire*. Calvinism became "of all Christian theologies the least hospitable to the existence of a profane as opposed to a sacred memory... Because human works play no role in salvation, they do not deserve to be remembered."[11] This distinctive theology-based deflection of attention from human works may have been among the reasons why Huguenots long stayed away from commemorations of individual lives, in the form of personal memoirs.

A complementary strategic reason may also help explain the rarity of Huguenot memoirs before the Revocation. Catholic controversialists routinely used attacks on the personal lives of early Reform leaders as a means of discrediting their religious beliefs. On the defensive, Huguenot strategists denied that histories of personal virtues or vices had any bearing on religious truths,

---

8 Ruth Whelan, "From the Other Side of Silence: Huguenot Life-writing, a Dialogic Art of Narrating the Self," in *Narrating the Self*, (eds.) Tribout and Whelan, 140.

9 Calvin reproved the pardon tale, for example, told by defendants in court proceedings to deny, justify or excuse the transgression of which they were accused. Natalie Zemon Davis, *Fiction in the Archives: Pardon Tales and their Tellers in Sixteenth-Century France* (Stanford: 1987): "Human remission would mean telling a false or dubious story and benefiting from a this-worldly indulgence that fed sin. This was of a piece with the deceptions of Catholic confession and the priest's absolution." (61, 114).

10 Richard Stauffer, "Les Discours à la première personne dans les sermons de Jean Calvin," in *Regards contemporains sur Jean Calvin* (Paris: 1965), 206–38.

11 Philippe Joutard, "The Museum of the Desert: The Protestant Minority," in *Realms of Memory: Rethinking the French Past*, (ed.) Pierre Nora, trans. Arthur Goldhammer, vol. 1 (New York: 1996–1998), 354.

which God alone, not the actions of men, revealed: "the character and actions of their leaders have nothing to do with their leaders' doctrines."[12] They "maintained a prudent silence...the effort of the Reformed controversialists—in conformity with their ecclesiology—rested upon the distinction between the person of the Reformers and the Reform of the Church."[13] Only toward the end of the 17th century did Huguenot advocacy begin to include personal histories in its armory of polemical weapons, alongside doctrine. Pierre Jurieu, Elie Benoist, and Pierre Bayle, writing in the Refuge, came to see that personal histories of those willing to suffer for it could testify to the truth of their religion.[14] Jurieu, for the *Lettres pastorales* he smuggled back into France in the 1680s,[15] collected the personal stories of those arriving in the Refuge as a way to publicize the iniquities of Louis XIV and honor the steadfast faith of the exiles.[16] Benoist, for the massive *Histoire de l'Edit de Nantes* he published in 1693–95, mixed the eyewitness accounts of persecution in Poitou-Charentes collected by Abraham Tessereau with what refugees told him, as a way to vindicate the innocence of the Huguenots and persuade host countries of their worthiness for welcome.

In the Refuge, autobiographical memoirs, too, began to flow from Huguenot pens in unprecedented numbers. The Huguenot exodus was indeed the first of Europe's great migrations to produce first-hand memoirs. But just as the dearth of early Huguenot memoirs has been largely unexplained, so, too, has this turn to memoir writing only begun to be probed. What in the experience of persecution, emigration and exile turned French Protestant writers toward writing personal histories? And how did the forms in which they wrote their memoirs make them congruent with Protestant doctrine despite Calvin's own theological

---

12   Elisabeth Israels Perry, *From Theology to History: French Religious Controversy and the Revocation of the Edict of Nantes* (The Hague: 1973), 130. Marion Deschamp extends this chronology backward, to see the Catholic attacks as responses to early partisan Protestant biographies, in "Recueils et miroirs de l'infamie: Les stratégies d'écriture de Vies dans la littérature de controverse confessionnelle (XVIe–XVIIe siècles)," *BSHPF* 157 (2011), 133–45.

13   Jean-Robert Armogathe, "Les Vies de Calvin aux XVIe et XVIIe siècles," in *Historiographie de la réforme*, (ed.) Philippe Joutard (Paris: 1977), 48, 51.

14   Jacques Solé, "Pierre Bayle, historien de la réforme," in *Historiographie de la réforme*, (ed.) Joutard, 71–80.

15   Pierre Jurieu, *Lettres pastorales adressées aux fidèles de France qui gémissent sous la captivité de Babylon* (Rotterdam: 1686–87).

16   Élie Benoist, *Histoire de l'Edit de Nantes, contenant les choses les plus remarquables qui se sont passées en France avant et après sa publication, à l'occasion de la diversité des Religions* (5 vols. Delft: 1693–95).

disapproval of personal histories? Study of these texts can be expected to illuminate the causes and character of this turnabout in the relationship between French Protestantism and autobiographical memoirs.

2   Reading the Memoirs

The numbers of memoirs written by Huguenots in the years surrounding the Revocation are difficult to estimate. Those that survive number only in the dozens but are no doubt the remnants of a much larger corpus of writings— "the odd messages in bottles that happen to have washed up onto our shores."[17] Their existence suggests that many of the 180,000 or so Protestants who left France and at least a few of those who stayed as New Converts committed to paper some autobiographical account of their conversion under pressure or their escape and resettlement abroad. To date the only concerted search for memoirs has focused on accounts of clandestine escape, of which more than 50 have been identified, and a search needs to be undertaken for additional Revocation-era memoirs written by persons who stayed in France, left with permission, or were expelled.[18] Many of the known memoirs were unearthed and published by Protestant historians in the 19th century, especially in the *Bulletin de la Société de l'Histoire du Protestantisme Français* or in the *Proceedings of the Huguenot Society of London*. Others survive in libraries in France and in the Refuge, or lie among descendants' family papers. The texts identified to date range from less than a page in length to more than 300; they recount their author's experience of persecution for their religion, variously, as part of a more extensive life story or as a freestanding tale. They encompass a remarkable variety of formats: some are arranged as genealogies, others mimic travel accounts or judicial factums or even fairy tales. The authors were obscure refugees rather than professional writers: ministers, country noblemen, schoolteachers, and a tiny handful of women.

Over the years, Huguenot memoirs have been read as much for inspiration and celebration as for insight into the experience of persecution, flight, and resettlement. One reader of an escape account wrote that it "makes me feel great respect for the energy and courage of those fine people who never

---

17   Amelang, "Room of One's Own," 179.
18   The Appendix below lists Huguenot memoirs from the Revocation era as a first pass toward a list that other scholars might in the future expand through additions or refine through subtraction of texts that, upon closer scrutiny, only appear to be firsthand memoirs.

allowed themselves to go down...those gallant old Huguenots."[19] A reader of another escape memoir christened it "a monument to true Huguenot devotion to God, prudence, and determination."[20] Historians who have looked at Huguenot memoirs have sometimes read them uncritically, as objective eyewitness testimonies to the events of the Revocation. But though these texts can help illuminate numerous dimensions of the Refuge that historians commonly pursue—including acculturation/assimilation, religion and *patrie*, hardship and heroism—memoir is a genre that reshapes the past that it renders into narrative, as recent scholarship has recognized. And that reshaping constitutes much of its value. As Leslie Stephen said long ago, "An autobiography, alone of all books, may be more valuable in proportion to the amount of misrepresentation it contains."[21] Identifying that reshaping—which is the term we would use in place of Stephen's "misrepresentation"—is the key to unlocking the multiple levels of meaning in Huguenot memoirs.[22]

Three overlapping approaches have contributed strongly to moving Huguenot memoirs into the terrain Natalie Zemon Davis called "the field between the true and the plausible."[23] A literary approach focuses on the language, rhetorical strategies, tropes, symbolisms, and implied genres employed by the author, to enhance the meanings lying on the surface of these autobiographical texts. A more global approach, based on recognition that "In every story is a story not told,"[24] embraces the structure of the account as well as its linguistic character, to reveal meanings not accessible from semantic content alone: seeking clues in patterns of inclusion and exclusion, juxtapositions, strategic silences, puzzling exaggerations, curious placements, the unexpected "'circumstantial' detail...these guileful tricks on the part of the storyteller...

---

19   Huguenot Library (London), Ms. T1/5/2.
20   Henri Tollin, *Geschichte der französischen Colonie von Magdeburg* (Magdeburg: 1886), III¹B: 50.
21   Leslie Stephen, *Hours in a Library*, vol. 3 (London: 1892), 237.
22   Foundational works in the study of autobiography include Paul John Eakin, *Fictions in Autobiography: Studies in the Art of Self-Invention* (Princeton: 1985); Philippe Lejeune *Le Pacte autobiographique* (Paris: 1975); Philippe Ariès, "Pourquoi écrit-on des mémoires?," in *Les Valeurs chez les mémorialistes français, du XVIIe siècle avant la Fronde*, (eds.) Noémi Hepp and Jacques Hennequin (Paris: 1979), 13–20; James Olney, *Memory and Narrative: The Weave of Life-Writing* (Chicago: 1998); Nicholas D. Paige, *Being Interior: Autobiography and the Contradictions of Modernity in Seventeenth-Century France* (Philadelphia: 2001).
23   Davis, *Fiction in the Archives*, 58. Davis speaks here of the way storytelling in petitions for pardon should be understood, but the phrase is equally illuminating with respect to memoir.
24   Kim Chernin, *In My Mother's House* (1983; repr. New York: 1994), viii.

this *extra* element hidden in the felicitous stereotypes [that]...makes the commonplace produce other effects."[25] Finally, a historical approach relates texts to their immediate social and political context, including the audience to which they were, or claimed to be, addressed. No matter how much is individual in the narration and how therapeutic the writing may have been for the self, the text is never entirely self-contained; it can be enriched by placing text and life, as it can be accessed through extra-textual sources, in one another's light.

To date, few Huguenot memoirs have been read in these ways. The texts have generally been neglected except by a few scholars who focus on French Protestantism. They were excluded from the generally recognized canon of Old Regime memoirs, perhaps due to the obscurity of their authors, by comparison with the well-known statesmen whose memoirs appear in such canonical collections at those compiled by Petitot and Monmerqué or Michaud and Poujoulat.[26] Likely as well, they were ignored because their content disputed the *gloire* of the king who betrayed them; "they contested the image of France those collections were designed to promote." Present and future study of these memoirs is, then, an act of recuperation: "While Huguenot memoirs may not be central to the grand tapestry of the history of France, they do provide insight into another symbolic world, that is simultaneously part of the 'grand siècle,' and yet apart from it."[27]

Three of the longest and richest Huguenot memoirs—those by Isaac Dumont de Bostaquet,[28] Jacques Fontaine[29] and Jean Migault[30]—have received most of the attention from scholars to date. The remaining dozens of shorter texts, once studied, will round out the picture of Huguenot memoirs that can presently be seen only in outline. In the meantime, these three works illustrate the multiple approaches that have been applied to them and provide preliminary answers to the two principal questions posed above: What in the experience of persecution, emigration and exile turned French Protestant

---

25 Michel de Certeau, *The Practice of Everyday Life*, trans. Steven Rendall (Berkeley: 1984), 89.
26 Alexandre Petitot and L.J.N. Monmerqué (eds.), *Collection des mémoires relatifs à l'histoire de France* (130 vols. Paris: 1819–1829); J.F. Michaud and Jean Joseph François Poujoulat (eds.), *Nouvelle collection des mémoires pour servir à l'histoire de France, depuis le XIIIe siècle jusqu'à la fin du XVIIIe* (32 vols. Lyon: 1836–54).
27 Ruth Whelan, "From the Other Side of Silence," 141.
28 *Mémoires d'Isaac Dumont de Bostaquet sur les temps qui ont précédé et suivi la révocation de l'Edit de Nantes*, (ed.) Michel Richard (Paris: 1968).
29 *Mémoire d'une famille huguenote victime de la révocation de l'édit de Nantes*, (ed.) Bernard Cottret (Montpellier: 1992).
30 *Journal de Jean Migault ou malheurs d'une famille protestante du Poitou victime de la révocation de l'édit de Nantes (1682–1689)*, (ed.) Yves Krumenacker (Paris: 1995).

writers toward writing personal histories? And how did the forms in which they wrote their memoirs make them congruent with Protestant doctrine despite Calvin's own theological disapproval of personal histories?

3   Isaac Dumont de Bostaquet

The well-known autobiographical memoir of Isaac Dumont de Bostaquet (1632–1709) was written in eight segments over the course of six years, beginning after his escape to Holland in 1687 and ending in 1693 when he settled definitively in Ireland. His several hundred pages of reminiscence on his lost life in France and commentary on his years of service (1688–1692) in England and Ireland with the troops of William III have been recognized as an exceptionally valuable source on military history. As "the only substantial eyewitness account of an officer in one of the three Huguenot regiments which played a significant role in William III's victory in Ireland,"[31] they were used selectively (omitting Dumont's negative portrayals of English behavior during the Irish campaigns) by Thomas Babington Macaulay for his *History of England from the Accession of James II*.[32]

Even the most straightforward reading of the memoir as "a largely factual account of Dumont's life"[33]—his idyllic days as a privileged nobleman in Normandy, the engaging adventure story of his multiple attempts at escape, his military service from Torbay to The Boyne—finds lying on its very surface the emotional experience of bereavement and the psychological need to make sense of the involuntary transformation of life that provoked Huguenot refugees to write memoirs. "He looked back with longing and nostalgia to his extended family, his estates in Normandy, and to the children left behind… [with] deep sadness and yearning for his lost and lovely life there." In numerous ways, what Dumont relates about his experience echoes what is known of

---

31   Unless otherwise indicated, the following discussion is drawn from Dianne W. Ressinger, "Good Faith: The Military and the Ministry in Exile, or the Memoirs of Isaac Dumont de Bostaquet and Jaques Fontaine," in *From Strangers to Citizens: The Integration of Immigrant Communities in Britain, Ireland and Colonial America, 1550–1750*, (eds.) Randolph Vigne and Charles Littleton (London: 2001), 457–58, 452. This article offers a useful synopsis of Dumont's biography, 451–62.

32   Thomas Babington Macaulay, *History of England from the Accession of James II* (London: 1849–61), Chapters 14–16.

33   Derek A. Watts, "Testimonies of Persecution: Four Huguenot Refugees and their Memoirs," in *Studies in Eighteenth-Century French Literature Presented to R. Niklaus*, (eds.) J.H. Fox, M.H. Waddicor and D.A. Watts (Exeter: 1975), 321.

other Huguenots' experiences from non-memoir sources: his indecision whether to stay and convert or flee, his fall into abjuring, his devastation at the prospect of having to leave. It echoes as well the "extraordinary faith in God's plan which he trusted in spite of the disruptions and discomforts of life in exile." God was a constant presence for Dumont, and his explanation for his dispossession rested upon his conception of Providence: "I regarded these repeated blows as the effect of God's anger toward me. I reflected on them as much as my human weakness was capable of, and throwing myself into the arms of His divine providence, I tried to endure all my unhappiness with constancy." His sense of loss and his trust in Providence converge at the end of the memoir in a prayer for the deliverance of his family still in France and for reunion with them.

Reading Dumont not only for the story he tells, however, but for how he tells his story—its narrative form, its overall shaping, its dialogic dynamic, the temporal closeness of his writing to events in the Refuge—yields deeper insights into the experience of exile that provoked Huguenots to begin recording their personal lives in memoirs.[34] Though chronology seems to order the account, a closer look at the pattern of waxing and waning emotional intensity in the narrative reveals a single turning-point from which subsequent episodes cascade into "a kaleidoscopic narrative reconstruction of lost identity and a narrative rehabilitation of a lost self." The moment of rupture that gives an arc to the account—the forced abjuration of his religion, which he experiences as loss of identity—is the crisis that impels Dumont to engage in writing. By writing, he not only expressed but performed his "quest for a moral order capable of providing the structures to enable him to understand his life and redeem it from incoherence." From this perspective, the large portion of the opening section that Dumont devoted to a seemingly mundane or even tiresome tracing of kinship and friendship networks back in Normandy betokens a trauma much more profound than nostalgia: his need to recover from loss of cultural and religious as well as political identity. Putting together his story was therapeutic: "narrating the self also constructed the self that was being narrated."[35] He needed to "save the self, and the cultural identity of that self, from oblivion."[36] He must re-establish coherence through recall before he could move on to recount his escape and his adventures in exile.

---

34 Unless indicated otherwise, the following discussion is drawn from Ruth Whelan, "Writing the Self: Huguenot Autobiography and the Process of Assimilation," in *From Strangers to Citizens*, (eds.) Vigne and Littleton, 465, 468–69, 471.

35 Whelan, "From the Other Side of Silence," 140.

36 Whelan, "Writing the Self," 466.

Similarly, the shaping of the memoir's emotional intensity to its apogee in abjuration lays bare the "moral and theological narrative frame" that pervades the text—and Dumont's sensibility—to an extent far beyond what is suggested by mere verbal exposition of overwhelmingly secular activities. To take one example of meaning deepened by attention to the memoir's use of allegory, Dumont summons up The Flood to convey the depths of horror with which French Protestants experienced the Revocation as "a cataclysmic event bringing a whole world to an end." Resonances from this single Biblical reference—sounding notes of sin, guilt, divine punishment and yet Providential care—spill through Dumont's pages, to turn them into much more than "a largely factual account of Dumont's life." They become a "spiritual autobiography with a Calvinist tone." Through introspective self-examination in writing, "Dumont re-establishes continuity with a more authentic self—the one preceding abjuration—and rehabilitates it." Reading in this way demonstrates that "memoirs are a site of rehabilitation and reconstruction of lost identity, brought about by storytelling."

If, then, literary analysis brings new meanings to the fore in Dumont's memoir, so too does social analysis that sets it in the context in which it was written.[37] The identity Dumont needed to reconstruct in the Refuge was not only psychological, familial, and religious but also military and professional. Indeed, it is probable that the first writing Dumont did after reaching the Refuge was a petition for employment to William of Orange—"illustrious protector of the refugees"—that he reworked into the section of his memoir that speaks of Holland. If so, then his case exemplifies one way in which practical needs particular to Huguenots in exile made storytellers of them.

Writing in April 1688, ten months after he received his first pension, Dumont recounted the difficulties he had faced as he sought a military commission. He had not had proofs of his identity and social status, nor certificates proving the duration and rank of his earlier military service. What he lacked in exile was not virtue, not religion, not memory, but documentation of social place. Bereft of written documentation, he turned to writing new versions of what he needed. To revive his persona in exile, he had to create new papers, to write his identity—that is, become a memorialist.

Dumont de Bostaquet's problem—establishing social identity—faced Huguenot refugees generally after their escape. How could they prove who they were to the persons they met in exile? How could they lay claim to what they deserved? The usual way of proving identity and privilege was through parchments and stamped papers held in private hands, usually by the head of

---

37   Elaboration of the following can be found in Lougee, "Paper Memories and Identity Papers."

the family, in "a coffer of notarized family contracts and deeds."³⁸ But it was precisely such material confirmations of identity that refugees had lost when they escaped or were expelled. For this reason, the writing of memoirs became a practical necessity; Huguenot memoirs, while dedicated to family and as such ostensibly private, were to be *used* and used *in public*, as substitute identification papers. In them, refugees had to set forth the details that made their identity credible and their claims persuasive. Or better, they had to perform their identity through their remembrance of persons, places, and experiences that readers could verify by their own memory. Memory performed by both writer and reader validated social identity and social place.

The transition from what Dumont wrote for the prince—"a memorandum... my petition"—to the text of the memoir as he inscribed it in his parchment "Registre" is detectable within the text of the memoir. He tells of showing a version of his petition to the commissioners in charge of the pensions he sought: "They found it both very respectful and well-crafted but a bit too extended, so they advised me to rewrite it if I wished the prince to read it; which I did, reducing my petition to just a few lines." It seems reasonable to think that his verbose version of his autobiographical self-justification became inscribed in the "Registre" as memoir. Indeed, it may be that petitioning for patronage was a key to all three times from which the memoir emerged—The Hague in 1688, Greenwich in 1689, Dublin in 1693—for these were three times when, as his text indicates, he was seeking patronage and pensions. The fact that he wrote no more after his final resettlement in Ireland, which secured his final pension for him, would seem to confirm that the writings he did for patronage purposes melded to become his memoir.

4 Jacques Fontaine

The story told by Jacques Fontaine (1658–1728) in the memoir he wrote in 1722, just a few months after the death of his wife, contains "the familiar ingredients of the Huguenot memoirs: a circumstantial account of the *dragonnades* and other forms of persecution that the Protestants suffered; and some lively narratives, which make good reading despite the limited literary skill, of arrest, imprisonment, escape and armed combat."³⁹ The storyline begins with his

---

38   Natalie Zemon Davis, "Ghosts, Kin, and Progeny: Some Features of Family Life in Early Modern France," *Daedalus* 106 (1977), 97.

39   A synopsis is offered in Watts, "Testimonies of Persecution," 323–25. The observations and quotations in this paragraph are taken from Ressinger, "Good Faith," 452, 455 and from Watts, "Testimonies of Persecution," 325–26, 330.

childhood in France—"more detailed and more absorbing than almost any to be found in French autobiographical writing before Rousseau"—and continues through his adult years in England and Ireland. His display of personality offers one of the most compelling portraits of the emotional and psychological impact of the deprivations inseparable from exile on a man whose resourcefulness and determination could be expected to meet better outcomes in other circumstances. Like Dumont de Bostaquet, he was a man "of outstanding mental stamina and resourcefulness, the salt of the Huguenot earth." But Fontaine's is an uncomfortable text, an end-of-life story markedly different in tone from Dumont's late-penned retrospective, dipped in "bitterness and frustration," vituperation and blame toward the corrupted churches and inhospitable communities that blocked his success. Irascible, volatile, "arrogant and uncompromising," Fontaine uses his text to distance himself from and display his contempt for both his host societies.

And yet, looking at how Fontaine's story is told uncovers, between and beneath the lines, not an antagonistic rejection of host society and home country but rather a remarkable blending, in the mind of the writer, of resources he imported from his childhood and those he found in the Refuge.[40] The shape of the story as a three-generation male epic and the centrality of compact to Fontaine's values reveal a psychological mutation in exile by which he substituted an innovative religious and familial lineage for the social lineage he had both rejected and been dispossessed of.

Fontaine sacralizes the family, setting the concept of binding promise at its religious and secular heart. The generations of fathers and sons evoke the heavenly father and son—"between fathers and the Father exists a dialectic of memory and piety." The paterfamilias functions as the pastor transmitting to his children "the gifts of God to his people," in particular to his family, which the ordeals of exile show to be "a family chosen by God." "Here we encounter this extraordinary case in which the family compensates for the shortfalls of society or of the Church. The Fontaine family becomes an elect people or Church in its turn." And the promise binds relationships on earth even as it binds earth to heaven. "In exile or more generally in times of trial, the people become conscious of the promise." The family compact resting upon lateral good faith—promises kept—which Fontaine imposes from above on his sons sits at the center of his memoir's meaning, for it fuses the patriarchy of the stem family traditional in Saintonge with the innovative contract theory then resonating in Locke's England: "two complementary principles: hierarchy and

---

40 The following is drawn from Bernard Cottret, "La Religion du père: Jacques Fontaine, mémorialiste protestant (1658–1728)," *Etudes théologiques et religieuses* 71 (1996), 511–22.

equality." "It is not individualism that triumphs with Jacques Fontaine, but the family. The 'children' and the 'fathers,' a religion centered on the household make it possible to overcome the institutional void of the Revocation."

If, then, Fontaine reconceptualized his family to fill a psychological void hollowed out by emigration, the outsized emphasis in his text on writing, on the memoir itself as an instrument of the family's salvation points more precisely to a way in which exile provoked not merely new ways of thinking but new practices of inscribing.[41] Fontaine needed memoir because emigration had meant the loss of lineage, loss of the safety that only lineage can assure. He must recreate lineage through writing "with my own hand." He had already narrated the family story orally to the children (as he notes at the outset of his memoir), but a written version was required for the same reason that his family had recently "sworn, written and signed" a paper contract that he calls "this union": because oral communication, oral promises, even family sentiment or blood ties did not suffice in the diaspora as they had for earlier generations in France (though not for his own). Once geographical place did not provide family with a center, in diaspora only paper could offer the material grounding for family that face-to-face communications had previously provided. Fontaine was far from alone among emigrant memorialists in believing he had lost his safety during the persecutions because his family disintegrated and that the only safety in the Refuge would come from family solidarity "passed from father to son down to the end of the world." His memoir would, he hoped, create a renewed kinship solidarity "so it will not be suffered that any one of my children or grandchildren should ever be tempted to return into the Babylon from which [God] withdrew me," nor would suffer in the Refuge the intra-familial perfidy that he blames for forcing his emigration from France.

For this reason, the first third of Fontaine's book reconstitutes his genealogy, and the rest reads like an annotated inventory of his accumulated papers, culminating in page upon page of little other than details of the writing, signing by each child, and acting out of the family union. The memoir itself, then, was to serve, through writing, as the tangible and lasting bond of mutual obligation, a trans-generational binder:

> I hope by the grace of God that what is contained therein may be a commitment, both for you and for your posterity, to hold all of yourselves closely united in a true reciprocal love, each toward the others and all toward God. If the Lord, whose benediction I beg for my work, wishes it to produce this effect, I shall believe myself more than repaid for all my pains.

---

41   Elaboration of the following can be found in Lougee, "Emigration and Memory."

5 Jean Migault

Jean Migault (1645–1706), a schoolmaster from Poitou, began to write his story of persecution and escape while still in France and finished it just after arriving in the Refuge.[42] As soon as the first *dragonnade* displaced him from his home in 1681, he wrote the first section of what would become a "precious testimony on the persecutions endured by the Protestants of Poitou." Migault shows himself to be "a particularly engaging man," a gentle father and devoted husband. In contrast to Fontaine, whose bitterness never lacked for targets, Migault "possessed what today would be called an ecumenical spirit." His memoir is at once a catechism—"a text that reveals who God is"—and a "written memorial" to his wife, who died in childbirth just after the onset of persecution. The two genres converge whenever Migault speaks of her: extolling her virtues, exhorting the children to imitate them, and ascribing to her the love of God that the rest of the text will show to be his own. Optimism permeates his pages. For Migault, the sufferings he and the family endured were the good news of Providence's care for the faithful: God preserved them in safety, never abandoned them, and led them into peace in the Refuge.

It is the timing of Migault's turn to memoir that leads the reader beyond the surface story of plight and flight.[43] That he recorded his experiences so close to the events and that he did so before he could be influenced by the process of consensus-building in the Refuge make the text uniquely useful to historians as a source on the persecutions. Once thousands of refugees began pouring out of France after the Revocation, Huguenot leaders like Jurieu and Benoist saw the need to persuade public opinion in the principal host countries—Holland, Prussia, England—that the refugees merited welcome: that they were oppressed innocents whose disobedience was justified, not rebels, as Louis XIV and his officials claimed. Because tales of the *dragonnades* were effective in raising indignation, they came to occupy a central place in the apologiae; *dragonnades* were said to have been ubiquitous and uniformly cruel, and it was their violence that produced the abjurations of would-be-faithful Huguenots in the thousands. Once formulated in the Refuge, this "myth of a martyred people, of the faithful ready to live their faith far from home and of brothers who gave in only under violence" would become a staple of refugee memoirs and continue to color Huguenot history down to the present.

---

42 The following is drawn from Yves Krumenacker's introduction and epilogue to his 1995 reprint of Migault's *Journal*, 7–11, 145–71.

43 The following is drawn from Yves Krumenacker, "Les Dragonnades du Poitou: leur écho dans les mémoires," *BSHPF* 131 (1985): 405–22.

But Migault's firsthand account of the *dragonnades* he experienced, when read closely, serves as a corrective to this "Manichaean schema...cosmic struggle of Good and Evil." Migault did not argue the point: he merely framed stories of what he saw, and in his careful telling, the *dragonnades*, while tragic for their direct victims, were neither widespread nor usually destructive. Their impact was more commonly financial loss than physical violence, and the abjurations, which vastly surpassed the *dragonnades* in the region, were attributable more to fear than to actual violence. Nor, in Migault's stories, was the conflict a contest between two communities, Catholic and Protestant. As he struggled to survive and depart, some Catholic neighbors, friends, and kin protected him; in the end he was able to escape only with the help of a trusted neighbor: "a papist but a good man."

Migault's memoir was, then, only partly a response to actual exile. Nonetheless, the use to which he put his text suggests yet another way in which the context of the Refuge generated needs that could be met by memoirs. Migault said in his text that he wrote for his children. Readers cognizant that he made no effort to publish his memoir have held that he wanted to "keep the contents of his narrative secret beyond the family circle."[44] "Jean Migault would have wanted no one other than his children to read this text."[45] But single texts can be moves in many games at once. Memoirs require what Roger Chartier has called "plural reading": awareness that within a given text, multiple purposes can layer upon one another so closely that each draws upon and redounds upon all.[46] Taking these memoirs as private family accounts, as written for "the darkness of intended privacy,"[47] obscures the way their use was shaped by the Refuge and overlooks the contribution they made (or, at least, were intended to make) to constructing the Huguenot diaspora.

What Migault wrote for "my dear children" was meant at the same time for a second audience, as becomes clear in the instructions for using the memoir with which he prefaced it when he sent it from Amsterdam to his son Gabriel in Celle (Germany) at New Year's 1691. "In a word, when you have read it all, my son, if you do not find it appropriate to share it with another, keep it for yourself." Migault's precise phrasing provides that if and only if the son did not want to show it to others, then he might keep it to himself. Indeed Migault *père*

---

44 Tricard, "Des secrets politiques," 142.
45 Yves Krumenacker, "Jean Migault, ou les dragonnades fondatrices," afterword to his 1995 reprint of Migault's *Journal*, 171.
46 Roger Chartier, "Texts, Printing, Readings," in *The New Cultural History*, (ed.) Lynn Hunt (Berkeley: 1989), 155.
47 Amelang, "Room of One's Own," 181.

suggested that son Gabriel show it to some of the people where he was, specifically naming Louis de la Forest, who had been their pastor in Poitou and had found refuge in Celle, even suggesting the son read it aloud to him "to divert him with it of an evening." And the father says he himself would have read it aloud to Anne de Chauffepié, another Poitevin refugee, if they had ended up traveling together to Celle, as they once had planned.

And why read it aloud? Why was the memoir not to be wholly private? Because, as Migault points out to his son, he has written in his memoir of obligations he had to "many persons who are at your court." He would like it shown to others, such as his former patrons in Poitou madame d'Olbreuse and madame de La Bessière, both now in Celle, whom he has named lavishly in his story. On the surface, Migault, by making into major actors in his story the patrons to whom he had been attached in Poitou, was avowing "the great obligations" he had to them and counseling his children to express gratitude to them through the words he had composed. But such namings ribboning through the memoir as a whole are also reminiscent not only of book dedications in which authors praise grandees who are their patrons (or who the author hopes will become their patrons) but reminiscent as well of the traditional practice of reading a work aloud before the prince, lord, or institution to which it was dedicated.[48] Migault's memoir, then, was intended as an homage from client to patron, as a means of reinforcing a traditional relationship that had been valuable to the Migault family in France and that Migault was concerned to transfer into the diaspora, in part by means of the memoir he wrote. The diaspora was a network of patronage relations in Migault's conception as it was in practice, and this written text intended for oral sharing was a vehicle for binding together Protestant notables residing beyond the borders of France.

6   A Great Store of Memoirs

Memoirs other than those by Dumont de Bostaquet, Fontaine, and Migault contribute importantly to the history of the Refuge. The escape account that Marie de la Rochefoucauld wrote in 1690 of her 1687 escape from Saintonge suggests the importance of refugee institutions and rites in making each

---

48 Wolfgang Leiner, *Der Widmungsbrief in der französischen Literatur (1580–1715)* (Heidelberg: 1965); Roger Chartier, "Princely Patronage and the Economy of Dedication," in his *Forms and Meanings: Texts, Performances, and Audiences from Codex to Computer* (Philadelphia: 1995), 25–42.

fugitive a storyteller, perhaps planting a taste for telling one's own story and hearing others': the *reconnaissance* that required arriving Protestants to narrate the circumstances of their life and faith "in the presence of the entire flock"; the stories those asking for charity wove to convince the *Bourse française* in Geneva or the Estates-General in The Hague of "their steadfastness in the Protestant Religion"; the confessions before consistories of strangers passing through.[49] The memoir by Marie de la Rochefoucauld's daughter, Susanne de Robillard de Champagné, bares intra-familial tensions among refugees and the burdens borne by young persons who lost their expected futures at emigration.[50] Three Huguenot galley slaves—Jean Marteilhe,[51] Elie Neau,[52] and Louis de Marolles[53]—used their pens to denounce as an abuse of power the "baroque theatre" in which Louis XIV confined them for the purpose of magnifying his own glory.[54] Madame Du Noyer's deft sociologist's eye illuminates the customs and everyday practices not only of her fellow refugees but of the hosts in each Refuge country she experiences. She weaves her autobiographical account of her personal struggles into philosophical demands of "indisputable originality": for freedom of conscience grounded on concepts of natural law and for "the sanctity of maternal authority" that allows mothers to raise their own children in families based upon contract between free and autonomous individuals.[55] Jean Cavalier's memoir, like those of Dumont de Bostaquet and Fontaine, displays the anti-papist attitudes carried by Huguenots into the Refuge that underlay, in places like the Ireland in which they settled, "the ease with which they shifted from persecuted victim to colonizer."[56]

---

49   Elaboration of this point can be found in Lougee, "Writing the Diaspora."
50   See Lougee, "Pains I Took."
51   Jean Marteilhe, *Mémoires d'un galérien du Roi Soleil*, (ed.) André Zysberg (Paris: 1982).
52   Elie Neau, *Des Galères de Louis XIV à New York*, (eds.) Didier Poton and Bertrand Van Ruymbeke (Paris: 2014).
53   Louis de Marolles, *Histoire des souffrances du bienheureux martyr Louis de Marolles* (The Hague: 1699).
54   Ruth Whelan, "Turning to Gold: The Role of the Witness in French Protestant Galley Slave Narratives," *Seventeenth-Century French Studies* 32 (2010), 3–18; Ruth Whelan, "From the Other Side of Silence"; Watts, "Testimonies of Persecution."
55   Henriette Goldwyn, "Mme du Noyer: Dissident Memorialist of the Huguenot Diaspora," in *Women Writers in Pre-Revolutionary France: Strategies of Emancipation*, (eds.) Colette H. Winn and Donna Kuizenga (New York: 1997), 117–26. See also Régine Reynolds-Cornell, *Fiction and Reality in the Mémoires of the Notorious Anne-Marguerite Petit Du Noyer* (Tübingen: 1999).
56   Ruth Whelan, "Persecution and Toleration: the Changing Identities of Ireland's Huguenot Refugees," *PHSL* 27 (1998): 20–35.

7 Concluding Remarks

Reasons specific to the post-Revocation emigration, then, encouraged or required refugees to tell their individual personal histories and in some cases write them down in the form of memoirs. Those who wrote of their escape and resettlement invented the genre of refugee memoir out of their experience of exile and their understanding of their own unprecedented needs. No single pattern characterized their writings, but certain features are common to many of the autobiographical accounts Huguenots began to write at the end of the 17th century, and those common features—expression of distinctively Huguenot religiosity, focus on everyday life, and celebration of family—bring into play alternative Calvinist values that implicitly neutralized and superseded Calvin's own theological disapproval of personal histories.

The form of Huguenot religiosity present in nearly all of the memoirs brought personal history inside the umbrella of Calvinist orthodoxy, even as the texts themselves recounted events and actions that were overwhelmingly secular and this-worldly. Readers familiar with contemporaneous English Puritan spiritual memoirs will be surprised by the way quotidian life events, rather than religious meta-narrative, structure Huguenot memoirs. The details of genealogy, friendships, escape, and renewal of social bonds are rarely subsumed to a cosmic pilgrimage and spiritual renewal in conversion as in John Bunyan's *Pilgrim's Progress* or Mary Rowlandson's captivity narrative.[57] Not that the memoirs of those who left France for their religion—as Marie de la Rochefoucauld said, for "liberty to worship God"—omitted religion from their personal histories. Fontaine came the closest of any escape memorialist to writing in an English meta-narrative style: "the message of the work is spiritual…the slow unveiling of Providence's design for the elect."[58] Jean Migault wrote to help his children understand that the persecution of the Elect (i.e. their fellow exiles) and their apostasy under pressure were not a sign of God's abandonment, but rather "chastisements and afflictions that he gave us to remind you that the disregarding of his holy Word was the principal object of his wrath and the just subject of our dispersion." Dumont bemoaned his shameful abjuration back in Normandy, "this criminal signature" and considered writing his memoir as, in part, a means to "making public redress for my

---

57   John Bunyan, *The Pilgrim's Progress from This World to That Which is to Come: Delivered under the Similitude of a Dream* (London: 1678); Mary Rowlandson, *The Sovereignty and Goodness of God* (Cambridge, MA: 1682).

58   Bernard Cottret, "Postface: Jacques Fontaine, ou la providence dans le texte," in Fontaine, *Mémoires*, 233.

crime of having signed the renunciation of my religion." Many Huguenot memorialists attached their personal experiences to Old Testament stories of exodus and deliverance that they heard told and retold in Sunday sermons.

It was precisely the quotidian content of the Huguenot memoirs that served to cloak personal history in the distinctive cast of French Calvinist religiosity: "The central drama of a Huguenot's life was not the progress from conviction of sin through conversion to the gradual movement toward full assurance. It was the demonstration of genuine conviction by remaining firm to the true faith in the face of pressure to abjure."[59] The mundane details of the escape and the challenges of resettlement for refugees could be considered precisely religious material because they demonstrated fidelity to the faith. "The repression that fell upon the French Protestants, the exile it engendered, could serve as signs of belonging to the true flock."[60] Profane narration could tell a religious story congenial to the Calvinist message in its French form. The genre of Huguenot memoir wrapped expressions of the writer's fidelity to Protestant religion around the written personal histories that served their practical needs as refugees.

Celebration of family, too, pervaded and structured the stories told by Dumont de Bostaquet, Fontaine, and Migault. Dumont pulled together his genealogy at great length, in part to clarify for his children their origins in France that had been charted in documentation left back home and now inaccessible to them. Fontaine compiled a permanent record of stories previously told to his children in order to create family identity that would bond his kin across the diaspora and keep them out of France. Migault hand-wrote at least three copies of his memoir as gifts to two sons and a daughter, and these became family treasures; they only survive because they were preserved by his descendants—as was the case generally for known Huguenot memoirs.

This focus on family, anchored by the stated dedication to "my dear children," whether or not the children were the sole, or even the primary, audience, seems to have served a multiplicity of purposes. For one, the dedication to children set the genre of the Huguenot memoir apart from the openly circulated *mémoire-histoire* with its self-justificatory authorial stance and associated it with the wholly accepted and conventional *livre de raison*, which was discreetly "reserved for family use, not for the outside world."[61] But more importantly, the dedication to the writer's children and the structuring by family story wrapped the memoir in the cloak of family that stood at the heart of Calvinism, burnishing

---

59   Benedict, "Two Calvinisms," 228.
60   Hubert Bost, *Ces Messieurs de la R.P.R.: histoires et écritures de huguenots, XVIIe–XVIIIe siècles* (Paris: 2001), 110.
61   Tricard, "Des secrets politiques," 136.

personal history with a central Calvinist value that could implicitly justify the cultivation of human memory that Calvin himself had disapproved. Passing along to a new generation the wisdom gained from experience could be construed as a parent's duty, even as a pastoral function, for Protestants, who regarded the family itself as a religious space. This unstated purpose may be one reason why the dedication to "my dear children" was among the few nearly universal features of the many-layered memoirs in this corpus.

As this celebration of family demonstrates, memoirs in the era of the Revocation served to recuperate not only identity but community. Though their words reveal something of their authors' personalities and characters, these Huguenot self-narratives bespeak their authors' longing for social embeddedness and their drive to reconstruct and strengthen social relationships, including but not limited to family ties. A century later, autobiography would change and so would representations of Huguenots. Autobiography would become an "egodocument" celebrating its protagonist as a unique individual at odds with the social, the distinctive genre of modernity. Huguenot apologetics modernized, too, developing a picture of the refugees as harbingers of modernity, including individualism. A reading of even a fraction of the corpus of Revocation-era memoirs, whose stories so strongly center on the importance of social bonds, corrects this anachronistic picture of Huguenot values and Huguenot experience in the period of their most dire need. These writers did not celebrate their own individual heroism but the heroism of their religion, their religious group, and their families. In so doing, Huguenot memorialists succeeded in transforming personal history into a central and valued part of their Calvinist religion.

Appendix: Additional Memoirs

These firsthand accounts of persecution, escape and resettlement offer an as-yet-unexplored window on the experiences of Huguenots in France and in the Refuge during the era of the Revocation.

Bibliography

Aigaliers, Jacques Jacob Roussel, baron d.' *Mémoires d'un gentilhomme huguenot au temps des Camisards*, (ed.) baronne de Charnisay (Mialet: 1935). Original in Papiers Court no. 30, Bibliothèque de Genève.

Allix, Pierre. *Escape from France in 1685*. Excerpts reprinted in *PHSL* 13 (1928–29), 625–27. Original in the hands of descendants.

Anonymous. *Récit des souffrances d'un protestant dieppois de 16 ans, persécuté en 1685–1686*. Reprinted in *BCEW* 4 (1890), 73–80.

Arbaud, Baronne d'. *Mémoire à messieurs de Berne sur sa fuite miraculeuse de France*. Excerpts reprinted in Eugène Arnaud (ed.), *Histoire des protestants de Provence*, vol. 1 (Paris: 1884), 483–87.

Astier, Alexandre. *Extrait naïf et fidèle des souffrances arrivées à Alexandre Astier, natif d'un village nommeé le Vigna en Vivarez*. Reprinted in *BSHPF* 29 (1880), 460–71, 500–11. Original in Papiers Court no. 13/vol.2, Bibliothèque de Genève.

Aulnis, Pierre d'. *Journal [du] sorti du royaume de France par voie de mer, le 14 novembre 1685*. Reprinted in *BCEW* 4 (1890), 81–86 and in *BSHPF* 31 (1882), 62–66. Original in the Bibliothèque wallonne (Leiden).

Babault, Jacob. *Journal d'un réfugié, 1686–1726*, (ed.) Louis Dufour (Geneva: 1880).

Baudouin de la Bruchardière, Frédéric. *Relation de la fuite de Baudouin de la Bruchardière et de sa famille, 6 décembre 1686*, in *BSHPF* 18 (1869), 424–28.

Boisrond, René de Saint-Légier de. *Mémoires*. Reprinted in *Recueil de la Commission des arts et monuments historiques de la Charente-Inférieure* 9 (1890): 304–24, 338–55, 396–426; 10 (1891): 176–91, 237–43, 280–88, 344–51, 410–38.

Bonbonnoux, Jacques. *Mémoires*. Reprinted as *Mémoires de Jacques Bonhonnoux, Chef Camisard et Pasteur du Désert*, (ed.) J. Vielles (Anduze: 1883).

Bouhéreau, Elie. *Diary, 1689–1719*. Excerpts reprinted in *PHSL* 15 (1933–34): 46–68. Original in Marsh's Library, Dublin.

Brousson, Claude. *Relation de la sortie de France du sieur Daniel Brousson et de sa famille pour cause de Religion, ecritte par Claude Brousson, son Fils*, (ed.) N. Weiss (Paris: 1885).

Cabrit, Jacques. *Histoire de la vie de J. Cabrit ecrite par lui-même*, in *BSHPF* 39 (1890), 530–45, 587–98, 635–45; 40 (1891), 89–96, 213–17, 360–65, 481–87, 584–90, 641–51.

Cabrol, Jean. *Mémoire de l'origine du sr Jean Cabrol, natif de Nismes, en Languedoc, et de ce qui lui est arrivé de plus remarquable dans sa famille*. Reprinted in *BSHPF* 44 (1895), 530–36.

Cambolive, Estienne. *Histoire de divers évènemens contenans en abrégé les persécutions exercées en France* (Amsterdam: 1698).

Catel, Jean. *Relation fidèle des procédés de l'Inquisition à Grenade*. Reprinted in *Revue d'histoire et de philosophie religieuses* 67 (1987), 1–17.

Chaillaud, Taré. *Journal*. Excerpts reprinted in *BSHPF* 15 (1866), 317–24.

Chalmot, Jacques de, *Journal*. Original at the University of Groningen Library; Ms. 193$^{1-2}$ at the BPF is a copy from this original.

Changuion, Pierre. *Biographie (1685–1690)*. Reprinted in *BSHPF* 14 (1865), 139–58.

Chauffepié, Anne de. *Journal*. Reprinted in *BSHPF* 6 (1857–58), 57–68, 257–68. Manuscript is Ms. 468$^{1-2}$ at the BPF.

Chauffepié, Samuel de. *Abrégé des principaux événemens de ma vie*. Reprinted in *BSHPF* 52 (1903), 240–54. Manuscript versions are B36 and F19 in the Bibliothèque wallonne (Leiden).

Chenu de Chalezac, Guillaume. *Narrative of His Experiences as a Huguenot Refugee, 1686–89*, (ed.) Randolph Vigne (Cape Town: 1993).

Collot d'Escury, Daniel and Henri. *Livre de ma genealogie*. Extracts reprinted in *BSHPF* 10 (1861), 306–18. Original is Familiearchief Collot d'Escury 390, Nationaal Archief, The Hague.

Cosne, Pierre de. *Memoirs*. Extracts reprinted in *PHSL* 9 (1910), 530–44. Original was owned in 1910 by E.B. Vignoles.

Coulan, Antoine. *Journal*. Excerpted in Papiers Court no. 17/D, Bibliothèque de Genève.

Du Bois, Marie. *Relation, 28. Novembre, 1687*. Printed in Pierre Jurieu, *Lettres pastorales*, 15 January 1688. Reprinted in Maurice Thirion, *Etude sur l'histoire du protestantisme à Metz et dans le pays Messin* (Nancy: 1884), 357–61.

Du Hamel, Josias. *Mésmoire de Josias Duhamel, marchandt a Amsterdam a ses Enfans*. Reprinted as *Mémoires de Josias Duhamel*, (ed.) L.P. Reyss. Original is B18 in the Bibliothèque wallonne (Leiden), and a handwritten copy is in the Winterthur Library (Delaware).

Dumont de Bostaquet, Isaac. *Récit fidelle de ce qui s'est passé dans ma vie de plus essentiel*. Reprinted in French as *Mémoires d'Isaac Dumont de Bostaquet sur les temps qui ont précédé et suivi la Revocation de l'Edit de Nantes*, (ed.) Michel Richard (Paris: 1968) and in English as *Memoirs of Isaac Dumont de Bostaquet: A Gentleman of Normandy*, (ed.) Dianne W. Ressinger (London: 2005). Original in The Royal Irish Academy (Dublin).

Du Noyer, Anne Marguerite Petit, madame. *Mémoires*, vol. 6 of *Lettres historiques et galantes de madame Du Noyer* (London: 1739). Reprinted as Madame du Noyer, *Mémoires*, (ed.) Henriette Goldwyn (Paris: 2005).

Durand de Dauphiné. *Voyages d'un françois exilé pour la religion, avec une description de la Virgine et Marilan dans l'Amérique*, (ed.) Gilbert Chinard (Paris: 1932).

Ebruy, Jean-Paul. *Mémoire sur les affaires de la religion en Vivarais*. Reprinted as *Mémoire de Jean-Paul Ebruy* (Privas: 2000). Original in Papiers Court no. 17/B, Bibliothèque de Genève.

Etienne, Jakob. *Die Memoiren des Buchhändlers Jakob Etienne*. Reprinted in Jochen Desel and Walter Mogk (eds.), *Wege in eine neue Heimat: Fluchtberichte von Hugenotten aus Metz* (Lahr-Dinglingen: 1987).

Faisses, Jeanne. *La Fin heureuse de Jeanne Faisses, détenue pour la religion et ensuite délivrée, réfugiée et morte en Suisse*. Reprinted in *BSHPF* 26 (1877), 461–72; 27 (1878), 155–70. Original in Papiers Court no. 43, Bibliothèque de Genève.

Faisses, Pierre. *Livre de mémoire pour l'usage de ma famille*. Reprinted in *BSHPF* 27 (1878), 451–59. Original in Papiers Court no. 43, Bibliothèque de Genève.

Fauché, *Mémoires*. Extracts reprinted in *BSHPF* 30 (1881), 551–59.

Fontaine, Jacques. *Mémoires*. A fragment of a 1722 manuscript in Fontaine's hand and an 1825 transcription taken from the 1722 manuscript before its partial destruction are in the Special Collections Department, Alderman Library, University of Virginia. Reprinted in French as *Mémoires d'une famille huguenote victime de la révocation de l'édit de Nantes*, (ed.) Bernard Cottret (Montpellier: 1992) and in English as *Memoirs of the Reverend Jaques Fontaine, 1658–1728*, (ed.) and trans. Dianne W. Ressinger (London: 1992).

Gamond, Blanche. *Récit des persécutions que Blanche Gamond, de Saint-Paul-Trois-Châteaux, en Dauphiné, âgée d'environ vingt et un ans, a endurées pour la cause de l'Evangile.* Reprinted in *Deux héoïnes pour la foi: Blanche Gamond et Jeanne Terrasson*, (eds.) Th. Claparède and Ed. Goty (Paris: 1880). Original in Papiers Court no. 17/D, Bibliothèque de Genève.

Gayet, Paul. *Journal inédit d'un fidèle de l'ancienne église réformée de Metz.* Reprinted in *BSHPF* 11 (1862), 163–79, 281–99.

Giraud, Jean. *Recueil des percecussions quy nous sont arivées a la communauté de La Grave.* Excerpted in *BSHPF* 14 (1865), 251–58. A copy in the Archives départementales de l'Isère.

Giton, Judith. *Relasions de notre sortyee de france.* Reprinted in *Transactions of the Huguenot Society of South Carolina* 59 (1954), 24–27.

Guyon. *Relation de ma sortie de France.* Original in private hands.

Lacoste, Benjamin. *Genealogie de moy Benjamin Lacoste et de Louise Duluc, ma femme*, with his son's *Detail de mes etudes, voyages, campagnes et avanteures.* Original in the Bodleian Library (Oxford).

Lambert de Beauregard, Pierre. *Relation de ce qui a été fait soufrir a moy pour la religion en le 69ᵉ année de mon âge.* Reprinted in *BSHPF* 22 (1873), 433–71. Original is Ms. 459 at the BPF.

La Motte Fouqué, Charles de. *Autre Relation de la sortie de France de Messire Charles de La Motte Fouqué, écrite de sa propre main et trouvée dans ses papiers après son décès.* Reprinted in *Preussische Jahrbücher* 59 (1887), 25–26.

Lamp, Henry. *Autobiography: Written by Himself For the Information of His Own Children.* Reprinted as *Curriculum Vitae, or the Birth, Education, Travels, and Life of Henry Lamp, M.D.*, (ed.) Joseph J. Green (London: 1895). Handwritten copy is XH7 LAM at the Huguenot Library (London).

Lamy, Jacob. *Journal.* Reprinted in *BCEW* 4 (1890), 337–58.

La Rochefoucauld, Marie de. *Ce 10 Ienvier 1690 nostre sortie de france.* Reprinted in *French Historical Studies* 22 (1999), 39–46. Original manuscript is Champagné Papers A49, Special Collections, Stanford University Library.

Lautère, Raoul François de [Franz Lotter]. *Etlich merveilleuse Nachrichten übber mein Leben.* Reprinted in *Deutsche Hugenott* 4 (1955), 115–19.

Lislemarais. *Relation de la Sortie de m. de Lisle Marais de Montacier du royaume de France, pour la persécution de la religion.* Reprinted in *BSHPF* 31 (1882), 261–72, 310–25. Original is A3 in the Bibliothèque wallonne (Leiden).

Marion, Elie. *Mémoires*. Reprinted in *Mémoires inédits d'Abraham Mazel et d'Elie Marion sur la guerre des Cévennes, 1701–1708*, (ed.) Charles Bost (Paris: 1931).

Marolles, Louis de. *Histoire des souffrances du bienheureux martyr Louis de Marolles* (The Hague: 1699).

Marteilhe, Jean. *Mémoires d'un Protestant condamné aux galères de France* (1757). Reprinted as *Mémoires d'un galérien du Roi Soleil*, (ed.) André Zysberg (Paris: 1982).

Massanes, Antoine de. *Relation de ce qui m'est arrivé et à ma famille depuis la Révocation de l'Edit de Nantes en octobre 1685*. Reprinted in *BSHPF* 88 (1939), 394–417; 89 (1940), 40–72.

Migault, Jean. *Journal*. Reprinted as *Journal de Jean Migault ou malheurs d'une famille protestante du Poitou victime de la révocation de l'édit de Nantes (1682–1689)*, (ed.) Yves Krumenacker (Paris: 1995). The originals that Migault sent to his children are at the BPF (Ms. 227), at the Huguenot Library (London), and in the hands of descendants in Germany.

Minet, Isaac. *Narrative of Isaac Minet's Escape from France*. Reprinted in *PHSL* 2 (1887), 428–45. Original is Mss. 224 and 88 at The Huguenot Library (London).

Mirmand, Henri de. *Mémoires*. Reprinted in *Henri de Mirmand et les réfugiés de la révocation de l'Edit de Nantes, 1650–1721*, (ed.) Madame Alexandre de Chambrier (Neuchâtel: 1910), Appendix I, 1–32.

Molinier, Marie. *Mémoires pour mes enfants*. Reprinted in *PHSL* 10 (1912), 156–75 and in *BSHPF* 62 (1913), 435–56; 63 (1914), 277–79. Original is T 8/5/10 at the Huguenot Library (London).

Morin, Jean. *Histoire de mes prisons*. Reprinted as *Journal d'un pasteur wallon dans les prisons de Louis XIV (1685)*, (ed.) L.P. Reyss (Leiden: 1947).

Neau, Elie. *Histoire abbregée des souffrances du sieur Elie Neau, sur les galères et dans les cachots de Marseille* (1701). Reprinted as *Des Galères de Louis XIV à New York*, (eds.) Didier Poton and Bertrand Van Ruymbeke (Paris: 2014).

Nissolle, Jean. *Ce qui est arrivé au sieur Jean Nissolle, marchand de la ville de Ganges, en Languedoc*. Reprinted as *Jean Nissolle, Marchand, de Ganges en Languedoc, son évasion hors de France*, (ed.) Matthieu Lelievre (Paris: 1907).

Olry, Jean. *La Persécution de l'église de Metz*. Reprinted as *La Persécution de l'église de Metz décrite par le sieur Jean Olry*, (ed.) Othon Cuvier (Paris: 1859).

Pechels, Samuel de. *Mémoires*. Reprinted as *Mémoires de Samuel de Pechels, 1685–1692*, Robert Garrisson (Mialet: 1936).

Pelet, François de. *Mémoires*. Reprinted in *BSHPF* 29 (1880), 73–85, 120–30, 178–88.

Perigal, Jean. *Relation de ce qui est arrivé à Jean Perigal, jeune homme de la ville de Dieppe*. Reprinted in *La Seconde Partie de l'histoire de l'église réformée de Dieppe, 1660–1685*, (eds.) Guillaume Daval and R. Garreta. 2 vols. (Rouen: 1902–03), 2:1–117. Original is Add. Ms. 37214 in the British Library.

Pineton de Chambrun, Jacques. *Larmes*. Reprinted as *Les Larmes de Jacques Pineton de Chambrun*, (ed.) Ad. Schaeffer (Paris: 1854).

Rebotier, Elias. *Autobiography*. Reprinted in *Proceedings of the Somersetshire Archaeological and Natural History Society* 40 (1894), 91–112.

Rival, Pierre. *Apologie de Pierre Rival, ministre de la Chapelle françoise au Palais de St James* (London: 1716). Original in the Huguenot Library (London).

Robert, Mr. *Relation de ce qui s'est passe de remarquable dans les Vallees de Luserne en l'annee 1689 et 1690*. Original is B33 in the Bibliothèque wallonne (Leiden).

Robillard de Champagné, Susanne de. *Récit abrégé de ma sortie de France, pour venir dans les païs étrangers chercher la liberté de ma conscience et l'exercice de notre sainte religion*. Reprinted in *French Historical Studies* 22 (1999), 47–64. Manuscript copies are Ms. 3613 in the Hessische Landes- und Hochschulbibliothek (Darmstadt) as well as Ms. 55.682 and 55.683 at the Deutsches Literaturarchiv/Schiller-Nationalmuseum (Marbach am Neckar).

Rochegude de Barjac, Jacques de. *Réponse au Baron de****. Reprinted in *BSHPF* 38 (1889), 528–49.

Rou, Jean. *Mémoires*. Reprinted as *Mémoires inédits et opuscules*, (ed.) Francis Waddington. 2 vols. (Paris: 1857). Original in the Nationaal Archief, The Hague.

Savois, Alexandre. *Histoire abrégée de mon origine, de ma sortie de France, et de ma vie*. Reprinted in *BSHPF* 54 (1905), 38–83.

Serres, Etienne. *Quatre Relations véritables*. Reprinted in *Un Déporté pour la foi*, (ed.) Matthieu Lelièvre (Paris: 1881).

Terrasson, Jeanne. *Recueil des choses qui me sont arrivées en France, dans le temps des persécutions et des maux qu'on m'y a fait souffrir, à moi*. Reprinted in *Deux héoïnes pour la foi: Blanche Gamond et Jeanne Terrasson*, (eds.) Th. Claparède and Ed. Goty (Paris: 1880).

Valat, Jean. *Mémoire au sujet de la persécution que nous avons souffert en France et des circonstances de ma sortie dudit royaume*. Reprinted as *Mémoires d'un protestant du Vigan. Des dragonnades au Refuge (1683–1686)*, (ed.) Eckart Birnstiel and Véronique Chanson (Paris: 2011).

Vieusseux-Léger, Pierre. *Relation à ses enfants de son départ de S-Anthonin pour Genève en 1688*. Reprinted in *BSHPF* 25 (1876), 275–78.

CHAPTER 13

Histories of Martyrdom and Suffering in the Huguenot Diaspora

David van der Linden

1   **Introduction**

Stories of martyrdom and suffering have always been perceived as central to the Huguenot exile experience. Indeed, as soon as Huguenot refugees reached the countries of the Refuge they began writing down histories of the persecutions they had endured in France. Arguably, the most recurrent event in these stories was the *dragonnades*. Starting in Poitou in 1681, French authorities quartered dragoons on Huguenot families to force them to convert to Catholicism.[1] As the soldiers often used excessive violence and even torture to extract an abjuration, it is not surprising that this traumatic moment stood out in many refugee memoirs. The history of Jean Migault, a refugee schoolmaster from Poitou, is a case in point. After the Revocation, Migault had fled to Amsterdam, where he composed a memoir of the sufferings that had befallen his family, including the *dragonnades* that had taken place in his home town of Mougon in August 1681. Whereas most Huguenot families had quickly signed their abjuration, Migault and his wife Elisabeth had suffered the abuse of the soldiers because they refused to convert. The dragoons had kicked Elisabeth and threatened to push her into the fire if she did not abjure her faith. Although the Migault eventually managed to escape the soldiers with the help of their Catholic neighbors, Jean suffered many more ordeals before he went into exile. His beloved wife passed away in 1683 and he himself was ultimately forced to convert to Catholicism at the Revocation.[2]

The reason that Migault's trials and tribulations, along with many similar stories of plight, continue to be cited as prime examples of religious intolerance and Huguenot suffering has much to do with the memorialization practices of

---

1   Yves Krumenacker, *Les protestants du Poitou au XVIIIe siècle, 1681–1789* (Paris: 1998), 62–83; Roy L. McCullough, *Coercion, Conversion and Counterinsurgency in Louis XIV's France* (Leiden: 2007), 125–79.
2   Yves Krumenacker (ed.), *Journal de Jean Migault ou malheurs d'une famille protestante du Poitou victime de la révocation de l'Edit de Nantes, 1682–1689* (Paris: 1995). See also the essay by Carolyn Lougee in this volume.

the refugees and their descendants. Already in the first decades following the Revocation, refugee authors such as Pierre Jurieu and Elie Benoist included the most brutal examples of persecution in their printed histories, stressing the suffering of the Huguenots in order to denounce the discriminatory policies of the French state. Large-scale interest in the fate of the French Protestants reemerged in the 19th century when Huguenot descendants all over Europe created societies to extoll their past. The reaffirmation of a Huguenot identity was most visible in France, where in April 1852 a group of prominent Protestants founded the *Société de l'Histoire du Protestantisme Français*, together with their own library and a review, the *Bulletin*. The Society had a clear emancipatory mission: Protestants were to reclaim their rightful place in French history, which, the founding fathers argued, had always stigmatized them as rebels and heretics.[3]

As part of this campaign Protestant authors soon turned their attention to the years surrounding the Revocation, publishing histories that glorified the refugees and their suffering. During the first general assembly of the *Société* in 1853, for instance, vice-president Charles Weiss gave a lecture in which he praised the heroic decision of the Huguenots to flee religious oppression in France. His two-volume *Histoire des réfugiés protestants de France*, which appeared later that year, even referred to the refugees as "martyrs of their faith."[4] Likewise, many of the articles published in the *Bulletin* during the first decades of its existence focused disproportionally on Huguenot suffering and martyrdom. The persecution of the Huguenots during the French Wars of Religion and under the rule of Louis XIV took center stage, with particular attention being paid to the St. Bartholomew's Day massacre of 1572 and the *dragonnades* associated with the Revocation.[5]

Since the 1980s, however, historians have begun to research the Refuge with a more critical attitude. As a result, stories of heroic suffering are no longer

---

3 Patrick Harismendy, "'Post tenebras lux,' ou cent ans de la Société de l'Histoire du Protestantisme Français," *Revue d'Histoire de l'Eglise de France* 86 (2000), 717–33; Roger-Armand Weigert, "Cent ans d'érudition nationale: La Société de l'Histoire du Protestantisme Français, 1852–1952," *BSHPF* 98 (1952), 219–50. See also the chapter by Bertrand Van Ruymbeke in the present volume.

4 Weigert, "Cent ans d'érudition nationale," 240; Charles Weiss, *Histoire des réfugiés protestants de France depuis la révocation de l'Edit de Nantes jusqu'à nos jours* (2 vols. 1853, repr. Paris: 2007).

5 André Encrevé, "Les premières années du Bulletin de la Société de l'Histoire du Protestantisme Français," *BSHPF* 148 (2002), 709–33; Anne Reichert, "La Société de l'Histoire du Protestantisme Français et son Bulletin: Un regard protestant sur l'histoire du protestantisme français," *BSHPF* 143 (1997), 63–97.

taken at face value. Rather than reading them as clear-cut news reports that allow us to get at the heart of the Huguenot exile experience—as was often argued in the 19th century—scholars are currently analyzing memoirs and histories as constructed narratives, which tell us something about the way refugees perceived their own past and created a new identity in exile. Without dismissing the centrality of suffering and martyrdom in the Huguenot diaspora, historians are more interested in the formulation and uses of this widespread vocabulary of victimhood. This shift in focus can be attributed, first of all, to postmodern theories of self-fashioning, which were developed in the field of literary studies to underscore the notion that texts do not necessarily communicate a true version of the past, but are purposefully constructed narratives, shaped by literary genres and the objectives of their authors. In this sense, Huguenot autobiographies reveal more about the narrative strategies of their authors than about the lived experience of exile.[6] The recent boom in memory studies also accounts for a reappraisal of Huguenot suffering. As memory scholars have argued, examining the ways in which early modern communities such as Huguenots remembered their past helps us understand how group identities were formed in this period.[7] Instead of reading Huguenot histories for their factual information, we should analyze how their authors presented a particular version of the past to define the refugees as a suffering yet strong-minded community.

Because it falls outside the scope of a single chapter to offer a comprehensive overview of victimhood narratives in the Huguenot diaspora, attention will focus on the many published histories that were produced in exile,[8] analyzing how their authors crafted a Huguenot past permeated by martyrdom. The focus

---

6   Carolyn Chappell Lougee, "The Pains I Took to Save My/His Family: Escape Accounts by a Huguenot Mother and Daughter after the Revocation of the Edict of Nantes," *French Historical Studies* 22 (1999), 1–64. Ruth Whelan, "Writing the Self: Huguenot Autobiography and the Process of Assimilation," in *From Strangers to Citizens: The Integration of Immigrant Communities in Britain, Ireland and Colonial America, 1550–1750*, (eds.) Randolph Vigne and Charles Littleton (Brighton: 2001), 463–77.

7   Recent examples include Philip Benedict, "Divided Memories? Historical Calendars, Commemorative Processions and the Recollection of the Wars of Religion During the Ancien Regime," *French History* 22 (2008), 381–405; idem, "Shaping the memory of the French Wars of Religion: The first centuries," in *Memory before Modernity: Practices of Memory in Early Modern Europe*, (eds.) Erika Kuijpers et al. (Leiden: 2013), 111–26; David van der Linden, *Experiencing Exile: Huguenot Refugees in the Dutch Republic, 1680–1700* (Aldershot: 2015), Chapter 7.

8   For an analysis of private memoirs, see the chapter by Carolyn Chappell Lougee in this volume.

will be on the Dutch Republic, which not only was the principal destination for Huguenot refugees, but also witnessed the largest production of histories and martyrologies in the decades following the Revocation. At the same time, it is clear that more research needs to be done on comparable histories from other refugee destinations before we can assess the true importance of the Dutch Republic, both in sense of output and content. For purposes of clarity and analysis this chapter has been divided into four parts, each of which discusses a different aspect of these printed histories: the tradition of martyrdom, which provided the framework for narratives of suffering; the *Lettres pastorales* by the refugee minister Pierre Jurieu, who acknowledged suffering Huguenots as martyrs and reproduced the most brutal stories to exhort Protestants to persevere; the *Histoire de l'Edit de Nantes* by Elie Benoist, who offered a judicial perspective on Huguenot victimhood by tracing the dismantlement of Protestants communities over the course of the 17th century; and his re-appropriation of stories on suffering Protestants to dramatize Huguenot victimhood.

2   The Tradition of Martyrdom

Huguenots habitually perceived their own suffering and that of their ancestors in terms of martyrdom. This religious tradition stretched back to medieval times, when the Church of Rome celebrated as saints those men and women, who during the first centuries of Christianity, had been executed by the Roman authorities on charges of heresy. When the Reformation split Europe along confessional lines in the 16th century, Protestants and Catholics were quick to canonize the victims of religious persecution as martyrs for their own cause. Authors began compiling martyrologies that detailed the lives of those executed by their confessional opponents. Among the most famous of these early martyrologies were John Foxe's massive *Acts and Monuments* (1563), later known as the *Book of Martyrs*, which catalogued the fate of Protestant martyrs from the British Isles, and from a Catholic perspective the *Theatre of the Cruelties of the Heretics of Our Time* (1587) by the Antwerp publisher and author Richard Verstegan, who included Catholic martyrs from France, England and the Low Counties.[9]

---

[9] Brad Gregory, *Salvation at Stake: Christian Martyrdom in Early Modern Europe* (Cambridge, Mass.: 1999); John N. King, *Foxe's Book of Martyrs and Early Modern Print Culture* (Cambridge: 2006); Romana Zacchi, "Words and Images: Verstegan's 'Theatre of Cruelties,'" in *Richard Rowlands Verstegan: A Versatile Man in an Age of Turmoil*, (eds.) Massimiliano Morini and Romana Zacchi (Turnhout: 2012), 53–75.

The first and most influential Huguenot martyrology was produced by the Genevan-based publisher Jean Crespin, who collected stories of Huguenot martyrs for his *Livre des Martyrs* (1554). Although the book included martyrs' stories from across Europe, even those of Hussites, Waldensians and Lutherans, Crespin devoted ample space to the sufferings of French Protestants. The book was clearly aimed at a Huguenot audience, as Crespin wrote in the French vernacular and printed the first edition in a portable octavo format, which facilitated its clandestine circulation in France. The martyrology was expanded with each successive edition, and from 1564 onwards the book appeared in huge folio volumes. After Crespin's death in 1572, the Genevan minister Simon Goulart continued to add material, so that when the final edition of the *Livre des Martyrs* appeared in 1619 it stretched to almost 1,800 pages.[10]

Crespin's martyrology, read by French Protestants throughout the 17th century, was to have a lasting impact on Huguenot consciousness. In the city of Metz, for example, the *Livre des Martyrs* was the most widely owned book by Protestant households around 1650, after the Bible and the Huguenot Psalter.[11] On the eve of the Revocation its popularity had not diminished: Jean Migault noted in his journal that his wife Elisabeth was an avid reader of Crespin.[12] The book also circulated outside France. In 1684, Daniel Desmarets, a minister in the Walloon Church of The Hague, published an abridged version that included only the French martyrs, entitled *Histoire abregée des martirs francois du tems de la Reformation*. Reflecting on the recent persecutions in France, Desmarets argued that the Huguenots should follow in the footsteps of their ancestors and remain steadfast in their faith, even if this entailed their death.[13] By 1685, the tradition of martyrdom was thus deeply rooted in Huguenot mentality, offering the refugees a well-established framework to narrate stories of adversity and suffering.

Yet the notion of martyrdom also presented problems. In particular, martyrologists found it difficult to agree on who qualified as a martyr, and who did not. The most obvious definition—surely, all those who had suffered at the

---

10   Jean-François Gilmont, *Jean Crespin: Un éditeur réformé du XVIe siècle* (Geneva: 1981), 165–90; Arthur Piaget and Gabrielle Berthoud, *Notes sur le livre des martyrs de Jean Crespin* (Neuchâtel: 1930); David El Kenz, *Les bûchers du roi: La culture protestante des martyrs, 1523–1572* (Seyssel: 1997), 121–84.

11   Philip Benedict, "Protestant and Catholic Book Ownership in Seventeenth-Century Metz," in *The Faith and Fortunes of France's Huguenots, 1600–85*, (ed.) Philip Benedict (Aldershot: 2001), 166–67 and 173.

12   Krumenacker (ed.), *Journal de Migault*, 50.

13   Daniel Desmarets, *Histoire abregée des martirs francois du tems de la Reformation* (Amsterdam: 1684). See also Piaget and Berthoud, *Notes sur le livre des martyrs*, 67–72.

hands of their confessional opponent should be considered as martyrs—was in fact deeply contested. Since the 16th century, Protestants and Catholics had continuously clashed over the definition of "true" and "false" martyrs. Some authors came up with circumstantial evidence, such as the martyrs' willingness to die, their brutal punishment, or even the number of executions. Others, including Crespin, adhered to Augustine's famous dictum that it was "not the punishment, but the cause, that makes the martyr." Yet because Catholics and Protestants held fundamentally different views on what constituted a true religious cause, applying Augustine's definition hardly solved the problem.[14]

One of the first refugee authors who tried to re-define martyrdom was Pierre Jurieu, a professor of theology and refugee minister in the Walloon Church of Rotterdam.[15] In 1683 he published the *Histoire du Calvinisme*, (see figure 13.1) written in response to a history of Protestantism by the Jesuit priest and church historian Louis Maimbourg. In his book, Jurieu firmly rejected Augustine's definition of martyrdom, as he spotted the obvious problem that "each sect in Christendom, claiming to be the true Church, will pretend with this argument that its martyrs are true martyrs." Hence his alternative was to look for "particular characteristics in those who suffer for justice and truth."[16] The more people went to their death, Jurieu argued, the more likely it was that they defended a true cause. Constancy and devotion at the stake also marked them as martyrs, as did the calm or even joyful acceptance of one's imminent death. Jurieu finally ranked women, children and otherwise simple folk among true martyrs. Although they lacked sophisticated religious training, they were nonetheless often willing to die for their beliefs.[17]

The widespread *dragonnades* made Jurieu change his mind. What about all the Protestants who had suffered, but never died as martyrs? Martyrologies typically included stories of people who had been arrested, sentenced and executed. Crespin, for instance, only acknowledged as martyrs those Protestants who had been formally convicted, while he designated the victims of massacres during the French Wars of Religion simply as "persecuted believers." Simon

---

14 Gregory, *Salvation at Stake*, 315–32. For a discussion of Augustine's dictum by French martyrologists, see Frank Lestringant, *Lumière des martyrs: Essai sur le martyre au siècle des réformes* (Paris: 2004), 62–72.

15 On Jurieu, see: F.R.J. Knetsch, *Pierre Jurieu: Theoloog en politikus der Refuge* (Kampen: 1967); Robin Howells, *Pierre Jurieu: Antinomien radical* (Durham: 1983).

16 Pierre Jurieu, *Histoire du Calvinisme & celle du Papisme mises en parallele, ou Apologie pour les Reformateurs, pour la Reformation, et pour les Reformez, divisée en quatre parties; contre un libelle intitulé l'Histoire du Calvinisme par Mr Maimbourg*, vol. 1 (Rotterdam: 1683), 169.

17 Jurieu, *Histoire du Calvinisme*, 1:164–69.

FIGURE 13.1 *Frontispiece of Pierre Jurieu's* Histoire du Calvinisme, *depicting the crucifixion of the true Church in the form of a woman. The Latin text encourages martyrdom: "If we suffer with Him, we shall be glorified together" (Rom. 8:17)*
COURTESY OF THE KONINKLIJKE BIBLIOTHEEK, THE HAGUE, KW 1791F 101

Goulart blurred this distinction in later editions of the *Livre des Martyrs*, because he felt that those murdered during the St. Bartholomew's Day massacre of 1572 also deserved inclusion.[18] Jurieu likewise understood that a narrow definition would deprive the Huguenots of many valid martyrs. After all, during the *dragonnades* Protestants had fallen victim to persecution in their own homes rather than on the scaffold, while those who refused to abjure were imprisoned rather than executed. Jurieu labeled these men and women as "confessors," Protestants who had suffered because they bravely clung to their religious beliefs, but who had not perished in the persecutions.[19] Jurieu actually admired these confessors more than formal martyrs: "In my opinion, it is a far more serious matter to sustain a terrible and intense struggle for several months or years, than to suffer the prospect of dying for only a few moments."[20] The persecutions in France thus forced Jurieu to rethink his conception of martyrdom and to concede that Augustine was right after all. In 1688 he concluded that "it is not the punishment, but it is the cause that makes the martyr."[21]

3   Martyrdom in Jurieu's *Lettres pastorales*

Jurieu's reflections on martyrdom also prompted him to document systematically stories of Huguenot suffering, and to publish the most brutal examples in what was arguably one of his most successful publications: the *Lettres pastorals addressées aux fidèles de France qui gémissent sous la captivité de Babylon* (*Pastoral Letters to the Faithful in France Groaning in Babylonian Captivity*). As the title suggested, Jurieu addressed his letters to the Protestants who had stayed behind in France, encouraging them to persevere in their faith despite their forced conversion to Catholicism. The letters appeared every fortnight from September 1686 to July 1689, when Jurieu had to abandon his project because of illness, although he would briefly resume the project between November 1694 and January 1695. Jurieu had his letters printed in inexpensive installments of just eight pages in quarto by the refugee bookseller Abraham

---

18   Amy C. Graves, "Martyrs manqués: Simon Goulart, continuateur du martyrologue de Jean Crespin," *Revue des Sciences Humaines* 269 (2003), 53–86.
19   Pierre Jurieu, *Lettres pastorales adressées aux fidèles de France qui gémissent sous la captivité de Babylon*, (ed.) Robin Howells (Hildesheim: 1988), 15 December 1686, 62.
20   Jurieu, *Lettres pastorales*, 1 January 1687, 72. See also Hubert Bost, "La conscience martyre des Eglises sous la croix au XVIIIe siècle," *Revue des Sciences Humaines* 269 (2003), 251–53.
21   Jurieu, *Lettres pastorales*, 1 April 1688, 114.

Acher. The latter smuggled the letters from Rotterdam in casks of dried herring and secretly sold them in France.[22]

The *Lettres pastrorales* offered readers lengthy theological arguments against the doctrines taught by the Church of Rome, but Jurieu also included numerous reports and original letters sent by Huguenots from France and across the Refuge. He believed that these stories would encourage Protestants in the kingdom to persevere. These documents all revolved around the theme of martyrdom, as Jurieu mostly reproduced stories by Huguenots who had suffered religious persecution in the wake of the Revocation. "Letters are reaching us from our confessors who are in chains, on the galleys, in dungeons a hundred feet down, in the darkest prisons, in torture," he wrote. "From them, I say, arrive letters that excite us, that revive the ancient times, and that show that the greater the torments are to which you are exposed, the more God will give you the strength and the courage to overcome them."[23] Jurieu's observation that letter-writers were "reviving the ancient times" clearly shows that he intended these stories as a martyrology. Amid the tribulations of 17th-century Huguenots, he saw a reflection of the early Christian martyrs.

Jurieu was especially interested in a specific category of confessors—the many Protestant galley slaves. Between 1685 and 1748, roughly 38,000 Frenchmen were sent to serve on the Mediterranean galleys. Some 1550 were Protestants arrested on their escape from France or during secret assemblies. Besides the strenuous labor aboard the Protestant galleys, slaves had to contend with priests trying to convert them to Catholicism.[24] In the eyes of Jurieu, these men therefore ranked foremost among the Protestant martyrs. In 1686, for example, he included two letters written by Louis des Marolles, "one of our most illustrious confessors," who had been arrested during an escape attempt near Strasbourg and subsequently sent to the galleys. Before he was marched to the port of Marseille, Des Marolles wrote Jurieu two letters detailing his plight. He shared a small cell with 52 other men, he was chained around both his neck and feet, and he had suffered no less than five fever attacks.[25] In his

---

22   The best introduction is given by Robin Howells in his edition of Jurieu's *Lettres pastorales*, vii-lix. See also Knetsch, *Pierre Jurieu*, 219–43; Elisabeth Labrousse, "Les Pastorales de Pierre Jurieu," in *Conscience et conviction: Etudes sur le XVIIe siècle*, (ed.) Elisabeth Labrousse (Oxford: 1996), 230–37. On Acher's clandestine trade, see the report from Louis XIV to Feydeau de Brou, Versailles, 27 February 1688, Paris, AN, O1/32, fols. 58v–59r.

23   Jurieu, *Lettres pastorales*, 1 September 1686, 3.

24   André Zysberg, *Les galériens: Vies et destins de 60,000 forçats sur les galères de France, 1680–1748* (Paris: 1987), 102–11 and 172–93; Gaston Tournier, *Les galères de France et les galériens protestants des XVIIe et XVIIIe siècles* (3 vols. Montpellier: 1943–49).

25   Jurieu, *Lettres pastorales*, 15 September 1686, 15–16, and 1 November 1686, 39–40. On Des Marolles, see also: Tournier, *Les galériens protestants*, vol. 2, 46–49.

first pastoral letter of 1687 Jurieu could reassure Des Marolles that his suffering was not in vain, as he compared him to another Protestant captive and wrote that "both of them follow with equal courage the glorious course of their martyrdom."[26]

To obtain these pitiful stories, Jurieu relied on a vast epistolary network that stretched across the Huguenot diaspora, and even reached into France. In his very first letter, dated 1 September 1686, Jurieu issued a call for papers, asking readers to send him memoirs on the persecutions in France: "Since we have the intention to enter in these letters the major acts of our confessors and martyrs, may those who know something for certain take the pains to inform us about them."[27] Before long, Jurieu was flooded with letters. Some Huguenots wrote to him directly, such as Marie du Bois from Metz, who explained from her refuge in Germany how she had courageously escaped the Catholic convent in which she had been locked up.[28] Most letters, however, reached Jurieu through the large network of refugee ministers, many of whom were still in touch with their former communities. In 1686, reports by Protestants from Béarn, claiming that they had heard angels singing Psalms from the skies, reached Jurieu via Arnaud Majendie and Jacob Garcin, two ministers from Orthez who had taken refuge in Amsterdam but still corresponded with their flock in France.[29]

That ministers were the intermediaries upon whom Jurieu relied for his *Lettres pastorales* can be seen most clearly in the case of Blanche Gamond, a Protestant woman imprisoned at the hospital of Valence. Although hospital director La Rapine was known to convert even the most stubborn Protestants through brutal torture, Gamond managed to persevere because she exchanged regular letters with her godfather François Murat, a refugee minister living in Geneva, who encouraged her to remain a proud Protestant.[30] Having read Jurieu's letters, Murat realized that Gamond's story also merited inclusion in the *Lettres pastorales*. A letter he received from her in October 1687 was especially useful, as Gamond detailed how La Rapine and his aides had beaten her with wooden sticks until she was bleeding. Praising her "spirit of martyrdom,"

---

26 Jurieu, *Lettres pastorales*, 1 January 1687, 72.

27 Jurieu, *Lettres pastorales*, 1 September 1686, 2.

28 Jurieu, *Lettres pastorales*, 15 January 1688, 79–80.

29 Jurieu, *Lettres pastorales*, 1 December 1686, 49–56. See also Hubert Bost, "L'Apocalypse et les Psaumes dans l'arsenal des Pastorales de Jurieu," in *Ces Messieurs de la R.P.R.: Histoires et écritures de huguenots, XVIIe–XVIIIe siècles*, (ed.) Hubert Bost (Paris: 2001), 175–213. Short biographies of both ministers can be found in Albert Sarrabère, *Dictionnaire des pasteurs basques et béarnais, XVIe–XVIIe siècles* (Pau: 2001), 130 and 187.

30 Théodore Claparède, "Une héroïne protestante: Blanche Gamond de Saint-Paul-Trois-Châteaux, 1686–1687," *BSHPF* 16 (1867), 366–77.

Murat asked Gamond to supply him with a detailed account of her sufferings, but when she was unexpectedly released he decided to send off her last letter instead, which Jurieu duly included in his *Lettres pastorales*.[31]

Jurieu was not the only refugee minister who relied on epistolary networks to publish histories of Huguenot suffering. Many exiled ministers were still corresponding with their former communities and individual Huguenots in France, and ultimately used these stories to publish their own histories of martyrdom, focusing in particular on the fate of the galley slaves.[32] The letters written by Louis des Marolles, for example, who served on the galleys until his death in 1692, were turned into a history by refugee minister Isaac Jaquelot in 1699.[33] Jaquelot may well have hit on the idea in February 1699, when the consistory of the Walloon Church in The Hague organized a collection for "our poor brothers who are on the galleys" and asked Jacquelot to draw attention to their miserable life in his Sunday sermon.[34] Other epistolary bestsellers were the *Histoire des souffrances et de la mort du fidèle confesseur et martyr, M. Isaac le Febvre*, compiled by refugee minister Etienne Girard from Utrecht, and the *Histoire abrégée des souffrances du Sieur Elie Neau sur les galères et dans les cachots de Marseille* by Jean Morin, a refugee minister in Bergen-op-Zoom. Both books, incidentally, were published by Abraham Acher, who also printed Jurieu's *Lettres pastorales*.[35] The refugee minister Daniel de Superville in Rotterdam was even working on a comprehensive history of the Huguenot

---

[31] Jurieu, *Lettres pastorales*, 1 April 1688, 119. The letters between Gamond and Murat are published in Théodore Claparède (ed.), "Récit des persécutions de Blanche Gamond," *BSHPF* 16 (1867), 497 and 502–05.

[32] Ruth Whelan, "Résistance et spiritualité dans les témoignages des galériens pour la foi," *BSHPF* 156 (2010), 231–46; idem, "Turning to Gold: The Role of the Witness in French Protestant Galley Slave Narratives," *Seventeenth-Century French Studies* 32 (2010), 3–18.

[33] Isaac Jaquelot, *Histoire des souffrances du bien-heureux martyr Mr Louis de Marolles, Conseiller du Roy, Receveur des Consignations au Baillage de Sainte-Menehoult en Champagne* (The Hague: 1699). See also Ruth Whelan, "Diamants dans les ténèbres: La fortune en France et en Angleterre des mémoires de Louis de Marolles, galérien protestant," in *La réception des mémoires d'Ancien Régime: Discours historique, critique, littéraire*, (ed.) Jean-Jacques Tatin-Gourier (Paris: 2009), 75–99.

[34] Consistory minutes Walloon Church The Hague, 1 February 1699, The Hague, Gemeentearchief, EW 1, fol. 223.

[35] Etienne Girard, *Histoire des souffrances et de la mort du fidele Confesseur et Martyr, M. Isaac le Febvre, de Châtelchignon en Nivernois, Advocat en Parlement* (Rotterdam: 1703); Jean Morin, *Histoire abrégée des souffrances du Sieur Elie Neau sur les galères et dans les cachots de Marseille* (Rotterdam: 1701). For a modern edition, see: *Histoire des souffrances du sieur Elie Neau, sur les galères, et dans les cachots de Marseille*, (eds.) Didier Poton and Bertrand Van Ruymbeke (Paris: 2014).

galley slaves, based on the many letters he had received from them, although the work was still unfinished when he passed away in 1728.[36]

Unfortunately, we shall never be able to know whether Jurieu also edited the memoirs he received, because the original documents have largely been lost. Jurieu himself always maintained that he did not polish the texts he published. In 1687, he promised to include only unabridged letters in an attempt to silence critics who argued that "everything one reads in the *Lettres pastorales* are fables invented by the author."[37] Concern about the veracity of his reports also showed in a pastoral letter from December 1687. Everyone knew about the horrific persecutions in the Poitou, Jurieu wrote, but since he lacked written memoirs to back up these stories, he would not report on the basis of hearsay evidence.[38] Yet even if Jurieu did not rewrite the memoirs he received, his writing strategy clearly transformed individual stories into a collective narrative of Huguenot martyrdom. He consciously asked readers to supply him with accounts of their plight. Huguenots throughout the Refuge drafted memoirs that were shaped by Jurieu's narrative of suffering, as they consistently framed their experiences as tales of perseverance in the face of persecution.

4   Elie Benoist and the Archeology of Persecution

Whereas Jurieu was mostly interested in recent examples of Huguenot suffering, other refugee ministers took a long-term perspective on the persecution of French Protestants. The most impressive of these Huguenot histories was the five-volume *Histoire de l'Edit de Nantes*, written by Elie Benoist, a minister from Alençon who had left France after the Revocation and found a position in the Walloon Church of Delft.[39] Scholars of French Protestantism have often cited Benoist's magnum opus to reconstruct the history of the Huguenots under the Edict of Nantes. Yet in 1985 Elisabeth Labrousse warned that despite his factual accuracy, Benoist had written a "militant" history that stresses Huguenot

---

36   Court to Superville the Younger, Lausanne, 11 April 1733, BGE, Court 1, vol. 8, fol. 209r; Superville the Younger to Court, Rotterdam, 16 September 1733, BGE, Court 1, vol. 9, fol. 16.
37   Jurieu, *Lettres pastorales*, 15 September 1687, 15.
38   Jurieu, *Lettres pastorales*, 15 December 1687, 64.
39   On Benoist see Paul Pascal, *Elie Benoist et l'Eglise Réformée d'Alençon, d'après des documents inédits* (Paris: 1892). The full title of his book is *Histoire de l'Edit de Nantes, contenant les choses les plus remarquables qui se sont passées en France avant & après sa publication, à l'occasion de la diversité des Religions, et principalement les Contraventions, Inexécutions, Chicanes, Articles, Violences & autres Injustices, que les Reformez y ont souffertes, jusques à l'Edit de Révocation, en Octobre 1685*, 5 vols (Delft: 1693–95).

victimhood.[40] Following her lead, several scholars have taken a closer look at Benoist's history, focusing on the aims, composition and sources of the *Histoire de l'Edit de Nantes*.[41] This section will summarize some of their findings, but also explore the content of the book and the ways in which Benoist gathered his information, as these aspects are revealing of his belief that history could convince the world that the Huguenots had been unjustly persecuted.

The *Histoire de l'Edit de Nantes* differed markedly in scope from Jurieu's *Lettres pastorales*, because Benoist charted the entire history of French Protestantism, from the Reformation of the 16th century until his present day. The idea for this grand project came to Benoist only after the Revocation, and may well have been prompted by a letter from the Walloon consistory in Amsterdam. In November 1685, one of the elders raised the question whether "given the great and extraordinary persecutions in France against those of our religion, it would not be a good idea to write some history about it." The consistory discussed the project with all French ministers living in Amsterdam, but also resolved to write letters to those in other Dutch towns.[42] By September 1687, Benoist was seriously contemplating such a Huguenot history. His friend Pieter Teding van Berkhout, a burgomaster in Delft, noted in his diary that Benoist had come to see him "about his history of the persecution, which he is considering." Van Berkhout also discussed the project with pensionary Gaspar Fagel, who persuaded the States of Holland to accord Benoist a secret annual subsidy of 315 guilders to cover research expenses.[43]

When the book was finally published, it numbered well over 3500 pages in quarto, spread out over three parts and five volumes (see Table 13.1). Parts one and two rolled off the presses in 1693, each in a separate volume, and covered the Wars of Religion, the promulgation of the Edict of Nantes and the reigns of

---

40 Elisabeth Labrousse, *"Une foi, une loi, un roi?" Essai sur la Révocation de l'Edit de Nantes* (Geneva: 1985), 25–26.

41 Hubert Bost, "Elie Benoist et l'historiographie de l'édit de Nantes," in *Coexister dans l'intolérance: L'édit de Nantes, 1598,* (ed.) Michel Grandjean and Bernard Roussel (Geneva: 1998), 371–84; Frank van Deijk, "Elie Benoist (1640–1728), historiographer and politician after the revocation of the Edict of Nantes," *Nederlands Archief voor Kerkgeschiedenis* 69 (1989), 54–92; Charles Johnston, "Elie Benoist, Historian of the Edict of Nantes," *Church History* 55 (1986), 468–88.

42 Consistory minutes Walloon Church Amsterdam, 11 November 1685, Amsterdam, Gemeentearchief, EW 5.

43 Teding van Berkhout, Journal de mes occupations, 20 September 1687, The Hague, Koninklijke Bibliotheek, 129 D 16; Secret resolution Gecommitteerde Raden States of Holland, 6 November 1687, The Hague, Nationaal Archief, GR 3037, fol. 203r-v. On Teding van Berkhout and his diary, see Jeroen Blaak, *Literacy in Everyday Life: Reading and Writing in Early Modern Dutch Diaries* (Leiden: 2009), 113–87.

TABLE 13.1 *Contents of the* Histoire de l'Edit de Nantes *by volume*

Vol.	Year of publication	Page length chapters	Page length compendium	Period covered	Main events
1	1693	544	100	1517–1610	Wars of Religion; Edict of Nantes; reign of Henry IV
2	1693	646	98	1610–43	Reign of Louis XIII; revolt of 1610–29
3	1695	686	197	1643–65	Regency of Queen Anne and Mazarin; the Fronde
4	1695	630	0	1665–83	Reign of Louis XIV; "Cold War" against the Huguenots
5	1695	422	201	1683–86	Reign of Louis XIV; the Revocation and its aftermath

Note: Benoist integrated the compendium of laws covering the years 1665–83 into volume 5.
Source: Elie Benoist, *Histoire de l'Edit de Nantes*, 5 vols (Delft: 1693–95).

Henry IV and Louis XIII. Part three appeared in 1695, presenting readers with the history of the Edict under Mazarin, Queen Anne and Louis XIV.

Benoist's history was not an ordinary chronology of events, but a legal history of the Edict of Nantes and its dismantlement by the French state. Rather than emphasize the suffering of the Huguenots through exemplary stories of martyrs and confessors in the years surrounding the Revocation, Benoist argued that Huguenot victimhood stretched back to the beginning of the 17th century. He demonstrated that prior to the *dragonnades* of the 1680s, French Protestants had suffered a more subtle form of persecution. The French state had first and foremost relied on legal discrimination to harass the Huguenots, gradually robbing them of their civil and religious rights. According to the general preface of the *Histoire de l'Edit de Nantes*, the book served to unmask this steady erosion of Huguenot liberties, and to safeguard the memory of persecution for generations to come. Benoist wrote that

> If history be properly devoted to preserve for posterity the memory of the most remarkable things that happen in the world, it cannot be denied that the sorry end of the liberties, which the Reformed have so long enjoyed in France, is one of the most memorable events, which merits to be taken in hand to instruct those in times to come.[44]

---

44 Benoist, *Histoire de l'Edit de Nantes*, vol. 1, preface, sig. b3.

FIGURE 13.2   *Frontispiece to the first volume of the* Histoire de l'Edit de Nantes, *depicting French Protestantism as a woman assailed from all sides.*
COURTESY OF THE KONINKLIJKE BIBLIOTHEEK, THE HAGUE, KW 3067 A 1 (1)

Benoist thus took a different approach than Jurieu in his *Lettres pastorales*. Rather than collecting examples of Huguenot martyrdom, Benoist sought out legal documents to hammer home the argument that church and crown had worked in tandem to undermine Protestantism in France. His method can best be described as the "archeology of persecution," because Benoist deconstructed the origins, mechanisms and effects of what Elisabeth Labrousse has termed the "judicial Cold War" against French Protestants: the series of royal declarations, arrests and edicts that gradually tore apart the fabric of the Huguenots' civil and religious rights.[45] To unearth the historical roots of anti-Protestant legislation, Benoist discussed in great detail the creation of laws that targeted Protestantism, analyzing their content and describing the effects on local communities. The importance Benoist attached to law-making is obvious not only from the detailed discussion of each successive law, but also from the lengthy appendices he included in each volume, which offered readers an unabridged anthology of anti-Protestant laws under the heading "Compendium of edicts, declarations, arrests, petitions, memories, and other authentic pieces serving as proof of the reported facts" (see Table 1). The compendium was essential to Benoist's conception of history, as he believed that readers should be able to see for themselves that Protestants were the victim of royal policies.

To trace the evolution of anti-Protestant law-making, Benoist borrowed heavily from the histories written by other refugee ministers, who had already detailed the discriminatory policies against French Protestants and their churches. In 1687, for example, refugee minister Jean Claude in The Hague published *Les plaintes des Protestans*, which listed all the methods employed by the French state to convert Huguenots, with a heavy focus on restrictive laws.[46] Most of Benoist's material, however, came from the *Histoire apologétique* by François Gaultier de Saint-Blancard, a refugee minister from Montpellier who had become court chaplain to the elector of Brandenburg in Berlin. In his book, Gaultier stressed that the Revocation was the result of a decade-long campaign against the Huguenots, and in 1687 he published a compendium of all the edicts, declarations and arrests issued against the Huguenots since 1652.[47] Finally, in 1689, Benoist obtained the papers of

---

45   Labrousse, "*Une foi, une loi, un roi?*", 119–24.

46   Jean Claude, *Les plaintes des Protestans, cruellement opprimez dans le Royaume de France* (Cologne: 1686). On Claude's career, see David van der Linden, "Predikanten in ballingschap: De carrièrekansen van Jean en Isaac Claude in de Republiek," *De Zeventiende Eeuw* 27 (2011), 141–61.

47   François Gaultier de Saint-Blancard, *Histoire apologetique, ou Défense des libertez des Eglises Réformées de France* (2 vols. Mainz: 1687–88). The compendium appeared as

Abraham Tessereau, a former royal secretary and lawyer in the *parlement* of Paris, who had amassed a large number of state papers, including royal edicts, declarations and arrests.[48]

Benoist's legal approach is evident throughout the *Histoire de l'Edit de Nantes*, but as the book progressed into the reign of Louis XIV, his main focus in describing the judicial campaign against French Protestants was the attack on their churches. Benoist meticulously analyzed the series of royal laws that allowed the authorities to put ministers on trial and close their churches, and he supplied readers with examples from all over France to illustrate how these laws had cost congregations the destruction of their temples. The most important of these laws was issued in 1661, when Louis XIV dispatched into the provinces bipartisan commissions, composed of one Catholic—usually the local intendant—and one Huguenot. Their task was to ask Protestant consistories to supply evidence that their community had already existed in the years 1596–1597, otherwise their church would be closed.[49]

In Benoist's home town of Alençon, for example, the commissioners arrived in 1664. The Protestant consistory soon supplied documents proving that its community had been worshipping in town since 1597, including an ordinance issued in 1600 that formalized Protestant worship at Alençon. Pressured by the Catholic commissioner, however, a handful of local Catholics testified that more than a century ago some Protestants had been arrested for mistreating the nuns from the nearby convent of Saint Claire. As a result, the royal council ruled that the Protestant temple in the center of Alençon was to be closed, although the Huguenots were allowed to construct a new temple in the *faubourg* Lancrel.[50]

Most Protestant churches were closed down only in the 1680s, when the king issued a new set of laws. In June 1680, for example, Louis XIV decreed that Protestants who had abjured their faith were no longer allowed to reconvert to

---

Recueil de Plusieurs Edits, Declarations et Arrets, et de quelques autres Pieces, qui servent à justifier les Principaux faits, qu'on avance dans cette Histoire Apologétique (Mainz: 1687). On Gaultier, see Hubert Bost, "De Montpellier à Berlin: L'itinéraire du pasteur François Gaultier de Saint-Blancard (1639–1703)," in *Hugenotten zwischen Migration und Integration: Neue Forschungen zum Refuge in Berlin und Brandenburg*, (eds.) Manuela Böhm, Jens Häseler and Robert Violet (Berlin: 2005), 179–204.

48 Thomas Philip Le Fanu, "Mémoires inédits d'Abraham Tessereau," PHSL 15 (1937), 566–85. Benoist paid tribute to Tessereau's research in the third volume of his book: Benoist, *Histoire de l'Edit de Nantes*, vol. 3, preface, sig. ***2.

49 Labrousse, "*Une foi, une loi, un roi?*", 125–26.

50 Benoist, *Histoire de l'Edit de Nantes*, vol. 3, 597–99. See also Luc Daireaux, "*Réduire les Huguenots.*" *Protestants et pouvoirs en Normandie au XVIIe siècle* (Paris: 2010), 355–65.

Calvinism—the so-called *crime de relaps*. If they returned to worship at a Protestant church, the serving minister would be removed from office and see his temple demolished.[51] The *Histoire de l'Edit de Nantes* contains numerous examples of communities that suffered under this law. In 1684, for instance, the pastor Pierre du Bosc from Caen was accused of allowing a lapsed woman, Elisabeth Vaultier, into his church. Although she had married a Catholic in 1664, she continued to attend services at the Protestant temple. The local priest actually produced an attestation showing that Elisabeth had converted to Catholicism, as well as a statement from her daughter claiming that her mother had recently taken communion at the Protestant church. This sealed the fate of the church at Caen. In June 1685 a local court ordered the church to be closed and had the building razed to the ground.[52]

5 Martyrdom in the *Histoire de l'Edit de Nantes*

Although the main focus of the *Histoire de l'Edit de Nantes* was the judicial campaign against the Huguenots, Benoist occasionally included stories of individual Protestants and specific communities to illustrate how royal and ecclesiastical policies had affected them. Especially in the last two volumes, which covered the years before the Revocation, the emphasis shifted from an almost exclusive focus on legal texts to a narrative interspersed with touching stories of Huguenot suffering. The fifth and final volume of the *Histoire de l'Edit de Nantes* even contained a long list of all the victims of the *dragonnades*, whom Benoist praised as "confessors."[53] Despite his legal analysis, he certainly agreed with Jurieu that history could supply Huguenots with noteworthy examples that they should emulate. In a pastoral letter of 1686 addressed to his former congregation at Alençon, Benoist urged them to follow in the footsteps of their forefathers, who had bravely suffered persecution in the decades of the Reformation. "Go through the history of your fathers," he wrote. "Many, to be sure, were weaklings and cowards, but many also were steadfast and faithful witnesses who lost their peace, fortune and even their lives for the Reformation that you have abandoned."[54]

---

51 The law is published in Léon Pilatte, *Recueil des Edits, Déclarations et arrests concernans la Religion P. Réformée, 1662–1751, précédés de l'Edit de Nantes* (Paris: 1885), 51–53.

52 Benoist, *Histoire de l'Edit de Nantes*, 5: 774–76; Daireaux, "Réduire les huguenots," 556–62.

53 The non-paginated list of victims, which comprises 22 pages, is attached as an appendix to volume 5.

54 Elie Benoist, *Lettre d'un pasteur banni de son pays, à une Eglise qui n'a fait pas son devoir dans la dernière Persécution* (Delft: 1686), 22–23.

To obtain inspiring stories for his book, Benoist first enlisted the epistolary network of the Huguenot Refuge. In 1688, the Walloon synod encouraged all ministers in the Dutch Republic to conduct a thorough inquiry among their flocks, asking that "if there be some people that have memoirs concerning the persecution of the churches in France, let them have the charity to address them to our most beloved brother, Monsieur Elie Benoist."[55] Benoist also circulated a letter to all refugee communities across Europe, soliciting original documents on the persecutions.[56] But the results were disappointing. In 1695, Benoist complained that he had hardly received any reports on the sufferings of Protestants who had been executed, banished, or sentenced to serve on the galleys.[57]

Benoist relied instead on the histories of specific Huguenot communities that had been published by other refugee ministers, selecting from these books the cruelest episodes to demonstrate the fate of the Huguenots in France. Gaultier's *Histoire apologétique*, for example, not only offered an overview of royal laws, but also included an account of the persecutions in Montpellier, where he had served as a pastor before the Revocation. The story that Benoist took straight from this book was the remarkable episode of an eleven-year old Protestant boy who refused to convert to Catholicism, even though his father had already done so. When two noblemen tried to trick the boy into a conversion with a fake order to hang him at the gallows if he did not abjure his faith, he threw himself from the nearest window—a fall he miraculously survived because the neighbors had spread sheets across the street to create some shade during the hot summer. Benoist recounted this story in the *Histoire de l'Edit de Nantes* to illustrate how royal laws had made life miserable for French Protestants, in this case an edict issued in June 1681 that allowed children to convert to Catholicism from the age of seven, even without their parents' consent.[58]

Benoist also mined an exemplary tale of perseverance from a book written by the refugee minister Jacques Pineton de Chambrun, who in 1687 published his autobiography under the title *Les larmes de Jacques Pineton de Chambrun*.

---

55   E. Bourlier (ed.), *Livre Synodal contenant les articles résolus dans les Synodes des Eglises Wallonnes des Pays-Bas*, vol. 2 (The Hague: 1896–1904), 48.

56   Michel Nicolas, "Appèl d'un historien du XVIIe siècle demandant des matériaux pour une histoire des protestants de France, sous les règnes de Henri IV, Louis XIII et Louis XIV," BSHPF 7 (1859), 274–90; Van Deijk, "Benoist, historiographer and politician," 62, n. 33.

57   Benoist, *Histoire de l'Edit de Nantes*, vol. 3, preface, sig. ****2.

58   Gaultier, *Histoire apologétique*, 1: 251–53; Benoist, *Histoire de l'Edit de Nantes*, 4: 511–12. For the 1681 edict, see: Pilatte, *Receuil des édits*, 88–90.

FIGURE 13.3 Jan Luyken, *The whipping of Louis de Neuville in Orange*, engraving from Elie Benoist, Historie der Gereformeerde Kerken van Vrankryk (*Amsterdam: 1696*), vol. 2.
COURTESY OF UNIVERSITY LIBRARY LEIDEN, BWA 147

Besides an account of his conversion to Catholicism in the wake of the Revocation and subsequent repentance in Geneva, the book also gave a detailed chronology of the persecutions that had taken place in the principality of Orange, where Chambrun had preached since 1658.[59] The episode that caught Benoist's eye was that of Louis de Villeneuve, a nine-year-old boy who had been accused in 1663 of urinating in a bottle of wine used during Mass at the Capuchin chapel of Orange. After two months in prison, the boy was released, though not before a public whipping on Sunday morning, which

---

59 Jacques Pineton de Chambrun, *Les larmes de Jacques Pineton de Chambrun, qui contiennent les Persecutions arrivées aux Eglises de la Principauté d'Orange, depuis l'an 1660* (The Hague: 1687). On Chambrun, see: Amanda Eurich, "Les occupations françaises de la principauté d'Orange entre 1660 et 1685: Controverse religieuse, tolérance et les écrits de Jacques Pineton de Chambrun," in *Entre calvinistes et catholiques: Les relations religieuses entre la France et les Pays-Bas du Nord, XVIe–XVIIIe siècles*, (ed.) Yves Krumenacker (Rennes: 2010), 259–73.

prompted Pineton to canonize Louis as a martyr for the Huguenot cause (see figure 13.3). "I have regarded him all my life as an illustrious confessor," he observed.[60] This was probably the reason why Benoist included the episode in his book, as he argued that Louis' tribulations clearly demonstrated the "inhumane" treatment of French Protestants. Not even the children were spared.[61]

Benoist's account of enduring victimhood struck a chord with refugees throughout the Huguenot diaspora. They framed their own experiences within the larger narrative of suffering provided by the *Histoire de l'Edit de Nantes*. Some readers wrote letters to Benoist, responding to his complaint in 1695 that he lacked detailed reports on the suffering of individual Huguenots. Among these letter-writers was Jacques de Barjac, marquis de Rochegude, who had been banished to Switzerland in 1688. De Rochegude had clearly read the *Histoire de l'Edit de Nantes* as a martyrology, as he sent Benoist an account of his own sufferings, which, he hoped, "would contribute something to the edification of the Church." The marquis explained that because of his refusal to convert to Catholicism he had been thrown into prison. Yet despite frequent maltreatment, sickness, and regular pressure from priests he had held on to his Protestant beliefs.[62]

Refugee pastor François Bancelin likewise related his experiences as a tale of victimhood. Writing to Benoist from Berlin, he recalled that only three months after his confirmation as fifth minister of Metz in 1662, the authorities had forbidden him to preach, on the grounds that there had never been more than four ministers. The consistory protested that French law did not restrain the number of ministers preaching in Protestant temples, but in 1663 the king formally fixed the maximum at four ministers. Bancelin was forced to leave Metz, until in 1669 the death of his father-in-law, pastor Paul Ferry, paved the way for his return.[63] Bancelin consciously placed these experiences within the legal narrative of the *Histoire de l'Edit de Nantes*. Having read the book, he argued that events in Metz provided another fine example of the judicial campaign against the Huguenots prior to the Revocation, because he had been deposed on the basis of laws invented to undermine Protestant liberties. He therefore hoped that Benoist would "take from this little story that I have just

---

60 Chambrun, *Larmes de Pineton de Chambrun*, 5–6.
61 Benoist, *Histoire de l'Edit de Nantes*, 5: 920.
62 De Rochegude to Benoist, Vevey, 18 April 1698, BGE, Court 48, fols. 5–6. On De Rochegude, see E. Jaccard, *Le marquis de Rochegude et les protestants sur les galères* (Lausanne: 1898).
63 Bancelin to Benoist, Berlin, 23 October 1697, BGE, Court 48, fols. 8r-9r. See also Maurice Thirion, *Etude sur l'histoire du protestantisme à Metz et dans le Pays messin* (Nancy: 1884), 254–58 and 459–63.

told you whatever you shall deem appropriate, to show the injustices committed against me, as well as against the Church of Metz." Bancelin even included a copy of the ordinance issued against him in 1662, which, he suggested, could be added to the compendium of legal documents.[64]

Finally, the Huguenot merchant Jacques Barbaud, who had fled from La Rochelle to the Dutch city of Kampen in 1687, forwarded Benoist a memoir written by a refugee officer called Delbecque. The memoir recounted Delbecque's life and subsequent escape to the Dutch Republic—he had also settled in Kampen—as well as the sufferings of his son, who had died in a French prison because he refused to convert. The son's letters from prison and the father's replies certainly merited publication, Barbaud argued, as he agreed with Benoist that "other confessors, or those who have extraordinarily suffered during the persecutions, had not taken care to put in order all the tribulations, sorrows and sufferings that have happened to them."[65] The *Histoire de l'Edit de Nantes*, in sum, defined Huguenot suffering in two complementary ways. On the one hand, Benoist deconstructed the long-term campaign of the French state to undermine French Protestantism, detailing the many laws and court procedures that had targeted Huguenot communities. On the other, he illustrated his narrative with touching examples of suffering Huguenots, whom he proudly labeled "confessors."

6   Conclusion

Stories of martyrdom and suffering circulated widely in the Huguenot diaspora, as refugees all had their own account of the persecutions they had suffered in France and their subsequent escape abroad. These stories only became known on a wider scale, however, through the efforts of refugee pastors, who selected and publicized in printed histories the most gruesome episodes of suffering. Ministers such Jacques Pineton de Chambrun and François Gaultier de Saint-Blancard documented the fate of their former communities on the basis of eyewitness accounts and their own memory, consciously presenting their readers with stories of persecution to hammer home the message that Protestants were the innocent victims of Catholic fanaticism. Refugee ministers also functioned as go-betweens in networks of correspondence that

---

64   Bancelin to Benoist, Berlin, 23 October 1697, BGE, Court 48, fols. 9r-v.
65   Barbaud to Benoist, Kampen, March 1696, BGE, Court 48, fol. 11r. On Barbaud, see Elisabeth Forlacroix, *L'Église Réformée de La Rochelle face à la Révocation*, vol. 2 (PhD diss., Université de Montpellier III: 1996), 50–51.

stretched across the Huguenot world, as they collected letters and memoirs from their brethren in France, publishing epistolary bestsellers on the fate of the galley slaves, or forwarding accounts to Jurieu for inclusion in his *Lettres pastorales*. Elie Benoist came toward the end of this process. Although he collected some material himself, he mostly exploited the histories of other refugee ministers to illustrate the campaign against the Protestant churches in France in his *Histoire de l'Edit de Nantes*. However different their aims may have been, what united all these ministers was the sifting of individual stories to construct a narrative of Huguenot victimhood. It was this story that would mark Huguenot identity from the Revocation until the late 20th century, as stories of persecution and suffering became the main focus of histories dealing with the Refuge. Yet as scholars are nowadays deconstructing Huguenot histories of suffering and martyrdom, they are also setting a clear research agenda for the future: to explore exile histories throughout the Huguenot diaspora; to compare them to those of other refugee waves, including Catholics; and to use them as a point of entry to understand the formation of refugee identities in early modern Europe.

CHAPTER 14

Huguenot Congregations in Colonial New York and Massachusetts: Reassessing the Paradigm of Anglican Conformity

Paula Wheeler Carlo

1   Introduction

A recurring theme in many studies of the Huguenots who sought refuge in the British Atlantic World is their rapid assimilation into the British majority. Another frequent and closely-related premise is their swift and eager conformity to the Church of England. Although these assertions have not been completely dismissed by recent scholarship, a growing body of research has called for more nuanced interpretations of these aspects of the Huguenot experience. Accordingly, this essay explores Anglican conformity as it pertains to Huguenot congregations in the British colonies of New York and Massachusetts in the late-17th and 18th centuries.

2   General Background

The Huguenot diaspora was one of the largest involuntary migrations of the early modern period. Some 180,000 Huguenots left France between 1680 and 1710 as persecution intensified in the years immediately surrounding the 1685 revocation of the Edict of Nantes.[1] Most Huguenots remained in European places of refuge, with probably no more than 4000 migrating to North America during the 17th and 18th centuries.[2] Even Huguenots who came to North America did so after spending several years in a European refuge. For example, the Huguenots who went to South Carolina had first settled in England. This was also the case for the founders of New Rochelle, New York. The founders of New Paltz, New York resided for several years in the German Palatinate, while

---

1   Bertrand Van Ruymbeke, *From New Babylon to Eden: The Huguenots and Their Migration to Colonial South Carolina* (Columbia: 2006), xv.
2   Van Ruymbeke, "Refuge or Diaspora? Historiographical Reflections on the Huguenot Dispersion in the Atlantic World," in *Religious Refugees in Europe, Asia and North America (6th–21st Century)*, (ed.) Susanne Lachenicht (Hamburg: 2007), 161–62.

many of the Huguenot settlers of Manakintown, Virginia had lived in Ireland. Although the European Refuge offered religious toleration for Huguenots, America was perceived as a place that also offered greater economic opportunities. As Jon Butler put it, "few Protestants left France with America in mind. Rather America came into mind as their first places of exile turned sour."[3]

In North America the Huguenots were scattered among fourteen communities in five colonies.[4] Over time they became even more widely dispersed. Nevertheless, several settlements were founded by and for French-speaking Protestants—New Rochelle and New Paltz, New York, Narragansett, Rhode Island, Oxford, Massachusetts, and Manakintown, Virginia. During the 18th century Huguenots in the settlements that endured (New Paltz, New Rochelle, and Manakintown) were joined by other ethnic groups. But most Huguenots who came to North America settled in more diverse communities in cities such as New York, Boston, and Charleston. This relatively small migration coupled with far-flung settlements, often among non-Huguenots, prompted Robert M. Kingdon to suggest that these factors helped to account for the Huguenots' swift assimilation into Anglo-American society and their easy embrace of the Church of England.[5]

Approximately 1000 French-speaking Protestants were living in the British colonies of New York and Massachusetts in the early 18th century. Over 800 lived in New York, making it one of the most popular destinations in North America for Huguenot refugees. Most of these Francophone Protestants lived in New York City (317 people), followed by New Rochelle (184), Staten Island (172), and New Paltz (121).[6] They established French-speaking Reformed churches in these settlements soon after their arrival. Huguenots who settled in the New England region initially were divided among several locations, including

---

3   Jon Butler, "The Huguenots and the American Immigrant Experience," in *Memory and Identity: The Huguenots in France and the Atlantic Diaspora*, (eds.) Bertrand Van Ruymbeke and Randy J. Sparks (Columbia: 2003), 198.
4   Van Ruymbeke, "Refuge or Diaspora?" 162.
5   Robert Kingdon "Why Did the Huguenot Refugees in the American Colonies become Episcopalians?" *Historical Magazine of the Protestant Episcopal Church* 49 (1980), 317–18. An earlier version was published in French, "Pourquoi les Réfugiés Huguenots aux colonies américaines, sont-ils devenus épiscopaliens?" BSHPF 115 (1969), 487–509. After the American Revolution the Church of England became the Episcopal Church in the United States.
6   Figures based on census data analyzed by Jon Butler, *The Huguenots in America: A Refugee People in New World Society* (Cambridge, Mass.: 1983), 47–48. Huguenot children born in New York were nearly 50 per cent of the total. For locations of census materials see Butler, 229–30, notes 13 and 15.

Boston and Oxford, Massachusetts and Narragansett, Rhode Island.[7] By the early 1700s some had relocated to Boston after the collapse of Huguenot congregations in the smaller, more rural settlements in Oxford and Narragansett. Thus, about 200 Huguenots lived in the New England region, with most attending the French Church of Boston in the early 18th century. While all of these Francophone Protestant settlements and their congregations shared similarities, they also evinced striking differences.

Many of the French-speaking Protestants who settled New Paltz in the late 1670s were not from places along the southwestern coast of France, such as La Rochelle, where the majority of Huguenots who settled in North America had originated.[8] Instead, most were Walloons from what is now known as Belgium and, therefore, were not Huguenots. Yet, they are often referred to as Huguenots, even by modern-day descendants of the founding families. Moreover, they arrived in North America in the 1660s and 1670s—more than a decade before most of the Huguenots arrived.[9] Several New Paltz founders were from Calais (in northwestern France) which had been incorporated into France in the mid 1500s. During the 18th century the population of New Paltz was augmented by the arrival of additional Huguenots (who had been born in France or were born to Huguenot parents while they were living in a European refuge) and by an even larger number of Dutch settlers.

Most Francophone Protestants who arrived in New Amsterdam before it became English-controlled New York City in 1664 were Walloons rather than Huguenots. Indeed, Walloons were among the earliest settlers of this Dutch colony. This was also the case for many French-speaking Protestants who settled in Staten Island during the 1660s. This earlier Walloon migration was much smaller than the Huguenot exodus which occurred primarily in the decade surrounding the 1685 revocation of the Edict of Nantes. Thus, Walloon migration and identity have often been overshadowed by the larger and better-known Huguenot dispersion. In addition to their common use of the French language, both the Walloon Protestants and Huguenots shared the experience of persecution in Catholic-controlled regions of Europe because of their Calvinist beliefs. Nevertheless, some studies produced over the past thirty years have appropriately differentiated between these two groups.

---

7 New England included Massachusetts, Rhode Island, New Hampshire, and Connecticut.
8 For origins of North American Huguenots see Charles Baird, *History of the Huguenot Emigration to America* (2 vols. New York: 1885).
9 Eric Roth, "'where ye walloens dwell': Rethinking the Ethnic Identity of the Huguenots of New Paltz and Ulster County, New York," *New York History* (Fall 2008). http://www.historyco operative.org/journals/nyh/89.4/roth.html (1 Jun. 2012).

3   Anglican Conformity: Sources and Issues

There are hundreds of secondary studies about the Huguenot diaspora. Some are excellent, while others are mediocre or outdated. With few exceptions, most examinations of the North American Huguenots that were published before the 1980s have limited use for researchers today.[10] The following is an overview of the most salient problems and debates concerning Huguenot conformity and assimilation as well as some of the pertinent sources essential for future research.

Jon Butler's 1983 monograph *The Huguenots in America: A Refugee People in New World Society* is indispensable as a starting point for research on the North American Refuge. It is a modern analysis of the Huguenots' rapid assimilation into Anglo-American society and culture. Butler focused on three major areas where Huguenots settled—Massachusetts, New York, and South Carolina—with significant emphasis on the urban settlements of Boston, New York City, and Charleston. He also concentrated on migration before 1700, thereby eliminating later arrivals such as some 700 Huguenots who settled in Manakintown, Virginia around 1700.[11] While these settlements were quite different, the outcome for the Huguenots was the same according to Butler. "By 1750 Huguenots no longer existed as a significant religious, national, or ethnic minority in most of their places of exile; by 1800 they had disappeared in all of them."[12] Some subsequent studies have reassessed Butler's thesis and have advanced more nuanced explanations of the assertion that the Huguenots disappeared as a distinctly recognizable ethnic and religious group in North America and in other places of refuge.[13] Although one of Butler's specialties is American religious history, his study of the Huguenots placed considerable emphasis

---

10   Baird's *History of the Huguenot Emigration to America* is a notable exception. Although it presumes the rapid assimilation of Huguenots into their host societies, its identification of Huguenot places of origin remains essential. The publication coincided with the two-hundredth anniversary of the revocation of the Edict of Nantes and the founding of several Huguenot heritage societies.

11   Concerning this migration, see David Lambert, *The Protestant International and the Huguenot Migration to Virginia* (New York: 2010).

12   Butler, *Huguenots in America*, 211.

13   Susanne Lachenicht, for one, compared Huguenot experiences in several European places of refuge and North America and concluded that "the role Huguenots chose to play within the hosting nations was altogether more complex than has been suggested" by Butler and others. Lachenicht, "Huguenot Immigrants and the Formation of National Identities, 1548–1787," *The Historical Journal* 50 (2007), 311.

on patterns of exogamy and their political and economic integration into Anglo-American society. To this end he relied extensively on demographic sources (such as census, tax, birth, marriage, and death records) rather than sources like manuscript sermons, which illuminate their religious beliefs and practices. This partly explains why some of Butler's conclusions are at odds with those of subsequent researchers who have relied on different sources. Still, Butler's work continues to be a significant contribution that has stimulated new research on the North American Huguenots.

Robert M. Kingdon's essay "Why did the Huguenot Refugees in the American Colonies become Episcopalians?" is another essential analysis, particularly for people who are investigating the Huguenot propensity for conformity to the Church of England. Kingdon noted that there were numerous motivations for Anglican conformity and for the subsequent disappearance of the Huguenots as a distinct religious group. Motivations included financial incentives, social, economic and political advantages, gratitude for toleration and a place of refuge, and perhaps even an attraction to Anglican doctrines and a desire for Christian unity. Since its publication this essay, like Butler's monograph on the Huguenots, has inspired further research and debate. Nevertheless, the general pattern of conformity that Kingdon outlined depicts the experience of many, but not all, Huguenots in colonial America.

To help explain the Huguenot attraction to Anglicanism, Kingdon cited the Reverend André Le Mercier (1692–1764), the last minister of the French Church in Boston. Kingdon described him as "perhaps the most literate of the Huguenots to come to America." Le Mercier had written the following in a 1732 publication: "As to Articles of Discipline, we must be of a sociable spirit, and submit to the order of the Churches among which we live..."[14] For Kingdon this phrase suggested that American Huguenots did not consider church organization to be something that was unalterable: in other words, they may have advocated "a kind of adiaphorism."[15] This implies that many Huguenots did not believe that conformity to the Church of England meant a betrayal or abandonment of their essential religious beliefs and practices. As Bertrand Van Ruymbeke observed, conformity to Anglicanism "must not be confused with conversion since the Church of England, although Episcopalian in character

---

14 Kingdon, 334–35. Le Mercier's quotation is from *Church History of Geneva, in Five Books* (Boston: 1732), A2. Available through an online subscription database available at many large research libraries, *Early American Imprints*, Series I: Evans, 1639–1800, # 3557, 182–83.

15 Kingdon, 335.

and in polity, was in essence a Protestant church, that is, in the eyes of the Huguenots, one born of the Reformation."[16]

On the surface this quotation from Le Mercier appears to be very appropriate. But André Le Mercier is an unusual choice as a presumed standard-bearer for Huguenot conformity to the Church of England since he never conformed to Anglicanism and the French Church of Boston, of which he was the minister, did not conform either! Instead, Le Mercier's comment is more relevant to his cooperative efforts with Scots-Irish Presbyterian ministers in New England. Along with these ministers, Le Mercier created the Presbytery of New England (also known as the Presbytery of Londonderry).[17] Information about the presbytery is limited and it did not wield significant power although it exercised some disciplinary measures. The presbyters also debated questions about a candidate's suitability for ordination and ordained candidates they deemed appropriate. For example, when arguments over a controversial ordination divided the presbytery in 1736, the disagreement led to published materials that openly discussed the dispute.[18] Another cooperative effort was preaching since member ministers occasionally preached to one another's congregations. One published sermon strove to demonstrate Huguenot and Scots-Irish Presbyterian support of British military endeavors against the French in the 1740s. Thus, one did not have to conform to Anglicanism in order to express support for British rule. Moreover, public affirmations of that allegiance reinforced the notion of Protestant solidarity against the French papists.[19]

---

16   Van Ruymbeke, *From New Babylon to Eden*, 97–98. For further discussion of issues surrounding conformity see Paula Wheeler Carlo, *Huguenot Refugees in Colonial New York: Becoming American in the Hudson Valley* (Brighton: 2005), 78–83.

17   Presbyterian and French Reformed churches had presbyteries composed of ministers who oversaw local congregations under their auspices. English Calvinist churches were governed by a congregational system that did not have a body outside of the local church to impose discipline, mediate disputes, or interfere with the church in any way.

18   The disputed candidate, James Hillhouse, was a Congregational minister who was locked out of his church by his irate flock. Consequently, he sought Presbyterian ordination. Le Mercier responded publicly since one of Hillhouse's supporters had published a pamphlet criticizing Le Mercier and other opposing presbyters. Le Mercier explained that the ordination had been pushed through the presbytery when most of the opponents were absent. He argued that Hillhouse's Presbyterianism was weak and that he sought this ordination merely to secure another position. Le Mercier, "Remarks on the Preface of a Pamphlet Published by John Presbyter" (Boston: 1737), 8. *Early American Imprints*, I, # 41908.

19   At least three sermons were published and were preached at the "French Meeting-House in Boston" in 1742 and 1745. The speakers were the Rev. John Caldwell and the Rev. William McClenachan. One of Caldwell's sermons was "On the Scripture Characters of False

Despite Le Mercier's intelligence, energy, and cooperative spirit, the French Church of Boston did not survive beyond the mid-18th century. By the 1740s only seven families continued to attend the French Church and the building was sold in 1748.[20] The deed of sale mandated that the building could only be used by another Protestant congregation.[21] Since the Church of England played a limited role in Boston, most Huguenots defected to English-speaking Calvinist churches as they contracted exogamous marriages, entered local politics, and developed business connections with non-Huguenots.[22] Some Huguenots, like the wealthy and politically ambitious Faneuils, even supported Anglican King's Chapel after 1720. Meanwhile they helped to maintain the French Church building and "contributed to Le Mercier's salary." Other Boston Huguenots seemingly had multiple church affiliations as well.[23]

André Le Mercier was the only Huguenot minister in the British colonies who worked with Presbyterian ministers to form a presbytery in the 18th century.[24] The three Huguenot congregations in New England had formed a *colloque* (presbytery) in the late 1600s but it did not survive beyond the collapse of the short-lived congregations in Oxford, Massachusetts and Narragansett, Rhode Island.[25] A common presbytery for Huguenot churches in the colonies

---

Prophets." Another concerned "Rash and Uncharitable Judging," in which Caldwell criticized popular revivalist preachers including Gibert Tennent. McClenachan's sermon, "The Christian Warrior," was preached in honor of General William Pepperell, who was the commander-in-chief of the army sent from New England against the French-controlled, fortified town of Louisbourg on Cape Breton Island, Nova Scotia. Sermons are available electronically in *Early American Imprints*, I, # 4909, 4910, 5622. It is possible that there were more instances of cooperative preaching, but the sermons were not published.

20 Butler, *Huguenots in America*, 88. Butler uses the word subscribers, which implies the head of a family, so presumably there were more than seven members. The records of the French Church in Boston are not extant so numbers are difficult to ascertain.

21 For additional discussion and sources, see Paula Wheeler Carlo, "Huguenot Identity and Protestant Unity in Colonial Massachusetts: The Reverend André Le Mercier and the 'Sociable Spirit,'" *Historical Journal of Massachusetts* 40 (2012), 140. The building was used by a Congregational Church until 1788.

22 Congregationalism was the established church in Massachusetts, where Anglicans were dissenters.

23 Butler, *Huguenots in America*, 84–85.

24 For more on the presbytery see Carlo, "Huguenot Identity and Protestant Unity," 137–38.

25 Van Ruymbeke, *From New Babylon to Eden*, 328, note 22. Also see Van Ruymbeke "Le Refuge en Amérique du Nord britannique: périodisation, caractéristiques, problématiques," in *Les Huguenots et l'Atlantique: Fidélités, Racines et Mémoires*, (eds.) Mickaël Augeron, Didier Poton and Bertrand Van Ruymbeke, vol. 2 (Paris: 2012), 34.

might not have been effective because of the widely-dispersed settlements, but regional presbyteries for churches in the south and in the north might have been feasible. Instead, Huguenot congregations usually relied on transatlantic connections to refugee communities and to Reformed church polity in Europe. In some cases the Huguenot church on Threadneedle Street in London sent potential ministers to the colonies. Le Mercier, for one, was recruited from London by André Faneuil, a wealthy Huguenot merchant in Boston.[26] Another source for French-speaking ministers was the Walloon synod in the Netherlands, which sent the Reverend Louis Rou (whose parents were Huguenots born in France) to the French Church of New York in the 1720s. Sometimes candidates were recruited and sent from Geneva. In several cases the candidates were people of the highest caliber. Sometimes they were not.

By the mid-18th century it became increasingly difficult to enlist competent ministers for the independent Huguenot churches in the colonies. Considering this, cooperation with Presbyterians would appear to have been a sensible solution for Huguenots in British North America, because many were proficient in English by then. But the situation was far more complex. As Bernard Cottret has explained, many Huguenots in Britain (and presumably in British North America as well) were reluctant to maintain Presbyterian forms of church governance because of their potential for republicanism.[27] In contrast, Huguenot churches that conformed to Anglicanism were able to secure financial, ministerial, and other types of assistance from the Church of England without incurring suspicion or hostility. Additionally, the Bishop of London served as an advocate and overseer for Anglican churches in the colonies because there was no Anglican bishop in North America. And, as Kingdon observed, Anglican conformity had the potential to secure social, economic, and financial benefits for individuals as well.

A growing body of work on the Protestant International demonstrates that Huguenots were not the only Protestants who were willing to overlook minor theological differences. This cooperative spirit was largely driven by "the need to unite against the persecuting papists" who threatened Protestantism in both Europe and North America.[28] This sense of Protestant unity surged after the

---

26 Carlo, "Huguenot Identity and Protestant Unity," 127. The Reverend Pierre Stouppe was also sent by the Threadneedle Street Church at the request of the nonconforming church in Charleston, South Carolina. Van Ruymbeke, *From New Babylon to Eden*, 141.

27 Bernard Cottret, *The Huguenots in England: Immigration and Settlement c. 1550–1700*, trans. Peregrine and Adriana Stevenson (Cambridge: 1991), 265.

28 Owen Stanwood, "Catholics, Protestants, and the Clash of Civilizations in Early America," in *The First Prejudice: Religious Tolerance and Intolerance in Early America*, (eds.) Chris Beneke and Christopher Grenda (Philadelphia: 2011), 234.

1680s—the decade of the Glorious Revolution in England and the revocation of the Edict of Nantes in France—when it seemed that the Protestant cause was under siege. Meanwhile, in British North America Native American attacks on settlers were believed to be incited by French Jesuit priests in nearby New France. Hence, territorial disputes between France and England increasingly assumed a robust religious component or were regarded as "battle[s] for the soul of the continent."[29] Some excellent studies that explore the Protestant International include, but are not limited to, works by J.F. Bosher, Robin Gwynne, and Thomas Kidd.[30] Thus, literature on the Protestant International provides another possible explanation for Huguenot willingness to conform to the established church of the one European nation that was capable of leading an assault against the purported evils and threats of popery and of Catholicism in general.

Anglican religious institutions also forged cooperation among different Protestant groups. In this connection, the Society for Promoting Christian Knowledge (SPCK) worked with foreign Protestants, including Huguenots, who were living in England in the early 1700s. While the SPCK fostered a sense of Protestant unity, it did not require these foreign Protestants to conform to Anglicanism.[31]

Anglican conformity among Huguenots in England has been the topic of much recent research. Some of these works can serve as excellent models for studies of conformity in British North America. Robin Gwynn is one of the leading proponents of the argument that Huguenot conformity in England "cannot simply be equated with Anglican orthodoxy."[32] Gwynn argued that

---

29   Stanwood, "Catholics, Protestants, and the Clash of Civilizations," 231.

30   J.F. Bosher, "Huguenot Merchants and the Protestant International in the Sixteenth Century," *William and Mary Quarterly*, 3rd series, 52 (1995), 77–102; Robin Gwynn, "The Huguenots in Britain, the 'Protestant International' and the Defeat of Louis XIV," in *From Strangers to Citizens: The Integration of Immigrant Communities in Britain, Ireland and Colonial America, 1550–1750*, (eds.) Randolph Vigne and Charles Littleton (Brighton: 2001), 412–24; Thomas Kidd, "'Let Hell and Rome Do Their Worst': World News, Anti-Catholicism, and International Protestantism in Early-Eighteenth-Century Boston," *New England Quarterly* 76 (2003), 265–91.

31   Katherine Carté Engel, "The SPCK and the American Revolution: The Limits of International Protestantism," *Church History* 81 (2012), 77–103. The SPCK was founded in 1698. Engel notes that the early eighteenth century was the apogee of international Protestant cooperation and these ties were weakened by the time of the American Revolution.

32   Robin Gwynn, "Strains of Worship: The Huguenots and Non-conformity," in *The Huguenots: History and Memory in Transnational Context*, (ed.) D.J.B. Trim (Leiden: 2011), 148.

they created their own version of Anglicanism that was a "half-way house between the French Reformed and Anglican churches."[33] Moreover, Bernard Cottret asserted that conforming Huguenot churches in England were highly selective in their use of ritual: ministers did not wear a surplice or make the sign of the cross and the laity did not kneel at communion.[34] Susanne Lachenicht further noted that "both conforming and non-conforming churches in London and Dublin still had a consistory," which was typical of Presbyterian rather than Anglican governance.[35] These and other differences from Anglican orthodoxy persisted in both cities until the early-19th century.[36]

Idiosyncrasies in Huguenot conformity to the Church of England were also manifest in the British North American colonies. In 1713 Anglican Commissary Gideon Johnston, who represented the Bishop of London in the Carolinas, reported that conforming Huguenot churches there were playing "fast and loose with the Canons and Rubrick." Johnston wrote that the minister of the French parish at Goose Creek "baptized with and without the sign of the Cross… and would administer the Communion kneeling, sitting, or standing as People would have him."[37] Evidently, the conforming Huguenots in England were not alone in their selective use of ritual. Several modern studies of colonial Anglicanism have made similar observations by noting that Calvinists who conformed to Anglicanism tended to retain certain Calvinist proclivities. John F. Woolverton noted that many "Episcopalian ministers in South Carolina [where Huguenots were 10 per cent of the population at one point] were theological Calvinists and were not high churchmen."[38] More recently John K. Nelson

---

33 Robin Gwynn, *Huguenot Heritage: The History and Contribution of the Huguenots in Britain*. 2nd rev. ed. (Brighton: 2001), 128.

34 Cottret, *Huguenots in England*, 178.

35 "Huguenots in Ireland, Britain and Brandenburg-Prussia (1660–1750)," in *Religious Refugees in Europe, Asia and North America*, (ed.) Lachenicht, 107–20. The consistory was composed of the minister and elected elders within Calvinist churches. It exercised discipline within the church and decided who could be admitted to membership and to communion. It was also charged with making financial decisions.

36 Lachenicht, "Huguenots in Ireland, Britain and Brandenburg, Prussia," 115. Raymond Hylton also studied the Huguenots in Ireland and saw the conflict between conformity and non-conformity as a "natural outgrowth" of the earlier tensions in France between the Huguenot "*Politiques*" who were willing to compromise and more militant Calvinists who advocated resistance. *Ireland's Huguenots and Their Refuge. 1662–1745: An Unlikely Haven* (Brighton: 2005), 179–80.

37 Amy Friedlander (ed.), "Commissary Johnston's Report, 1713," *South Carolina Historical Magazine* (1982), 260. The Bishop of London oversaw Anglican churches in the colonies.

38 John Woolverton, *Colonial Anglicanism in North America* (Detroit: 1984), 163–64.

argued that conforming Huguenots in colonial Virginia also diverged from standard Anglican practices.[39] This was despite the fact that Virginia was one of the colonies where the Church of England was the established church.

A growing number of important scholarly works devoted to the North American Huguenots have emerged in the past decade or so. Bertrand Van Ruymbeke is the leading voice among this new generation of scholars of the North American Refuge. Although most of his research has focused on the South Carolina Huguenots, he has framed this experience in a broader Atlantic world perspective and has done significant research in French, British, and American sources. The author of numerous articles and a scholarly monograph, Van Ruymbeke has also edited several volumes of collected essays devoted to various aspects of the Huguenot experience. All are excellent sources and models for further research.

In his scholarly monograph *From New Babylon to Eden: The Huguenots and Their Migration to Colonial South Carolina*, Van Ruymbeke asserted that Kingdon's "interpretation is insightful yet incomplete." According to Van Ruymbeke, it "does not explain why the Charleston Huguenots, the wealthiest and most Anglicized refugees in the colony opted for nonconformity, at least collectively." Meanwhile, smaller, rural congregations were more likely to conform because they encountered difficulty in "recruiting and maintaining French-speaking Calvinist pastors." Rather than shut their doors, they sought assistance from the Church of England. Through the auspices of the Society for the Propagation of the Gospel (SPG), the Church of England was eager to send pastors and to help defray expenses for congregations that conformed.[40] Van Ruymbeke also argued that the Church of England gave Huguenots the opportunity to transfer their sense of allegiance from Louis XIV to the British monarch. Thus, "conformity provided them with invaluable compensation for the post-Revocation loss of their legitimate monarchy."[41] As Van Ruymbeke and others have observed, the lack of a resident bishop in the colonies gave conforming churches greater ecclesiastical flexibility to forge a low church Anglican-Huguenot hybrid.[42] Therefore, while most Huguenot churches

---

39 John Nelson. *A Blessed Company: Parishes, Parsons, and Parishioners in Anglican Virginia, 1690–1776* (Chapel Hill: 2001), 98.

40 These observations coincide with mine for the conforming Huguenot congregation in New Rochelle. Carlo, *Huguenot Refugees*, 55–59.

41 Van Ruymbeke, *From New Babylon to Eden*, 97–99.

42 "High church" and "low church" are used to differentiate between different forms of Anglicanism. Low church Anglicanism was popular in the American colonies. The more ritualistic high church Anglicanism "stressed historical continuity with Catholic Christianity and upheld a 'high' conception of the authority of the Church, of the claims

conformed in South Carolina, the foundations of Huguenot-Anglican religious life "were...erected...on existing Calvinist congregational structures." But, in the 18th century these churches "all went through crises of varying seriousness until the Huguenots and their descendants finally became full-fledged members of the Church of England.[43]

Conforming Huguenots in New Rochelle, New York also played "fast and loose with the canons and rubric."[44] The Reverend Pierre Stouppe, who was educated at the Geneva Academy, had been recommended in 1717 by the Threadneedle Street Church in London to become the pastor of the independent French church in Orange Quarter, South Carolina. He soon left this quarrelsome congregation to become the pastor of the Huguenot church in Charleston. In 1723 he conformed to the Church of England and went to London to be ordained as an Anglican priest by the Bishop of London. The following year he returned to the colonies, this time to the Anglican-Huguenot congregation in New Rochelle, New York. This church had conformed in 1709 and its minister had recently passed away. Stouppe remained as pastor of this church until he died in 1760.

Stouppe's French manuscript sermons provide important insights into his theology, which was virtually unchanged since his days as the pastor of the Huguenot Church in Charleston. Indeed, in New Rochelle on 2 May 1725 he preached almost verbatim the same sermon on I John 3:10 that he had previously delivered in Charleston on 24 January 1720. Stouppe asserted that faith alone was needed for justification, but that good works should follow justification. These good works made it possible to identify a child of God.[45] Van Ruymbeke concurs with this analysis and wrote that repeated use of this sermon "most significantly shows that conformity did not in the least alter [Stouppe's] theological message...that [was] essentially Calvinistic."[46] Stouppe's discussion of the need for good works was very similar to what Calvinists

---

of the episcopate and of the nature of the Sacraments." In the 17th century High Churchmen supported the divine right of kings and were closely allied with the Stuart dynasty. *Oxford Dictionary of the Christian Church*, (eds.) F.L. Cross and E.A. Livingstone (Oxford: 1974), s.v. High Churchmen. Concerning the Anglican-Huguenot church in New Rochelle, see Carlo, *Huguenot Refugees*, 81–102.

43   Van Ruymbeke, *From New Babylon to Eden*, 131–32.
44   Paula Wheeler Carlo, "'Playing Fast and Loose with the Canons and Rubrick': French Anglicanism in Colonial New Rochelle, New York" *Journal of the Canadian Church Historical Society* 44 (2002), 35–50.
45   Seventy-eight sermons are extant. Pierre Stouppe, "Sermons," 1724–1741. Library, Huguenot Society of America, New York, New York. For further analysis of sermons see Carlo, *Huguenot Refugees*, 85–94.
46   Van Ruymbeke, *From New Babylon to Eden*, 153–54.

referred to as signs of election or visible sainthood. Additional references underscoring Stouppe's Calvinism appear in later sermons. For instance, he frequently mentioned *les Elus* (the Elect). Another characteristic of Stouppe's lingering Calvinism was his view of the sacraments. Many Anglicans, like Roman Catholics, acknowledge the existence of seven sacraments. But Anglicans accord higher status to baptism and communion (which are observed by nearly all Protestants) and usually refer to the remaining sacraments as "the lesser five."[47] Stouppe went beyond this categorization and derisively referred to the Anglican "lesser five" as *les cinq prétendus sacrements*. Moreover, in at least one sermon he criticized signing of the cross, which was typical in the Church of England as well as in the Roman Catholic Church.[48]

Further evidence of lingering Calvinism among Anglican-Huguenots in New Rochelle is apparent in the church records. After the church conformed in 1709, the records continued to use the Calvinist term *ancien* (elder) rather than the Anglican term "churchwarden" until Stouppe's death in 1760.[49] Also, the records were written almost exclusively in French until then, despite the fact that Stouppe was proficient in English. Stouppe's command of English was evident in his letters to the Secretary of the Society for the Propagation of the Gospel in London. Unlike his sermons and the church records, these letters do not suggest that Stouppe was still a Calvinist whose interpretation of Anglican doctrines and rituals was more in line with conforming Huguenots elsewhere in the British Atlantic world.[50]

---

47 Eighteenth-century Anglicanism was evolving and may have been understood differently by different people, especially in the American colonies where there was no resident bishop. Still, the trend within high church Anglicanism was to consider Baptism and Communion "sacraments of the Gospel," while the lesser five were often called "sacraments" but because they were not sacraments of the Gospel ordained by Christ, they did not have the same nature as the other two and were partly "apostolic corruptions" as the 1571 version of Article 25 of the Thirty-Nine Articles states. Since the 19th century, Anglican theologians and subsequent versions of the Thirty-Nine Articles have usually regarded the lesser five more positively as "sacraments of the church."

48 Stouppe, "Section 48 of the Catechism," in "Sermons." *Les cinq prétendus sacrements* is a play on words. In France, Protestantism was contemptuously referred to as *la religion prétendue réformée*, signifying Stouppe's contempt for the five "pretend" sacraments.

49 Manuscript records are at Trinity-St. Paul Episcopal Church, New Rochelle.

50 Society for the Propagation of the Gospel in Foreign Parts, "Records." (1701ff.) Series "A," vols. 1–26; Series "B," vols. 1–3, 10–21; Series "C," vol. 1. (Yorkshire, England: Microform Academic Publishers, 1964). These records are available at major academic and research libraries. The letters are arranged chronologically, so letters from the Anglican-Huguenots in New Rochelle are scattered throughout the collection. References to pertinent letters appear in Carlo, *Huguenot Refugees*, 58–69, 164–65.

Anglican conformity was financially beneficial for the French Church in New Rochelle and its minister. The minister received a yearly salary from the Society for the Propagation of the Gospel, which supplemented the meager amount that the congregation was able to pay him. Soon after conformity the congregation received a license to construct a new church. Prominent Anglican politicians in New York sent contributions for this purpose. Even Queen Anne sent a royal patent along with a solid silver chalice to be used for communion. Whenever the need arose, the SPG sent Bibles, prayer books, and catechisms.[51] The SPG also expected the minister to Christianize African slaves in New Rochelle. Indeed, the Church of England was more active in its ministry to slaves than most other Protestant denominations in the colonies, including the French and Dutch Reformed.[52] Conformity, however, did not confer any obvious financial advantages for individuals in New Rochelle. Assessment of New Rochelle tax lists from the 1690s through the 1760s indicates an ongoing pattern of humble living standards for most residents and several ministers noted that their congregations were not prosperous.[53] So Kingdon's analysis only has limited applicability for individual New Rochelle Anglican Huguenots.

There was also a non-conforming French church in New Rochelle. Although a majority of church members voted to conform to Anglicanism in 1709, this decision provoked significant controversy from a determined and influential minority. They maintained a separate, non-conforming congregation in New Rochelle for most of the 18th century.[54] Initially they met in the home of Alexandre Allaire, who had been a church elder at the time of conformity. This congregation was able to survive as long as it did because of financial and ministerial assistance from the French Church of New York. Moreover, the numbers of non-conformists increased as couples produced children. In 1725 Pierre Stouppe reported that thirty families in New Rochelle had not conformed. He also wrote that they mocked the liturgy and ceremonies of the Church of England and threatened to disassociate themselves from anyone who joined

---

51   Carlo, *Huguenot Refugees*, 59, 203 notes 100–104.
52   Carlo, *Huguenot Refugees*, 161–66.
53   Carlo, *Huguenot Refugees*, 132–34. See 218–19, fn. 63 for contemporary primary sources attesting to the limited financial resources of New Rochelle residents.
54   They did not have a full- or part-time minister after 1764. In the 1770s Methodists and Presbyterians held services in the non-conforming church. In 1808 a Presbyterian congregation took over the former non-conforming church. Today the First Presbyterian Church of New Rochelle tries to preserve the memory of the Huguenot roots of the town and of its congregation.

the conforming church.[55] By that time they had built their own church about 200 yards from the conforming church and were engaged in a land dispute with the Anglican-Huguenot congregation.[56]

The Église Française du St. Esprit in New York was more prosperous than the financially-strapped congregation in New Rochelle. Indeed, the church maintained two ministers in the 1690s and again in the early 1700s. The minister of St. Esprit was expected to visit the nonconforming church in New Rochelle four times a year to perform baptisms and marriages and to administer communion. Some ministers accepted this responsibility without complaint. But the Reverend Louis Rou (pastor of St. Esprit from 1710 to 1750) chafed at the task and insisted that the non-conformists should attend the conforming church to mitigate dissention in New Rochelle. In contrast, the Reverend Jean Joseph Brumeau de Moulinars eagerly embraced this activity after the elders of the New York church hired him as an assistant minister in 1718. Eventually legal conflicts between Rou and the church elders prompted Moulinars to leave New York to become the full-time minister to the non-conformists in New Rochelle from 1725 until his death in 1741.[57] After his death the non-conformists relied on the part-time services of the minister of St. Esprit, which did not hire a second minister after the departure of Moulinars.

Since there were more families of Huguenot ancestry in New York City, St. Esprit was better positioned to survive as an independent French Reformed congregation. Another advantage was that some Huguenot families in New York were prosperous and better able to support a church than were the New Rochelle Huguenots. As Jon Butler noted, "the city's richest Huguenots...competed for business with the city's richest Dutch and English merchants, while

---

55 Anglican-Huguenot churches in England and in the colonies used French translations of the *Book of Common Prayer* and of the Anglican catechism. The prayer book and the catechism had been translated by Jean Durel who was born in 1625 in the French-speaking, English-controlled island of Jersey, where many Huguenots settled before 1685. Durel wanted to facilitate Huguenot connections with Anglicanism. He later became pastor of the French Church of the Savoy, one of the largest conforming churches in London. Robin Gwynn observed that in the 1680s some people noted that Durel's *La Liturgie* was at variance with the English version. Moreover, both Anglican and French Calvinist forms of worship were blended in the Savoy and in other conforming churches in England, prompting Gwynn to refer to them as "amphibious." Gwynn, *Huguenot Heritage*, 127.

56 Stouppe, Letter to the SPG Secretary, May 12, 1725, "SPG Records," ser. A, vol. 19, no. 156–159.

57 For further discussion Paula Wheeler Carlo, "The Huguenot Soul: the Calvinism of Reverend Louis Rou," in *The Religious Culture of the Huguenots, 1660–1750*, (ed.) Anne Dunan-Page (Aldershot: 2006), 110–12.

poor refugees...took charity to survive." Still, Butler's assessment of New York City Huguenot tax categories between 1695 and 1735 indicates a decrease of Huguenots in the bottom third and an increase in Huguenots in the middle and top third of city taxpayers.[58] This is in stark contrast to the modest and even poor incomes of New Rochelle residents for several decades after conformity. Obviously, Anglican conformity did not alter an individual's socio-economic status in New Rochelle. What remains unclear is if the New York Huguenots became more successful (financially, socially, and politically) after they began to attend Trinity Church or if they switched their allegiance to Trinity after achieving some success and they simply wanted to move in the predominantly-English circles that they deemed appropriate for their affluent status.[59] In this connection, Carla Gardina Pestana has asserted that "rural Huguenots and those less well off financially seemed to have been less inclined to assimilate into the local established church."[60] But this statement warrants further examination. For instance, relatively-prosperous Huguenot congregations in Charleston and in New York City remained independent, while the financially-strapped congregation in New Rochelle conformed to the Church of England as did rural congregations in South Carolina. In short, Huguenot conformity to Anglicanism is a multi-faceted issue that defies simple explanations and generalizations.

Several conditions in New York City presented challenges to an independent Huguenot church. Huguenots who were dissatisfied with conditions in St. Esprit or with its minister had a wide variety of churches to choose from. The legal conflict with Louis Rou in the 1720s initiated a pattern of attrition in church membership as evidenced by a dramatic decline in the number of baptisms after 1730.[61] Despite these defections, particularly to nearby Trinity Church (an Anglican congregation), St. Esprit endured as an independent French Reformed church until the American Revolution. During that war St. Esprit was seized by the British and the building fell into disrepair. When the congregation reassembled in 1796, they found that the church building needed to be replaced. They also lacked a minister. Six years later they were still unable to afford to build a new church and to find a French-speaking Calvinist minister. Hence, the Église Française du St. Esprit decided to become Episcopalian in 1802 so that the church could claim a financial bequest from a deceased

---

58   Butler, *Huguenots in America*, 157.
59   Precise analysis is difficult because early records from Trinity Church have been lost.
60   Carla Gardina Pestana, *Protestant Empire: Religion and the Making of the British Atlantic World* (Philadelphia: 2009), 162.
61   Jon Butler analyzed the declining numbers. *Huguenots in America*, 194–98.

parishioner and to facilitate the search for a resident full-time minister.[62] Services at St. Esprit today blend Anglican and Huguenot worship traditions and one or more French-language services are conducted every month.[63]

The situation differed in New Paltz, located in the Hudson Valley about halfway between New York City and Albany. Here, the Church of England made fewer inroads than it did in New York City or in New Rochelle. Instead, the Dutch Reformed Church and Dutch language and culture influenced the Huguenots and Walloons of New Paltz during the 17th and 18th centuries. Consequently, whenever the New Paltz Church lacked a minister it usually relied on the minister of the Dutch Reformed Church in Kingston, New York to perform marriages, baptisms, and communion. Kingston was about sixteen miles away, so it is likely that the faithful only trekked there when they required the services of an ordained minister.[64] Apparently they attended services in the Reformed Church in New Paltz where sermons were read by a lay reader, who was probably the schoolmaster, an elder, or a deacon. This practice was common in various denominations, especially in rural communities in colonial America, because it was difficult to recruit and maintain qualified ministers.[65] Additionally, most ministers (unless they were desperate or had a questionable past) preferred to accept positions with larger, more prosperous congregations in cities.

Unlike many Huguenot congregations in the British colonies, the New Paltz Church did not rely on the Threadneedle Street Church in London when they sought a minister. This is not surprising, because most of the founders of New Paltz did not come to British North American colonies via England. Rather

---

62 For additional analysis and sources see Carlo, "Anglican Conformity and Nonconformity among the Huguenots of Colonial New York," *From Strangers to Citizens*, 313–21. For discussions concerning these problems and decisions, see New-York Historical Society, Manuscript Collection, "Proceedings of the Trustees of l'Église Réformée Protestante Française à la Nouvelle York, 1796–1802." The classic history of the New York Church is John Maynard, *The Huguenot Church of New York: A History of the French Church of Saint Esprit* (New York: 1938). Although this book is short on modern historical analysis and methods, it continues to be an invaluable source of narrative information on the New York Church and its ministers. Many of the church's records have been published in Alfred Wittmeyer (ed.), *Registers of the Births, Marriages, and Deaths of the Église Française á la Nouvelle York from 1688 to 1804* (1886; repr. Baltimore: 1968).
63 For more information, see http://stesprit.org/.
64 Communion was observed four times annually in Reformed churches. Anglican churches in colonial America adhered to this pattern.
65 For further discussion of the French Church of New Paltz and sources, see Carlo, *Huguenot Refugees*, 44–54.

they had spent several years in the German Palatinate before migrating to America. Although several New Paltz founders came to the colonies via England, their stay in England was brief. During the 18th century increasing numbers of people who were either Dutch or of Dutch ancestry moved into New Paltz. They were not joined by significant numbers of people who were English or of English descent until the late-18th and 19th centuries. Hence, the Dutch and French languages were more prevalent than English in this area for most of the 18th century. Because of these factors, Anglican conformity was not an issue in the shift of religious allegiances for the Huguenots and Walloons of New Paltz. Like French-speaking Calvinists elsewhere in the colonies they found it difficult to find and recruit Francophone Reformed ministers, but they sought assistance from Dutch Reformed bodies, such as the Classis of Amsterdam, to meet their religious needs.[66]

Huguenots and Walloons had a fairly strong presence in the late-17th century in Staten Island, located just south of New York City.[67] A French-speaking congregation was established in Staten Island around 1663. At that time the French-speaking population was poor and their numbers were few; accordingly they did not have a full-time resident minister. Instead they relied on the Reverend Samuel Drisius of New York, who was proficient in both French and Dutch, to visit every two months to administer communion and perform marriages and baptisms.[68] The Huguenot population in Staten Island increased significantly after 1685, which led to the construction of a larger church building in 1698 to accommodate the expanding population. In fact, this Huguenot church was constructed before either the Dutch or English built churches on Staten Island. Consequently, in the 1690s the Reverend David de Bonrepos (a former pastor of the Huguenot Church in New Rochelle) was the only resident clergyman in Staten Island. He served as the minister to thirty-six French, forty English, and forty-four Dutch persons, in what seems to have been a thriving congregation.[69]

---

66   For more discussion see Carlo, *Huguenot Refugees*, 74–78. A recent dissertation places greater emphasis on Dutch influences during the 1720–1760 period than my work did, but it also supports the relatively late (post-1760) English influence. Kenneth Shefsiek, "Stone House Days: Constructing Cultural Hybridity in the Hudson Valley" (Ph.D. diss., University of Georgia, 2010).

67   Today Staten Island is one of five boroughs, along with Manhattan, Brooklyn, Queens, and the Bronx, which compose New York City. In the 17th and 18th centuries New York City meant Manhattan.

68   Charles Leng and William Davis, *Staten Island and its People: A History*, vol. 1 (New York: 1930), 105.

69   Leng and Davis, *Staten Island*, 1: 136, 139.

De Bonrepos never conformed to the Church of England, but he was cordial and supportive of Anglican initiatives in Staten Island. "He allowed the Anglican missionary Aeneas MacKenzie to conduct services in the French Church in 1709, the year New Rochelle's congregation conformed to the Church of England, and in 1711 he allowed Huguenot children to attend MacKenzie's catechism classes."[70] De Bonrepos lost English parishioners after St. Andrew's Church, an Anglican congregation, was constructed in Staten Island in 1712. Four years later, he lost Dutch members to the newly-constructed Dutch Reformed Church.[71] French membership began to decline in the 1720s as the aging de Bonrepos permitted William Harrison, the new Anglican minister, to preach to the Huguenot congregation. By the time of de Bonrepos's death in 1734, many Huguenots were already attending St. Andrew's Church and the elders decided to close the Staten Island French Church.[72] Unfortunately, the records of the French Church in Staten Island are not extant, making it difficult to recreate congregational life. Accordingly, the best way to trace religious allegiances of Huguenots and their descendants is through the extant records of other churches. St. Andrew's Church, in particular, attracted many Huguenot descendants. The Dutch Reformed and Moravian churches were other options. So far, the movement of Staten Island Huguenots to different congregations has not undergone a rigorous analysis.[73]

Since 2000 the New York Huguenots have received increased attention from several researchers. Neil Kamil utilized a multi-disciplinary methodology, including interpretation of material culture, to challenge the thesis of rapid assimilation and widespread conformity to Anglicanism. Using an Atlantic perspective, he explained how Huguenots in southwestern France developed clandestine worship following the devastating siege of La Rochelle in 1628. He traced their exodus to Great Britain and later to New York, where secretive patterns developed in France continued. Kamil argued that the presumed disappearance of the Huguenots in their places of refuge was instead a tactic deliberately cultivated by Huguenots as a means of survival. Despite this, a sense of identity was maintained by Huguenot artisans whose handiwork,

---

70 Butler, *Huguenots in America*, 191.
71 Leng and Davis, *Staten Island*, 1: 434–35.
72 Butler, *Huguenots in America*, 191–92.
73 The published version of the records of St. Andrew's Church is William Davis, Charles Leng and Royden Vosburgh, *The Church of St. Andrew, Richmond, Staten Island: Its History, Vital Records, and Gravestone Inscriptions* (Staten Island: 1925). Family genealogies, some of which are published, are often helpful for tracing changes in religious affiliation. Changes were often prompted by exogamous marriages.

such as wooden cabinets, often displayed symbolic details and secret compartments that were emblematic of their underground existence in France. This seeming disappearance helped to reduce potential conflicts with host populations in their places of refuge. Instead of emphasizing Huguenot conformity to Anglicanism, Kamil explored the attraction that some Huguenots in the New York area developed for Quakerism.[74] Like the Huguenots, many Quakers were artisans and they had endured persecution in Great Britain and in some British colonies in the mid-17th century.

Catharine Randall studied the radical and unorthodox tendencies among those French Protestants known as Camisards. In *From a Far Country*, she began the story in the midst of persecution in France in the late-17th and early-18th centuries. Randall then examined the writings and activities of several of these more mystical Protestants in British North America—Elias Neau in New York, Gabriel Bernon in Massachusetts and Ezéchiel Carré in Narragansett, Rhode Island and later Massachusetts.[75] Although she did not follow the story of the Camisards and Huguenots beyond the early 1700s, Randall asserted that their religious beliefs and practices persisted. She also argued that they exercised a broader influence outside French Protestant circles. For example, the Puritan leader Cotton Mather promoted the Huguenots and their allegedly steadfast devotion in the face of persecution as a model for Puritans whose own piety had declined by the late-17th century.

The Massachusetts Huguenots have received less attention from researchers than their co-religionists in South Carolina, New York, or even Virginia. This is partly due to the comparatively small Huguenot population in the New England region. Source limitations, such as the lack of records for the French Church of Boston, also play a role in this relative neglect. Despite these drawbacks, the Huguenot experience in New England deserves further investigation and analysis. The most viable research option for this community is to utilize Butler's model that relies heavily on secular records supplemented by models like Randall's or mine that focus on the religious writings of prominent Huguenot individuals like Le Mercier, Bernon and Carré.

Numerous essay collections concerning Huguenots in the Atlantic world have been published since 2000. Some of these can serve as information sources and models for future research. One such publication is *From Strangers to Citizens: The Integration of Immigrant Communities in Britain, Ireland, and*

---

74 Neil Kamil, *Fortress of the Soul: Violence, Metaphysics, and Material Life in the Huguenots' New World, 1517–1751* (Baltimore: 2005).

75 Catharine Randall, *From a Far Country: Camisards and Huguenots in the Atlantic World* (Athens, GA: 2009).

Colonial America, 1550–1750, edited by Randolph Vigne and Charles Littleton.[76] Another essential collection is *Memory and Identity: The Huguenots in France and the Atlantic Diaspora*, edited by Bertrand Van Ruymbeke and Randy J. Sparks.[77] *The Religious Culture of the Huguenots, 1660–1750*, edited by Anne Dunan-Page, is also useful.[78] *The Huguenots: History and Memory in Transnational Context*, edited by David J.B. Trim is another fine source.[79] *Les Huguenots et l'Atlantique*, prepared under the direction of Mickaël Augeron, Didier Poton, and Bertrand Van Ruymbeke is a fascinating, lavishly-illustrated collection.[80]

Several general essay collections or monographs are worth consulting. *Religious Refugees in Europe, Asia and North America (6th–21st Century)* provides a broad historical perspective for Huguenots and other refugee populations. Susanne Lachenicht's essay compared the Huguenot experience in Ireland, Britain, and Brandenburg-Prussia to refute the notion of their complete and rapid assimilation.[81] Instead of abandoning their mother tongue, she asserted that the Huguenots instead adopted a "pragmatic bilingualism" and possessed "hybrid identities" well into the 18th century. Nevertheless, Lachenicht conceded that "at the end of the 19th century, they seem to have blended into the hosting society." Even so Huguenot descendants to this day often take pride in their ancestry, thus belying the notion of disappearance or loss of identity.[82] *The First Prejudice: Religious Tolerance and Intolerance in Early America*, edited by Chris Beneke and Christopher Grenda, contains

---

76 Vigne and Littleton, *From Strangers to Citizens*. Parts VI, VII, VIII, and IX are the most pertinent.

77 Van Ruymbeke and Sparks, *Memory and Identity*. Essays by Van Ruymbeke, Littleton, Butler, Goodfriend, and Cottret are the most relevant for conformity.

78 Dunan-Page (ed.), *The Religious Culture of the Huguenots*. The most pertinent essays are those by Gwynn, Lachenicht, Larminie, and Carlo and the editor's introduction.

79 Trim, *The Huguenots: History and Memory in Transnational Context*. The essays by Gwynn and McGraw are particularly useful.

80 Augeron, et al., *Les Huguenots et l'Atlantique*. All essays are worthwhile, but the selections by Van Ruymbeke, Henneton, Hylton, Chabrol, and Carlo and Boyden are the most relevant.

81 "Huguenots in Ireland, Britain and Brandenburg-Prussia (1660–1750)," in *Religious Refugees in Europe, Asia and North America*, (ed.) Lachenicht, 107–20. The essay by Van Ruymbeke and the commentaries by Canny and Schnurmann are also essential reading.

82 Lachenicht, *Religious Refugees*, 119–20. In "Huguenot Immigrants and the Formation of National Identities," Lachenicht compared the Huguenot experience in several European Protestant states and North America and concluded that Huguenots "preserved their distinct Calvinist faith and French cultural identity for at least two to three generations" (331).

several essays that provide useful background material.[83] Finally, Carla Gardina Pestana's *Protestant Empire: Religion and the Making of the British Atlantic World* provides an overview of various religious groups, including the Huguenots, within an imperial context from around 1500 until after the American Revolution.

4   Conclusion

Conformity to the Church of England was not typical for individual Huguenots or for Huguenot congregations in New England, where Calvinist churches predominated during the colonial era. In New York the situation was more complex, varying from congregation to congregation. In the early 18th century the French Church in New Rochelle split into two congregations: one conformed but retained many French Calvinist beliefs and practices, while the other congregation did not conform. During the 18th century the church in New Paltz gradually became a Dutch Reformed congregation. In Staten Island the Huguenot Church disintegrated and individuals were dispersed among several denominations, with the Church of England being one of the leading choices. Finally, the Église Française du St. Esprit in New York City became Episcopalian (the American counterpart of the Church of England) in 1802. Today the church blends Anglican and Huguenot worship traditions.

When we examine Anglican conformity in New York or Massachusetts, we must consider the respective differences from other colonies where Huguenots settled. In contrast to South Carolina and Virginia, the Church of England was not established in New York or Massachusetts. The earliest European settlers of New York were sent by the Dutch West India Company and the Calvinist Dutch Reformed Church maintained a strong presence in the colony when it was known as New Netherland. Following the English takeover of the colony in 1664, Dutch influences remained strong and even persisted into the 1800s. The Dutch had also established religious toleration which prompted a wide variety of religious and ethnic groups to settle in 17th-century New Netherland. Since toleration and diversity continued under English control, it is not surprising that the Church of England was never established in New York. Massachusetts and New England in general were dominated by English Calvinists (Congregationalists) during the colonial period. Congregationalism was even the established church in several colonies. Consequently, the Church

---

83 Beneke and Grenda (eds.), *The First Prejudice*. The essays by Landsman, Goodfriend, Stanwood, and the introduction by the editors are especially useful.

of England made even fewer inroads in New England than in New York. Because of these factors, the model of Huguenot conformity to Anglicanism was not as prominent or compelling in New York and Massachusetts as it was in Virginia and South Carolina or in Great Britain itself. Nevertheless, further research is warranted to ensure a more accurate and comprehensive understanding of this complex topic.[84]

---

[84] Robin Gwynn reached a similar conclusion: "More studies are needed to show how assimilation took place during the 18th century; the nature of the English-speaking congregations in which the descendants of refugees ended up; and how the strong memory of the first refugees was dulled and (in some cases) their resistance to conformity gradually eroded." "Strains of Worship," 151.

CHAPTER 15

The Huguenot Refuge and European Imperialism

Owen Stanwood

1   Introduction

The creation of the Huguenot Refuge occurred during an age of empire. While the *dragonnades* roamed France and thousands of refugees crossed the English Channel and the Alps, representatives of European states attempted to settle new lands and exert their power in the farthest reaches of the world, from North America to East Asia. Not surprisingly, more than a few refugees joined the ranks of European who sought to colonize and conquer other lands. By the middle of the 18th century descendants of the refugees lived throughout British America, in the Dutch Cape Colony, in Suriname and various Caribbean islands, and even, in smaller numbers, in the Far East. The Huguenot Refuge, therefore, was a global phenomenon, and the consequences of Louis XIV's revocation of the Edict of Nantes stretched far beyond Europe.

While historians have long acknowledged the global dimensions of the Refuge, however, its contours remain poorly understood. To be sure, many historians, from the 19th century to the present, have narrated the histories of refugee communities overseas. Thanks to the genealogical interest of their descendants, for instance, the small refugee communities in colonial America are among the best documented in the world, and the several hundred Huguenots who landed in South Africa have received similar attention.[1] At the same time, historians have spent far less time examining the larger structure and purpose of these communities, or the links that existed between them. Historians of the Refuge have tended to view overseas communities as aberrations—understandably so, as only a small percentage of migrants, perhaps two per cent at most, ventured beyond Europe.[2] Scholars of empires, meanwhile, have rarely viewed the Huguenots as significant actors in their histories, since

---

[1] On the historiography of Huguenots in America see especially Geneviève and Philippe Joutard, "L'Amerique huguenote est-elle un paradoxe?" *BSHPF* 151 (2005), 65–90; and on South Africa, Philippe Denis, "The Cape Huguenots and Their Legacy in Apartheid South Africa," in *Memory and Identity: The Huguenots in France and the Atlantic Diaspora*, (eds.) Bertrand Van Ruymbeke and Randy J. Sparks (Columbia, S.C.: 2003), 285–309.

[2] For the estimate of numbers see Bertrand Van Ruymbeke, "Le Refuge dans les marches atlantiques: Les huguenots du nouveau monde," *Diasporas: Histoire et sociétés* 18 (2012), 17–18.

the many communities of refugees in the Atlantic and beyond tended to remain small and quickly assimilate into their respective host cultures.³

Nonetheless, territories beyond Europe played a key role in the history of the Refuge, and Huguenots had a significant impact on imperial histories. While their numbers were far less than their coreligionists in Germany, Britain, or the Netherlands, Huguenots constituted a significant percentage of the smaller settler populations in many of the places they ventured. Beyond that, the promise of new worlds played a substantial role in the lives even of those refugees who never left Europe. Schemes for overseas colonies appeared as early as the 1550s, proliferated during the 1680s and 90s, and continued well into the 18th century, especially during times, like the 1760s, when French authorities cracked down on Protestant worship. Thus, many refugees understood overseas emigration as an option—even if they did not themselves take advantage of it. Finally, a focus on Huguenots overseas allows us to better note how imperial statesmen attempted to utilize a European crisis to transform their states. Looking down on the Refuge from a vantage point far above the Atlantic Ocean, we see Huguenots setting off on any number of quixotic tasks, from making wine in Virginia to converting Indians in New England, to setting up agricultural and shipping entrepots in southern Africa and the Mascarene Islands. These efforts all fit into a common imperial context: leaders of the British and Dutch empires believed that the skills of these luckless refugees could help to transform global politics and economics.

At the heart of this global refuge was a tension between the Huguenots and their sponsors, between dreams of Eden and desires for empire. Like other Europeans, French Protestants had been raised on stories of the wonders—and dangers—that lay beyond Europe, and indeed, Huguenots had been disproportionately represented in early French colonial efforts. Moreover, as Myriam Yardeni has aptly noted, French Protestants were masters of utopian literature, and often situated their ideal societies in mythic lands beyond Europe.⁴ The real Huguenot colonies that appeared after the revocation of the Edict of Nantes bore the marks of these utopian ambitions. Colonial projectors from Henri Duquesne to Charles de Rochefort represented overseas colonies as earthly paradises where refugees could live simply

---

3 For an attempt to place the Huguenots in imperial history see Owen Stanwood, "Between Empire and Eden: Huguenot Refugees and the Promise of New Worlds," *American Historical Review* 118 (2013), 1319–44.

4 Myriam Yardeni, *Utopie et révolte sous Louis XIV* (Paris: 1980); Yardeni, "Protestantisme et utopie en France aux XVIe et XVIIe siècles," *Diasporas: Histoire et sociétés* 1 (2002), 51–58.

in the peace of the gospel—and where French Protestants could control their own destinies. However benevolent their intentions may have been, imperial leaders cared more about strategy than utopia, and more about advancing their own state interests than supporting the French Protestant church in exile. Huguenots began arguing with their sponsors—and amongst themselves—about what these new worlds meant, and what duties they owed to their sponsors. The tensions between ideals and realities meant that few of these experiments lived up to their great promise. At the same time, however, many refugees became adept imperial subjects who learned to gain advantages for themselves and their families by making themselves useful to their powerful patrons.

2   Engineering the Global Refuge

From the time of the Reformation onward Protestants played leading roles in French overseas exploration and settlement. Huguenots dominated many of the places that faced the Atlantic—Norman towns like Dieppe and Honfleur as well as La Rochelle—and a disproportionate number of merchants and mariners embraced the Reformed religion. Their leadership in navigation gave Huguenots an important role in the French state, and Protestant leaders like the Admiral of France Gaspard de Coligny hoped that by proving their mettle in overseas endeavors Protestants would prove their importance to the king and realm. Even Catholics could not deny the Huguenots' usefulness on the world stage. At the same time, Atlantic trade and colonization opened up another possibility for French Protestants, that of escape. New worlds opened up the promise of new societies and polities, and perhaps the chance to build French Protestant places where Huguenots could be dominant rather than merely tolerated. These visions did not come to pass, but continued to influence Huguenot perceptions of the worlds beyond Europe for centuries.[5]

Driven by these two contradictory goals, to prove themselves to their king and to flee persecution, Huguenots traveled the world in the 16th and 17th centuries.

---

5   The key works on Huguenot global endeavors in the 16th century are those of Frank Lestringant, especially *Le huguenot et le sauvage: L'Amérique et la controverse coloniale en France au temps des guerres de religion (1555–1589)* (Geneva: 2004); and Mickaël Augeron and Laurent Vidal, "Réseaux ou refuges? Logiques d'implantation du Protestantisme aux Amériques au XVIe siècle," in *D'un rivage à l'autre: villes et protestantisme dans l'aire atlantique (XVIe–XVII siècles)*, (eds.) Guy Martinière, Didier Poton, and François Souty (Paris: 1999), 31–61.

Protestants directed or participated in overseas endeavors in Brazil, Florida, and Canada, and while all of these ventures met untimely ends, Protestant reports about these new worlds remained popular, both in and beyond Protestant circles.[6] In the 17th century, after the Wars of Religion ended, Protestants returned in great numbers to global trade. With the exception of the short-lived colony in Tortuga during the 1640s, there were no more Huguenot colonies under the auspices of the French state, but Protestants remained active in overseas colonies. They made up a significant part of the population of Guadeloupe and Saint-Christophe, and while official edicts prevented them from being year-round residents of New France, many Huguenots lived discretely there as well. Others traveled the world and became some of the most famous French travel writers—like Jean-Baptiste Tavernier, Jean Chardin, or Jean Barbot.[7]

These global connections meant that when persecution returned under Louis XIV, many Huguenots were in good position to consider moving overseas—a fact illustrated by the story of Charles de Rochefort. In 1681, as *dragonnades* terrorized Huguenots in Poitou and Louis XIV concocted new legal strictures against Protestantism, the Rotterdam minister published a third edition of his guide to the Caribbean. Entitled *Histoire naturelle et morale des îles Antilles de l'Amérique*, Rochefort's work drew on his experience in the islands during the 1650s, when he had served as a chaplain in the Huguenot colony in Tortuga. The first two editions combined practical descriptions of the French and English islands with some fanciful flourishes—most notably a long digression about the Apalachites, a mythical native empire in the southeastern part of North America that had played host to several groups of French and English migrants. In the new edition, Rochefort added a section of an entirely different nature. Called the "Recit de l'Estate Present des Celebres Colonies De la Virginia, de Marie-Land, de la Caroline, du nouveau Duché d'York, de Pennsylvania, & de la nouvelle Angleterre," the book took a hypothetical journey from Carolina to New England, laying out the various advantages that emigrants would find in the colonies. These were not places for easy riches, Rochefort stressed, but for those who "suffered elsewhere under the shame of

---

[6] For brief overviews of these colonies see Frank Lestringant, "Geneva and America in the Renaissance: The Dream of the Huguenot Refuge, 1555–1600," *SCJ* 26 (1995), 285–95; John T. McGrath, *The French in Early Florida: In the Eye of the Hurricane* (Gainesville, Fla.: 2000).

[7] Gérard Lafleur, *Les protestants aux Antilles françaises du vent sous l'ancien régime* (Basse-Terre, Guadeloupe: 1988); Leslie Choquette, "A Colony of 'Native French Catholics'? The Protestants of New France in the Seventeenth and Eighteenth Centuries," in *Memory and Identity*, (eds.) Van Ruymbeke and Sparks, 255–66.

poverty," there was no place better. "Those who work," the minister wrote, "will be rewarded with bread."[8]

While Rochefort studiously avoided any reference to France's political situation, he clearly aimed his tract at the Huguenots who crowded into cities like Rotterdam, London, and Geneva during the 1680s. The numbers of newcomers were staggering. In Rochefort's home of Rotterdam, for instance, which enjoyed close trading links to France, migrants trickled in during the early-1680s, and that trickle became a flood after the revocation of the Edict of Nantes. By 1686, claimed the Norman Isaac Dumont de Bostaquet, the Dutch port was "almost a French city" because so many refugees, especially from Dieppe, crowded its streets. Rotterdam was not alone; in Geneva 350 refugees passed through each day during the summer of 1687, while London's Threadneedle Street Church hosted dozens of new arrivals who gave testimony of their Protestant beliefs in hopes of gaining aid and acceptance.[9]

The thousands of new arrivals created logistical problems nearly without precedent in 17th-century Europe. In Switzerland, for instance, hordes of refugees inundated small towns, demanding food, lodging, and in many cases medical care. Leaders of the Refuge attempted to make their coreligionists' plight easier by mounting a massive public relations campaign. Powerful Huguenots lobbied European courts to grant land and aid to their people, who they promoted as Protestant heroes. In a characteristic appeal from 1688, a group of refugee ministers targeted "kings, princes, magistrates, and all other evangelical Protestant Christians," calling for a "union and communion of saints." The key outcome of this union would be relief for Huguenots; "give our poor people retreats," the petition requested, "and lands to cultivate wherever they are available."[10]

---

8   For a modern edition see Charles de Rochefort, *Histoire naturelle et morale des îles Antilles de l'Amérique*, (eds.) Bernard Grunberg, Benoît Roux and Josiane Grunberg, vol. 2 (Paris: 2012), 254. (The "Recit" appears on 2: 254–84.) On Rochefort's authorship and life see Everett C. Wilkie, "The Authorship and Purpose of the *Histoire naturelle et morale des îles Antilles*, an Early Huguenot Emigration Guide," *Harvard University Library Bulletin* 38 (1991), 27–82.

9   Dianne W. Ressinger (ed.), *Memoirs of Isaac Dumont de Bostaquet, a Gentleman of Normandy, before and after the Revocation of the Edict of Nantes* (London: 2005), 143; Philippe Joutard, "The Revocation of the Edict of Nantes: End or Renewal of French Protestantism?" in *International Calvinism, 1541–1715*, (ed.) Menna Prestwich (Oxford: 1985), 355; Robin Gwynn (ed.), *Minutes of the Consistory of the French Church of London, 1679–1692* (London: 1994), esp. 184–205.

10 "Les pasteurs, anciens, et autres chrétiens protestants de France réfugiés en Suisse pour le cause de l'Evangile, aux rois, princes, magistrats et tous autres chrétiens protestants évangeliques," BSHPF 9 (1860), 151–52.

The best solution to this problem, leaders of the Refuge determined, was the creation of Huguenot colonies: autonomous French Protestant enclaves within other European states. Mere days after the Revocation the elector of Brandenburg issued the Edict of Potsdam, inviting refugees into his realm, and over the next few years thousands of Huguenots negotiated settlements in German territories. Organizers intended these "colonies" as remnants of the French Protestant church under the protection of benevolent protectors. By remaining autonomous and distinct from their non-French neighbors, these colonies would help refugees retain their language and church structure in preparation for an eventual return to France. At the same time, their presence in strategic or underpopulated territories would provide a boon to their host states. As one petition outlined, the refugees would "augment the number of their subjects," which was "the principal power of States."[11] Or as one English political economist put it, "The Numbers of Refugees here, and in other Countreys near us, are Objects in this Case, both for our Charity to them, and Advantage to ourselves."[12]

These colonial visions abounded in corners of Protestant Europe during the 1680s, but they could also be extended beyond the continent. They key theorist of Huguenot overseas colonization was Henri Duquesne, the son of Louis XIV's leading admiral. Looking out from his perch in the Swiss town of Aubonne on Lac Léman, Duquesne noticed problems with colonization within Europe. While he appreciated the benevolence of Protestant allies, Huguenots would prefer "to live among men of the same Language, of the same Nation, and of the same Religion, [among] which the humors would consequently be less incompatible, than among those who were born in different countries, which is almost always a source of divisions, of quarrels, and of many other inconveniences." In short, true independence was impossible in someone else's land. In addition, Duquesne believed, unlike allies such as the minister Pierre Jurieu, that a return to France was impractical and unwise. He believed a "general persecution in all of Europe" to be more likely than "an imminent deliverance of the Church." And even if they did succeed in convincing Louis to tolerate them, they would remain a minority, "only tolerated, and not dominant." The only solution, Duquesne claimed, was to strike off to new worlds and found new, French Protestant societies,

---

11   Mémoire pour le dessein des colonies, BGE, Collection Court, 17L, fols. 105–08. For an overview of these colonies in Germany and beyond see Susanne Lachenicht, "Intégration ou coexistence? Les huguenots dans les îles britanniques et le Brandebourg," *Diasporas: Histoires et sociétés* 18 (2012), 108–22.

12   Francis Brewster, *Essays on Trade and Navigation* (London: 1695), 18.

independent from both the tyranny of Louis XIV and the influence of foreign allies.[13]

Duquesne sought to realize these ambitions in the Indian Ocean, in a place he called "the Isle of Eden." His descriptions of the place for his prospective colony—eventually revealed to be Île Bourbon (present-day Réunion)—drew heavily from French travel writing and utopian literature, claiming that the island's "bounty and its beauty could make it pass for an earthly paradise." Duquesne envisioned creating a sort of French Calvinist aristocratic utopia in the tropics, a "république" run by a "chef" (clearly Duquesne himself) with the aid of a senate of notables. Missing, however, was any sense of economic objectives. His new Eden was a land of plenty, but not a land of profit. He had no time for colonists who searched for "pearls or precious stones," but sought to create "a society composed of honest men, established in a fertile and agreeable place with the blessings of health, liberty, tranquility of conscience, justice, charity, and above all the hope of safety."[14]

Duquesne's utopian vision represented one half of the impetus for Huguenot overseas expansion. His proposals drew on the colonial vision that originated in Europe itself, but perfected it, allowing the refugees a theoretical independence in Edenic lands beyond the seas. No wonder that many ordinary refugees flocked to such schemes; in 1689 in Amsterdam, for example, hundreds of Huguenots reportedly gathered, ready to take off for Duquesne's tropical republic. At the same time, it took more than just utopian visions to make these overseas ventures happen. As Duquesne himself learned quickly, overseas colonization was expensive, and he needed powerful patrons to provide the necessary ships and supplies. As it happened, however, many of Europe's leaders were all too happy to help Huguenots move overseas—though often with conditions and interests that diverged in significant ways from the visions of Duquesne and Rochefort.

If Duquesne and some of his followers dreamed of Eden, imperial leaders across Europe had visions of profit. The late-1600s saw a proliferation of imperial plans in both the East and West Indies, plans that required both new people and new products. The coming of the Huguenots, therefore, occurred

13   Henri Duquesne, *Recueil de quelques mémoires servant d'instruction pour l'établissement de l'Île d'Eden* (Amsterdam: 1689), reprinted as an appendix in François Leguat, *Voyage et aventures de François Leguat et ses compagnons en deux îles désertes des Indes orientales*, (eds.) Jean-Michel Racault and Paolo Carile (Paris: 1995), 242.

14   Duquesne, *Recueil*, 244, 247. On Duquesne's influences see Paolo Carile, *Huguenots sans frontières: Voyage et écriture à la Renaissance et à l'Âge classique* (Paris: 2001), 97–103; and Jean-Michel Racault, *L'Utopie narrative en France et en Angleterre, 1675–1761* (Oxford: 1991), 63–67.

at a fortuitous time. The refugees came in large numbers; they were desperate to go almost anywhere they could gain good advantages. They also had special skills. Many were artisans and merchants, but in imperial capitals they became known especially for their facility with two important commodities, silk and wine. In England especially, these two luxury goods drained the national coffers, and damaged the kingdom's trade balance. Projectors had long wanted to produce these goods in England's overseas colonies, many of which were on the same latitude as southern France, Italy, and the Middle East, but with little success.[15] Large numbers of Huguenots, however, had experience with silk and wine, and now were desperate for new retreats. Many were more than willing to play up their skills as silk and wine experts, even if they had no direct experience in producing them. Thus the imperial refuge stemmed from a number of ambitions: the search for Eden; the search for autonomy; and from an imperial perspective, the search for profit and power. As both the refugees and their patrons discovered, these goals often contradicted each other.

3   The British Empire

Most refugees who ventured beyond Europe ended up in the far reaches of the British Empire. Given the demographics of European imperialism, this was not a surprising development. Of the Protestant empires, none attracted as many migrants as the British did, and colonial authorities had a history of reaching out to foreign settlers, especially other Protestants. When the Virginia Company sought possible paths to profit in the 1610s, it invited several Huguenots to the colony to jumpstart the colony's wine and silk industries. Sadly, the French families "neglected to plant any vynes" and the design failed.[16] In 1629 a Huguenot gentleman named the baron of Sancé attempted to restart the plan, proposing to create a colony of French Protestants in Virginia that would "plant vines and olives there and make silk." Sancé's plan, like so many others, led to no stable establishment, but over the first half-century a small number of Huguenots traveled or settled in English colonies, though not in coherent French communities.[17]

---

15   For one part of the story see Ben Marsh, "Silk Hopes in Colonial South Carolina," *Journal of Southern History* 78 (2012), 807–54.

16   William Waller Hening (ed.), *The Statutes at Large of Virginia*, vol. 1 (Richmond and New York: 1819–23), 161.

17   Antoine de Ridouet, baron de Sancé to [Sec. Dorchester], [June?] 14, 1629, TNA, CO 1/5, no. 14.

As persecution heated up in the 1680s the old dreams of Huguenots in the empire resurfaced. Thanks to the beneficence of Charles II and his bishop of London, Henry Compton, Huguenots began arriving in England well before the Revocation occurred. The king issued a brief welcoming these "distressed Strangers" and "Persecuted Protestants" in 1681, as England was still reeling from the revelations of the ultimately fictional "Popish Plot" of 1678.[18] The refugee cause enjoyed wide support across the political spectrum, from personages as diverse as Compton and the Presbyterian Roger Morrice, but at the same time the arrival of so many strangers created practical problems. The refugees tended to crowd into certain cities and towns, especially London, taxing local resources and inviting the ire of local artisans and laborers who viewed the French newcomers as competitors for jobs. Champions of the refugees like Compton sought to send them elsewhere, to "poor and depopulated" parts of the realm that could benefit from "industrious strangers."[19] One possible location was Ipswich in East Anglia, where a number of refugee families settled, but proposals abounded from one end of the kingdom to the other. Even in North Wales, for instance, the local bishop raised the possibility of settling 20 to 30 families to "teach our people Art & Industry," asking especially for "fishers or makers of French stuffs."[20]

While most refugees stayed in England, these schemes quickly turned imperial in nature. The 1680s, after all, was a time of imperial consolidation in England, as political economists theorized about how overseas colonies could improve the metropole. For Sir Josiah Child, for instance, the president of the East India Company and a key advocate of colonization, plantations could improve England's balance of trade by producing items that England's climate would not allow—like the silk and wine desired by the Virginia Company decades before. This could only be done by transporting people to the colonies, and Child advocated allowing persecuted religious minorities, both foreign and domestic, to settle overseas. The Huguenots fit Child's purposes exactly, since they had special skills and had recently deserted one of the nation's key competitors.[21]

---

18   "Brief, 1681," PHSL 7 (1901–1904), 164–66. On Huguenots in Britain see especially Bernard Cottret, *The Huguenots in England: Immigration and Settlement, c. 1550–1700* (Cambridge: 1992); and Robin Gwynn, *Huguenot Heritage: The History and Contributions of the Huguenots in Britain* (London: 1985).

19   Newsletter to Roger Garstell, 3 September 1681, *Calendar of State Papers, Domestic Series, 1680–81* (London: 1860), 437.

20   William Lloyd, Bishop of St. Asaph, to Thomas Mostyn, 14 April 1685, Bangor University Library, Mostyn Mss. 9069, no. 28.

21   Josiah Child, *A New Discourse of Trade* (London: 1693).

As in so many other instances, the first and most robust of these imperial schemes concerned not America or Asia but Ireland. That troubled island was ground zero for state-sponsored schemes during the Restoration period, as various Protestant leaders attempted to encourage agriculture and industry while bringing in Protestant settlers to counteract the Catholic majority. As early as 1681 Irish lords produced tracts calling for Huguenots to settle in vacant parts of the island, which the tracts described as lands of milk and honey.[22] Many refugees took the bait. In one petition a group of Huguenots promoted themselves as perfect settlers in a place that was "naturally one of the most fertile countries in Europe," but lacked "good and faithful subjects." The refugees could be these subjects: increasing the population of Ireland while providing important skills and a good example for the lazy and bigoted Catholics.[23] In fact, several thousand refugees did end up in Ireland, especially after the Williamite Wars further depopulated the country during the 1690s.[24]

If Ireland was relatively close, England's more distant colonies in North America seemed to provide greater promise for refugees. After all, Mediterranean crops like silk and wine seemed far more appropriate in temperate American colonies than in cold and rocky Ireland. In addition, the colonies had large quantities of land free for the taking, and in a few cases desperate proprietors willing to grant particular advantages to any Protestant settlers willing to relocate. Refugee leaders actively courted these opportunities; the papers of the Lords of Trade and Plantations abound with proposals from refugees asking for land and tax relief. A characteristic entreaty came from one James Guibal in 1683, who petitioned the Lords on behalf of a group of French Protestants who had left France "because of the persecutions which are there exercised against the Protestants," and requested transportation for fifteen men to Virginia, "to lay the foundation of a new Colony; that soe they may be in a condition for the future to land their assisting hand to their poor afflicted brethren."[25]

An earlier, more detailed petition—that of Jacob Guérard and René Petit for land in Carolina—perfectly outlined the views of Huguenots who chose colonial settlements over those closer to home. The two men expressed their

---

22 Ruth Whelan, "Promised Land: Selling Ireland to French Protestants," *PHSL* 29 (2008), 37–50.
23 Copie of the Remonstrance of the Protestants in France to Remove into Ireland, Bodleian Library, Oxford, Rawl. Mss. A 478, fol. 30.
24 For the full story of these refugees see Raymond Hylton, *Ireland's Huguenots and their Refuge, 1662–1745: An Unlikely Haven* (Brighton: 2005).
25 Petition of French Gentlemen, read 10 January 1683, TNA, CO 1/51, no. 2.

heartfelt thanks to English authorities for giving "peace and liberty" to those who suffered under French persecution. Their status as "strangers" made life difficult, however; the "natural English" were jealous of their "privileges," and defined the French as "strangers who came to take away their subsistence." In a colony overseas, the French could gain the rights of naturalized subjects, and become "one people" with the English there while "increasing [the king's] power and his glory by increasing the number of his Subjects," who would "bring to these places their arts and their sciences and even their goods and who will cultivate the land."[26] In particular, the two men promised to lend their expertise in making silk and wine, the two magical commodities so desired by imperial planners. Their petition succeeded, and the two men's colony provided the basis for South Carolina's small but important refugee settlement.[27]

While refugee industry helped to begin the migration, proprietary propaganda accelerated the movement of Huguenots overseas. During the 1680s leaders of Carolina and Pennsylvania competed for the refugees' attention, producing a number of French-language promotional tracts. William Penn promised cheap land, tax relief, and liberty of conscience in a colony that was "close to the same latitude as Montpellier in France, and Naples in Italy."[28] The Carolina tracts were more numerous and glowing, describing the colony as something akin to a new Eden, "one of the most beautiful countries in the world," where people lived in health and plenty.[29] As an afterthought that must have piqued the curiosity of many a French reader, one author noted that "the vine grows naturally in Carolina, and one can make good wine from the grapes that it produced without cultivation."[30]

These tracts tempted many refugees to consider moving overseas. A testament to their value appeared in a later pamphlet written by a traveler known only as Durand of Dauphiné. He fled southern France in 1686, and en route to

---

26 Humble Proposition faite au Roy et à Son Parlement pour donner retraite aux Etrangers protestans et au proselites dans ses Colonies de L'amerique et sur tout en la Carolina, March 1679, in A.S. Salley (ed.), *Records in the British Public Record Office Relating to South Carolina, 1663–1684* (Columbia: 1928), 62–64.

27 The definitive work on South Carolina's Huguenots is Bertrand Van Ruymbeke, *From New Babylon to Eden: The Huguenots and Their Migration to Colonial South Carolina* (Columbia: 2006).

28 *Recüeil de Diverses Pieces, Concernant la Pensylvanie* (The Hague: 1684), 19.

29 *Description du Pays nommé Caroline* (London: 1679), 1. In general see Bertrand Van Ruymbeke, "Vivre au paradis? Représentations de l'Amérique dans les imprimés de propagande et les lettres des réfugiés," BHSPF 153 (2007), 343–58.

30 *Nouvelle Relation de la Caroline par Un Gentil-homme François arrivé, depuis deux mois, de ce nouveau pais* (The Hague: 1686), 36.

London read tracts expounding the advantages of Carolina. His ambitions were renewed when he sampled the weather in London, and resolved to partner with a woman he met in his travels and devote himself to raising silkworms. As it happened Durand's ship ended up in Virginia rather than Carolina, which was all the better since he learned from other travelers that the pamphlets were wrong, and that the southern colony was a humid, unhealthy place.[31] Durand's journey from booster to skeptic mirrored that of many refugees. For instance, a manuscript set of "questions and answers" regarding Carolina specifically answered the frequent query "if all that is said in the printed relations is true." They were true "in general and in particular," the anonymous author insisted, and perhaps even downplayed the advantages of the colony.[32] But the reports of witnesses like Durand had an effect, as "Carolina fever" faded markedly during the 1690s.

While several hundred migrants settled in Carolina and a score in Virginia during the 1680s, other establishments took hold in the northern colonies. New England's Huguenot community owed its fortunes to the efforts of Gabriel Bernon, a Rochelais merchant with ties to New France. In 1685 Bernon was in Quebec City, attempting to negotiate toleration with the French governor there. After this design failed he chose the closest English alternative, working with authorities in London and Boston to settle refugees in Massachusetts. Rather than silk, Bernon dreamed of tar and turpentine, conceiving a colony in the inland town of Oxford that would serve as a center for the naval stores industry.[33] Between Oxford and settlements in Boston and Rhode Island, several hundred refugees came to the region. One manuscript report related that while New England fell short of Eden, it was an "exceedingly cheap" place to live, and "with a little one can make a good Settlement."[34]

The final center of Huguenot settlement in British North America was in the colony of New York. After the Revocation a number of Huguenot families moved to the city from the French colony of Saint-Christophe, many of them

---

31 Durand of Dauphiné, *A Huguenot Exile in Virginia; or Voyages of a Frenchman Exiled for His Religion with a Description of Virginia and Maryland*, (ed.) Gilbert Chinard (New York: 1934), 86–87, 98.

32 Questions et reponces faites au sujet de la Caroline, Mediathèque Michael Crepeau, La Rochelle, MS 1909, fol. 51v.

33 Lettre de Denonville au ministre, 13 novembre 1685, Archives nationales d'Outre-Mer, C^{11}A 7, fol. 100v–101; The Humble Petition of Gabriel Bernon of Boston in New England, Rhode Island Historical Society, Gabriel Bernon Papers.

34 *Report of a French Protestant Refugee, in Boston, 1687*, trans. E.T. Fisher (Brooklyn, NY: 1868), 25–26. For a survey of the New England Huguenots see Jon Butler, *The Huguenots in America: A Refugee People in New World Society* (Cambridge, Mass.: 1983), 71–143.

leading merchants. Soon other refugees settled in the newly incorporated town of New Rochelle, settling near a group of French-speaking Protestants who had earlier established the town of New Paltz. These refugees stood somewhat aloof from the imperial establishments to the north and south, as they came on their own volition and there was little concerted effort to attract refugees to New York. Nonetheless, the community became one of the most influential in the colonies, with Huguenots in positions of political and economic power soon after their arrival.[35]

While most Huguenots in the British Empire settled in North America, the East Indies hosted several proposed projects involving refugees. Probably because of the prominence of John Chardin, a refugee and East Indies expert who joined the East India Company's employ, the Company sponsored a number of plans to move Huguenots to Asia. In 1688 they suggested sending a number of French soldiers to Bombay and Madras to strengthen the Company's regiments there, but the soldiers (and ministers to tend to their spiritual needs) seem never to have reached India.[36] The following year Company ambitions switched to St. Helena, a small island in the Atlantic that functioned as a provisioning station for Company ships heading to the East Indies. Company leaders aimed to settle refugees on the island to engage in "planting of the vine." They sent a gentleman named Stephen Poirier with a number of French Protestant "vinerons" who would hopefully bring some profits to make up for the "prodigious charge" the company put out to keep the provisioning station operational. The men did settle on the island, but the attempts to make wine failed. By the end of the 1690s all of the men had returned to England except Poirier, who eventually became the island's governor.[37]

For the hundreds of Huguenots living on its edges, life in the British Empire offered opportunities and dangers. In many places the refugees received land and aid, but often in places where they had to labor to make land productive under harsh conditions. In addition, while many English subjects welcomed the refugees, they faced suspicion as well, especially during the 1690s when England and France were at war. The series of official pronouncements about the refugees from Massachusetts offers a case in point. As early as 1682 the

---

35   Butler, *Huguenots in America*, Ch. 5; Paula Wheeler Carlo, *Huguenot Refugees in Colonial America: Becoming American in the Hudson Valley* (Brighton: 2005). See also the chapter by Paula Carlo in this volume.

36   Court of Committees, 11 May 1688, BL, IOR B/39, fol. 128. When the ship that supposedly carried the French soldiers reached Madras no one noted the refugees' presence on it; see *Records of Fort St George: Letters from Fort St George for 1689* (Madras: 1916), 63, 65.

37   London to St. Helena, 5 April 1698, BL, IOR E/3/92, fol. 17v; Hudson Ralph Janisch (ed.), *Extracts from the St. Helena Records* (Jamestown, St. Helena: 1885), 49, 73–75.

colony's legislature, the General Court, declared it "for the credit of Religion" to grant refuge to Huguenots. Several years later, however, several refugees came to Salem "for the sake of their Religion to avoid the great persecution against the Protestants in France," but authorities seized their ship, since foreigners were not permitted to traffic in New England. Some years later, after the start of King William's War, things got even worse. In 1692 the General Court noted that many of the French in New England "pretend to be Protestants" but were in fact "papists & Enemies to their Majesties." As a result, the Court ordered all French people to give a satisfactory account of themselves, with the risk of losing their goods if they could not prove their Protestantism. In short, Huguenots could be objects of suspicion, as French Protestants were hard to distinguish from the other, worse variety of French people.[38]

In some ways the problems of the Huguenots in North America vindicated Henri Duquesne's statements about the difficulties of getting along with people of other nationalities, cultures, and religions. To retain their communal identity, the Huguenots needed independence, which was hardly possible during the 1690s. The last major project of the decade sought to remedy the situation, and while it ultimately failed to live up to its high ambitions, it did bring in the largest single number of refugees to a town in the backcountry of Virginia, a place called Manakin Town.[39]

The origins of Manakin Town lay in a new European crisis. After the end of the War of the League of Augsburg (King William's War in America) Louis XIV did nothing to relax his stance on Protestantism, even as in some places, especially Switzerland, authorities had fewer and fewer resources for refugees. In these new straitened circumstances foreign plantations seemed one of the few options left, and an English colonial projector named Daniel Coxe sought to create such a colony in a place he called Carolana, a colony on the Gulf of Mexico. Carolana combined the older dreams of silk and wine with Huguenot ambitions for their own community, but it was not to be. A reconnaissance trip met French ships near the mouth of the Mississippi, and through a convoluted series of events the refugees ended up instead on the Virginia frontier, on the site of an abandoned Indian town.[40] The thousand or so refugees there had no easier a time than their counterparts around North America, in spite of royal

---

38 Massachusetts State Archives, Boston, Massachusetts Archives Collection, 11: 22a, 41, 65.
39 The best overview of this colony is David E. Lambert, *The Protestant International and the Huguenot Migration to Virginia* (New York: 2010).
40 Daniel Coxe, *A Description of the English Province of Carolana: By the Spaniards call'd Florida, and by the French La Louisiane* (London: 1722); "Opinion of the Board of Trade," TNA, CO 5/1288, 139.

protection and free land. Indeed, by the early 18th century the community had split, with some people relocating to North and South Carolina. Virginia authorities, in the meantime, chided Manakin Town's leaders for referring to themselves as "the French colony," reminding them that whatever ambitions for autonomy they possessed, they had to answer to colonial leaders. Also, officials added, they should write their appeals and entreaties to the governor in English rather than French.[41]

By the dawn of the 18th century Huguenots played an outsized role in the British Empire. Many had found great advantages there, from merchants like Peter Faneuil and Thomas Bayeux, to statesmen like Stephen Poirier and Jean-Paul Mascarene. At the same time, their communities had failed to remain together. Like many migrants to the edges of empire, Huguenots frequently preferred to go off on their own rather than stay in communities that were often located in less than ideal places. They also made tactical choices, like joining the Church of England or marrying into powerful non-French families, placing them closer to avenues of power but compromised the dreams of preserving the church in exile espoused by leaders of the Refuge.[42]

4   The Dutch Empire

There was another option for Huguenots who wanted to settle overseas in the late-1600s. They could set out for one of the many overseas colonies and outposts of the United Provinces of the Netherlands. Those who did so, however, would find themselves in a very different kind of empire: indeed, one that some scholars insist was not a real empire at all.[43] Dutch expansion rested in the hands of two powerful companies, the East India Company (VOC) and the West India Company (WIC). The two companies controlled the trade of vast swaths of the world, and had trading posts everywhere, but they did not maintain many extensive settlement colonies. The companies provided many

---

41 A Collection of Several Matters Relating to the French Refugees from the 12th of March 1701/2, TNA, CO 5/1312, no. 40.lxi. In general see R.A. Brock (ed.), *Documents, Chiefly Unpublished, Relating to the Huguenot Migration to Virginia and to the Settlement at Manakin-Town* (Richmond: 1886).

42 The most influential scholar to posit Huguenot assimilation is Jon Butler, *The Huguenots in America*. On Anglicanism in particular see also Robert M. Kingdon, "Pourquoi les réfugiés huguenots aux colonies américaines sont-ils devenus épiscopaliens?" *BHSPF* 115 (1969), 487–509.

43 Pieter C. Emmer and Wim Klooster, "The Dutch Atlantic, 1600–1800: Expansion without Empire," *Itinerario* 23 (1999), 48–69.

possible opportunities to refugees, and while most Huguenots who went abroad on Dutch ships did not intend to spend their lives overseas, a few did end up finding a permanent refuge in Dutch colonies and outposts.

As in England, French Protestants had a long history in the Netherlands and their colonies well before the Revocation. During the Dutch Revolt thousands of Walloons (French-speakers from modern-day Belgium and northern France) settled in the provinces that became the Dutch Republic, and these refugees formed churches and networks in a number of Dutch cities. They also were active in overseas trade. The most storied example involved the first settlers of the outpost of New Amsterdam, many of whom were Walloons—including the first director Peter Minuit. In addition, small numbers of French-speaking Protestants ended up in other Dutch outposts, from the "Wild Coast" of South America to the Caribbean islands of Curaçao and the VOC headquarters in Batavia. Refugees from France in the 1680s followed in the footsteps of their Walloon forbears. They first flooded into the old Walloon Churches—as in Rotterdam where the world traveler Charles de Rochefort served as minister. Then they became involved in overseas endeavors as well. The East and West India Companies proved especially attractive to young men looking for employment, but such postings tended to be solitary and temporary. At the same time, however, Dutch leaders and prominent refugees began to plan for more permanent Huguenot settlements on the fringes of the Dutch Empire that closely resembled refugee communities in British possessions.[44]

The first experiment was one of the most obscure. In 1664 the Dutch had acquired the English colony of Suriname on the northern coast of South America. While the tropical plantation had great potential as a sugar colony, it suffered from an acute population shortage, and leaders attempted to locate new sources of people. In 1682 the colony passed to a coalition that included the States of Zeeland, the city of Amsterdam, and the Aarssen van Sommelsdijks, a prominent family. As it happened, the colony's incoming governor, Cornelis Aarssen van Sommelsdijk, had married a Huguenot and had connections to the Dutch refugee community. Nearly 300 refugees accompanied him to Suriname in 1683, while more followed in 1685, to the point that nearly 20 per cent of plantation owners in the early-1700s had French surnames. While details remain murky, the Huguenot migration to Suriname represented a

---

44 There is little scholarship dedicated to Walloons in the Dutch colonies, but for New Netherland see Jaap Jacobs, *New Netherland: A Dutch Colony in Seventeenth-Century America* (Leiden: 2005), Ch. 2. On Huguenots in the Dutch Republic itself see Willem Frijhoff, "Uncertain Brotherhood: The Huguenots in the Dutch Republic," in *Memory and Identity*, (eds.) Van Ruymbeke and Sparks, 128–71.

classic trope: Sommelsdijk and his wife used their position to grant charity to the refugees in a way that would also bring financial advantages to investors and the state.[45]

In addition to working the land, French settlers in Suriname served another important purpose: they acted as a defensive bastion against other empires, especially the French. This became clear in 1686, when the colony apparently received a new influx of refugees from nearby Cayenne. Five sailors deserted their ship, and when the French captain traveled from Cayenne to Suriname to negotiate their return, the Dutch governor demurred, claiming that some of the men "were there in the liberty of their Religion." Suriname's leaders had learned a valuable lesson: that by opening their doors to refugees they could acquire soldiers and settlers for their somewhat unattractive border colony.[46]

The other major refugee center in the Dutch Empire—and one with much better documentation—existed across the Atlantic Ocean at the Cape of Good Hope.[47] Unlike Suriname, which existed in its early years outside the powerful company networks, the Cape Colony was an outpost of the VOC, intended as a way station to provision ships heading from the Netherlands to the East Indies. While the VOC never imagined building a large settler colony at the Cape, from the 1660s onward they attempted to move farmers there who could provide grain and perhaps other necessaries like wine and brandy for passing ships. Much like Suriname, however, the Company had trouble finding anyone willing to settle so far from home. After surveying the persecution in France, the Company's Assembly of the Seventeen saw a great opportunity. They resolved to target "French Refugees of the reformed religion" as potential colonists, "especially those understanding the cultivation of the vine, the making of vinegar and the distilling of brandy."[48]

In order to attract settlers the VOC conducted a promotional campaign that was subtler than but nearly as effective as that of the Carolina proprietors.

---

45 Cornelis Ch. Goslinga, *The Dutch in the Caribbean and in the Guianas, 1680–1791* (Assen: 1985), 275–76; Jean-Louis Poulalion, "Les français dans l'histoire du Suriname," *Mondes et cultures* 46 (1986), 780–81; S. Kalff, "Franschen in Suriname," *De West-Indische Gids* 11 (1929–30), 316–34.

46 Relation du Voyage de Cayenne à Surinam fait par Isaac Maret Maitre du Navire le Marin de Bourdeaux, à la poursuite de cinq hommes de Son equipage qui ont deserté de Son Bord, 1687, Archives Nationales d'Outre-Mer, C^{14}, vol. 2, fol. 179.

47 The most recent history of this community is Pieter Coertzen, *The Huguenots of South Africa, 1688–1988* (Cape Town: 1988).

48 Extract from the Resolutions of the Assembly of the Seventeen, 3 October 1685, in C. Graham Botha, *The French Refugees at the Cape*, 3d ed. (Cape Town: 1970), 126.

Soon after the Company issued its resolution to find Huguenot settlers, a printer distributed a description of the advantages they would find on the Cape around the refugee community. The tract said nothing of Eden; indeed, it was silent about actual conditions in the colony. It did provide many details about the benefits the company would provide to prospective migrants. In return for signing an oath and agreeing to remain five years, refugees would receive free transport to the Cape and help setting up in whatever profession they chose, whether as an artisan or a farmer. The provenance of the printed tract, which now sits in a collection of correspondence from Huguenot ministers in Switzerland, demonstrates how the VOC set out to advertise the opportunity.[49] Another letter provides further clues. Around the time the tract came out Zurich's French minister, Paul Reboulet, noted in a letter to a colleague of a new opportunity for their distressed brethren. The VOC aimed to relocate "thousands of families" to the Cape, and aimed to publish a tract laying out the advantages. Clearly a representative of the Company sent advance word to Reboulet so he could advertise the opportunity to his flock. It was a good choice, as the minister was enthusiastic. "The country produces everything," Reboulet reported, "and especially wine."[50]

After some false starts, several boatloads of refugees did end up in Cape Town in 1688. Governor Simon van der Stel sent the newcomers to the Drakenstein Valley a few leagues east of the capital, where he hoped they would set up farms. Life in the refugee settlement was far from easy. In a remarkable letter to VOC officials, the minister Pierre Simond described "the sad state of our refugees" on the African frontier. Much of the land was of poor quality, and transporting food and building materials from Cape Town proved time consuming and expensive. The VOC provided free grain, but refugees had to travel two days to procure it, and usually had to hire a Dutch burgher to provide transport. In addition, the refugees' landholdings were scattered, making it difficult for the French to support each other and maintain a community. Simond urged authorities to allow them to take new land closer together and establish their own church consistory.[51]

---

49 Reglement, De l'assemblée des Dix-sept, qui representent la Compagnie des Indes Orientales des Païs-Bas, suivant lequel les Chambres de le ditte Compagnie auront pouvoir de transporter au Cap de Bonne Esperance des Personnes de tout sexe de la Religion reformée, entre autres les refugies de France, & des Vallees de Piedmont [n.p.: 1687], BGE, Collection Court, 17U, fols. 207–08.
50 Paul Reboulet to Jacques Tronchin, 4 octobre 1687, BGE, Archives Tronchin, vol. 50.
51 Pierre Simond aux directeurs de la Compagnie d'Orient, 15 juin 1689, Nationaal Archief, The Hague VOC 4026, ff. 1298–304.

Despite great challenges, the Cape Huguenots did survive—and the colony proved far more successful than any other in an at least one common goal of Huguenot imperial projects. While the prospective wine industry in British America failed to develop, grapes grew well in the Cape's Mediterranean climate. By the mid-1690s the "extensive business of the Company" in the Cape Colony was "the cultivation of wine and corn," officials reported back to Amsterdam.[52] An English visitor credited those "sent hither by the *French Persecution*" with at least some of the wine production. The colony's vineyards were "now able to supply their Ships, and to furnish the *Indies* with some quantity," the witness reported, though he questioned the quality of the wine, claiming it was "much harder and less palatable" than its European equivalent.[53] A French traveler agreed that the wine was not the best, but still raved about the conditions in the Huguenot community. In particular he mentioned one Isaac Taillefer, who had an extensive garden and "the best Wine in the Country, which is not unlike our small Wines of *Champagne*."[54]

While the Cape Huguenot community was itself one of the larger overseas schemes, it was merely part of a larger design that had it come to pass would have changed the face of the Refuge. In 1689, just as he wrote his tract attracting settlers to his new French Protestant Eden in the Indian Ocean, Henri Duquesne visited the Dutch States General looking for a patron. His scheme was expensive, and only by finding powerful allies could he hope to be able to transport thousands of refugees to the far end of the world. While Duquesne's tracts claimed his intentions were peaceful, his agreement with the States General told a different story. To attract Dutch support Duquesne promised to make his scheme a plank in the VOC's strategy to combat French pretensions in the East. He pledged to "arm several ships" in order to "seize a small island that is close to Madagascar, that the French have occupied for several years and is named Ile Bourbon." The island was adjacent to the existing Dutch colony of Mauritius, so taking it would serve a key strategic purpose in securing the Mascarene Islands for the Dutch—an important outcome if they wanted to maintain control of the shipping lanes between the Cape and India. Probably for this reason, the VOC and the States General offered their support to the expedition, offering a ship to transport the first settlers to their new Eden.[55]

52   Cape to the Seventeen, 23 January 1696, in H.C.V. Liebbrandt (ed.), *Precis of the Archives of the Cape of Good Hope. Letters Dispatched, 1696–1708* (Cape Town: 1896), 3.
53   John Ovington, *A Voyage to Suratt* (London: 1696), 503.
54   François Leguat, *The Voyage of François Leguat of Bresse to Rodriguez, Mauritius, Java, and the Cape of Good Hope*, vol. 2 (London: 1891), 287.
55   Requesten van den Marquis du Quesne en geassocieerden, om permissie tot het doen van sen equipagie om het eylant Bourbon ofte Mascarenhas op de franschon te ucuperen,

The scheme appealed to dozens if not hundreds of potential settlers who gathered in Amsterdam in 1689. One of them was a middle-aged gentleman named François Leguat. Duquesne's published tract on the Isle of Eden "made me conceive so good an Opinion of it," Leguat later wrote, "that I was tempted to give it a Visit, resolving to end my Days there in Peace, and out of the Care and Confusion of the World." Probably because of his high position, Duquesne made Leguat the leader of one of two ships "about which all the French Protestants, who were willing to be of this Colony, were received *gratis*." The ships never left, however. Hearing rumors of French warships ranging in the Indian Ocean, Duquesne decided to merely send a small advance guard of colonists on the ship *Hirondelle*, including Leguat and nine others. The ship's captain, a Huguenot named Antoine Valleau, received the commission to bring back information on the islands, and in the meantime to leave the ten men to make an early establishment, "in expectation of the rest of the Colony, who were to come after, in two Years Time at Farthest, and then to possess themselves of the Isle of *Eden*, under the Protection, and by the Assistance of *Messieurs* of the Company."[56]

While the details are difficult to recover, some evidence suggests that Amsterdam was not the only possible source of settlers. The *Hirondelle* stopped at the Cape on the way to the Mascarene Islands, where the Huguenot passengers made contact with their coreligionists. At this time they may have tried to bring the Cape Huguenots into the scheme, hoping that they would serve as the bulk of the force that would take Île Bourbon for the VOC and the refugees. The spotty evidence comes from an odd deposition from Antoine Valleau himself. After encountering French ships, Valleau dropped his ten passengers off on nearby Rodrigues Island. He then returned to Bourbon, where he gathered information about its condition and kidnapped a black man named Arré to be his guide. After a stop at the Cape he attempted to return to Amsterdam to pass his intelligence to Duquesne and the States General, but along the way the *Hirondelle* fell into French hands. The French interrogated the captain, who gave details of his travels, including among the Cape Huguenots, but claimed that "he knew only two men among the French who had the intention of offering their services to the said Sr Duquesne." Valleau's companion Arré told a different story, alleging "That the said Valleau had told him Sr. Duquesne had

---

met een advis van de Oostinde compe. daer op, overgegeven in den jaere 1689, Nationaal Archief, The Hague, Staten Generaal 12581.40. For an account of how all these schemes connected see Randolph Vigne, "Huguenots to the Southern Oceans: Archival Fact and Voltairian Myth," in *The Huguenots: France, Exile, and Diaspora*, (eds.) Jane McKee and Randolph Vigne (Brighton: 2013), 113–24.

56 Leguat, *The Voyage of François Leguat*, 1: 3–5.

the design to seize the said Île Bourbon, and that he had taken him to present him to the said Sr. Duquesne in order to inform him about the state of the island." In addition, "there are 400 French refugees" at the Cape, Arré added, "who say that they await the said Sr. Duquesne in order to offer themselves to him to go and conquer Île Bourbon."[57] In other words, the Cape and the Mascarenes were part of a larger strategy to use Huguenots to secure all sorts of strategic territories for the VOC.

If it existed at all, this grand design did not survive Valleau's capture. A manuscript note on the frontispiece of Duquesne's tract suggests that the VOC withdrew its financial support for the measure, leaving Leguat and his men stranded on a remote island with no vessel and no means to communicate with the outside world.[58] In a remarkable episode, the men built a boat and somehow reached Dutch Mauritius, where they immediately came into dispute with the VOC governor over a piece of ambergris. Through a convoluted series of events the men came under suspicion of treason. (Two of the men had decided to try and escape their imprisonment by stealing a boat and heading to Île Bourbon.) It was only after more than four years and an acquittal by a court in Batavia that the four survivors eventually made their way back to Europe in 1698. One of them, Jacques de La Case, apparently had not traveled enough, as he soon moved again, this time to the refugee colony in Manakin Town, Virginia.[59]

While the Huguenot colony in the Mascarenes met its sad end, similar problems appeared in the Cape. The issue there was autonomy. After the refugees struggled to build a community in the Drakenstein Valley, they requested the right to "have their own Magistrate, Commander and Prince to be chosen from the people," and that to better do this "they appealed to the Commander to allow them to settle all together, and not among the Dutch people at Stellenbosch and Drakenstein" and also sought to create their own church council or consistory, something that Pierre Simond had earlier raised as well. All of these requests would have looked routine in many of the Huguenot colonies in Europe, especially Germany, where some degree of self-determination

---

57   Interrogatoire du nommé Valleau de l'Isle de Rhé, 20 may 1692, Archives Nationales d'Outre-Mer, C³1, ff. 185–86.

58   The manuscript note, probably from the 18th century, appears immediately after the title page of Duquesne, *Recueil de quelques mémoires servant d'instruction pour l'établissement de l'île d'Eden* in the Bibliothèque Nationale de France, Paris.

59   The episode is detailed in Leguat, vol. 2, and in *Diverse papieren de 3 Fransche persoonen van den Marquies du Quesne wegens de mishandelingh haer aen 't eijlant mauritiun aengedaen volgens apart register*, 1697, Nationaal Archief, VOC 1588, fols. 909–1042.

was the norm. In this case the commander angrily denied the request, arguing that it constituted a violation of their oath to the Company.[60] By the end of the 1690s VOC officials had soured on the refugees entirely. Governor van der Stel warned his son and successor that the French were not to be trusted, and local leaders implored the Company to send farmers from Zeeland rather than more Huguenots. After Pierre Simond's departure in 1701 the Dutch restricted the use of French and attempted to force the refugees to integrate into the Dutch population.[61] The wine may have been palatable, but in other ways South Africa failed to become a French Eden.

The Dutch Empire attracted fewer Huguenot migrants than its British counterpart, but in some ways those who were there more clearly illustrated the opportunities and pitfalls of settlement on the edge of an empire. Huguenots like Duquesne and Leguat hoped to be partners of the VOC and the States General, lending their talents to the imperial cause in exchange for territories where they could realize their dreams of building a new Protestant France overseas. In the end, however, that was not to be. The Dutch viewed Huguenots as subjects rather than partners, and when they failed to live up to their promise they were easily discarded or forgotten.

5   18th-Century Projects

In the standard telling of the history of the American and South African refugees, Huguenot communities quickly disappeared in the 18th century. "Everywhere they fled, everywhere they vanished," wrote Jon Butler of the colonial North American Huguenots, but versions of the same story appear for South Africa, Great Britain, Germany, and nearly every other place where refugees settled. Within two generations, in most cases, the descendants of refugees gradually abandoned the French language, the distinctive Calvinism of French Protestantism, and the practice of marrying within the community.[62] While the contours of this narrative remain more or less correct, it is important not to end the story too soon. In fact, the imperial Refuge lived on in the 18th century in

---

60   Resolutions, 1686–1699, in Botha, *The French Refugees at the Cape*, 151–52.
61   Botha, *The French Refugees at the Cape*, 57; Letter to Chamber Middelburg, 2 July 1699, in Botha, *The French Refugees at the Cape*, 160.
62   Butler, *The Huguenots in America*, 199. For an account that extends the argument to South Africa as well see Thera Wijsenbeck, "Identity Lost: Huguenot Refugees in North America and South Africa, 1650 to 1750—A Comparison," *South African Historical Journal* 59 (2007), 79–102.

several ways. First, a number of studies have tempered the old story of Huguenot assimilation. In fact, many refugees maintained much of their distinctiveness in private, while outwardly conforming to the dominant culture. Additionally, some Huguenots, like those in New Rochelle, New York, officially became Anglicans while maintaining distinctive Calvinist elements in their church services.[63]

Even when individuals became less distinctively French and refugee "colonies" dispersed, the 18th century abounded with new refugee settlement projects. Indeed, the political economic objectives that inspired the first colonies remained important right up to the era of the American and French Revolutions, and inspired dozens of real and projected colonies, mostly in North America but occasionally in places as far-flung as South Australia. This was, as Daniel Defoe famously argued, "the Projecting Age," when people "rack[ed] their Wits for New Contrivances, New Inventions, New Trades, Stocks, Projects, and anything to retrieve the desperate Credit of their Fortunes."[64] Huguenots were prominent in these projects, both as sponsors and objects of them, and many of the schemes involved overseas settlements. The numbers of migrants in the 18th century were fairly modest, compared both to the Huguenot migration of the 1680s and the contemporary migration of other European groups, such as Germans. Nonetheless, imperial projects remained an important possibility for refugees seeking advantages in an uncertain world, and imperial leaders, especially in Britain, still looked to Huguenots to help them build their empires.

Perhaps the greatest exemplar of this new projecting age was Jean-Pierre Purry, a wine merchant from Neuchâtel, Switzerland. After meeting some misfortunes in his business, Purry served as a chaplain in the Dutch East Indian capital of Batavia, and while there he came upon what he considered a brilliant plan. Based on his travels, he deduced that his favored commodity, grapes for wine, grew best at thirty-three degrees north and south latitude. He presented a proposal to the VOC to form a settlement that could become the "Repository of the Wine and Corn" for all the East Indies somewhere on that line of latitude. These countries abounded "not only in Milk and Honey, but in General with all Sorts of things that minister to our Pleasure." His profitable Eden would benefit the Dutch state while also proving attractive to prospective settlers. In this sense Purry's proposals did not depart that heavily from

---

63   The most important works to question Butler's thesis have been Van Ruymbeke, *From New Babylon to Eden*; Carlo, *Huguenot Refugees in Colonial America* and her chapter in this volume; Neil Kamil, *Fortress of the Soul: Violence, Metaphysics, and Material Life in the Huguenots' New World, 1517–1751* (Baltimore: 2005).

64   [Daniel Defoe], *An Essay upon Projects* (London: 1697), 1, 6.

those of earlier Huguenot colonies in North America and South Africa, and there was another important parallel. Purry aimed to look for prospective settlers in and around his hometown of Neuchâtel, especially to refugees who, still some decades later, taxed resources in the economically struggling Swiss cantons. Now the Huguenots were not alone; they would be joined by other German and French-speaking Swiss looking for opportunities overseas.[65]

Purry had immense troubles finding either a proper location or sponsorship for his bold project. In his initial appeal to the VOC he suggested either "Cafrerie" (the part of South Africa just east of the existing Cape Colony) or the "Land of Nuyts," present-day South Australia. The VOC had no interest in Purry's proposals, so he moved on to France, which in the 1710s was suffering from "Mississippi fever" until John Law's schemes led to a collapse of the French financial state in 1720. Luckily, while in Paris Purry found a new patron, the British ambassador Horace Walpole. In 1724 Purry sent several letters to Walpole detailing his proposals to settle a colony in Carolina that would help improve Britain's balance of trade with its French and Spanish rivals.[66] This time Purry had found the right audience; his dreams of wine and silk fit perfectly with British imperial objectives.

In a breathless tract Purry used his climatic theories to argue for new establishments in South Carolina. At that point most of the colony's population remained in the Lowcountry. New settlers could expand—always keeping close to the magic thirty-third degree of latitude—moving all the way across the continent and seizing the underpopulated colony of French Louisiana. Purry advocated a number of industries in South Carolina, but especially the old standards, wine and silk. These things grew best at thirty-three degrees, which meant that Carolina silk would necessarily surpass even that from Languedoc and Italy, located farther north. Moreover, Purry had a large number of migrants who could produce these crops and not even drain Britain's own population. He pointed to refugees from all over Europe, but especially in Switzerland and Protestant France. "[M]any Protestants remain in France, enduring tyranny and persecution," Purry wrote, but would be happy for "a sure and honest retreat where they may, by cultivating their own lands, guard themselves against poverty, and dispense with the charity of their brethren."[67]

---

65 John Peter Purry, *A Method for Determining the Best Climate of the Earth, on a Principle to which All Geographers and Historians have been Hitherto Strangers* (London: 1744), 1, 14.

66 Walpole to Newcastle, 7 June 1724, and Purry to Walpole, 6 June 1724, BL, Add. Mss. 32739, ff. 39, 41.

67 Jean Pierre Purry, *Memorial Presented to His Grace My Lord the Duke of Newcastle, Chamberlain of His Majesty King George, &c., and Secretary of State: Upon the Present Condition of Carolina, and the Means of Its Amelioration* (Augusta: 1880), 19–20.

It took nearly a decade for Purry to move from eccentric theorizing to building an actual community: a town called Purrysburgh overlooking the Savannah River on South Carolina's southern border. The venture took place during a time of transition in South Carolina, with proprietary rule slowly giving way to a royal government. During the 1720s the proprietors pledged support but then withdrew it—causing riots in the streets of Neuchâtel when potential migrants realized that they would not be going to America after all. The settlement finally took hold the next decade with royal grants of assistance, and several hundred migrants worked to make Purry's vision a reality. Obviously, his theories had some major holes; the South Carolina climate bore little resemblance to most silk and wine producing places. Nonetheless, the French, Swiss, and Germans who settled in Purrysburgh did dedicate themselves to silk culture, with some modest success. By mid-century settlers sent large quantities of cocoons for production at the government-sponsored silk filature in nearby Savannah, Georgia.[68]

While it was far less than a complete success, the example of Purrysburgh inspired many imitators over the subsequent decades. Projects involving refugees abounded throughout the British empire, from the Mediterranean to America. Many of these proposed settlements targeted places that the British conquered in various mid-century wars against France and Spain. Officials tried, for instance, to settle "a numerous Colony of substantial and Industrious Protestants" on the island of Menorca, captured from the Spanish in 1708, to counteract the "indolent" character of its Catholic inhabitants. The design led to nothing.[69] A similar impulse inspired attempts to settle Huguenots in Nova Scotia (formerly Acadia), a colony dominated by the "French Neutrals," or Catholic Acadians. While a few refugees did travel to Halifax and Lunenburg, Nova Scotia's poor reputation discouraged migration. As London's French minister Jacques Serces noted of his flock, "the very name [of Nova Scotia] makes them tremble."[70] Somewhat later, administrators in East and West Florida hatched similar plans to attract French Protestants, who they considered

---

68 The story of the settlement is told most completely in Arlin C. Migliazzo, *To Make This Land Our Own: Community, Identity, and Cultural Adaptation in Purrysburgh Township, South Carolina, 1732–1865* (Columbia: 2007).

69 A Plan for settling the Island of Menorca with a Sett of Substantial and industrious Inhab[itants], TNA, CO 174/1, no. 65.

70 Jacques Serces to Antoine Court, 29–30 septembre 1752, *Correspondence of Jaques Serces*, vol. 2 (Frome: 1952), 228. On the Huguenots who did end up in Nova Scotia see Winthrop Pickard Bell, *The "Foreign Protestants" and the Settlement of Nova Scotia: The History of a Piece of Arrested British Colonial Policy in the Eighteenth Century* (Toronto: 1961), 41–42, 212–14.

"the most valuable colonists," though in these cases the refugees would settle not among Spanish Catholics but alongside a motley crew of various migrants, few of whom lasted long in the fetid swamps of the far Southeast.[71]

The most significant settlement, however, formed in the South Carolina upcountry just upriver from Purrysburgh. The saga of New Bordeaux, founded there by two French ministers in 1764, provides a great indication of the continuing relevance of Huguenot refugees in the British empire right up to the eve of the American Revolution. The colony owed its origins to the efforts of Jean-Louis Gibert, a minister from Languedoc who played a leading role in building clandestine churches in France during the 1740s in an attempt to revive the fortunes of French Protestantism. Like many Protestant leaders in 18th-century France, Gibert used the threat of emigration in an attempt to win concessions from the monarchy; in effect, he hoped to blackmail French leaders into tolerating his religion.[72] Unlike many of his friends, however, Gibert followed through on his threat. In 1763 he traveled to London to gain sponsors for his project to move as many of 60,000 refugees to British America.[73]

Gibert sold his plan in London by using the same political economic language that had abounded in Huguenot appeals for decades. He told his main ally, the Archbishop of Canterbury William Secker, that the townspeople in his new colony would devote themselves to "the making of silk and…coarse cloth," and this talk of sericulture undoubtedly raised the ears of leaders of South Carolina, who were still eager to develop alternative crops that could help the imperial economy, especially in the colony's exposed backcountry areas. In the end, only 112 French people accompanied Gibert to South Carolina, and few besides Gibert showed any interest in silk, but the town survived nonetheless.[74] In 1772 a new troupe arrived under the leadership of Louis de Mesnil de Saint-Pierre, a Norman gentleman who preferred wine to silk, and earned the support of Governor William Bull. Saint-Pierre hoped to lead efforts to make the South a giant vineyard. "The Vine is a native of America," wrote the Frenchman in a tract he published in London during a tour there in 1774 to gain sponsors, "And this divine plant may be found throughout that vast continent,

---

71   James Grant to John Pownall, 30 July 1763, TNA, CO 5/540, p. 2.
72   On these activities and how they fit in France's religious landscape see Myriam Yardeni, "La France protestante et le Refuge," in idem, *Le Refuge huguenot: Assimilation et culture* (Paris: 2002), 163–76.
73   Francis Waddington, "Projet d'émigration de la Saintonge et des provinces voisines, d'après des documents inédits, 1761–1764," *BSHPF* 6 (1858), 371–72.
74   Janie Revill (ed.), *A Compilation of the Original Lists of Protestant Immigrants to South Carolina, 1763–1773* (Columbia: 1939), 30.

from the mouth of the Mississippi to that of the St. Lawrence, where it is as common as now, and much more so than formerly in France and Italy."[75] He offered to lend his own talents, and those of his countrymen, to making the American wine industry take off, but despite the support of the governor and a well-placed lord, he was unable to win much support for his scheme. New Bordeaux lived on, but South Carolina wine never gained many adherents.

6   The End of Empire, the End of the Refuge

By the time of the American Revolution, British and Dutch colonies were filled with Huguenots and their descendants. To be sure, many of these people had stopped speaking French at home or worshiping in French churches, and most of the Huguenot *colonies* envisioned by the early leaders had faded away. But still, the Huguenots had in many ways adapted well to the world of empires. They had learned to speak the language of political economy, to make themselves useful to foreign patrons, and while dreams of Eden rarely came to pass, many individual refugees built impressive lives on the far ends of European empires.

The coming of the Age of Revolution brought an end to the first age of empires and with it the story of the global Refuge. One story provides some indication of how this occurred. In 1766 Hector de Bérenger, baron de Beaufain died in Charleston, South Carolina. A native of Orange, Beaufain had moved to the colony with Jean-Pierre Purry over thirty years before, and become a wealthy and important man, a member of the colony's council and the collector of customs. Dying childless, he left his property to his nephew Jean Henry de Bérenger, a retired Prussian officer living in the German city of Bayreuth. Jean Henry sought to collect his inheritance by appealing to the same networks of patronage that had always worked for Huguenots in the past. He allied with the London merchant Pierre Simond—the South African-born son of the Cape Colony's former minister—and made contacts in South Carolina. In 1769 he arranged through his contacts to sell his uncle's land, but as often happens, the transfer of the money dragged on for years. Jean Henry pled his case to the Hanoverian ambassador in London, and in turn the appeal made it, in July 1776, to South Carolina's Governor William Bull, the man who had the authority to

---

75   Louis de Saint-Pierre, *The Art of Planting and Cultivating the Vine; as Also, of Making, Fining, and Preserving Wines &c. according to the Most Approved Methods in the Most Celebrated Wine-Countries in France* (London: 1772), xx–xxi.

settle the matter. Being a Huguenot—especially one with such strong connections—ensured that his letters received prompt attention.⁷⁶

But something else happened in July 1776, and by the time Bull responded to his letter some years later the world had changed. The former royal governor could no longer help, and to make matters worse the guardian of Beaufain's property had been a loyalist, so much of it had been confiscated. Jean Henry continued to try to work his connections. He wrote to the Hanoverian ambassador again, to George III, and when the king could not solve matters to the patriot and Huguenot descendant Henry Laurens. Increasingly desperate, he cast his net wider, petitioning Lord North, Benjamin Franklin, and John Rutledge, beginning in each case with a narrative of his family's story of persecution. Finally, in April 1786, he made the most desperate plea, writing to Louis XVI. Since the American states were "indebted to Your Majesty," Bérenger wrote, perhaps they would listen if French ambassadors intervened on his behalf.⁷⁷

None of these measures worked, and Bérenger never secured his fortune. While just one story, it serves as a fitting end to the story of Huguenots in European empires. The baron of Beaufain and his nephew were creatures of the *ancien régime* world of states and empires, and they learned to use their global connections, as well as their stories of persecution, to win advantages under very difficult circumstances. With the world of empires in ruin, the global Refuge came to an end. Individual Huguenots remade themselves once again, this time as heroes in the various national histories of the *pays d'accueil*, but never again would they play as prominent a role in global history.

---

76   Mémoire Pour servir d'information dans les affaires et d'intérêts à régler dans l'hoirie de feu Hector de Bérenger Baron de Beaufain, Huguenot Library, University College London, de Bérenger Papers, F Br 4.

77   Bérenger to Louis XVI, 3 avril 1786, Huguenot Library, de Bérenger Papers, F Br 4. The rest of his petitions and entreaties are scattered in the same collection.

CHAPTER 16

Le Refuge: History and Memory from the 1770s to the Present

Bertrand Van Ruymbeke

1 Introduction: Huguenot Memory a Century after the Dispersion (1770s–1790s)

A century after the Revocation and the clandestine flight of thousands of Huguenots, descendants of these refugees began to reflect on the experience of their forebears and how it affected their worldview. The world had radically changed since the days of the Revocation. Absolutism and religious bigotry were being condemned in this new Age of Enlightenment philosophy, deism, and revolution. Louis XIV's policy of religious unification and forced conversion seemed terribly obsolete. While visiting Philadelphia in 1780, the aristocrat François-Jean de Chastellux, one of Rochambeau's aides-de-camp, told Anthony Benezet, the Huguenot-born Quaker philanthropist, "intolerance and persecution, these two enemies of the human race...they are no longer fashionable."[1] Republicanism and toleration were the order of the day. In France itself, Voltaire successfully campaigned for the rehabilitation of Jean Calas, a Huguenot condemned by the Catholic *parlement* of Toulouse in 1762, with the publication of his *Treaty on Toleration*.[2] In 1787, the Huguenots saw their civil rights restored by an enlightened French monarchy through the Edict of Toleration or Édit de Versailles. In the same years and same Voltairean spirit of toleration and condemnation of the Louis Quatorzian monarchy, the Abbé Raynal, famous for his *Histoire philosophique et politique des établissements et du commerce des Européens dans les deux Indes*, planned, as announced in the 1780 edition of this seminal work, to write a

---

1 Howard C. Rice, Jr, (ed.), *Travels in North America in the Years 1780, 1781 and 1782 by the Marquis de Chastellux*, vol. 2 (Chapel Hill: 1963), 166.
2 In ancien régime France, *parlements* were regional courts of justice, not elected assemblies. Janine Garrisson, *L'Affaire Calas. Miroir des passions françaises* (Paris: 2004). Benoît Garnot, *Voltaire et l'affaire Calas. Les faits, les interprétations, les enjeux* (Paris: 2013). On the Enlightenment context see Geoffrey Adams, *The Huguenots and French Opinion 1685–1787. The Enlightenment Debate on Toleration* (Waterloo, Ontario: 1991), especially Chapters 15 and 20.

"Histoire de la révocation de l'édit de Nantes" in which he would follow the French refugees "over the entire globe."³ Following the method he used for his successful *Histoire des deux Indes*, Raynal did prepare (and sent) a questionnaire to gather information on the refugees who had settled in Northern Europe. Raynal received completed questionnaires, mostly from German and Swiss towns and states, and his initiative sparked an international debate on the value of such a study.⁴

With the Revolution, the law of return of December 1790 allowed descendants of Huguenot refugees to return to France and obtain full citizenship.⁵ Although understandably very few refugee families took advantage of this opportunity—descendants of refugees were fully integrated into host societies by then—the law embodied a revolutionary denunciation of the Revocation, which was in concert with the contemporaneous full-blown attack on the Catholic Church with the *Constitution Civile du Clergé*. In Charleston, South Carolina, where a few hundred refugees had settled in the 1680s, a parade headed by the French republican consul, Michel Ange Mangourit, along with the "Huguenot" pastor, the Swiss Jean Paul Coste, walked victoriously through town in January 1793 and stopped by the French Church. There the consul "to atone for Louis XIV's persecution against the Protestants...took off his hat and saluted the church with the national colors."⁶

In the same decades, the first accounts of the dispersion by descendants of Huguenot refugees were published. The best example is the *Mémoires pour servir à l'histoire des Réfugiés françois dans les Etats du Roi (1782–1799)* published

---

3   Gilles Bancarel, *Raynal ou le devoir de vérité* (Paris: 2004), 187. Raynal never wrote the history.
4   Patrick Cabanel, *Histoire des protestants en France XVIe-XXIe siècle* (Paris: 2012), 781–82.
5   Of the 50,000 expected, 250 family names have been identified, which means that 1000 Protestants, not necessarily descendants of refugees for that matter, at the most returned to France. Eckart Birnstiel, "Le retour des huguenots du Refuge en France, de la Révocation à la Révolution," BSHPF 135 (1989), 763–90 and idem, "La France en quête de ses enfants perdus. Mythe et réalité du retour au 'pays des ancêtres' des huguenots du Refuge de la Réforme à la Révolution," *Diasporas. Histoire et Sociétés* 8 (2006), 22–44; Patrick Cabanel, "Une loi du retour (15 décembre 1790). Réparations nationales et crispations nationalistes sur le thème du retour des huguenots," *Diasporas. Histoire et Sociétés* 8 (2006), 49–73.
6   Charles Fraser, *Reminiscences of Charleston: lately published in the* Charleston Courier, *and now revised and enlarged by the author* (Charleston, SC: 1854) and Bertrand Van Ruymbeke, "Fêtes révolutionnaires et clubs jacobins: Vivre la Révolution à Charleston, en Caroline du Sud, 1792–1797," in *Cosmopolitisme, patriotisme, Europe-Amériques, 1773–1802*, (eds.) Marc Belissa and Bernard Cottret (Rennes: 2005), 125–39.

in Prussia by Jean-Pierre Erman and Pierre Chrétien Frédéric Reclam.[7] This book is the expression of a burgeoning dual identity French (Huguenot) and Prussian, and a first history of a Huguenot settlement in a country of the dispersion. Incidentally, its publication proves how illusory it was on the part of France to expect a massive return of descendants of refugees in the 1790s.

The American Revolution was also a time of travel and reflection on the part of Huguenot descendants. John Jay, future first Supreme Court chief justice and one of the American negotiators for the 1783 Treaty of Paris, openly rooted his Francophobia in the flight of his ancestors out of France.[8] In his diary John Adams, another peace negotiator, recorded that "[Jay] says they [the French] are not a moral people" and that "he doesn't like any Frenchman," further noting that according to Jay "The Marquis de La Fayette is clever but he's a Frenchman."[9] The other peace negotiator of Huguenot origins, Henry Laurens, from Charleston, South Carolina, and former President of the Continental Congress in 1777 and 1778, had traveled in 1772 to Poitiers and La Rochelle, birthplace of his grandfather André Laurent, in search of cousins and ancestral coats of arms. Laurens returned from France empty-handed and despondent. Two years later the fortuitous reception of a letter from the Laurence family in Poitiers while he was in London restored his confidence. It gave him the opportunity to compare the coats of arms he had designed in South Carolina to those of the French branch of his family. Thus, he wrote in a letter to "Monsieur et Madame Laurence": "When I was at La Rochelle in December 1772 being informed that there was none of my Name in that City, nor any Register of Family Arms, I despaired of tracing my Ancestry" but "Perhaps by a Comparison of our Arms our Alliance may be further Confirmed... The Crest was a lion couchant or passant but I have adopted a new Crest which will appear over the Cypher of the Initial Letters of my Name, also fixed to this Letter."[10] This Huguenot memorial quest was individual and aristocratic and is

---

7 Viviane Rosen-Prest, *L'historiographie des Huguenots en Prusse au temps des Lumières. Entre mémoire, histoire et légende: J.P. Erman et P.C.F. Reclam, Mémoires pour servir à l'histoire des Réfugiés françois des Etats du Roi (1782–1799)* (Paris: 2002). Erman and Reclam met with Raynal when he traveled to Berlin in 1782.

8 Julian P. Boyd, "Two Diplomats between Revolutions: John Jay and Thomas Jefferson," *The Virginia Magazine of History and Biography* 66 (1958), 134. See also Ronald Hoffman and Peter J. Albert (eds.), *Peace and Peacemakers. The Treaty of 1783* (Charlottesville: 1986).

9 John Adams Diaries, Massachusetts Historical Society, Electronic Archives, November 5, 1782.

10 "To Messieurs and Madame Laurence," (London, February 25, 1774), in George C. Rogers, Jr, et al. (eds.), *The Papers of Henry Laurens* (Columbia, SC: 1981), vol. 9, *April 19, 1773–December 12, 1774*, 309 and 311.

not representative of the descendants of refugees at large. It shows however—and this applies to nearly all descendants at the end of the 18th century—that they were interested in France only inasmuch as it gave them information on their origins. Not at all to ever return there.

2 Mid-19th-century Renaissance (1850s–1860s)

While in 1802 Protestantism received full state recognition in France under the Concordat, the Huguenots were reintegrated into the national historical narrative only in the mid-19th century. The 1850s were a crucial decade in France from that respect. In 1852 the Protestants founded their historical society, the *Société de l'Histoire du Protestantisme Français* (SHPF) in Paris along with the publication of a journal, the *Bulletin*.[11] The founders wished to collect manuscripts and books on Huguenot history, as well as oral traditions, in France but also to gather information on the refugees' influence wherever they settled. With the help of local associations they also started commemorating events and places in France's historically Protestant regions. Their intention was to show that French religious history was not limited to Catholicism and to reintegrate the Huguenots into the national past. The *Société* also aimed at making 19th-century Huguenots aware of their own history and the place it should occupy in local and national memory.

The following year, the Alsatian historian Charles Weiss published his seminal and monumental two-volume study of the Refuge, entitled *Histoire des réfugiés protestants de France depuis la révocation de l'Edit de Nantes jusqu'à nos jours*. Weiss coined the term "refuge" to designate the post-revocation exodus.[12] In a footnote Weiss acknowledged that "the word refuge applied to all refugees settled in the countries that offered them asylum is not French…" and explained that he borrowed it from "expatriated authors" forced to invent new terms.[13] In this sweeping survey Weiss discussed refugees in Brandenburg, England, the Netherlands, Switzerland, Denmark, Sweden, and Russia, but

---

11   See the special issue of the *Bulletin* on the 150th anniversary of the Société, *1852–2002: numéro spécial du cent-cinquantenaire de la SHPF*, 148/4 (2002) and in that issue Thierry Du Pasquier, "Les sociétés huguenotes, relais de l'histoire du protestantisme français dans le monde," 735–44.

12   Whereas the term *"réfugiés"* or "refugees" had been in use since the time of the migration except in France where refugees were labeled *fugitifs*. Weiss spelled refuge with a lower case "r" whereas French historians now use a capital.

13   Charles Weiss, *Histoire des réfugiés protestants de France depuis la révocation de l'Edit de Nantes jusqu'à nos jours*, (1853; repr. Paris: 2007), 5.

also more surprisingly for the time period America, South Africa, and Suriname. Yet Weiss aspired to much more. Beyond the Refuge he wished to "in some ways fill a void in our national history." As early as 1854, Weiss's study was translated into English and published in New York "with an American appendix by a descendant of the Huguenots." The translator, Henry William Herbert, was a historical novelist (one of his novels dealt with the *Fronde*[14]) and translator of Alexandre Dumas and Eugène Sue. This translation guaranteed Weiss wide readership at least in the English-speaking countries of the dispersion. In America, Herbert placed the "expatriated Huguenots" on the pantheon of the country's founders in adding them to the famed George Bancroft list enumerating "the adventurous companions of Smith, the Puritan felons that freighted the fleet of Winthrop, [and] the Quaker outlaws that fled from jails with a Newgate prisoner as their sovereign"![15]

Soon after, in 1860, the great French historian Jules Michelet, professor at the prestigious Collège de France, published his *Louis XIV et la Révocation de l'édit de Nantes* in which the Huguenots are depicted as victims of Louis XIV's absolutism. Considering the phenomenal impression of Michelet's work on France's collective memory and perception of history this condemnation of Louis XIV and rehabilitation of the Huguenots, fueled by the historian's republicanism, is noteworthy. Michelet exhumed the history of French Protestants from "under the ashes of oblivion," as his biographer Paul Viallaneix nicely put it.[16] In his opening words he even declared that the Revocation held the place for the 17th century as the Revolution did for the 18th.[17] One could not give more visibility to the Protestants and their emigration in French history.

In 1867, in the wake of Michelet's saga, Scottish reformer and educator Samuel Smiles published his thorough *The Huguenots: Their Settlement, Churches and Industries in England and Ireland*.[18] Smiles's intention was to show how much England had benefited from the Huguenots' industry and skills. Thus, whereas Weiss underlined the cultural benefits of the dispersion on the European-wide influence of French culture and language and Herbert made Huguenots founders of the American republic, Smiles emphasized the economic impact of the Huguenot immigration on England. All stressed the loss to France.

---

14   Weiss, *Histoire des réfugiés*, 1.
15   George Bancroft, *History of the United States from the Discovery of the American Continent*, vol. 2 (Boston: 1859), 453.
16   Jules Michelet, *De la Révocation de l'Edit de Nantes à la Guerre des Cévennes* (Paris: 1985), foreword, iv.
17   Michelet, *De la Révocation*, v.
18   Samuel Smiles, *The Huguenots: Their Settlements, Churches and Industries* (London: 1867).

3 The "Huguenot Race" (1880s)

The 1880s, which culminated with the bicentenary of the Revocation, were a decisive decade for the history and the memory of the Refuge. The 1885 commemoration, along with the contemporaneous founding of Huguenot societies, launched a series of publications and events that gave international visibility to the dispersion and the descendants of the refugees. As early as 1883, New York Huguenots founded the *Huguenot Society of America*. The name was not, as one might think, a sign of New York arrogance. Simply put, it was then the only Huguenot Society in America. It was a surprisingly precocious foundation when one considers that the American colonies were marginal to the dispersion with a total of no more than 3000 refugees out of at least 180,000. This development can only be explained by the wave of ethnic and patriotic pride that followed the 1876 centennial in the United States.[19] There, Huguenot memory was one of an ethno-religious group among many. It carried prestige nonetheless due to the early arrival of the refugees on American shores and to the no less early foundation of their genealogical societies.[20]

The 1880s corresponded to the beginning of the professionalization of history. At the time, all historical societies were also genealogical and patriotic. It was in this spirit that the Huguenot Society of America was founded. It was a way for Huguenot descendants to be part of American mainstream memory. Although Huguenot refugees were persecuted Calvinists, and consequently potential heroes, they were nonetheless French, that is not "Anglo-Saxon." This was the time when the pastor Josiah Strong deified the "Anglo-Saxon race," meaning Anglo-American, and delineated its world mission in his book *Our Country. Its Possible Future and its Present Crisis* published in 1885. In 1912 an American chronicler wrote that "the Huguenot was a French Puritan, in substance identical to the English Puritans [and] not fundamentally different

---

19 Bertrand Van Ruymbeke and François Weil, "Du *melting-pot* à l'histoire atlantique. Historiographie du Refuge et mémoire huguenote aux États-Unis (1880–2006)," in *Les huguenots et l'Atlantique*, vol.2 *Fidélités, racines et mémoires*, (eds.) M. Augeron, D. Poton, and B. Van Ruymbeke (Paris: 2012), 217–29; and *Huguenot Society of America. History, Organization, Activities, Membership, Constitution, Huguenot Ancestors, and Other Matters of Interest* (New York: 1963).

20 As evidence of this prestige in the mid-19th century, South Carolina Unionist James Pettigrew "huguenotted" his name into Petigru as told by Mary Boykin Chesnut in her Civil War diary. C. Vann Woodward (ed.), *Mary Chesnut's Civil War* (New Haven: 1981), 366. See also William Henry Pease and Jane H. Pease, *James-Louis Petigru: Southern Conservative, Southern Dissenter* (Columbia, SC: 2002).

from a Catholic Frenchman, except that he averaged higher."[21] Calvinism thus became a redeeming quality for Protestants of Latin extraction and their migration acted as a selective process.

Late 19th-century descendants of refugees forged what they called the "Huguenot race." In this form of genealogical eugenics, cultural and personal characteristics are transmitted through the blood. For the Huguenots, these were industry, honesty, nobility, and faith.[22] These traits formed the basis of what Etienne François, referring to the Berlin Huguenots, called *"le légendaire Huguenot."*[23] It is striking that Huguenot memory, be it in the United States, Germany, Britain or South Africa, has sanctified the same characteristics: faith, industry, nobility, courage, and patriotism.[24] In the United States, Huguenot ethnic self-celebration preceded that of other groups of non-English stock. The Dutch founded the Holland Society in New York in 1886, the Scotch-Irish met in a Congress in 1889, and the American-Irish Historical Society was created in 1897. As François Weil notes, these groups "used genealogy to attempt to counterbalance what they perceived as the undue weight of Anglo-Saxonism" in America.[25]

4   American Huguenot Memory: North and South

As early as 1885, the New York Huguenots suggested that their brethren in Charleston form a local, meaning southern branch of their Society. Twenty years after the end of the Civil War, the Huguenot ancestor served as a mediator between two former enemies. These men had all lived through the deadly maelstrom of the Civil War. Honoring a common ancestor—the émigré—was

---

21   *Transactions of the Huguenot Society of South Carolina*, 19 (1912), 29. See also Bernard Cottret, "Frenchmen by Birth, Huguenots by the Grace of God. Some Aspects of the Huguenot Myth," in *Memory and Identity. The Huguenots in France and the Atlantic Diaspora*, (eds.) Bertrand Van Ruymbeke and Randy J. Sparks (Columbia: 2003), 310–24.

22   Bertrand Van Ruymbeke, "*Cavalier* et *Puritan*: l'ancêtre huguenot au prisme de l'histoire américaine," *Diasporas. Histoire et Sociétés* 5 (2004), 12–22.

23   Etienne François, "Du patriote prussien au meilleur des Allemands," in *Le Refuge huguenot*, (eds.) Michèle Magdelaine and Rudolf von Thadden (Paris: 1985), 229.

24   In France, since Michelet, the Huguenots have been associated with republicanism. Michelet wrote that with their first synod in 1559 the Huguenots gave France "la République, l'idée et la chose et le mot." Quoted in Paul Viallaneix, in foreword Michelet, *De la Révocation*, ii. A parallel can be made with George Bancroft and his followers who rooted American democracy in the Puritan (Calvinist) 1620 *Mayflower Compact*.

25   François Weil, *Family Trees. A History of Genealogy in America* (Cambridge, Mass.: 2013), 135.

their way to participate in the process of reunion that was at play in the nation at large in the post-Civil War era.[26]

In the midst of the Civil War, South Carolina planter Samuel Porcher Gaillard had included a brief account entitled "First Huguenot Emigrants" in his plantation ledger. The opening words state:

> Men & Women, old & young, strove together in the most menial & laborious occupations. But, as courage and virtue usually go hand in hand with industry, the three are apt to triumph together. Such was the history in the case of the Carolina Huguenots. If the labor & the suffering were great, the fruits were prosperity.[27]

Gaillard implicitly mentioned the colonial era when life was difficult yet all was possible. He highlighted three of the four pillars of 19th-century Huguenot identity outside of France: courage, virtue, and industry. Faith is missing but later Gaillard alluded to it in evoking "the Popish persecution in [his ancestors'] native land."[28] In 1866, when Gaillard finished his account, the South was ruined and everything needed to be rebuilt. Gaillard lived an inward exile, a defeat, and looked for better times. To construct his new post-Civil War identity, Gaillard invoked the perils and exile, this time literal, his Huguenot ancestors had lived through.

When in February 1885, upon the occasion of the bicentennial commemorations, E.F. Delancy, president of the Huguenot Society of America, wrote to W.G. DeSaussure in Charleston, he invited South Carolina Huguenots to individually join the Huguenot Society in order to form a "General Committee of Gentlemen of French Protestants" representing the fourteen historical Huguenot settlements.[29] This invitation raised much enthusiasm in Charleston but instead of joining the New York society South Carolina Huguenots founded their own society a month later. Reunion, yes, absorption, no! After all there were limits to what Southerners were ready to do even on behalf of the heroic colonial ancestors.[30]

---

26 On this fascinating issue, see David W. Blight, *Race and Reunion: The Civil War in American Memory* (Cambridge, Mass.: 2001).

27 Samuel Gaillard, "First Huguenot Emigrants," Plantation ledger, 1863–1866, Columbia, South Caroliniana Library, Gaillard Collection, Ms. 781, [1].

28 Gaillard, "First Huguenot Emigrants," [3].

29 "Correspondence leading to the Organization of the Huguenot Society of South Carolina," *The Transactions of the Huguenot Society of South Carolina*, 4 (1899), 3.

30 Various Huguenot Societies were created in the United States in the first half of the 20th century. One of the largest was the Huguenot Society of the Founders of Manakin in the Colony of Virginia (1922). Today the *National Huguenot Society*, founded in 1951, has over forty state chapters.

5 The 1885 Anniversary and the Launching of World-wide Huguenot History

The year 1885 can be seen as the starting point of Huguenot history outside of France inasmuch as history and memory, along with genealogy, were not then perceived as distinct.[31] In fact, state historical journals in America, such as the *South Carolina Historical and Genealogical Magazine*, founded in 1900, or the *Virginia Magazine of History and Biography*, founded in 1893, were as much genealogical as historical. In South Carolina, the Huguenot Society publication, called *Transactions*, whose first issue preceded that of the *South Carolina Historical and Genealogical Magazine*, carried much local prestige. It would be anachronistic to sideline it as a minor publication simply because its aim was genealogical and, to some extent, denominational. Local memory, especially in the South, was in the hands of prestigious families, a sort of genealogical aristocracy. Not everybody could claim a passenger of the *Mayflower* as an ancestor but nearly all Huguenots could assert descent from a family settled in North America before 1720. Quite a prestigious pedigree if ever.

Thus American Huguenots led the way.[32] This was due to America's love for local history and genealogy as well as to the particular importance an early arrival on the continent carried in an age when the country was traversed by Nativist preoccupations concerning the maintenance of its WASP identity. In 1885, Huguenots in Britain founded the Huguenot Society of London.[33] There also, emulating their American counterparts, descendants of refugees claimed the honor of belonging to a "Huguenot race." This concept is fascinating to observe in its implied nationalistic, even "racial" in the sense it carried then, meanings. It superbly reveals how Huguenot descendants were profoundly integrated in their countries. British or American Huguenots were not, despite

---

31 In the United States the 1685 Revocation was celebrated by the Huguenot Societies as a founding moment with the arrival of Huguenot settlers in America when the colonies, except Massachusetts, Virginia and marginally New York, were nascent. In France as well the Revocation was seen as a founding moment in the history of Protestantism as the Huguenots, a religious minority fatally attracted to dominant Catholicism, found the resources to remain a minority through persecution and resilience.

32 The term "Huguenot," as in *Huguenot Societies*, to refer to French Protestants also came into France in the late 19th century from abroad, especially from the Anglo-American world. Conversation with Patrick Cabanel, Berlin, November 2013.

33 Renamed in 1986 the Huguenot Society of Great Britain and Ireland. The Huguenot Society of Great Britain and Ireland has been very active in publishing sources (denization and naturalization lists, consistory records, correspondence, and so forth) on the Refuge in Britain in its quarto series.

all their claims, speaking as Huguenots, meaning French Protestants, precisely because they were not French. Make no mistake, claiming to be a Huguenot or to have "Huguenot blood" did not mean being Francophile or for that matter Francophone. In 19th-century America or Britain, being French meant essentially being a Catholic peasant. This is the ambiguity which lay at the core of 19th-century Huguenot identity. Huguenot descendants were no doubt proud of being of French Protestant ancestry yet they were prouder of being American or British.

A case in point is Lucian J. Fosdick's 1906 book called *The French Blood in America*. Despite the generic word "French" the book is a narrative and simple (there are no notes) account of the Huguenot migration to America. In a very telling way the Huguenots are brandished as an example to the (Catholic) Québécois who were then settling in New England. In his introduction Fosdick wrote:

> It is the author's conviction that the French who of late years have been pouring into New England...may be greatly stimulated by the example of their fellow countrymen of an earlier day...[for] it was the distinction and one source of the wide spread influence of the early French settlers that they assimilated thoroughly and rapidly...becoming American instead of striving to perpetuate race prejudice and peculiarity.[34]

Beyond the amalgam of French Protestants and Catholic Québécois as "fellow countrymen" and the confusion between colonial settlers and 19th-century immigrants, the message is clear.

Fosdick's book was meant to be a simplified version of Charles W. Baird's *History of the Huguenot Emigration to America* published in 1885.[35] Baird was a New York Presbyterian minister. He had accompanied his father, the Reverend Robert Baird, in his missionary activities in Europe. Charles W. Baird was particularly sensitive to the cause of a Protestant minority in a Catholic country. Hence the story of the Huguenots' flight appealed to him.[36] Translated into French a year after its publication, Charles Baird's two-volume study of the Huguenot migrations across the Atlantic still stands as an important work on the Refuge.[37] Baird wrote in the biased, anti-Catholic, and hagiographical style

---

34 Lucian, J. Fosdick, *The French Blood in America* (New York: 1906), 12.
35 Charles W. Baird, *History of the Huguenot Emigration to America* (2 vols. New York: 1885).
36 His father Robert Baird included a chapter on the Huguenots in his 1842 *Religion in America* and his brother Henry Martyn Baird also published books on the French Reformation and the Revocation.
37 Charles W. Baird, *Histoire des réfugiés huguenots en Amérique* (Toulouse: 1886).

of his days but he relied meticulously on archival sources. His book is full of information on individual refugees and transcriptions of documents. A little before Baird, British historian and archivist Reginald Lane Poole published his *A History of the Huguenots of the Dispersion at the Recall of the Edict of Nantes*.[38] Poole's tone is even more anti-Catholic than Baird's and decidedly anti-Louis XIV with chapters as "The Tyranny" and "Commercial Decadence" in reference to the widespread yet erroneous belief in Huguenot circles, then and now, that the exodus caused France's economic collapse.[39] Poole surveyed all places within the Refuge and concluded his book with chapters on "The Power of the Refugees." Baird and Poole rode the wave of late 19th-century dominant "Anglo-Saxonism" and wrote books with a militant Protestant spirit. Their tone is unapologetic, almost vindictive, and certainly confident.

In Berlin, the journal *Die französische Colonie*, founded in 1887, successfully called for the creation of a Huguenot Society (*Deutsch Hugenotten-Verein*) based in Frankfurt. The announcement also praised the Huguenots in saying: "In the history of Protestantism there has existed no name that sounds as beautiful, as pure, as noble as that of the Huguenots. The Huguenots were a blessing for the world."[40] As in London, the creation of the *Deutsch Hugenotten-Verein* was the result of the 1885 commemorations and the publication of books on the Refuge in Germany.

In the United States, the British Isles, and Germany the term "Huguenot" actually includes more than the Protestants who left France.[41] "Huguenot" also refers to the Walloons, the Swiss Calvinists, the Waldenses, and the Orangeois. The word Huguenot means French-speaking Protestants, even if the Huguenots proper, that is Calvinists from the kingdom of France, far outnumbered other refugees. Probably because of sheer numbers, and the prestige carried in some places by having an ancestor who escaped clandestinely from absolutist France, the Huguenot absorption of other groups' memory has gone unnoticed. Only in New York, did it lead to an intense rivalry. In their quest for founders, the Huguenot Society of America and the Holland Society coveted the Walloons who arrived in the Hudson River in 1624. They were French-speaking Protestants,

---

38 Reginald L. Poole, *A History of the Huguenots of the Dispersion at the Recall of the Edict of Nantes* (London: 1880).

39 On this point see Myriam Yardeni, "Naissance et essor d'un mythe: la révocation de l'Edit de Nantes et le déclin économique de la France," BSHPF 139 (1993), 76–96.

40 Quoted in Friedrich Centurier, "Les descendants de huguenots et l'association des huguenots allemands," in *Le Refuge huguenot*, (eds.) Magdelaine and von Thadden, 247.

41 Hence the use of the redundant association "French Huguenots." On the disputed origin of the word Huguenot see Janet G. Gray, "The Origin of the Word Huguenot," SCJ 14 (1983), 349–59.

therefore Huguenots, yet they were sent across the Atlantic by the Dutch West India Company. Who could therefore boast of having founded New York: the Huguenot or Holland Society? To complicate matters, "Were not the Walloons rather from Belgium?" began to ask French-speaking Belgian historians. In the 1920s, Lucy Green wrote about the "Walloon founding of New Amsterdam," but William E. Griffis wrote of "the Belgic Pilgrim Fathers of the Middle States."[42] Sixty years later Robert Goffin in his *Les Wallons, fondateurs de New York*—suggesting that New York was a more impressive name than New Amsterdam—still described the Dutch settlement in the 1620s as "a Walloon village in a corner of the New World"![43] Eventually the Huguenots won. The New York Walloon legacy was claimed by the Huguenot Society.

The exception to this trend is the Netherlands, where Huguenot memory has conversely long been eclipsed by that of the Walloons, more numerous and present earlier on Dutch soil than the French. In fact, the migration of these French-speaking Protestants from the Spanish Netherlands is coterminous with the foundation of the United Provinces, which gives it a higher visibility in Dutch national memory than that of the Huguenots. In 1878, a century before the Dutch Huguenot Society (*Nederlandse Huguenoten Stichting*), the *Commission pour l'histoire des Églises wallonnes* was founded at Leiden. Similarly, a Huguenot Society of South Africa (*Hugenote Stigting van Suid-Afrika*) was only founded in 1953, precisely because Huguenot memory was an integral part of Afrikaner identity celebrated with the founding of the Society of True Afrikaners (*Genootskap vir Regte Afrikaners*) in 1875 as a reaction to the anglicizing of white South Africa.[44]

---

42   William E. Griffis, *The Story of the Walloons, at Home, in Lands of Exiles and in America* (Boston: 1923) and Lucy G. Green, *The De Forests and the Walloon Founding of New Amsterdam* (New York: 1924). See also Bertrand Van Ruymbeke, "The Huguenot and Walloon Elements in New Netherland and Seventeenth-Century New York: Identity, History, and Memory," in *Revisiting New Netherland. Perspectives on Early Dutch America*, (ed.) Joyce D. Goodfriend (Leiden: 2005), 41–54.

43   Robert Goffin, *Les wallons, fondateurs de New York* (Gilly, Belgium: 1970), 95. This book was inspired by a larger hymn to the Belgians in the United States written by Goffin while he had taken refuge in New York during WWII entitled *De Pierre Minuit aux Roosevelt, l'épopée belge aux États-Unis* (New York: 1943).

44   Marilyn Garcia-Chapleau, "Le Refuge huguenot du cap de Bonne-Espérance. Genèse, assimilation, heritage," (Doctoral diss., Université de Montpellier: 2013), 379–83. To be published as *Le Refuge au Cap de Bonne-Espérance* (Paris: 2016). On the Huguenots in the Netherlands from a dual migratory and memorial perspective, see the recent study by David van der Linden, *Experiencing Exile: Huguenot Refugees in the Dutch Republic, 1680–1700* (Aldershot: 2015).

6   Early 20th-century Historiography and Commemorations (1920s)

In North America, the 1920s were an eventful decade regarding Huguenot memory and history. In 1924, the Tercentenary Huguenot-Walloon Commission celebrated the founding of New Amsterdam. This prestigious body counted among its members President Calvin Coolidge, French President Gaston Doumergue, the King of Belgium, the Queen of the Netherlands, and the French ambassador to the United States Jules Jusserand.[45] The commemoration gave the Huguenots considerable national and international visibility. The Council of the Belgian Province of Hainaut gave a Walloon Settlers Monument to the city of New York. It still stands at Battery Park. Two years later, the Huguenot Society of South Carolina organized a commemorative event at Parris Island, where Charlesfort stood in 1562. "La Floride Huguenote," a brief French colonization attempt in the American Southeast under the late Valois kings, became the symbol of a sort of Huguenot discovery of America.[46] It did not matter that the archeological remnants that had been located actually belonged to a Spanish fort. European founders had to be Protestant, even Calvinist for that matter.

In 1927, Jean Ribaut's account *The Whole and True Discoverye of Terra Florida* was published with a preface by Jeannette T. Connor, who collected and transcribed documents (mostly Spanish) on early Florida history as well as co-founded the Florida State Historical Society in 1921.[47] In her preface, Connor proudly stated that "the landing of the first Protestants on the soil of North America mark[ed] the birth of religious freedom in our country, forty-five years before…the beginning of Jamestown, and fifty-eight years before the Pilgrims came to Plymouth."[48] Beyond this Huguenot commemoration,

---

45   Caroline-Isabelle Caron, "Une fondation française de New York? Le tricentenaire Huguenot-Wallon de 1624," in *De Québec à l'Amérique française: histoire et mémoire*, (eds.) Yves Frenette, Thomas Wien and Cécile Vidal (Québec: 2007), 175–91.

46   On this brief yet eventful historical moment, see Frank Lestringant, *Le huguenot et le sauvage. La controverse coloniale en France au temps des guerres de Religion (1555–1589)* (Geneva: 2004); John McGrath, *The French in Early Florida. In the Eye of the Hurricane* (Gainesville: 2000); and Mickaël Augeron, John de Bry and Annick Notter (eds.), *Floride, un rêve français (1562–1565)* (La Rochelle: 2013).

47   Jean Ribault, *The Whole and True Discoverye of Terra Florida*, (ed.) Jeannette T. Connor (Deland, Fla.: 1927). This publication was reprinted in 1964 by the University of Florida Press, Gainesville, for the quatercenteny of the foundation of Fort Caroline (1564–1964). Connor's edition contained a facsimile of the 1563 London original edition of Ribaut's account in addition to a transcription and notes by M.H. Biggar of a manuscript version then recently discovered at the British Museum.

48   Ribault. *The Whole and True Discoverye*, (ed.) Connor, x.

Ribaut's account—the word "discoverye" in the title being most opportune 360 years later—served to give Florida an early Protestant founding. A southern state could claim precedence over New England.

As part of the ceremonies, columns, replicas of those left by the Huguenot captains Ribaut and Laudonnière, were erected on Parris Island and on a bluff near Mayport on the coast of Florida, south of Jacksonville where Fort Caroline (1564–1565) was until very recently thought to be located.[49] Adapted from a Portuguese usage along the coast of Africa, the French left the columns, as visible from the sea as possible, with the triple objective of marking the territory in the eyes of other European explorers, helping other French captains locate the settlement, and impressing local inhabitants. These columns attracted the attention of the various American commemorative committees in the 1920s as unusual since the English did not leave columns at Jamestown or Plymouth.[50]

In 1925, in the midst of these commemorations, French historian and Johns Hopkins professor Gilbert Chinard opportunely published his *Les réfugiés huguenots en Amérique*, which remained for decades the only study on the topic available in French besides the 1886 translation of Baird's monograph.[51] Chinard, originally a literary scholar, offered in his post-WWI study of the North American Refuge a fascinating historical introduction on *"le mirage américain"* or the deceptions of the image of America in Europe since the time of its "discovery."[52] Regarding the Huguenot settlements in the United States, this book did not add much to what was then known. Its principal merit was to make the Huguenot migration to North America better known in France. Three years later, Arthur Hirsch published *The Huguenots of South Carolina*.[53] This work was based on a 1916 dissertation defended at the University of Chicago. Hirsch thus was trained in the burgeoning Chicago immigration history school.

---

49 "Programme, ceremonies at Parris Island, South Carolina, on March 27, 1926," *Transactions of the Huguenot Society of South Carolina*, 31, 1926, 7–41. A similar column was even erected at Dieppe, Ribaut's hometown, in 1935. Mickaël Augeron, Didier Poton, and Bertrand Van Ruymbeke (eds.), *Les Huguenots et l'Atlantique*, vol. 1, *Pour Dieu, la Cause ou les affaires* (Paris: 2009), 144–47. Recent efforts have located Fort Caroline in southeast Georgia near the mouth of the Altamaha River. Barry Ray, "Oldest Fortified Settlement ever found in North America? Location of Fort Caroline may be in Georgia," Florida State University, *Science Daily* 21 (February 2014).

50 Bertrand Van Ruymbeke, "Musées et lieux de mémoire huguenots aux États-Unis et en Afrique du Sud," special issue "Les Musées du Protestantisme" of the BSHPF 157 (2011), 597–618.

51 Gilbert Chinard, *Les réfugiés huguenots en Amérique* (Paris: 1925).

52 Chinard, *Les réfugiés huguenots*, introduction, *Le mirage américain*, v–xxxvii.

53 Arthur H. Hirsch, *The Huguenots of South Carolina* (1928; repr. Columbia, SC: 1999).

Based on archival sources, the book had many transcribed documents appended at the end. Still, Hirsch's study, like Chinard's, added little to what Baird and Weiss had written. The scope was different since Hirsch focused only on South Carolina and this was especially welcome since Baird had planned a book on the Huguenots in the southern colonies but passed away before writing it. Hirsch's conclusions were not the least original or innovative. In essence, the Huguenots settled in large number in South Carolina where they quickly and thoroughly assimilated and prospered.

7   The Refuge as a Historical Object (1980s)

For the next sixty years Huguenot historiography on the Refuge was moribund. The Huguenot Diaspora was deemed of no particular interest to professional historians in France or elsewhere.[54] The history of the refugees was for all intents and purposes in the hands of genealogists, antiquarians, and Huguenot Societies.[55] The 1985 tercentenary of the Revocation brought the Huguenot Diaspora suddenly into the limelight. Two major exhibits were organized in Paris and London: "Les Huguenots" at the Archives Nationales and "The Quiet Conquest: The Huguenots 1685–1985" at the Museum of London.[56] International academic conferences, which led to quality publications, were held in most countries of the dispersion (Great Britain, Ireland, the Netherlands, Switzerland, and Germany) and monographs were published in the others (the United States and South Africa).[57] The historical profession and the world of academia

---

54   Notable exceptions to this trend are Warren Scoville, *The Persecutions of Huguenots and French Economic Development, 1680–1720* (Berkeley: 1960); Émile-G. Léonard, *Histoire générale du protestantisme* (3 vols. Paris: 1961–1964); Samuel Mours, *Essai sommaire de géographie du protestantisme réformé français au XVIIe siècle* (Paris: 1966); Daniel Ligou, *Le protestantisme en France de 1598 à 1715* (Paris: 1968); *Le Refuge Huguenot*, special issue of the BSHPF 115 (1969); and Philippe Wolff (ed.), *Histoire des Protestants en France* (Toulouse: 1977).

55   An illustration of this trend is G. Elmore Reaman, *The Trail of the Huguenots in Europe, the United States, and Canada*, originally published in Toronto in 1963 and reprinted by the Genealogical Publishing Co. in 1986. A book of "interest [to] all descendants of Huguenots" according to a review by the president of the [US] National Huguenot Society printed on the back flap.

56   "Les Huguenots," Archives Nationales (October 1985–January 1986) and Tessa Murdoch, "The Quiet Conquest: The Huguenots 1685–1985," *History Today* 35:5 (1985).

57   J.A.H. Bots and G.H.M. Posthumus Meyjes (eds.), *La révocation de l'Édit de Nantes et les Provinces-Unies/The Revocation of the Edict of Nantes and the Dutch Republic*

at last decided to treat the Refuge as an important historical development. Much was learned regarding the total number of refugees (200,000 was the consensual figure), the local factors that led Huguenots to flee France, the much-debated economic impact of the exodus, the escape routes out of France, where the refugees went and in what proportions, as well as what factors led to their integration into the various host societies. Interestingly, this went along with a reexamination by major French historians, Catholic and Protestant alike, of Louis XIV's religious policy and the causes of the Revocation, which the 1985 commemorations called for.[58]

In the United States, Jon Butler's prize-winning book, *The Huguenots in America*, addressed the Huguenot migration for the first time with full academic objectivity. Butler's conclusions appalled proponents of Huguenot religious heroism and hagiographers. According to Butler, the Huguenots were few in America (less than 2000 by 1700), owned slaves extensively, and were unable to maintain group identity as they massively converted to Anglicanism (although an Episcopal church), married British and in New York Dutch settlers, and quickly lost the use of their mother tongue. "Everywhere they went

---

(Amsterdam: 1986); Jon Butler, *The Huguenots in America: A Refugee People in New World Society* (Cambridge, Mass.: 1983); Bernard Cottret, *Terre d'exil. L'Angleterre et ses réfugiés français et wallons, 1550–1700* (Paris: 1985) [English version: *The Huguenots in England immigration and settlement c.1550–1700*, Peregrine and Adriana Stevenson, trans., (Cambridge: 1991)]; R.M. Golden (ed.), *The Huguenot Connection. The Edict of Nantes, its Revocation, and Early French Migration to South Carolina* (Dordrecht: 1988); Robin D. Gwynn, *Huguenot Heritage. The History and Contribution of the Huguenots in Britain* (London: 1985); Magdelaine and Rudolf von Thadden (eds.), *Le Refuge Huguenot*; Irene Scouloudi (ed.), *Huguenots in Britain and their French Background, 1550–1800* (Totowa, NJ: 1987); Edric Caldicott, Hugh Gough and Jean-Paul Pittion (eds.), *The Huguenots in Ireland. Anatomy of an Emigration* (Dublin: 1987); O. Fatio, O.M. Grandjean, L. Martin, and L. Mottu-Weber, *Genève au temps de la Révocation de l'édit de Nantes, 1680–1705* (Geneva: 1985); Maurice Boucher, *French Speakers at the Cape in the First Hundred Years of Dutch East Company Rule, the European Background* (Pretoria: 1981); Pieter Coertzen, *The Huguenots of South Africa, 1688–1988* (Cape Town: 1988); Myriam Yardeni, *Le refuge protestant* (Paris: 1985); Marie-Jeanne Ducommun and Dominique Quadroni, *Le Refuge protestant dans le pays de Vaud (Fin XVIIe-début XVIIe s.). Aspects d'une migration* (Geneva: 1991). See also Liliane Crété, *Coligny* (Paris: 1985).

58 Emmanuel Le Roy Ladurie "Glorieuse Révolution, Révocation honteuse," foreword to Cottret, *Terre d'exil*; Jean-Robert Armogathe, *Croire en la liberté: l'Église catholique et la révocation de l'Édit de Nantes* (Paris: 1985); Janine Garrisson, *L'Édit de Nantes et sa révocation. Histoire d'une intolérance* (Paris: 1985); Élisabeth Labrousse, *"Une foi, un roi, une loi?" Essai sur la révocation de l'édit de Nantes* (Paris: 1985); Jean Quéniart, *La révocation de l'Édit de Nantes. Protestants et catholiques français de 1598 à 1685* (Paris: 1985).

they vanished" seems to be the key message of the book. Thus, the Huguenots, contrary to Baird and Hirsch's visions, were antithetical to the essence of the American experience as seen in the 1980s. In America, the Huguenots could have taken advantage of religious freedom and space to remain Huguenots, that is, Calvinists. Instead they disappeared.[59]

Wrested from the hands of hagiographers and antiquarians, the Huguenot dispersion received the intellectual treatment it merited.[60] The Refuge must be studied as the most important international migration in early modern Europe along with that of the Jews and the Moriscos from Spain in respectively 1492 and 1609. In more ways than one, the 1985 commemorations were a success and much of what we know about the Refuge and the Revocation draws from works published on this occasion.

The 1998 quatercentenary commemorations of the Edict of Nantes (1598–1998) also brought much academic and public attention to Huguenot history, mostly in France, but the focus was understandably on the French Reformation, the Wars of Religion, Henry IV, and the Edict itself. Although the focus was different, clearly 1998 was given birth by 1985.[61]

8   Recent Trends (since 2000)

Since 2000, the Huguenot dispersion has been regularly studied by professional historians. It has become a full-fledged (although not quite mainstream) historical subject. No approach has influenced the historiography more than

---

59   Butler, *The Huguenots in America*.
60   High-level, meticulous, and rigorous genealogy should not be discarded as it remains useful to the historian of the Refuge. See for example the recent Olivier Le Dour and Grégoire Le Clech, *Les Huguenots Bretons en Amérique du Nord* (2 vols. Rennes: 2012–2013).
61   Richard L. Goodbar (ed.), *The Edict of Nantes: Five Essays and a New Translation* (Bloomington, Minn.: 1998); Pierre Joxe, *L'édit de Nantes. Réflexions pour un pluralisme religieux* (Paris: 1998); Thierry Wanegffelen, *L'Édit de Nantes. Une histoire européenne de la tolérance du XVIe au XXe siècle* (Paris: 1998); and Bernard Cottret, *1598. L'Edit de Nantes. Pour en finir avec les guerres de religion* (Paris: 1997). Additionally, the historiography of the Refuge has had a strong traditional interest in the history of ideas, with an emphasis on the Netherlands that has endured. See, for example, Gerald Cerny, *Theology, Politics and Letters at the Crossroads of European Civilization: Jacques Basnage and the Baylean Huguenot Refugees in the Dutch Republic* (Dordrecht: 1987), Jens Häseler and Antony McKenna, *La Vie intellectuelle aux Refuges protestants* (Paris: 1999), idem, *Huguenots traducteurs* (Paris: 2002) and Hubert Bost, *Pierre Bayle* (Paris: 2006).

Atlantic history.⁶² Born in the 1990s, Atlantic history has radically changed our perception of the Refuge and has made it part of an Atlantic phenomenon. In the late 1990s, I developed the idea of a *"Refuge atlantique."*⁶³ My intention was to show that the traditional dichotomy Europe/colonies was not only historically inaccurate, but was also conceptually flawed. The Refuge was only partially a continental phenomenon, even if most refugees remained on the continent. There existed another diasporic space that included the British Isles, the coastal Netherlands, the North American colonies, and to a lesser extent the Cape colony. It was mostly centered around London. The Atlantic refugees shared many characteristics: they were predominantly merchants, came from the quadrangle Poitou-Aunis-Saintonge-Normandy, and maintained epistolary as well as commercial ties among themselves. In addition, most churches founded in distant lands overseas relied on the London Threadneedle Street consistory for advice and pastors, thus creating a sort of "Atlantic *colloque*" [presbytery] in the Huguenot fashion.

In 2003, the University of South Carolina Press published an edited volume, *Memory and Identity. The Huguenots in France and the Atlantic Diaspora*, based on a 1997 Huguenot conference organized in Charleston by the Program in Carolina Lowcountry and Atlantic World.⁶⁴ For the first time, Huguenot history

---

62   Bernard Bailyn, *Atlantic History: Concept and Contours* (Cambridge, Mass.: 2005). Alongside Atlantic history, a renewed interest in religious migration history, particularly in Germany, has also fostered publications on the Refuge. See for instance, Susanne Lachenicht (ed.), *Religious Refugees in Europe, Asia and North America (6th–21st century)*, (Hamburg: 2007); Susanne Lachenicht and Kirsten Heinsohn (eds.), *Diaspora Identities. Exile, Nationalism, and Cosmopolitanism* in *Past and Present* (Frankfurt: 2009); Olivier Forcarde and Philippe Nivet (eds.), *Les réfugiés en Europe du XVIe au XXe siècle* (Paris: 2008); and the 2005 Berlin exhibition entitled *Zuwanderungsland Deutschland: Die Hugenotten*.

63   Bertrand Van Ruymbeke, "Le Refuge atlantique: la diaspora huguenote et l'Atlantique anglo-américain," in Guy Martinière, Didier Poton, and François Souty (eds.), *D'un rivage à l'autre. Villes et protestantisme dans l'aire atlantique (XVIe-XVIIe siècles)* (Paris: 1999), 195–204.

64   Bertrand Van Ruymbeke and Randy J. Sparks (eds.), *Memory and Identity. The Huguenots in France and in the Atlantic Diaspora* (Columbia, SC: 2003). French historians, unlike Americans, have been traditionally reluctant to use the term diaspora generically. Therefore, the word "Refuge" is still the norm. See nonetheless the exception Eckard Birnstiel and Chrystel Bernat (eds.), *La Diaspora des Huguenots. Les réfugiés protestants de France et leur dispersion dans le monde (XVI–XVIIIe siècles)* (Paris: 2001). On this reluctance see Cabanel, *Histoire des protestants en France*, 710–11 and 1291, note 6; and Élisabeth Labrousse, quoted by Cabanel, "Le Refuge, ou comme disent les historiens américains, la diaspora huguenote," *XVIIe siècle* 80 (1967), 75.

in France and in the dispersion was studied through an Atlantic history lens. Another innovation was to use the concept of integration, not only outside of France but also in France itself. The Huguenots were, in this narration, victims of assimilationist policies aimed at making them full-fledged French subjects through forced conversion to Catholicism. Beyond the Refuge, the Atlantic approach came to full fruition with the publication of the extensive two-volume *Les Huguenots et l'Atlantique* (2009–2012).[65] With over sixty contributors from France, Great Britain, Germany, Switzerland, Ireland, South Africa, Canada, the United States, Brazil, Israel, and Spain this work revisits the history of French Protestantism from the earliest days of the Reformation to Huguenot memory today all around the Atlantic basin.

In the wake of Butler's book and inspired by Atlantic history, American and French historians have recently published a number of works on the Huguenot migration and settlement in North America.[66] The Refuge in America is now well mapped. These historians have nuanced Butler's work in several respects. Huguenots were more numerous than Butler had calculated, excluding Virginia from his totals because the refugees who settled there were younger and therefore did not belong to the post-revocation dispersion. They have also revised his notion of the full and quick (not to say desperate) integration—disintegration?—of the Huguenots. In America refugees resisted conformity to Anglicanism, kept the use of French through bilingualism at least up to the third generation, and tried to find marriage partners within the group as long as it was possible. If the overall picture remained the same, the integration process was slower and less linear than Butler had suggested.

---

65   Mickaël Augeron, Didier Poton, and Bertrand Van Ruymbeke (eds.), *Les Huguenots et l'Atlantique*, vol. 1 *Pour Dieu, la Cause et les affaires* and vol. 2 *Fidélités, racines et mémoires* (Paris: 2009–2012).

66   Paula W. Carlo, *Huguenot Refugees in Colonial New York: Becoming American in the Hudson Valley* (Brighton: 2005); Neil Kamil, *Fortress of the Soul: Violence, Metaphysics, and Material Life in the Huguenots' New World, 1517–1751* (Baltimore: 2005); Bertrand Van Ruymbeke, *From New Babylon to Eden. The Huguenots and Their Migration to Colonial South Carolina* (Columbia, SC: 2006); Catharine Randall, *From a Far Country. Camisards and Huguenots in the Atlantic World* (Athens, GA: 2009); David E. Lambert, *The Protestant International and the Huguenot Migration to Virginia* (New York: 2010). See also Geneviève and Philippe Joutard, *De la francophilie en Amérique. Ces Américains qui aiment la France* (Paris: 2006), Ch. 2, 41–53. It is a most welcome book courageously published in the wake of the tense Franco-American crisis over the Iraq war. P. Joutard and G. Joutard, "L'Amérique huguenote est-elle un paradoxe?" *BSHPF* 151 (2005), 65–91 and the special issue of the Toulouse-based *Diasporas, Les Huguenots* 18 (2011).

Beyond Atlantic history the latest—and most welcome—historiographical trend is the study of the Huguenot dispersion in a global perspective. In her *Hugenotten in Europa und Nordamerika* (2010), German historian Susanne Lachenicht compared the experience of Huguenot refugees in Brandenburg, England, Ireland, and North America.[67] Similarly, Owen Stanwood in his *American Historical Review* article (2013), "Between Eden and Empire: Huguenot Refugees and the Promise of New Worlds," not only drew comparisons between actual overseas Huguenot settlements in the Atlantic and Indian Oceans, but also between projects whether or not they led to anything concrete.[68] Stanwood, in addition, articulated an understanding of the history of the dispersion linked to the notion of empire building. This approach promises to yield a global and comprehensive vision of the Huguenot dispersion, devoid of the limitations imposed by a national or regional angle. Like all diasporas, the Refuge was in essence a transnational phenomenon and should be studied as such. Finally, the Companion volume at hand advances the historiographical integration and expansion process initiated in the late 1990s. The essays address a series of critical issues relating to Huguenot life and worship in and outside of France from the Reformation to beyond the Revocation, while expanding geographically as well as topically our vision of the Refuge.

---

67 Susanne Lachenicht, *Hugenotten in Europa und Nordamerika. Migration und Integration in der Frühen Neuzeit* (Frankfurt: 2010). As seen above in note 61 Lachenicht has also edited two volumes on religious migrations that have included the Huguenots, thus placing the Refuge in a salutary comparative perspective worldwide and *dans la longue durée*. See also Birnsteil and Bernat (eds.), *La Diaspora des Huguenots* and Myriam Yardeni, *Le Refuge huguenot. Assimilation et Culture* (Paris: 2002).

68 Owen Stanwood, "Between Eden and Empire: Huguenot Refugees and the Promise of New Worlds," *American Historical Review*, 115 (2013), 1319–44. On the Refuge, utopias, and prophecies see the doctoral thesis of Laetitia Cherdon, "L'imaginaire comme refuge. Utopies et prophéties protestantes à l'époque de la Révocation de l'Édit de Nantes" (Université de Liège, Belgium: 2009). See also Paolo Carile, *Huguenots sans frontières. Voyage et écriture à la renaissance et à l'Âge classique* (Paris: 2001), a study of Huguenot explorers, travelers, and writers at the margins of the Refuge.

Bibliography

Published Primary Sources

Ancillon, Charles, *Mélange critique de littérature recueilli des conversations de feu Monsieur (David) Ancillon avec un Discours sur la vie de feu Monsieur (David) Ancillon et ses dernières heures*, 3 vols. (Basel: 1698).
Apologie ou defence des bons chrestiens contre les ennemis de l'Eglise catholique (n.p.: 1558).
Avertissement aux protestants des provinces, (ed.) Élisabeth Labrousse (Paris: 1986).
Aymon, Jean (ed.), *Tous les synodes nationaux des églises réformées de France*, 2 vols. (The Hague: 1710).
Baron (avocat au Conseil), *Dialogue entre un père et son fils* (Paris: 1658).
Basnage de Beauval, Henri, *Tolérance des religions*, (ed.) Élisabeth Labrousse (New York: 1970).
Bayle, Pierre, *Ce que c'est que la France toute catholique*, (ed.) Élisabeth Labrousse (Paris: 1973).
———, *De la tolérance. Commentaire philosophique sur ces paroles de Jésus-Christ "Contrains-les d'entrer,"* (ed.) Jean-Michel Gros (Paris:1992).
Benedict, Philip and Nicolas Fornerod (eds.), *L'organisation et l'action des églises reformées de France (1557–1563): synodes provinciaux et autres documents* (Geneva: 2012).
Benoist, Élie, *Histoire de l'Edit de Nantes, contenant les choses les plus remarquables qui se sont passées en France avant et après sa publication, à l'occasion de la diversité des Religions*, 5 vols. (Delft: 1693–95).
Bernier, Jean, *Histoire de Blois, contenant les antiquitez et singularitez du comté de Blois* (Paris: 1682).
Boisson, Didier (ed.), *Actes des synodes provinciaux. Anjou-Touraine-Maine (1594–1683)* (Geneva: 2012).
Bosquet, Georges, *Histoire de la délivrance de la ville de Toulouse (1562)*, repr. in *Pièces historiques relatives aux guerres de Religion de Toulouse* (Paris: 1872),
Brewster, Francis, *Essays on Trade and Navigation* (London: 1695).
Brock, R.A. (ed.), *Documents, Chiefly Unpublished, Relating to the Huguenot Migration to Virginia and to the Settlement at Manakin-Town* (Richmond: 1886).
Brousson, Claude, *Estat des Reformez de France* (Cologne: 1684).
——— *La manne mystique du désert* (Amsterdam: 1695).
———, *Lettres et opuscules de feu Mons. Brousson, ministre et martyr du saint Evangile* (Utrecht: 1701).
Calvin, John, *A Commentarie of John Calvine, upon the first booke of Moses called Genesis* (London: 1578).

———, *Institution de la religion chrétienne* (*1559*), in *Ioannis Calvini Opera quae supersunt omnia*, (eds.) G. Baum, E. Cunitz and E. Reuss, vol. 2 (59 vols. Brunswick: 1863–1900).

———, *Institutes of the Christian Religion*, (ed.) John T. McNeill, trans. Ford Lewis Battles, 2 vols. (Philadelphia: 1960).

———, *Calvin's Old Testament Commentaries. Ezekiel I (Chapters 1–12)*, trans. D. Foxgrover and D. Martin (Grand Rapids, Mich.: 1994).

Cato ou reproche à Pompée, se rapportant aux troubles présentes: avec une imprécation à Dieu vengeur (Orléans: 1568).

Chambrun, Jacques Pineton de, *Les larmes de Jacques Pineton de Chambrun, qui contiennent les Persecutions arrivées aux Eglises de la Principauté d'Orange, depuis l'an 1660* (The Hague: 1687).

Chandieu, Antoine de, *Histoire des persecutions et martyrs de l'Eglise de Paris, depuis l'an 1557 iusques au temps du Roy Charles neufviesme* (Lyon: 1563).

Chevalier, Françoise (ed.), *Actes des synodes nationaux. Charenton (1644) – Loudon (1659)* (Geneva: 2012).

Child, Josiah, *A New Discourse of Trade* (London: 1693).

Claude, Jean, *Les plaintes des Protestans, cruellement opprimez dans le Royaume de France* (Cologne: 1686).

———, *An Essay on the Composition of a Sermon*, trans. Robert Robinson (Cambridge: 1778).

Coena Domini I. Die Abendmahlsliturgie der Reformationskirchen in 16./17. Jahrhundert, (ed.) Irmgard Pahl (Freiburg: 1983).

Commission expédiée par le Roy pour envoyer par les provinces de ce royaume certains commissaires pour faire entretenir l'edict et traicté sur la pacification des troubles advenuz en iceluy (Paris: 1563).

Coras, Jean de, *Arrest memorable du parlement de Tholose contenant une Histoire prodigieuse d'un supposé mary, advenüe de nostre temps: enrichie de cent & onze belles & doctes annotations* (Paris: 1572; lst ed. 1560).

———, *Question politique: s'il est licite aux subjects de capituler avec leur prince*, (ed.) Robert M. Kingdon (Geneva: 1989).

Court, Antoine, *Mémoires pour servir à l'histoire et à la vie d'Antoine Court*, (ed.) P. Duley-Haour (Paris: 1995).

———, *Le Patriote français et impartial*, (ed.) Otto H. Selles (Paris: 2002).

Coxe, Daniel, *A Description of the English Province of Carolana: By the Spaniards call'd Florida, and by the French La Louisiane* (London: 1722).

Daillé, Jean, *Melange de sermons prononcés par Jean Daillé à Charenton pres de Paris, en divers temps, & sur differents sujets* (Amsterdam: 1658).

Dentière, Marie, *Epistle to Marguerite de Navarre and Preface to a Sermon by John Calvin*, trans. Mary B. McKinley (Chicago: 2007).

Desmarets, Daniel, *Histoire abregée des martirs francois du tems de la Reformation* (Amsterdam: 1684).

Deux requestes de le part des fidèles de France, qui desirent vivre selon la reformation de l'Evangile, données pour présenter au Conseil tenu à Fontainebleau au mois d'aoust 1560 (n.p.: n.d.).

Duke, Alistair, Gillian Lewis and Andrew Pettegree (eds.), *Calvinism in Europe, 1540–1610: A Collection of Documents* (Manchester: 1992).

Duley-Haour, P. (ed.), *Mémoires pour servir à l'histoire et à la vie d'Antoine Court* (Paris: 1995).

Dumont de Bostaquet, Isaac, *Mémoires d'Isaac Dumont de Bostaquet sur les temps qui ont précédé et suivi la Révocation de l'Édit de Nantes*, (ed.) Michel Richard (Paris: 1968).

——, *Memoirs of Isaac Dumont de Bostaquet, a Gentleman of Normandy, before and after the Revocation of the Edict of Nantes*, (ed.) Dianne W. Ressinger (London: 2005).

Du Moulin, Charles, *Apologie de M. Charles Du Moulin, contre un livret intitulé: "la Deffense civile et militaire des innocens et de l'Église de Christ"* (Lyon: 1563).

Du Moulin, Pierre, *Conseil fidele et salutaire sur les mariages entre personnes de contraire religion* (n.p.: 1620).

Duquesne, Henri, *Recueil de quelques mémoires servant d'instruction pour l'établissement de l'Ile d'Eden* (Amsterdam: 1689).

Erman, Jean-Pierre and Pierre Chrétien Frédéric Reclam, *Mémoires pour servir à l'histoire des réfugiés françois dans les états du Roi de Prusse*, 8 vols. (Berlin: 1782–1799).

Fatio, Olivier (ed.), *Confessions et catéchismes de la foi réformée* (Geneva: 1986).

Félibien, André, *Entretiens sur les vies et sur les ouvrages des plus excellens peintres anciens et modernes*, 6 vols. (1725, repr. Geneva: 1967).

Félice, Paul de, *La Réforme en Blaisois, documents inédits. Registre du consistoire (1665–1677)* (1885: repr. Marseille: 1979).

Fléchier, Esprit, *Fanatiques et insurgés du Vivarais et des Cévennes*, (ed.) Daniel Vidal (Grenoble: 1997).

Fontaine, Jacques, *Mémoires d'une famille huguenote victime de la révocation de l'édit de Nantes*, (ed.) Bernard Cottret (Montpellier: 1992).

Fraser, Charles, *Reminiscences of Charleston: Lately Published in the* Charleston Courier, *and Now Revised and Enlarged by the Author* (Charleston, SC: 1854).

Gassot, Jules, *Sommaire mémorial (souvenirs) de Jules Gassot secrétaire du roi (1555–1623)* (Paris: 1934).

Gaultier de Saint-Blancard, François, *Histoire apologetique, ou Défense des libertez des Eglises Réformées de France*, 2 vols. (Mainz: 1687–88).

Girard, Etienne, *Histoire des souffrances et de la mort du fidele Confesseur et Martyr, M. Isaac le Febvre, de Châtelchignon en Nivernois, Advocat en Parlement* (Rotterdam: 1703).

Grévin, Jacques, *Sonnets d'Angleterre et de Flandre* (Paris: 1898),
Gwynn, Robin (ed.), *Minutes of the Consistory of the French Church of London, Threadneedle Street: 1679–1692* (London: 1994).
Histoire ecclésiastique des églises réformées au royaume de France, (eds.) G. Baum, Ed. Cunitz and Rodolphe Reuss, 3 vols. (1883–89; repr. Nieuwkoop: 1974).
Hotman, François, *L'histoire du tumulte d'Amboyse advenu au moys de mars 1560. Ensemble un avertissement et une complainte au peuple François* (n.p.: 1560).
———, *Epistre envoiée au Tigre de la France* (n.p.: n.d. [Strasbourg: 1560]).
Huber, M. and C.C.H. Rost, *Manuel des curieux et des amateurs de l'art, contenant une notice des principaux graveurs*, 9 vols. (Zurich: 1797–1808),
Huisseau, Isaac d', *La Discipline des Eglises réformées de France ou l'ordre par lequel elles sont conduites et gouvernées* (Geneva: 1666).
Jaquelot, Isaac, *Histoire des souffrances du bien-heureux martyr Mr. Louis de Marolles, Conseiller du Roy, Receveur des Consignations au Baillage de Sainte-Menehoult en Champagne* (The Hague: 1699).
Janisch, Hudson Ralph (ed.), *Extracts from the St. Helena Records* (Jamestown, St. Helena: 1885).
Jarrige, Pierre de, *Journal historique de Pierre de Jarrige, viguier de la ville de St Yrieix (1560-1574)* (Angoulême: 1868).
Jurieu, Pierre, *Histoire du Calvinisme & celle du Papisme mises en parallele, ou Apologie pour les Reformateurs, pour la Reformation, et pour les Reformez, divisée en quatre parties; contre un libelle intitulé l'Histoire du Calvinisme par Mr. Maimbourg*, 4 vols. (Rotterdam: 1683).
———, *Lettres pastorales adressées aux fidèles de France qui gémissent sous la captivité de Babylon*, (ed.) Robin Howells (Hildesheim: 1988).
———, *L'accomplissement des prophéties*, (ed.) Jean Delumeau (Paris: 1994).
La Beaumelle, Laurent Angliviel de, *Deux traités sur la tolérance. L'Asiatique tolérant (1748). Requête des protestants français au roi (1763)*, (ed.) H. Bost (Paris: 2012).
La Haize, Jean de (ed.), *Quarante-sept sermons de M. Jean Calvin sur les huict derniers chapitres des prophéties de Daniel, recueillis fidèlement de sa bouche, selon qu'il les preschoit* (La Rochelle: 1565).
———, *Declaration et Protestation de ceux de la religion reformee de La Rochelle, sur la prise et capture des armes qu'ils ont fait le neufieme de Ianuier dernier* (La Rochelle: 1568).
La Place, Pierre de, *Commentaires de l'estat de la religion et république sous les rois Henry et François seconds et Charles neufieme* (n.p. [Orléans]: 1565).
La Planche, Louis Régnier de, *Histoire de l'Estat de France, tant de la République que de la Religion sous le règne de François II* (n.p.: 1576).
Leguat, François, *The Voyage of François Leguat of Bresse to Rodriguez, Mauritius, Java, and the Cape of Good Hope*, 2 vols. (London: 1891).

———, *Voyage et aventures de François Leguat et ses compagnons en deux îles désertes des Indes orientales*, (eds.) Jean-Michel Racault and Paolo Carile (Paris: 1995).

Lemoine, Jean (ed.), *Mémoires des évêques de France sur la conduite à tenir à l'égard des Réformés* (Paris: 1902).

Le Vasseur, Josué, *Sermon sur la premiere Epistre de Saint Paul Apostre aux Corinthien Chap. 6. Vers. 10. Prononcé à Sedan* (Geneva: 1678).

Livre des délibérations de l'Église réformée de l'Albenc (1606–1682). Édition du manuscrit conservé à la Bibliothèque d'Etude et d'Information Fonds Dauphinois. Grenoble Cote R 9723, (ed.) François Francillon (Paris: 1998).

Louis XIV, *Mémoires pour l'instruction du Dauphin*, (ed.) Pierre Goubert (Paris: 1992).

Marion, Élie, *Avertissements prophétiques*, (ed.) Daniel Vidal (Grenoble: 2003).

Marolles, Louis de, *Histoire des souffrances du bienheureux martyr Louis de Marolles* (The Hague: 1699).

Marteilhe, Jean, *Mémoires d'un galérien du Roi Soleil*, (ed.) André Zysberg (Paris: 1982).

Méjan, François (ed.), *Discipline de l'Eglise Réformée de France annotée et précédée d'une introduction historique* (Paris: 1947).

Mémoires d'un calviniste de Millau (1560–1582), (ed.) J.-L. Rigal (Rodez: 1911).

Michaud, J.F. and Jean Joseph François Poujoulat (eds.), *Nouvelle collection des mémoires pour servir à l'histoire de France, depuis le XIIIe siècle jusqu'à la fin du XVIIIe*, 32 vols. (Lyon: 1836–54).

Migault, Jean, *Journal de Jean Migault ou malheurs d'une famille protestante du Poitou victime de la révocation de l'édit de Nantes (1682–1689)*, (ed.) Yves Krumenacker (Paris: 1995).

Misson, Maximilien, *Le théâtre sacré des Cévennes*, (ed.) Jean-Pierre Richardot (Paris:1996).

Morin, Jean, *Histoire abrégée des souffrances du Sieur Elie Neau sur les galères et dans les cachots de Marseille* (Rotterdam: 1701).

Mylius, Christian Otto, *Recueil des édits, ordonnances, règlements et rescrits contenant les privilèges et les droits attribués aux françois réfugiés dans les États du Roy de Prusse* (Berlin: 1750).

Neau, Elie, *Histoire des souffrances du sieur Élie Neau, sur les galères, et dans les cachots de Marseille*, (eds.) Didier Poton and Bertrand Van Ruymbeke (Paris: 2014).

Nouvelle Relation de la Caroline par Un Gentil-homme François arrivé, depuis deux mois, de ce nouveau pais (The Hague: 1686).

Ordonnances Ecclésiastiques (Genevan), in *Registres de la Compagnie des Pasteurs de Genève du temps de Calvin*, (ed.) J.-F. Bergier, vol. 1, *1546–1553* (Geneva: 1964). In English translation: "Ecclesiastical Ordinances," in *The Register of the Company of Pastors of Geneva in the Time of Calvin*, (ed.) and trans. Philip Edgcumbe Hughes (Grand Rapids, Mich.: 1966).

Pajon, Claude, *Remarques sur l'Avertissement pastoral, avec une Relation de ce qui se passa au consistoire d'Orléans assemblé à Bionne, quand il y fut signifié* (Amsterdam: 1685).

Papier pour le Consistoire de Barbezieux (Angoulême: 1990).

Petitot, Alexandre and L.J.N. Monmerqué (eds.), *Collection des mémoires relatifs à l'histoire de France*, 130 vols. (Paris: 1819–1829).

Pilatte, Léon, *Édits, déclarations et arrests concernans la Religion P. Réformée (1662–1751)* (Paris: 1885).

Pithou, Nicolas, *Chronique de la ville de Troyes et de la Champagne durant les guerres de Religion (1524-1594)*, 3 vols (Reims: 2000).

Pradel, Charles (ed.), *Lettres de Jean de Coras, sa femme et ses amis* (Albi: 1880).

Procès-verbaux de l'Académie Royale de peinture et de sculpture 1648–1793, (eds.) Anatole de Montaiglon and Paul Cornu, 11 vols. (Paris: 1875–1909).

Purry, John Peter, *A Method for Determining the Best Climate of the Earth, on a Principle to Which All Geographers and Historians Have been Hitherto Strangers* (London: 1744).

———, *Memorial Presented to His Grace My Lord the Duke of Newcastle, Chamberlain of His Majesty King George, &c., and Secretary of State: Upon the Present Condition of Carolina, and the Means of Its Amelioration* (Augusta: 1880).

Quick, John (ed.), *Synodicon in Gallia Reformata, or the Acts, Decisions, Decrees, and Canons of Those Famous National Councils of the Reformed Churches in France*, 2 vols. (London: 1692).

Rabaut Saint-Étienne, Jean-Paul, *Du Désert au Royaume. Parole publique et écriture protestante (1765–1788). Édition critique du "Vieux Cévenol" et de sermons de Rabaut Saint-Étienne* (ed.) Céline Borello (Paris: 2013).

Requeste et remonstrance du peuple, addressante au Roy (Orléans: 1567).

Revill, Janie (ed.), *A Compilation of the Original Lists of Protestant Immigrants to South Carolina, 1763–1773* (Columbia: 1939).

Ribault, Jean, *The Whole and True Discoverye of Terra Florida*, (ed.) Jeannette T Connor (Deland, Fla.: 1927).

Rice, Howard C. Jr., (ed.), *Travels in North America in the Years 1780, 1781 and 1782 by the Marquis de Chastellux*, vol. 2 (Chapel Hill: 1963).

Rochefort, Charles de, *Histoire naturelle et morale des îles Antilles de l'Amérique*, (eds.) Bernard Grunberg, Benoît Roux and Josiane Grunberg (Paris: 2012).

Rubys, Claude de, *Histoire veritable de la ville de Lyon* (Lyon: 1604).

Saint-Pierre, Louis de, *The Art of Planting and Cultivating the Vine; As Also, of Making, Fining, and Preserving Wines &c. according to the Most Approved Methods in the Most Celebrated Wine-Countries in France* (London: 1772).

Salvaire, Élie, *Relation sommaire des désordres commis par les Camisards des Cévennes*, (ed.) Didier Poton (Montpellier: 1997).

Schaff, Philip (ed.), *Creeds of Christendom*, 3 vols. (1931; repr. Grand Rapids, Mich.: 1998).

Schurman, Anna Maria van, *Whether a Christian Woman Should be Educated and Other Writings from Her Intellectual Circle*, trans. Joyce Irwin (Chicago: 2007).

Sentence redoutable et arrest rigoureux du jugement de Dieu, à l'encontre de l'impiété des tyrans, recueillies tant des sainctes escriptures, comme de toutes autres histoires (Lyon: 1564).

Thou, Jacques-Auguste de, *Histoire universelle* (London: 1734).

Trento, Jean-Baptiste and Pierre Eskrich, *Mappe-Monde Nouvelle Papistique. Histoire de la Mappe-Monde Papistique, en laquelle est declairé tout ce qui est contenu et pourtraict en la grande table, ou carte de la Mappe-Monde* (Geneva: 1566), (eds.) Frank Lestringant and Alessandra Preda (Geneva: 2009).

Trouillard, Pierre, *Deux sermons faits pour le jeune celebré le 29 Juin 1667* (Sedan: 1667).

Voltaire, *Traité sur la tolérance*, (ed.) John Renwick (Oxford: 2000).

Wittmeyer, Alfred (ed.), *Registers of the Births, Marriages, and Deaths of the Église Française á la Nouvelle York from 1688 to 1804* (1886; repr. Baltimore: 1968).

Secondary Literature

Adams, Geoffrey, *The Huguenots and French Opinion 1685–1787. The Enlightenment Debate on Toleration* (Waterloo, Ontario: 1991).

Alazard Florence (ed.), *La Plainte à la Renaissance* (Paris: 2008).

Alsina, Dominique (ed.), *Louyse Moillon: Paris, vers 1610–1696: la nature morte au Grand Siècle: catalogue raisonné* (Dijon: 2009).

Altrock, Georg et al. (eds.), *Migration und Modernisierung* (Frankfurt am Main: 2006).

Amalou, Thierry, *Une Concorde urbaine: Senlis au temps des Réformes, vers 1520-vers 1580* (Limoges: 2007).

Anquez, Léonce, *Histoire des assemblées politiques des réformés de France, 1573–1622* (1859; repr. Geneva: 1970).

Arendt, Hannah, *La Condition de l'homme moderne* (1961; French edition, Paris: 1983).

Armogathe, Jean-Robert, *Croire en la liberté: l'Église catholique et la révocation de l'Édit de Nantes* (Paris: 1985).

Armstrong, Brian G., *Calvinism and the Amyraut Heresy: Protestant Scholasticism and Humanism in Seventeenth-Century France* (Madison: 1969).

Asche, Matthias, *Neusiedler im verheerten Land: Kriegsfolgenbewältigung, Migrationssteuerung und Konfessionspolitik im Zeichen des Landeswiederaufbaus: Die Mark Brandenburg nach den Kriegen des 17. Jahrhunderts* (Münster: 2006)

Astoul, Guy and P. Chareyre (eds.), *Le protestantisme et la cité* (Montauban: 2013).

Audisio, Gabriel, *Les vaudois. Histoire d'une dissidence. XIIe–XVIe siècle* (Paris: 1998).

Auer, Peter et al. (eds.), *Dialect Change. Convergence and Divergence in European Languages* (Cambridge: 2005).

Augeron, Mickaël, Didier Poton and Bertrand Van Ruymbeke (eds.), *Les Huguenots et l'Atlantique*, 2 vols. (Paris: 2009–2012).

Augeron, Mickaël, John de Bry and Annick Notter (eds.), *Floride, un rêve français (1562–1565)* (La Rochelle: 2013).

Avènement d'Henri IV. Quatrième centenaire, Coutras, 1987 (Pau: 1989).

Baeumerth, Angelika, *300 Jahre Friedrichsdorf 1687–1987* (Friedrichsdorf: 1987).

Bahlcke, Joachim (ed.), *Glaubensflüchtlinge: Ursachen, Formen und Auswirkungen frühneuzeitlicher Konfessionsmigration in Europa* (Münster: 2008).

Baird, Charles W., *History of the Huguenot Emigration to America*, 2 vols. (1885; repr. Baltimore: 1973).

Badstübner-Gröger, Sibylle, Klaus Brandenburg, Rainer Geissler et al. (eds.), *Hugenotten in Berlin* (Berlin: 1988).

Bancarel, Gilles, *Raynal ou le devoir de vérité* (Paris: 2004).

Beer, Mathias et al. (eds.), *Migration und Integration. Aufnahme und Eingliederung im historischen Wandel* (Stuttgart: 1997).

Beil, Ralf (ed.), *Le Monde selon François Dubois: peintre de la Saint-Barthélemy* (Lausanne: 2003).

Belissa, Marc and Bernard Cottret (eds.), *Cosmopolitisme, patriotisme, Europe-Amériques, 1773–1802* (Rennes: 2005).

Bell, Winthrop Pickard, *The "Foreign Protestants" and the Settlement of Nova Scotia: The History of a Piece of Arrested British Colonial Policy in the Eighteenth Century* (Toronto: 1961).

Benbassa, Esther and Aron Rodrigue, *Sephardi Jewry: A History of the Judeo-Spanish Community, 14th–20th Centuries* (Berkeley: 2000).

Benedict, Philip, *Rouen during the Wars of Religion* (Cambridge: 1981).

———, *The Huguenot Population of France, 1600–1685: The Demographic Fate and Customs of a Religious Minority* (Philadelphia: 1991).

———, *The Faith and Fortunes of France's Huguenots, 1600–1685* (Aldershot: 2001).

———, *Christ's Churches Purely Reformed: A Social History of Calvinism* (New Haven: 2002).

———, *Graphic History. The Wars, Massacres and Troubles of Tortorel and Perrissin* (Geneva: 2007).

Benedict, Philip, Guido Marnef, Henk van Nierop and Marc Venard (eds.), *Reformation, Revolt and Civil War in France and the Netherlands 1555–1585* (Amsterdam: 1999).

Benedict, Philip, Silvana Seidel Menchi and Alain Tallon (eds.), *La Réforme en France et en Italie. Contacts, comparaisons et contrastes* (Rome: 2007).

Benedict, Philip, Hugues Daussy and Pierre-Olivier Léchot (eds.), *L'Identité huguenote. Faire mémoire et écrire l'histoire (XVIe–XXIe siècle)* (Geneva: 2014).

Beneke, Chris and Christopher Grenda (eds.), *The First Prejudice: Religious Tolerance and Intolerance in Early America* (Philadelphia: 2011).

Beneke, Sabine and Hans Ottomeyer (eds.), *Zuwanderungsland Deutschland. Die Hugenotten. Ausstellungskatalog des Deutschen Historischen Museums* (Wolfratshausen: 2005).

Benezit, E. et al. (eds.), *Dictionary of Artists*, 14 vols. (Paris: 2006).

Berbig, Roland et al. (eds.), *Berlins 19. Jahrhundert. Ein Metropolen-Kompendium* (Berlin: 2011).

Bernard, Gildas, *Les familles protestantes en France, XVIe siècle-1792. Guide des recherches biographiques et généalogiques* (Paris: 1987).

Bernard, Mathilde, *Ecrire la peur à l'époque des guerres de Religion. Une étude des historiens et mémorialistes contemporains des guerres civiles en France (1562–1598)* (Paris: 2010).

Bernat, Chrystel (ed.), *Enoncer/dénoncer l'autre. Discours et représentations du différend confessionnel à l'époque moderne* (Turnhout: 2012).

Berriot-Salvadore, Evelyne, *Les femmes de la société de la Renaissance* (Geneva, 1999).

Bertrand, Pascal-François (ed.), *Nicolas Tournier et la peinture caravagesque en Italie, en France et en Espagne* (Toulouse: 2003).

Bertrand, Pierre, *Genève et la Révocation de l'Edit de Nantes* (Geneva: 1965).

Beuleke, Wilhelm, *Studien zum Refuge in Deutschland und zur Ursprungsheimat seiner Mitglieder* (Obersickte/Braunschweig: 1966).

Bezzina, Edwin, *After the Wars of Religion: Protestant–Catholic Accommodation in the French Town of Loudun, 1598–1665* (PhD diss., University of Toronto, 2004).

Bieler, André, *L'Homme et la femme dans la morale calviniste* (Geneva: 1963).

Bien, David, *The Calas Affair: Persecution, Toleration, and Heresy in Eighteenth-Century Toulouse* (Princeton: 1960).

Birnstiel, Eckart and Chrystel Bernat (eds.), *La diaspora des huguenots: les réfugiés protestants de France et leur dispersion dans le monde, XVIe–XVIIIe siècles* (Paris: 2001).

Bischoff, Johannes E., *Lexikon deutscher Hugenotten-Orte* (Bad Karlshafen: 1994).

Blet, Pierre, *Les Assemblées du clergé et Louis XIV, de 1670 à 1693* (Rome: 1972).

Blight, David W., *Race and Reunion: The Civil War in American Memory* (Cambridge, Mass.: 2001).

Böhm, Manuela, *Sprachenwechsel. Akkulturation und Mehrsprachigkeit der Brandenburger Hugenotten vom 17. bis 19. Jahrhundert* (Berlin: 2010).

Böhm, Manuela, Jens Häseler and Robert Violet (eds.), *Hugenotten Zwischen Migration und Integration: Neue Forschungen tum Refuge in Berlin und Brandenburg* (Berlin: 2005).

Boisson, Didier, *Les protestants de l'ancien colloque du Berry de la révocation de l'Édit de Nantes à la fin de l'Ancien régime (1679–1789), ou l'inégale résistance de minorités religieuses* (Paris: 2000).

Boisson, Didier and Hugues Daussy, *Les protestants dans la France moderne* (Paris: 2006).

Boisson, Didier and Yves Krumenacker (eds.), *La coexistence confessionnelle à l'épreuve: Études sur les relations entre protestants et catholiques dans la France moderne* (Lyon: 2009).

―――― (eds.), *Justice et protestantisme* (Lyon: 2011).

Bolliger, Daniel, Marc Boss, Mireille Hébert and Jean-François Zorn (eds.), *Jean Calvin. Les visages multiples d'une réforme et de sa réception* (Lyon: 2009).

Borello, Céline, *Les protestants de Provence au XVIIe siècle* (Paris: 2004).

——— (ed.), *Les œuvres protestantes en Europe* (Rennes: 2013).

Bosc, Henri, *La guerre des Cévennes, 1702–1710* (Montpellier: 1985).

Bost, Ami, *Histoire de l'église protestante de Mâcon* (Mâcon: 1977).

Bost, Charles, *Les prédicants des Cévennes et du Bas-Languedoc, 1684–1700*, 2 vols. (Paris:1912).

Bost, Hubert, *Un "intellectuel" avant la lettre: le journaliste Pierre Bayle (1647–1706)* (Amsterdam: 1994).

———, *Ces Messieurs de la R.P.R. Histoires et écritures de Huguenots, XVIIe–XVIIIe siècles* (Paris: 2001).

———, *Pierre Bayle* (Paris: 2006).

Bost, Hubert and Claude Lauriol (eds.), *Entre Désert et Europe. Le pasteur Antoine Court (1695–1760)* (Paris: 1998).

——— (eds.), *Refuge et Désert. L'évolution théologique des huguenots de la Révocation à la Révolution française* (Paris: 2003).

Botha, C. Graham, *The French Refugees at the Cape*, 3d ed. (Cape Town: 1970).

Bots, J.A.H., *La République des Lettres* (Paris: 1997).

Bots, J.A.H. and G.H.M. Posthumus Meyjes (eds.), *La Révocation de l'Edit de Nantes et les Provinces-Unies, 1685. The Revocation of the Edict of Nantes and the Dutch Republic* (Amsterdam: 1986).

Boucher, Maurice, *French Speakers at the Cape in the First Hundred Years of Dutch East Company Rule, the European Background* (Pretoria: 1981).

Braun, Guido and Susanne Lachenicht (eds.), *Hugenotten und deutsche Territorialstaaten: Immigrationspolitik und Integrationsprozesse. Les États allemands et les huguenots. Politique d'immigration et processus d'intégration* (Munich: 2007).

Bregulla, Gottfried (ed.), *Hugenotten in Berlin* (Berlin: 1988).

Broomhall, Susan, *Women and the Book Trade in Sixteenth-Century France* (Aldershot: 2002).

———, *Women and Religion in Sixteenth-Century France* (London: 2006).

Bruhns, Hinnerk (ed.), *Féodalité, capitalisme et Etat moderne en France. Essais d'histoire sociale comparée* (Paris: 1991).

Bucher, Bernadette, *Icon and Conquest. A Structural Analysis of the Illustrations of the De Bry's Great Voyages* (Chicago: 1981).

Burke, Peter, *The Fabrication of Louis XIV* (London: 1992).

Burnett, Amy (ed.), *John Calvin, Myth and Reality: Images and Impact of Geneva's Reformer* (Grand Rapids: 2010).

Butler, Jon, *The Huguenots in America: A Refugee People in New World Society* (Cambridge, Mass.: 1983).

Bourchenin, Pierre-Daniel, *Etude sur les académies protestantes en France au XVIe et au XVIIe siècle* (1882; repr. Geneva: 1969).

Boyer, Henri (ed.), *Dix siècles d'usages et d'images de l'occitan* (Paris: 2001).
Cabanel, Patrick, *Histoire des protestants en France: XVIe–XXIe siècle* (Paris: 2012).
Cabanel, Patrick and Philippe Joutard (eds.), *Les Camisards et leur mémoire 1702–2002* (Montpellier: 2003).
Caldicott, C.E.J., H. Gough and J.-P. Pittion (eds.), *The Huguenots and Ireland: Anatomy of an Emigration* (Dun Laoghaire: 1987).
Cameron, Keith, *Henri III, a Maligned or Malignant King? (Aspects of the Satirical Iconography of Henri de Valois)* (Exeter: 1978).
Canny, Nicholas, *Kingdom and Colony. Ireland in the Atlantic World 1560–1800* (Baltimore: 1988).
Capot, Stéphane, *Justice et religion en Languedoc au temps de l'Edit de Nantes: la chambre de l'Edit de Castres (1579–1679)* (Paris: 1998).
Carile, Paolo, *Huguenots sans frontières. Voyage et écriture à la renaissance et à l'Âge classique* (Paris: 2001).
Carlo, Paula W., *Huguenot Refugees in Colonial New York: Becoming American in the Hudson Valley* (Brighton: 2005).
Cassan, Michel, *Le temps des guerres de Religion. Le cas du Limousin (vers 1530–vers 1630)* (Paris: 1996).
Cerny, Gerald. *Theology, Politics and Letters at the Crossroads of European Civilization. Jacques Basnage and the Baylean Huguenot Refugees in the Dutch Republic* (Dordrecht: 1987).
Chambrier, Alexandre de, *Henri de Mirmand et les réfugiés de la Révocation de l'Edit de Nantes, 1650–1721* (Neuchâtel: 1910).
Chareyre, Philippe, *Le consistoire de Nîmes 1561–1685*, 4 vols. (Doctoral diss., Université de Montpellier III, 1987).
Chareyre, Philippe and Claudie Martin-Ulrich (eds.), *Jeanne d'Albret et sa cour. Actes du colloque international de Pau 17–19 mai 2001* (Paris: 2001).
Chareyre, Philippe and Hugues Daussy (eds.), *La France huguenote. Histoire institutionnelle d'une minorité religieuse (XVIe–XVIIIe siècles)* (Rennes: 2016).
Charonnet, Charles, *Les guerres de Religion et la société protestante dans les Hautes-Alpes (1560-1789)* (Gap: 1861).
Chevalier, Françoise, *Prêcher sous l'Edit de Nantes: la prédication réformée au XVIIe siècle en France* (Geneva: 1994).
Chinard, Gilbert, *Les réfugiés huguenots en Amérique* (Paris: 1925).
Cholakian, Patricia F. and Rouben C. Cholakian, *Marguerite de Navarre (1492–1459): Mother of the Renaissance* (New York: 2005).
Christin, Olivier, *Une révolution symbolique. L'iconoclasme huguenot et la reconstruction catholique* (Paris: 1991).
———, *La paix de religion: l'autonomisation de la raison politique au XVIe siècle* (Paris: 1997).

Clark, Peter (ed.), *The Crisis of the 1590s* (London: 1985).
Coertzen, Pieter, *The Huguenots of South Africa, 1688–1988* (Cape Town: 1988).
Cohen, Robin, *Global Diasporas: An Introduction* (London: 1999).
Colin, Pierre, Élisabeth Germain, Jean Joncheray and Marc Venard (eds.), *Aux origines du catéchisme en France* (Paris: 1989).
Condition (La) juridique de l'étranger hier et aujourd'hui. Actes du Colloque organisé à Nimègue 8–11 mai 1988 (Nijmegen: 1988).
Conlon, Pierre M., *Jean-François Bion et sa Relation des tourments soufferts par les forçats protestants* (Geneva: 1966).
Conner, Philip, *Huguenot Heartland: Montauban and Southern French Calvinism during the Wars of Religion* (Aldershot: 2002).
Coon, Lynda et al. (eds.), *That Gentle Strength: Historical Perspectives on Women in Christianity* (Charlottesville: 1990).
Cosmos, Georgia, *Huguenot Prophecy and Clandestine Worship in the Eighteenth Century: "The Sacred Theatre of the Cévennes"* (Aldershot: 2005).
Coster, Will and Andrew Spicer (eds.), *Sacred Space in Early Modern Europe* (Cambridge: 2005).
Cottin, Jérôme, *Le Regard et la Parole. Une théologie protestante de l'image* (Geneva: 1994).
Cottret, Bernard, *Terre d'exil. L'Angleterre et ses réfugiés français et wallons, 1550–1700* (Paris: 1985).
———, *The Huguenots in England: Immigration and Settlement, c. 1550–1700*, trans. Peregrine and Adriana Stevenson (Cambridge: 1991).
———, *1598. L'Edit de Nantes. Pour en finir avec les guerres de religion* (Paris: 1997).
Crété, Liliane, *Coligny* (Paris: 1985).
Croq, Laurence and David Garrioch (eds.), *La religion vécue. Les laïcs dans l'Europe moderne* (Rennes: 2013).
Crouzet Denis, *Les guerriers de Dieu. La violence au temps des troubles de religion, vers 1525–vers 1610*, 2 vols. (Paris: 1989).
———, *La Nuit de la Saint-Barthélemy. Un rêve perdu de la Renaissance* (Paris: 1994).
———, *Le haut cœur de Catherine de Médicis, une raison politique aux temps de la Saint-Barthélemy* (Paris: 2005).
Daireaux, Luc, *"Réduire les huguenots." Protestants et pouvoirs en Normandie au XVIIe siècle* (Paris: 2010).
Daubresse, Sylvie, *Le Parlement de Paris ou la voix de la raison (1559–1589)* (Geneva: 2005).
Daumas, Maurice (ed.), *Le plaisir et la transgression en France et en Espagne aux XVIe et XVIIe siècles* (Orthez: 1999).
Daussy, Hugues, *Les huguenots et le roi. Le combat politique de Philippe Duplessis-Mornay (1572–1600)* (Geneva: 2002).

———, *Le parti huguenot. Chronique d'une désillusion (1557–1572)* (Geneva: 2014).
Davis, Natalie, *Society and Culture in Early Modern France: Eight Essays by Natalie Zemon Davis* (Stanford: 1975).
———, *Fiction in the Archives: Pardon Tales and their Tellers in Sixteenth-Century France* (Stanford: 1987).
Delaborde, Jules, *Eléanor de Roye, princesse de Condé, 1534–1564* (Paris: 1876).
Delumeau, Jean (ed.), *Histoire vécue du peuple chrétien*, vol. 1 (Toulouse: 1979).
——— (ed.), *La Religion de ma mère: les femmes et la transmission de la foi* (Paris: 1992).
Denis, Vincent, *Une Histoire de l'Identité. France, 1715–1815* (Seyssel: 2008).
Desel, Jochen and Walter Mogk, *Hugenotten und Waldenser in Hessen-Kassel* (Kassel: 1978).
Deursen, Arie Theodorus van, *Professions et métiers interdits, un aspect de l'histoire de la Révocation de l'édit de Nantes* (Groningen: 1960).
Deyon, Solange, *Du loyalisme au refus: les protestants français et leur député général entre la Fronde et la Révocation de l'édit de Nantes* (Lille: 1976).
Diefendorf, Barbara, *Beneath the Cross: Catholics and Huguenots in Sixteenth-Century Paris* (Oxford: 1991).
Dixon, C. Scott, Dagmar Freist and Mark Greengrass (eds.), *Living with Religious Diversity in Early Modern Europe* (Aldershot: 2009).
Dölemeyer, Barbara, *Aspekte zur Rechtsgeschichte des deutschen Refuge* (Sickte: 1988).
———, *Die hessen-homburgischen Privilegien für französisch-reformierte Glaubensflüchtlinge* (Bad Karlshafen: 1990).
———, *Die Hugenotten* (Stuttgart: 2006).
Dompnier, Bernard, *Le venin de l'hérésie. Image du protestantisme et combat politique au XVIIe siècle* (Paris: 1985).
Douglass, E. Jane Dempsey, *Women, Freedom and Calvin* (Philadelphia: 1985).
Ducommun, Marie-Jeanne and Dominique Quadroni, *Le refuge protestant dans le pays de Vaud, fin XVIIe-début XVIIIe s.: aspects d'une migration* (Geneva: 1991).
Dunan-Page Anne (ed.), *The Religious Culture of the Huguenots, 1660–1750* (Aldershot: 2006).
Dupont, André, *Rabaut Saint-Etienne, 1743–1793. Un protestant défenseur de la liberté religieuse* (Geneva: 1989).
Duro, Paul, *The Academy and the Limits of Painting in Seventeenth-Century France* (Cambridge: 1997).
Ebrard, Friedrich K., *Die französisch reformierte Gemeinde in Frankfurt am Main. 1554–1904* (Frankfurt am Main: 1906).
Eire, Carlos M.N., *War against the Idols. The Reformation of Worship from Erasmus to Calvin* (Cambridge: 1986).

Elias, Norbert, *Über den Prozess der Zivilisation* (1939; English trans. *The Civilizing Process*, Oxford: 1994).

El Kenz, David, *Les bûchers du roi: La culture protestante des martyrs, 1523–1572* (Seyssel: 1997).

El Kenz, David and Claire Gantet, *Guerres et paix de religion en Europe, XVIe–XVIIe siècles* (Paris: 2003).

Elyada, Ouzi and Jacques Le Brun (eds.), *Conflits politiques, controverses religieuses* (Paris: 2002).

Engammare, Max, *L'Ordre du temps. L'invention de la ponctualité au XVIe siècle* (Geneva: 2004).

Eschmann, Jürgen (ed.), *Hugenottenkultur in Deutschland* (Tübingen: 1989).

Eurich, S. Amanda, *The Economics of Power: The Private Finances of the House of Foix-Navarre-Albret during the Religious Wars* (Kirksville, Mo.: 1994).

Faré, Michel, *La Nature morte en France. Son histoire et son évolution du XVIIe au XXe siècle* (Geneva: 1962).

Fatio, Olivier, *Méthode et théologie: Lambert Daneau et les débuts de la scolastique réformée* (Geneva: 1976).

Fatio, Olivier, M. Grandjean, L. Martin and L. Mottu-Weber, *Genève au temps de la Révocation de l'édit de Nantes, 1680–1705* (Geneva: 1985).

Félice, Paul de, *Les protestants d'autrefois: vie intérieure des églises, mœurs et usages*, 4 vols. (Paris: 1896–1902).

Ferguson, Gary and Mary McKinley (eds.), *A Companion to Marguerite de Navarre* (Leiden: 2013).

Finney, Paul Corby (ed.), *Seeing beyond the Word. Visual Arts and the Calvinist Tradition* (Grand Rapids, Mich.: 1999).

Fishman, Joshua A., *Reversing Language Shift. Theoretical and Empirical Foundations of Assistance to Threatened Languages* (Clevedon: 1991).

Foa, Jérémie, *Le tombeau de la paix: Une histoire des édits de pacification, 1560–1572* (Limoges: 2015).

Forcarde, Olivier and Philippe Nivet (eds.), *Les réfugiés en Europe du XVIe au XXe siècle* (Paris: 2008).

Forcey, Linda (ed.), *Peace: Meanings, Politics, Strategies* (New York: 1989).

Fouilleron, Joël and Henri Michel (eds.), *Mélanges à la mémoire de Michel Péronnet*, 2 vols. (Montpellier: 2003–2006).

Fragonard, Marie-Madeleine and Michel Péronnet (eds.), *Catéchismes et Confessions de foi* (Montpellier: 1995).

François, Etienne, *Protestants et Catholiques en Allemagne. Identités et pluralisme, Augsbourg, 1648–1806* (Paris: 1993).

Frenette, Yves, Thomas Wien and Cécile Vidal (eds.), *De Québec à l'Amérique française: histoire et mémoire* (Québec: 2007).

Fuhrich-Grubert, Ursula, *Die Französische Kirche zu Berlin. Ihre Einrichtungen. 1672–1945* (Bad Karlshafen: 1992).

Galland, Alfred, *Essai sur l'histoire du protestantisme à Caen et en Basse-Normandie de l'édit de Nantes à la Révolution* (Paris: 1991).

Gantet, Claire, *Discours et images de la paix dans les villes d'Allemagne du Sud aux XVIIe et XVIIIe siècles* (Doctoral diss.: Université de Paris I, 1999).

Garnot, Benoît, *Voltaire et l'affaire Calas. Les faits, les interprétations, les enjeux* (Paris: 2013).

Garrioch, David, *The Huguenots of Paris and the Coming of Religious Freedom, 1685–1789* (Cambridge: 2014)

Garrisson, Francis, *Essai sur les commissions d'application de l'Edit de Nantes*, part 1: *Le règne d'Henri IV* (Montpellier: 1964).

Garrisson, Janine, *Protestants du Midi* (Toulouse: 1980).

———, *L'Édit de Nantes et sa révocation. Histoire d'une intolérance* (Paris: 1985).

———, *L'Affaire Calas: miroir des passions françaises* (Paris: 2004).

Gilmont, Jean-François, *Jean Crespin: un éditeur réformé du XVIe siècle* (Geneva: 1981).

Glozier, Matthew, *The Huguenot Soldiers of William of Orange and the Glorious Revolution of 1688: The Lions of Judah.* (Brighton: 2002).

Glozier, Matthew and David Onnekink, *War, Religion and Service: Huguenot Soldiering, 1685–1713* (Aldershot: 2007).

Glück, Helmut, *Deutsch als Fremdsprache in Europa vom Mittelalter bis zur Barockzeit* (Berlin: 2002).

——— (ed.), *Metzler-Lexikon Sprache* (Stuttgart: 2000).

Goffin, Robert, *De Pierre Minuit aux Roosevelt, l'épopée belge aux États-Unis* (New York: 1943).

———, *Les wallons, fondateurs de New York* (Gilly, Belgium: 1970).

Golden, Richard M. (ed.), *The Huguenot Connection. The Edict of Nantes, Its Revocation, and Early French Migration to South Carolina* (Dordrecht: 1988).

Goldstein, Carl, *Print Culture in Early Modern France. Abraham Bosse and the Purposes of Print* (Cambridge: 2012).

Gonthier, Ursula Haskins and Alain Sandrier (eds.), *Multilinguisme et multiculturalité dans l'europe des lumières* (Paris: 2007).

Goodbar, Richard L. (ed.), *The Edict of Nantes: Five Essays and a New Translation* (Bloomington, Minn.: 1998).

Goodfriend, Joyce D. (ed.), *Revisiting New Netherland. Perspectives on Early Dutch America* (Leiden: 2005).

Gootjes, Albert, *Claude Pajon (1626–1685) and the Academy of Saumur: The First Controversy over Grace* (Leiden: 2014).

Gordon, Bruce and Peter Marshall (eds.), *The Place of the Dead: Death and Remembrance in Late Medieval and Early Modern Europe* (Cambridge: 2000).

Goslinga, Cornelis Ch., *The Dutch in the Caribbean and in the Guianas, 1680–1791* (Assen: 1985).
Grafton, Anthony, *New Worlds, Ancient Texts. The Power of Tradition and the Shock of Discovery* (Cambridge, Mass.: 1992).
Graham, Fred W. (ed.), *Later Calvinism: International Perspectives* (Kirksville, Mo.: 1994).
Grandjean, Michel and Bernard Roussel (eds.), *Coexister dans l'intolérance: l'édit de Nantes (1598)* (Geneva: 1998).
Green, Michael, *The Huguenot Jean Rou (1638–1711): Scholar, Educator, Civil Servant* (Groningen: 2013).
Gregory, Brad, *Salvation at Stake: Christian Martyrdom in Early Modern Europe* (Cambridge, Mass.: 1999).
Grell, Ole Peter and Bob Scribner (eds.), *Tolerance and Intolerance in the European Reformation* (Cambridge: 1996).
Grell, Ole Peter, Jonathan I. Israel and Nicholas Tyacke (eds.), *From Persecution to Toleration. The Glorious Revolution in England* (Oxford: 1991).
Grintchenko, Marie-Hélène, *Catherine de Bourbon (1559–1604): influence politique, religieuse et culturelle d'une princesse calviniste* (Paris: 2009).
Grosse, Christian, *Les rituels de la Cène. Le culte eucharistique réformé à Genève (XVIe–XVIIe siècles)* (Geneva: 2008).
Guillemain, Hervé, Stéphane Tison and Nadine Vivier (eds.), *La foi dans le siècle. Mélanges offerts à Brigitte Waché* (Rennes: 2009).
Guiraud, Louise, *La Réforme à Montpellier* (Montpellier: 1918).
Gwynn, Robin D., *The Huguenots of London* (Brighton: 1998).
———, *Huguenot Heritage: The History and Contribution of the Huguenots in Britain*, 2nd ed. (Brighton: 2001).
Haag, Eugène and Emile, *La France Protestante, ou Vies des Protestants Français*, 9 vols. (Paris: 1846–59).
Haase, Erich, *Einführung in die Literatur des Refuge. Der Beitrag der französischen Protestanten zur Entwicklung analytischer Denkformen am Ende des 17. Jahrhunderts* (Berlin: 1959).
Halvorsen, Michael and Karen Spierling (eds.), *Defining Community in Early Modern Europe* (Aldershot: 2008).
Hanlon, Gregory, *Confession and Community in Seventeenth-Century France: Catholic and Protestant Coexistence in Aquitaine* (Philadelphia: 1993).
Hartweg, Frédéric and Steffi Jersch-Wenzel (eds.), *Die Hugenotten und das Refuge. Deutschland und Europa. Beiträge zu einer Tagung* (Berlin: 1990).
Häseler, Jens and Antony McKenna (eds.), *La vie intellectuelle aux refuges protestants* (Paris: 1999).
Heinich, Nathalie, *Du peintre à l'artiste. Artisans et académiciens à l'âge classique* (Paris: 1993).

Herluison, Henri, *Actes d'état-civil d'artistes, musiciens et comédiens extraits des registres de l'Hôtel-de-Ville de Paris, détruits dans l'incendie du 24 mai, 1871* (Orléans: 1876).

Heyd, Michael, *Between Orthodoxy and the Enlightenment: Jean-Robert Chouet and the Introduction of Cartesian Science in the Academy of Geneva* (The Hague: 1982).

———, *"Be Sober and Reasonable": The Critique of Enthusiasm in the Seventeenth and Early Eighteenth Centuries* (Leiden: 1995).

Hirsch, Arthur Henry, *The Huguenots of Colonial South Carolina* (1928; repr. Columbia, SC: 1999).

Holt, Mack, *The French Wars of Religion, 1562–1629*, 2nd ed. (Cambridge: 2005).

Howells, Robin, *Pierre Jurieu: Antinomien radical* (Durham: 1983).

Hsia, R. Po-Chia and Henk van Nierop (eds.), *Calvinism and Religious Toleration in the Dutch Golden Age* (Cambridge: 2002).

Hugues, Edmond, *Antoine Court. Histoire de la restauration du protestantisme français au XVIIIe siècle*, 2 vols. (Paris: 1872).

———, *Les synodes du Désert*, 3 vols. (Paris: 1886).

Hulton, Paul (ed.), *The Work of Jacques Le Moyne de Morgues. A Huguenot Artist in France, Florida and England*, 2 vols. (London: 1977).

Hunt, Lynn, Margaret C. Jacob and Wijnand Mijnhardt, *The Book that Changed Europe: Picart and Bernard's Religious Ceremonies of the World* (London: 2010).

Hylton, Raymond Pierre, *Ireland's Huguenots and Their Refuge, 1662–1745: An Unlikely Haven* (Brighton: 2005).

Imberdis, André, *Histoire des guerres religieuses en Auvergne pendant les XVIe et XVIIe siècles* (Riom: 1848).

Jaccard, E., *Le marquis de Rochegude et les protestants sur les galères* (Lausanne: 1898).

Jacobs, Jaap, *New Netherland: A Dutch Colony in Seventeenth-Century America* (Leiden: 2005).

Jacobson, Karen (ed.), *The French Renaissance in Prints from the Bibliothèque Nationale de France* (Los Angeles: 1994).

Janse, Wim and Barbara Pitkin (eds.), *The Formation of Clerical Confessional Identities in Early Modern Europe* (Leiden: 2005).

Jersch-Wenzel, Stefi, *Juden und "Franzosen" in der Wirtschaft des Raumes Berlin/Brandenburg zur Zeit des Merkantilismus* (Berlin: 1978).

Jersch-Wenzel, Stefi and Barbara John (eds.), *Von Zuwanderern zu Einheimischen. Hugenotten, Juden, Böhmen, Polen in Berlin* (Berlin: 1990).

Joblin, Alain, *Dieu, le juge et l'enfant. L'enlèvement des enfants protestants en France (XVIIe–XVIIIe siècles)* (Arras: 2010).

Joby, Christopher R., *Calvinism and the Arts: A Re-assessment* (Leuven: 2007).

Join-Lambert, Sophie and Maxime Préaud (eds.), *Abraham Bosse. Savant graveur. Tours, vers 1604–1676, Paris* (Paris: 2004).

Jouanna, Arlette, *Le devoir de révolte. La noblesse française et la gestation de l'État moderne, 1559–1661* (Paris: 1989).

Jouanna, Arlette and Michel Péronnet (eds.), *L'Edit de Nantes: sa genèse, son application en Languedoc*. Special issue of the *Bulletin historique de Montpellier* 23 (1999).

Jourda, Pierre, *Marguerite d'Angoulême, duchesse d'Alençon, reine de Navarre (1492–1549): étude biographique et littéraire*, 2 vols. (Paris: 1930).

Joutard, Philippe, *Les Camisards* (Paris: 1976).

——— (ed.), *Historiographie de la réforme* (Paris: 1977).

———, *La légende des Camisards* (Paris: 1978).

Joutard, Philippe and Geneviève Joutard, *De la francophilie en Amérique. Ces Américains qui aiment la France* (Paris: 2006).

Joxe, Pierre, *L'Édit de Nantes. Réflexions pour un pluralisme religieux* (Paris: 2011).

Kadell, Franz-Anton, *Die Hugenotten in Hessen-Kassel* (Darmstadt: 1980).

Kamil, Neil, *Fortress of the Soul: Violence, Metaphysics, and Material Life in the Huguenots' New World, 1517–1751* (Baltimore: 2005).

Kang, Nam Soo, *La Première période de coexistence religieuse en France: entre la paix d'Amboise (mars 1563) et la deuxième guerre de religion (septembre 1567)* (Doctoral diss.: Paris X-Nanterre, 1995).

Kaplan, Benjamin *Calvinists and Libertines: Confession and Community in Utrecht, 1578–1620* (Oxford: 1995).

———, *Divided by the Faith. Religious Conflict and the Practice of Toleration in Early Modern Europe* (Cambridge: 2007).

Karant-Nunn, Susan, *The Reformation of Ritual: An Interpretation of Early Modern Germany* (London: 1997).

Keefe, Thomas and Ron Roberts, *Realizing Peace: An Introduction to Peace Studies* (Ames, IA: 1991).

King, John N., *Foxe's Book of Martyrs and Early Modern Print Culture* (Cambridge: 2006).

Kingdon, Robert M., *Geneva and the Consolidation of the French Protestant Movement* (Geneva: 1967).

———, *Geneva and the Coming of the Wars of Religion in France, 1555–1563* (1956; repr. Geneva: 2007).

Kingdon, Robert M. and Thomas Lambert, *Reforming Geneva: Discipline, Faith and Anger in Calvin's Geneva* (Geneva: 2012).

Kirchner, Frédéric, *Entre deux guerres 1563–1567. Essai sur la tentative d'application à Lyon de la politique de "Tolérance"* (Lyon: 1952).

Klingebiel, Thomas, *Weserfranzosen: Studien zur Geschichte der Hugenottengemeinschaft in Hameln (1690–1757)* (Göttingen: 1992).

Knecht, Robert, *The French Civil Wars, 1562–1598* (Harlow: 2000).

Knetsch, F.R.J., *Pierre Jurieu: Theoloog en politikus der Refuge* (Kampen: 1967).

Köbler, Gerhard, *Historisches Lexikon der deutschen Länder. Die deutschen Territorien und reichsunmittelbaren Geschlechter vom Mittelalter bis zur Gegenwart*, 7th ed. (Munich: 2007).

Konnert, Mark, *Civic Agendas and Religious Passion: Châlons-sur-Marne during the French Wars of Religion* (Kirksville, Mo.: 1997).

Koselleck, Reinhart, *Le règne de la Critique* (French edition, Paris: 1979).

Kramer, Johannes (ed.), *Das Französische in Deutschland. Eine Einführung* (Stuttgart: 1992).

Kretzer, Hartmut, *Calvinismus und französische Monarchie im 17. Jahrhundert. Die politische Lehre der Akademien Sedan und Saumur mit besonderer Berucksichtigung von Pierre Du Moulin, Moyse Amyraut und Pierre Jurieu* (Berlin: 1975).

Krippendorff, Ekkehart (ed.), *Friedensforschung* (Cologne and Berlin:1968).

Krumenacker, Yves, *Les protestants du Poitou au XVIIIe siècle (1681–1789)* (Paris: 1998).

———, *Les protestants au siècle des Lumières: le modèle lyonnais* (Paris: 2002).

——— (ed.), *Entre calvinistes et catholiques: Les relations religieuses entre la France et les Pays-Bas du Nord, XVIe–XVIIIe siècles* (Rennes: 2010).

Kuijpers, Erika et al. (eds.), *Memory before Modernity: Practices of Memory in Early Modern Europe* (Leiden: 2013).

Kuperty-Tsur, Nadine, *Se dire à la Renaissance* (Paris: 1997).

Labov, William, *Principles of Linguistic Change*, 3 vols. (Oxford: 1994),

Labrousse, Élisabeth, *"Une foi, une loi, un roi?" Essai sur la Révocation de l'édit de Nantes* (Paris: 1985).

———, *Pierre Bayle* (Paris: 1996).

——— (ed.), *Conscience et conviction: Etudes sur le XVIIe siècle* (Oxford: 1996).

Lachenicht, Susanne (ed.), *Religious Refugees in Europe, Asia and North America, 6th–21st century* (Hamburg: 2007).

———, *Hugenotten in Europa und Nordamerika: Migration und Integration in der Frühen Neuzeit* (Frankfurt: 2010).

Lachenicht, Susanne and Kirsten Heinsohn (eds.), *Diaspora Identities. Exile, Nationalism and Cosmopolitanism in Past and Present* (Frankfurt: 2009).

Lafage, Valérie Leclerc, *Montpellier au temps des troubles de Religion. Pratiques testamentaires et confessionnalisation (1554–1622)* (Paris: 2010).

Lafleur, Gérard, *Les Protestants aux Antilles françaises du vent sous l'Ancien Régime* (Basse-Terre: 1988).

Lambert, David E., *The Protestant International and the Huguenot Migration to Virginia* (New York: 2010).

Laplanche, François, *Orthodoxie et prédication: l'œuvre d'Amyraut et la querelle de la grâce universelle* (Paris: 1965).

———, *L'évidence du Dieu chrétien: religion, culture et société dans l'apologétique protestante de la France classique (1576–1670)* (Strasbourg: 1983).

———, *L'écriture, le sacré et l'histoire: érudits et politiques protestants devant la Bible en France au XVIIe siècle* (Amsterdam: 1986).

Lasserre, Claude, *Le Séminaire de Lausanne (1726–1812), instrument de la restauration du protestantisme français* (Lausanne: 1997).

Lauriol, Claude, *La Beaumelle. Un protestant cévenol entre Montesquieu et Voltaire* (Geneva: 1978).

Laursen, John Christian (ed.), *New Essays on the Political Thought of the Huguenots of the Refuge* (Leiden: 1995).

Le Dour, Olivier and Grégoire Le Clech, *Les Huguenots Bretons en Amérique du Nord*, 2 vols. (Rennes: 2012–2013).

Lee, Grace Lawless, *Huguenot Settlers in Ireland* (1936; repr. Baltimore: 1993).

Lehmann, Hartmut, Hermann Wellenreuther and Renate Wilson (eds.), *In Search of Peace and Prosperity: New German Settlements in Eighteenth-Century Europe and America* (University Park, Pa.: 2000).

Léonard, Émile G., *Histoire générale du protestantisme*, 3 vols. (Paris: 1961–1964).

Léonard, Julien, *Être pasteur au XVIIe siècle. Le ministère de Paul Ferry à Metz (1612–1669)* (Rennes: 2015).

LePage, Robert B. and Andree Tabouret-Keller, *Acts of Identity: Creole-Based Approaches to Language and Ethnicity* (New York: 1985).

Le Roux, Nicolas, *La faveur du roi. Mignons et courtisans au temps des derniers Valois (vers 1547–vers 1589)* (Seyssel: 2000).

Le Roy Ladurie, Emmanuel, *Les paysans de Languedoc*, 2 vols. (Paris: 1966),

Lestringant, Frank, *Le huguenot et le sauvage. L'Amérique et la controverse coloniale en France au temps des guerres de Religion (1555–1589)*, 3rd ed. (Geneva: 2004a).

———, *Lumière des martyrs: Essai sur le martyre au siècle des réformes* (Paris: 2004b).

Ligou, Daniel, *Le protestantisme en France de 1598 à 1715* (Paris: 1968).

Lipscomb, Suzannah, *Maids, Wives and Mistresses: Disciplined Women in Reformation Languedoc* (D.Phil., University of Oxford, 2009).

Lodge, Anthony R., *French. From Dialect to Standard* (London: 1993).

Lorimer, Emma, *Huguenot General Assemblies in France, 1579–1622* (PhD diss., Oxford University: 2004).

Louthan, Howard and Randall Zachman (eds.), *Conciliation and Confession: The Struggle for Unity in the Age of Reform, 1415–1648* (Notre Dame: 2005).

Luria, Keith, *Sacred Boundaries. Religious Coexistence and Conflict in Early Modern France* (Washington: 2005).

Luthy, Herbert, *La banque protestante en France, de la Révocation de l'Édit de Nantes à la Révolution*, 2 vols. (Paris: 1959).

Maag, Karin, *Seminary or University? The Genevan Academy and Reformed Higher Education, 1560–1620* (Aldershot: 1994).

Magdelaine, Michelle and Rudolf von Thadden (eds.), *Le Refuge huguenot* (Paris: 1985).

Magdelaine, Michelle, Maria-Christina Pitassi, RuthWhelan and Antony McKenna (eds.), *De l'humanisme aux Lumières, Bayle et le protestantisme: mélanges en l'honneur d'Elisabeth Labrousse* (Oxford: 1996).

Manetsch, Scott, *Theodore Beza and the Quest for Peace in France, 1572–1598* (Leiden: 2000).

Marandet, François (ed.), *Daniel Sarrabat (1666–1748)* (Saint-Étienne: 2011).

Margolf, Diane, *Religion and Royal Justice in Early Modern France: The Paris Chambre de l'Edit, 1598–1665* (Kirksville, Mo.: 2003).

Marshall, John, *John Locke, Toleration and the Early Enlightenment: Religious Intolerance and Arguments for Religious Toleration in Early Modern and "Early Enlightenment" Europe* (Cambridge: 2006).

Martinière, Guy, Didier Poton and François Souty (eds.), *D'un rivage à l'autre. Villes et protestantisme dans l'aire atlantique (XVIe–XVIIe siècles)* (Paris: 1999).

Maynard, John, *The Huguenot Church of New York: A History of the French Church of Saint Esprit* (New York: 1938).

Mayo, Ronald, *The Huguenots in Bristol* (Bristol: 1985).

McCabe, Ina Baghdiantz, Gelina Harlaftis and Ioanna Pepelasis Minoglou (eds.), *Diaspora Entrepreneurial Networks. Four Centuries of History* (Oxford: 2005).

McCullough, Roy L., *Coercion, Conversion and Counterinsurgency in Louis XIV's France* (Leiden: 2007).

McFadin, Christopher, *The Fiscal Reformation in Rural France, 1598–1685* (PhD diss., University of Iowa, 2015).

McGrath, John, *The French in Early Florida: In the Eye of the Hurricane* (Gainesville: 2000).

McKee, Rebecca Jane and Randolph Vigne (eds.), *The Huguenots: France, Exile and Diaspora* (Portland: 2013).

Mellet, Paul-Alexis, *Les traités monarchomaques: confusion des temps, résistance armée et monarchie parfaite (1560–1600)* (Geneva: 2007).

Mentzer, Raymond, *Heresy Proceedings in Languedoc, 1500–1560* (Philadelphia: 1984).

———, *Blood and Belief: Family Survival and Confessional Identity among Provincial Huguenot Nobility* (Lafayette, In.: 1994)

——— (ed.), *Sin and the Calvinists: Morals Control and the Consistory in the Reformed Tradition* (Kirksville, Mo.: 1994)

———, *La construction de l'identité réformée aux 16e et 17e siècles: le rôle des consistoires* (Paris: 2006).

———, *Les registres des consistoires des Églises réformées de France, XVIe–XVIIe siècles. Un inventaire* (Geneva: 2014).

Mentzer, Raymond and Andrew Spicer (eds.), *Society and Culture in the Huguenot World, 1559–1685* (Cambridge: 2002)

Mentzer, Raymond and Philippe Chareyre (eds.), *La mesure du fait religieux: l'approche méthodologique des registres consistoriaux dans l'espace calvinien XVI–XVIIIe siècle,* special issue of *Bulletin de la Société de l'Histoire du Protestantisme Français* 153: 4 (octobre–novembre–décembre 2007).

Mentzer, Raymond and Didier Poton (eds.), *Agir pour l'Église: ministères et charges ecclésiastiques dans les Églises réformées (XVIe–XIXe siècles)* (Paris: 2014).

Mentzer, Raymond, Philippe Chareyre and Françoise Moreil (eds.), *Dire l'interdit: The Vocabulary of Censure and Exclusion in the Early Modern Reformed Tradition* (Leiden: 2010).

Merlin, Hélène, *L'absolutisme dans les lettres et la théorie des deux corps. Passions et politique* (Paris: 2000).

Mérot, Alain, *French Painting in the Seventeenth Century* (New Haven: 1995).

Meyer, Judith Pugh, *Reformation in La Rochelle: Tradition and Change in Early Modern Europe, 1500–1568* (Geneva: 1996).

Michalski, Sergiusz, *The Reformation and the Visual Arts: The Protestant Image Question in Western and Eastern Europe* (London: 1993).

Michelet, Jules, *De la Révocation de l'Edit de Nantes à la Guerre des Cévennes* (Paris: 1985).

Middell, Katharina, *Hugenotten in Leipzig* (Leipzig: 1989).

Mieck, Ilja, *Toleranzedikt und Bartholomäusnacht. Französische Politik und europäische Diplomatie, 1570–1572* (Göttingen: 1969).

Migliazzo, Arlin C., *To Make This Land Our Own: Community, Identity, and Cultural Adaptation in Purrysburgh Township, South Carolina, 1732–1865* (Columbia: 2007).

Minerbi Belgrado, Anna, *L'avènement du passé: la Réforme et l'histoire* (Paris: 2004).

Mironneau, Paul and Isabelle Pébay-Clottes (eds.) *Paix des armes, paix des âmes*, (Paris: 2000).

Monter, William, *Judging the French Reformation: Heresy Trials in Sixteenth-Century Parlements* (Cambridge, Mass.: 2002).

Morini, Massimiliano and Romana Zacchi (eds.), *Richard Rowlands Verstegan: A Versatile Man in an Age of Turmoil* (Turnhout: 2012).

Mours, Samuel, *Le protestantisme en Vivarais et en Velay des origines à nos jours* (1948; repr. Montpellier: 2001).

———, *Les Églises réformées en France: tableaux et cartes* (Paris: 1958).

———, *Le protestantisme en France au XVIe siècle* (Paris: 1959).

———, *Essai sommaire de géographie du protestantisme réformé français au XVIIe siècle* (Paris: 1966).

———, *Le protestantisme en France au XVIIe siècle (1598–1685)* (Paris: 1967).

Mours, Samuel and Daniel Robert, *Le protestantisme en France du XVIIIe siècle à nos jours (1685–1970)* (Paris: 1972).

Mousnier, Roland and Jean Mesnard (eds.), *L'âge d'or du Mécénat* (Paris: 1985).

Munns, Jessica and Penny Richards (eds.), *Gender, Power and Privilege in Early Modern Europe* (London: 2003).

Murdock, Graeme, Penny Roberts and Andrew Spicer (eds.), *Ritual and Violence. Natalie Zemon Davis and Early Modern France*, Past and Present Supplement 7 (Oxford: 2012).

Murdoch, Tessa, *The Quiet Conquest: The Huguenots, 1685 to 1985* (London: 1985).

Muret, Edouard, *Geschichte der Französischen Kolonie in Brandenburg-Preußen, unter besonderer Berücksichtigung der Berliner Gemeinde* (Berlin: 1885).

Naef, Henri, *La conjuration d'Amboise et Genève* (Paris: 1922).

Naphy, William, *Calvin and the Consolidation of the Genevan Reformation* (Manchester: 1994).

Nolde, Dorothea and Claudia Opitz (eds.), *Grenzüberschreitende Familienbeziehungen. Akteure und Medien des Kulturtransfers in der Frühen Neuzeit* (Cologne: 2008).

Notter, Annick (ed.), *Les Mays de Notre Dame de Paris* (Arras: 1999).

Ollier, D. *Eglises wallonnes de la Barrière, Tournai, Armentières, Menin, Ypres et Namur* (Le Cateau: 1894).

Olson, Todd P., *Poussin and France. Painting, Humanism and the 'Politics of Style'* (New Haven: 2002).

Orcibal, Jean, *Louis XIV et les protestants* (Paris: 1951).

Otterness, Philip, *Becoming German: The 1709 Palatine Migration to New York* (Ithaca: 2004).

Pannier, Jacques, *L'Église réformée de Paris sous Louis XIII de 1621 à 1629 environ* (Paris: 1932).

——, *Les origines de la Confession de foi et de la Discipline des Églises réformées de France* (Paris: 1936).

Pascal, Paul, *Elie Benoist et l'Eglise Réformée d'Alençon, d'après des documents inédits* (Paris: 1892).

Paul, Céline, *Les Mystérieux du XVIIe siècle. Une enquête au cabinet d'art graphique* (Paris: 2002).

Pérès, Jacques-Noël (ed.), *Pratiques autour de la mort. Enjeux œcuméniques* (Paris: 2012).

Péronnet, Michel (ed.), *Les Églises et leurs institutions au XVIe siècle. Actes du Vème Colloque de Centre d'Histoire de la Réforme et du Protestantisme* (Montpellier: 1978).

Perry, Elisabeth Israels, *From Theology to History: French Religious Controversy and the Revocation of the Edict of Nantes* (The Hague: 1973).

Pestana, Carla Gardina, *Protestant Empire: Religion and the Making of the British Atlantic World* (Philadelphia: 2009).

Pettegree, A., A. Duke and G. Lewis (eds.), *Calvinism in Europe, 1540–1620* (Cambridge: 1994).

Piaget, Arthur and Gabrielle Berthoud, *Notes sur le livre des martyrs de Jean Crespin* (Neuchâtel: 1930).

Pidoux, Pierre, *Le psautier huguenot du XVIe siècle, mélodies et documents*, 2 vols. (Basel: 1962).

Pitassi, Maria-Cristina, *Entre croire et savoir: le problème de la méthode critique chez Jean Le Clerc* (Leiden: 1987).

—— (ed.), *Édifier ou instruire? Les avatars de la liturgie réformée du XVIe et XVIIe siècle* (Paris: 2000).

Pitou, Frédérique and Jacqueline Sainclivier (eds.), *Les affrontements. Usages, discours et rituels* (Rennes: 2008).

Plank, Ezra L., *Creating Perfect Families: French Reformed Churches and Family Formation, 1559–1685* (PhD diss., University of Iowa, 2013).

Poivre, Joël, *Jérémie Ferrier (1576–1626). Du protestantisme à la raison d'état* (Geneva: 1990).

Poole, Reginald L., *A History of the Huguenots of the Dispersion at the Recall of the Edict of Nantes* (London: 1880).

Poton, Didier, *Saint-Jean-de-Gardonnenque. Une communauté réformée à la veille de la Révocation (1663–1685)* (Gap: 1985).

——, *De l'Edit à sa Révocation: Saint Jean de Gardonnenque 1598–1686*, 2 vols. (Doctoral diss., Université Paul-Valéry – Montpellier III, 1988).

Pott, Sandra, Martin Mulsow and Lutz Danneberg (eds.), *The Berlin Refuge, 1680–1780: Learning and Science in European Context* (Leiden: 2003).

Prestwich, Menna (ed.), *International Calvinism, 1541–1715* (Oxford: 1985).

Prodi, Paolo, *Christianisme et monde moderne. Cinquante ans de recherches* (Paris: 2006).

Quéniart, Jean, *La révocation de l'Édit de Nantes. Protestants et catholiques français de 1598 à 1685* (Paris: 1985).

Rabut, Elisabeth, *Le Roi, l'Église et le Temple: l'exécution de l'Edit de Nantes en Dauphiné* (Grenoble: 1987).

Racault, Jean-Michel, *L'Utopie narrative en France et en Angleterre, 1675–1761* (Oxford: 1991).

Racaut, Luc, *Hatred in Print: Propaganda and Huguenot Identity during the French Wars of Religion* (Aldershot: 2002).

Rambeaud, Pascal, *De La Rochelle vers l'Aunis: l'histoire des réformés et de leurs Églises dans une province française au XVIe siècle* (Paris: 2003).

Randall, Catharine, *From a Far Country: Camisards and Huguenots in the Atlantic World* (Athens, Ga.: 2009).

Reid, Jonathan, *King's Sister—Queen of Dissent: Marguerite de Navarre (1492–1549) and Her Evangelical Network*, 2 vols. (Leiden: 2009).

Rémond, R. (ed.), *Pour une histoire politique* (Paris: 1996).

Reymond, Bernard, *L'architecture religieuse des protestants* (Geneva: 1996).

Reynies, Nicole de and Sylvain Lavessière (eds.), *Isaac Moillon 1614–1673. Un peintre du roi à Aubusson* (Aubusson: 2005).

Rex, Walter, *Essays on Pierre Bayle and Religious Controversy* (The Hague: 1965).
Ricalens, Henry, *Castelnaudary au temps de Catherine de Médicis Comtesse de Lauragais* (Toulouse: 1999).
Ricoeur, Paul, *La Mémoire, l'Histoire, l'Oubli* (Paris: 2000).
Rimbault, Lucien, *Pierre Du Moulin, 1568–1658, un pasteur classique à l'âge classique: étude de théologie pastorale sur des documents inédits* (Paris: 1966).
Roberts, Penny, *Peace and Authority during the French Religious Wars, c.1560–1600* (Basingstoke: 2013).
Robbins, Kevin, *City on the Ocean Sea: La Rochelle, 1530–1650. Urban Society, Religion, and Politics on the French Atlantic Frontier* (Leiden: 1997).
Roelker, Nancy, *Queen of Navarre, Jeanne d'Albret, 1528–1572* (Cambridge, Mass.: 1968).
Romier, Lucien, *Le royaume de Catherine de Médicis. La France à la veille des guerres de religion*, 2 vols. (Paris: 1925).
Roosen, Franziska, *"Soutenir notre Église." Hugenottische Erziehungskonzepte und Bildungseinrichtungen im Berlin des 18. Jahrhunderts* (Bad Karlshafen: 2008).
Rosen-Prest, Viviane, *L'Historiographie des Huguenots en Prusse au temps des Lumières: entre mémoire, histoire et légende: J.P. Erman et P.C.F. Reclam, Mémoires pour servir à l'histoire des Réfugiés françois des Etats du Roi (1782–1799)* (Paris: 2002).
Rosenberg, Pierre, *France in the Golden Age. Seventeenth-Century Paintings in American Collections* (New York: 1982).
Ruel, Marianne, *Les chrétiens et la danse dans la France moderne, XVIe–XVIIIe siècle* (Paris: 2006).
Sacquin, Michèle, *Entre Bossuet et Maurras. L'antiprotestantisme en France de 1814 à 1870* (Paris: 1998).
Salmons, Joseph, *A History of German: What the Past Reveals about Today's Language* (Oxford: 2012).
Sarrabère, Albert, *Dictionnaire des pasteurs basques et béarnais, XVIe–XVIIe siècles* (Pau: 2001).
Saupin, Guy (ed.), *La tolérance. Colloque international de Nantes* (Rennes: 1999).
Schapira, Nicolas, *Un professionnel des lettres au XVIIe siècle. Valentin Conrart: une histoire sociale* (Seyssel: 2003).
Schmitt, Carl, *Hamlet ou Hécube* (1956; French trans. Paris: 1992),
Schmitt, Hans Joachim, *Der französische Wortschatz der Waldenser in Deutschland. Archivstudien* (Tübingen: 1996).
Schnur, Roman, *Die französischen Juristen im konfessionellen Bürgerkrieg d. 16. Jh.s. Ein Beitrag z. Entstehungsgeschichte d. modernen Staates* (Berlin: 1962).
Schultz, Helga (ed.), *Berlin 1650–1800. Sozialgeschichte einer Residenz* (Berlin: 1992).
Scoville, Warren C., *The Persecutions of Huguenots and French Economic Development, 1680–1720* (Berkeley: 1960).

Scouloudi, Irene (ed.), *Huguenots in Britain and their French Background, 1550–1800* (London: 1987).

Serr, Gaston, *Une église protestante au XVIe siècle: Montauban* (Aix-en-Provence: 1958).

Shepardson, Nikki, *Burning Zeal: The Rhetoric of Martyrdom and the Protestant Community in Reformation France, 1520–1570* (Bethlehem, Pa.: 2007).

Sheridan, Geraldine and Viviane Rosen-Prest (eds.), *Les Huguenots éducateurs dans l'espace européen à l'époque moderne* (Paris: 2011).

Skinner, Quentin, *The Foundations of Modern Political Thought*, 2 vols. (Cambridge: 1978).

Sottocasa, Valérie, *Mémoires affrontées. Protestants et catholiques face à la Révolution dans les montagnes du Languedoc* (Rennes: 2004).

Souriac, Pierre-Jean, *Une guerre civile. Affrontements religieux et militaires dans le Midi toulousain (1562–1596)* (Seyssel: 2008).

Sowa, Helen Chastain, *Louise Moillon: Seventeenth Century Still-Life Artist. An Illustrated Biography* (Chicago: 1998).

Spicer, Andrew, *Calvinist Churches in Early Modern Europe* (Manchester: 2007).

Stein, Peter (ed.), *Frankophone Sprachvarietäten. Variétés linguistiques francophones* (Tübingen: 2000).

Stephenson, Barbara, *The Power and Patronage of Marguerite of Navarre* (Burlington, Vt.: 2004).

Strauss, Bettina, *La Culture française à Francfort au XVIIIe siècle* (Paris: 1914).

Sunshine, Glenn S., *Reforming French Protestantism: The Development of Huguenot Ecclesiastical Institutions, 1557–1572* (Kirksville, Mo.: 2003).

Sutherland, N.M., *The Huguenot Struggle for Recognition* (New Haven: 1980).

Swetschinski, Daniel M., *Reluctant Cosmopolitans. The Portuguese Jews of Seventeenth-Century Amsterdam* (Oxford: 2004).

Thirion, Maurice, *Etude sur l'histoire du protestantisme à Metz et dans le Pays messin* (Nancy: 1884).

Thompson, Bard, *Liturgies of the Western Church* (New York: 1961).

Thompson, John, *John Calvin and the Daughters of Sarah* (Geneva: 1992).

Thuillier, Jacques et al. (eds.), *Vouet* (Paris: 1990).

——— (ed.), *Sébastien Bourdon, 1616–1671. Catalogue critique et chronologique de l'œuvre complet* (Paris: 2000).

Tilly, Charles, *Contrainte et capital dans la formation de l'Europe de 990 à 1990* (Paris: 1992).

Tournier, Gaston, *Les trois frères Serres de Montauban, forçats pour la foi de 1686 à 1713 et 1714* (Mas-Soubeyran: 1937).

———, *Les galères de France et les galériens protestants des XVIIe et XVIIIe siècles*, 3 vols. (Montpellier: 1943–49).

Toynbee, Arnold J., *A Study of History*, (ed.) David Churchill Somervell (London: 1957).
Treasure, Geoffrey, *The Huguenots* (New Haven: 2013).
Trim, D.J.B. (ed.), *The Huguenots: History and Memory in Transnational Context: Essays in Honour of Walter C. Utt* (Leiden: 2011).
Tulchin, Allan A., *That Men Would Praise the Lord: The Triumph of Protestantism in Nîmes, 1530–1570* (Oxford: 2010).
Van der Linden, David, *Experiencing Exile: Huguenot Refugees in the Dutch Republic, 1680–1700* (Aldershot: 2015).
Van Ruymbeke, Bertrand, *From New Babylon to Eden: The Huguenots and Their Migration to Colonial South Carolina* (Columbia: 2006).
Van Ruymbeke, Bertrand and Randy J. Sparks (eds.), *Memory and Identity: The Huguenots in France and the Atlantic Diaspora* (Columbia: 2003).
Velder, Christian, *300 Jahre französisches Gymnasium Berlin* (Berlin: 1989).
Verdi, Richard and Pierre Rosenberg (eds.), *Nicolas Poussin, 1594–1665* (London: 1995).
Verdier, Raymond (ed.), *Le Serment*, 2 vols. (Paris: 1991).
Vigne, Randolph and Charles Littleton (eds.), *From Strangers to Citizens: The Integration of Immigrant Communities in Britain, Ireland and Colonial America, 1550–1750* (Brighton: 2001).
Vinols, Jean-Baptiste de, *Histoire des guerres de Religion dans le Velay* (Le Puy:1862).
Vitet, L., *L' l'Académie Royale de peinture et de la sculpture. Étude historique* (Paris: 1861).
Vray, Nicole, *Catherine de Parthenay, duchesse de Rohan: protestante insoumise, 1554–1631* (Paris: 1998).
Waele, Michel de (ed.), *Lendemains de guerre civile: Réconciliations et restaurations en France sous Henri IV* (Quebec: 2011).
Wandel, Lee P. (ed.), *History Has Many Voices* (Kirksville, Mo.: 2003).
Wanegffelen, Thierry, *Ni Rome ni Genève. Des fidèles entre deux chaires en France au XVIe siècle* (Paris: 1997).
———, *L'Édit de Nantes. Une histoire européenne de la tolérance du XVIe au XXe siècle* (Paris: 1998).
Warmbrunn, Paul, *Zwei Konfessionen in Einer Stadt: Das Zusammenleben von Katholiken und Protestanten in den paritätischen Reichsstädten Augsburg, Biberbach, Ravensburg, und Dinkelsbühl von 1548 bis 1648* (Wiesbaden: 1983).
Weinreich, Uriel, *Languages in Contact. Findings and Problems* (New York: 1953).
Weil, François, *Family Trees. A History of Genealogy in America* (Cambridge, Mass.: 2013).
Weiss, Charles, *Histoire des réfugiés protestants de France depuis la révocation de l'édit de Nantes jusqu'à nos jours*, 2 vols. (1853; repr. Paris: 2007).
Wellman, Kathleen, *Queens and Mistresses of Renaissance France* (New Haven: 2013).
Whaley, Joachim, *Religious Toleration and Social Change in Hamburg, 1529–1819* (Cambridge: 1985).

Willis-Watkins, David, *The Second Commandment and Church Reform. The Colloquy of St. Germain-en-Laye, 1562* (Princeton: 1994).

Wilson, Christie Sample, *Beyond Belief: Surviving the Revocation of the Edict of Nantes* (Bethlehem, Pa.: 2011).

Wolfe, Michael (ed.), *Changing Identities in Early Modern France* (Durham, NC: 1997).

Wolff, Philippe (ed.), *Histoire des Protestants en France* (Toulouse: 1977).

Wright, Christopher, *The French Painters of the Seventeenth Century* (London: 1985).

Wunderli, Peter, *Die okzitanischen Bibelübersetzungen des Mittelalters. Gelöste und ungelöste Fragen* (Frankfurt: 1969).

Yardeni, Myriam, *Utopie et révolte sous Louis XIV* (Paris: 1980).

———, *Le Refuge protestant* (Paris: 1985).

———, *Le Refuge huguenot. Assimilation et culture* (Paris: 2002).

Zuber, Roger and Laurent Theis (eds.). *La Révocation de l'édit de Nantes et le protestantisme français en 1685* (Paris: 1986).

Zysberg, André, *Les galériens. Vies et destins de 60,000 forçats sur les galères de France* (Paris: 1987).

Index

Aarssen van Sommelsdijks, Cornelis   409
Abbeville   93
Acadia   418
Acher, Abraham   356, 358
Adams, John   424
Agar, Jacques d'   203
Agard, Jacob d'   170, 219
Aigues-Mortes   27, 229, 239
Aimargues   27
Aix   110
Alard, Madeleine   152
Albenc, L'   26–27
Albret, Henry d'   122
Albret, Jeanne d' (Queen of Navarre)   8, 68, 77, 122, 145, 147–48
Alençon   227, 359, 364–65
Alençon, Duchy of   81
Alès   27, 51, 152, 154, 221
Allaire, Alexandre   384
Alsace   30, 227
Amboise   2, 71, 90–91, 93–94, 98–99, 102, 105, 112–13, 122
Amiens   87, 102, 113
Amsterdam   37, 227, 238, 270, 272, 274, 279–81, 290, 337, 348, 357, 360, 388, 400, 409, 412–13
Amyraut, Moïse   54
Ancillon, Charles   284
Ancillon, Jean Pierre Frédéric   284
Andelot (*see* Coligny, François de)
Andros, Edmund   268
Anduze   81
Angenoust, Jerosme   105
Angers   229
Angoumois   68, 82
Anjou   26, 105–06
Anjou, François d'Alençon, Duke of   84
Anne, Queen   257, 272, 384
Anne of Austria   197, 202, 361
Arbaleste, Charlotte d'   122, 125, 138–39, 141, 146–47
Archdale, John   268
Armagnac, Cardinal d'   145
Asia   394, 403, 406
Aubigné, Agrippa d'   142, 324
Aunis   105, 226, 233–34, 139

Authore   183–84
Auvergne   105–06
Avignon   158
Aymon, Jean   26

Baird, Charles W.   431–32, 435–36, 438
Baird, Robert   431
Bancelin, François   368–69
Bancroft, George   426
Bar, Duke of   123
Barbados   261
Barbaud, Jacques   369
Barbot, Jean   397
Barjac, Jacques de (marquis de Rochegude)   368
Barjot, Philibert   98
Baron   63
Barrière, La   241
Barthez   244
Barton   244
Basnage de Beauval, Henri   227
Basel   285
Batavia   409, 414, 416
Bauge-en-Bresse   98
Bauquemare, Jacques de   105
Bauquemare, Jessé de   105–06
Bâville, Nicolas de Lamoignon de   231
Bayeux, Thomas   408
Bayle, Pierre   227, 241–42, 280, 326
Bayly, Lewis   58
Bayreuth   420
Beauce   81
Béarn   37, 88–89, 122–23, 132, 135, 152–53, 226, 235, 357
Beaune   193
Beauregard   103
Belfast   266
Belgium   373, 409, 433
Belot, Jehan de   106
Benedict, Philip   26, 140, 152, 173
Benezet, Anthony   422
Benoist, Elie   12–13, 227, 326, 336, 349, 351, 359–61, 363–70
Bérenger, Hector de (baron de Beaufain)   420–21

Berlin   258, 260, 276, 282–84, 304–08, 310–14, 316–22, 363, 368, 428, 432
Bern (Berne)   1, 256–57, 264, 266, 285–86
Bernard, Gildas   25
Bernard, Samuel   170–71, 174, 204–05, 208–09, 211, 215
Bernon, Gabriel   390, 405
Berriot-Salvadore, Evelyne   125, 140–41
Berry   105
Berton, Barthélemy   78
Bertrand, David   134
Besançon   185
Bethmann   244
Beza, Theodore   22, 43, 49, 50–51, 54–55, 78, 80, 121, 147, 159
Béziers   110
Bezzina, Edwin   40–41
Bieler, André   118
Birnstiel, Eckart   274, 303
Blaisdell, Charmarie   120–21
Blois   110
Bocage (Normandy)   243
Böhm, Manuela   11
Boisson, Didier   9, 26
Bombay   406
Bonnaffé   244
Bonrepos, David de   388–89
Bordeaux   74, 233, 240, 244, 261, 272, 302
Bosher, John   253, 261, 379
Bosquet, Georges   113
Bosse, Abraham   173–74, 177, 210–12, 215, 217–19
Boston   261, 287–88, 372–78, 390, 405
Boucard, François de   78
Boucher, Arnoul   105
Bouchu   230
Bouillon, Henri de La Tour d'Auvergne, Duke of   89
Bourbon, Antoine de, King of Navarre   68
Bourbon, Catherine de   123, 146, 148
Bourbonnais   105–06
Bourdon, Sébastien   171–74, 177, 186–90, 192, 202–03, 205, 212, 218–19
Bourges   230
Bourgneuf, René   105
Boutecou, Daniel   288
Brandenburg   11, 250, 254, 256, 258, 263–65, 267, 271, 275, 278, 282–83, 285–86, 293–97, 307–07, 310–311, 363, 391, 399, 425, 441
Brantôme   124
Brazil   397, 440
Breteuil, baron de   424
Briançon   110
Briçonnet, François   105
Briçonnet, Guillaume   120
Brie   105, 243
Bremen   284
Bretagne (*see* Brittany)
Bristol   277
British Isles   4, 236, 272–73, 275–77, 285, 351, 432, 439
Brittany   105–07
Broomhall, Susan   124–26, 128, 130–31, 138–39, 144, 146–48
Brosse, Salomon de   173
Brousson, Claude   64, 225, 230
Brumeau de Moulinars, Jean Joseph   385
Bry, Theodor de   183, 185
Bryson, David   122
Bucer, Martin   54, 59
Bugé, Aaron   172
Bull, William   419–21
Bunel, François   194–95
Bunel, Jacob   192, 195
Bunyan, John   340
Burgundy   105–06, 226
Burke, Peter   194
Bussy, Jacquette de   125–26
Butler, Jon   13, 372, 374–75, 385–86, 390, 415, 437, 440

Cabanel, Patrick   6
Caen   240, 365
Caesar   79
Cahors   93
Calais   233, 373
Calas, Jean   221, 239, 422
Callot, Jacques   210
Calvin, John   6, 9, 12, 19, 21–22, 43–45, 48–51, 53–55, 57, 59, 61–67, 70, 78, 118, 120–21, 129, 133, 135, 138, 159, 174–75, 185, 192–93, 201, 206, 220, 252, 303, 325, 330, 342
Calvisson   35
Cameron, John   154
Canada   397, 440

INDEX 473

Canny (François de Barbançon, seigneur de) 69
Canny, Nicholas 266
Canterbury 277
Cape Colony (South Africa) 287, 394, 410, 412, 420, 439
Carolina (North America) 397, 403–05, 410, 417
Carolinas (North America) 13, 267, 268, 380
Caravaggio, Michelangelo Merisi da 188
Carbonnier-Burkard, Marianne 6
Carlo, Paula 13
Carolus Gustavus, King of Sweden 203
Caron, Anthoine 183
Carré, Ezéchiel 390
Cassan, Michel 95
Castellio, Sebastien 49
Castres 17, 74, 76, 224, 239
Catel, Henri Samuel 319
Cavalier, Jean 232, 339
Cayenne 410
Cecil, William 68
Celle (Germany) 284, 337–38
Cévennes Mountains 3, 129, 226, 231–35, 237, 258
Chamier, Adrien 152–53
Chamier, Daniel 152–53, 176
Chamier, Madeleine 153
Chamier, Marguerite 153
Chamier, Pierre 153
Champagne 104–06, 165, 233, 308, 412
Chandieu, Antoine de 44, 61, 66, 69–70
Channel Islands 277
Chantecler, Pierre de 105
Chardin, Jean 397, 406
Charenton 26, 37, 53, 56, 58–60, 157, 161–62, 173, 177, 196, 211, 219, 225
Chareyre, Philippe 6, 26, 39–41, 137
Charlemagne 2
Charles I 208
Charles II 268, 402
Charles IX 7–8, 50, 72, 79, 90–91, 93, 97, 100, 102, 108, 113–14, 116–17
Charleston 14, 261, 372, 374, 381–82, 386, 420, 423–24, 428–29, 439
Charlet, Estienne 105
Chartier, Mathieu 105
Chartier, Roger 337

Chartres 188, 308
Chastellux, François-Jean 422
Châtillon, Cardinal de (*see* Coligny, Odet de)
Chauffepié, Anne de 338
Cherfils, Laure 134
Chéron, Louis 177, 187, 219
Chevalier, Françoise 26, 160
Child, Sir Josiah 402
Chinard, Gilbert 435–36
Christian V, King of Denmark 203
Christin, Olivier 95, 101
Christina, Queen of Sweden 202–03
Cholakian, Patricia 120
Claude, Jean 37, 64, 150, 236, 363
Clement VIII 190
Clermont 97, 111
Cohen, Robin 249
Colbert, Jean-Baptiste 170, 201, 227
Coligny, François de 67, 75
Coligny, Gaspard I de 67
Coligny, Gaspard II de, Admiral of France 67, 69, 74–75, 77, 146, 183, 396
Coligny, Louise de 122, 125, 141, 146
Coligny, Odet de 67
Compton, Henry 267–69, 402
Condé, Henri de Bourbon, Prince of 50, 67, 72, 75, 77, 79
Condé, Louis de Bourbon, Prince of 77
Condé, le Grand (Louis II de Bourbon-Condé) 88, 202, 215
Condé-sur-Noireau 243
Condorcet, Nicolas 242
Conrart, Valentin 54
Constantinople 45, 286
Coolidge, Calvin 434
Copenhagen 132
Coras, Jean de 79, 125–26
Cork 267, 279
Corregio, Antonio 212
Corteiz, Pierre 324
Coste, Jean-Paul 423
Cottret, Bernard 378, 380
Couchman, Jane 125, 146
Court, Antoine 53, 234, 236–38, 240–42, 258
Court de Géblin, Antoine 240, 242, 244
Courthézon 134
Coxe, Daniel 407
Cranach, Lucas the Elder 178

Crenne, Hélisenne de   145
Crespin, Jean   143–44, 352–53
Crespin, René   106–07
Crest   231
Crussol, Antoine de   76
Curaçao   409

Daguesseau, Henri   222
Daillé, Jean   37, 161–62, 164–65
Daillon, Benjamin   279
Daneau, Lambert   36
Dauphiné   3, 68, 75–76, 94, 105–06, 176, 226, 230–31, 233–35, 237, 243–44, 274, 294, 308
Daussy, Hugues   7
Davis, Natalie Z.   118–19, 141, 144–45, 328
Defoe, Daniel   416
DeJean, Joan   143
Delancy, E.F.   429
Delft   359–60
Delmé, Sir Peter   276
Denmark   254, 259, 425
Dentière, Marie   127–28
Des Gallars, Nicolas   66, 70
Des Marolles, Louis   356–58
Des Roches, Catherine   145
Des Roches, Madeleine   145
DeSaussure, W.G.   429
Desmarets, Daniel   352
Dey de Séraucourt, Louis François   230
Die   153
Dieppe   233, 396, 398
Dieulefit   135
Dijon   125
Diodati, Jean   211
Dolan, Frances   143
Douglass, Jane Dempsey   118
Douxsaintz, Gilbert   111
Dover   277
Drelincourt, Charles   6, 37, 53, 62, 211, 236, 238
Drelincourt, Peter   279
Drisius, Samuel   388
Du Bois, Marie   357
Du Bosc, Pierre   365
Du Cerceau   173
Du Chaila, Abbé   232
Du Guernier, Alexander   185
Du Guernier, Louis   171, 174, 185, 202, 205, 219

Du Moulin, Charles   78
Du Moulin, Pierre   154, 162–66
Dublin   266–67, 279, 333, 380
Dubois, François   182–83, 185
Dubourdieu, Jean-Armand   276
Dumont de Bostaquet, Isaac   12, 329–34, 338–39, 340–41, 398
Dumoustier   244
Duplessis-Mornay, Philippe   80, 84, 87–89, 138, 141, 147, 183
Duquesne, Henri   395, 399, 400, 407, 412–15
Durand, Pierre   234
Durand du Dauphiné   404–05
Düsseldorf   304
Dutch Republic   11, 171, 178, 261, 279–82, 351, 366, 369, 409

Ekman, Mary   145
Elias, Norbert   94
Elisabeth I   122, 253
Elizabeth, Princess (daughter of Elector of the Palatinate)   142
Elle, Ferdinand   170, 195–96, 198–99
Elle, Louis Ferdinand (père)   170–71, 195–96, 198, 202
Elle, Louis Ferdinand (fils)   170, 196, 204
Elster, Jon   104
England   11, 94, 153, 170, 177, 185, 209, 236, 253–57, 261–62, 266–69, 271, 276–78, 281, 289, 294, 330, 334, 336, 351, 371, 379–80, 387–88, 401–03, 406, 409, 424–26, 441
English Channel   324, 394
Ercole II   121
Erman, Jean-Pierre   424
Eskrich, Pierre   178
Espagnandel, Mathieu   170
Esternay, Jean Raguier d'   69
Eude, Nicolas   170, 202
Eurich, Amanda   8, 122, 135

Fagel, Gaspar   360
Faneuil, Andrew   288, 377–78
Faneuil, Peter   288, 377, 408
Farel, Guillaume   54
Faulcon, Claude   106
Félibien, André   172, 187, 219
Ferguson, Gary   120–21
Ferry, Paul   36, 368

INDEX

Figeac   62
Figuieyres, Donne, dite La Sauvage   129
Finley-Crosswhite, Annette   125
Florida   183, 185, 397, 418, 434–35
Foa, Jérémie   7–8
Fontaine, Jacques   12, 329, 333–36, 338–41
Formey, Jean Henri Samuel   258, 260, 316, 319
Fornerod, Nicolas   26
Fosdick, Lucian J.   431
Foucault, Nicolas   222
Francillon, François   26
Francis I   120, 303
Francis II   2, 69, 77
François, Etienne   254, 282, 428
Francourt (Gervais Barbier, seigneur de)   69
Frankfurt-am-Main   14, 183, 233, 274, 282, 296, 306, 308–11, 313–14, 316–18, 320, 322, 432
Franklin, Benjamin   421
Frederick William, Great Elector   262–63
Frizeau   244
Fumée, Anthoine   105–06

Gaillard, Samuel Porcher   429
Gallargues   27
Gamond, Blanche   357–58
Ganges   130
Gap   110
Garcin, Jacob   357
Garnier, François   207–09
Garnier, Isabelle   120
Garrisson, Janine   39, 41
Gascony   95
Gassot, Jules   115
Gaultier de Saint-Blancard, François   316, 363, 366, 369
Geneva   2, 19, 22, 29, 43–44, 49, 53–56, 58, 60–67, 107, 127–28, 133, 136, 155, 158–59, 167, 173, 178–79, 181–82, 185, 211, 236, 238, 242, 252, 256, 266, 283, 285–87, 295, 339, 357, 367, 378, 382, 398
George III   421
Georgia   271, 418
Gergeau   58
Germany   4, 37, 171, 244, 282–83, 290, 293, 310, 337, 357, 395, 414–15, 418, 432, 436, 440
Gibert, Jean-Louis   419
Gilbert de Voisins   242

Girard, Etienne   358
Girardot   244
Girardot, Etienne   207, 244
Goffin, Robert   433
Goldstein, Carl   211
Gonesse   215
Goulart, Simon   352, 355
Gourreau de la Proustière, Philippe   106
Grant, Alison   261
Green, Lucy   433
Greengrass, Mark   122, 125, 274
Greenwich   256, 333
Grenoble   26, 109, 114, 302
Grieco Matthews, Sara   147
Griffis, William E.   433
Grintchenko, Marie-Hélène   122
Groningen   270, 280–81
Guadeloupe   397
Guérard, Jacob   267, 403
Guise family   2, 71–72, 84–85, 107, 179
Guise, François, Duke of   71–72, 75
Gulf of Mexico   407
Guyenne   3, 68, 74, 105–06
Gwynn, Robin   253, 277, 379

Halifax   418
Hamburg   284, 286
Harrington, James   278
Head, Thomas   142–43
Hébert, Christine   111
Hegel, Georg Wilhelm Friedrich   92, 94
Heinich, Nathalie   171
Henry II   50
Henry III   85, 179
Henry IV (Henry of Navarre)   7–8, 85–88, 108, 116–17, 123, 148, 152, 158, 173, 181, 195, 197, 361, 438
Hesse   11, 293, 295, 305–07
Hesse-Darmstadt   284, 294
Hesse-Homburg   308, 314
Hesse-Kassel   264, 282, 284, 294–97
Hirsch, Arthur   435–36, 438
Hobbes, Thomas   94, 211
Holy Roman Empire   253, 263–65, 293
Honfleur   396
Hôpital, Michel de l'   106
Hotman, François   71, 80, 85
Huber, Marie   238
Hugues (Hugon), King   2

Ignatius of Loyola 211
Île Bourbon (Île de la Réunion) 400, 412–14
Ile-de-France 68, 81, 105–06
India 249, 406, 412
Ireland 11, 13–14, 254–56, 259, 262, 266–67, 270–71, 278,79, 285, 290, 330, 333–34, 339, 372, 391, 403, 436, 440–41
Irwin, Joyce 142
Israel 231, 440
Italy 67, 187, 192, 401, 404, 417, 420

Jamaica 261, 272
James, Duke of York 202
Jamestown (Virginia) 434–35
Jaquelot, Isaac 358
Jarnac 77
Jarrige, Pierre de 92
Jay, John 424
Johnston, Gideon 380
Joly de Fleury 242
Jouanna, Arlette 94, 117
Jouy 244
Jurieu, Pierre 12, 231, 326, 336, 349, 351, 353, 355–60, 363, 365, 370, 399
Jusserand, Jules 434
Jussie, Jeanne de 127

Kamil, Neil 389–90
Kampen (The Netherlands) 369
Karant-Nunn, Susan 188–19
Kingdon, Robert M. 13, 22, 133, 372, 375, 378, 381, 384
Kirchner, Frédéric 93
Koselleck, Reinhart 94
Kuperty-Tsur, Nadine 147

La Bastide, Marc-Antoine 54
La Beaumelle, Laurent Angliviel de 241
La Case, Jacques de 414
La Grande Mademoiselle (Anne-Marie-Louise d'Orléans) 198
La Guesle, Jehan de 105, 111
La Haize, Jean de 78–79
La Rochefoucauld, François de 68, 75
La Rochefoucauld, Marie de 338–40
La Rochelle 17, 50, 58, 61, 77–79, 82, 89, 105, 124, 148, 176, 233, 240, 288, 369, 373, 389, 396, 424
La Tour, Claude de, dame de Turenne 124
La Tour d'Auvergne, Marie de 123, 132
La Trémoille, Charlotte-Brabantine, duchesse de 123, 125
Labé, Louise 145
Labauche 244
Labrousse, Elisabeth 227, 359
Lachenicht, Susanne 10, 303, 380, 391, 441
Lafayette, Marquis de 424
Lallemant de Voulzay, Estienne 105–06
Lamoignon, Charles de 102, 105–07
Langres 97
Languedoc 3, 35, 38, 68, 74–77, 81–82, 100, 105–06, 176, 222, 226, 231, 234–35, 237, 244, 308, 417, 419
Laudonnière, René G. 183, 435
Laurens, Henry 421, 424
Lausanne 65, 158, 237, 256, 285–86
Lavau, Jehan de 105
Le Bret 230
Le Brun, Charles 170, 172
Le Challeux, Jacques 178
Le Cirier, François 102, 105
Le Mans 25–26, 29
Le Mercier, André 375–78, 390
Le Moyne, Jacques 183–85
Le Nain (three brothers : Antoine, Louis and Mathieu) 177
Le Roy Ladurie, Emmanuel 4
Le Tellier, Michel (chancellor) 226–27
Le Vasseur, Josué 167–68
Lectoure 95
Lefevre, Gabrielle 135
Lefèvre, Isaac 229
Leiden 37, 153, 155, 270, 433
Leipzig 290, 296
Léonard, E.-G. 273
Lesdiguières, François de Bonne, sieur de 89
Lieburg, Fred van 37
Limerick 266
Limoges 95
Limousin 95, 302
Linden, David van der 12–13
Lipscomb, Suzannah 31, 41, 134–35, 137
Lisieux 111
Locke, John 242, 334
Loménie de Brienne 242
London 13–14, 185, 238, 258, 261, 268–69, 271, 276–77, 286, 378, 380, 382–83, 387, 398, 402, 405, 418–20, 424, 430, 432, 436, 439

INDEX

Longueil, Pierre de   105
Lorient   286
Lorraine   72–73, 85, 104
Lorraine, Cardinal Charles of (Guise, Charles de)   71
Loudun   23, 26, 29, 33, 35, 38, 40, 53–54, 58, 86–88, 156
Lougee, Carolyn Chappell   12
Louis XI   77
Louis XII   77, 121
Louis XIII   88–89, 173, 197, 215, 221, 361
Louis XIV   18, 24, 166, 170, 173, 195, 198, 200–02, 209, 215, 221–22, 227–28, 232, 234–35, 237, 242, 250, 254, 256–57, 266, 270, 273–74, 283, 326, 336, 339, 349, 361, 364, 381, 394, 397, 399–400, 407, 422–23, 426, 432, 437
Louis XV   242
Louis XVI   221, 242, 421
Louisiana   417
Louvois, François Michel Le Tellier, Marquis de   227
Lübeck   284
Lun, Philippe de   131
Luria, Keith   123, 131–32, 142–43
Luther, Martin   18, 46, 51, 61, 303, 305
Lyon   75, 77–78, 93, 109–10, 178–79, 181, 238, 261
Lyonnais   76, 105–06

Maag, Karin   8–9
Machault, Baptiste de   105
Mâcon   98–100
Madagascar   412
Madeleine   110
Madras   406
Magdeburg   284, 294
Maimbourg, Louis   353
Maine   26, 81, 105
Mailly, Madeleine de   67
Maintenon, Madame de   198, 227
Majendie, Arnaud   357
Malesherbes, Chrétien Guillaume de Lamoignon de   242
Manakintown (Manakin Town) (Virginia)   289, 372, 374, 407–08, 414
Manetsch, Scott L.   22
Mangourit, Michel Ange   423
Mantes   86
Marguerite de Navarre   120–22, 127, 145

Marillac, René de   223, 225
Marie-Thérèse of Austria, Queen of France   198
Marly   209, 219
Marot, Clément   43, 54–55
Marseille   240, 244, 356
Marteilhe, Jean   229, 339
Martin-Ulrich, Claudie   145
Marion, Elie   232
Mascarene Islands   13, 395, 412–14
Mascarene, Jean Paul   408
Masparraulte, Pierre de   105
Massachusetts   13, 371–74, 377, 390, 392–93, 405–06
Massue, Henri, Marquis de Ruvigny   256, 266
Mather, Cotton   390
Mauritius   412, 414
Mazarin, Cardinal Jules   215, 222, 361
Mazel, Abraham   231–32
McKinley, Mary   120–21, 127
Meaux   120
Mechelen (southern Netherlands)   195
Medici, Catherine de   50, 69, 72, 106, 117, 126, 145, 183, 194
Medici, Marie de   88–89, 192
Mentzer, Raymond A.   6, 25, 27, 33, 35, 40–41, 128–29, 132–34, 136, 141
Mesmes, Jean-Jacques de   105, 109
Mesnil de Saint Pierre, Louis de   419
Mestrezat, Jean   37
Metz   28, 36, 152, 276, 302, 308, 352, 357, 368–69
Meyer, Judith   138
Michaud, J. F.   329
Michelet, Jules   426
Michelin, Jean   170–71, 219
Middelburg   281
Middle East   401
Midi   82, 131, 133, 226, 234, 237, 241
Migault, Jean   12, 329, 336–38, 340–41, 348, 352
Milan   67, 189
Millau   81–82, 84, 109–110
Minuit, Peter   409
Miremont, Armand de Bourbon, Marquis de   257
Mirmand, Henri de   256, 263, 266, 286
Mississippi   407, 417, 420
Moigneville, Simon de Piennes, seigneur de   69

Moillon, Isaac   173, 193, 201
Moillon, Louise   207–210, 219
Moissard, Antoinette   152
Molé, Edouard   106
Molesworth, Robert   262
Monceaux, Jehan de   105
Monmerqué, L.J.N.   329
Montargis   121
Montauban   17, 24–25, 27, 74, 82, 109, 138–39, 152, 154, 158, 222, 245
Montbéliard   185
Montdoulcet, Robert de   106
Montélimar   152–53
Montenay, Georgette de   147
Monter, E. William   136, 144
Montmorency, Anne, Duke of (Constable of France)   72
Montmorency, Louise de   67
Montpellier   17, 39, 54, 74, 89, 100, 110, 159, 173, 176, 190, 203, 218, 230, 363, 366, 404
Moreil, Françoise   134–35
Morel, François de   66, 71
Morély, Jean   128
Munster   255
Murat, François   357–58
Murdock, Graeme   139
Myron, Gabriel   105–06

Namur   241
Nantes   103–04
Narragansett (Rhode Island)   372–73, 377, 390
Nash, R. C.   261
Navarre   123
Neau, Elie   339, 390
Nelson, John K.   380
Nemours, Marie de   285
Netherlands, The (*see* also United Provinces)   4, 11, 38, 136–37, 253–54, 256, 265–66, 270, 272–73, 275, 280–81, 285, 294, 378, 395, 408–10, 425, 433–34, 436, 439
Neuchâtel   53, 238, 285–86, 416–18
Neuschel, Kristen   124
New Amsterdam   288, 373, 409, 433–34
New Bordeaux (South Carolina)   419–20
New England   13, 372–73, 376–77, 390, 392–93, 395, 397, 405, 407, 431, 435
New Paltz (New York)   268, 288, 371–73, 387–88, 392, 406

New Rochelle (New York)   268, 304, 371–72, 382–89, 392, 406, 416
New York   13–14, 258, 261, 268, 270, 287–88, 371–74, 378, 382, 384–90, 392–93, 405–06, 416, 426–29, 431–34, 437
Nîmes   17, 25–29, 31, 33, 35–40, 74–76, 82, 110, 137, 139, 153, 158, 224–25, 240, 245, 256, 277
Niort   229
Nivernais   105
Normandy   68–69, 81, 105–06, 233–35, 243, 277, 330–31, 340, 439
North America   4, 13, 249, 254, 262, 267–68, 270–71, 371–75, 378–81, 387, 390, 394, 397, 403, 405–07, 415–17, 430, 434–35, 439–41
North Carolina   408
Northern Ireland   97
Norwich   277
Nova Scotia   418

Oberkampf, Christophe-Philippe   244
Orange, principality and city of   134, 153, 158, 294, 367, 420
Orléanais   105–06
Orléans   62, 70, 77, 176, 308
Orléans, Philippe d'   198
Orthez   89, 153, 357
Ostervald, J.-F.   53, 65, 238
Ostervald, Jean-Rodolphe   236
Oxford, Massachusetts   372–73, 377, 405

Pain, François   106
Palatinate   35, 253–54, 265–66, 270, 272, 294–95, 307, 309, 371, 381
Paloque, Pierre   157
Pannier, Jacques   173
Paradis, Nicolas   318
Paris   6, 14, 18, 20, 23, 25, 44, 50, 53, 56, 63, 70–71, 75, 106, 113, 122, 161, 165, 170, 172–73, 177–79, 183, 185–86, 188, 192–93, 195, 201, 203, 207, 209, 215, 220, 225, 227, 238–40, 242, 244, 256, 281, 302, 308, 364, 417, 424–25, 436
Parris Island (South Carolina)   434–35
Parthenay, Catherine de, duchesse de Rohan   122–23, 125, 146, 148
Pas de Calais   307
Pau   27, 41

INDEX

Pays Chartrain   81
Pays de Caux   82
Pays de Vaud   285–86
Pellisson, Paul   224
Pelloutier, Simon   290
Penn, William   404
Pennsylvania   260, 404
Perche   81
Perrissin, Jean   9, 173, 177, 179. 181–82, 185
Pestana, Carla Gardina   386, 392
Petit, René   267, 403
Petitot, Alexandre   329
Phellypeaux, Jacques   105
Phélypeaux, Louis   192
Philadelphia   286, 422
Philip of Hesse   253
Picardy   68–69, 81, 105–06, 233, 243, 294, 306–07
Picart, Bernard   178
Picart, Etienne   177, 211
Pictet, Bénédict   236
Pinagier, Thomas   171
Pineton de Chambrun, Jacques   366, 368–69
Pithou, Nicolas   104
Pittion, Jean-Paul   155
Plymouth (England)   277
Plymouth (Massachusetts)   434–35
Poirier, Stephen   406, 408
Poissy   73
Poitiers   19, 50, 69–70, 73, 223, 424
Poitou   68, 94, 105–07, 143, 225, 230, 233–35, 243, 277, 326, 336, 338, 348, 359, 397, 439
Pollmann, Judith   41, 136–37, 139
Pompey   79
Pondicherry   286
Pont-de-Montvert   232
Pont-de-Veyle   224
Pontoise   70, 73
Poole, Reginald Lane   432
Portarlington   266–67, 279
Pot de Chemault   110
Potier, Nicolas   106
Poton, Didier   39–41, 391
Poujoulat, Jean Joseph François   329
Poupart   244
Pourbus, Frans   195
Pourtalès, Jacques Louis   286
Poussin, Nicolas   172–73

Prestwich, Menna   173
Provence   105–06
Purry, Jean-Pierre   416–18, 420
Purrysburgh   418–19
Prussia   11, 250, 254, 258, 263–67, 271, 275, 283–85, 294–97, 305–08, 310–11, 336, 391, 424

Quebec   287
Quebec City   405
Quelain, Michel   105
Quick, John   27

Rabaut, Paul   240, 244
Rabaut Saint-Etienne, Jean-Paul   240, 242, 245
Racaut, Luc   142
Randall (Coats), Catherine   138, 147, 390
Raynal, Abbé   422–23
Réalmont   126
Reboulet, Paul   411
Reclam, Pierre Chrétien Frédéric   251, 424
Reid, Jonathan   120
Reinhard, Wolfgang   31
Renée de France   121–22
Reni, Guido   211
Rhode Island   372–73, 377, 390, 405
Ribault, Jean   183–84
Richelieu, Cardinal   89, 324
Riesener, J.-H.   244
Ritter, Raymond   148
Rivet, André   142
Roberts, Penny   96, 102
Rochambeau   422
Rochefort, Charles de   395, 397–98, 400, 409
Rochette, François   239
Rocquière, Anne   135
Rodrigues Island   413
Roelker, Nancy   118, 122
Roger, Jacques   234
Roger, Simon   106
Rohan, Henri, Duke of   88–89
Romans   110
Romilly (pastor)   242
Roper, Lyndal   118–19
Rotterdam   13, 227, 280, 353, 356, 358, 397–98, 409
Rou, Louis   378, 385–86
Rouen   185, 227, 308

Rouergue 106
Roujault de Villeman, Etienne-Nicolas 230
Rousseau, Jacques 170–71, 209, 219
Rousseau, Jean-Jacques 242, 334
Roussel, Bernard 27
Rowlandson, Mary 240
Roye, Charlotte de 67
Roye, Éléonore de, princesse de Condé 67, 122, 146
Rubens, Peter Paul 201
Rubys, Claude de 109
Russia 254, 271, 425
Rutledge, John 421
Ruvigny, Marquis de 224, 256, 266–67, 278

Sadoleto, Cardinal Jacopo 22
Saint-André, Marshal de 72
Saint-Cloud 209, 219
Saint-Cyr 198
Saint-Christophe 397, 405
Saint Gall 285
Saint-Germain-des-Prés 177
Saint Helena 406
Saint-Jean-d'Angély 75, 84
Saint-Jean-du-Bruel 130
Saint-Jean-du-Gard 30, 38–40
Saint-Maixent 111, 155, 230
Saint-Malo 229
Saint Petersburg 259
Saint-Quentin 67, 243–44
Sainte-Foy 55, 74, 82, 86
Sainte-Marie-aux-Mines 30
Saintonge 68, 75, 105, 226, 234–35, 334, 338, 439
Sancé, baron de 401
Sandberg, Brian 124
Sarrabat, Daniel 174, 177
Saumur 86–88, 153–54, 159, 238
Savannah 418
Savoy 294
Savoy, Duke of 1
Saxony 284, 295
Scandinavia 203, 254, 265
Scherer 244
Schilling, Heinz 31
Schmitt, Carl 94, 107
Schmitt, Hans Joachim 304–05
Schroeder, Joy 135
Schurman, Anna Maria van 142

Scoville, Warren C. 233
Séant-en-Othe 104
Secker, William 419
Sedan 152–54, 165, 167, 244, 308
Seignoret, Baudouin 261
Serces, Jacques 418
Serres, Jean de 158–59
Shepardson, Nikki 134, 144
Simond, Pierre 287, 411, 414–15, 420
Sirven, Pierre-Paul 239
Sixtus V 85
Smiles, Samuel 426
Sollicoffre 244
Soubise 78
Soubise, Benjamin 88–89
South Africa 5, 13, 97, 254, 260–61, 394–95, 411, 415, 417, 420, 426, 428, 433, 436, 440
South Carolina 14, 287–89, 371, 374, 380–82, 386, 390, 392–93, 404, 408, 417–20, 423–24, 429–30, 434, 436
Spain 85, 227, 273, 418, 438, 440
Spanish Netherlands 82, 253, 433
Spicer, Andrew 6, 9
Stanwood, Owen 13–14, 441
Staten Island (New York) 372–73, 388–89, 392
Stellenbosch 414
Stouppe, Pierre 382–84
Strasbourg 54–55, 59, 71, 227, 356
Strasburg (Germany) 306–07, 309–13, 315–21
Strong, Josiah 427
Sully, Maximilien de Béthune, Duke of 89, 324
Superville, Daniel de 303, 358
Surinam 14, 260–61, 272, 287, 394, 409–10, 426
Swanevelt, Herman van 209
Sweden 241, 254, 259, 425
Switzerland (Swiss cantons) 4, 11, 37–38, 54, 234, 236–37, 239, 253–54, 256–58, 266–67, 273–75, 278, 282, 285–86, 368, 398, 407, 411, 416–17, 425, 436, 440

Taffin, Jean 37
Taillefer, Isaac 412
Tarente, prince de 132
Tavannes, Sieur de, Governor 98
Tavernier, Jean-Baptiste 397
Teding van Berkhout, Pieter 360

Tessereau, Abraham   326, 364
Testelin, Henri   170–71, 199–201, 219
Testelin, Louis   171, 187–88, 192, 211, 215, 219
The Hague   64, 281, 333, 339, 352, 358, 363
Thelusson   244
Thiérarche   243
Thompson, John   135
Tortorel, Jacques   9, 173, 179, 185
Toulouse   74, 114, 125–26, 239, 422
Touraine   2, 26, 105
Tournai   127, 241
Tournier, Nicolas   174, 177, 185
Tours   2, 101, 106, 173, 193
Toynbee, Arnold   251
Treasure, Geoffrey   6
Tronchin, Madeleine   153
Trouillard, Pierre   165–67
Troyes   104, 109
Turgot, Anne Robert Jacques   242

Ulster   255
United Provinces, The (*see* also Netherlands)   82, 224, 227, 236, 241, 273, 276, 280, 287, 408, 433
United States   94, 290, 427–28, 432, 434–37, 440
Utrecht   41, 254, 257, 270, 273, 358

Valence   75, 101, 327
Valleau, Antoine   413–14
Van der Stel, Simon   411, 415
Van Ruymbeke, Bertrand   6, 14, 288, 375, 381–82, 391
Vaultier, Elisabeth   365
Venard, Marc   94
Vergerio, Pier Paulo   121
Vermandois   243
Vernet   244
Versailles   209
Verstegan, Richard   351
Vevey   285
Vexin   82
Viallaneix, Paul   426
Viart, Jacques   105

Vielhenx, Charles   142
Vienne   110
Viennot, Elaine   124
Villemur   129
Villeneuve, Jehan de   113
Villeneuve, Louis de   367
Villerman, Jean   124
Vincent, Isabeau   231
Viole, Jacques   105, 107, 111
Viret, Pierre   78, 121, 127
Virginia   287–89, 372, 374, 381, 390, 392–93, 395, 397, 401–03, 405, 407–08, 414, 440
Vitry-le-François   233, 283
Vivarais   76, 226, 232, 234–35, 237, 258
Voltaire   239, 241–42, 422
Von Haller, Albrecht   260
Von Spanheim, Ezekiel   258
Vouet, Simon   173
Vray, Nicole   123, 148

Waele, Michel de   123
Wales   402
Walpole   417
Wanegffelen, Thierry   95
Weber, Max   94
Wellman, Kathleen   123
Wiesner, Merry   118–19
Weiss, Charles   14, 349, 425–26, 436
William III (William III of Orange)   210, 256–57, 263, 278, 281, 266, 330
William of Orange (William the Silent)   37, 146
Winn, Colette   146
Wolff, Christian   260
Woolverton, John F.   380
Württemberg, Duke of   185, 294–95, 297

Yardeni, Myriam   11, 13, 253, 395
Yverdon   285–86

Zeeland   409–15
Zwingli, Huldrych   56, 61
Zurich   55–56, 256–57, 266, 285–86, 411

Printed in the United States
By Bookmasters